*Reference
Library of*

EUROPEAN

AMERICA

Reference Library of

EUROPEAN AMERICA

VOLUME **I**

Ethnic Essays

Acadians
to
Hungarian Americans

Distributed by
AFRO AMERICAN PRESS
AFRICAN AMERICAN PUBLICATIONS
PROTEUS ENTERPRISES

Reference Library of European America
ISBN 0-7876-2965-0 (set)
ISBN 0-7876-2966-9 (volume 1)
ISBN 0-7876-2967-7 (volume 2)
ISBN 0-7876-2968-5 (volume 3)
ISBN 0-7876-2969-3 (volume 4)

∞™ This book is printed on acid-free paper that meets the minimum requirements of American National Standard for Information Sciences-Permanence Paper for Printed Library Materials, ANSI Z39.48-1984.

Printed in the United States of America.

10 9 8 7 6 5 4 3 2 1

CONTENTS

Volume 4

PREFACE

The *Reference Library of European America* supports the interests of the many descendants of immigrants from Europe and of those researching them. It offers lengthy essays on the experiences of more than 40 ethnic and ethnoreligious groups and detailed profiles of 45 countries of origin.

SCOPE

The ethnic and ethnoreligious groups that are covered in volumes one and two of the *Reference Library of European America* were selected according to two principal criteria: the magnitude of each ethnic group based on the 1990 U.S. Census, and the recommendations of an advisory board regarding widely studied groups in high schools and universities. To meet the needs of students and researchers, the editors and advisory board therefore chose to include some groups that have relatively small populations. The majority of the articles were written by scholars and writers with a special interest in and knowledge of the ethnic groups about which they were writing. Once the ethnic essays were completed, additional scholars were asked to review the ethnic essays for comprehensiveness, factual accuracy, and objectivity.

In compiling data on European countries that are covered in volumes three and four of the *Reference Library of European America*, substantial efforts were made to enlist the assistance of the government of every European nation, as well as of all pertinent United Nations agencies, who cooperated by supplying data and by revising and updating materials relevant to their sphere of interest. Material received from official sources was reviewed and critically assessed by the editorial staff as part of the process of incorporation. Materials and publications of the United Nations family and of intergovernmental and nongovernmental organizations throughout the world provided a major fund of geographic, demographic, economic, and social data.

In compiling historical, economic, and political data also found in volumes three and four, primary materials generated by governments and international agencies were supplemented by data gathered from numerous other sources including newspapers (most notably *The European*, the *Financial Times*, the *New York Times*, and the *Wall Street Journal*); periodicals (most notably *Current History*, *Elections Today*, *The Economist*, and *World Press Review*); and over 150 worldwide Websites hosted by government agencies and embassies.

FORMAT

While each ethnic essay contained in volumes one and two of the *Reference Library of European America* includes information on the country of origin and circumstances surrounding major immigration waves (if applicable), the primary focus of these ethnic essays is on that group's experiences in the United States, specifically in the areas of acculturation and assimilation, family and community dynamics, language, religion, employment and economic traditions, politics and government, and significant contributions. Wherever possible, each ethnic essay also features directory listings of periodicals, radio and television stations, organizations and associations, and museums and research centers to aid the user in conducting additional research. Each ethnic essay also contains sources for further study that are both useful and accessible.

Volumes three and four of the *Reference Library of European America* provide information on 45 European countries within individual chapters. Introductory matter for each European country includes coat of arms, capital, flag, anthem, monetary unit, weights and measures, holidays, and time zone. All other information within a country chapter appears under one of fifty-numbered subject headings. (For a listing of these headings, consult the "Guide to Country Articles" page found at the beginning of volumes three and four.) A bibliography section appears at the end of each chapter as a guide to further reading on the country in question. Effort was made to provide a broad sampling of works in the bibliography on major subjects and topics covered by the chapter.

The ethnic essays and country chapters in the *Reference Library of European America* are designed for ease of use with the information divided into clearly marked headings and subheadings. This method of organization makes it easy to find specific types of information, and it also facilitates comparative studies among ethnic groups and countries.

ADDITIONAL FEATURES

In addition to a general subject index that provides reference to significant terms, people, places, movements, events, and organizations, the *Reference Library of European America* contains a general bibliography of over 80 books and periodicals, compiled by Vladimir Wertsman of the Ethnic Materials Information Exchange Round Table, American Library Association. These sources supplement those listed in the text; they are more general works in the field of multicultural studies. The text is highlighted by numerous photographs, maps, flags, and national emblems.

CREDITS

The editorial staff wishes to thank the permissions managers of the companies that assisted us in securing reprint rights. The following list acknowledges the copyright holders who have granted us permission to reprint material in this edition of the *Reference Library of European America*. Every effort has been made to trace the copyright holders, but if omissions have been made, please contact the editorial staff.

COPYRIGHTED PHOTOGRAPHY

The photographs and illustrations appearing in the *Reference Library of European America* were received from the following sources:

Village Historique Acadien: page 3; **Corbis-Bettmann:** pages 17, 335, 517, 548; **AP/Wide World Photos, Inc.:** pages 20, 31, 40, 48, 72, 255, 264, 319, 364, 463, 480, 509, 575, 586, 615; **Nathan Nourok/Photo Edit:** page 358; **Aneal Vohra/Unicorn Stock Photos** : pages 121, 135, 149; **UPI/Corbis-Bettmann:** pages 132, 161, 188, 252, 288, 296, 314, 374, 376, 386, 393, 418, 425, 432, 458, 475, 557, 573, 583, 598, 601; **Dana College, Blair Nebraska:** page 147; **Dennis MacDonald/Photo Edit:** page 165; **Gale Zucker:** page 179; **Rich Baker/Unicorn Stock Photos:** page 182; **Library of Congress/Corbis:** page 195; **The Tuomi Family Photographs/Balch Institute for Ethnic Studies:** page 210; **Gary Conner/Photo Edit:** page 204; **Joe Sohm/Unicorn Stock Photos:** page 219; **Kelly-Mooney Photography/Corbis:** page 271; **Russell Grundke/Unicorn Stock Photos:** page 280; **Special Collections and University Archives, Rutgers University:** page 303; **Robert Brenner/PhotoEdit:** pages 340, 401, 447; **Jeff Greenberg/Photo Edit:** page 412; **Gale Zucker:** page 450; **Tony Freeman/Photo Edit:** page 488; **Jim Shiopee/Unicorn Stock Photos:** page 491.

Advisory Board

Kay A. Averette
Head Librarian, Philosophy, Religion, and
   Education Division, Akron/Summit County
   Public Library

Patricia F. Beilke
Director, Library and Information Science and
   Secondary Education Programs, Ball State
   University

Araxie Churukian
Librarian and Lecturer, University of California,
   Riverside

David Cohen
Director, Ethnic Materials Information
   Exchange, American Library Association;
   Adjunct Professor of Library Science,
   Queens College

Frank L. Ellsworth
President, Independent Colleges of Southern
   California; Visiting Professor of Library
   Science, Loyola Marymount University

Rudolph J. Vecoli
Director, Immigration History Research Center,
   University of Minnesota, St. Paul

Vladimir Wertsman
Chair of Publishing in Multicultural Materials,
   Ethnic Materials Information Exchange,
   American Library Association

CONTRIBUTORS

Victor Alba
Author, *Transition in Spain: From Franco to Democracy*

June Granatir Alexander
Adjunct Assistant Professor
Russian and East European Studies
University of Cincinnati
Cincinnati, Ohio

Donald Altschiller
Freelance Writer
Cambridge, Massachusetts

Diane Andreassi
Freelance Writer
Livonia, Michigan

Charles W. Arnade
Professor, Department of History
University of South Florida

Douglas E. Ashford
Department of Political Science
Cornell University

Carl L. Bankston III
Professor, Department of Sociology
Louisiana State University
Baton Rouge, Louisiana

William J. Barber
Associate Professor, Department of Economics
Wesleyan University

Muriel T. Barron

Elizabeth M. Bass
Economist-Editor

Norman Bennett
Professor, Department of History
Boston University
Boston, Massachusetts

Elliot J. Berg
Professor, Department of Economics
University of Michigan
Ann Arbor, Michigan

Nancy Guinlock Berg

Marvin Bernstein
Professor, Department of History
State University of New York at Buffalo
Buffalo, New York

Barbara Bigelow
Freelance Writer
White Lake, Michigan

D.L. Birchfield
Editor and Writer
Oklahoma City, Oklahoma

Laurence R. Birns
Director
Council on Hemispheric Affairs

R. W. Bradbury
Professor, Department of Economics
College of Business Administration
University of Florida

Herbert Brinks
Professor, Department of History
Calvin College
Grand Rapids, Michigan

Alan J. Brody
Department of Political Science
Cleveland State University

Sean Buffington
Professor, Department of Ethnic Studies
University of Michigan
Ann Arbor, Michigan

Phyllis Burson
Independent Consultant
Silver Spring, Maryland

Richard Butwell
Dean for Arts and Sciences
State University of New York at Fredonia
Fredonia, New York

Helen Caver
Associate Professor and Librarian
Jacksonville State University
Jacksonville, Alabama

Cida S. Chase
Professor of Spanish
Oklahoma State University
Stillwater, Oklahoma

Clark Colahan
Professor of Spanish
Whitman College
Walla Walla, Washington

Robert O. Collins
Professor, Department of History
University of California, Santa Barbara
Santa Barbara, California

Robert J. Conley
Freelance Writer
Tahlequah, Oklahoma

Jane Cook
Freelance Writer
Green Bay, Wisconsin

José Descárrega Corderas
Royal Geographical Society
Valverde, Spain

Bruce G. Cumings
Professor, Department of Political Science
Swarthmore College

Laszlo Czirjak
Associate Professor
Columbia University

Rosetta Sharp Dean
Counselor and Writer
Anniston, Alabama

Charles F. Dunbar
President
Cleveland Council on World Affairs

John R. Dunkle
Associate Professor of Geography and Physical
   Science
University of Florida

Allen Englekirk
Professor of Spanish
Gonzaga University
Spokane, Washington

Laurence Evans
Professor, Department of History
Harpur College

Gunther F. Eyek
Professorial Lecturer, History and International
   Relations
American University

Marianne Fedunkiw
Freelance Writer
Toronto, Ontario, Canada

Evelyn Feretti
Department of Agricultural Economics
Cornell University

Willard Allen Fletcher
Professor and Chair, Department of History
College of Arts & Sciences
University of Delaware

Mary Gillis
Freelance Writer
Huntington Woods, Michigan

Edward Gobetz
Executive Director
Slovenian Research Center of America, Inc.
Willoughby Hills, Ohio

Rodger M. Govea
Associate Professor, Department of Political
    Science
Cleveland State University

Mark A. Granquist
Assistant Professor of Religion
Saint Olaf College
Northfield, Minnesota

Derek Green
Freelance Writer
Ann Arbor, Michigan

Ralph Greenhouse
US Information Agency

Kenneth W. Grundy
Marcus A. Hanna Professor of Political Science
Case Western Reserve University

John W. Guendelsberger
Professor of Law
The Claude W. Pettit College of Law,
Ohio Northern University

Nese Guendelsberger
Attorney at Law
Ada, Ohio

Herbert G. Hagerty
Foreign Service Officer (ret.)
US Department of State

Paula Hajar
Freelance Writer
New York, New York

Loretta Hall
Freelance Writer
Albuquerque, New Mexico

Sheldon Hanft
Professor, Department of History
Appalachian State University
Boone, North Carolina

James J. Heaney
Managing Editor
Webster's New World Dictionary

Evan Heimlich
Assistant Coordinator
Multicultural Resource Center
The University of Kansas
Lawrence, Kansas

Mary A. Hess
Teaching Assistant
Integrated Arts and Humanities
Michigan State University
Lansing, Michigan

Laurie Hillstrom
Freelance Writer
Pleasant Ridge, Michigan

George W. Hoffman
Professor of Geography
University of Texas at Austin
Austin, Texas

Maria Hong
Freelance Writer
Austin, Texas

Ed Ifkovic
Writer and Lecturer
Hartford, Connecticut

Kenneth Ingham
Director of Studies
Royal Military Academy, Sandhurst

**International Institute for Aerial Survey and
    Earth Sciences**
F. J. Ormeling, Head of Cartography Department,
    C. A. de Bruijn, P. Hofstee, A. B. M. Hijl,
    Department of Urban Surveys

Syd Jones
Freelance Writer and Novelist
Aptos, California

Gail Junion-Metz
President
Information Age Consultants

Jane Jurgens
Assistant Professor
Learning Resources Center
St. Cloud State University
St. Cloud, Minnesota

Jim Kamp
Freelance Writer and Editor
Royal Oak, Michigan

Harry Kantor
Professor, Department of Political Science
Marquette University

Fredric M. Kaplan

Mark N. Katz
Associate Professor of Government and Politics
George Mason University

Oscar Kawagley
Assistant Professor of Education
College of Liberal Arts, UAF
Fairbanks, Alaska

Robert C. Kingsbury
Assistant Professor of Geography
Indiana University

Vituat Kipel
Librarian, Slavic and Baltic Division
The New York Public Library
New York, New York

George Kish
Professor of Geography
University of Michigan
Ann Arbor, Michigan

John I. Kolehmainen
Chair, Department of Political Science
Heidelberg College

Charles J. Kolinski
Professor, Department of History
Florida Atlantic University

Huey Louis Kostanick
Professor of Geography
University of Southern California

Walter Kranz
Press and Information Officer
Principality of Liechtenstein

Donald B. Kraybill
Professor, Department of Sociology
Elizabethtown College
Elizabethtown, Pennsylvania

Ken Kurson
Freelance Writer
New York, New York

Robert H.G. Lee
Assistant Professor, Department of History
State University of New York at Stony Brook

Emil Lengyel
Professor, Department of History
Fairleigh Dickinson University

H.A. Lewis
G.O.B.E. Fellow
Royal Geographical Society

William H. Lewis
Department of Anthropology and Sociology
American University

Odd S. Lovoll
Professor of Scandinavian American Studies
Saint Olaf College
Northfield, Minnesota

William R. Lux
Assistant Professor, Department of History
University of Alabama

Catherine Lynch
Assistant Professor, Department of History
Case Western Reserve University

Henry S. Marks
Professor, Department of History
Northeast Alabama State Junior College

Carl McGuire
Professor, Department of Economics
University of Colorado

Vincent McHale
Chair, Department of Political Science
Case Western Reserve University

Robert C. McIntire
Associate Professor and Chair, Department of
      Political Science
Millikin University

Robert S. McLellan
US Information Agency

Jacqueline A. McLeod
Freelance Writer
Michigan State University
East Lansing, Michigan

Glenn McLoughlin
Specialist in Science and Technology Policy
Congressional Research Service
Library of Congress

H. Brett Melendy
University Archivist
San Jose State University
San Jose, California

Marcia Eigen Mendell

Raymond E. Metz
Interim Director
University Libraries
Case Western Reserve University

Nathan Miller
Associate Professor, Department of History
University of Wisconsin, Milwaukee
Milwaukee, Wisconsin

Allan R. Millett
Mason Professor of Military History
The Mershon Center
Ohio State University

Christine Molinari
Manuscript Editor
The University of Chicago Press
Chicago, Illinois

Molly Mortimer
Former Commonwealth Correspondent
The Spectator
London

Edward Moseley
Assistant Professor, Department of History
University of Alabama

Lloyd Mulraine
Professor of English
Jacksonville State University
Jacksonville, Alabama

Jeremy Mumford
Assistant News Editor
Courtroom Television Network
New York, New York

Amy Nash
Freelance Writer
Minneapolis, Minnesota

New York University Department of Politics
I. William Zartman, Editor; John Entelis, Oladipo
    Coles, Jeffrey Knorr, Marie-Daniele Harmel,
    Contributors

John Mark Nielson
Professor of English
Dana College
Blair, Nebraska

Ernest E. Norden
Professor, Division of Spanish and Portuguese
Baylor University
Waco, Texas

Andrew C. O'Dell
Professor of Geography
University of Aberdeen

John K. Oh
Professor, Department of Political Science
Marquette University

Martha Brill Olcott
Professor, Department of Political Science
Colgate University

Robert T. Oliver
Head, Department of Speech
Pennsylvania State University

John F. Packel, II
Freelance Writer
Brooklyn, New York

DDR Panorama
Berlin

Raphael Patai
Editor, The Herzl Press

Tinaz Pavri
Freelance Writer
Columbus, Ohio

Walter A. Payne
Professor, Department of History
University of the Pacific

Richard Perrin
Librarian, Reference and Instructional
    ServicesTimme Library
Ferris State University
Big Rapids, Michigan

Peter L. Peterson
Professor of History
West Texas A&M
Canyon, Texas

Victor P. Petrov
Professor of Geography
California State College

Embassy of Poland
Washington D.C.

William R. Polk
Director
Adlai E. Stevenson Institute
University of Chicago

George E. Pozzetta
Professor, Department of History
University of Florida
Gainesville, Florida

Pragopress
Prague, Czech Republic

Henry Precht
Adjunct Associate Professor, Department of
    Political Science
Case Western Reserve University

John Ranahan
Lake Ridge Academy

Brendan Rapple
Reference Librarian/Education Bibliographer
O'Neill Library
Boston College
Boston, Massachusetts

Megan Ratner
Freelance Writer
New York, New York

Bernard Reines

La Vern J. Rippley
Professor of German
Saint Olaf College
Northfield, Minnesota

Kenneth E. Robinson
Director, Institute of Commonwealth Studies
Professor of Commonwealth Affairs
University of London

Julio César Rodríguez
Freelance Writer
Walla Walla, Washington

Carl G. Rosberg, Jr.
Associate Professor of Political Science
University of California

Robert I. Rotberg
Professor of Political Science and History
MIT

Lorene Roy
Associate Professor and Minority Liaison Officer
The University of Texas at Austin
Austin, Texas

Robert A. Rupen
Associate Professor, Department of Political
    Science
University of North Carolina

Vladimir Rus
Department of Slavic Literature (ret.)
Case Western Reserve University

Maria J. Santos
Senior Evaluator
United States General Accounting Office

Kwasi Sarkodie-Mensah
Chief Reference Librarian
O'Neill Library
Boston College
Boston, Massachusetts

Leo Schelbert
Professor, Department of History
University of Illinois at Chicago
Chicago, Illinois

Mary C. Sengstock
Professor, Department of Sociology
Wayne State University
Detroit, Michigan

George Shepherd
Professor, Department of Political Science
University of Denver

Stefan Smagula
Freelance Writer
Austin, Texas

Soviet Encyclopedia Publishing House

Bosiljka Stevanovic
Principal Librarian
Donnell Library Center
World Languages Collection
The New York Public Library
New York, New York

Joseph W. Stoll
Supervisor
Cartography Laboratory
University of Akron

Andris Straumanis
Freelance Writer
New Brighton, Minnesota

Pamela Sturner
Freelance Writer
New Haven, Connecticut

Mark Swartz
Manuscript Editor
The University of Chicago Press
Chicago, Illinois

Syracuse University, Foreign and Comparative
    Studies Program
Peter Dalleo; Thomas C.N. Evans; Robert G.
    Gregory, Professor of History; Elisabeth
    Hunt; Roderick J. Macdonald, Professor of
    History; Thomas F. Taylor

Harold T. Takooshian
Professor, Division of Social Sciences
Fordham University
New York, New York

Felix Unaeze
Head Librarian
Reference and Instructional Services Department
Timme Library
Ferris State University
Big Rapids, Michigan

Amry Vandenbosch
Director Emeritus
Patterson School of Diplomacy and International
    Commerce
University of Kentucky

Steven Béla Várdy
Professor and Director, Department of History
Duquesne University
Pittsburgh, Pennsylvania

K. Marianne Wargelin
Freelance Writer
Minneapolis, Minnesota

Manfred W. Wenner
Associate Professor, Department of Political
    Science
University of Northern Illinois

Frederick L. Wernstedt
Associate Professor of Geography
Pennsylvania State University

Vladimir Wertsman
Chair of Publishing in Multicultural Materials
Ethnic Materials Information Exchange
American Library Association
New York, New York

Mary T. Williams
Associate Professor
Jacksonville State University
Jacksonville, Alabama

Martin W. Wilmington
Professor, Department of Economics
Pace College

Elaine Winters
Freelance Writer
Berkeley, California

Gregory D. Wolfe
Portland State University

Winthrop R. Wright
Professor, Department of History
University of Maryland

Yugoslav Federal Committee for Information

INTRODUCTION

RUDOLPH J. VECOLI, DIRECTOR
IMMIGRATION HISTORY
RESEARCH CENTER,
UNIVERSITY OF MINNESOTA, ST. PAUL

The term multiculturalism has recently come into usage to describe a society characterized by a diversity of cultures. Religion, language, customs, traditions, and values are some of the components of culture, but more importantly culture is the lens through which one perceives and interprets the world. When a shared culture forms the basis for a "sense of peoplehood," based on consciousness of a common past, we can speak of a group possessing an ethnicity. As employed here, ethnicity is not transmitted genetically from generation to generation; nor is it unchanging over time. Rather, ethnicity is invented or constructed in response to particular historical circumstances and changes as circumstances change. "Race," a sub-category of ethnicity, is not a biological reality but a cultural construction. While in its most intimate form an ethnic group may be based on face-to-face relationships, a politicized ethnicity mobilizes its followers far beyond the circle of personal acquaintances. Joined with aspirations for political self-determination, ethnicity can become full-blown nationalism. In this essay, ethnicity will be used to identify groups or communities that are differentiated by religious, racial, or cultural characteristics and that possess a sense of peoplehood.

The "Multicultural America" to which this encyclopedia is dedicated is the product of the mingling of many different peoples over the course of several hundred years in what is now the United States. Cultural diversity was characteristic of this continent prior to the coming of European colonists and African slaves. The indigenous inhabitants of North America who numbered an estimated 4.5 million in 1500 were divided into hundreds of tribes with distinctive cultures, languages, and religions. Although the numbers of "Indians," as they were named by Europeans, declined precipitously through the nineteenth century, their population has rebounded in the twentieth century. Both as members of their particular tribes (a form of ethnicity), Navajo, Ojibwa, Choctaw, etc., and as American Indians (a form of panethnicity), they are very much a part of today's cultural and ethnic pluralism.

Most Americans, however, are descendants of immigrants. Since the sixteenth century, from the earliest Spanish settlement at St. Augustine, Florida, the process of repeopling this continent has gone on apace. Some 600,000 Europeans and Africans were recruited or enslaved and transported across the Atlantic Ocean in the colonial period to what was to become the United States. The first census of 1790 revealed the high degree of diversity that already marked the American population. Almost 19 percent were of African ancestry, another 12 percent Scottish and Scotch-Irish, ten percent German, with smaller numbers of French, Irish, Welsh, and Sephardic Jews. The census did not include American Indians. The English, sometimes described as the "founding people," only comprised 48 percent of the total. At the time of its birth in 1776, the United States was already a "complex ethnic mosaic," with a wide variety of communities differentiated by culture, language, race, and religion.

The present United States includes not only the original thirteen colonies, but lands that were subsequently purchased or conquered. Through this territorial expansion, other peoples were brought within the boundaries of the republic; these included, in addition to many Native American tribes, French, Hawaiian, Inuit, Mexican, and Puerto Rican, among others. Since 1790, population growth, other than by natural increase, has come primarily through three massive waves of immigration. During the first wave (1841-1890), almost 15 million immigrants arrived: over four million Germans, three million each of Irish and British (English, Scottish, and Welsh), and one million Scandinavians. A second wave (1891-1920) brought an additional 18 million immigrants: almost four million from Italy, 3.6 million from Austria-Hungary,

and three million from Russia. In addition, over two million Canadians, Anglo and French, immigrated prior to 1920. The intervening decades, from 1920 to 1945, marked a hiatus in immigration due to restrictive policies, economic depression, and war. A modest post-World War II influx of refugees was followed by a new surge subsequent to changes in immigration policy in 1965. Totalling approximately 16 million—and still in progress, this third wave encompassed some four million from Mexico, another four million from Central and South America and the Caribbean, and roughly six million from Asia. While almost 90 percent of the first two waves originated in Europe, only 12 percent of the third did.

Immigration has introduced an enormous diversity of cultures into American society. The 1990 U.S. Census report on ancestry provides a fascinating portrait of the complex ethnic origins of the American people. Responses to the question, "What is your ancestry or ethnic origin?," were tabulated for 215 ancestry groups. The largest ancestry groups reported were, in order of magnitude, German, Irish, English, and African American, all over 20 million.

Other groups reporting over six million were Italian, Mexican, French, Polish, Native American, Dutch, and Scotch-Irish, while another 28 groups reported over one million each. Scanning the roster of ancestries one is struck by the plethora of smaller groups: Hmong, Maltese, Honduran, Carpatho-Rusyns, and Nigerian, among scores of others. Interestingly enough, only five percent identified themselves simply as "American"—and less than one percent as "white."

Immigration also contributed to the transformation of the religious character of the United States. Its original Protestantism (itself divided among many denominations and sects) was both reinforced by the arrival of millions of Lutherans, Methodists, Presbyterians, etc., and diluted by the heavy influx of Roman Catholics—first the Irish and Germans, then Eastern Europeans and Italians, and more recently Hispanics. These immigrants have made Roman Catholicism the largest single denomination in the country. Meanwhile, Slavic Christian and Jewish immigrants from Central and Eastern Europe established Judaism and Orthodoxy as major American religious bodies. As a consequence of Near Eastern immigration—and the conversion of many African Americans to Islam—there are currently some three million Muslims in the United States. Smaller numbers of Buddhists, Hindus, and followers of other religions have also arrived. In many American cities, houses of worship now include mosques and temples as well as churches and synagogues. Such religious pluralism is an important source of American multiculturalism.

The immigration and naturalization policies pursued by a country are a key to understanding its self-conception as a nation. By determining whom to admit to residence and citizenship, the dominant element defines the future ethnic and racial composition of the population and the body politic. Each of the three great waves of immigration inspired much soul-searching and intense debate over the consequences for the republic. If the capacity of American society to absorb some 55 million immigrants over the course of a century and a half is impressive, it is also true that American history has been punctuated by ugly episodes of nativism and xenophobia. With the possible exception of the British, it is difficult to find an immigrant group that has not been subject to some degree of prejudice and discrimination. From their early encounters with Native Americans and Africans, Anglo-Americans established "whiteness" as an essential marker of difference and superiority. The Naturalization Act of 1790, for example, specified that citizenship was to be available to "any alien, being a free white person." By this provision not only were blacks ineligible for naturalization, but also future immigrants who were deemed not to be "white." The greater the likeness of immigrants to the Anglo-American type (e.g., British Protestants), the more readily they were welcomed.

Not all Anglo-Americans were racists or xenophobes. Citing Christian and democratic ideals of universal brotherhood, many advocated the abolition of slavery and the rights of freedmen—freedom of religion and cultural tolerance. Debates over immigration policy brought these contrasting views of the republic into collision. The ideal of America as an asylum for the oppressed of the world has exerted a powerful influence for a liberal reception of newcomers. Emma Lazarus's sonnet, which began "Give me your tired, your poor, your huddled masses yearning to breathe free, the wretched refuse of your teeming shore," struck a responsive chord among many Anglo-Americans. Moreover, American capitalism depended upon the rural workers of Europe, French Canada, Mexico, and Asia to man its factories and mines. Nonetheless, many Americans have regarded immigration as posing a threat to social stability, the jobs of native white

workers, honest politics, and American cultural—even biological—integrity. The strength of anti-immigrant movements has waxed and waned with the volume of immigration, but even more with fluctuations in the state of the economy and society. Although the targets of nativist attacks have changed over time, a constant theme has been the danger posed by foreigners to American values and institutions.

Irish Catholics, for example, were viewed as minions of the Pope and enemies of the Protestant character of the country. A Protestant Crusade culminated with the formation of the American (or "Know-Nothing") Party in 1854, whose battle cry was "America for the Americans!" While the Know-Nothing movement was swallowed up by sectional conflict culminating in the Civil War, anti-Catholicism continued to be a powerful strain of nativism well into the twentieth century.

Despite such episodes of xenophobia, during its first century of existence, the United States welcomed all newcomers with minimal regulation. In 1882, however, two laws initiated a progressive tightening of restrictions upon immigration. The first established qualitative health and moral standards by excluding criminals, prostitutes, lunatics, idiots, and paupers. The second, the Chinese Exclusion Act, the culmination of an anti-Chinese movement centered on the West Coast, denied admission to Chinese laborers and barred Chinese immigrants from acquiring citizenship. Following the enactment of this law, agitation for exclusion of Asians continued as the Japanese and others arrived, culminating in the provision of the Immigration Law of 1924, which denied entry to aliens ineligible for citizenship (those who were not deemed "white"). It was not until 1952 that a combination of international politics and democratic idealism finally resulted in the elimination of all racial restrictions from American immigration and naturalization policies.

In the late nineteenth century, "scientific" racialism, which asserted the superiority of Anglo-Saxons, was embraced by many Americans as justification for imperialism and immigration restriction. At that time a second immigrant wave was beginning to bring peoples from eastern Europe, the Balkans, and the Mediterranean into the country. Nativists campaigned for a literacy test and other measures to restrict the entry of these "inferior races." Proponents of a liberal immigration policy defeated such efforts until World War I created a xenophobic climate that not only insured the passage of the literacy test, but prepared the way for the Immigration Acts of 1921 and 1924. Inspired by racialist ideas, these laws established national quota systems designed to drastically reduce the number of southern and eastern Europeans entering the United States and to bar Asians entirely. In essence, the statutes sought to freeze the biological and ethnic identity of the American people by protecting them from contamination from abroad.

Until 1965 the United States pursued this restrictive and racist immigration policy. The Immigration Act of 1965 did away with the national origins quota system and opened the country to immigration from throughout the world, establishing preferences for family members of American citizens and resident aliens, skilled workers, and refugees. The unforeseen consequence of the law of 1965 was the third wave of immigration. Not only did the annual volume of immigration increase steadily to the current level of one million or more arrivals each year, but the majority of the immigrants now came from Asia and Latin America. During the 1980s, they accounted for 85 percent of the total number of immigrants, with Mexicans, Chinese, Filipinos, and Koreans being the largest contingents.

The cumulative impact of an immigration of 16 plus millions since 1965 has aroused intense concerns regarding the demographic, cultural, and racial future of the American people. The skin color, languages, and lifestyles of the newcomers triggered a latent xenophobia in the American psyche. While eschewing the overt racism of earlier years, advocates of tighter restriction have warned that if current rates of immigration continue, the "minorities" (persons of African, Asian, and "Hispanic" ancestry) will make up about half of the American population by the year 2050.

A particular cause of anxiety is the number of undocumented immigrants (estimated at 200,000-300,000 per year). Contrary to popular belief, the majority of these individuals do not cross the border from Mexico, but enter the country with either student or tourist visas and simply stay—many are Europeans and Asians. The Immigration Reform and Control Act (IRCA) of 1986 sought to solve the problem by extending amnesty for undocumented immigrants under certain conditions and imposing penalties on employers who hired undocumented immigrants, while making special provisions for temporary agricultural migrant workers. Although over three million persons qualified for consideration for amnesty, employer sanctions failed for lack of effective enforcement, and the number of undocumented immigrants has not decreased. Congress subsequently enacted the Immigration Act of 1990, which established a cap of 700,000 immigrants per year, maintained preferences based on family reunification, and expanded the number of skilled workers to be admitted. Immigration, however, has continued to be a hotly debated issue. Responding to the nativist mood of the country, politicians have advocated measures to limit access of legal as well as undocumented immigrants to Medicare and other welfare benefits. A constitutional amendment was even proposed that would deny citizenship to American-born children of undocumented residents.

Forebodings about an "unprecedented immigrant invasion," however, appear exaggerated. In the early 1900s, the rate of immigration (the number of immigrants measured against the total population) was ten per every thousand; in the 1980s the rate was only 3.5 per every thousand. While the number of foreign-born individuals in the United States reached an all-time high of almost 20 million in 1990, they accounted for only eight percent of the population as compared with 14.7 per cent in 1910. In other words, the statistical impact of contemporary immigration has been of a much smaller magnitude than that of the past. A persuasive argument has also been made that immigrants, legal and undocumented, contribute more than they take from the American economy and that they pay more in taxes than they receive in social services. As in the past, immigrants are being made scapegoats for the country's problems.

Among the most difficult questions facing students of American history are: how have these tens of millions of immigrants with such differing cultures incorporated into American society?; and what changes have they wrought in the character of that society? The concepts of acculturation and assimilation are helpful in understanding the processes whereby immigrants have adapted to the new society. Applying Milton Gordon's theory, acculturation is the process whereby newcomers assume American cultural attributes, such as the English language, manners, and values, while assimilation is the process of their incorporation into the social networks (work, residence, leisure, families) of the host society. These changes have not come quickly or easily. Many immigrants have experienced only limited acculturation and practically no assimilation during their lifetimes.

Among the factors that have affected these processes are race, ethnicity, class, gender, and character of settlement.

The most important factor, however, has been the willingness of the dominant ethnic group (Anglo-Americans) to accept the foreigners. Since they have wielded political and social power, Anglo-Americans have been able to decide who to include and who to exclude. Race (essentially skin color) has been the major barrier to acceptance; thus Asians and Mexicans, as well as African Americans and Native Americans, have in the past been excluded from full integration into the mainstream. At various times, religion, language, and nationality have constituted impediments to incorporation. Social class has also strongly affected interactions among various ethnic groups. Historically, American society has been highly stratified with a close congruence between class and ethnicity, i.e., Anglo-Americans tend to belong to the upper class, northern and western Europeans to the middle class, and southern and eastern Europeans and African Americans to the working class. The metaphor of a "vertical mosaic" has utility in conceptualizing American society. A high degree of segregation (residential, occupational, leisure) within the vertical mosaic has severely limited acculturation and assimilation across class and ethnic lines. However, within a particular social class, various immigrant groups have often interacted at work, in neighborhoods, at churches and saloons, and in the process have engaged in what one historian has described as "Americanization from the bottom up."

Gender has also been a factor since the status of women within the general American society, as well as within their particular ethnic groups, has affected their assimilative and acculturative experiences. Wide variations exist among groups as to the degree to which women are restricted to traditional roles or have freedom to pursue opportunities in the larger society. The density and location of immigrant settlements have also influenced the rate and character of incorporation into the mainstream culture. Concentrated urban settlements and isolated rural settlements, by limiting contacts between the immigrants and others, tend to inhibit the processes of acculturation and assimilation.

An independent variable in these processes, however, is the determination of immigrants themselves whether or not to shed their cultures and become simply Americans. By and large, they are not willing or able to do so. Rather, they cling, often tenaciously, to their old world traditions, languages, and beliefs. Through chain migrations, relatives and friends have regrouped in cities, towns, and the countryside for mutual assistance and to maintain their customary ways. Establishing churches, societies, newspapers, and other institutions, they have built communities and have developed an enlarged sense of peoplehood. Thus, ethnicity (although related to nationalist movements in countries of origin) in large part has emerged from the immigrants' attempt to cope with life in this pluralist society. While they can not transplant their Old Country ways intact to the Dakota prairie or the Chicago slums, theirs is a selective adaptation, in which they have taken from American culture that which they needed and have kept from their traditional culture that which they valued. Rather than becoming Anglo-Americans, they became ethnic Americans of various kinds.

Assimilation and acculturation have progressed over the course of several generations. The children and grandchildren of the immigrants have retained less of their ancestral cultures (languages are first to go, customs and traditions often follow) and have assumed more mainstream attributes. Yet many have retained, to a greater or lesser degree, a sense of identity and affiliation with a particular ethnic group. Conceived of not as a finite culture brought over in immigrant trunks, but as a mode of accommodation to the dominant culture, ethnicity persists even when the cultural content changes.

We might also ask to what have the descendants been assimilating and acculturating. Some have argued that there is an American core culture, essentially British in origin, in which immigrants and their offspring are absorbed. However, if one compares the "mainstream culture" of Americans today (music, food, literature, mass media) with that of one or two centuries ago, it is obvious that it is not Anglo-American (even the American English language has undergone enormous changes from British English). Rather, mainstream culture embodies and reflects the spectrum of immigrant and indigenous ethnic cultures that make up American society. It is the product of syncretism, the melding of different, sometimes contradictory and discordant elements. Multiculturalism is not a museum of immigrant cultures, but rather this complex of the living, vibrant ethnicities of contemporary America.

If Americans share an ideological heritage deriving from the ideals of the American Revolution, such ideals have not been merely abstract principles handed down unchanged from the eighteenth century to the present. Immigrant and indigenous ethnic groups, taking these ideals at face value, have employed them as weapons to combat ethnic and racial prejudice and economic exploitation. If America was the Promised Land, for many the promise was realized only after prolonged and collective struggles. Through labor and civil rights movements, they have contributed to keeping alive and enlarging the ideals of justice, freedom, and equality. If America transformed the immigrants and indigenous ethnic groups, they have also transformed America.

How have Americans conceived of this polyglot, kaleidoscopic society? Over the centuries, several models of a social order, comprised of a variety of ethnic and racial groups, have competed for dominance. An early form was a society based on caste—a society divided into those who were free and those who were not free. Such a social order existed in the South for two hundred years. While the Civil War destroyed slavery, the Jim Crow system of racial segregation maintained a caste system for another hundred years. But the caste model was not limited to black-white relations in the southern states. Industrial capitalism also created a caste-like structure in the North. For a century prior to the New Deal, power, wealth, and status were concentrated in the hands of an Anglo-American elite, while the workers, comprised largely of immigrants and their children, were the helots of the farms and the factories. The caste model collapsed in both the North and the South in the twentieth century before the onslaught of economic expansion, technological change, and geographic and social mobility.

Anglo-conformity has been a favored model through much of our history. Convinced of their cultural and even biological superiority, Anglo-Americans have demanded that Native Americans, African Americans, and immigrants abandon their distinctive linguistic, cultural, and religious traits and conform (in so far as they are capable) to the Anglo model. But at the same time that they demanded conformity to their values and lifestyles, Anglo-Americans erected barriers that severely limited social intercourse with those they regarded as inferior. The ideology of Anglo-conformity has particularly influenced educational policies. A prime objective of the American public school system has been the assimilation of "alien" children to Anglo-American middle class values and behaviors. In recent years, Anglo-conformity has taken the form of opposition to bilingual education. A vigorous campaign has been waged for a constitutional amendment that would make English the official language of the United States.

A competing model, the Melting Pot, symbolized the process whereby the foreign elements were to be transmuted into a new American race. There have been many variants of this ideology of assimilation, including one in which the Anglo-American is the cook stirring and determining the ingredients, but the prevailing concept has been that a distinctive amalgam of all the varied cultures and peoples would emerge from the crucible. Expressing confidence in the capacity of America to assimilate all newcomers, the Melting Pot ideology provided the rationale for a liberal immigration policy. Although the Melting Pot ideology came under sharp attack in the 1960s as a coercive policy of assimilation, the increased immigration of recent years and the related anxiety over national unity has brought it back into favor in certain academic and political circles.

In response to pressures for 100 percent Americanization during World War I, the model of Cultural Pluralism has been offered as an alternative to the Melting Pot. In this model, while sharing a common American citizenship and loyalty, ethnic groups would maintain and foster their particular languages and cultures. The metaphors employed for the cultural pluralism model have included a symphony orchestra, a flower garden, a mosaic, and a stew or salad. All suggest a reconciliation of diversity with an encompassing harmony and coherence. The fortunes of the pluralist model have fluctuated with the national mood. During the 1930s, when cultural democracy was in vogue, pluralist ideas were popular. Again during the period of the "new ethnicity" of the 1960s and the 1970s, cultural pluralism attracted a considerable following. In recent years, heightened fears that American society was fragmenting caused many to reject pluralism for a return to the Melting Pot.

As the United States approaches the twenty-first century its future as an ethnically plural society is hotly contested. Is the United States more diverse today than in the past? Is the unity of society threatened by its diversity? Are the centrifugal forces in American society more powerful than the centripetal? The old models of Anglo-conformity, the Melting Pot, and Cultural Pluralism have lost their explanatory and symbolic value. We need a new model, a new definition of our identity as a people, which will encompass our expanding multiculturalism and which will define us as a multiethnic people in the context of a multiethnic world. We need a compelling paradigm that will command the faith of all Americans because it embraces them in their many-splendored diversity within a just society.

SUGGESTED READINGS

On acculturation and assimilation, Milton Gordon's *Assimilation in American Life: The Role of Race, Religion, and National Origins* (1964) provides a useful theoretical framework. For a discussion of the concept of ethnicity, see Kathleen Neils Conzen, et al. "The Invention of Ethnicity: A Perspective from the USA," *Journal of American Ethnic History*, 12 (Fall 1992). *Harvard Encyclopedia of American Ethnic Groups*, ed. Stephan Thernstrom (Cambridge, MA, 1980) is a standard reference work with articles on themes as well as specific groups; see especially the essay by Philip Gleason. "American Identity and Americanization." Roger Daniels' *Coming to America: A History of Immigration and Ethnicity in American Life* (New York, 1991) is the most comprehensive and up-to-date history. For a comparative history of ethnic groups see Ronald Takaki's *A Different Mirror: A History of Multicultural America* (1993). On post-1965 immigration, David Reimers' *Still the Golden Door: The Third World Comes to America* (1985), is an excellent overview. A classic work on nativism is John Higham's, *Strangers in the Land: Patterns of American Nativism: 1860-1925*(1963), but see also David H. Bennett's *The Party of Fear: From Nativist Movements to the New Right in American History* (1988). On the Anglo-American elite see E. Digby Baltzell's *The Protestant Establishment: Aristocracy and Caste in America* (1964).

ACADIANS

by

Evan Heimlich

Acadians brought a solidarity with them to Louisiana. As one of the first groups to cross the Atlantic and adopt a new identity, they felt connected to each other by their common experience.

OVERVIEW

Acadians are the descendants of a group of French-speaking settlers who migrated from coastal France in the late sixteenth century to establish a French colony called Acadia in the maritime provinces of Canada and part of what is now the state of Maine. Forced out by the British in the mid-sixteenth century, a few settlers remained in Maine, but most resettled in southern Louisiana and are popularly known as Cajuns.

HISTORY

Before 1713, Acadia was a French colony pioneered mostly by settlers from the coastal provinces of Brittany, Normandy, Picardy, and Poitou—a region that suffered great hardships in the late sixteenth and early seventeenth centuries. In 1628, famine and plague followed the end of a series of religious wars between Catholics and Protestants. When social tensions in coastal France ripened, more than 10,000 people left for the colony founded by Samuel Champlain in 1604 known as "La Cadie" or Acadia. The area, which included what is now Nova Scotia, New Brunswick, Prince Edward Island, and part of Maine, was one of the first European colonies in North America. The Company of New France recruited colonists from coastal France as indentured servants. Fishermen, farmers, and trappers served for five years to repay the company with their labor for the transportation and materials it had provided. In the New World, colonists forged alliances with local Indians, who generally preferred the settlers from France over those from Britain because, unlike the British who took all the land they could, the coastal French in Acadia did not invade Indian hunting grounds inland.

The early French settlers called themselves "Acadiens" or "'Cadiens" (which eventually became Anglicized as "Cajuns") and were among the first Old World settlers to identify themselves as North Americans. The New World offered them relative freedom and independence from the French upper class. When French owners of Acadian lands tried to collect seignorial rents from settlers who were farming, many Acadians simply moved away from the colonial centers. When France tried legally to control their profit from their trade in furs or grain, Acadians traded illegally; they even traded with New England while France and England waged war against each other.

As French colonial power waned, Great Britain captured Acadia in 1647; the French got it back in 1670 only to lose it again to the British in the 1690s. Acadians adapted to political changes as their region repeatedly changed hands. Before the British took the Nova Scotia region, they waged the Hundred Year War against French colonial forces in a struggle over the region's territory. The Treaty of Utrecht in 1713, which failed to define realistic boundaries for the French and English territories after Queen Anne's War, converted most of the peninsula into a British colony. Despite British attempts to impose its language and culture, Acadian culture persisted. Large families increased their numbers and new settlers spoke French. The British tried to settle Scottish and other Protestant colonists in Acadia to change the region's French-Catholic culture to a British-Protestant one. The French-speaking Acadians, however, held onto their own culture.

In 1745 the British threatened to expel the Acadians unless they pledged allegiance to the King of England. Unwilling to subject themselves to any king (especially the King of England who opposed the French and Catholics), Acadians refused, claiming that they were not allied with France. They also did not want to join the British in fights against the Indians, who were their allies and relatives. To dominate the region militarily, culturally, and agriculturally without interference, the British expelled the Acadians, dispersing them to colonies such as Georgia and South Carolina. This eventually led the British to deport Acadians in what became known as *Le Grand Dérangement*, or the Expulsion of 1755.

The roundup and mass deportation of Acadians, which presaged British domination of much of North America, involved much cruelty, as indicated by letters from British governor, Major Charles Lawrence. In an attempt to eliminate the Acadians from Acadia, the British packed them by the hundreds into the cargo holds of ships, where many died from the cold and smallpox. At the time, Acadians numbered about 15,000, however, the Expulsion killed almost half the population. Of the survivors and those who escaped expulsion, some found their way back to the region, and many drifted through England, France, the Caribbean, and other colonies. Small pockets of descendants of Acadians can still be found in France. In 1763 there were more than 6,000 Acadians in New England. Of the thousands sent to Massachusetts, 700 reached Connecticut and then escaped to Montreal. Many reached the Carolinas; some in Georgia were sold as slaves; many eventually were taken to the West Indies as indentured servants. Most, however, eventually made their way down the Mississippi River to Louisiana. At New Orleans and other southern Louisiana ports, about 2,400 Acadians arrived between 1763 and 1776 from the American colonies, the West Indies, St. Pierre and Miquelon islands, and Acadia/Nova Scotia.

According to *Cajun Country*, after Spain gained control of Louisiana in the mid-1760s, Acadian exiles "who had been repatriated to France volunteered to the king of Spain to help settle his newly acquired colony." The Spanish government accepted their offer and paid for the transport of 1,600 settlers. When they arrived in Louisiana in 1785, colonial forts continued Spain's services to Acadian pioneers (which officially began with a proclamation by Governor Galvez in February of 1778). Forts employed and otherwise sponsored the settlers in starting their new lives by providing tools, seed corn, livestock, guns, medical services, and a church.

A second group of Acadians came 20 years later. Louisiana attracted Acadians who wanted to rejoin their kin and Acadian culture. After decades of exile, immigrants came from many different regions. The making of "Acadiana" in southern Louisiana occurred amid a broader context of French-speaking immigration to the region, including the arrival of European and American whites, African and Caribbean slaves, and free

Reenactment of an early Acadian kitchen scene at the Babineau House in Caraquet, New Brunswick, Canada.

Blacks. Like others, such as Mexicans who lived in annexed territory of the United States, Cajuns and other Louisianans became citizens when the United States acquired Louisiana from Napoleon through the Louisiana Purchase in 1803.

SETTLEMENT PATTERNS

The diaspora of Acadians in the United States interweaves with the diaspora of French Canadians. In 1990, one-third as many Americans (668,000) reported to the U.S. Census Bureau as "Acadian/Cajun" as did Americans reporting "French Canadian" (2,167,000). Louisiana became the new Acadian homeland and "creolized," or formed a cultural and ethnic hybrid, as cultures mixed. French settlers in Louisiana adapted to the subtropics. Local Indians taught them, as did the slaves brought from Africa by settlers to work their plantations. When French settlers raised a generation of sons and daughters who grew up knowing the ways of the region—

unlike the immigrants—Louisianans called these native-born, locally adapted people "Creoles." Louisianans similarly categorized slaves—those born locally were also "Creoles." By the time the Acadians arrived, Creoles had established themselves economically and socially.

French Creoles dominated Louisiana, even after Spain officially took over the colony in the mid-eighteenth century and some Spanish settled there. Louisiana also absorbed immigrants from Germany, England, and New England, in addition to those from Acadia. Spanish administrators welcomed the Acadians to Louisiana. Their large families increased the colony's population and they could serve the capital, New Orleans, as a supplier of produce. The Spanish expected the Acadians, who were generally poor, small-scale farmers who tended to keep to themselves, not to resist their administration.

At first, Spanish administrators regulated Acadians toward the fringes of Louisiana's non-Indian settlement. As Louisiana grew, some

Cajuns were pushed and some voluntarily moved with the frontier. Beginning in 1764, Cajun settlements spread above New Orleans in undeveloped regions along the Mississippi River. This area later became known as the Acadian coast. Cajun settlements spread upriver, then down the Bayou Lafourche, then along other rivers and bayous. People settled along the waterways in lines, as they had done in Acadia/Nova Scotia. Their houses sat on narrow plots of land that extended from the riverbank into the swamps. The settlers boated from house to house, and later built a road parallel to the bayou, extending the levees as long as 150 miles. The settlement also spread to the prairies, swamps, and the Gulf Coast.

INTERNAL MIGRATION

Soon after the Louisiana Purchase, the Creoles pushed many Acadians westward, off the prime farmland of the Mississippi levees, mainly by buying their lands. Besides wanting the land, many Creole sugar-planters wanted the Cajuns to leave the vicinity so that the slaves on their plantations would not see Cajun examples of freedom and self-support.

After the Cajuns had reconsolidated their society, a second exodus, on a much smaller scale, spread the Cajuns culturally and geographically. For example, a few Acadians joined wealthy Creoles as owners of plantations, rejecting their Cajun identity for one with higher social standing. Although some Cajuns stayed on the rivers and bayous or in the swamps, many others headed west to the prairies where they settled not in lines but in small, dispersed coves. As early as 1780, Cajuns headed westward into frontier lands and befriended Indians whom others feared. By the end of the nineteenth century, Cajuns had established settlements in the Louisiana-Texas border region. Texans refer to the triangle of the Acadian colonies of Beaumont, Port Arthur, and Orange as Cajun Lapland because that is where Louisiana "laps over" into Texas.

Heading westward, Cajuns first reached the eastern, then the western prairie. In the first region, densely settled by Cajuns, farmers grew corn and cotton. On the western prairie, farmers grew rice and ranchers raised cattle. This second region was thinly settled until the late 1800s when the railroad companies lured Midwesterners to the Louisiana prairies to grow rice. The arrival of Midwesterners again displaced many Cajuns; however, some remained on the prairies in clusters of small farms. A third region of Cajun settlement, to the south of the prairies and their waterways, were the coastal wetlands—one of the most distinctive regions in North America and one central to the Cajun image. The culture and seafood cuisine of these Cajuns has represented Cajuns to the world.

CAMPS

Life for Cajuns in swamps, which periodically flood, demanded adaptations such as building houses on stilts. When floods wrecked their houses, Cajuns rebuilt them. In the late 1800s, Cajun swamp dwellers began to build and live on houseboats. Currently, mobile homes with additions and large porches stand on stilts ten feet above the swamps. Cajuns and other Louisianans also established and maintained camps for temporary housing in marshes, swamps, and woods. For the Acadians, many of whom were hunters and trappers, this was a strong tradition. At first, a camp was only a temporary dwelling in order to make money. Eventually, Cajuns did not need to live in camps, because they could commute daily from home by car or powerboat. By that time, however, Cajuns enjoyed and appreciated their camps. As settlements grew, so did the desire to get away to hunt and fish; today, many Cajun families maintain a camp for recreation purposes.

ACCULTURATION AND ASSIMILATION

Cajuns have always been considered a marginal group, a minority culture. Language, culture, and kinship patterns have kept them separate, and they have maintained their sense of group identity despite difficulties. Cajun settlement patterns have isolated them and Cajun French has tended to keep its speakers out of the English-speaking mainstream.

Acadians brought a solidarity with them to Louisiana. As one of the first groups to cross the Atlantic and adopt a new identity, they felt connected to each other by their common experience. Differences in backgrounds separated the Acadians from those who were more established Americans. Creole Louisianans, with years of established communities in Louisiana, often looked down on Acadians as peasants. Some

Cajuns left their rural Cajun communities and found acceptance, either as Cajuns or by passing as some other ethnicity. Some Cajuns became gentleman planters, repudiated their origins, and joined the upper-class (white) Creoles. Others learned the ways of local Indians, as Creoles before them had done, and as the Cajuns themselves had done earlier in Acadia/Nova Scotia.

Because Cajuns usually married among themselves, as a group they do not have many surnames; however, the original population of Acadian exiles in Louisiana grew, especially by incorporating other people into their group. Colonists of Spanish, German, and Italian origins, as well as Americans of English-Scotch-Irish stock, became thoroughly acculturated and today claim Acadian descent. Black Creoles and white Cajuns mingled their bloodlines and cultures; more recently, Louisiana Cajuns include Yugoslavs and Filipinos.

Economics helped Cajuns stay somewhat separate. The majority of Cajuns farmed, hunted, and/or fished; their livelihoods hardly required them to assimilate. Moreover, until the beginning of the twentieth century, U.S. corporate culture had relatively little impact on southern Louisiana. The majority of Cajuns did not begin to Americanize until the turn of the twentieth century, when several factors combined to quicken the pace. These factors included the nationalistic fervor of the early 1900s, followed by World War I. Perhaps the most substantial change for Cajuns occurred when big business came to extract and sell southern Louisiana's oil. The discovery of oil in 1901 in Jennings, Louisiana, brought in outsiders and created salaried jobs. Although the oil industry is the region's main employer, it is also a source of economic and ecological concern because it represents the region's main polluter, threatening fragile ecosystems and finite resources.

Although the speaking of Cajun French has been crucial to the survival of Cajun traditions, it has also represented resistance to assimilation. Whereas Cajuns in the oilfields spoke French to each other at work (and still do), Cajuns in public schools were forced to abandon French because the compulsory Education Act of 1922 banned the speaking of any other language but English at school or on school grounds. While some teachers labeled Cajun French as a low-class and ignorant mode of speech, other Louisianans ridiculed the Cajuns as uneducable. As late as 1939, reports called the Cajuns "North America's last unassimilated [white] minority;" Cajuns referred to themselves, even as late as World War II, as "*le français*," and all English-speaking outsiders as "*les Americains*."

The 1930s and 1940s witnessed the education and acculturation of Cajuns into the American mainstream. Other factors affecting the assimilation of the Cajuns were the improvement of transportation, the leveling effects of the Great Depression, and the development of radio and motion pictures, which introduced young Cajuns to other cultures. Yet Cajun culture survived and resurged. After World War II, Cajun culture boomed as soldiers returned home and danced to Cajun bands, thereby renewing Cajun identity. Cajuns rallied around their traditional music in the 1950s, and in the 1960s this music gained attention and acceptance from the American mainstream. On the whole, though, the 1950s and 1960s were times of further mainstreaming for the Cajuns. As network television and other mass media came to dominate American culture, the nation's regional, ethnic cultures began to weaken. Since the 1970s, Cajuns have exhibited renewed pride in their heritage and consider themselves a national resource. By the 1980s, ethnicities first marginalized by the American mainstream became valuable as regional flavors; however, while Cajuns may be proud of the place that versions of their music and food occupy in the mainstream, they—especially the swamp Cajuns—are also proud of their physical and social marginality.

TRADITIONS, CUSTOMS, AND BELIEFS

Cajun society closely knits family members and neighbors who tend to depend on each other socially and economically, and this cooperation helps to maintain their culture. According to *Cajun Country*, "The survival—indeed the domination—of Acadian culture was a direct result of the strength of traditional social institutions and agricultural practices that promoted economic self-sufficiency and group solidarity." Cajuns developed customs to bring themselves together. For example, before roads, people visited by boat; before electrical amplification and telephones, people sang loudly in large halls, and passed news by shouting from house to house. And when Cajuns follow their customs, their culture focuses inwardly on the group and maintains itself.

Cajuns maintain distinctive values that predate the industrial age. Foremost among these, perhaps, is a traditional rejection of protocols of social hierarchy. When speaking Cajun French, for instance, Cajuns use the French familiar form of address, *tu*, rather than *vous* (except in jest) and do not address anyone as *monsieur*. Their *joie de vivre* is legendary (manifested in spicy food and lively dancing), as is their combativeness. Cajun traditions help make Cajuns formidable, mobile adversaries when fighting, trapping, hunting, or fishing. Cajun boaters invented a flatboat called the *bateau*, to pass through shallow swamps. They also built European-style luggers and skiffs, and the *pirogue*, based on Indian dugout canoes. Cajuns often race *pirogues*; or, two competitors stand at opposite ends on one and try to make each other fall in the water first. Fishermen hold their own competitions, sometimes called "fishing rodeos."

Cajuns value horses, too. American cowboy culture itself evolved partly out of one of its earliest ranching frontiers on Louisiana's Cajun prairies. Cajun ranchers developed a tradition called the barrel or buddy pickup, which evolved into a rodeo event. Today, Cajuns enjoy horse racing, trail-riding clubs, and Mardi Gras processions, called *courses*, on horseback.

Cajuns also enjoy telling stories and jokes during their abundant socializing. White Cajuns have many folktales in common with black Creoles—for example, stories about buried treasure abound in Louisiana. One reason for this proliferation was Louisiana's early and close ties to the Caribbean where piracy was rampant. Also, many people actually did bury treasure in Louisiana to keep it from banks or, during the Civil War, from invading Yankees. Typically, the stories describe buried treasure guarded by ghosts. Cajuns relish telling stories about moonshiners, smugglers, and contraband runners who successfully fool and evade federal agents.

Many Cajun beliefs fall into the mainstream's category of superstition, such as spells (*gris-gris*, to both Cajuns and Creoles) and faith healing. In legends, Madame Grandsdoigts uses her long fingers to pull the toes of naughty children at night, and the werewolf, known as *loup garou*, prowls. Omens appear in the form of blackbirds, cows, and the moon. For example, according to *Cajun Country:* "When the tips of a crescent moon point upward, [the weather] is supposed to be dry for a week. A halo of light around a full moon supposedly means clear weather for as many days as there are stars visible inside the ring."

CUISINE

Cajun cuisine, perhaps best known for its hot, red-pepper seasoning, is a blend of styles. Acadians brought with them provincial cooking styles from France. Availability of ingredients determined much of Cajun cuisine. Frontier Cajuns borrowed or invented recipes for cooking turtle, alligator, raccoon, possum, and armadillo, which some people still eat. Louisianans' basic ingredients of bean and rice dishes—milled rice, dried beans, and cured ham or smoked sausage—were easy to store over relatively long periods. Beans and rice, like gumbo and crawfish, have become fashionable cuisine in recent times. They are still often served with cornbread, thus duplicating typical nineteenth-century poor Southern fare. Cajun cooking is influenced by the cuisine of the French, Acadian, Spanish, German, Anglo-American, Afro-Caribbean, and Native American cultures.

Gumbo, a main Cajun dish, is a prime metaphor for creolization because it draws from several cultures. Its main ingredient, okra, also gave the dish its name; the vegetable, called "*guingombo*," was first imported from western Africa. Cayenne, a spicy seasoning used in subtropical cuisines, represents Spanish and Afro-Caribbean influences. Today Louisianans who eat gumbo with rice, usually call gumbo made with okra *gumbo févi*, to distinguish it from *gumbo filé*, which draws on French culinary tradition for its base, a *roux*. Just before serving, *gumbo filé* (also called *filé gumbo*) is thickened by the addition of powdered sassafras leaves, one of the Native American contributions to Louisiana cooking.

Cajuns thriftily ate many animals and parts of animals. *Gratons*, also known as cracklings, were made of pig skin. Internal organs were used in the sausages and *boudin*. White *boudin* is a spicy rice and pork sausage; red *boudin*, which is made from the same rice dressing but is flavored and colored with blood, can still be found in neighborhood *boucheries*. Edible pig guts not made into *boudin* were cooked in a *sauce piquante de débris* or entrail stew. The intestines were cleaned and used for sausage casings. Meat was carefully removed from the head and congealed for a spicy *fromage de tête de cochon* (hogshead cheese). Brains were cooked in a pungent brown sauce. Other Cajun specialties include *tasso*, a spicy Cajun version of jerky, smoked beef and pork sausages (such as *andouille* made from the large intestines), *chourice* (made from the small intestines), and *chaudin* (stuffed stomach).

Perhaps the most representative food of Cajun culture is crawfish, or mudbug. Its popularity is a relatively recent tradition. It was not until the mid-1950s, when commercial processing began to make crawfish readily available, that they gained popularity. They have retained a certain exotic aura, however, and locals like to play upon the revulsion of outsiders faced for the first time with the prospect of eating these delicious but unusual creatures by goading outsiders to suck the "head" (technically, the thorax). Like lobster, crawfish has become a valuable delicacy. The crawfish industry, a major economic force in southern Louisiana, exports internationally. However, nearly 85 percent of the annual crawfish harvest is consumed locally. Other versions of Cajun foods, such as pan-blackened fish and meats, have become ubiquitous. Chef Paul Prudhomme helped bring Cajun cuisine to national prominence.

Cooking is considered a performance, and invited guests often gather around the kitchen stove or around the barbecue pit (more recently, the butane grill) to observe the cooking and comment on it. Guests also help, tell jokes and stories, and sing songs at events such as outdoor crawfish, crab, and shrimp boils in the spring and summer, and indoor gumbos in winter.

MUSIC

The history of Cajun music goes back to Acadia/Nova Scotia, and to France. Acadian exiles, who had no instruments such as those in Santo Domingo, danced to *reels à bouche*, wordless dance music made by only their voices at stopping places on their way to Louisiana. After they arrived in Louisiana, Anglo-American immigrants to Louisiana contributed new fiddle tunes and dances, such as reels, jigs, and hoedowns. Singers also translated English songs into French and made them their own. Accordi to *Cajun Country*, "Native Americans contributed a wailing, terraced singing style in which vocal lines descend progressively in steps." Moreover, Cajun music owes much to the music of black Creoles, who contributed to Cajun music as they developed their own similiar music, which became zydeco. Since the nineteenth century, Cajuns and black Creoles have performed together.

Not only the songs, but also the instruments constitute an intercultural gumbo. Traditional Cajun and Creole instruments are French fiddles, German accordians, Spanish guitars, and an assortment of percussion instruments (triangles, washboards, and spoons), which share European and Afro-Caribbean origins. German American Jewish merchants imported diatonic accordians (shortly after they were invented in Austria early in the nineteenth century), which soon took over the lead instrumental role from the violin. Cajuns improvised and improved the instruments first by bending rake tines, replacing rasps and notched gourds used in Afro-Caribbean music with washboards, and eventually producing their own masterful accordians.

During the rise of the record industry, to sell record players in southern Louisiana, companies released records of Cajun music. Its high-pitched and emotionally charged style of singing, which evolved so that the noise of frontier dance halls could be pierced, filled the airwaves. Cajun music influenced hillbilly/country music; moreover, for a period, Harry Choates' string band defined Western swing music. Beginning in 1948, Iry Lejeune recorded country music and renditions of Amée Ardoin's Creole blues, which Ardoin recorded in the late 1920s. Lejeune prompted "a new wave of old music" and a postwar revival of Cajun culture. Southern Louisiana's music influenced Hank Williams—whose own music, in turn, has been extremely influential. "Jambalaya" was one of his most successful recordings and was based on a lively but unassuming Cajun two-step called "Grand Texas" or "L'Anse Couche-Couche." In the 1950s, "swamp pop" developed as essentially Cajun rhythm and blues or rock and roll. In the 1960s, national organizations began to try to preserve traditional Cajun music.

HOLIDAYS

Mardi Gras, which occurs on the day before Ash Wednesday, the beginning of Lent, is the carnival that precedes Lent's denial. French for "Fat Tuesday," Mardi Gras (pre-Christian Europe's New Year's Eve) is based on medieval European adaptations of even older rituals, particularly those including reversals of the social order, in which the lower classes parody the elite. Men dress as women, women as men; the poor dress as rich, the rich as poor; the old as young, the young as old; black as white, white as black.

While most Americans know Mardi Gras as the city of New Orleans celebrates it, rural Cajun Mardi Gras stems from a medieval European procession in which revelers traveled through the countryside performing in exchange for gifts. Those in a Cajun procession, called a *course* (which traditionally did not openly include women), masquerade across lines of gender, age, race, and class. They also play at crossing the line of life and death with a ritual skit, "The Dead Man Revived," in which the companions of a fallen actor revive him by dripping wine or beer into his mouth. Participants in a Cajun Mardi Gras *course* cross from house to house, storming into the yard in a mock-pillage of the inhabitant's food. Like a trick-or-treat gang, they travel from house to house and customarily get a series of chickens, from which their cooks will make a communal gumbo that night. The celebration continues as a rite of passage in many communities.

Carnival, as celebrated by Afro-Caribbeans (and as a ritual of ethnic impersonation whereby Euro- and Afro-Caribbean Americans in New Orleans chant, sing, dance, name themselves, and dress as Indians), also influences Carnival as celebrated in southern Louisiana. On one hand, the mainstream Mardi Gras celebration retains some Cajun folkloric elements, but the influence of New Orleans invariably supplants the country customs. Conversely, Mardi Gras of white, rural Cajuns differs in its geographic origins from Mardi Gras of Creole New Orleans; some organizers of Cajun Mardi Gras attempt to maintain its cultural specificity.

Cajun Mardi Gras participants traditionally wear masks, the anonymity of which enables the wearers to cross social boundaries; at one time, masks also provided an opportunity for retaliation without punishment. *Course* riders, who may be accompanied by musicians riding in their own vehicle, might surround a person's front yard, dismount and begin a ritualistic song and dance. The silent penitence of Lent, however, follows the boisterous transgression of Mardi Gras. A masked ball, as described in *Cajun Country*, "marks the final hours of revelry before the beginning of Lent the next day. All festivities stop abruptly at midnight, and many of Tuesday's rowdiest riders can be found on their knees receiving the penitential ashes on their foreheads on Wednesday."

Good Friday, which signals the approaching end of Lent, is celebrated with a traditional procession called "Way of the Cross" between the towns of Catahoula and St. Martinville. The stations of the cross, which usually hang on the walls of a church, are mounted on large oak trees between the two towns.

On Christmas Eve, bonfires dot the levees along the Mississippi River between New Orleans and Baton Rouge. This celebration, according to *Cajun Country*, has European roots: "The huge bonfires ... are descendants of the bonfires lit by ancient European civilizations, particularly along the Rhine and Seine rivers, to encourage and reinforce the sun at the winter solstice, its 'weakest' moment." Other holidays are uniquely Cajun and reflect the Catholic church's involvement in harvests. Priests bless the fields of sugar cane and the fleets of decorated shrimp boats by reciting prayers and sprinkling holy water upon them.

HEALTH AND MENTAL HEALTH ISSUES

Professional doctors were rare in rural Louisiana and only the most serious of conditions were treated by them. Although the expense of professional medical care was prohibitive even when it was available, rural Cajuns preferred to use folk cures and administered them themselves, or relied on someone adept at such cures. These healers, who did not make their living from curing other Cajuns, were called *traiteurs*, or treaters, and were found in every community. They also believed that folk practitioners, unlike their professional counterparts, dealt with the spiritual and emotional—not just the physiological—needs of the individual. Each *traiteur* typically specializes in only a few types of treatment and has his or her own cures, which may involve the laying-on of hands or making the sign of the cross and reciting of prayers drawn from passages of the Bible. Of their practices—some of which have been legitimated today as holistic medicine—some are pre-Christian, some Christian, and some modern. Residual pre-Christian traditions include roles of the full moon in healing, and left-handedness of the treaters themselves. Christian components of Cajun healing draw on faith by making use of Catholic prayers, candles, prayer beads, and crosses. Cajuns' herbal medicine derives from post-medieval French homeopathic medicine. A more recent category of Cajun cures consists of patent medicines and certain other commercial products.

Some Cajun cures were learned from Indians, such as the application of a poultice of chewing tobacco on bee stings, snakebites, boils, and headaches. Other cures came from French doctors or folk cures, such as treating stomach pains by putting a warm plate on the stomach, treating ringworm with vinegar, and treating headaches with a treater's prayers. Some Cajun cures are unique to Louisiana: for example, holding an infection over a burning cane reed, or putting a necklace of garlic on a baby with worms.

Cajuns have a higher-than-average incidence of cystic fibrosis, muscular dystrophy, albinism, and other inherited, recessive disorders, perhaps due to intermarriage with relatives who have recessive genes in common.

LANGUAGE

Cajun French, for the most part, is a spoken, unwritten language filled with colloquialisms and slang. Although the French spoken by Cajuns in different parts of Louisiana varies little, it differs from the standard French of Paris as well as the French of Quebec; it also differs from the French of both white and black Creoles.

Cajun French-speakers hold their lips more loosely than do the Parisians. They tend to shorten phrases, words, and names, and to simplify some verb conjugations. Nicknames are ubiquitous, such as "'tit joe" or "'tit black," where "'tit" is slang for "petite" or "little." Cajun French simplifies the tenses of verbs by making them more regular. It forms the present participle of verbs—e.g., "is singing"—in a way that would translate directly as "is after to sing." So, "Marie is singing," in Cajun French is "Marie est apres chanter." Another distinguishing feature of Cajun French is that it retains nautical usages, which reflects the history of Acadians as boaters. For example, the word for tying a shoelace is amerrer (to moor [a boat]), and the phrase for making a U-turn in a car is virer de bord (to come about [with a sailboat]).

Generally, Cajun French shows the influence of its specific history in Louisiana and Acadia/Nova Scotia, as well as its roots in coastal France. Since Brittany, in northern coastal France, is heavily Celtic, Cajun French bears "grammatical and other linguistic evidences of Celtic influence." Some scattered Indian words survive in Cajun French, such as "bayou," which came from the Muskhogean Indian word, "bayuk," through Cajun French, and into English.

Louisiana, which had already made school attendance compulsory, implemented a law in the 1920s that constitutionally forbade the speaking of French in public schools and on school grounds. The state expected Cajuns to come to school and to leave their language at home. This attempt to assimilate the Cajuns met with some success; young Cajuns appeared to be losing their language. In an attempt to redress this situation, the Council for the Development of French in Louisiana (CODOFIL) recently reintroduced French into many Louisianan schools. However, the French is the standard French of Parisians, not that of Cajuns. Although French is generally not spoken by the younger generation in Maine, New England schools are beginning to emphasize it and efforts to repeal the law that made English the sole language in Maine schools have been successful. In addition, secondary schools have begun to offer classes in Acadian and French history.

In 1976, Revon Reed wrote in a mix of Cajun and standard French for his book about Cajun Louisiana, Lâche pas la patate, which translates as, "Don't drop the potato" (a Cajun idiom for "Don't neglect to pass on the tradition"). Anthologies of stories and series of other writings have been published in the wake of Reed's book. However, Cajun French was essentially a spoken language until the publication of Randall Whatley's Cajun French textbook (Conversational Cajun French I [Baton Rouge: Louisiana State University Press, 1978]).

In the oilfields, on fishing boats, and other places where Cajuns work together, though, they have continued to speak Cajun French. Storytellers, joke tellers, and singers use Cajun French for its expressiveness, and for its value as in-group communication. Cajun politicians and businessmen find it useful to identify themselves as fellow insiders to Cajun constituents and patrons by speaking their language.

FAMILY AND COMMUNITY DYNAMICS

Cajuns learned to rely on their families and communities when they had little else. Traditionally they have lived close to their families and villages. Daily visits were usual, as were frequent parties and dances, including the traditional Cajun house-party called the fais-dodo, which is Cajun baby talk for "go to sleep," as in "put all the small kids in a back bedroom to sleep" during the party. Traditionally, almost everyone who would come to a party would be a neighbor from the same community or a family member. Cajuns of all ages and abilities participated in music-making and dancing since almost everyone was a dancer or a player.

In the 1970s, 76 percent of the surnames accounted for 86 percent of all Cajuns; each of those surnames reflected an extended family which functioned historically as a Cajun subcommunity. In addition to socializing together, a community gathered to do a job for someone in need, such as building a house or harvesting a field. Members of Cajun communities traditionally took turns butchering animals and distributing shares of the meat. Although *boucheries* were essentially social events, they were a useful way to get fresh meat to participating families. Today, *boucheries* are unnecessary because of modern refrigeration methods and the advent of supermarkets, but a few families still hold *boucheries* for the fun of it, and a few local festivals feature *boucheries* as a folk craft. This cooperation, called *coups de main* (literally, "strokes of the hand"), was especially crucial in the era before worker's compensation, welfare, social security, and the like. Today such cooperation is still important, notably for the way it binds together members of a community.

A challenge to a group's cohesiveness, however, was infighting. Fighting could divide a community, yet, on the other hand, as a spectator sport, it brought communities together for an activity. The *bataille au mouchoir*, as described in *Cajun Country*, was a ritualized fight "in which the challenger offered his opponent a corner of his handkerchief and the two went at each other with fists or knives, each holding a corner, until one gave up." Organized bare-knuckle fights persisted at least until the late 1960s. More recently, many Cajuns have joined boxing teams. Neighboring communities maintain rivalries in which violence has historically been common. A practice called *casser le bal* ("breaking up the dance") or *prendre la place* ("taking over the place") involved gangs starting fights with others or among themselves with the purpose of ending a dance. Threats of violence and other difficulties of travel hardly kept Cajuns at home, though. According to *Cajun Country*, "As late as 1932, Saturday night dances were attended by families within a radius of fifty miles, despite the fact that less than a third of the families owned automobiles at that time."

Cajun family relations are important to all family members. Cajun fathers, uncles, and grandfathers join mothers, aunts, and grandmothers in raising children; and children participate in family matters. Godfathering and godmothering are still very important in Cajun country. Even non-French-speaking youth usually refer to their godparents as *parrain* and *marraine*, and consider them family. Nevertheless, traditionally it has been the mother who has transmitted values and culture to the children. Cajuns have often devalued formal education, viewing it as a function of the Catholic church—not the state. Families needed children's labor; and, until the oil boom, few jobs awaited educated Cajuns. During the 1920s many Cajuns attended school not only because law required it and jobs awaited them, but also because an agricultural slump meant that farming was less successful then.

COURTSHIP

Although today Cajuns tend to date like other Americans, historically, pre-modern traditions were the rule. Females usually married before the age of 20 or risked being considered "an old maid." A young girl required a chaperon—usually a parent or an older brother or uncle, to protect her honor and prevent premarital pregnancy, which could result in banishment until her marriage. If a courtship seemed to be indefinitely prolonged, the suitor might receive an envelope from his intended containing a coat, which signified that the engagement was over. Proposals were formally made on Thursday evenings to the parents, rather than to the fiancee herself. Couples who wanted to marry did not make the final decision; rather, this often required the approval of the entire extended family.

Because Cajuns traditionally marry within their own community where a high proportion of residents are related to one another, marriages between cousins are not unusual. Pairs of siblings frequently married pairs of siblings from another family. Although technically forbidden, first-cousin marriages have occurred as well. Financial concerns influenced such a choice because intermarriage kept property within family groupings. One result of such marriages is that a single town might be dominated by a handful of surnames.

WEDDINGS

Cajun marriage customs are frequently similar to those of other Europeans. Customarily, older unmarried siblings may be required to dance barefoot, often in a tub, at the reception or wedding dance. This may be to remind them of the poverty awaiting them in old age if they do not begin families of their own. Guests contribute to the new household by pinning money to the bride's veil in exchange for a dance with her or a kiss. Before the wedding dance is over, the bride will often be wearing a headdress of money. Today, wedding guests have extended this practice to the groom as well, covering his suit jacket with bills.

One rural custom involved holding the wedding reception in a commercial dance hall and giving the entrance fees to the newlyweds. Another Cajun wedding custom, "flocking the bride," involved the community's women bringing a young chick from each of their flocks so that the new bride could start her own brood. These gifts helped a bride establish a small measure of independence, in that wives could could sell their surplus eggs for extra money over which their husbands had no control.

RELIGION

Roman Catholicism is a major element of Cajun culture and history. Some pre-Christian traditions seem to influence or reside in Cajun Catholicism. Historians partly account for Cajun Catholicism's variation from Rome's edicts by noting that historically Acadians often lacked contact with orthodox clergymen.

Baptism of Cajun children occurs in infancy. Cajun homes often feature altars, or shrines with lawn statues, such as those of Our Lady of the Assumption—whom Pope Pius XI in 1938 declared the patroness of Acadians worldwide—in homemade grottoes made of pieces of bathtubs or oil drums. Some Cajun communal customs also revolve around Catholicism. For decades, it was customary for men to race their horses around the church during the sermon. Wakes call for mourners to keep company with each other around the deceased so that the body is never left alone. Restaurants and school cafeterias cater to Cajuns by providing alternatives to meat for south Louisiana's predominantly Catholic students during Ash Wednesday and Lenten Fridays. Some uniquely Cajun beliefs surround their Catholicism. For example, legends say that "the Virgin will slap children who whistle at the dinner table;" another taboo forbids any digging on Good Friday, which is, on the other hand, believed to be the best day to plant parsley.

EMPLOYMENT AND ECONOMIC TRADITIONS

Coastal Louisiana is home to one of America's most extensive wetlands in which trapping and hunting have been important occupations. In the 1910s extensive alligator hunting allowed huge increases in *rat musqué* (muskrat) populations. Muskrat overgrazing promoted marsh erosion. At first the muskrats were trapped mainly to reduce their numbers, but cheap Louisiana muskrat pelts hastened New York's capture of America's fur industry from St. Louis, and spurred the rage for muskrat and raccoon coats that typified the 1920s. Cajuns helped Louisiana achieve its long-standing reputation as America's primary fur producer. Since the 1960s, Cajuns in the fur business have raised mostly nutria.

The original Acadians and Cajuns were farmers, herders, and ranchers, but they also worked as carpenters, coopers, blacksmiths, fishermen, shipbuilders, trappers, and sealers. They learned trapping, trading, and other skills for survival from regional Indians. Industrialization has not ended such traditions. Workers in oilfields and on oil rigs have schedules whereby they work for one or two weeks and are then off work for the same amount of time, which allows them time to pursue traditional occupations like trapping and fishing.

Because present-day laws ban commercial hunting, this activity has remained a recreation, but an intensely popular one. Louisiana is located at the southern end of one of the world's major flyways, providing an abundance of migratory birds like dove, woodcock, and a wide variety of ducks and geese. A wide range of folk practice is associated with hunting—how to build blinds, how to call game, how to handle, call and drive packs of hunting dogs, and how to make decoys. Cajun custom holds that if you hunt or fish a certain area, you have the clear-cut folk right to defend it from trespassers. Shooting a trespasser is "trapper's justice." Certain animals are always illegal to hunt, and some others are illegal to hunt during their off-season. Cajuns sometimes circumvent restrictions on hunting illegal game, which is a practice called "outlawing."

According to some claims, the modern American cattle industry began on the Cajun prairie almost a full century before Anglo-Americans even began to move to Texas. Learning from the Spanish and the Indians, Cajuns and black Creoles were among the first cowboys in America, and they took part in some of this country's earliest cattle drives. Cattle rearing remains part of prairie Cajun life today, but the spread of agriculture, especially rice, has reduced both its economic importance and much of its flamboyant ways. In the nonagricultural coastal marshes, however, much of the old-style of cattle rearing remains.

Cajuns catch a large proportion of American seafood. In addition to catching their own food, many Cajuns are employees of shrimp companies, which own both boats and factories, with their own brand name. Some fisherman and froggers catch large catfish, turtles, and bullfrogs by hand, thus preserving an ancient art. And families frequently go crawfishing together in the spring.

The gathering and curing of Spanish moss, which was widely employed for stuffing of mattresses and automobile seats until after World War II, was an industry found only in the area. Cajun fishermen invented or modified numerous devices: nets and seines, crab traps, shrimp boxes, bait boxes, trotlines, and frog grabs. Moss picking, once an important part-time occupation for many wetlands Cajuns, faded with the loss of the natural resource and changes in technology. Dried moss was replaced by synthetic materials used in stuffing car seats and furniture. Now there is a mild resurgence in the tradition as moss is making a comeback from the virus which once threatened it and as catfish and crawfish farmers have found that it makes a perfect breeding nest.

Cajuns learned to be economically self-reliant, if not completely self-sufficient. They learned many of southern Louisiana's ways from local Indians, who taught them about native edible foods and the cultivation of a variety of melons, gourds, and root crops. The French and black Creoles taught the Cajuns how to grow cotton, sugarcane, and okra; they learned rice and soybean production from Anglo-Americans. As a result, Cajuns were able to establish small farms and produce an array of various vegetables and livestock. Such crops also provided the cash they needed to buy such items as coffee, flour, salt, and tobacco, in addition to cloth and farming tools. A result of such Cajun agricultural success is that today Cajuns and Creoles alike still earn their livelihood by farming.

Cajuns traded with whomever they wanted to trade, regardless of legal restrictions. Soon after their arrival in Louisiana, they were directed by the administration to sell their excess crops to the government. Many Cajuns became bootleggers.

One of their proudest historical roles was assisting the pirate-smuggler Jean Lafitte in an early and successful smuggling operation.

In the twentieth century, the Cajuns' trading system has declined as many Cajuns work for wages in the oil industry. In the view of some Cajuns, moreover, outside oilmen from Texas—or "Takes-us"—have been depriving them of control over their own region's resource, by taking it literally out from under them and reaping the profits. Some Cajun traders have capitalized on economic change by selling what resources they can control to outside markets: for example, fur trappers have done so, as have fishermen, and farmers such as those who sell their rice to the Budweiser brewery in Houston.

POLITICS AND GOVERNMENT

Cajuns, many of whom are conservative Democrats today, have been involved at all levels of Louisiana politics. Louisiana's first elected governor, as well as the state's first Cajun governor, was Alexander Mouton, who took office in 1843. Yet perhaps the most well known of Louisiana's politicians is Cajun governor Edwin Edwards (1927-), who has served for more than ten years in that office—the first French-speaking Catholic to do so in almost half a century. In recent decades, more Cajuns have entered electoral politics to regain some control from powerful oil companies.

MILITARY

Historically, Cajuns have been drafted and named for symbolic roles in pivotal fights over North America. In the mid-1700s in Acadia/Nova Scotia, when the French colonial army drafted Acadians, they weakened the Acadians' identity to the British as "French Neutrals," and prompted the British to try to expel all Acadians from the region. In 1778, when France joined the American Revolutionary War against the British, the Marquis de Lafayette declared that the plight of the Acadians helped bring the French into the fight. The following year, 600 Cajun volunteers joined Galvez and fought the British. In 1815, Cajuns joined Andrew Jackson in preventing the British from retaking the United States. Cajuns were also active in the American Civil War;

General Alfred Mouton (1829-1864), the son of Alexander Mouton, commanded the Eighteenth Louisiana Regiment in the Battle of Pittsburgh Landing (1862), the Battle of Shiloh (1863), and the Battle of Mansfield (1864), where he was killed by a sniper's bullet.

INDIVIDUAL AND GROUP CONTRIBUTIONS

ACADEMIA

Thomas J. Arceneaux, who was Dean Emeritus of the College of Agriculture at the University of Southwestern Louisiana, conducted extensive research in weed control, training numerous Cajun rice and cattle farmers in the process. A descendent of Louis Arceneaux, who was the model for the hero in Longfellow's *Evangeline*, Arceneaux also designed the Louisiana Cajun flag. Tulane University of Louisiana professor Alcé Fortier was Louisiana's first folklore scholar and one of the founders of the American Folklore Society (AFS). Author of *Lâche pas la patate* (1976), a book describing Cajun Louisiana life, Revon Reed has also launched a small Cajun newspaper called *Mamou Prairie*.

ART

Lulu Olivier's traveling "Acadian Exhibit" of Cajun weaving led to the founding of the Council for the Development of French in Louisiana (CODOFIL), and generally fostered Cajun cultural pride.

CULINARY ARTS

Chef Paul Prudhomme's name graces a line of Cajun-style supermarket food, "Chef Paul's."

MUSIC

Dewey Balfa (1927-), Gladius Thibodeaux, and Louis Vinesse Lejeune performed at the 1964 Newport Folk Festival and inspired a renewed pride in Cajun music. Dennis McGee performed and recorded regularly with black Creole accordionist and singer Amédé Ardoin in the 1920s and 1930s; together they improvised much of what was to become the core repertoire of Cajun music.

SPORTS

Cajun jockeys Kent Desormeaux and Eddie Delahoussaye became famous, as did Ron Guidry, the fastballer who led the New York Yankees to win the 1978 World Series, and that year won the Cy Young Award for his pitching. Guidry's nicknames were "Louisiana Lightnin'" and "The Ragin' Cajun."

MEDIA

PRINT

Acadiana Catholic.
Formerly *The Morning Star*, it was founded in 1954 and is primarily a religious monthly.

Contact: Barbara Gutierrez, Editor.
Address: 1408 Carmel Avenue, Lafayette, Louisiana 70501-5215.
Telephone: (318) 261-5511.
Fax: (318) 261-5603.

Acadian Genealogy Exchange.
Devoted to Acadians, French Canadian families sent into exile in 1755. Carries family genealogies, historical notes, cemetery lists, census records, and church and civil registers. Recurring features include inquiries and answers, book reviews, and news of research.

Contact: Janet B. Jehn.
Address: 863 Wayman Branch Road, Covington, Kentucky 41015.
Telephone: (606) 356-9825.

Acadiana Profile.
Published by the Acadian News Agency since 1969, this is a magazine for bilingual Louisiana.

Contact: Trent Angers, Editor.
Address: Acadian News Agency, Inc., Box 52247, Oil Center Station, Lafayette, Louisiana 70505.
Telephone: (800) 200-7919.

Cajun Country Guide.
Covers Cajun and Zydeco dance halls, Creole and Caju restaurants, swamp tours, and other sites in the southern Louisiana region.

Contact: Macon Fry or Julie Posner, Editors.

Address: Pelican Publishing Co., 1101 Monroe Street, P.O. Box 3110, Gretna, Louisiana 70054.

Telephone: (504) 368-1175; or, (800) 843-1724.

Fax: (504) 368-1195.

Mamou Acadian Press.
Founded in 1955, publishes weekly.

Contact: Bernice Ardoin, Editor.

Address: P.O. Box 360, Mamou, Louisiana 70554.

Telephone: (318) 363-3939.

Fax: (318) 363-2841.

Rayne Acadian Tribune.
A newspaper with a Democratic orientation; founded in 1894.

Contact: Steven Bandy, Editor.

Address: 108 North Adams Avenue, P.O. Box 260, Rayne, Louisiana 70578.

Telephone: (318) 334-3186.

Fax: (318) 334-2069.

The Times of Acadiana.
Weekly newspaper covering politics, lifestyle, entertainment, and general news; founded in 1980.

Contact: Richard Baudouin, Editor.

Address: 201 Jefferson Street, P.O. Box 3528, Lafayette, Louisiana 70502.

Telephone: (318) 237-3560.

Fax: (318) 233-7484.

RADIO

KAFB-FM (97.7).
This station, which has a country format, plays "Cajun and Zydeco Music" from 6:00 a.m. to 9:00 a.m. on Saturdays.

Contact: Johnny Bordelon, Station Manager.

Address: 100 Chester, Box 7, Marksville, Louisiana 71351.

Telephone: (318) 253-9331.

KDLP-AM (1170).
Country, ethnic, and French-language format.

Contact: Paul J. Cook.

Address: 182 Pluto Street, Bayou Vista, Louisiana 70381.

Telephone: (504) 395-2853.

KJEF-AM (1290), FM (92.9).
Country, ethnic, and French-language format.

Contact: Bill Bailey, General Manager.

Address: 122 North Market Street, Jennings, Louisiana 70545.

Telephone: (318) 824-2934.

Fax: (318) 824-1384.

KQKI-FM (95.3).
Country, ethnic, and French-language format.

Contact: Paul J. Cook.

Address: 182 Pluto Street, Morgan City, Louisiana 70380.

Telephone: (504) 395-2853.

Fax: (504) 395-5094.

KROF-AM (960).
Ethnic format.

Contact: Garland Bernard, General Manager.

Address: Highway 167 North, Box 610, Abbeville, Louisiana 70511-0610.

Telephone: (318) 893-2531.

Fax: (318) 893-2569.

KVOL-AM (1330), FM (105.9).
Blues, ethnic format.

Contact: Roger Cavaness, General Manager.

Address: 123 East Main Street, Lafayette, Louisiana 70501.

Telephone: (318) 233-1330.

Fax: (318) 237-7733.

KVPI-AM 1050.
Country, ethnic, and French-language format.

Contact: Jim Soileau, General Manager.

Address: 809 West LaSalle Street, P.O. Drawer J, Ville Platte, Louisiana 70586.

Telephone: (318) 363-2124.

Fax: (318) 363-3574.

ORGANIZATIONS AND ASSOCIATIONS

The Center for Acadian and Creole Folklore.
Located at the University of Southwestern Louisiana (*Université des Acadiens*), the center organizes festivals, special performances, and television and radio programs; it offers classes and

workshops through the French and Francophone Studies Program; it also sponsors musicians as adjunct professors at the university.

The Council for the Development of French in Louisiana (CODOFIL).

A proponent of the standard French language, this council arranges visits, exchanges, scholarships, and conferences; it also publishes a free bilingual newsletter.

Address: *Louisiane Française, Boite Postale 3936, Lafayette, Louisiana 70502.*

The International Relations Association of Acadiana (TIRAA).

This private-sector economic development group funds various French Renaissance activities in Cajun country.

The Madawaska Historical Society.

Promotes local historical projects and celebrates events important in the history of Acadians in Maine.

MUSEUMS AND RESEARCH CENTERS

Visitors can see preservations and reconstructions of many nineteenth-century buildings at the Acadian Village and Vermilionville in Lafayette; at the Louisiana State University, Rural Life Museum in Baton Rouge, and at the Village Historique Acadien at Caraquet.

Researchers can find sources at Nichols State University Library in Thibodaux; at the Center for Acadian and Creole Folklore of the University of Southwestern Louisiana; and at the Center for Louisiana Studies at the University of Southwestern Louisiana.

SOURCES FOR ADDITIONAL STUDY

Ancelet, Barry, Jay D. Edwards, and Glen Pitre (with additional material by Carl Brasseaux, Fred B. Kniffen, Maida Bergeron, Janet Shoemaker, and Mathe Allain). *Cajun Country*. Jackson: University of Mississippi Press, 1991.

Ancelet, Barry, and Elemore Morgan, Jr. *The Makers of Cajun Music*. Austin: University of Texas Press, 1984.

Brasseaux, Carl. *Founding of New Acadia, 1765-1803; In Search of Evangeline: Birth and Evolution of the Myth*. Thibodaux, Louisiana: Blue Heron Press, 1988.

Cajuns: Essays on Their History and Culture, edited by Glenn Conrad. Lafayette, Louisiana: Center for Louisiana Studies, University of Southwestern Louisiana, 1978.

Comeaux, Malcolm. *Attchafalaya Swamp Life: Settlement and Folk Occupations*. Baton Rouge: Louisiana State University, Geoscience Publications, 1972.

The First Franco-Americans: New England Life Histories From the Federal Writers Project, 1938-1939, edited by C. Stewart Doty. Orono: University of Maine at Orono Press, 1985.

Griffiths, Naomi Elizabeth Saundaus. *The Acadians: Creation of a People*. New York, McGraw-Hill Ryerson, 1973.

Hallowell, Christopher L. *People of the Bayou: Cajun Life in Lost America*, illustrations by Joe Deffes. New York: Dutton, 1979.

Reed, Revon Reed. *Lâche pas la patate*. Montreal: Parti Pris, 1976.

Rushton, William Faulkner. *The Cajuns: From Acadia to Louisiana*. New York: Farrar, Straus, Giroux, 1979.

ALBANIAN AMERICANS

by
Jane Jurgens

OVERVIEW

Albania is a mountainous country, 28,748 square miles in size, slightly larger than the state of Maryland. It is located in southeastern Europe and borders Montenegro, Serbia, and Macedonia on the north and east, Greece in the south and southeast, and the Adriatic Sea on the west. The name Albania was given by the Romans in ancient times (after a port called Albanopolis); but the Albanians themselves call their country Shiqiptare ("Sons of the Eagle"). The majority of the country's population of 3,360,000 consists of Albanians (more than 85 percent) in addition to assorted minorities: Greeks, Bulgarians, Gypsies, Macedonians, Serbs, Jews, and Vlachs. More than two million Albanians live in neighboring Balkan countries (e.g., Kosovo Region in Yugoslavia, Macedonia, and Turkey) as well as in other countries. The country's capital is Tirana; the Albanian flag is red with a black double-edged eagle, the symbol of freedom. The national language is Albanian.

HISTORY

Albanians descend from the ancient Illyrians. Conquered by the Romans in the third century A.D., they were later incorporated into the Byzantine Empire (395 A.D.) and were subjected to foreign invasions by Ghots, Huns, Avars, Serbs,

Croats, and Bulgarians. In 1468 Albania became part of the Ottoman Empire despite strong resistance by Gjergj Kastrioti Skenderbeu (George Castrioti Skanderbeg, 1403-1468), who is the most outstanding hero of Albania's fight against foreign subjugation. At the beginning of the nineteenth century, Albania's fight for independence intensified under the leadership of Naim Frasheri (1846-1900), Sami Frasheri (1850-1904), and Andon Zaki Cajupi (1866-1930). During World War I, Albania became a protectorate of the Great Powers after a short period of independence in 1912. It once again gained full independence in 1920, first as a republic and since 1928 as a monarchy under King Ahmet Zogu (1895-1961). In 1939, Albania was invaded and occupied by Italy; it regained independence after World War II, but under a Communist regime (led by Enver Hoxha, 1908-1985) which outlawed religion and suppressed the people. After the collapse of communism in 1991, Albania became a free and democratic country with a multi-party parliamentarian system under President Sali Berisha.

THE FIRST ALBANIANS

Few Albanians came to the United States before the twentieth century. The first Albanian, whose name is lost, is reported to have come to the United States in 1876, but soon relocated to Argentina. Kole Kristofor (Nicholas Christopher), from the town of Katundi, was the first recorded Albanian to arrive in the United States, probably between 1884 and 1886. He returned to Albania and came back to the United States in 1892. In *The Albanians in America,* Constantine Demo records the names of 16 other Albanians who either came with Kole or arrived soon after. They came from Katundi, located in southern Albania.

SIGNIFICANT IMMIGRATION WAVES

Albanians are the most recent group of Europeans to immigrate to the United States and their numbers have remained small. Prior to World War I, Albanians migrated to America because of poor economic conditions, political concerns, or to escape military conscription in the Turkish army. Many Albanians (between 20,000 and 30,000) who fled Albania for political reasons returned to Albania between 1919 and 1925. Many of these same Albanians re-migrated to the United States, intending to remain permanently in America. Another wave immigrated after Albania came

under Communist control in 1944. After the fall of communism, Albanians began entering the United States in increasing numbers between 1990 and 1991. There are no accurate immigration statistics on the most recent immigration.

According to U.S. immigration statistics, between the years 1931 and 1975, the total number of Albanians entering the United States was 2,438. After 1982, the official number of Albanians entering the United States is as follows: 1983 (22); 1984 (32); 1985 (45); 1986 (n/a); 1987 (62); 1988 (82) 1989 (69); 1990 (n/a); 1991 (141). These immigration figures do not reflect accurately the number of Albanians living in the United States. The 1990 population census reports the number of people claiming at least one ancestor as Albanian at 47,710, although the total population in the United States may range from 75,000 to 150,000 or more.

SETTLEMENT PATTERNS

Early Albanian immigrants settled around Boston and then moved to other parts of Massachusetts where unskilled factory labor was plentiful. Prior to 1920, most of the Albanians who migrated to the United States were Orthodox Tosks from the city of Korce in southern Albania. Most were young males who either migrated for economic gain or were seeking political asylum and did not intend to remain permanently in the United

States. They lived in community barracks or *konaks*, where they could live cheaply and send money home. The *konak* gradually gave way to more permanent family dwellings as more women and children joined Albanian men in the United States. Early Massachusetts settlements were established in Worcester, Natick, Southbridge, Cambridge, and Lowell. The 1990 census reveals that the largest number of Albanians live in New York City with a high concentration in the Bronx, followed by Massachusetts, Michigan, New Jersey, Illinois, California, Ohio, and Pennsylvania. Settlements of Albanians can be found in Chicago, Los Angeles, Denver, Detroit, New Orleans, Miami, Pittsburgh, and Washington, D.C.

ACCULTURATION AND ASSIMILATION

Current studies that fully record the experiences and the contributions of Albanian Americans in the United States do not exist. Albanian neighborhoods have tended to resist assimilation in the United States. The communities in New York and Massachusetts have tended to be restricted and interaction with other groups has been infrequent. Other groups of Albanians in the Midwest may have assimilated more quickly. In 1935, a newspaper reported that the Albanians were "not a clannish people ... [they] associate freely with other nationalities, do business with them, partake of their common culture, and participate in a typically middle class way to the general life of the city" (Arch Farmer, "All the World Sends Sons to Become Americans," *Chicago Sunday Tribune*, July 28, 1935). Albanians have often been confused with other ethnic groups, such as Greeks or Armenians. They have succeeded in preserving a sense of communal identity, customs, and traditions in the numerous clubs, associations and coffee-houses (*vatra*) that have been organized wherever Albanians live.

Most of the early Albanians who immigrated to the United States were illiterate. According to Denna Page in *The Albanian-American Odyssey*, it was estimated that of the 5,000 Albanians in America in 1906, only 20 of them could read or write their own language. Due to the strong efforts of community leaders to make books, pamphlets, and other educational materials (especially the newspaper, *Kombi*) available in the *konaks*, the rate of illiteracy declined significantly. By 1919, 15,000 of 40,000 Albanians could read and write their own language. Albanians remained suspicious of American ways of life and were often reluctant to send their children to American schools. Gradually, they accepted the fact that an education provided the foundation for a better way of life in America.

CUISINE

Albanian dishes have been heavily influenced by Turkey, Greece, Armenia, and Syria. Recipes have often been adapted and altered to suit American tastes. Albanians enjoy a variety of appetizers, soups, casseroles, pilaf, pies, stews, and desserts. Salads (*sallate*) are made with cabbage, lettuce, onions, peppers, olives, and feta cheese. *Sallate me patate* is a potato salad. Soups are made with a variety of ingredients such as beans, chicken, lentils, and fish. *Pace*, a soup made with lamb's tripe, is served at Easter. Albanian pies, *lakror-byrek*, are prepared with a variety of *gjelle* ("filling"). Fillings may be lamb, beef, cabbage, leeks, onions, squash, or spinach, combined with milk, eggs, and olive oil. A *lakror* known as *brushtul lakror* is made with a cottage and feta cheese filling, butter and eggs. *Domate me qepe* is a *lakror* made with an onion and tomato filling. Stews are made with beef, rabbit, lamb, veal, and chicken, which are combined with cabbage, spinach, green beans, okra, or lentils. Favorites include *mish me patate* (lamb with potatoes), *comblek* (beef with onions) and *comblek me lepur* (rabbit stew). A popular dish with Albanian Italians living in Sicily is Olives and Beef Albanesi-Siciliano, which consists of brown, salted beef cubes in a sauce of tomatoes, parsley, garlic, olives, and olive oil and served with *taccozzelli* (rectangles of pasta and goat cheese). *Dollma* is a term applied to a variety of stuffed dishes, which consist of cabbage, green peppers, or vine leaves, and may be filled with rice, bread, onions, and garlic. An Albanian American variation of the traditionally Greek lasagna-like dish, *moussaka*, is made with potatoes and hamburger instead of eggplant. Albanians enjoy a variety of candies, cookies, custards, sweet breads, and preserves. They include *halva*, a confection made with sugar, flour, butter, maple syrup, water, oil, and nuts; *te matur*, a pastry filled with butter and syrup; *baklava*, a filo pastry made with nuts, sugar, and cinnamon; *kadaif*, a pastry made with shredded dough, butter, and walnuts; and *lokume*, a Turkish paste. Popular cookies include *kurabie*, a butter cookie made without liquid; *finique*, a filled cookie with many variations; and *kuluraqka-kulure*, Albanian "tea cookies." *Te dred-*

hura, bukevale, and *brustull* are hot sweet breads. Family members will announce the birth of a child by making and distributing *petulla,* pieces of fried dough sprinkled with sugar or dipped in syrup. Albanians enjoy Turkish coffee or Albanian coffee (*kafe*), Albanian whiskey (*raki*) and wine. *Kos,* a fermented milk drink, is still popular.

TRADITIONAL COSTUMES

Albanian costumes have been influenced by Turkey, Greece, and Persian-Tartar designs. Albanian traditional costumes vary depending on the region. In countries where Albanians have established themselves, traditional costumes often distinguish the region in Albania from which the Albanian originally came. A man's costume from Malesia (Malcija Vogel area), for example, consists of close-fitting woolen trousers with black cord trim, an apron of wool with a leather belt buckled over it, and a silk jacket with long dull red sleeves with white stripes. A long sleeveless coat may be worn over the jacket along with an outer, short-sleeved jacket (*dzurdin*). The head and neck may be covered with a white cloth. A style of male dress most often seen in the United States is the *fustanella,* a full, white pleated skirt; a black and gold jacket; a red flat fez with a large tassel (*puskel*); and shoes with black pompoms.

Women's clothing tends to be more colorful than the men's clothing. Northern Albanian costumes tend to be more ornamental and include a distinctive metal belt. Basic types of costume include a wide skirt (*xhublete*), long shirt or blouse (*krahol*), and a short woolen jacket (*xhoke*). The traditional costume of Moslem women may include a tightly pleated skirt (*kanac*) or large woollen trousers (*brekeshe*). Aprons are a pervasive feature in every type of women's costume and great variety is seen in their shape and embroidery. Many Albanian Americans often wear traditional costumes during Independence Day celebrations and other special occasions and social events.

HOLIDAYS AND CELEBRATIONS

Since Albanian Americans are members of either Roman Catholic, Orthodox, or Islamic faiths, many religious festivals and holy days are observed. November 28 is celebrated as Albanian Independence Day, the day that Albanians declared their independence from the Ottoman Empire in 1912. Many Albanian Albanians also recognize the Kosova declaration of independence from Serbia on July 2, 1990.

MUSICAL TRADITIONS

Although the Albanian musical tradition has been influenced by neighboring countries such as Greece, much of the musical folklore remains distinct. Albania has had a rich tradition of musical and theatrical activities. In 1915, Albanian Americans organized the Boston Mandolin Club and the Albanian String Orchestra. They also had amateur groups perform plays by Albanian authors. Because the heroic sense of life has always been part of Albanian life, ballads are often recited and sung in an epic-recitative form that celebrates not only fantastic heroes of the past but also more recent heroes and their deeds in modern history. Songs may be accompanied by traditional instruments such as the two stringed *cifteli,* a lute instrument, and a*lahuta,* a one-stringed violin.

LANGUAGE

Albanian is probably part of the Illyrian branch of eastern Indo-European. It is a descendant of Dacian, one of the ancient languages that were among the Thraco-Phrygian group once spoken in Anatolia and the Balkan Peninsula. Its closest modern relative is Armenian. Today, Albanian is spoken in two major dialects (with many subdialects) in Albania and in neighboring Kosova—*Tosk* (about two-thirds of the population) and *Gheg* (the remaining one-third). A third dialect (*arberesh*) is spoken in Greece and southern Italy. Throughout the centuries, Albania has endured numerous invasions and occupations of foreign armies, all of whom have left their influence on the language. Despite outside influence, a distinct Albanian language has survived. Albanians call their language "*shqip.*"

Until the early twentieth century, Albanians used the Greek, Latin, and Turko-Arabic alphabets and mixtures of these alphabets. In 1908, Albania adopted a standard Latin alphabet of 26 letters, which was made official in 1924. During the 1920s and 1930s, the government tried to establish a mixed Tosk and Gheg dialect from the Elbascan region as the official language. In 1952, a standardized Albanian language was adopted, which is a mixture of Gheg and Tosk but with a prevailing Tosk element. In addition to the letters of the Latin alphabet, the Albanian language adds: "dh," "gf," "ll," "nj," "rr," "sh," "th," "xh," and "zh." Albanian is taught at such universities as the University of California-San Diego, University of Chicago, University of North Carolina-

Harry Bajraktari poses in his Bronx, New York, office. He is the publisher of *Illyria,* an Albanian/English newspaper.

Chapel Hill, and Cleveland State University. Libraries with Albanian language collections include the Library of Congress, Chicago Public Library, Boston Public Library, New York Public Library (Donnel Library Center), and Queens Borough Public Library.

GREETINGS AND OTHER POPULAR EXPRESSIONS

Some common expressions in the Albanian language include: *Po* ("Yes"); *Jo* ("No"); *Te falemnderit/Ju falemnderit* ("Thank you"); *Po, ju lutem* ("Yes, please"); *Miredita* ("Hello" or "Good day"); *Miremengjes* ("Good Morning"); *Si jeni?* ("How are you?"); *Gezohem t'ju njoh* ("Pleased to meet you" or "morning"); *Mirembrema* ("Good evening"); *Naten e mire* ("Good night"); *Mirupafshim* ("Goodbye"); *Me fal/Me falni* ("Excuse me"); *Ne rregull* ("All right" or "Okay"); *S'ka perse* ("Don't mention it"); *Gjuha vete ku dhemb dhemballa* ("The tongue follows the toothache"); *Shqiptare* ("Albanians").

FAMILY AND COMMUNITY DYNAMICS

THE CODE OF LEKE DUKAGJINI (*Kanuni I Leke Dukagjinit*)

The Kanun is an ancient set of civil, criminal, and family laws that still exerts influence on the lives of many Albanian Americans. The Kanun is traditionally ascribed to Leke Dukagjini (1460-1481), a compatriot and contemporary of Skanderberg. It sets forth rights and obligations regarding the church, family, and marriage. The code is based on the concepts of honor (*bessa*) and blood; the individual is obligated to guard the honor of family, clan, and tribe. The rights and obligations surrounding the concept of honor have often led to the blood feud (*gjak*), which frequently lasts for generations. At the time of King Zog in the 1920s, the blood feud accounted for one out four male deaths in Albania. This code was translated into English and published in a bilingual text in

1989 in the United States. American attorneys brought the code to the attention of Albanian lawyers to help Albania codify their new legislation after the collapse of communism. According to a newspaper article, the code is "the central part of their legal and cultural identity" (*New York Times*, November 11, 1994, p. B-20).

The Kanun defines the family as a "group of human beings who live under the same roof, whose aim is to increase their number by means of marriage for their establishment and the evolution of their state and for the development of their reason and intellect." The traditional Albanian household is a patriarchy in which the head of the household is the eldest male. The principal roles of the wife are to keep house and raise the children. The children have a duty to honor their parents and respect their wishes.

THE ROLE OF WOMEN

Although the Kanun considers a woman a superfluity in the household, many Albanian American women in the United States would strongly disagree. Historically, Albanian American women have borne the responsibility of preserving the memories, customs, and traditions of the Albanian homeland. A woman's first obligation is to marry and raise a family. Girls have not been allowed as much freedom as boys and were not encouraged "to go out." Instead, girls have been kept at home and taught domestic skills. Girls were sent through high school but not encouraged to pursue higher education and a career. After graduation and before marriage, women have often helped with the family business. Albanian women have usually married at an early age.

During the 1920s and 1930s, Albanian men outnumbered Albanian women in the United States by about three to one. Many Albanian men considered their stay in America temporary and therefore left their wives in Albania with the intent of making enough money to return home. During this period, when Albanian women were in short supply, Albanian men in the United States began to "order" wives from Albania. The man usually supplied the dowry, which compensated the girl's parents for her fare to the United States.

Today many Albanian American women feel caught between two worlds. They often feel obligated to conform to the standards and mores of their community but, at the same time, are pressured to "Americanize." Although many Albanian American women have pursued higher education and careers outside the home, many in the community still view these pursuits as inappropriate.

Albanian American women have only recently begun to organize. The *Motrat Qirijazi* (Sisters Qirjazi), the first Albanian-American women's organization, was founded on March 27, 1993. The principal founder and current president is Shqipe Baba. This organization serves all Albanian women in the United States, assisting and supporting them in the pursuit of unity, education, and advancement.

WEDDINGS

Traditionally, Albanian weddings are arranged by parents or by an intermediary or matchmaker. The festivities may begin a week before the wedding (*jav' e nuses*—"marriage week"). Usually, an engagement ceremony is held between the two families and the bride is given a gold coin as a token of the engagement. A celebration is held at the home of the bride's parents and the future bride is given gifts and sweets. Refreshments are usually served. A second celebration is given by the family of the groom and the bride's family attends. At these celebrations, small favors of candy-coated almonds (*kufeta*) are exchanged. In Albania, a dowry is usually given but this custom is not followed in the United States.

A week before the ceremony, wedding preparations began. During this week, relatives and friends visit the homes of the couple and food preparation begins. A chickpea bread (*buke me qiqra*) is usually prepared. Gifts to the groom and the bride's trousseau and wedding clothes are displayed. A party is given in which family and friends attend. Members of the groom's family come to the house of the bride and invite her to the festivities. They carry wine, flowers, and a plate of rice, almond candy, and coins with a cake on top. The groom also invites the *kumbare* (godfather) and *vellam* (best man). The bride gives similar gifts. The party is a time of great rejoicing with food, drink, dancing, and singing. Around midnight, the bride and groom, with family and friends, go in opposite directions to three different bodies of water to fill two containers. Coins are thrown into the air at each stop for anyone to pick up.

On the day of the wedding, the bride is dressed, given a sip of wine by her parents along with their good wishes. Other family members give her money. The *vellam* brings in the bride's shoes, filled with rice and almond candy, wrapped in a silk handkerchief. Accompanied by singing women, the *vellam* puts the shoes on the bride and gives money to the person who assisted the bride in dressing. The *vellam* is encouraged to give everybody money. He throws coins into the air three times and everyone tries to get one coin. The groom's family accompanies the bride to the ceremony. The ceremony is followed by a reception. On the following day, the bride may be visited by her family, who bring sweets (*me peme*). One week after the ceremony, the couple is visited by friends and relatives. This is called "first visit" (*te pare*). After a few weeks, the bride's dowry may be displayed (in Albania) and the bride, in turn, distributes gifts to the groom's family. The couple is sent off with good wishes: "*te trashegojen e te plaken; jete te gjate me dashuri*" or "a long, happy, healthy life together" ("Albanian Customs," *Albanian Cookbook* [Worcester, Massachusetts: Women's Guild, St. Mary's Albanian Orthodox Church, 1977).

BIRTH AND BIRTHDAYS

Traditionally, the one who tells friends and relatives that a child has been born receives a *siharik* (tip). Within three days after the birth, the family makes *petulla* (fried dough or fritters) and distributes them to friends and family. A hot sweet bread (*buevale*) may also be prepared for guests who visit the mother and child. A celebration is usually held on the third day where friends and relatives bring *petulla* and other gifts. In the Orthodox Church, this celebration may be delayed until the child is baptized. Traditionally, for Albanians of the Orthodox faith, the *kumbare* and *ndrikull* (godparents) choose the name of the child to be baptized. Many superstitions surround the birth of an Albanian child. Among older Albanian Americans may of these superstitions may still exist. Infants are especially vulnerable to the "evil eye" and many Albanian mothers will place a *kuleta* (amulet) on a new-born child. For Christians, the *kuleta* may be a small cross, and among Muslims, it may be a small triangular silver form (*hajmali*). Garlic may also ward off evil. A person who touches an Albanian child or offers a compliment is required say "*Mashalla*" (as God wishes) to ward off the misfortune of the evil eye.

Among Orthodox Christians, birthdays are not traditionally observed. Instead, the family observes a "name's day" for the saint after whom the person is named. Family and friends may gather together and wish the person a "happy nameday" and "good health and long life." The family may serve guests fruit preserves (*liko*), pastries (*te embla*), Albanian whiskey (*raki*), and coffee (*kafe*). Guests would be formally served in the reception room (*ode*) or the living room (*vater*). The guests are treated with great courtesy and all formalities are observed.

RELIGION

Albanians in the United States are primarily Orthodox Christians, Roman Catholics, or Muslims. Currently, the Albanian Orthodox Church in the United States is divided into two ecclesiastical jurisdictions. The Albanian Orthodox Archdiocese in America (OCA) is an autocephalous church established in 1908 by Fan S. Noli, a major religious and political figure in the Albanian community. With a membership of around 45,000, it currently has 16 parishes nationwide. The current Primate is Metropolitan Theodosius. The headquarters of the Archdiocese, St. George Albanian Orthodox Cathedral, is located in South Boston. One of the oldest chapters of the St. George Cathedral was organized in Worcester, Massachusetts, in 1911. This chapter became the Church of Saint Mary's Assumption in 1915. The Albanian Orthodox Archdiocese of America, established in 1950 by Bishop Mark Lipa, is under the jurisdiction of the ecumenical Patriarch of Constantinople. This Archdiocese currently administers two churches, Saint Nicholas in Chicago and Holy Trinity in South Boston.

Albanian Roman Catholics began coming to the United States in the 1960s and 1970s. At present, three Albanian Catholic churches exist in the United States: Church of Our Lady of Shkodra, located in the Bronx, New York City, founded in 1969 and has a membership of 1,350; St. Paul Catholic Church, located in Warren, Michigan; and Our Lady of the Albanians, located in Beverly Hills, Michigan.

Albanian Muslims came to the United States around 1913. Currently, there are between 25,000 and 30,000 Albanian Muslims in the United States, primarily of the Sunni division within Islam. The Presidency of Albanian Muslim Community Centers in the United States and Canada was founded in 1992 by Imam Vehbi Ismail (1919-) in an attempt to provide unity for Muslims of Albanian heritage. The Presidency comprises 13 community centers or mosques located in Connecticut, Philadelphia, Toronto,

New York, New Jersey, Florida, and Michigan. Albanian Americans of all faiths are welcome at these centers (for more information on Albanian Muslims, contact Imam Vehbi Ismail, Albanian Islamic Center, 20426 Country Club Road, Harper Woods, Michigan 48236).

A small sect of Muslims of the Bektaski Order, the First Albanian Teke Bektashiane in America, is located in Taylor, Michigan. The Order was founded in 1954. They have a small library and publish *The Voice of Bektashism*.

EMPLOYMENT AND ECONOMIC TRADITIONS

The Albanians who came to the United States prior to 1920 were from rural backgrounds and worked as farmers, while others from the urban areas worked as small shopkeepers and tradesmen. The large population of Albanians who settled in Massachusetts found work with the American Optical Company of Southbridge and the textile mills of New Bedford. Others worked as cooks, waiters, and bellhops. Albanians soon began opening their own businesses. The most successful Albanian businesses were fruit stores and restaurants. "By 1925 ... most Albanians of Greater Boston could claim ownership of over three hundred grocery and fruit stores" (Dennis Lazar, *Ethnic Community as it Applies to a Less Visible National Group: The Albanian Community of Boston, Massachusetts* [Rensselaer Polytechnic Institute, doctoral dissertation, 1982], p. 6). Today Albanians are employed in a variety of professional and enterprises. The Ghegs and Kosovars have been especially successful in the Bronx area of New York City, selling and managing real estate.

POLITICS AND GOVERNMENT

Albanian Americans have always felt a strong attachment to Albania and have supported events that occur in the homeland. Both the Orthodox church and the Albanian press have played important roles in the awakening of Albanian nationalism in the United States. The early political efforts of Albanian Americans centered upon furthering the cause of Albania's independence from the Ottoman Empire by instilling a sense of pride in Albanian heritage. Early names in the nationalist movement were Petro Nini Luarasi, who founded the first Albanian national organization in America, the *Mali i Memedheut* ("Longing for the Homeland"), and Sotir Petsi, who founded *Kombi*, the first known Albanian weekly newspaper. *Kombi* actively supported an independent Albania, run by Albanians, within the Turkish empire. The circulation of this early newspaper was instrumental in reducing the rate of illiteracy among Albanians in the United States. Fan S. Noli was one of the most influential figures in the Albanian Nationalist movement in the United States. On January 6, 1907, he founded *Besa-Besen* ("Loyalty"), the first Albanian Nationalist organization in the United States. The founding of the Albanian Orthodox Church in America in 1908 was also a significant event in the life of Albanian Americans. To further Albania's freedom, Fan Noli began publication of *Dielli* ("The Sun") in 1909. A successor to *Kombi*, *Dielli* supported liberation for Albania. Faik Konitza became the first editor of *Dielli*. To further strengthen the cause, a merger of many existing Albanian organizations occurred in April 1912, becoming the Pan-Albanian Federation of America (*Vatra*). Vatra became the principal organization to instill Albanians with a sense of national purpose.

Since the end of World War II, Albanian Americans have shown an increasing interest in American politics, as the process relates to Albanian issues. The Albanian Congressional Caucus has recently been formed with the support of congressional members Elliot Engle (New York), Susan Molinare (New York), and others. Its purpose is to promote Albanian causes with a focus on the plight of Albanians in Kosova. With the defeat of communism in Albania, many new immigrants have arrived in the United States. Several new immigrant aid societies, such as the New England Albanian Relief Organization, Frosinia Organization, and the Albanian Humanitarian Aid Inc., have been organized to assist newly arrived Albanian immigrants. Such organizations have also worked to assist Albanians in Albania.

INDIVIDUAL AND GROUP CONTRIBUTIONS

ACADEMIA

Arshi Pipa (1920-), born in Scutari, Albania, taught humanities, philosophy, and Italian at various colleges and universities in Albania and in the United States. Nicholas Pano (1934-) is a professor of history and has served as the Dean of Arts and Sciences at Western Illinois University; he has made contributions to scholarly journals on the subject of Albania and is the author of *The People's Republic of Albania* (1968). Peter R. Prifti (1924-), author and translator, has made significant contributions to Albanian studies and has published widely on a variety of Albanian topics; he is the author of *Socialist Albania Since 1944* (1978). Stavro Skendi (1906-1989), born in Korce, Albania, was Emeritus Professor of Balkan Languages and Culture at Columbia University from 1972 until his death.

BUSINESS

Anthony Athanas (1912-) is a community leader and has been a restauranteur for over 50 years.

COMMUNITY LEADERS

Constantine A. Chekrezi, an early supporter of the nationalist movement in Albania, briefly served as editor of *Dielli* in 1914 and published *Illyria* from March to November 1916; he is the author of *Albania Past and Present* (1919), which is considered to be the first work in English on Albania written by an Albanian, *A History of Europe—Ancient, Medieval and Modern* (1921), an early history of Europe written in Albanian, and an English-Albanian Dictionary (1923). Christo Dako, an educator and a key figure in the early nationalist movement, is the author of *Albania, the Master Key to the Near East* (1919). Faik Konitza (1876-1942), was one of the more influential leaders of the Albanian community in America in the early twentieth century; he published the magazine *Albania* from 1897-1909 and was the editor of *Dielli* from 1909-1910, and 1921-1926; he also co-founded the Pan-American Federation of America in 1912, serving as its president from 1921-1926; he served as Minister Plenipotentiary of Albania from 1926-1939. Fan Stylian Noli (1865-1964) was one of the most well-known and distinguished historical personalities in the Albanian community; a major figure in the Albanian nationalist movement, Noli founded the Albanian Orthodox Church In America in 1908. Eftalia Tsina (1870-1953), the mother of physician Dimitra Elia, was an early promoter of Albanian social and cultural issues; in the 1920s, she founded *Bashkimi*, the first Albanian women's organization in Boston.

ENTERTAINMENT

John Belushi (1949-1982), actor and comedian, is best known for his work on the original television series *Saturday Night Live* (1975-1979); his movies include: *Goin' South* (1978), *National Lampoon's Animal House* (1978), *Old Boyfriends* (1979), *The Blues Brothers* (1980), *Continental Divide* (1981), and *Neighbors* (1981). His brother, James (Jim) Belushi (1954-) is an actor and comedian who has been in films since 1978; his best-known films include: *The Principal* (1987), *Red Heat* (1988), *K-9* (1989), *Mr. Destiny* (1990), *Only the Lonely* (1991), *Curly Sue* (1991), and *Diary of a Hitman* (1992). Stan Dragoti (1932-) is a prominent director and producer who is best known for his work in movies and television; his best-known work as a movie director includes: *Dirty Little Billy* (1973), *Love at First Bite* (1979), *Mr. Mom* (1983), *The Man with One Red Shoe* (1985), *She's Out of Control* (1989), and *Necessary Roughness* (1991).

JOURNALISM

Gjon Mili (1904-1984), a photographer for *Life* magazine and other magazines from 1939, is best known for his innovative and visionary work with color and high speed photography. His vivid images are well known to readers of *Life*; collections of his work are housed in the Museum of Modern Art (New York), Time-Life Library (New York), Massachusetts Institute of Technology (Cambridge), and the Bibliotheque Nationale (Paris). Donald Lambro (1940-) is a writer, political analyst, and investigative reporter whose writings include *The Federal Rathole* (1975), *Conscience of a Young Conservative* (1976), *Fat City: How Washington Wastes Your Taxes* (1980), *Washington—City of Scandals: Investigating Congress and Other Big Spenders* (1984) and *Land of Opportunity: The Entrepreneurial Spirit in America* (1986).

MEDICINE

Andrew and Dimitra Tsina Elia were early pioneers in the Albanian community in the field of medicine. Andrew Elia (1906-1991) graduated from Boston University Medical School in 1935 and was a practicing obstetrician and gynecologist in the Boston area. Dimitra Elia (1906-1965) was one of the first Albanian American women to practice general medicine in the United States.

MUSIC

Thomas Nassi (1892-), musician and composer, graduated from the New England Conservatory of

Music in 1918; he trained choirs for the Cathedral of St. George in Boston and for churches in Natick, Worcester, and Southbridge, Massachusetts, between 1916-1918. He also arranged Byzantine liturgical responses in Albanian for mixed choirs.

POLITICS

Steven Peters (1907-1990) served as a research analyst in the U.S. State Department in 1945 and the Foreign Service in 1958; he is the author of *The Anatomy of Communist Takeovers* and the government publications, *Area Handbook for the Soviet Union* and *Area Handbook for Albania*. Rifat Tirana (c. 1907-1952), an economist, was a member of the staff of the League of Nations in the 1930s; at the time of his death, he was serving as deputy chief of the U.S. Security Agency Mission to Spain; he authored *The Spoil of Europe* (1941). Bardhyl Rifat Tirana (1937-) served as co-chair of the Presidential Inaugural Committee (1976-1977) and director of the Defense Civil Preparedness Agency (1977-1979).

SPORTS

Lee Constantine Elia (1937-), baseball player, coach, and manager, managed the Chicago Cubs (1982-1983) and the Philadelphia Phillies (1987-1988).

WRITERS

Shqipe Malushi, poet, essayist, media information specialist and an active community leader, has published fiction, nonfiction, translations, essays, and newspapers articles; her works of poetry, written in Albanian and in English, include: *Memories of '72* (1972, in Kosova), *Exile* (1981), *Solitude* (1985), *Crossing the Bridges* (1990), and *For You* (1993); she has published *Beyond the Walls of the Forgotten Land* (1992), a collection of short stories, and *Transformation* (1988), a book of essays. She has also written and collaborated on several plays and screenplays. Loretta Chase (1949-), born in Worcester, Massachusetts, is a popular writer of romance novels for Regency and Avon Presses; her novels include: *Isabella* (1987), *Viscount Vagabond* (1988), and *Knaves Wager* (1990). Nexmie Zaimi is the author of *Daughter of the Eagle: The Autobiography of an Albanian Girl* (1937), which describes her immigrant experience, customs, and practices.

PRINT

Albanian Herald.

Albanian and English. Begun in 1993, the *Herald* is one the newest Albanian newspapers with a nationwide circulation. Less political than either *Liria* or *Illyria*, the paper covers a wide variety of cultural, social, and historical topics as well as political events.

Contact: Gjok Martini, Editor.
Address: 11661 Joseph Campau, Hamtramck, Michigan 48212.
Telephone: (313) 365-1133.

Albanica.

Journal devoted to Albanian culture on a scholarly level.

Contact: Arshi Pipa, Editor.
Address: 134 G Street, N.W., Washington, D.C. 20024.
Telephone: (202) 479-0633.

Dielli.

Albanian and English weekly, one of the oldest Albanian newspapers, published by the Pan Albanian Federation of America, *Vatra*. It publishes articles on social, cultural, and political events of interest to Albanians.

Contact: Agim Karagjozi, Editor.
Address: 167 East 82nd Street, New York, New York 10028.
Telephone: (718) 347-6470.

Illyria.

Albanian and English bi-weekly published by the Illyrian Publishing Company featuring international news with a focus on news from the Balkans. Emphasis is currently on political events of interest to Albanian Americans; however, the paper is beginning to focus on local community events as well.

Contact: Hajdar Bajraktari.
Address: 232 Hughes Avenue, Bronx, New York 10452.
Telephone: (718) 220-2000.

Liria.

Albanian and English monthly published by the Free Albania Organization. Features local and national news on Albanian community life and events and news from Albania.

Contact: Shkelqim Begari, Editor.

Address: 409 West Broadway, South Boston, Massachusetts 02127.

Telephone: (617) 269-5192.

RADIO

WCUW-FM.

"Albanian Hour" is the oldest continuous Albanian radio program in the country; it airs on Saturday from 8:30 to 9:30 p.m. It broadcasts local community news and events and international news from Albania. Lately, it focuses on concerns of new immigrants from Albania.

Contact: Demetre Steffon.

Address: 910 Main Street, Worcester, Massachusetts 01602.

Telephone: (508) 753-1012.

WKDM-AM.

"LDK Radio Program" ("Democratic League of Kosova") airs on Friday, 7:00 to 8:00 p.m. It presents local news, community events, and international news.

Contact: Rooster Mebray, Producer.

Address: 449 Broadway, Second Floor, New York, New York 10013.

Telephone: (212) 966-1059; or (718) 933-6202.

WKDM-AM.

"Voice of Malesia" airs on Monday from 7:00 to 8:00 p.m. It features community events, music, interviews, and news from Albania.

Contact: Gjeto Sinishtaj.

Address: 449 Broadway, Second Floor, New York, New York 10013.

Telephone: (212) 966-1059; or (718) 898-0107.

WMEX-AM.

"Albanian Hour of Boston," formerly, "Voice of Albania," airs every Sunday evening from 8:00 to 9:00 p.m. It features local community news and events, music, and interviews as well as news from Albania.

Contact: David Kosta.

Address: P.O. Box 170, Cambridge, Massachusetts 02238.

Telephone: (617) 666-4803.

WNWK-FM.

"Festival of the Albanian Music" airs on Sundays, 8:30 to 9:00 p.m. and features music from Albania.

Contact: Louis Shkreli.

Address: 449 Broadway, New York, New York 10013.

Telephone: (212) 966-1059; or (718) 733-6900.

TELEVISION

WNYE (Channel 25, Brooklyn, New York).

"T.V. Victoria" airs Sunday, 4:00 to 5:00 p.m. and features local and international news, local and community events, and sports. Commentary is provided in Albanian and English on news from Albania.

Contact: Terrence O'Driscoll, Station Manager; or Esat Osmani.

Address: 112 Tillary Street, Brooklyn, New York 11201.

Telephone: (718) 935-4480; or (718) 939-4838.

ORGANIZATIONS AND ASSOCIATIONS

At present, Albania is undergoing rapid changes and Albanian Americans are responding. Since the fall of the Communist government in Albania (1990-1992), several new relief organizations such as the Frosinia Organization (New York City), New England Albanian Relief Organization (Worcester, Massachusetts), and Albanian Humanitarian Aid Inc. (New York City) have been formed within the Albanian community to assist newly arrived immigrants. Second, many long standing Albanian organizations and associations in the United States are redefining their function in view of the new political order that now exists in Albania.

Albanian American Civic League.

Founded in 1986, the organization is dedicated to informing the American public about the political and social problems in Albania.

Contact: Joseph DioGuardi.

Address: 717 Second Street, N.E., Washington, D.C. 20003.

Telephone: (202) 547-3637.

Albanian American National Organization (AANO).

Founded in 1938 as the Albanian Youth Organization, it is a non-denominational cultural organization open to all Albanians and Americans of Albanian descent.

Contact: Andrew Tanacea.

Address: 22 Dayton Street, Worcester, Massachusetts 10609.

Telephone: (508) 754-9440.

Albanian Catholic Institute (ACI).

Gathers and disseminates information on the state of religion in Albania; conducts research on Albania's religious and cultural history; maintains collection of materials pertaining to Albanian history.

Contact: Gjon Sinishta.

Address: University of San Francisco, Xavier Hall, San Francisco, California 94117-1080.

Telephone: (415) 666-6966.

Albanian National Council.

Founded in 1988, the organization provides assistance to all people of Albanian descent regardless of religion.

Contact: Gjok Martini.

Address: 11661 Hamtramck, Michigan 48212.

Telephone: (313) 365-1133.

Free Albania Organization (FAO).

A nonprofit organization that has kept the Albanian community informed about political and social events in Albania through the newspaper *Liria* since 1941.

Contact: William Johns, President.

Address: 409 West Broadway, South Boston, Massachusetts 02127.

Telephone: (617) 269-5192.

Pan-Albanian Organization, "Vatra."

Founded in 1912, *Vatra* is a national organization open to all Albanians 18 years of age and older. The organization is well known to all Albanians and has played an active political and cultural role in the community. It has sponsored many charitable, cultural, and social events and publishes books on Albanian culture. The organization has provided scholarships for students of Albanian descent. *Vatra* has recently relocated from South Boston to New York. It continues to publish the newspaper *Dielli*.

Contact: Agim Karagjozni.

Address: 167 East 82nd Street, New York, New York.

Telephone: (516) 354-6598 or (718) 482-2002.

MUSEUMS AND RESEARCH CENTERS

Fan S. Noli Library.

The library and archives contain the papers of Fan S. Noli.

Address: Albanian Orthodox Archdiocese in America, St. George Albanian Orthodox Cathedral, 529 East Broadway, South Boston, Massachusetts 02127.

Telephone: (617) 268-1275.

SOURCES FOR ADDITIONAL STUDY

Demo, Constantine. *The Albanians in America: The First Arrivals*. Boston: Society of Fatbardhesia of Katundi, 1960.

Federal Writers Project of Massachusetts. *The Albanian Struggle in the Old World and the New*. Boston: Federal Writers Project of Massachusetts, 1939.

Noli, Fan S. *Fiftieth Anniversary Book of the Albanian Orthodox Church in America, 1908-1958*. Boston: Pan-Albanian Federation of America, 1960.

Page, Denna L. *The Albanian-American Odyssey: A Pilot Study of the Albanian Community of Boston, Massachusetts*. New York: AMS Press, 1987.

Roucek, Joseph. "The Albanian and Yugoslav Immigrants in America," *Revue Internationale Des Etudes Balkaniques*, 3, 1938; pp. 499-519.

———. "Albanian Americans." In *One America*, edited by Francis Brown and Joseph S. Roucek. New York: Prentice Hall, 1952; pp. 232-239.

If the Amish can educate and retain their children, make a living, and restrain interaction with the larger world, they will likely flourish into the twenty-first century.

AMISH

by
Donald B. Kraybill

OVERVIEW

The year 1993 marked the existence of 300 years of Amish life. Extinct in their European homeland, today they live in more than 200 settlements in 22 states and the Canadian province of Ontario. The Amish are one of the more distinctive and colorful cultural groups across the spectrum of American pluralism. Their rejection of automobiles, use of horse-drawn farm machinery, and distinctive dress set them apart from the high-tech culture of modern life.

HISTORY

Amish roots stretch back to sixteenth-century Europe. Impatient with the pace of the Protestant Reformation, youthful reformers in Zurich, Switzerland, outraged religious authorities by baptizing each other in January 1525. The rebaptism of adults was then a crime punishable by death. Baptism, in the dissidents' view, was only meaningful for adults who had made a voluntary confession of faith. Because they were already baptized as infants in the Catholic Church, the radicals were dubbed Anabaptists, or rebaptizers, by their opponents. Anabaptism, also known as the Radical Reformation, spread through the Cantons of Switzerland, Germany, and the Netherlands.

The rapid spread of Anabaptist groups threatened civil and religious authorities. Anabaptist hunters soon stalked the Reformers. The first martyr was drowned in 1527. Over the next few decades, thousands of Anabaptists burned at the stake, drowned in rivers, starved in prisons, or lost their heads to the executioner's sword. A 1,200-page *Martyrs Mirror*, first published in Dutch in 1660 and later in German and English, records the carnage. Many Amish have a German edition of the *Martyrs Mirror* in their homes today.

The Swiss Anabaptists sought to follow the ways of Jesus in daily life, loving their enemies, forgiving insults, and turning the other cheek. Some Anabaptist groups resorted to violence, but many repudiated force and resolved to live peaceably even with adversaries. The flames of execution tested their faith in the power of suffering love, and although some recanted, many died for their faith. Harsh persecution pushed many Anabaptists underground and into rural hideaways. Swiss Anabaptism took root in rural soil. The sting of persecution, however, divided the church and the larger society in Anabaptist minds. The Anabaptists believed that the kingdoms of this world anchored on the use of coercion clashed with the peaceable kingdom of God.

By 1660 some Swiss Anabaptists had migrated north to the Alsace region of present-day France, which borders southwestern Germany. The Amish came into the picture in 1693 when Swiss and South German Anabaptists split into two streams: Amish and Mennonite. Jakob Ammann, an elder of the Alsatian church, sought to revitalize the Anabaptist movement in 1693. He proposed holding communion twice a year rather than the typical Swiss practice of once a year. He argued that Anabaptist Christians in obedience to Christ should wash each others' feet in the communion service. To promote doctrinal purity and spiritual discipline Ammann forbade fashionable dress and the trimming of beards, and he administered a strict discipline in his congregations. Appealing to New Testament teachings, Ammann advocated the shunning of excommunicated members. Ammann's followers, eventually called Amish, soon became another sect in the Anabaptist family.

SIGNIFICANT IMMIGRATION WAVES

Searching for political stability and religious freedom, the Amish came to North America in two waves—in the mid-1700s and again in the first half of the 1800s. Their first settlements were in southeastern Pennsylvania. Eventually they followed the frontier to other counties in Pennsylvania, then to Ohio, Indiana, and to other Midwestern states. Today Amish settlements are primarily located in the mid-Atlantic and the Midwest regions of the United States. Very few Amish live west of the Mississippi or in the deep south. In Europe, the last Amish congregation dissolved about 1937.

SETTLEMENT PATTERNS

Flowing with the rising tide of industrialization in the late nineteenth century, some clusters of Amish formed more progressive Amish-Mennonite churches. The more conservative guardians of the heritage became known as the Old Order Amish. In the twentieth century some Old Order Amish, hankering again after modern conveniences, formed congregations of New Order Amish in the 1960s. The small numbers of New Order Amish groups sometimes permit their members to install phones in their homes, use electricity from public utilities, and use tractors in their fields.

At the turn of the twentieth century the Old Order Amish numbered about 5,000 in North America. Now scattered across 22 states and Ontario they number about 150,000 children and adults. Nearly three quarters live in Ohio, Pennsylvania, and Indiana. Other sizeable communities are in Iowa, Michigan, Missouri, New York, and Wisconsin. A loose federation of some 900 Amish congregations, the Amish function without a national organization or an annual convention. Local church districts—congregations of 25 to 35 families—shape the heart of Amish life.

ACCULTURATION AND ASSIMILATION

The Amish have been able to maintain a distinctive ethnic subculture by successfully resisting acculturation and assimilation. The Amish try to maintain cultural customs that preserve their identity. They have resisted assimilation into American culture by emphasizing separation from the world, rejecting higher education, selectively using technology, and restricting interaction with outsiders.

TRADITIONS, CUSTOMS, AND BELIEFS

The word Amish evokes images of buggies and lanterns. At first glance Amish groupings across North America appear pressed from the same cultural mold. A deeper look reveals many differences among Amish groups. Some affiliations forbid milking machines while others depend on them. Mechanical hay balers widely used in some areas are taboo in others. Prescribed buggy tops are gray or black in many affiliations but other groups have white or yellow tops. Buttons on clothing are banished in many groups, but acceptable in others. The dead are embalmed in one settlement but not in another. Some bishops permit telephones in small shops, but others do not. Artificial insemination of livestock is acceptable in one district but not in another. In some communities virtually all the men are farmers, but in others many adults work in small shops and cottage industries. In still other settlements Amish persons work in rural factories operated by non-Amish persons. Practices vary between church districts even within the same settlement. Diversity thrives behind the front stage of Amish life.

Several distinctive badges of ethnic identity unite the Old Order Amish across North America: horse-and-buggy transportation; the use of horses and mules for field work; plain dress in many variations; a beard and shaven upper lip for men; a prayer cap for women; the Pennsylvania German dialect; worship in homes; eighth-grade, parochial schooling; the rejection of electricity from public utility lines; and taboos on the ownership of televisions and computers. These symbols of solidarity circumscribe the Amish world and bridle the forces of assimilation.

Amish life pivots on *Gelassenheit* (pronounced Ge-las-en-hite), the cornerstone of Amish values. Roughly translated, this German word means submission, yielding to a higher authority. In practice it entails self-surrender, resignation to God's will, yielding to others, self-denial, contentment, and a quiet spirit. The religious meaning of Gelassenheit expresses itself in a quiet and reserved personality and places the needs of others above self. It nurtures a subdued self, gentle handshakes, lower voices, slower strides, a life etched with modesty and reserve. Children learn the essence of Gelassenheit in a favorite verse: "I must be a Christian child, / Gentle, patient, meek, and mild, / Must be honest, simple, true, / I must cheerfully obey, / Giving up my will and way."

Another favorite saying explains that JOY means Jesus first, Yourself last, and Others in between. As the cornerstone of Amish culture, Gelassenheit collides with the bold, assertive individualism of modern life that seeks and rewards personal achievement, self-fulfillment, and individual recognition at every turn.

The spirit of Gelassenheit expresses itself in obedience, humility, and simplicity. To Amish thinking, obedience to the will of God is *the* cardinal religious value. Disobedience is dangerous. Unconfessed it leads to eternal separation. Submission to authority at all levels creates an orderly community. Children learn to obey at an early age. Disobedience is nipped in the bud. Students obey teachers without question. Adults yield to the regulations of the church. Among elders, ministers concede to bishops, who obey the Lord.

Humility is coupled with obedience in Amish life. Pride, a religious term for unbridled individualism, threatens the welfare of an orderly community. Amish teachers also remind students that the middle letter of pride is I. Proud individuals display the spirit of arrogance, not Gelassenheit. They are pushy, bold, and forward. What non-Amish consider proper credit for one's accomplishments the Amish view as the hankerings of a vain spirit. The Amish contend that pride disturbs the equality and tranquility of an orderly community. The humble person freely gives of self in the service of community without seeking recognition.

Simplicity is also esteemed in Amish life. Simplicity in clothing, household decor, architecture, and worship nurtures equality and orderliness. Fancy and gaudy decorations lead to pride. Luxury and convenience cultivate vanity. The tools of self-adornment—make-up, jewelry, wrist watches, and wedding rings—are taboo and viewed as signs of pride.

AMISH SURVIVAL

The Amish do not actively evangelize. They do welcome outsiders, but few make the cultural leap. Membership in some settlements doubles about every 20 years. Their growth is fueled by a robust birth rate that averages seven children per family. The defection rate varies by settlement, but is usually less than 20 percent. Thus, six out of seven children, on the average, remain Amish.

Beyond biological reproduction, a dual strategy of resistance and compromise has enabled the Amish to flourish in the modern world. They have resisted acculturation by constructing social fences around their community. Core values are translated

This group of Amish boys is watching a horse and mule auction in Lancaster, Pennsylvania. This annual event attracts Amish farmers from throughout the Midwest.

into visible symbols of identity. Badges of ethnicity—horse, buggy, lantern, dialect, and dress—draw sharp contours between Amish and modern life.

The Amish resist the forces of modernization in other ways. Cultural ties to the outside world are curbed by speaking the dialect, marrying within the group, spurning television, prohibiting higher education, and limiting social interaction with outsiders. Parochial schools insulate Amish youth from the contaminating influence of worldly peers. Moreover, ethnic schools limit exposure to threatening ideas. From birth to death, members are embedded in a web of ethnicity. These cultural defenses fortify Amish identity and help abate the lure of modernity.

Their survival strategy has also involved cultural compromises. The Amish are not a calcified relic of bygone days, for they change continually. Their willingness to compromise often results in odd mixtures of tradition and progress. Tractors may be used at Amish barns but not in fields. Horses and mules pull modern farm machinery in some settlements. God smiles on 12-volt electricity from batteries but not when it comes from public utility lines. Hydraulic and air pressure are used instead of electricity to operate modern machines in many Amish carpentry and mechanical shops. Members frequently ride in cars or vans, but are not permitted to drive them. Telephones, found by farm lanes and shops, are missing from Amish homes. Modern gas appliances fill Amish kitchens in some states and lanterns illuminate modern bathrooms in some Amish abodes.

These riddles of Amish life often baffle and, indeed, appear downright silly to outsiders. In reality, however, they reflect delicate bargains that the Amish have struck between their desire to maintain tradition while enjoying the fruits of progress. The Amish are willing to change but not at the expense of communal values and ethnic identity. They use modern technology but not when it disrupts family and community stability.

Viewed within the context of Amish history, the compromises are reasonable ways of achieving community goals. Hardly foolish contradictions, they preserve core values while permitting selective modernization. They bolster Amish identity while reaping many benefits of modern life. Such flexibility boosts the economic vitality of the community and also retains the allegiance of Amish youth.

CUISINE

Food preferences among the Amish vary somewhat from state to state. Breakfast fare for many families includes eggs, fried potatoes, toast, and in some communities, commercial cereals such as Cornflakes and Cheerios. Typical breakfast foods in Pennsylvania also include shoofly pie, which is sometimes dipped in or covered with coffee or milk, stewed crackers in warm milk, mush made from corn meal, and sausage. Puddings and scrapple are also breakfast favorites. The puddings consist of ground liver, heart, and kidneys from pork and beef. These basic ingredients are also combined with flour and corn meal to produce scrapple.

For farm families the mid-day dinner is usually the largest meal of the day. Noontime dinners and evening suppers often include beef or chicken dishes, and vegetables in season from the family garden, such as peas, corn, green beans, lima beans, and carrots. Mashed potatoes covered with beef gravy, noodles with brown butter, chicken potpie, and sauerkraut are regional favorites. For side dishes and deserts there are applesauce, corn starch pudding, tapioca, and fruit pies in season, such as apple, rhubarb, pumpkin, and snitz pies made with dried apples. Potato soup and chicken-corn-noodle soup are commonplace. In summer months cold fruit soups consisting of strawberries, raspberries, or blueberries added to milk and bread cubes appear on Amish tables. Meadow tea, homemade root beer, and instant drink mixes are used in the summer.

Food preservation and preparation for large families and sizeable gatherings is an enormous undertaking. Although food lies beyond the reach of religious regulations, each community has a traditional menu that is typically served at large meals following church services, weddings, and funerals. Host families often bake three dozen pies for the noontime meal following the biweekly church service. Quantities of canned food vary by family size and preference but it is not uncommon for a family to can 150 quarts of applesauce, 100 quarts of peaches, 60 quarts of pears, 50 quarts of grape juice, and 50 quarts of pizza sauce.

More and more food is purchased from stores, sometimes operated by the Amish themselves. In a more progressive settlement one Amishwoman estimates that only half of the families bake their own bread. The growing use of instant pudding, instant drinks, snack foods, and canned soups reflects growing time constraints. The use of commercial food rises as families leave the farm and especially as women enter entrepreneurial roles.

TRADITIONAL COSTUMES

The Amish church prescribes dress regulations for its members but the unwritten standards vary considerably by settlement. Men are expected to wear a wide brim hat and a vest when they appear in public. In winter months and at church services they wear a black suit coat which is typically fastened with hooks and eyes rather than with buttons. Men use suspenders instead of belts.

Amish women are expected to wear a prayer covering and a bonnet when they appear in public settings. Most women wear a cape over their dresses as well as an apron. The three parts of the dress are often fastened together with straight pins. Various colors, including green, brown, blue, and lavender, are permitted for men's shirts and women's dresses, but designs and figures in the material are taboo. Although young girls do not wear a prayer covering, Amish children are typically dressed similar to their parents.

HOLIDAYS

Sharing some national holidays with non-Amish neighbors and adding others of their own, the Amish calendar underscores both their participation in and separation from the larger world. As conscientious objectors, they have little enthusiasm for patriotic days with a military flair. Memorial Day, Veterans Day, and the Fourth of July are barely noticed. Labor Day stirs little interest. The witches and goblins of Halloween run contrary to Amish spirits: pumpkins may be displayed in some settlements, but without cut faces. And Martin Luther King, Jr.'s birthday slips by unnoticed in many rural enclaves.

Amish holidays earmark the rhythm of the seasons and religious celebrations. A day for prayer and fasting precedes the October communion service in some communities. Fall weddings provide ample holidays of another sort. Amish without wedding invitations celebrate Thanksgiving Day with turkey dinners and family gatherings. New Year's Day is a quiet time for family gatherings. In many communities a second day is added to the celebrations of Christmas, Easter, and Pentecost. The regular holiday, a sacred time, flows with quiet family activities. The following day, or second Christmas, Easter Monday, and Pentecost Monday, provides time for recreation, visiting, and sometimes shopping. Ascension day, the day prior to Pentecost, is a holiday for visiting, fishing, and other forms of recreation.

Christmas and Easter festivities are spared from commercial trappings. Families exchange Christmas cards and gifts. Some presents are homemade crafts and practical gifts, but are increasingly store bought. Homes are decorated with greens but Christmas trees, stockings, special lights, Santa Claus, and mistletoe are missing.

Although eggs are sometimes painted and children may be given a basket of candy, Easter bunnies do not visit Amish homes. These sacred holidays revolve around religious customs, family gatherings, and quiet festivities rather than commercial trinkets and the sounds of worldly hubbub. Birthdays are celebrated at home and school in quiet, pleasant ways, with cakes and gifts. Parents often share a special snack of cookies or popsicles with school friends to honor a child's birthday.

HEALTH AND MENTAL HEALTH ISSUES

Contrary to popular misconceptions the Amish use modern medical services to some extent. Lacking professionals within their ranks, they rely on the services of dentists, optometrists, nurses, and physicians in local health centers, clinics, and hospitals. They cite no biblical injunctions against modern health care nor the latest medicine, but they do believe that God is the ultimate healer. Despite the absence of religious taboos on health care, Amish practices differ from prevailing patterns.

The Amish generally do not subscribe to commercial health insurance. Some communities have organized church aid plans for families with special medical costs. In other settlements special offerings are collected for members who are hit with catastrophic medical bills. The Amish are unlikely to seek medical attention for minor aches or illnesses and are more apt to follow folk remedies and drink herbal teas. Although they do not object to surgery or other forms of high-tech treatment they rarely employ heroic life-saving interventions.

In addition to home remedies, church members often seek healing outside orthodox medical circles. The search for natural healing leads them to vitamins, homeopathic remedies, health foods, reflexologists, chiropractors, and the services of specialized clinics in faraway places. These cultural habits are shaped by many factors: conservative rural values, a preference for natural antidotes, a lack of information, a sense of awkwardness in high-tech settings, difficulties accessing health care, and a willingness to suffer and lean on the providence of God.

Birthing practices vary in different settlements. In some communities most babies are born at home under the supervision of trained non-Amish midwives. In other settlements most children are born in hospitals or at local birthing clinics. Children can attend Amish schools without immunizations. Some parents follow the advice of family doctors or trained midwives and immunize their children, but many do not. Lax immunization is often due to cost, distance, misinformation, or lack of interest. Occasional outbreaks of German measles, whooping cough, polio, and other contagious diseases prompt public health campaigns to immunize Amish children. Amish elders usually encourage their people to cooperate with such efforts. In recent years various health providers have made special efforts to immunize Amish children.

Marriages within stable geographical communities and the influx of few converts restricts the genetic pool of Amish society. Marriages sometimes occur between second cousins. Such intermarriage does not always produce medical problems. When unique recessive traits are common in a closed community certain diseases simply are more likely to occur. On the other hand, a restricted gene pool may offer protection from other hereditary diseases.

A special type of dwarfism accompanied by other congenital problems occurs at an exceptionally high rate in some settlements. Higher rates of deafness have also been found. In the late 1980s, Dr. Holmes Morton identified *glutaric aciduria* in the Lancaster, Pennsylvania, Amish community. Unrecognized and untreatable before, the disease is a biochemical disorder with symptoms similar to cerebral palsy. Approximately one in every 200 Amish infants inherits the disease. By 1991, Dr. Morton had organized a special clinic that tested some 70 percent of Amish infants and treated those diagnosed with the disease in the Lancaster settlement.

LANGUAGE

The Amish speak English, German, and a dialect known as Pennsylvania German or Pennsylvania Dutch. The dialect is the Amish native tongue and should not be confused with the Dutch language of the Netherlands. Originally a German dialect, Pennsylvania Dutch was spoken by Germanic settlers in southeastern Pennsylvania. The folk pronunciation of the word *German*, *Deutsche*, gradually became *Dutch* in English, and eventually the dialect became known as Pennsylvania Dutch. Even the Amish who live outside of Pennsylvania speak the Pennsylvania German dialect. In Amish culture, the dialect is used mainly as a form of oral communication: it is the language of work, family, friendship, play, and intimacy.

Young children live in the world of the dialect until they learn English in the Amish school. Students learn to read, write, and speak English from their Amish teachers, who learned it from their Amish teachers. But the dialect prevails in friendly banter on the playground. By the end of the eighth grade, young Amish have developed basic competence in English although it may be spoken with an accent. Adults are able to communicate in fluent English with their non-Amish neighbors. When talking among themselves, the Amish sometimes mix English words with the dialect, especially when discussing technical issues. Letters are often written in English, with salutations and occasional phrases in the dialect. Competence in English varies directly with occupational roles and frequency of interaction with English speakers. Ministers are often the ones who are best able to read German. Idioms of the dialect are frequently mixed with German in Amish sacred writings. Although children study formal German in school they do not speak it on a regular basis.

GREETINGS AND OTHER POPULAR EXPRESSIONS

Common Pennsylvania Dutch greetings and other expressions include: *Gude Mariye*—Good morning; *Gut-n-Owed*—Good evening; *Wie geht's?*—How are you?; *En frehlicher Grischtdsaag*—a Merry Christmas; *Frehlich Neiyaahr*—Happy New Year; *kumm ball widder*—come soon again. When inviting others to gather around a table to eat, a host might say *Kumm esse*.

FAMILY AND COMMUNITY DYNAMICS

The *immediate family*, the *extended family*, and the *church district* form the building blocks of Amish society. Amish parents typically raise about seven children, but ten or more children is not uncommon. About 50 percent of the population is under 18 years of age. A person will often have more than 75 first cousins and a typical grandmother will count more than 35 grandchildren. Members of the extended family often live nearby, across the field, down the lane, or beyond the hill. Youth grow up in this thick network of family relations where one is rarely alone, always embedded in a caring community in time of need and disaster. The elderly retire at home, usually in a small apartment built onto the main house of a homestead. Because the Amish reject government aid, there are virtually no families that receive public assistance. The community provides a supportive social hammock from cradle to grave.

SOCIAL ORGANIZATION

A church district comprises 25 to 35 families and is the basic social and religious unit beyond the family. Roads and streams mark the boundaries of districts. Members are required to participate in the geographic district in which they live. A district's geographic size varies with the density of the Amish population. As districts expand, they divide.

A bishop, two preachers, and a deacon share leadership responsibilities in each district without formal pay or education. The bishop, as spiritual elder, officiates at baptisms, weddings, communions, funerals, ordinations, and membership meetings. The church district is church, club, family, and precinct all wrapped up in a neighborhood parish. Periodic meetings of ordained leaders link the districts of a settlement into a loose federation.

The social architecture of Amish society exhibits distinctive features. Leisure, work, education, play, worship, and friendship revolve around the immediate neighborhood. In some settlements, Amish babies are born in hospitals, but they are also born at home or in local birthing centers. Weddings and funerals occur at home. There are frequent trips to other settlements or even out of state to visit relatives and friends. But for the most part the Amish world pivots on local turf. From home-canned food to homemade haircuts, things are likely to be done near home. Social relationships are multi-bonded. The same people frequently work, play, and worship together.

Amish society is remarkably informal and the tentacles of bureaucracy are sparse. There is no centralized national office, symbolic national figurehead, or institutional headquarters. Apart from schools, a publishing operation, and regional historical libraries, formal institutions simply do not exist. A loosely organized national committee handles relations with the federal government for all the settlements. Regional committees funnel the flow of Amish life for schools, mutual aid, and historical libraries, but bureaucracy as we know it in the modern world is simply absent.

The conventional marks of modern status (education, income, occupation, and consumer goods) are missing and make Amish society relatively homogeneous. The agrarian heritage places everyone on common footing. The recent rise of cottage industries in some settlements and factory work in others threatens to disturb the social equality of bygone years, but the range of occupations and social differences remains relatively small. Common costume, horse and buggy travel, an eighth-grade education, and equal-size tombstones embody the virtues of social equality.

The practice of mutual aid also distinguishes Amish society. Although the Amish own private property, like other Anabaptists they have long emphasized mutual aid as a Christian duty in the face of disaster and special need. Mutual aid goes beyond barn raisings. Harvesting, quilting, birthing, marriages, and funerals require the help of many hands. The habits of care encompass all sorts of needs triggered by drought, disease, death, injury, bankruptcy, and medical emergency.

GENDER ROLES

Amish society is patriarchal. Although school teachers are generally women, men assume the helm of most leadership roles. Women can nominate men to serve in ministerial roles but they themselves are excluded from formal church roles; however, they can vote in church business meetings. Some women feel that since the men make the rules, modern equipment is permitted more readily in barns and shops than in homes. In recent years some women have become entrepreneurs who operate small quilt, craft, and food stores.

Although husband and wife preside over distinct spheres of domestic life, many tasks are shared. A wife may ask her husband to assist in the garden and he may ask her to help in the barn or fields. The isolated housewife is rarely found in Amish society. The husband holds spiritual authority in the home but spouses have considerable freedom within their distinctive spheres.

SOCIAL GATHERINGS

Various social gatherings bring members together for times of fellowship and fun beyond biweekly worship. Young people gather in homes for Sunday evening singing. Married couples sometimes gather with old friends to sing for shut-ins and the elderly in their homes. Work frolics blend work and play together in Amish life. Parents gather for preschool frolics to ready schools for September classes. End-of-school picnics bring parents and students together for an afternoon of food and games.

Quilting bees and barn raisings mix goodwill, levity, and hard work for young and old alike. Other moments of collective work (cleaning up after a fire, plowing for an ill neighbor, canning for a sick mother, threshing wheat, and filling a silo) involve neighbors and extended families in episodes of charity, sweat, and fun. Adult sisters, sometimes numbering as many as five or six, often gather for a sisters day, which blends laughter with cleaning, quilting, canning, or gardening.

Public auctions of farm equipment are often held in February and March and attract crowds in preparation for springtime farming. Besides opportunities to bid on equipment, the day-long auctions offer ample time for farm talk and friendly fun. Games of cornerball in a nearby field or barnyard often compete with the drama of the auction. Household auctions and horse sales provide other times to socialize. Family gatherings at religious holidays and summer family reunions link members into familial networks. Single women sometimes gather at a cabin or a home for a weekend of fun. Special meetings of persons with unique interests, often called reunions, are on the rise and attract Amish from many states: harnessmakers, cabinetmakers, woodworkers, blacksmiths, businesswomen, teachers, the disabled, and the like. The disabled have gathered annually for a number of years.

Among youth, seasonal athletics are common: softball, sledding, skating, hockey, and swimming. Volleyball is a widespread favorite. Fishing and hunting for small game are preferred sports on farms and woodlands. In recent years some Amishmen have purchased hunting cabins in the mountains where they hunt white-tailed deer. Deep-sea fishing trips are common summertime jaunts for men in Pennsylvania. Others prefer camping and canoeing. Pitching quoits is common at family reunions and picnics.

Leisure and pleasure have long been suspect in Amish life. Idleness is viewed as the devil's workshop. But the rise of cottage industries and the availability of ready cash has brought more recreational activities. Amish recreation is group oriented and tilted more toward nature than toward taboo commercial entertainment. The

Amish rarely take vacations but they do take trips to other settlements and may stop at scenic sites. Some couples travel to Florida for several weeks in the winter and live in an Amish village in Sarasota populated by winter travelers from settlements in several states. Trips to distant sites in search of special medical care sometimes include scenic tours. Although some Amish travel by train or bus, chartered vans are by far the most popular mode. Traveling together with family, friends, and extended kin these mobile groups bond and build community life.

INTERACTION WITH OTHER ETHNIC GROUPS

Amish culture and religion stresses separation from the world. Galvanized by European persecution and sanctioned by scripture, the Amish divide the social world into two pathways: the straight, narrow way to life, and the broad, easy road to destruction. Amish life embodies the narrow way of self-denial. The larger social world symbolizes the broad road of vanity and vice. The term world, in Amish thinking, refers to the outside society and its values, vices, practices, and institutions. Media reports of greed, fraud, scandal, drugs, violence, divorce, and abuse confirm that the world teems with abomination.

The gulf between church and world, imprinted in Amish minds by European persecution, guides practical decisions. Products and practices that might undermine community life, such as high school, cars, cameras, television, and self-propelled farm machinery, are tagged worldly. Not all new products receive this label, only those that threaten community values. Definitions of worldliness vary within and between Amish settlements, yielding a complicated maze of practices. Baffling to outsiders, these lines of faithfulness maintain inter-group boundaries and also preserve the cultural purity of the church.

WEDDINGS

The wedding season is a festive time in Amish life. Coming on the heels of the harvest, weddings are typically held on Tuesdays and Thursdays from late October through early December. The larger communities may have as many as 150 weddings in one season. Fifteen weddings may be scattered across the settlement on the same day. Typically staged in the home of the bride, these joyous events may involve upwards of 350 guests, two meals, singing, snacks, festivities, and a three-hour service. The specific practices vary from settlement to settlement.

Young persons typically marry in their early twenties. A couple may date for one to two years before announcing their engagement. Bishops will only marry members of the church. The church does not arrange marriages but it does place its blessing on the pair through an old ritual. Prior to the wedding, the groom takes a letter signed by church elders to the bride's deacon testifying to the groom's good standing in his home district. The bride's deacon then meets with her to verify the marriage plans.

The wedding day is an enormous undertaking for the bride's family and for the relatives and friends who assist with preparations. Efforts to clean up the property, paint rooms, fix furniture, pull weeds, and pave driveways, among other things, begin weeks in advance. The logistics of preparing meals and snacks for several hundred guests are taxing. According to custom, the day before the wedding the groom decapitates several dozen chickens. The noontime wedding menu includes chicken roast—chicken mixed with bread filling, mashed potatoes, gravy, creamed celery, pepper cabbage, and other items. Deserts include pears, peaches, puddings, dozens of pies, and hundreds of cookies and doughnuts.

The three-hour service—without flowers, rings, solos, or instrumental music—is similar to an Amish worship service. The wedding includes congregational singing, prayers, wedding vows, and two sermons. Four single friends serve the bride and groom as attendants: no one is designated maid of honor or best man. Amish brides typically make their own wedding dresses from blue or purple material crafted in traditional styles. In addition to the groom's new but customary black coat and vest, he and his attendants often wear small black bow ties.

Several seatings and games, snacks, and singing follow the noon meal. Young people are paired off somewhat randomly for the singing. Following the evening meal another more lively singing takes place in which couples who are dating pair off—arousing considerable interest because this may be their first public appearance. Festivities may continue until nearly midnight as guests gradually leave. Some guests, invited to several weddings on the same day, may rotate between them.

Newly married couples usually set up housekeeping in the spring after their wedding. Until then the groom may live at the bride's home or continue to live with his parents. Couples do not take a traditional honeymoon, but visit relatives on weekends during the winter months. Several newlywed couples may visit together, sometimes staying overnight at the home of close relatives. During these visits, family and friends present gifts to the newlyweds to add to the bride's dowry, which often consists of furniture. Young men begin growing a beard, the functional equivalent of a wedding ring, soon after their marriage. They are expected to have a "full stand" by the springtime communion.

FUNERALS

With the elderly living at home, the gradual loss of health prepares family members for the final passage. Accompanied by quiet grief, death comes gracefully, the final benediction to a good life and entry into the bliss of eternity. Although funeral practices vary from community to community, the preparations reflect core Amish values, as family and friends yield to eternal verities.

The community springs into action at the word of a death. Family and friends in the local church district assume barn and household chores, freeing the immediate family. Well-established funeral rituals unburden the family from worrisome choices. Three couples are appointed to extend invitations and supervise funeral arrangements: food preparation, seating arrangements, and the coordination of a large number of horses and carriages.

In the Lancaster, Pennsylvania, settlement a non-Amish undertaker moves the body to a funeral home for embalming. The body, without cosmetic improvements, returns to the home in a simple, hardwood coffin within a day. Family members of the same sex dress the body in white. White garments symbolize the final passage into a new and better eternal life. Tailoring the white clothes prior to death helps to prepare the family for the season of grief. Women often wear the white cape and apron worn at their wedding.

Friends and relatives visit the family and view the body in a room on the first floor of the home for two days prior to the funeral. Meanwhile, community members dig the grave by hand in a nearby family cemetery as others oversee the daily chores of the bereaved. Several hundred guests attend the funeral in a barn or home typically on the morning of the third day after death. During the simple hour-and-a-half-long service,

ministers read hymns and scriptures, offer prayers, and preach a sermon. There are no flowers, burial gowns, burial tents, limousines, or sculpted monuments.

The hearse, a large, black carriage pulled by horses, leads a long procession of other carriages to the burial ground on the edge of a farm. After a brief viewing and graveside service, pallbearers lower the coffin and shovel soil into the grave as the bishop reads a hymn. Small, equal-sized tombstones mark the place of the deceased in the community of equality. Close friends and family members then return to the home for a meal prepared by members of the local congregation. Bereaved women, especially close relatives, may signal their mourning by wearing a black dress in public settings for as long as a year. A painful separation laced with grief, death is nevertheless received gracefully as the ultimate surrender to God's higher ways.

EDUCATION

The Amish supported public education when it revolved around one-room schools in the first half of the twentieth century. Under local control, the one-room rural schools posed little threat to Amish values. The massive consolidation of public schools and growing pressure to attend high school sparked clashes between the Amish and officials in several states in the middle of the twentieth century. Confrontations in several other states led to arrests and brief stints in jail. After legal skirmishes in several states, the U.S. Supreme Court gave its blessing to the eighth-grade Amish school system in 1972, stating that "there can be no assumption that today's majority is 'right' and the Amish and others are 'wrong.'" The court concluded that "a way of life that is odd or even erratic but interferes with no rights or interests of others is not to be condemned because it is different."

Today the Amish operate more than 850 parochial schools for some 24,000 Amish children. Many of the schools have one room with 25 to 35 pupils and one teacher who is responsible for teaching all eight grades. A few Amish children attend rural public schools in some states but the vast majority go to parochial schools operated by the Amish.

A scripture reading and prayer opens each school day, but religion is not formally taught in the school. The curriculum includes reading, arithmetic, spelling, grammar, penmanship, history, and geography. Both English and German are taught. Parents want children to learn German to enhance their ability to read religious writings, many of which are written in formal German. Science and sex education are missing in the curriculum as are the other typical trappings of public schools: sports, dances, cafeterias, clubs, bands, choruses, computers, television, guidance counselors, principals, strikes, and college recruiters.

A local board of three to five fathers organizes the school, hires a teacher, approves curriculum, oversees the budget, and supervises maintenance. Teachers receive about $25 to $35 per day. The cost per child is roughly $250 per year, nearly 16 times lower than many public schools where per pupil costs often top $4,000. Amish parents pay public school taxes and taxes for their own school.

Schools play a critical role in the preservation of Amish culture. They not only reinforce Amish values, but also shield youth from contaminating ideas. Moreover, schools restrict friendships with non-Amish peers and impede the flow of Amish youth into higher education and professional life. Amish schools promote practical skills to prepare their graduates for success in Amish society. Some selective testing indicates that Amish pupils compare favorably with rural peers in public schools on standardized tests of basic skills.

Amish teachers, trained in Amish schools, are not required to be certified in most states. Often the brightest and best of Amish scholars, they return to the classroom in their late teens and early twenties to teach. Amish school directors select them for their ability to teach and their commitment to Amish values. Frequently single women, they typically drop their occupation if wed. Periodic meetings with other teachers, a monthly teachers' magazine, and ample common sense prepare them for the task of teaching 30 students in eight grades. With three or four pupils per grade, teachers often teach two grades at a time. Pupils in other classes ponder assignments or listen to previews of next year's lessons or hear reviews of past work. Classrooms exhibit a distinct sense of order amidst a beehive of activity. Hands raise to ask permission or clarify instructions as the teacher moves from cluster to cluster teaching new material every ten or 15 minutes. Some textbooks are recycled from public schools while others are produced by Amish publishers. Students receive a remarkable amount of personal attention despite the teacher's responsibility for eight grades. The ethos of the classroom accents cooperative activity, obedience, respect, diligence, kindness, and the natural world. Despite the emphasis on order, playful pranks and giggles are commonplace. Schoolyard play in daily recesses often involves softball or other homespun games.

Amish schools exhibit a social continuity rarely found in public education. With many families sending several children to a school, teachers may relate to as few as a dozen households. Teachers know parents personally and special circumstances surrounding each child. In some cases, children have the same teacher for all eight grades. Indeed, all the children from a family may have the same teacher. Amish schools are unquestionably provincial by modern standards. Yet in a humane fashion they ably prepare Amish youth for meaningful lives in Amish society.

RELIGION

At first glance the Amish appear quite religious. Yet a deeper inspection reveals no church buildings, sacred symbols, or formal religious education even in Amish schools. Unlike most modern religions, religious meanings pervade all aspects of Amish life. Religion is practiced, not debated. Silent prayers before and after meals embroider each day with reverence. The Amish way of living and being requires neither heady talk nor formal theology.

The *Ordnung,* a religious blueprint for expected behavior, regulates private, public, and ceremonial behavior. Unwritten in most settlements, the Ordnung is passed on by oral tradition. A body of understandings that defines Amish ways, the Ordnung marks expected Amish behavior: wearing a beard without a mustache; using a buggy; and speaking the dialect. It also specifies taboos: divorce; filing a lawsuit; wearing jewelry; owning a car; and attending college. The understandings evolve over the years and are updated as the church faces new issues: embryo transplants in cattle; using computers and facsimile machines; and working in factories. Core understandings, such as wearing a beard and not owning a car, span all Old Order Amish settlements but the finer points of the Ordnung vary considerably from settlement to settlement.

Although ordained leaders update the Ordnung in periodic meetings, each bishop interprets it for his local congregation. Thus, dress styles and the use of telephones and battery-powered appliances may vary by church district. Once embedded in the Ordnung and established as tradition, the understandings rarely change. As new issues face the church, leaders identify those which may be detrimental to community life. Non-threatening changes such as weed-whackers and instant coffee may be overlooked and gradually slip into Amish life. Battery-powered video cameras, which might lead to other video entanglements with the outside world, would surely be forbidden.

Children learn the ways of the Ordnung by observing adults. The Ordnung defines the way things are in a child's mind. Teenagers, free from the supervision of the church, sometimes flirt with worldly ways and flaunt the Ordnung. At baptism, however, young adults between the ages of 16 and 22 declare their Christian faith and vow to uphold the Ordnung for the rest of their lives. Those who break their promise face excommunication and shunning. Those choosing not to be baptized may gradually drift away from the community but are welcome to return to their families without the stigma of shunning.

WORSHIP SERVICES

Worship services held in Amish homes reaffirm the moral order of Amish life. Church districts hold services every other Sunday. A group of 200 or more, including neighbors and relatives who have an "off Sunday," gather for worship. They meet in a farmhouse, the basement of a newer home, or in a shed or barn. A fellowship meal at noon and informal visiting follow the three-hour morning service.

The plain and simple but unwritten liturgy revolves around congregational singing and two sermons. Without the aid of organs, offerings, candles, crosses, robes, or flowers, members yield themselves to God in the spirit of humility. The congregation sings from the *Ausbund,* a hymnal of German songs without musical notations that date back to the sixteenth-century Anabaptists. The tunes passed across the generations by memory are sung in unison without any musical accompaniment. The slow, chant-like cadence means a single song may stretch over 20 minutes. Extemporaneous sermons, preached in the Pennsylvania German dialect, recount biblical stories as well as lessons from farm life. Preachers exhort members to be obedient to Amish ways.

Communion services, held each autumn and spring, frame the religious year. These ritual high points emphasize self-examination and spiritual rejuvenation. Sins are confessed and members reaffirm their vow to uphold the Ordnung. Communion is held when the congregation is at peace, when all members are in harmony with the Ordnung. The six- to eight-hour communion service includes preaching, a light meal during the service, and the commemoration of Christ's death with bread and wine. Pairs of members wash each others feet as the congregation sings. At the end of the communion service members give an alms offering to the deacon, the only time that offerings are collected in Amish services.

EXCOMMUNICATION

Baptism, worship, and communion are sacred rites that revitalize and preserve the Ordnung. But the Amish, like other human beings, forget, rebel, experiment, and stray into deviance. Major transgressions are confessed publicly in a members meeting following the worship service. Violations of the Ordnung—using a tractor in the field, posing for a television camera, flying on a commercial airline, filing a lawsuit, joining a political organization, or opening a questionable business—are confessed publicly. Public confession of sins diminishes self-will, reminds members of the supreme value of submission, restores the wayward into the community of faith, and underscores the lines of faithfulness which encircle the community.

The headstrong who spurn the advice of elders and refuse to confess their sin face a six-week probation. The next step is the *Meidung,* or shunning—a cultural equivalent of solitary confinement. Members terminate social interaction and financial transactions with the excommunicated. For the unrepentant, social avoidance becomes a lifetime quarantine. If their stubbornness does not mellow into repentance, they face excommunication.

EMPLOYMENT AND ECONOMIC TRADITIONS

Amish life is rooted in the soil. Ever since European persecution pushed them into rural areas, the Amish have been farmers. The land has nurtured their common life and robust families. Since the middle of the twentieth century, some of the older and larger Amish settlements in Indiana, Ohio,

This photograph, taken in 1986, features an Amish family from Lancaster, Pennsylvania. They are harvesting corn so that they may feed their livestock during the winter months.

and Pennsylvania have shifted to nonfarm occupations because of the pressure of urbanization. As urbanization devoured prime farmland, prices soared. Land, for example, in the heart of Pennsylvania's Lancaster Amish settlement sold for $300 an acre in 1940. In the 1990s, the same land sold for $8,000 to $10,000 an acre. If sold for development, prices can double or even triple.

The shrinking and expensive farmland in some of the older settlements has forced a crisis in the Amish soul. The Amish have also contributed to the demographic squeeze with their growing population. The community has coped with the crisis in several ways. First, farms have been subdivided into smaller units with intensive cropping and larger concentrations of livestock. Second, some families have migrated to the rural backwaters of other states where farms could be purchased at much lower prices. Third, in some settlements a majority of families no longer farms, but works in small shops, rural factories, or in various trades. But even ex-farmers insist that the farm remains the best place to raise a family.

The rise of cottage industries and small shops marks an historic turn in Amish life. Mushrooming since the 1970s, these new enterprises have reshaped Amish society. Amish retail shops sell dry goods, furniture, shoes, hardware, and wholesale foods. Church members now work as carpenters, plumbers, painters, and self-trained accountants. Professionals, like lawyers, physicians, and

veterinarians, are missing from Amish ranks because of the taboo on high school and college education. The new industries come in three forms. Home-based operations lodged on farms or by newly built homes employ a few family members and neighbors. Bakeshops, craft shops, hardware stores, health food stores, quilt shops, flower shops, and repair shops of all sorts are but a few of the hundreds of home-based operations. Work in these settings revolves around the family. A growing number of these small cottage industries cater to tourists but many serve the needs of Amish and non-Amish neighbors alike.

Larger shops and manufacturing concerns are housed in newly constructed buildings on the edge of farms or on commercial plots. These formal shops with five to ten employees manufacture farm machinery, hydraulic equipment, storage barns, furniture, and cabinetry. Some metal fabrication shops arrange subcontracts with other manufacturers. The larger shops are efficient and profitable. Low overhead, minimal advertising, austere management, modest wages, quality workmanship, and sheer hard work grant many shops a competitive edge in the marketplace.

Mobile work crews constitute a third type of industry. Amish construction groups travel to building sites for commercial and residential construction. The construction crews travel in hired vehicles and in some settlements they are permitted to use electric tools powered by portable generators and on-site electricity.

The rise of cottage industries may, in the long run, disturb the equality of Amish life by encouraging a three-tier society of farmers, entrepreneurs, and day laborers. Parents worry that youth working a 40-hour week with loose cash in their pockets will snub traditional Amish values of simplicity and frugality. The new industries also increase contact with the outside world which will surely prompt even more changes in Amish life. Despite the occupational changes, virtually no Amish are unemployed or receive government unemployment benefits.

POLITICS AND GOVERNMENT

The Amish view government with an ambiguous eye. Although they support and respect civil government, they also keep a healthy distance from it. On the one hand, they follow biblical admonitions to obey and pray for rulers and encourage members to be law-abiding citizens. On the other hand, government epitomizes worldly culture and the use of force. European persecutors of the Anabaptists were often government officials. Modern governments engage in warfare, use capital punishment, and impose their will with raw coercion. Believing that such coercion and violence mock the gentle spirit of Jesus, the Amish reject the use of force, including litigation. Since they regulate many of their own affairs they have less need for outside supervision.

When civil law and religious conscience collide, the Amish are not afraid to take a stand and will obey God rather than man, even if it brings imprisonment. They have clashed with government officials over the use of hard hats, zoning regulations, Workers' Compensation, and building codes for schools. However, as conscientious objectors many have received farm deferments or served in alternative service programs during times of military draft.

The church forbids membership in political organizations and holding public office for several reasons. First, running for office is viewed as arrogant and out of character with esteemed Amish values of humility and modesty. Second, office-holding violates the religious principle of separation from the world. Finally, public officials must be prepared to use legal force if necessary to settle civic disputes. The exercise of legal force mocks the stance of non-resistance. Voting, however, is viewed as a personal matter. Although the church does not prohibit it, few persons vote. Those who do vote are likely to be younger businessmen concerned about local issues. Although voting is considered a personal matter, jury duty is not allowed.

The Amish pay federal and state income taxes, sales taxes, real estate taxes, and personal property taxes. Indeed, they pay school taxes twice, for both public and Amish schools. Following biblical injunctions, the Amish are exempt from Social Security tax. They view Social Security as a national insurance program, not a tax. Congressional legislation, passed in 1965, exempts self-employed Amish persons from Social Security. Amish persons employed in Amish businesses were also exempted by congressional legislation in 1988. Those who do not qualify for the exemption, Amish employees in non-Amish businesses, must pay Social Security without reaping its benefits. Bypassing Social Security not only severs the Amish from old age payments, it also closes the spigot to Medicare and Medicaid.

The Amish object to government aid for several reasons. They contend that the church should assume responsibility for the social welfare of its own members. The aged, infirm, senile, disabled, and retarded are cared for, whenever possible, within extended family networks. To turn the care of these people over to the state would abdicate a fundamental tenet of faith: the care of one's brothers and sisters in the church. Furthermore, federal aid in the form of Social Security or Medicare would erode dependency on the church and undercut its programs of mutual aid, which the Amish have organized to assist their members with fire and storm damages and with medical expenses.

Government subsidies, or what the Amish call handouts, have been stridently opposed. Championing self-sufficiency and the separation of church and state, the Amish worry that the hand which feeds them will also control them. Over the years they have stubbornly refused direct subsidies even for agricultural programs designed for farmers in distress. Amish farmers do, however, receive indirect subsidies through agricultural price-support programs.

In 1967 the Amish formed the National Amish Steering Committee in order to speak with a common voice on legal issues related to state, and especially, federal government. The Steering Committee has worked with government officials to resolve disputes related to conscientious objection, zoning, slow-moving vehicle emblems, Social

Security, Workers' Compensation, and the wearing of hard hats at construction sites. Informally organized, the Steering Committee is the only Amish organization which is national in scope.

THE FUTURE OF AMISH SOCIETY

The future shape of Amish life escapes prediction. Particular outcomes will be shaped not only by unforeseen external forces, such as market prices, government regulations, and rates of urbanization, but also by internal politics and the sentiments of particular Amish leaders. Without a centralized decision-making process, let alone a strategic planning council, new directions are unpredictable. Migrations will likely continue to new states and to the rural areas of states where the Amish presently live.

The willingness of many Amish to leave their plows for shops and cottage industries in the 1970s and 1980s signalled a dramatic shift in Amish life. Microenterprises will likely blossom and bring change to Amish life as they increase interaction with the outside world. These business endeavors will probably alter the class structure and cultural face of Amish society over the years. But the love of farming runs deep in the Amish heart. Faced with a growing population, many families will likely migrate to more rural areas in search of fertile soil.

The cultural flavor of twenty-first century Amish life may elude forecast, but one pattern is clear. Settlements which are pressed by urbanization are the most progressive in outlook and the most updated in technology. Rural homesteads beyond the tentacles of urban sprawl remain the best place to preserve traditional Amish ways. If the Amish can educate and retain their children, make a living, and restrain interaction with the larger world, they will likely flourish into the twenty-first century. But one thing is certain: diversity between their settlements will surely grow, mocking the staid stereotypes of Amish life.

MEDIA

PRINT

Arthur Graphic Clarion.
Newspaper of the Illinois Amish country.

Contact: Allen Mann, Editor.
Address: P.O. Box 19, Arthur, Illinois 61911.

Telephone: (217) 543-2151.
Fax: (217) 543-2152.

Die Botschaft.
Weekly English newspaper with correspondents from many states that serves Old Order Mennonite and Old Order Amish communities.

Contact: Brookshire Publications, Inc.
Address: 200 Hazel Street, Lancaster, Pennsylvania 17608-0807.

The Budget.
Weekly Amish/Mennonite community newspaper.

Contact: George R. Smith, National Editor.
Address: Sugarcreek Budget Publishers, Inc., 134 North Factory Street, P.O. Box 249, Sugarcreek, Ohio 44681-0249.
Telephone: (216) 852-4634.
Fax: (216) 852-4421.

The Diary.
Monthly publication that lists migrations, marriages, births, and deaths. It also carries news and feature articles.

Contact: Pequea Publishers.
Address: P.O. Box 98, Gordonville, Pennsylvania 17529.

Family Life.
Monthly family magazine printed in English.

Contact: Pathway Publishers.
Address: Route 4, Aylmer, Ontario, N5H 2R3 Canada.

Mennonite Quarterly Review.
Scholarly journal covering Mennonite, Amish, Hutterian Brethren, Anabaptist, Radical Reformation, and related history and religious thought.

Contact: John E. Roth, Editor.
Address: Mennonite Historical Society, Goshen College, Goshen, Indiana 46526.
Telephone: (219) 535-7111.
Fax: (219) 535-7438.

Young Companion.
Monthly magazine for young people printed in English.

Contact: Pathway Publishers.
Address: Route 4, Aylmer, Ontario N5H 2R3, Canada.

ORGANIZATIONS AND ASSOCIATIONS

Lancaster Mennonite Historical Society (LMHS).
Individuals interested in the historical background, theology, culture, and genealogy of Mennonite and Amish related groups originating in Pennsylvania. Collects and preserves archival materials. Publishes the *Mirror* bimonthly.

Contact: Carolyn C. Wenger, Director.
Address: 2215 Millstream Road, Lancaster, Pennsylvania 17602-1499.
Telephone: (717) 393-9745.

National Committee for Amish Religious Freedom (NCARF).
Provides legal defense for Amish people, since the Amish are reluctant to defend themselves or seek court action.

Contact: Rev. William C. Lindholm, Chair.
Address: 30650 Six Mile Road, Livonia, Michigan 48152.
Telephone: (313) 427-1414.

MUSEUMS AND RESEARCH CENTERS

Heritage Historical Library.
Address: Route 4, Aylmer, Ontario N5H 2R3, Canada.

Mennonite Historical Library.
Address: Goshen College, Goshen, Indiana 46526.
Telephone: (219) 535-7000.

Ohio Amish Library.
Address: 4292 SR39, Millersburg, Ohio 44654.

Pequea Bruderschaft Library.
Address: P.O. Box 25, Gordonville, Pennsylvania PA 17529.

The Young Center for the Study of Anabaptist and Pietist Groups.
Address: Elizabethtown College, One Alpha Drive, Elizabethtown, Pennsylvania 17022.
Telephone: (717) 361-1470.

SOURCES FOR ADDITIONAL STUDY

The Amish and the State. Baltimore: Johns Hopkins University Press, 1993.

Amish Society, fourth edition. Baltimore: Johns Hopkins University Press, 1993.

The Amish Wedding and Other Special Occasions of the Old Order Communities. Intercourse, Pennsylvania: Good Books, 1988.

Hostetler, John A. *Amish Life.* Scottdale, Pennsylvania: Herald Press, 1983.

Kline, David. *Great Possessions: An Amish Farmer's Journal.* San Francisco: North Point Press, 1990.

Kraybill, Donald B. *The Riddle of Amish Culture.* Baltimore: Johns Hopkins University Press, 1989.

Kraybill, Donald B., and Marc A. Olshan. *The Amish Struggle with Modernity.* Hanover, New Hampshire: University Press of New England, 1994.

Nolt, Steven M. *A History of the Amish.* Intercourse, Pennsylvania: Good Books, 1992.

The Puzzles of Amish Life. Intercourse, Pennsylvania: Good Books, 1990.

Scott, Stephen. *Why Do They Dress That Way?* Intercourse, Pennsylvania: Good Books, 1986.

During the years 1901-1910 alone, over 2.1 million Austrian citizens arrived on these shores to become one of the ten most populous immigrant groups in the United States.

AUSTRIAN AMERICANS

by
Syd Jones

OVERVIEW

A mountainous landlocked country located in south-central Europe, Austria encompasses an area of 32,377 square miles, roughly the size of the state of Maine. Bordered to the west by Switzerland and Liechtenstein, to the south by Italy and the former Yugoslavia, to the east by Hungary, and to the north by the Czech and Slovak Republics as well as Germany, Austria lies at the center of political and geographic Europe. Two-thirds of Austria's land mass is located in the Alpine region, with its highest peak, the Grossglockner, reaching 12,457 feet.

With a population of 7,587,000, Austria has maintained zero population growth in the last half of the twentieth century. It is a German-speaking country. Eighty-five percent of its population are Roman Catholic while only six percent are Protestant. Vienna, the capital of the Federal Republic of Austria, also doubles as one of the nine autonomous provinces that constitute the federation. The Austrian flag is a simple red-white-red arrangement of horizontal stripes with the Austrian coat of arms in the center.

HISTORY

Austria's very name denotes its history. Ostmark or Ostarichi ("eastern provinces" or "borderland") as it was known in the time of Charlemagne, became over time the German Österreich, or Austria in Latin. As an eastern kingdom—more bulwark than principality, more fortress than palace—Austria bordered the civilized world. The first human inhabitants of this rugged environment were Stone Age hunters who lived 80,000 to 150,000 years ago. Permanent settlements were established in early Paleolithic times. Though little remains of that distant period, an early Iron Age settlement was unearthed at Hallstatt in the western lake district of present-day Austria. The Celts arrived around 400 B.C., and the Romans, in search of iron ore deposits, invaded 200 years later. The Romans established three provinces in the area by 15 B.C. They introduced the grape to the hills surrounding the eastern reaches of the Danube near a settlement they called Vindobona, later known as Wien, or Vienna in English.

For the next four centuries the Romans fought Germanic invasions, eventually losing, but establishing a fortification line along the Danube River, upon which many modern Austrian cities are built. With the fall of Rome, barbarian tribes such as the Bavarians from the west and Mongolian Avars from the east settled the region, bringing new cultural influences. One Germanic tribe, the Franks, were particularly interested in the area, and by the end of the eighth century, Charlemagne succeeded in subduing the other claimants, Christianizing the region and creating a largely Germanic province for his Holy Roman Empire. This Ostmark, or eastern borderland, did not hold long. Incursions from the east by the Magyars around 900 A.D. unsettled the region once again, until the Magyars too were subdued.

The political and territorial concept of Austria came about in 976 when the eastern province was granted to the house of Babenberg. For the next three centuries that family would rule the eastern borderland, eventually choosing Vienna as their seat. By the twelfth century Austria had become a duchy and a flourishing trade center. With the death of the line of Babenberg in 1246, the duchy was voted first to Ottokar II, king of Bohemia, who was defeated in battle by a member of a Swiss noble house, Rudolf IV of Habsburg. The Habsburgs would rule not only Austria, but large parts of Europe and the New World as well until 1918. The Habsburgs created a central European empire around the region of Austria and extending into Bohemia, Hungary, Yugoslavia, Poland, Spain, and the Netherlands. Throughout their rule, the empire acted as a bulwark against eastern invasion by Turks and Magyars, and through both diplomacy and strategic marriages, the Habsburgs established a civilization that would be the envy of the world. Under such emperors as Rudolf, Charles V, and the empress Maria Theresa, universities were established and Vienna became synonymous with music, fostering such composers as Franz Haydn, Wolfgang Mozart, Ludwig van Beethoven, Franz Schubert, and Johannes Brahms.

When the Napoleonic Wars ended the power of the Holy Roman Empire, the Austrian or Habsburg Empire took its place in central Europe and its foreign minister, Clemens Metternich-Winneburg, consolidated power to make a unified German state. The democratic revolutions of 1848 temporarily destabilized the country, but under the rule of Franz Joseph a strong government again rose to power. The Austrian Empire faced increasing nationalistic pressure, however. First the Magyars in Hungary won a compromise with Vienna, creating the Austro-Hungarian Empire in 1867. Other ethnic minorities in the polyglot empire pressed for independence, and eventually, with the assassination of Archduke Ferdinand in Sarajevo in 1914 by a Serbian extremist, the world was plunged into a war that destroyed the Austrian Empire.

In 1918, with the abdication of the last Habsburg, Karl I, the modern Republic of Austria was founded. Now a smaller country, it comprised only the original Germanic provinces with seven million inhabitants. Operating under severe economic hardship, Austria was annexed by Germany in 1938 led by Adolf Hitler, a former Austrian who had become chancellor of Germany. Until 1945, Austria was part of the Third Reich, an ambivalent ally to Germany in the Second World War. With the defeat of Germany, the republic was again restored in Austria, but the country was occupied jointly by the United States, Britain, France, and the Soviet Union until the state treaty of 1955 ensured Austria's permanent neutrality. Austria was no longer a bulwark against the east, but a buffer state between two competing ideologies. As a neutral country, Austria became the site of many United Nations organizations, and blending a market economy with a state partnership, its economy flourished. With the fall of the Soviet empire, Austria has rediscovered its former role as the geographic center of a new and revitalized Europe.

THE FIRST AUSTRIANS IN AMERICA

Austrian emigration patterns have been difficult to determine. There was no state known as Austria until 1918; prior to then the sprawling Habsburg Empire, an amalgam of a dozen nationalities, encompassed the idea of Austria. Thus Austrian immigration can rightly be seen as the immigration of Czech, Polish, Hungarian, Slovenian, Serbian, and Croatian peoples as well as a plethora of other national and ethnic groups. Additionally, immigrants themselves were often unclear about their countries of origin. A German-speaking person born in Prague in 1855, for example, was Czech, but also part of the larger Austrian Empire—Austrian, in fact, but may have considered himself German. Immigrants thus may have listed Czech, Austrian, and/or German as their country of origin. This study will confine itself to German Austrian emigration patterns.

The earliest documented German Austrian settlers in America were some 50 families of Protestants from Salzburg who arrived in the colony of Georgia in 1734 after fleeing religious persecution. Granted free passage and land, they established the settlement of Ebenezer near Savannah. Despite initial difficulties with poor land, sickness, and a relocation of their community, they grew and prospered as new families of immigrants arrived. Although the Revolutionary War witnessed the destruction of their settlements, one of these Austrian settlers, Johann Adam Treutlen, became the first elected governor of the new state of Georgia.

Few Austrians immigrated to the United States during the first half of the nineteenth century; fewer than 1,000 Austrians were listed in official surveys by 1850. Those who did come settled in Illinois and Iowa and were supported by 100 to 200 Catholic priests sent from both Germany and Austria to oversee the settlers' religious training and education. The Leopoldine Stiftung, an Austrian foundation that supported such missionaries, funded priests not only for the newly emigrated, but also for the Native Americans. Priests such as Francis Xavier Weninger (1805-1888) spread the Gospel to Austrian immigrants in the Midwest and black slaves in New Orleans. Bishop Frederic Baraga (1797-1868) was one of the most active priests among the Native Americans, working and preaching in northern Michigan. John Nepomuk Neumann (1811-1860) established numerous schools in the Philadelphia area and was a proponent of the retention of German culture and language.

Tyroleans provided a further segment of early nineteenth-century immigration to America. Mostly peasants, these Tyroleans came to the new world in search of land, yet few had the money they needed to turn their dreams into reality. Other early emigrants fled the oppressive Metternich regime, such as Dr. Samuel Ludvigh (1801-1869), a democratic intellectual who eventually founded *Die Fackel,* a well-known German-language periodical in Baltimore. The 1848 revolutions in Austria saw a small but influential tide of political refugees. These so-called Forty-eighters were mostly anticlerical and held strong antislavery views as well. Though they were few in number, they had a lasting influence on not only politics and journalism, but also in medicine and music. They were mostly free-thinking, well-educated liberals who found assimilation a wearisome process in their newly adopted country. Their presence also upset the conservative Americans. Among these Forty-eighters were many Austrian Jews. Most of the Forty-eighters became abolitionists in America, joining the new Republican party despite the fact that the Democratic party traditionally showed more openness to immigrants. It has been conjectured that their votes helped Abraham Lincoln win the 1860 presidential election.

SIGNIFICANT IMMIGRATION WAVES

Immigration statistics are difficult to interpret for the years between 1861 and 1910, as the U.S. Bureau of Immigration categorized all the inhabitants of the Austro-Hungarian Empire together. During these decades immigration swelled, with estimates of German-speaking Austrians in the United States reaching 275,000 by 1900. Immigrants were encouraged by relaxed emigration laws at home; by the construction of more railways, which allowed easy access to the ports of Europe from their mountainous homeland; by general overpopulation in Europe; and by migration from the farm to the city as Western society became increasingly industrialized. America thus became a destination for displaced Austrian agrarian workers. Many Austrians found employment in the United States as miners, servants, and common laborers. Others flocked to the cities of the Northeast and Midwest—New York, Pittsburgh, and Chicago—where many first- and second-generation Austrians still live. The 1880s witnessed massive immigration to the United States from all parts of Europe, Austria included, with over five million coming to America in that ten-year period. But if peasants were being displaced from the land in Austria, much the same situation was at play in the American midwest where mechanization was revolutionizing agriculture. Thus, newly arrived immigrants, dreaming of a plot of farm land, were largely disappointed. Many of these new arrivals came from Burgenland, an agricultural province to the southeast of Vienna.

During the years 1901-1910 alone, over 2.1 million Austrian citizens arrived on these shores to become one of the ten most populous immigrant groups in the United States. The Austrians—Catholic or Jewish and cosmopolitan—avoided rural Protestant conservative America. Fathers left families behind in Austria, hoping to save money working in Chicago stockyards and Pennsylvania cement and steel factories. More than 35 percent of them returned to their native home with their savings.

With the onset of the First World War, Austrian immigration stopped for a time. Even during the postwar period of 1919 to 1924, fewer than 20,000 Austrians came to the United States, most of them from Burgenland. The passage of a restrictive immigration law in 1924 further curtailed Austrian immigration, first to a limit of 785 and then to 1,413 persons per year. Austrian immigration slowed to a trickle during the years of the Depression.

A new wave of immigrants from Austria began arriving in the late 1930s. Unlike earlier immigrants who were largely unskilled laborers from the provinces, these new arrivals were mostly well-educated urban Jews fleeing Hitler's new regime. In 1938 Austria had become incorporated into the Third Reich and anti-Semitism had become a daily fact of life. In the three-year period between the *Anschluss*, or annexation by Germany, and the outbreak of all-out war in 1941, some 29,000 Jewish Austrians emigrated to the United States. These were generally highly skilled professionals in medicine, architecture, law, and the arts and included men of international renown: composers Arnold Schoenberg (1874-1951) and Erich Korngold (1897-1957); author Franz Werfel (1890-1945); and stage and film directors such as Max Reinhardt (1873-1943) and Otto Preminger (1906-1986). The Jewish Austrian intellectual elite was, in fact, scattered around the globe in the diaspora caused by the Second World War.

Some 40,000 Austrians entered the United States from 1945-1960. U.S. immigration quotas again limited and diverted immigration to other countries such as Canada and Australia. Recent Austrian immigration has been negligible, as Austria has built itself into a wealthy industrial state. The 1990 U.S. census listed 948,558 citizens of Austrian ancestry, only 0.4 percent of the total population. However, it is estimated that in the years from 1820 to 1960, 4.2 million or ten percent of the immigrants who arrived in America came from Austro-Hungary and the states succeeding it.

SETTLEMENT

The first sizable wave of Austrian immigrants tended to settle in the urbanized centers of the northeastern United States, especially in New York City. They were also populous in New Jersey, Pennsylvania, and Connecticut. Allentown, Pennsylvania, for example, had an Austrian-born population of 6,500 in 1930, the largest single ethnic minority in that town. Recent emigration has changed this trend somewhat. The 1990 census reports the largest single concentration in New York, followed by large contingents in both California and Florida.

ACCULTURATION AND ASSIMILATION

In general, Austrian immigrants have quickly assimilated in America. Part of a multi-ethnic melange in their original homeland, Austrians were accustomed to the melting pot and were quick to pick up new languages and customs once in America. Dr. Harry Zohn (1922-), professor of German literature at Brandeis University, voices a sentiment typical of many Austrian Americans: "I'm an American who just happened to be born in Vienna." Zohn, a refugee from Nazism, was one of the fortunate few whose entire family managed to escape. Once in the United States, Zohn quickly adapted to the culture and language, though never losing his intellectual and spiritual ties to Middle Europe, writing in both German and English about Austrian literature and culture (E. Wilder Spaulding, *The Quiet Invaders: The Story of Austrian Impact upon America* [Vienna: Österreichische Bundesverlag, 1968]).

On the whole, Austrians tend to differentiate themselves strongly from German immigrants whom they see as more chauvinistic and domineering. Austrians in America like to think of themselves as more cosmopolitan, sophisticated, and tolerant than their German neighbors. As a group, Austrian immigrants have not drawn attention to themselves. Moreover, they are, somewhat to their dismay, often lumped together with German immigrants and have thus suffered

from the same stereotypes as the Germans in America. Both world wars of this century resulted in Americans often having negative attitudes toward Germany. In the First World War, the two groups were derogatorily called Dutchy, from the German word *Deutsch*. Names sounding German, such as Braun and Schmidt, were changed overnight to Brown and Smith. Austrians and Germans became, for many Americans, the enemy within. Other stereotypes persisted even in peacetime, including the beer-swilling Austrian, and the pleasure-loving, wine-sipping, charming proponents of *Gemütlichkeit* or coziness.

TRADITIONS, CUSTOMS, AND BELIEFS

Austrian traditions, maintained most faithfully by those living in the mountainous region of Western Austria, center mainly around the seasons. *Fasching* is an old winter custom that traditionally takes place in February. In its pagan form, it was an attempt to drive out the evil spirits of winter

and prepare for spring. Processions of villagers dressed in varieties of masked costumes and ringing cow bells symbolized the fight of spring against winter. Some of these processions still take place in parts of Tyrol and Styria, but the *fasching* has generally evolved into a procession of carnival balls linked with Lent and the passion of Easter.

Similarly, the old spring festivals wherein village children would parade with boughs decorated with ivy and pretzels to celebrate the reawakening of the sun, have been replaced by Palm Sunday and Corpus Christi celebrations. May Day and the dance around the maypole is still a muchcelebrated event in villages all over Austria. The festival of the summer solstice, announced by bonfires on the hills, still takes place in parts of Salzburg, under the name of St. John's Night.

Harvest festivals of autumn, linked with apple and wine gathering, have a long tradition throughout Austria. Harvest fairs are still a vital part of the autumn season, and the wine harvest, from grape picking and pressing through the various stages of wine fermentation, is an affair closely monitored by many Austrians. The pine bough outside a winery signals customers that new wine is available. The thanksgiving festival of St. Leonard, patron saint of livestock, is a reminder of a pagan harvest celebration.

Perhaps best known and most retained by Austrian immigrants in America are traditions of the Christmas season, the beginning of which is marked by St. Nicholas Day on December 6. Good children are rewarded with apples and nuts in their stockings, while bad ones receive only lumps of coal. Caroling and the Christmas tree are but two of the Austrian and German contributions to the American celebrations of yuletide. One of the best-known Christmas carols, "Silent Night," was written by an Austrian.

As many customs and beliefs from Austria have been incorporated by the Catholic Church, many Austrian Americans have retained the feast days of their native country, though without the pageantry or connection to their original purpose. The Austrian custom of placing a pine tree atop newly constructed houses has become a traditional ceremony for American ironworkers as well, many of whom were of Central European origin. The fir tree, as mentioned, has become a staple of American Christmas. Yet overall, Austrian customs have become barely recognizable in America.

CUISINE

Austrian cuisine relies heavily on meat, especially pork. The famous dish *wienerschnitzel*, pork or veal fried in bread crumbs, is among the many recipes that were imported along with the immigrants. *Goulasch*, a spicy Hungarian stew, is another item that has found its way onto the American table, as has *sauerkraut*, both a German and Austrian specialty. Sausages, called *wurst* in German, have become so popular in America that names such as wiener (from *wienerwurst*) and frankfurter (from Frankfurt in Germany) are synonymous with a whole class of food. Pastries and desserts are also Austrian specialties; Austrian favorites include cake such as *Sachertorte*, a heavy chocolate concoction closely connected with Vienna's Hotel Sacher; *linzertorte*, more of a tart than cake, stuffed with apricot jam; and the famous pastry *apfelstrudel*, a flaky sort of pie stuffed with apples. The list of such sweets is lengthy, and many of them have found places, under different names, as staples of American cui-

sine. Breads are another Austrian contribution to the world's foods: the rye breads of both Germany and Austria are dense and longlasting with a hearty flavor.

Austrian beer, such as the light lagers and heavier *Bock*—brewed for Christmas and Easter—is on par with the better known German varieties. Early immigrants of both nationalities brought the fondness for barley and hops with them, and many Austrians founded breweries in the United States. Wines, especially the tart white wines of the Wachau region of the Danube and the refined, complex varietals of Gumpoldskirchen to the south of Vienna, have become world famous as well. The Austrian love for the new wine, or *heuriger*, is witnessed by dozens of drinking songs. The simple wine tavern, owned and operated by the vintner and his family, combines the best of a picnic with dining out.

TRADITIONAL COSTUMES

In Austria, the traditional costumes or *trachten*, are still fashionable, not only for the rural population, but for city-dwellers as well. Most typical and best known by those outside Austria is the *dirndl*. Both village girls and Viennese matrons can be seen wearing this pleated skirt covered by a brightly colored apron and surmounted by a tight-fitting bodice. White blouses are worn under the bodice, sometimes embroidered, sometimes with lace. For men the typical *trachten* is the *steirer anzug*, a collarless variation of a hunting costume, usually gray with green piping and trim, which can be worn for both formal and informal occasions. The *wetterfleck*, a long loden cape, is also still worn, as are knickers of elk hide or wool. *Lederhosen*, or leather shorts, associated with both Germany and Austria, are still typical summer wear in much of Austria.

AUSTRIAN MUSIC AND DANCES

From simple *lieder*, or songs, to symphonies and operas, Austrian music has enriched the cultural life of the Western world. Vienna in particular was the home of native Austrian and German composers alike who created the classical idiom. Men such as Haydn, Mozart, Beethoven, Schubert, and Brahms developed symphony and chamber music. More modern composers such as Anton Bruckner, Gustav Mahler, and Arnold Schoenberg—the latter immigrated to the United States—expanded the boundaries of tonality and structure in music composition.

Austria is also synonymous with the waltz, developed from an earlier peasant dance and made famous through the music of Johann Strauss and Joseph Lanner. The Viennese operetta has also influenced the musical taste of the world, helping to develop the form of the modern musical. Johann Strauss, Jr., is only one of many who pioneered the form, and a Viennese, Frederick Loewe, helped to transform it on Broadway by writing the lyrics to such famous musicals as *My Fair Lady* and *Camelot*.

HOLIDAYS CELEBRATED BY AUSTRIAN AMERICANS

Beyond such traditional holidays as Christmas, New Year's, and Easter, Austrian Americans cannot be said to celebrate various feast and seasonal days as a group. The more cosmopolitan immigrants from Vienna, for example, were and are much more internationalist in outlook than fellow Austrian immigrants from Burgenland, who hold to more traditional customs even in the United States. This latter group, former residents of a rural, agricultural area and generally Catholic, are more likely to observe such traditional feasts as St. Leonard's Day in November, St. Nicholas Day on December 6, and Corpus Christi in June, as well as such seasonal festivities as harvest festivals for wine in October.

HEALTH AND MENTAL HEALTH ISSUES

The medical tradition in Austria is long and noteworthy. The Viennese have contributed medical innovations such as antisepsis and new therapies such as psychoanalysis to the world. Austrian Americans place a high value on health care. They also bring with them the idea of medical care as a birthright, for in Austria such care has been part of a broad government-run social program during much of the twentieth century. There are no documented congenital diseases specific to Austrian Americans.

LANGUAGE

Austria and Germany are, to paraphrase Winston Churchill's famous quip about England and America, two countries separated by a common language. That Austria is a German-speaking country seems to come as a surprise to many Americans. Germans also have great fun scratch-

ing their heads over Austrianisms (e.g., the German *kartoffel* becomes *erdapfel*, or apple of the earth, in Austria). However, Austrian German, apart from a lighter, more sing-song accent and some regional words, is no different from true German than Canadian English is from American English. The umlaut (ä, ö, ü) is the primary diacritical mark over vowels, and is sometimes expressed by an "e" after the vowel instead of employing the diacritic.

As English is an offshoot of Old German, there are enough similarities between the two languages to make language assimilation a reasonably easy task for Austrian Americans. The "v" for "w" confusion is an especially difficult phonetic problem, as German has no unaspirated pronunciation of "w." Another pronunciation difficulty is the English diphthong "th" for which German has no equivalent, resulting in the thick "s" so caricatured by stage and screen actors.

GREETINGS AND OTHER POPULAR EXPRESSIONS

Typical Austrian greetings and farewells include the more formal Germanisms such as *Guten Tag* ("gooten tahg")—Good day; *Guten Abend* ("gooten ahbend")—Good evening; and *Auf Wiedersehen* ("ouf veedersayen")—Good-bye. More typically Austrian are *Grüss Gott* ("groos gote")—literally Greetings from God, but used as Hello or Hi; and *Servus* ("sairvoos")—both Hello and Good-bye, used by younger people and between good friends. Other polite expressions—for which Austrian German seems to have an overabundance—include *Bitte* ("bietuh")—both Please and You're welcome; *Danke Vielmals* ("dahnka feelmahls")—Thanks very much; and *Es tut mir sehr leid* ("es toot meer sair lied")—I'm very sorry. Seasonal expressions include *Frohe Weihnachten* ("frohuh vienahkten")—Merry Christmas; and *Prosit Neujahr* ("proezit noy yahr")—Happy New Year. *Zum wohl* ("tzoom vole")—To your health—is a typical toast.

FAMILY AND COMMUNITY DYNAMICS

Initially, many of the immigrants from Austria were males who came to America to earn and save money and then to return home. Most often, these early immigrants would live together in crowded rooming houses or primitive hostels in urban centers of the industrial northeastern United States. As permanent immigration patterns replaced this more nomadic style, the structure of the Austrian family became transplanted to America. Typically a tight nuclear family that seldom included a grandmother, the Austrian family has few of the characteristics of the extended Mediterranean family. The father ruled the economic life of the family, but the strong matriarch was boss at home. As in Austria, male children were favored. Sundays were a sacrosanct family time together. In general, few outsiders were allowed the informal "Du" greeting or even invited into the home.

This tight structure soon broke down, however, in the more egalitarian American environment. Austrian immigrants tended overall to assimilate rapidly into their new country, adapting to the ways of America and being influenced by the same cultural trends that affected native-born Americans: the increasing importance of the role of women in the twentieth century; the decline of the nuclear family, including a rising divorce rate; and the mobility of citizens—both geographically and economically. The variety of Austrian immigrants also changed in this century. Once mainly agrarian workers who congregated in urban areas despite their desire to settle on the land, immigrants from Austria—especially after the First World War—tended to be better educated with a larger world view. The flight of the Jewish Austrian intelligentsia during the Nazi period especially affected the assimilation patterns. These professional classes placed a high premium on education for both male and female children. Thus Austrian immigrants became skilled workers and professionals.

RELIGION

Mostly Roman Catholic, Austrians brought their religion with them to America. Austrian missionaries, mainly Jesuits, baptized Native Americans and helped chart the New World from the seventeenth century on. But by the nineteenth century that mission had changed, for newly arrived Austrian immigrants, disdained by Irish Catholic priests who spoke no German, were clamoring for Austrian priests. Partly to meet this need and partly to convert new souls to Catholicism, the Leopoldine Stiftung or Foundation was established in 1829. Collecting weekly donations throughout the Habsburg Empire, the foundation sent money and priests into North America to bring faith to the frontier. Through such contributions over 400 churches were built on the East Coast, in the Midwest, and in what was then known as Indian country further west. The Jesuits were especially active during this period in cities such as Cincinnati and St. Louis. The Benedictines and Franciscans were also represented by both priests and nuns. These priests founded bishoprics and built congregations in the thousands. One unfortunate reaction to this was an intensification of nativist tendencies, or anti-immigrant sentiments. This influx of priests was looked upon as a conspiracy to upset the balance of the population in America with Roman Catholics imported from Europe. For many years such nativist sentiments made it difficult for Austrian immigrants to fully assimilate into American society.

On the whole, the formal traditions and rights of the Church in the United States and in Austria were the same, but external pressures differed. Thus, as with the U.S. population in general, Austrian Americans in the twentieth century have become more secular, less faith-bound. New waves of Austrian immigrants, especially those fleeing Nazism, also changed the religious makeup of the groups as a whole. For the most part, arrivals between 1933 and 1945 were Jewish, and largely assimilated Jews.

EMPLOYMENT AND ECONOMIC TRADITIONS

As with all examinations of Austrian immigration, occupational statistics suffer from the inconsistent distinction between ethnic groups among the Austro-Hungarian immigrants. German-speaking Austrians did settle in the center of the country to become farmers, but in what numbers is unclear. Prior to 1900 Austro-Hungarian immigrants were also laborers, saloon keepers, waiters, and steel workers. Statistics that are available from 1900, however, indicate that a high proportion of later arrivals found work as tailors, miners, and peddlers. By the mid-twentieth century, these same occupational trends still prevailed, with tailoring and the clothing industry in general employing large numbers of Austrian Americans. The food industry was also heavily weighted with Austrians: bakers, restaurateurs, and meat packers. Mining was also a predominant occupation among Austrians.

In the half-century since then, Austrian Americans have branched out into all fields: medicine, law, entertainment, management, and technology, as well as the traditional service industries where many of them started as new immigrants.

POLITICS AND GOVERNMENT

The earliest notable political influence that Austrian Americans wielded came through the pens and the votes of the Forty-eighters. These liberal refugees from the failed revolts of 1848 were strongly abolitionist and pro-Lincoln. Later arrivals during the half-century of mass immigration from Austro-Hungary (1860-1910) packed the ranks of unskilled labor and of America's fledgling labor movement. Indeed, the deaths of ten Austro-Hungarian laborers during the 1897 mining strike in Lattimer, Pennsylvania, prompted a demand for indemnity by the embassy of Austro-Hungary.

Immigrants in the 1930s and 1940s tended to have strong socialist beliefs and formed organizations such as the American Friends of Austrian Labor to help promote labor issues. During World War II an Austrian government in exile was attempted in the United States, but fighting between factions of the refugees, specifically between Social Democrats and Christian Socialists, prevented any concerted action on that front. The creation of the Austrian battalion— the 101st Infantry Battalion—became the center of a debate that raged among Austrian Americans. Groups such as Austria Action and the Austrian Labor Committee opposed such a formation, anxious lest it become the vanguard of the restoration of the Habsburg monarchy under Otto von Habsburg after the war. On the other side, the Free Austrian Movement advocated such a battalion, even if it meant aligning the right with the left among the recruits. A scant six months after its formation, the Austrian battalion was disbanded. Despite this failure, the debate occasioned by the creation of the battalion had helped to bring to the forefront of American discussion the role of Austrian Americans and of Austria itself in the Second World War. Not only were Austrian Americans not interned, but Austria itself, in the Moscow Declaration of November 1, 1943, was declared one of the first victims of Nazism, and the restoration of its independence was made an Allied war aim.

Little information on Austrian American voting patterns exists, though early Jewish Austrian immigrants and Austrian socialists tended to vote Democrat rather than Republican. Interesting in this context is the career of Victor Berger (1860-1929), an Austrian who not only influenced Eugene V. Debs in becoming a socialist, but also became the first socialist to sit in the House of Representatives in Washington.

Austrians of the first generation, on the whole, maintain close links with Austria, returning periodically to their place of birth. Even Jewish Austrians who had to flee the Holocaust return to visit and sometimes to retire in their homeland.

INDIVIDUAL AND GROUP CONTRIBUTIONS

Austrian Americans have made lasting contributions in all fields of American life, though seldom is the emphasis on the fact of their Austrian roots. From the arts to the world of science, this immigrant population has made its mark.

ACADEMIA

Joseph Alois Schumpeter (1883-1950) was a well-known critic of Marxism and an authority on business cycles. Another notable Austrian American economist was Ludwig von Mises (1881-?), a critic of the planned economies of socialist countries. Other Austrian Americans in the fields of literature and history have done much to generate interest in Austria and Central Europe: Harry Zohn is a much-published professor of German literature at Brandeis University, and the Viennese Robert A. Kann's (1906-?) *A History of the Habsburg Empire* has become a standard reference. R. John Rath helped to centralize Austrian studies with his center at Rice University and then at the University of Minnesota. These are only a few of the many notable Austrian American historians at work in this country.

ART AND ARCHITECTURE

Austrian artists who came to the United States include the painter George Peter (1860-?), who immigrated to Milwaukee, Wisconsin, in 1885, painted Civil War themes, and eventually became director of the Milwaukee museum. Others include the artist and architect Joseph Urban (1872-1933); the sculptor and architectural designer Karl Bitter (1867-1915); Joseph Margulies, born in Austria in 1896, who painted and etched scenes of the New York ghetto; and René d'Harnoncourt (1901-?) from Vienna, who eventually became director of contemporary art at the Museum of Modern Art in New York. Max Fleischer (1885-?) was one of the pioneers of the animated cartoon on film whose creations include Betty Boop and Popeye. The exodus from Austria caused by the rise of Hitler brought to the United States such distinguished painters as the modernist Wilhelm Thoeny (1888-1949); the expressionist painters Franz Lerch (1895-?) and Max Oppenheimer (1885-1956); and the graphic artist, John W. Winkler (1890-?). Among architects of note are Karl Bitter, mentioned above, and John L. Smithmeyer (1832-1908), who was the architect of the Library of Congress. Best known of all Austrian American architects was Richard Neutra (1892-1970), whose name is synonymous with the steel and concrete structures he pioneered in California. Other more modern architects include R. M. Schindler (1887-1953) and Victor Gruen (1903-?), who emigrated in 1938 and whose environmental architecture helped transform such cities as Los Angeles, Detroit, and Fort Worth. Frederick John Kiesler (1896-1965) was known as an innovative architect, whose set designs, interiors, and bold floating architectural designs earned him a reputation as a maverick and visionary.

BUSINESS

Franz Martin Drexel (1792-1863), a native of Voralberg, founded the banking house of Drexel and Company in Philadelphia, which later gave rise to the House of Morgan. Another immigrant from Voralberg, John Michael Kohler (1844-1900), built one of the largest plumbing outfitters in the United States and introduced the enamel coated bathtub. August Brentano (1831-1886) was an impoverished Austrian immigrant who turned a newspaper stand into a huge bookshop chain. The development of department stores in America also owes a debt to Austrian Americans Nathan M. Ohrbach (1885-?), founder of the Ohrbach stores, and Joe Weinstein (1894-?), founder of the May stores. John David Hertz (1879-1961), an Austrian Czech, made his name synonymous with rental cars. Austrian American fashion designers have included Nettie Rosenstein (1893-?), a winner of the prestigious Coty award for clothing design, and the Vienna-born Rudi Gernreich (1922-) who created the topless

bathing suits of the 1960s. In the world of publishing, Frederick Ungar, a refugee from the Hitler era, created a well-respected New York house, as did Frederik Amos Praeger (1915-). Tourism in the United States has also been enhanced by the Austrian-style ski resorts and schools in Sun Valley developed by Felix Schaffgotsch, with a ski school operated by Hans Hauser. The Arlberg technique in skiing was promoted by Hannes Schneider (1890-1955) in Jackson, New Hampshire, and later resorts such as Aspen and Heavenly Valley were made famous by their Austrian instructors. In technology, the 1978 invention of a text scanner by the Austrian American Ray Kurzweil (1948-) has opened a new world for blind readers.

JOURNALISM

Among journalists, the foremost name is Joseph Pulitzer (1847-1911). Though claimed by both Hungarians and Austrians, Pulitzer spoke German and had a Hungarian father and an Austrian mother. The founder of the *St. Louis Post-Dispatch* and owner of the *New York World,* Pulitzer's name is remembered for the prize in journalism that he endowed. He was one of many Austro-Hungarians involved in journalism in nineteenth-century America. Others include Gustav Pollak (1848-1919), a contributor to *The Nation* and the *Evening Post,* and Joseph Keppler (1838-1894), an innovator in color cartoons and owner of the humorous magazine *Puck.* A more recent publishing venture involving an Austrian American is the *New Yorker,* whose founding president, Raoul H. Fleischmann (1885-1969), was born in Bad Ischl, Austria. Other more current Austrian American journalists include the one-time associate editor of the *Boston Globe,* Otto Zausmer; an editor for the *Christian Science Monitor,* Ernest S. Pisko; and Erwin Knoll (1928-1994), a Vienna-born journalist and longtime editor of *The Progressive.*

LAW AND SOCIETY

One of the best-known Austrian Americans in the law was Felix Frankfurter (1882-1965), a native of Vienna, who was a justice on the Supreme Court for 23 years. The Spingarn Medal, awarded yearly to an outstanding African American leader, was created by Joel Elias Spingarn (1875-1939), one of the founders of the National Association for the Advancement of Colored People (NAACP) and the son of an Austrian immigrant.

LITERATURE

Franz Werfel (1890-1945), though born in Prague, was a thoroughly Austrian writer. He and his wife fled the Nazis and came to the United States in 1940. His *Song of Bernadette* became a best seller in the United States, and the Werfels settled in Beverly Hills. The children's writer and illustrator Ludwig Bemelmans (1898-1962) was born in South Tyrol and settled in New York as a youth. His famous Madeline stories continue to charm young readers. Hermann Broch (1886-1951), one of the most influential of modern Austrian writers, known for such novels as *The Sleepwalkers* and *The Death of Virgil,* was another refugee from Hitler's Europe and taught at both Princeton and Yale. Frederic Morton (1925-), born in Vienna and educated in New York, has written many nonfiction books of renown, among them *The Rothschilds* and *A Nervous Splendor: Vienna 1888-1889.*

MEDICINE

Among Austrian American Nobel laureates in medicine were Karl Landsteiner (1868-1943), the discoverer of blood types, and the German Austrian Otto Loewi (1873-1961), a co-winner of the Nobel for his work in the chemical transmission of nerve impulses. Loewi came to New York University after he was driven out of Graz by the Nazis. Many other Austrian Americans have also left their mark in the United States both as practitioners and educators, but perhaps none so methodically as the psychoanalysts who spread Sigmund Freud's work to America. These include A. A. Brill (1874-1947), the Columbia professor and Freud translator; Heinz Werner (1890-1964); Paul Federn; Otto Rank (1884-1939), a Freud disciple; and Theodor Reik (1888-?), the New York psychoanalyst. This group of immigrants was not limited to Freudians, however. Alexandra Adler (1901-?), daughter of Alfred Adler, who is generally known as the second great Viennese psychoanalyst, came to the United States to work at both Harvard and Duke. Bruno Bettelheim (1903-1990) was also a native of Vienna; he became known for his treatment of autistic children and for his popular writings. The list of those both in medicine and mental health who were driven out of Austria during the reign of Hitler is long and impressive.

MUSIC

Arnold Schoenberg (1874-1951), creator of the 12-tone system and a pioneer of modern music,

fled the rise of Nazism in 1933 and continued composing and teaching at both the University of Southern California and the University of California, Los Angeles. Erich Wolfgang Korngold (1897-1957), a Viennese composer best known for his opera *Die tote Stadt,* immigrated to the United States in 1934 and composed and conducted film scores in Hollywood. Ernst Křenek (1900-1991), also a Viennese, was a modernist whose fame was built through his incorporation of jazz and opera in his *Jonny spielt auf.* He taught at Vassar for many years. Frederick Loewe (1904-?), a native Viennese, was the lyricist in the team of Lerner and Loewe who helped transform the American musical. The folk singer and actor Theodore Bikel (1924-) was born in Vienna and came to the United States via Israel and London. Paul Wittgenstein (1887-1961), brother of the philosopher and a pianist of note, settled in New York after 1938. Having lost his right arm in the First World War, Wittgenstein became famous for playing with one hand, and major composers such as Maurice Ravel wrote music for the left hand for him. The longtime general manager of New York's Metropolitan Opera, Rudolf Bing (1902-?), was also Austrian, born in Vienna. Bruno Walter (1876-1962), a German conductor who became a naturalized Austrian and then fled Hitler, was famous for his recordings of Mahler and Mozart and his conducting at the Met and with the New York Philharmonic. Another conductor, Erich Leinsdorf (1912-1993), also found fame in America with a longtime association with the Boston Symphony.

SCIENCE

Three of Austria's four Nobel Prize winners in physics immigrated to the United States. They include Victor Franz Hess (1883-1964), the discoverer of cosmic rays; Isidor Isaac Rabi (1898-1988), a physicist at Columbia; and Wolfgang Pauli (1900-1958). George Paul Sutton (1920-) immigrated to the United States in 1920 and contributed greatly to the development of rockets and missiles. Otto Halpern (1899-?) also contributed to the defense effort of his new homeland by his invention of a counter-radar device. A fair assortment of world class mathematicians also arrived in America from Austria. Among these, Richard von Mises (1883-1953) had a distinguished career at Harvard. Distinguished biologists include Spaeth Hauschka (1908-?) and Erna Altura Werber; among chemists are Ludwig F. Andrieth (1901-?), Oskar Paul Wintersteiner (1898-?), Ernst Berl

(1877-1946), who came to the United States to work on explosives and chemical warfare, and Hermann Francis Mark (1895-?), whose work in synthetic plastics led to the development of such materials as nylon and orlon.

STAGE AND SCREEN

The earliest contribution of Austrian Americans is found in the theater. Many of the earliest theater houses in this country were built by Austrian immigrants who brought their love for theater with them. Prominent arrivals from Austria include the impresario Max Reinhardt (1873-1943). Famous for his *Everyman* production at the Salzburg Festival and for a school of dramatics in Vienna, Reinhardt worked in Hollywood and New York after immigrating to escape the Nazis. Other Austrian Americans include such well-known stage and screen actors as Rudolph Schildkraut (1895-1964), who starred for De Mille in Hollywood, Paul Muni (1895-1967), Hedy Lamarr (1915-), Oscar Homolka (1898-1978), and Arnold Schwarzenegger (1947-). An impressive group of film directors also hail from Austria: Erich von Stroheim (1885-1957), whose film *Greed* is considered a modern masterpiece; Joseph von Sternberg (1894-1969), the father of gangster films; Fred Zinnemann (1907-), the director of *High Noon*; Billy Wilder (1906-) whose many accomplishments include *The Apartment* and *Sunset Boulevard*; and Otto Preminger (1906-1986), a boyhood friend of Wilder's in Vienna and director of such film classics as *Exodus* and *Anatomy of a Murder*.

MEDIA

PRINT

Austria Kultur.

This bimonthly publication is published by the Austrian Cultural Institute, an agency funded by the Austrian government to represent Austrian culture in the United States. It concentrates on cultural affairs such as exhibitions and exchanges.

Contact: Wolfgang Waldner, Editor.
Address: 11 East 52nd Street, New York, New York, 10022.
Telephone: (212) 759-5165.

Other regional German-language newspapers and magazines such as California's *Neue Presse* and the *Staats Zeitung* operate throughout the United States, though none are specifically oriented to or targeted at an Austrian readership.

RADIO AND TELEVISION

Though the short-wave broadcasts of the Austrian Broadcasting Company, ORF, can be picked up in the United States, and various cable networks air German-language programming on their international channels, there is no domestically produced programming that targets the Austrian American audience.

ORGANIZATIONS AND ASSOCIATIONS

In general, Austrian Americans, because of diverse interests and ethnic backgrounds, have tended to favor small regional organizations and clubs over national ones. Most of these societies are organized by province of origin, and those of the Burgenland contingent are the most pervasive. In addition, urban areas such as Chicago, New York, Los Angeles, and Miami Beach tend to have associations for the promulgation of Austrian culture. Other Austrian societies and organizations are united by such common themes as music or literature, or by shared history as with those who fled Austrian Nazism or Hitler. The following are a sampling of regional fraternal and cultural associations.

Austrian-American Federation, Incorporated.
Contact: Dr. Clementine Zernik, President.
Address: 31 East 69th Street, New York, New York, 10021.
Telephone: (212) 535-3261.

Austrian American Council Northeast.
The six chapters of this nonprofit organization have a common goal: to deepen the friendship and understanding between the United States and Austria. To this end, members facilitate cultural and educational exchange between the two countries and also participate in humanitarian efforts such as SOS *Kinderdorf*, an outreach to disadvantaged children in both Europe and the United States.

Contact: Juliana Belcsak, President.
Address: 5 Russell Terrace, Montclair, New Jersey 07042.
Telephone: (201) 783-6241.

Austrian American Council West.
Contact: Veronika Reinelt, Vice-President.
Address: 2701 Forrester Drive, Los Angeles, California 90064.
Telephone: (310) 559-8770.

Austrian American Council Midwest.
Contact: Gerhard Kaes, President.
Address: 5411 West Addison Street, Chicago, Illinois 60641-3295.
Telephone: (312) 685-4166.

Austrian American Council Southwest.
Contact: Christa Cooper, President.
Address: 1535 West Loop South, Suite 319a, Houston, Texas 77027.
Telephone: (713) 623-2233.

Austrian American Council Southeast.
Contact: Alfred Marek, President.
Address: P.O. Box 337, 33 Monsell Court, Roswell, Georgia 30077.

Austrian American Club, Los Angeles.
Contact: Othmar Friedler, President.
Address: P.O. Box 4711, North Hollywood, California 91607.
Telephone: (310) 634-0065.

Austrian-American "Enzian" Club, Colorado Springs.
Contact: Helga Jonas, President.
Address: 29 Circle Sea Road, Fountain, Colorado 80817.
Telephone: (719) 382-7639.

Austrian Society of Arizona.
Contact: Wolfgang Klien, President.
Address: 4501 North 22nd Street, Phoenix, Arizona 85016.
Telephone: (602) 468-1818.

MUSEUMS AND RESEARCH CENTERS

Austrian Cultural Institute.
Part of the cultural affairs section of the Austrian Consulate General, the institute is responsible for cultural and scientific relations between Austria and the United States. It maintains a reference library specializing in Austrian history, art, and folklore, and organizes lectures and panel discussions as well as educational exchanges.
Contact: Dr. Eichinger, Director; or, Friederike Zeitlhofer, Librarian.
Address: 11 East 52nd Street, New York, New York 10022.
Telephone: (212) 759-5165.

Center for Austrian Studies.
Located at the University of Minnesota, the center conducts research on Austrian history and publishes both a newsletter, three times annually, as well as the *Austrian History Yearbook*.
Contact: David Good.
Address: University of Minnesota, 314 Social Sciences Building, Minneapolis, Minnesota 55455.
Telephone: (612) 624-9811.

Society for Austrian and Habsburg History.
Focuses on central European history, and on Austria in particular. For scholars interested in research.
Contact: Ronald Coons.
Address: Department of History, University of Connecticut, 241 Glenbrook Road, Storrs, Connecticut 06269-2103.
Telephone: (203) 486-3722.

International Arthur Schnitzler Research Association.
Maintains a Schnitzler archive at the University of California, Riverside, and encourages and conducts research on that Austrian playwright and novelist as well as contemporaries of Schnitzler. It publishes the quarterly *Modern Austrian Literature*.
Contact: Professor Donald G. Daviau.
Address: Department of Literature and Languages, University of California, Riverside, Riverside, California 92521.
Telephone: (909) 787-5603.

SOURCES FOR ADDITIONAL STUDY

Goldner, Franz. *Austrian Emigration 1938 to 1945*. New York: Frederick Ungar, 1979.

Spaulding, E. Wilder. *The Quiet Invaders: The Story of the Austrian Impact upon America*. Vienna: Österreichische Bundesverlag, 1968.

BELARUSAN AMERICANS

by
Vituat Kipel

The Belarusan American Association, together with a number of other groups, developed a system of supplementary secondary schools in Belarusan communities where the American-born generations receive education in the language, culture, and religious traditions of Belarus.

OVERVIEW

The Republic of Belarus is a newly independent country which, prior to August 25, 1991, was known as the Byelorussian Soviet Socialist Republic. Since 1922 it had formed part of the Soviet Union. Geographically it is located in what is virtually the center of Europe, occupying 80,154 square miles (207,600 square kilometers). It is bounded by Poland to the west, Russia to the east, Ukraine to the south, and Lithuania/Latvia to the north and northwest. Belarus's capital city, Minsk, is situated along the railroad route linking Warsaw and Moscow and has a population of about two million. Other major cities of Belarus are Brest, Grodno, Vitebsk, Gomel, Mogilev, Polotsk, Baranovichy, Pinsk, and Slutsk.

The population of Belarus is over ten million people; over two million more Belarusans live in other parts of the former Soviet Union. About 80 percent of Belarusans in the Republic profess the Eastern Orthodox faith; about 15 to 18 percent are Roman Catholics. The remaining population is divided among Eastern Rite Catholics, (Uniates), Baptists, and Old Believers. There are also strong Muslim and Jewish minorities.

Because the Belarusans' ethnic territory is divided among several neighboring states, it is difficult to present a clear picture of a Belarusan state, nationhood, and historical development.

Part of the confusion stems from terminology. As political concepts, the terms "Byelorussia," "Byelorussian," and since 1991, "Belarus" and "Belarusans," are all relatively new. For most Americans, the term "Byelorussia" was not known until the end of World War II, when the then Byelorussian Soviet Socialist Republic became a charter member of the newly forming United Nations. Prior to World War II the terms more familiar to Americans were "White Russia" and "White Russians" or "White Ruthenia" and "White Ruthenians." The term "White" in these various formulations is simply the literal translation of "*byelo-*" or "*byela-*."

HISTORY

The tribes who were the antecedents of present-day Belarusans began to organize into individual principalities around such cities as Polotsk, Smalensk, and Turov as early as the ninth and tenth centuries. During the twelfth century these principalities moved closer, forming a unified structure and establishing the core of the Grand Duchy of Lithuania, which became an important political power as a commonwealth in eastern Europe over the next several centuries. As these Belarusan principalities gave rise to the Grand Duchy of Lithuania, Belarusan became recognized as the official language of this state. The city of Navahradak, in the earlier period, and the city of Vilna, in the later period, served as the capitals of this large, multinational, influential state.

Gradually the Grand Duchy of Lithuania came under the strong cultural influence of Poland. The upper strata of society became dissociated from the broader mass of the population, in part, by embracing Roman Catholicism, largely accepting the Polish forms of Catholicism, which in turn created religious inequality and social unrest. These factors destabilized the Grand Duchy, weakening it militarily and politically. Meanwhile in the east, the state known as Muscovy grew stronger and began its expansion westward. During the seventeenth and eighteenth centuries Muscovy moved into the territory of the Grand Duchy and farther west into Poland.

BELARUS UNDER RUSSIAN OCCUPATION

The beginnings of Russian domination over the Belarusan territories go back to the sixteenth and seventeenth centuries when the easternmost parts of Belarus were incorporated into the Russian Empire. Then, in a series of successful advances, Russia invaded and annexed the core of ethnic Belarusan lands in 1772, 1793, and 1795. Russian policies towards Belarus were uncompromising in their call for the territories to undergo Russian acculturation. Such Russification was systematically justified and encouraged. This approach remained vigorous through the reigns of successive tsars and the decades of the Soviet regime.

The nineteenth century witnessed an active implementation of Russian policies in Belarus. The term *Belarus* was abolished and replaced by the deliberately vague geographical concept, "Northwest Territory." The use of the Belarusan language was outlawed and all communication was ordered to be exclusively in Russian. Beginning in the 1830s the government adopted a policy of forced deportation of Belarusans to the northern regions of the Empire. Uprisings in Belarus in 1831 and 1863 to 1864 provoked policies of unprecedented harshness regarding Russification, exploitation of the land, and oppression of the populace. The result of these policies was the reduction of Belarus to the status of a colony; it was denied its own governmental bodies and was supervised in all things by appointed administrators. A further result was the creation of an enormous surplus of the local labor force which, in turn, caused a large wave of emigration. Thus, beginning with the last two decades of the nineteenth century and into the early years of World War I, hundreds of thousands of Belarusan peasants migrated out of their homeland to Siberia and the United States.

Although the Russian administrators exerted considerable effort to uproot any characteristics of Belarusan separateness—political or cultural—an ethnic awareness among Belarusans began to emerge toward the last quarter of the nineteenth century. From there on, the revival in self-awareness gained in numbers and in strength. In 1902 the first Belarusan political party, the Belarusan Revolutionary *Hramada*, was established. This was soon followed by numerous cultural and religious organizations, publishing groups, and a teachers' union. However, the real impetus for a widespread revival of Belarusan consciousness and development of a mass movement was the appearance of Belarusan-language newspapers: first, the short-lived *Nasa Dola* (1906), and then its successor, *Nasa Niva* (1906-15), both published in Vilna. This latter newspaper played a particularly important role in assembling the most active leaders of the Belarusan intelligentsia.

MODERN ERA

The high point of Belarusan political activities during the pre-war period and the World War I years was the convening of the all-Belarusan Congress in December 1917 in the capital city of Minsk. The Council, elected at this Congress in 1918, adopted a resolution declaring the independence of Belarus in the form of the Belarusan Democratic Republic. This new democratic state was short-lived, however. Bolshevik armed forces interrupted the Congress and overran the Republic.

The Bolsheviks moved quickly to catch up with the national aspirations of the people. On January 1, 1919, they proclaimed the Belarusan Soviet Socialist Republic (abbreviated as the BSSR). This event had a positive influence on the general populace as the leadership of the newly established Belarusan Soviet Republic improved the economy, political administration, educational system, and cultural life. Many Belarusan emigrants from Western Europe and the United States returned to their homeland. Unfortunately, according to the terms of the Treaty of Riga, signed in 1921, a significant part of Belarusan ethnic territory was given over to the new Polish state.

Belarusan national life in both halves—the eastern, under the Soviets, and the western, under the Poles—flourished during the early and mid-twenties. In both areas there were hundreds of Belarusan schools, publishing houses, and other expressions of cultural life. The Belarusan national movement reached its peak in eastern and western Belarus during the 1920s.

Uncomfortable with the growth of the Belarus national movement, Polish administrators in the middle of the 1920s began to curb Belarusan political activities, close Belarusan schools, outlaw Belarusan-language newspapers, and harass their religious communities. By the beginning of the 1930s the Belarusan movement in Poland had been totally crushed, with its leaders either imprisoned or emigrated—primarily to Soviet Belarus. The systematic persecution of nationally conscious Belarusan in Soviet Belarus began several years later. Soviet Belarus experienced several waves of intermittent purges, the peak years being 1930, 1933, and 1937 to 1938. The official explanation for these pogroms was that the party was struggling with the "National Democrats," i.e., with the Belarusan intelligentsia and nationally democratically minded citizens.

The major parts of the Belarusan nation—the Belarusan Soviet Socialist Republic and Western Belarus—were reunited into a single state in September 1939 when Soviet troops occupied the eastern part of the Polish state. The occupation of Western Belarus by the Soviet armed forces proved costly to the Belarusans: thousands of Belarusans were deported to Siberia, numerous leaders were shot, and all Belarusan activities were suppressed.

The German *Wehrmacht* occupied Belarusan territory within a few weeks after the beginning the German-Soviet War, on June 22, 1941. A number of Belarusan political leaders cooperated with the German occupiers, but any hope of new political freedom under German rule was dashed by the spring of 1944 when the Soviet army advanced westward and occupied Belarusan territory.

World War II devastated Belarus. Over nine thousand villages, two hundred towns, and approximately six million Belarusans were lost. The territory of Belarus was once again balkanized. Parts of Belarusan ethnic territory were included in Poland, Lithuania, and Latvia, with the largest portion given to the Russian Federation. Hundreds of thousands of Belarusans were resettled in Siberia, while thousands of others emigrated as a result of the war. Almost two decades would pass before Belarus could heal the material wounds resulting from World War II.

Surprisingly, despite the denigration and mistreatment of Belarusan culture, a sizable segment of the population and the intelligentsia resisted Russification. A powerful revival process became evident by 1985. Belarusan schools began to open, the Supreme Soviet adopted a Constitution proclaiming the Belarusan language the official language of the Republic, and numerous societies fostered a new esteem for the language and culture. The national revival also led to the emergence of the Belarusan Popular Front, a national political movement functioning as a democratic opposition party in the parliament of the republic. Many obstacles remain, however, before Belarus becomes a truly democratic state, as envisioned in the proclamation of August 25, 1991.

BELARUSAN IMMIGRANTS IN AMERICA

Some believe that the earliest Belarusan immigrants in America settled in the Colony of Virginia in the early 1600s. The reason is that Captain John Smith, who became the first Governor of Virginia in 1608, had visited Belarus in 1603. In his *True Travels*, Captain Smith recalls that he came to "Rezechica, upon the River Niper in the confines of Lithuania," and then he narrates how he traveled through southern Belarus, as Zora Kipel related in her article (*Zapisy*, Volume 16, 1978). Thus, it is possible that Smith brought Belarusans with him to Virginia, together with Polish or Ukrainian manufacturing specialists.

Mass emigration from Belarus began slowly during the final decades of the nineteenth century and lasted until World War I. At the outset emigration from Belarus was directed toward the industrial cities in Poland, to Riga, St. Petersburg, the mines in Ukraine and Siberia, and later, to the United States. Libava and northern Germany were the main points of departure while New York, Philadelphia, Boston, and Baltimore were the main gates of entry to the United States. Slightly over a million Belarusans came to the shores of America, but only about 650,000 immigrants settled here permanently. Unfortunately for the Belarusan immigrants, their ethnicity was not properly registered when they arrived. They were routinely registered as Russians (having Russian Imperial passports and being of the Eastern Orthodox religion) or as Poles, if they were Roman Catholics. Thus, American bureaucracy is partly responsible for creating "the Russian immigrant masses." Research has demonstrated that the majority of those "Russian masses" were of Belarusan background.

Belarusans who arrived in the United States after World War I were predominantly political immigrants, mainly from western Europe and Poland. They numbered only a few thousand persons but were able to found several Belarusan organizations. A few Belarusans, mainly the children of Jewish Belarusan marriages, came to the United States between the late 1930s and the end of 1941.

POSTWAR IMMIGRATION

Belarusans arrived in sizable numbers in the post-World War II period, from 1948 to the early 1950s. During this period about 50,000 Belarusans immigrated to the United States; for the most part, they were people with "displaced person" status who had left Europe for political reasons. They represented a very broad spectrum of the Belarusan nation, sharing one trait in common: fervent anti-Communism. The great majority of them were nationally conscious Belarusans filled with the political resolve to reestablish an independent democratic Belarusan state, the Belarusan Democratic Republic. They came from a variety of countries, the majority of them from West Germany and Austria, but many from Great

Britain, France, Italy, Belgium, Denmark, and other countries in South America and north Africa. These lands had been their first stop-overs after the events of World War II had prompted them to leave Belarus. These immigrants represented several distinct categories: former prisoners of war of the Polish and Soviet armies; former emigres who had left Belarus shortly after World War I or in 1939, when the Soviets invaded Poland; persons who had worked in Germany during the war as *Ostarbeiters*; refugees who had fled Belarus in 1943 or 1944; and post-World War II defectors and dissidents.

Emigration waves from Belarus during the 1980s and 1990s have been relatively small as compared with previous waves. People have emigrated for various reasons: political, economic, and filial (to reunite with families). Most of these immigrants are of Jewish Belarusan background. The political and economic situation in Belarus in the mid 1990s suggests that immigration should continue and increase in size, especially by individuals who are rejoining family members in the United States.

Because official databases in the United States are unable to provide accurate numbers of Belarusans entering the country, widely varying figures have appeared in print. Attempts have been made in Belarus by various researchers to calculate the number of Belarusans emigrating to the United States. While such calculations and estimates vary, they tend to range between one-half million to one million. The Belarusan Institute of Arts and Sciences in the United States has studied the problem and concluded that the total number of Belarusan immigrants who settled in the United States is somewhere between 600,000 and 650,000 persons.

SETTLEMENT

Since no one mapped the distribution of Belarusan immigrants to America when they arrived, it is impossible to reconstruct precise settlement patterns. Only general outlines are possible. The criteria for distribution and settlement tended to be based on the availability of unskilled jobs, proximity to landsmen, and the decision of the sending agent as to which port in the United States the immigrant should be sent. There is evidence of Belarusan settlement all over the United States, from Alaska to Florida, with the greatest numbers concentrated in the states between Illinois and New York. Belarusan population tends to be heaviest in industrial cities and mining regions. For the majority of immigrants, their first stops were New York City; Jersey City, Bayonne, the Amboys, Passaic, Newark, South River, and other small towns in New Jersey; cities such as Cleveland and Akron in Ohio; and Gary, Indiana, Chicago, Illinois, Detroit, Michigan, and Pittsburgh, Pennsylvania. A smaller number of Belarusans went to farms in New York, New Jersey, Connecticut, and Massachusetts.

ACCULTURATION AND ASSIMILATION

The Belarusan American Association, together with a number of other groups, developed a system of supplementary secondary schools in Belarusan communities where the American-born generations receive education in the language, culture, and religious traditions of Belarus. The task of representing Belarusan culture at various venues throughout the United States has been assumed by choirs, theatrical groups, musical and dance ensembles. One such dance ensemble, located in the New York metropolitan area, is headed by Dr. Alla Romano, a faculty member at the City University of New York. This group, *Vasilok,* has performed widely and often in the United States as well as in the Bielastok region and in Belarus itself.

TRADITIONS, CUSTOMS, AND BELIEFS

Many customs with roots in Belarus (some of which are shared with neighboring Slavic nations) are observed by Belarusan Americans. Belarusan customs typically interweave elements of nature, especially agriculture, with pagan and Christian components. Most customs are related to the calendar, ceremonial events, and games. Although the life styles of our modern, technological age are not conducive to maintaining many of these folk traditions, it is remarkable how many of them have survived. This is especially evident when one examines the 36 volumes on Belarusan ethnography published as *Bielaruskaja Narodnaja Tvorcasc* by the Academy of Sciences in Minsk, Belarus, between 1977 and 1993.

CUISINE

Cuisine plays an important role in manifesting the hospitality, cordiality, and friendliness implic-
it in the traditional Belarusan greeting, "A guest in the house is God in the house." Since Belarus is located in the forest, grain, and potato belts of eastern Europe, Belarusan cooking reflects the riches of the land. Favorite dishes include a wide variety of grains, a diversity of mushrooms, meats, and many kinds of fish dishes. There are, of course, a number of items which Belarusans share in common with their Slavic neighbors: *halubcy* (stuffed cabbage), borscht, and *kaubasa* (kielbasy). One popular comestible well known to many Americans is the bagel. The traditional bagel comes from the town of Smarhon in the northwestern part of Belarus. But unquestionably the most famous food of Belarus is the potato. The Belarusan housewife has close to one hundred ways of preparing potato dishes for every occasion. Traditional dishes are especially popular at holiday time in Belarusan American homes.

TRADITIONAL COSTUMES

The most visible and expressive Belarusan folk art is found in national apparel, where the predominant colors are red, white, black, and occasionally green. Symmetric and geometric designs are the most common features of Belarusan decorative patterns.

There are distinct patterns, designs, and materials for men and women. A woman's holiday dress of homespun material consists of a white linen blouse, always ornamented with embroidery or a woven design; an apron, usually of white linen with embroidery; a long pleated skirt of colorful woolen material; a vest, laced or buttoned in the front, often with slits from the waist down; and a headdress. The man's costume is composed of linen trousers and a shirt. The shirt is long, always embroidered, and worn with a hand-woven belt or sash.

SONGS AND DANCES

Scholars trace the origins of Belarusan music to pagan times. A national characteristic is the tendency to form instrumental groups. Every village in the home country has its own musicians and that pattern has been replicated in the United States, with virtually every Belarusan community having its own orchestra. The most commonly used instruments are the violin (*skrypka*), accordion (*bajan*), cymbals, pipe (*dudka*), and the tambourine.

An important part of the Belarusan musical heritage is the huge repertoire of songs, suitable for every occasion, including birth, marriage, death, entering military service, the change of seasons, work, and leisure. Belarusans sing solos, duets, and harmonize in ensembles and choirs. The rich and elaborately lyrical songs which form the basis of Belarusan folk music have a special appeal for Belarusans. Singing is often accompanied by one or more instruments, very often the *husli* (psaltery). The lullaby is especially popular in Belarusan families. Generations of children have grown up learning the lyrics to these songs sung to them by their mothers and grandmothers.

Dancing has similarly enjoyed a millennium-long life span in Belarus and this tradition continues in America. Belarusan folk dancing is characterized by the richness of its composition, uncomplicated movements, and small number of rapid steps. Folk dances are often accompanied by song expressing the feelings, work habits, and life style of the people. Ethnographers have identified over one hundred Belarusan folk dances, many of which are performed in America. The legacy of song and dance is an aspect of the native culture that is shared by both old and new immigrants, transcending chronological barriers.

HOLIDAYS

Holiday seasons are filled with traditional Belarusan practices and customs. The Christmas season, for example, includes many unique customs. One of the most cherished and carefully preserved traditions is the celebration of *kuccia*, a very solemn and elaborate supper on Christmas Eve. Twelve or more dishes are prepared and served. Each dish is served in a specific order, with a portion set aside for the ancestors. The pot holding the *kuccia* (a special barley confection) is placed in the corner of the room, under the icons. After the family says grace, the *kuccia* is the first course served. Another widely observed custom is the decoration of the Christmas tree with hand-made Belarusan ornaments. As a rule, the entire family takes part in the ceremony, with the oldest family members contributing most of the craftsmanship. Caroling, an old Christmas tradition, is solidly maintained by Belarusan Americans both of the older and younger generations, with the latter employing this custom as a means of fundraising for organizational purposes.

The Easter season is another occasion for the observance of many traditional customs. The season begins with a period of fasting, followed by

Vierbnica (Palm Sunday), and a competition of flower bouquets. Following the Easter Liturgy, the priest blesses colored eggs, sausage, *babka* (special Easter bread), and cheese. An Easter breakfast, *Razhavieny*, is held in the parish hall where traditional foods are served. Easter Sunday is given over to visiting friends and relatives, and to playing various games, such as cracking the Easter eggs.

Other "double-faith" observances include the celebration of *Kupalle*, marking the end of Spring and beginning of Summer. *Dziady* commemorates the departed and is one of four such feasts celebrated each year. Many Belarusan communities preserve the tradition of honoring army recruits. A special liturgy is celebrated, followed by a party where traditional draftee songs are sung. An Autumn observance, *Dazynki*, the harvest festival, is a joyous event concluding with a community dinner.

The most widely observed sanctified feastday is that of St. Euphrosynia of Polacak, the Patron Saint of Belarus. Her feast day, May 23, is traditionally celebrated by all Belarusans. Belarusan Americans also have a special devotion to St. Cyril of Turdu, whose feastday falls on April 28. The Mother of God of Zyrovicy is the patroness of many Belarusan churches. Her patronal feast is May 20. Other church-related customs and anniversaries observed by Belarusan Americans are the Smalensk Marian icon, *Adzihitrya* (Guide), observed on August 10, the Feast of Pentecost/Whitsunday, and the Feast of All the Saints of Belarus (the third Sunday after Pentecost). Belarusan Roman Catholics observe the feast of Our Lady of Vostraja Brama in Vilna on November 16; and St. Mary of Budslau on July 2, among others.

CRAFTS

Among the Belarusan crafts that are widespread in the United States are woven rugs and embroidered table covers and bedspreads. Hand-woven belts and embroidered towels are perhaps most prized. Towels have particular significance because of the numerous solemn occasions when they are employed—weddings, christenings, and adorning icons. Belarusan American families have dozens of towels for all types of events. Pottery, straw incrustations, and woodcarving are also popular age-old Belarusan crafts practiced throughout the United States. These items are typically adorned with simple geometric designs and are put to more practical uses, rather than kept as *objets d'art*.

LANGUAGE

The Belarusan language is a part of the East Slavic group of languages which includes Ukrainian and Russian. The language of Belarusan Americans has specific features. In everyday use many Americanisms have entered the Belarusan language, but are often so assimilated to the lexical and phonological patterns of Belarusan that they do not seem foreign to the language. A peculiar phenomenon is the language of thousands of Belarusan immigrants who came prior to World War I. These people claimed to speak Russian but were in fact speaking a Russified Belarusan, often with the admixture of Yiddish words. Unfortunately, because of the lack of language professionals working for the U.S. Census, this melange of languages stemming from a Belarusan base was recorded as Russian.

FAMILY AND COMMUNITY DYNAMICS

As in other Slavic cultures, the earlier Belarusan family was a large, communal group. Incorporating distant relatives or even strangers, the family was held together by the work each contributed to the farm rather than by blood relationships. A stranger (*zdolnik*) might join a family for life or for an agreed period; he and his heirs were accorded equal status with other members. Most often the father or grandfather acted as family head. He assigned the men jobs and acted as trustee for the family property, which was collectively owned. In modern times, such families have become rare, but some of the family leader's authority remains. At family gatherings, for example, the head sits in the place of honor, with the other men grouped by rank around him. Women sit at the other end of the table. The family head blesses the meal and serves himself first.

The sexes are also divided with respect to the jobs each performs. Washing clothes or preparing food, for example, is traditionally considered women's work, and no man would consider doing these tasks. Women also enjoy financial independence, within the limitations of family obligations. Like the men, they keep the money made from the sale of surplus vegetables. The women have unquestioned authority in the household, with complete responsibility for children younger than 14 years. As the male head of the household supervises the men, his wife directs the work of women within the parameters of the farm community. Belarusan women have long been respected for their willingness and ability to work.

FAMILY NAMES

Widespread and recognizable, Belarusan surnames include such names as Barsuk, Kalosha, Kresla, Savionak, and Sienka. Belarusan surnames are often based on geographical origin, e.g., Babruiski, Minskii, Mogilevskii, Slutski, Vilenski. Many others derive from baptismal names, e.g., Jakubau, Haponau, Kazimirau, or such diminutives as Jakubionak and Hapanionak. The most typical Belarusan surnames are those with the suffixes "ovich" or "ievich," such as Dashkievich, Mickievich, Zmitrovich. Others derive from occupations, e.g., Dziak, Hrabar, Mular.

RELIGION

Approximately 80 percent of modern-day Belarusans are Eastern Orthodox, about 15 to 18 percent are Roman Catholic, and the remaining population is divided among Eastern Rite Catholics, (Uniates), Baptists, and Old Believers. There are also strong Muslim and Jewish minorities.

Only after World War II did groups of believers begin to establish distinctly Belarusan churches in America. The majority of Belarusan immigrants were of the Eastern Orthodox faith. The formal organization of Belarusan Orthodox activities dates from 1949 to 1950, when parishes began to be founded as parishes of the Belarusan Autocephalous Orthodox Church (BAOC). Organizational work for the BAOC began in North America under the guidance of Archbishop Vasil, who established his residence in New York City. Archbishop Mikalaj of Toronto has become the Primate of this jurisdiction, which includes parishes in the states of New York, New Jersey, Ohio, and Michigan. Several Belarusan parishes in Illinois, New Jersey, and New York are within the jurisdiction of Archbishop Iakovos, the Exarch of the Ecumenical Patriarch for North and South America. The BAOC conducts an extensive school program and is involved in providing aid to Chernobyl victims. The liturgical services are conducted in Belarusan.

Belarusan Catholics of the Latin Rite have not formed parishes of their own in the United States. Consequently, Belarusan American Roman Catholics have devoted themselves to civic activities within the Belarusan Orthodox communities, while occasionally enjoying a visiting Catholic priest of Belarusan descent. Belarusan Catholics of the Byzantine-Slavic Rite (Uniates), organized their own parish in Chicago, primarily through the efforts of two Belarusan activists, Rev. John Tarasevich and his nephew Rev. Uladzimir Tarasevich.

POLITICS AND GOVERNMENT

RELATIONS WITH BELARUS

The idea of Belarusan statehood and separateness began to surface in non-Belarusan publications such as the newspapers *Novyi Mir*, *Russkii Golos*, and *Novoye Russkoye Slovo*. These Ukrainian American newspapers not only published materials of interest to Belarusan immigrants, but wholeheartedly supported Belarusan independence and the establishment of Belarusan ethnic organizations. In these ways—contacts with the homeland and through the printed word—the concepts of national separateness, national self-awareness, and Belarusan independence were communicated to the Belarusan American immigrant communities, inspiring them to come together and form specifically Belarusan ethnic organizations.

The political activities of Belarusan groups consist mainly of lobbying various political groups and individual political leaders to support the idea of a democratic and independent Belarusan state. The Belarusan American Association is a champion in this undertaking. For more than forty years this group has written thousands of memoranda and visited hundreds of legislators at all levels, soliciting political support for Belarus's movement for independence. During the past 20 years, under the leadership of Anton Shukeloyts, this organization has achieved an outstanding record of support for political dissidents and for the Belarusan National Front in the homeland.

INDIVIDUAL AND GROUP CONTRIBUTIONS

Several Belarusan Americans have made noteworthy contributions to American society and to the Belarusan community. An early attempt to form a Belarusan landsmen's circle was made by Dr. Aleksandr Sienkievich and some of his friends in Baltimore, Maryland, between 1910 and 1912. Although he recognized the need for such an organization, he soon became involved with the anarchist movement in the United States and was lost to the Belarusan movement. Viable Belarusan organizations were established in Chicago in the 1920s by such people as Anton and Jan Charapuks, Jazep Varonka, Rev. John Tarasevich, Makar Ablazhej, and a number of others who maintained contact with the Belarusan national movement in the homeland. Varonka, in particular, had already distinguished himself in Belarus by serving as the prime minister of the Belarusan National Republic before coming to the United States in 1923. He also started the first Belarusan newspaper in the United States, *The White Ruthenian Tribune* (1926) and pioneered radio broadcasts in the Belarusan language (1929).

MEDIA

PRINT

Bielarus/The Belarusan.

A monthly Belarusan-language newspaper, established in 1950 by the Belarusan American Association, that chronicles the Belarusan presence in the United States and promotes the idea of Belarusan independence.

Contact: Dr. Jan Zaprudnik, Editor.
Address: 166-34 Gothic Drive, Jamaica, New York 11432.
Telephone: (516) 627-0902.

Bielaruski Holas (Byelorussian Voice).

Byelorussian interest magazine.

Contact: Marian Ziniak, Editor and Publisher.
Address: 24 Tarlton Road, Toronto, Ontario, Canada, M5P 2M4.

Journals include *Belarusan Thought* (South River, New Jersey), *Polacak* (Cleveland, Ohio), and *Bielarusan Review* (Torrance, California).

ORGANIZATIONS AND ASSOCIATIONS

Immigrants arriving after World War II were anxious to establish organizations that would promote Belarusan consciousness and maintain their heritage here. They were active and vocal proponents of an independent Belarusan state and an independent Belarusan religious community. Among the first secular and religious organizations established by these immigrants were: United Whiteruthenian American Relief Committee, headquartered in South River, New Jersey (established in 1949); Belarusan American Association, Inc. (established in New York City in 1949 and chartered in Albany, New York, in 1950); the Byelorussian American Youth Organization (established in Cleveland, Ohio in 1951 and affiliated with the Belarusan American Association); the Belarusan American Congress Committee (established in 1951); the Belarusan American Academic Society, a student organization (established in 1951); the Association of Bielarusians in Illinois (established in 1953); several dozen women's organizations, veterans, various professional groups (physicians, poets, and writers); the Belarusan American Union (established in New York in 1965); and other smaller youth groups, such as scouts, YMCA groups, and several religious societies. These Belarusan organizations offer social, political, cultural, educational, recreational, and religious programs and activities. Over the past 40 years or more, about one hundred new Belarusan groups have been formed in dozens of states. These diverse organizations share two common characteristics: their anti-Communist stance; and their commitment to the goal of an independent and democratic Belarusan state.

The following is a list of some of the more prominent Belarusan organizations:

Belarusan American Association.
Address: 166-34 Gothic Drive, Queens, New York 11432.

Belarusian Congress Committee of America (BCCA).
Provides information about Belarus and Americans of Belarusian descent; supports the development of independent Belarus.
Contact: Russell R. Zavistovich, President.
Address: 724 West Tantallon Drive, Fort Washington, Maryland 20744.
Telephone: (301) 292-2610.

Belarusan Institute of Arts and Sciences.
Address: 230 Springfield Avenue, Rutherford, New Jersey 07070.

Telephone: (201) 933-6807.
Fax: (201) 438-4565.

Bielarusian American Union of New York.
Address: 104-29 Atlantic Avenue, Richmond Hill, New York 11419.
Telephone: (718) 625-9352.

Byelorussian American Women Association (BAWA).
Aims to preserve national identity, cultural heritage, and traditions.
Contact: Vera Bartul, President.
Address: 146 Sussex Drive, Manhasset, New York 11030.
Telephone: (516) 627-9195.

Byelorussian Autocephalous Orthodox Church.
Address: 9 River Road, Highland Park, New Jersey 08904.
Telephone: (908) 247-4490.

Byelorussian Congress Committee.
Address: Byelorussian American Community Center, South Whitehead Avenue, South River, New Jersey 08882.
Telephone: (908) 254-9594.

SOURCES FOR ADDITIONAL STUDY

Belarus: Then and Now (series). Minneapolis, Minnesota: Lerner Publications, 1993.

Byelorussian Cultural Tradition in America. New Brunswick, New Jersey: Rutgers University, 1983.

Kipel, Vitaut. "Byelorussians in the United States," *Ethnic Forum*, Volume 9, Nos. 1-2, 1989, pp. 75-90.

Novik, U. *Belarus: A New Land of Opportunity.* Minsk: Technology, 1993.

Zaprudnik, Jan. *Belarus: At a Crossroads in History.* Boulder, Colorado: Westview Press, 1993.

Belgian Americans

have excelled in

many fields,

especially in music,

science, medicine,

education, and

business.

BELGIAN AMERICANS

by
Jane Stewart Cook

OVERVIEW

Belgium, whose official name is the Kingdom of Belgium, is a densely populated country not much larger than the state of Maryland. It covers an area of 11,781 square miles (30,519 square kilometers), bounded on the north by The Netherlands, on the west by France, and on the east by Germany. The tiny nation of Luxembourg lies to the south. This strategic location has earned Belgium the sobriquet, "crossroads of Europe." Brussels, its capital city, is just a three-hour drive to The Hague, the capital of The Netherlands, and Paris, and the capital of France.

The country is divided into three regions: Northern Lowlands, Central Lowlands, and Southern Hilly Region. Its highest point is the Botrange Mountain (2,275 feet), and its major rivers are the Schelde, the Sambre, and the Meuse, which are important transportation routes. Approximately ten million people call Belgium home. The Flemish, those residing in Flanders, the northern half of the country, speak Dutch. They make up the majority of Belgium's population. Wallonia, the region closest to France, is occupied by the French-speaking Walloons. About one percent of the population speaks German, principally those who reside near the former West German border. About 98 percent of Belgians are Catholic. Protestants and those of the

Jewish and Muslim faiths make up the remainder. Belgium's political system is that of a constitutional monarchy, with the monarch having limited powers. The national flag, adopted in 1830, is a vertical tricolor of black, yellow, and red.

HISTORY

From approximately 57 B.C. to A.D. 431, Rome ruled over Gaul, an area of what is now France, Belgium, Luxembourg, and Germany. The land was then inhabited by independent tribes of Celtic origin. Julius Caesar's account of his efforts to subdue the area gives us the first written record of what came to be called Belgium. The Romans looked on Belgium as a defensive barrier to the Franks, Germanic tribes that eventually settled in what is now Flanders. Language patterns followed the settlement patterns. Germanic speech evolved into Dutch in the north, and the Latin of Rome developed into French in the south. These language patterns, which were established by the third century, A.D., have altered only slightly up to the present day.

With the collapse of the Roman Empire in the fifth century, the Franks held sway for more than 550 years. With the death of Charlemagne in 814, the country was divided into France, the Holy Roman Empire (Germany), and the "Middle Kingdom," a buffer state comprised of the Lowlands and Belgium. Feudal states developed, and in the later Middle Ages the dukes of Burgundy ruled the Low Countries. In 1516, Belgium became a possession of Spain and remained so until 1713, when the country was given to Austria as settlement in the War of the Spanish Succession. Belgium was annexed by France in 1795, and placed under the rule of The Netherlands after Napoleon's defeat in the Battle of Waterloo in 1815. In 1830, Belgium declared its independence, adopted a constitution, and chose its first king, Leopold I. He was succeeded in 1865 by his son, Leopold II.

MODERN ERA

During World War I, Belgium was overrun by Germany. More than 80,000 Belgians died. Under the personal command of their "soldier king," Albert I, Belgians managed to hold on until the arrival of the Allied forces in 1918. History repeated itself in World War II when Hitler bombed Belgium into submission and took its king, Leopold III, prisoner. The arrival of Allied forces in 1944 was followed by the Battle of the Bulge, which would decide the war's outcome. Belgium rebuilt its war-torn country, became a founding member of the United Nations and the North Atlantic Treaty Organization, and by the 1960s was enjoying a prosperous economy. Belgium has been a leader in the movement toward European economic integration, and in 1958 became a founding member of the European Economic Community.

THE FIRST BELGIANS IN AMERICA

It is said that when Henry Hudson sailed up the New York river that now bears his name, three Flemings were aboard the ship. Certainly the Belgians participated in the early settlement (seventeenth century) of what is now Manhattan. Many historians believe that Peter Minuit, who acted as purchasing agent for the West Indian Company when Manhattan Island was bought from the resident Native Americans, was a Walloon, or at least of Belgian heritage. And it is known that his secretary, Isaac de Rasiers, was a Walloon.

Henry C. Bayer, in his *The Belgians, First Settlers in New York and in the Middle States*, discusses Belgian settlements at Wallabout, Long Island, and Staten Island, as well as in Hoboken, Jersey City, Pavonia, Communipaw, and Wallkill, New Jersey. These place names are derived from both the Walloons who settled there, as well as from the Dutch version of Walloon words used to describe a locale. For example, Hoboken is named after a town in Belgium. Pavonia got its name when a Fleming, Michael Pauw, purchased land on the Jersey shore. Translating his own name, Pauw (which in Flemish and Dutch means "peacock") into Latin, he got "Pavonia." Wallkill is the Dutch word for "Walloon's Stream." Elsewhere, the Walloomsac River in Vermont derives its name from the Walloons who settled on the east branch of the Hoosac River in New York. Belgian settlements were also established during the seventeenth century in Connecticut, Delaware, and Pennsylvania. These were settled primarily by Walloons, many of whom came to America on ships owned by the West India Company, whose founder, William Usselinx, was Flemish.

A notable name connected with America's early history is Lord Baltimore, whose family were prominent aristocrats in Flemish Belgium. Belgian officers also fought during the Revolutionary War. To note a few: Charles De Pauw, a Fleming who accompanied Lafayette to America; Ensign

Thomas Van Gaasbeck, Captain Jacques Rapalje, and Captain Anthony Van Etten, all of New York; and Captain Johannes Van Etten of Pennsylvania.

SIGNIFICANT IMMIGRATION WAVES

Belgians came to America in greatest numbers during the nineteenth century. They came for reasons no different than many other Western Europeans—financial opportunity and a better life for their families. Belgian immigration records do not appear until 1820. From 1820 to 1910, immigration is listed at 104,000; from 1910 to 1950, 62,000 Belgians came to the United States. During the period 1847 to 1849, when disease and economic deprivation were the lot for many in Belgium, emigration numbers of those leaving for America reached 6,000 to 7,000 a year. During this time, most of those coming to the United States were small landowners (farmers), agricultural laborers, and miners; crafts people such as carpenters, masons and cabinetmakers; and other skilled tradespeople, such as glass blowers and lace makers. In later years, especially after the two World Wars, many middle class and urban professionals left Belgium for this country, seeking work in our universities, laboratories, and industrial corporations. Altogether, it is estimated that from 1820 to 1970, approximately 200,000 Belgian immigrants settled in the United States. Each year since 1950, a fixed quota of 1,350 has remained unfilled, and it is calculated that by 1981, Belgians represented no more than 0.4 percent of the foreign-born population.

SETTLEMENT PATTERNS

Nineteenth-century settlement patterns followed work opportunities. For example, the glass industry in the East attracted many to West Virginia and Pennsylvania. Detroit, Michigan, attracted building tradespeople. Door, Brown, and Kewaunee Counties in Wisconsin attracted those seeking farmland. Considerable numbers came to Indiana. Substantial pockets of Belgian Americans can also be found in Illinois, Minnesota, North Dakota, Ohio, Kentucky, Florida, Washington, and Oregon. Many towns and cities across the United States bear the names of their counterparts in Belgium: Liege, Charleroi, Ghent, Antwerp, Namur, Rosiere, Brussels.

Michigan and Wisconsin have the largest population of Belgian Americans, with the above-named Wisconsin counties having the largest rural settlement in the United States. The Belgian American settlement in Detroit took place mainly between 1880 and 1910. Most of these new arrivals were skilled Flemish crafts people. Detroit's early industrial and manufacturing growth was fueled in great part by their skills in the building trades and transportation. According to Jozef Kadijk, whose 1963 lecture at Loyola University in Chicago appears in *Belgians in the United States*, approximately 10,000 residents of Detroit at that time were born in Belgium. Taking their descendants into account is said to increase that figure to 50,000. Most of the Wisconsin Belgians were Walloons from the areas of Brabant and Liege, Belgium. They began arriving in substantial numbers by 1853, following the lure of farmland that could be purchased from 50 cents to $1.25 an acre. Here they cleared fields, felled trees, and built rude log shelters to house their families. Writing back home of their satisfaction with their new lives, they soon were joined by thousands of their fellow countrymen. The 1860 census shows about 4,300 foreign-born Belgians living in Brown and Kewaunee Counties.

ACCULTURATION AND ASSIMILATION

Belgians are also Western Europeans, and as such, presented a familiar religious and cultural background to others in their new homeland. Stereotypical notions as to traits of character often depict the Dutch-influenced Fleming as reserved, stubborn, practical, and vigorous, while the passion of France is observed in the Walloon's wit, extroversion, and quickness of mind and temper. It is true that whether Flemish or Walloon, the influences of The Netherlands, Germany and France upon their language, religion, and social customs were evident. This helped to make their assimilation easier—although they sometimes met with a strong anti-Catholic sentiment, which equated allegiance to the Church with disloyalty to America, and was prevalent in many parts of the United States. However, the Walloons who settled in Northeast Wisconsin found their way made easier because of the established French Catholic communities. In general, the Flemings, with higher education levels and sought-after job skills, suffered less prejudice than the Walloons, the majority of whom were poor, unskilled, and illiterate. But through their industry and thrift, these poor farmers soon won the respect of their neighbors. In time, Belgian Americans became admired not only for their industry and down-to-earth outlook, but also for their sociable character and friendly manner. Belgian hospitality and the retention of many old-world customs and traditions gave color and vitality to the communities in which they resided. Another factor which both hastened assimilation and fostered ethnic pride was the tragic experience of Belgium during the World Wars. The sympathy extended to Belgian Americans by others led them to re-emphasize their origins and culture.

TRADITIONS, CUSTOMS, AND BELIEFS

It is said that a Belgian, whether Fleming or Walloon, is an inveterate hand shaker. On meeting, greeting, and parting, prolonged handshakes are the rule. This custom is thought to stem from ancient times, when a man's handshake proved he held no weapon. The Belgians' belief in the value of the community and their sturdy outlook on life have helped them recover from plague, famine, two World Wars, and economic depression. Those characteristics have also contributed to the progress and well-being of Belgian Americans. For example, in 1871, a devastating forest fire in Wisconsin (known as the "Peshtigo Fire") destroyed land, farms, and residences in an area six miles wide and 60 miles long. The Belgian communities of northeast Wisconsin were swept away, leaving 5,000 homeless to face the coming winter. It is significant of their determination and resilience that by 1874 these communities were completely rebuilt. An interesting architectural variant can be found in Door County, Wisconsin, as a direct result of the disastrous fire. Up to that time, most homes were built of wood, because it was plentiful and cheap. Red brick homes and buildings began to appear—sturdy and square in design, trimmed in white, and reminiscent of the Belgium homeland. Even today, many fine examples of this form of architecture can be found throughout the Belgian farming communities in Wisconsin.

Many Belgian Americans lived long distances from hospitals or doctors; many could not afford medical services. Therefore folk remedies and home cures were common. A poultice made of flax seed and applied to the chest was thought to help with fever and colds. "King of Pain" liniment for aches and sprains, "Sunrise Herb Tea" for constipation, and cobwebs placed on wounds to stop bleeding were other remedies used.

Every ethnic group that came to America in the nineteenth century could not help but be influenced by other cultures. As ties with the old country weakened, these groups became more and more "Americanized." And, for the most part, they were eager to do so. But all groups, to some degree, kept land-of-origin customs and beliefs alive through religious and social practices. Belgian Americans have been very successful in preserving their secular and religious traditions.

INTERACTIONS WITH OTHER ETHNIC MINORITIES

In the early days, rural populations tended to remain homogeneous, separated mainly by distance from other communities. They relied on others of their own group to help them survive. Strong identification with one's own kind gave comfort and protection to those sharing a common language and heritage. Because of proximity, urban populations began to interact with other ethnic groups (mainly Catholics) earlier than those in rural areas. In time, greater access to transportation, employment and education, and the settlement of other nationalities nearby caused the sociable Belgians to seek interaction with others outside their group. Proud of their heritage, they have used it to enlighten and enrich their encounters with others.

CUISINE

Belgians have a love affair with food and revere the act of eating. To rush through a meal is thought to be uncivilized behavior. Belgian food is hearty and rich and often accompanied by beer. Indeed, there are more than 300 varieties of beer brewed in Belgium and the amount of beer consumed, per capita, is second only to Germany. Although many dishes in Belgian cooking are the same for the Flemish and the Walloons, there are differences. For example, Flemish cooking features sweet-salt and sweet-sour mixtures (sauerkraut and pickles). Nutmeg is a favored spice in Flemish cooking. Walloon cuisine is based on French techniques and ingredients. Garlic is a favored seasoning. As in Belgium, a typical Belgian American family meal begins with a thick vegetable soup, followed by meat and vegetables. Pork sausages made with cabbage and seasonings are called *tripes à l'djote* (or Belgian tripe); *boulettes* are meatballs. *Djote*, or "jut" is cooked cabbage and potatoes seasoned with browned butter, pepper, salt, and nutmeg, while *potasse* is a dish of potatoes, red cabbage and side pork. A homemade cottage cheese called *kaset* is often included with the meal. This spreadable cheese is cured in crocks and used like butter. For dessert, there is Belgian pie, which is an open-faced tart filled with custard or cottage cheese, then topped with layers of prunes or apples. A pastry called *cougnou* and shaped like the baby Jesus is a special Christmas treat for Walloons. A waffle-like cookie called *bona* or *guilette* is made with a special baking iron and is also served by Walloons at Christmas. The Belgian waffle, called *gället*, although a traditional food eaten on New Year's Day, has been Americanized and is commonly found on restaurant menus. Some traditional Flemish foods include: *geperste kop*, or head cheese, which is not cheese but the renderings from a pig's head, ears, and stomach made into a jelly-like product; *olie bollen*, a raised doughnut made with apples, and *advocaat*, a liqueur made of grain alcohol, vanilla, eggs, milk, and sugar.

Belgian women are known for their expertise in bread baking. Long ago, huge outdoor ovens were used for baking. The bakehouse was made of masonry and fieldstone, with walls two feet thick. The oven protruded from one end, and was also made of masonry and stone. The bakehouse chimney and interior of the oven were red brick. These whitewashed structures were often trimmed in green and their walls supported grape vines, whose fruit was used for making jelly. Their large ovens could bake as many as 50 loaves of bread at one time. And, after the bread was finished baking, the oven was just hot enough for baking pies. Some of these picturesque ovens still exist in rural Belgian American communities, although few of them are still in use.

TRADITIONAL COSTUMES

Wooden shoes called *sabots* (Walloon) or *klompen* (Flemish) were traditional footwear for men, women, and children. Like the people of Belgium, they wore these shoes outdoors; they were left by the door when entering the house. Some immigrants brought the knowledge and the tools for making wooden shoes with them from Belgium. Belgian Americans who could afford them wore wooden shoes decorated with carvings of leaves and flowers. Children sometimes used their wooden shoes as skates or sleds. The early immigrants were usually clothed in homespun cloth and caps. Belgian lace, the fine handwork which originated in sixteenth-century Flanders, was often used to trim religious vestments, altar cloths, handkerchiefs, table cloths, napkins, and bed linens. This fine art was practiced by Belgian

immigrants in every area of settlement in the United States. When celebrating the Kermiss, which is a Belgian harvest festival, the organizers of the Kermiss wore red, white, and blue sashes while leading the people of the community in a procession to the church to give thanks.

BELGIAN DANCES AND SONGS

At the Kermiss festivities (described below), revolutionary songs of the old country were sung, such as the Brabanconne and the Marseillaise. During the procession to the church, a dance called "Dance of the Dust" would be done on the dirt road. This dance honors the soil from which the harvest is reaped. At social get-togethers, drinking songs such as the Walloon song, "Society of the Long Clay Pipe," and songs of Belgium towns and cities, such as "Li Bia Bouquet," which honors the province of Namur, are sung. The local band, which usually consisted of cornets, slide trombone, violin, clarinet, and bass drum, played at weddings, festivals, and other social occasions, offering waltzes, quadrilles, and two-steps.

RECREATION

Archery clubs, pigeon racing, and bicycling clubs were forms of organized recreation for many Flemish Belgians. Gradually these organizations died out, but some existed until the 1960s and 1970s. Bowling, music societies, and drama clubs were formed by both Flemish and Walloon communities. Bowling is still a favorite form of recreation. A card game called "conion" was a popular pastime in taverns. The men fished, trapped, and hunted. Informally, women met to socialize and do needlework and sewing. Their work took on an additional aspect during World Wars I and II, when they supplied the Red Cross with articles of clothing and other needed materials for the war effort. Children skated, sledded, and played ball. Both boys and girls enjoyed games of chase and hide and seek. For rural children, berry picking in the company of their mothers was also recreation. Women enjoyed the preserving of fruits and berries, often gathering together as they did with their sewing groups.

HOLIDAYS CELEBRATED BY BELGIAN AMERICANS

The festival of Kermiss (also Kermis or Kermess) celebrates the abundant harvest. It generally lasted for six consecutive weeks. It is said that the first Kermiss in America was initiated in 1858 by Jean Baptiste Macaux, a native of Grand-Leez, Belgium. Masses were held to give thanks, and there was much feasting, dancing, and singing. Games were played—among them the card game called "conion" and a greased pole climb. The celebration of Kermiss has persisted to the present day in rural Belgian American communities.

Assumption Day on August 15 honors the Virgin Mary and her ascension into heaven. In the rural areas, a field mass was part of the celebration. This holiday celebration began in the morning, with clergy clad in white vestments and a choir singing Gregorian chant.

On the last Monday in May, people gathered to petition the Virgin for her blessings on their new plantings. This solemn holiday is called Rogation Day. A procession would be made to the church or shrine honoring the Virgin Mary. Young girls dressed in white with long veils would strew flowers along the way.

Belgian Americans celebrate traditional religious holidays such as Christmas and Easter. They also celebrate St. Nicholas Day, which comes on December 6. In the early days, men of the community would dress up like St. Nicholas (the Dutch version of our Santa Claus) and go from house to house, leaving candy and small presents for the children. Today, for many Belgian Americans, this holiday marks the beginning of the Christmas season.

HEALTH AND MENTAL HEALTH ISSUES

There are no documented physical or mental afflictions that affect Belgians any more than affect the general population. They have access to health and life insurance through their employers, or at their own expense. However, in the early days, beneficial societies were formed to provide this coverage, usually for a nominal monthly fee. These benefits often exist in some form today, to the extent that membership is held in various Belgian fraternal and religious organizations.

LANGUAGE

In Belgium, geographic circumstances determine which language is spoken. Those residing in northern Belgium speak Flemish, which is derived from Dutch and German. Those Belgians from the south speak Walloon, which is a French patois derived from Latin. Because of their proximity to France, Walloons hold the French language in high regard, using it as the standard for their own. On the other hand, the Flemings share many of the customs and beliefs, as well as the Dutch language, with the people of The Netherlands. A minority—about one percent of Belgium's population—speak German.

Because of geographic and cultural circumstances, a natural language boundary exists in Belgium. In the past, attempts to force an official adoption of either French or Dutch by towns along the language boundary caused great dissension among the people. To settle these disputes, laws were passed in the early 1960s making the language boundary permanent. As a result, both Dutch and French are the official languages, and two distinct cultures flourish side by side. Many Belgians switch back and forth between the two languages, using their native dialect with family and friends and either Dutch or French in public or formal situations. But even though both Dutch and French are the official languages of the country, they are still not regarded by Belgians as equal in value. The following proverbs illustrate how the two are viewed: French in the parlor, Flemish in the kitchen; You speak the language of the man whose bread you eat; It is necessary to cease being Flemish in order to become Belgian. Flemish proverbs include: *Stel niet uit tot morgen wat je heden kunt doen* (Delay not until tomorrow what you can do now); *Wie hierbinnen komt zijn onze vrienden* (Those who enter here are our friends); *Avondrood brengt water in de sloot* (Red sky at night brings water in the stream); *Beter een half ei dan een lege dop* (Better half an egg than an empty shell); *Zwijgen en denken kan niemand krenken* (Silence and thinking hurts no one).

Belgian immigrants in the United States used the primary language of their homeland in Belgium. The Flemish and Walloon languages were commonly used by first-generation Belgians until World War I. Gradually, most Belgian Americans lost the ability to speak either Walloon or Flemish. Immigrant parents were eager to have their children learn English, and today few retain more than a word or two in the old language. Individuals who were at least 50 years old in the middle 1970s spoke the Walloon language in a family environment but had to speak English in school. Punished by teachers when they did speak Walloon, they raised their own children to speak English and spoke Walloon with themselves only with people of their own generation (Françoise Lem-

pereur, "The Walloon Settlement of North-East Wisconsin," in *Belgians in the United States*, [Brussels, Belgium: Ministry of Foreign Affairs, 1976).

GREETINGS AND OTHER POPULAR EXPRESSIONS

The following greetings and expressions are in Dutch or French, depending upon whether the Belgian speaker is Flemish or Walloon. Dutch: *Goedemorgen* ("ghooderMORghern")—Good morning; *Goedemiddag* ("ghooderMIddahkh")—Good afternoon; *Dank u* ("dahnk ew")—Thank you; *Ja/Nee* ("yaa/nay")—Yes, No; *Vrolijk Kerstfeest* ("VROAlerk KEHRSTfayst")—Merry Christmas; *Veel geluk* ("vayl gherLURK")—Good luck. French: *Bonjour* ("bohng-zhoor")—Hello, good day; *Au revoir* ("ohr-vwahr")—Good bye; *Bonsoir* ("bohng-swahr")—Good evening; *A demain* ("ah duh-mahng")—Until tomorrow; *Eh bien* ("ay b'yahng")—Well; *Très bien* ("treh b'yahng")—Very well; *Voilà* ("vwah-lah")—Here you are; *Bon* ("bohng")—Good.

FAMILY AND COMMUNITY DYNAMICS

Belgian immigrants who arrived in America during the nineteenth century were immediately concerned with survival. Those who settled in the Midwest often came with only a few meager possessions. Often, they set down in what was then wilderness, and they needed all their mental and physical resources to make it through their first winter. The fact that there was no way for them to return to their homes in Belgium, and the comfort and assistance of the Catholic clergy pulled them through. These early families set to work clearing the land, building shelters, and planting crops. Men, women, and children all worked in the fields and tended the animals. Others, who lived in cities, took work where they could find it to support their families. The most fortunate were those that came with craft skills—a growing America needed these workers, and they readily found employment. As they became established in their new country, they began to form organizations to help the sick and poor among them. They also maintained ties with those they left behind in Belgium. As a result, many more came to join their friends and relatives in the new land. As years went by, the crude homesteads and rocky fields became productive family farms; job opportunities in the cities led many Belgian Americans to become business owners or to enter a profession.

Belgian American families tended to be large. There were strong social and religious taboos against divorce. Rural women were expected to work in the fields as well as in the home. Traditional roles for men and women were observed, and any deviation was often censured. Even though it was not uncommon for widows to carry on their deceased husband's occupation, especially that of farming, it was frowned upon if women assumed a community leadership role, except on a social basis. Children also had chores to do at an early age, and gender-based chores were commonly assigned. On farms, they also helped with planting and harvest, and as a result, were often absent from school during those times of the year. However, these early immigrants respected teachers and education. Parochial schools were established, but they also sent their children to the public schools. While most second-generation young women attended elementary school, most did not go on to high school. However, teaching was an approved vocation for women.

Belgian American populations are heavily concentrated in the Midwest. Whether rural or city dwelling, the second and third generations tended to carry on the work traditions of their forebears. Detroit, for example, has many Belgian descendants employed in the building and related trades. Well-kept Belgian farms dot small Wisconsin communities, even though many farmers may work second jobs at paper mills or at other occupations for their main source of income. As with most ethnic groups that arrived here during the nineteenth century, Belgian Americans have taken advantage of what America had to offer, combined it with their own unique talents and strengths, and enriched it with their contributions. Today, the grandchildren and great-grandchildren of nineteenth-century Belgian immigrants have assimilated fully into the educational and occupational roles of twentieth-century society.

WEDDINGS

The young (16 to 20 years was a common marrying age) bride prepared for her wedding by filling her hope chest with hand made quilts, tablecloths, and linens. Her friends often gave her a bridal shower. It was taken for granted that she would marry within the Catholic religion. Rural communities often held twilight wedding masses so the men would have time to be out of the fields.

A typical wedding celebration lasted all day and all night. It was common for 300 to 600 people to be invited. In the old days, the wedding couple went from house to house, extending a personal invitation. Once held in the bride's family home, the celebration is now often held at a local hall or country club. It was customary for neighbor women to help prepare the food, and preparation took many days. A very festive atmosphere surrounded the entire event. The guests ate and drank all day, and in the evening there was a wedding dance. The gift opening took place after the wedding dinner, and gifts were displayed for all the guests to see. Money was rarely given as a gift. Many of these same customs apply today, especially in the more homogeneous Belgian communities.

CATECHISM AND FIRST COMMUNION

Religious instruction for young people begins early. Catechism studies prepare children for first communion, which usually takes place at age 12. Children study under the guidance of a priest for about three years, and are confirmed in their teens. Boys often served as altar boys when they became communicants. Today, girls are allowed this privilege in some Catholic churches as well. These religious rites of passage are celebrated by family and friends with parties and gift-giving.

FUNERALS

After announcement of a death, a wake is held for friends and family. It is customary to have an open casket for viewing of the deceased. The body is taken to the church for a Catholic mass the following day. Funeral masses in memory of the dead person are held throughout the year, having been paid for by relatives and friends. A funeral dinner is held for all mourners. The dinner is usually put on by a group of church women, whose special task is supplying this service to members of the church. It is customary for friends and neighbors to send food to the home of the deceased. Other funeral customs from the past still persist in some form today. The rosary is still said at the wake. A procession of vehicles from the church to the cemetery is a usual occurrence. The wearing of dark, or black, clothing is observed today by only the most traditional mourners, but once was an expected ritual for the family. This usually went on for at least one year. During this time family members did not attend festive or social events. Tying a purple or black ribbon on the door of the dead person's home and the wearing of a black arm band by men in the family were other mourning customs of an earlier time.

RELIGION

The majority of Belgian Americans are of the Roman Catholic faith, although some are Presbyterians and Episcopalians. By 1900, Belgian religious orders were thriving in 16 states. The Sisters of Notre Dame, from Namur, Belgium, were successful in establishing bilingual schools in 14 of those states; the Benedictines built missions in the western part of the country, and the Jesuits, who founded St. Louis University in 1818, were able to expand the reach of the University through the use of Belgian teachers and benefactors. But Belgian immigrants often were without churches of their own, mainly because they assimilated at a faster rate in the more populous areas, attending Catholic churches founded by other ethnic Catholics, such as the German or French. However, two of the more homogeneous groups, those in Door County, Wisconsin, and those in Detroit, Michigan, were successful in establishing churches of their own.

In 1853, a Belgian missionary, Father Edward Daems, helped a group of immigrants establish a community in Northeast Wisconsin in an area called Bay Settlement. They called it *Aux premiers Belges*—The first Belgians. By 1860, St. Hubert's Church in Bay Settlement and St. Mary's in Namur were built. Other Belgian churches established during the nineteenth century in Door County were St. Michael's, St. John the Baptist, and St. Joseph's. In 1861, the French Presbyterian Church was established in Green Bay. Small roadside chapels were also built to serve those who lived too far away to attend parish churches regularly. The chapels were named by worshipers in honor of patron saints.

In 1834, Father Bonduel of Commnes, Belgium, became the first priest to be ordained in Detroit. The first Catholic College (1836) was operated by Flemish Belgian priests, and the first school for girls was founded by an order of Belgian nuns in 1834. By 1857, Catholics in Detroit were a sizable group. However, they had still had no church of their own and were, at that time, worshipping with other Catholics at St. Anne's Church. This was remedied in 1884, when the first Belgian parish was established.

With the consolidation of many Catholic parishes throughout the United States, even Belgian Americans in small, stable communities may no longer attend an ethnically affiliated church. As with, for example, the German Catholic and the French Catholic parish churches, many Belgian Catholic parishes have died out or have merged with other parishes in this age of priest shortages and financial hardship.

POLITICS AND GOVERNMENT

At first, little heed was paid to the American system of government. Exercising the right to vote and to have an influence in local affairs came gradually, as Belgian Americans learned the English language and began to establish leadership among themselves. Soon they began to draw upon these leaders for various offices—town assessor, justice of the peace, superintendent of schools. As a group, they realized the power of their vote, and as time went on, began to exert great influence in the communities where they resided. Independent of spirit, they were prone to band together politically to solve their problems, rather than passively waiting for outsiders to order their affairs.

On a national scale, Belgian Americans responded as a distinct group to Belgium's tragic experience during the two World Wars. The Flemings, especially, made a strong effort to avoid being associated in people's minds with the Germans. In general, assimilation was hastened by wartime experiences. Belgian American veterans'

and fraternal organizations came into being during this time.

MILITARY

Belgian Americans fought in America's War of Independence. The Civil War came shortly after the greatest influx of Belgian immigrants; and as American citizens, many were called to serve. In rural communities this caused great hardship, as women and children struggled to support themselves by working the farms alone. Belgian Americans fought in both World Wars. Their efforts were made more poignant by the fact that, in both Wars, Belgium was devastated by the German army. It is noted that during World War I, Belgian Americans gave so generously to the children who were victims of that war, that an official delegation from Belgium was sent to the United States in 1917 to honor their efforts. In a reverse effort, Edgar Sengier, the director of the Union Mine in Belgium, showed foresight in shipping all of Belgium's supply of radium and uranium ore to the United States. This kept this valuable material out of Hitler's hands. This ore was of tremendous value in the Manhattan project—America's plan to build the atomic bomb. Belgian Americans also served in subsequent military engagements in Korea and Vietnam.

RELATIONS WITH BELGIUM

Very few immigrants returned to Belgium, but the tie between the old country and the new has never been severed. From the beginning, letters went back and forth, telling of conditions in America and urging those left behind to join the new arrivals. As years went by, Belgians gradually became "Americanized." But even so, the connection with Belgium remained. The outpouring of aid from Belgians in the United States during World War I and World War II is certainly proof of that. Organizations such as the World War Veterans sent groups to Belgium and also received official delegations from there—often at the highest political and governmental levels. The Belgian American Educational Foundation grew out of the World War I Commission for the Relief of Belgium. This organization promotes and facilitates exchanges among the academic, artistic, and scientific communities of Belgium and the United States. The religious connection between the two countries remains strong, basically because of the ongoing work of Catholic missions in the United States by such Belgian Catholic orders as the Norbertines and the Crosiers (Holy Cross Fathers). Even more so, the modern-day interest in researching one's forebears has led many Belgian Americans to reconnect with their mother country. Whether Walloon or Fleming, pride in one's ancestry and customs is reflected in this interest. Since the 1970s, librarians across the country, and especially in the Midwest, note the rise in requests for genealogical information in this search for Belgian roots.

INDIVIDUAL AND GROUP CONTRIBUTIONS

Belgian Americans have excelled in many fields, especially in music, science, medicine, education, and business. Many are unsung, appreciated, and lauded only by their peers and in their own communities. Others have received national, and in some instances, international, recognition for their achievements. Some of their accomplishments are listed in the following sections.

ACADEMIA

Charles Raw was an important nineteenth-century archaeologist and museum curator whose career centered on the study of American archeology; in 1881, he was appointed curator of Archeology at the National Museum, where he established his reputation as the foremost American archaeologist. George Sarton (1884-1956) was a brilliant science historian, who traced the cultural and technical evolution of science from its beginnings to modern day. Others who made significant contributions to their academic specialty are economist Robert Triffin (b. 1911) and economic historian Raymond de Roover (1904-1972).

BUSINESS AND INDUSTRY

Washington Charles De Pauw (b. 1822) was an industrialist whose method of manufacturing plate glass secured his fortune; much of his wealth was used to benefit the city of New Albany, Indiana, where his plant was located. Peter Corteville (1881-1966) founded the Belgian Press, a Detroit printing company that published a prominent Belgian American weekly newspaper, the *Gazette van Detroit*, which at one point attained a circulation of almost 10,000.

EXPLORERS AND MISSIONARIES

Catholic missionary-explorers were active across America from the seventeenth century on. Two of the most notable are Father Louis Hennepin, a Franciscan, and Father Pierre-Jean de Smet, a Jesuit. Father Hennepin (1614-1705) joined the 1678 La Salle expedition to explore the Mississippi River; he was the first European to sketch and describe the Niagara Falls. In 1683, he wrote a comprehensive treatment of the Upper Mississippi Valley; 60 editions of this book were published in most of the major European languages. Father de Smet (1801-1873) was a notable pioneer in the exploration of the nineteenth-century frontier. From 1845 to 1873, he traveled thousands of miles in undeveloped Western territory. As a missionary, perhaps his most important work was with the Native Americans, and he played a prominent role in the final peace treaty with the Sioux leader, Sitting Bull.

LITERATURE

Georges Simenon (1903-) is famous for his psychological detective stories and is the creator of the popular Inspector Maigret. He is the author of more than 200 works. He came to the United States during World War II, and later lived in Switzerland.

MEDICINE

Father Joseph Damien De Veuster (1840-1889) devoted his life to the care of lepers in Hawaii; better known as Father Damien, he contracted leprosy himself in 1885. He was beatified by the Catholic Church in 1993, 104 years after his death. Albert Claude (1898-1983) was a joint recipient in 1974 of the Nobel Prize in Medicine for his work on the structure of the cell; he was also a pioneer in the development of the electronic microscope. Of more recent note: Charles Schepens (1919-) has made important contributions in the field of ophthalmology. Emile Boulpaep (1938-) discovered physicochemical characteristics of cell membranes that provided insight into a number of kidney and heart disorders. He was awarded the prestigious Christoffel Plantin prize in 1992, which honors the achievements of Belgians living in other countries.

MUSIC

Practitioners of the carillon art have flourished in the United States. The carillon is a bell tower comprised of fixed chromatically tuned bells which are sounded by hammers controlled from a keyboard. More than 150 carillons are located across the United States, on university campuses, botanical gardens, parks, and cathedrals. The 52-bell carillon in Ghent, Belgium, is 700 years old and was the largest in the world until it was surpassed in 1925 by the 53-bell carillon at the Park Avenue Baptist Church in New York City. Its present carillonneur, Jos D'hollander is one of the foremost in the country. Other famous carillonneurs were Antoon Brees, Riverside Church of New York and Cranbrook Church in the Detroit area, and Camiel Lefevre of Bok Tower in Florida. Lefevre was the first graduate of the world's first carillon school in Mechelen, Belgium, which was founded in 1922 and funded by the Belgian American Education Foundation. F. Gorden Parmentier, a Green Bay, Wisconsin native, is a world-recognized composer of symphonies and opera. Robert Gorrin (b. 1898) was a French language poet who lived in the United States during World War II. He created the National Jazz Foundation, and was one of the world's foremost jazz authorities.

SCIENCE AND TECHNOLOGY

Karel J. Van de Poele (1846-1895) is known as "the father of the electric trolley." By 1869, his electrical streetcars were operating in Detroit. He founded the Van de Poele Electric Light Company and invented the dynamo, which served to power American industry in its early days. Jean-Charles Houzeau de Lehaie (1820-1888) has been called the "Belgian von Humboldt" for his work in the fields of astronomy, mathematics, physics, botany, politics, journalism, and literature. He was born in Belgium and arrived in New Orleans in 1857. He was actively involved in politics at the time of the Civil War and campaigned against slavery. Ernest Rebecq Solvay (1838-1922) invented the process of manufacturing sodium carbonate with ammoniac. He built his first factory in a town named in his honor, Solvay, New York. Leo Baekeland (1863-1944) was a chemist who invented the substance bakelite, a synthetic resin which ushered in an industrial design revolution and was the forerunner of the modern plastics industry. He also invented the photographic paper called Velox. Karel Bossart (1904-1975) was called the father of the Atlas missile. His engineering work in the missile field culminated in 1958, when he received the U. S. Air Force's Exceptional Civilian Award for developing the first intercontinental ballistic missile. He was a graduate of Massachusetts Institute of Technology. Gaston De Groote (b. 1915) was the commander of the *Savannah*, the world's first nuclear-powered cargo passenger ship. George Washington Goethals (1858-1928) is known as the builder of the Panama Canal. An engineer, administrator, and soldier, he spent seven years overseeing its construction, and was the Canal Zone's first civil governor. Georges Van Biesbroeck (1880-1974) was an astronomer at Yerkes Observatory in Wisconsin. He is noted for verifying Einstein's theory that light is slightly distorted in the area of the solar corona.

MEDIA

PRINT

Two Flemish newspapers, the *Gazette van Moline* and *Gazette van Detroit*, were the largest Belgian publications in the early twentieth century. The *Gazette van Moline*, founded in 1907, was the first Flemish newspaper in the United States. It ceased publication in 1921. The *Gazette van Detroit* was founded in 1914, and was still publishing into the 1980s, although at a greatly reduced circulation. In 1964, the year of its fiftieth anniversary, its circulation was approximately 5,000. Newsletters are prevalent among Belgian associations and heritage societies in the United States. Listed below are two examples of the type:

Belgian Laces.
Official quarterly bulletin of the Belgian Researchers, Inc., and the Belgian American Heritage Society. Described as "the link between people of like ancestry and like interest on both sides of the ocean.

Contact: Leen Inghels, Editor.
Address: Fruitland Lane, LaGrande, Oregon 97850.
Telephone: (503) 963-6697.

Gazette Di Waloniye Wisconsin.
A French-language quarterly periodical that serves to connect the Belgian Americans of Northeastern Wisconsin with those in Belgium.

Contact: Willy Monfils, Editor.
Address: 770 Chemin de la Boscaille, B-7457, Walhain, Belgium.

RADIO AND TELEVISION

Belgian Radio and Television.
Broadcasts daily and frequency can be tuned in for listening anywhere in the United States and Canada.

Address: P.O. Box 26, B-1000, Brussels, Belgium.

ORGANIZATIONS AND ASSOCIATIONS

Belgian American Societies exist in areas of Belgian settlement throughout the United States. Most of these associations came into being in the early decades of the twentieth century, and served as social and cultural outlets for those of Belgian descent. In time, these local and state organizations formed regional federations, such as the Federation of Belgian American Societies of the Midwest and the United Belgians Societies. Many of these societies are still active, and the following state organization serves as an example of the type:

Belgian American Association.
Founded in 1945, the association has a membership of 4,000 individuals and firms united to better relationships between the United States and Belgium. Its focus is to foster awareness and appreciation between the two countries. Activities include a cultural conference, roundtable talks, organization of meetings for business people, film showings, luncheons and dinners in honor of important American visitors to Belgium, and organization of trips to the United States. The Association maintains liaison with similar groups abroad, informs members of available travel and education opportunities, operates exchange programs, sponsors fund raising and relief activities, and participates in related legislative activities. The Association also publishes a monthly newsletter.

Contact: Collette-Anne Stassey, Secretary General.
Address: 1201 Pennsylvania Avenue, N.W., Suite 500, Washington, D.C. 20044.

Belgian American Chamber of Commerce.
Founded in 1925, it has a membership of 500 Belgian exporters and American importers of Belgian products. It publishes the *Belgian American Trade Review*, a quarterly journal that contains company profiles, information on Belgian products, new members list, and Port of Antwerp news.

Contact: Robert Coles, Executive Director.
Address: Empire State Building, 350 Fifth Avenue, Suite 1322, New York, New York, 10118.
Telephone: (212) 967-9898.

Belgian American Education Foundation.
Founded in 1920, the foundation has 250 members. It promotes closer relations and exchange of intellectual ideas between Belgium and the United States through fellowships granted to graduate students of one country for study and research in the other. Assists higher education and scientific research. Commemorates the work of the Commission for Relief in Belgium and associated organizations during World War I.

Contact: Emile Boulpaep, President.
Address: 195 Church Street, New Haven, Connecticut 06510.
Telephone: (203) 777-5765.

Belgian American Heritage Society of West Virginia.
Founded in 1992, has as its purpose the social and intellectual advancement of West Virginia Belgians. Serves as a resource for those interested in Belgian genealogy, history, and culture.

Contact: Rene V. Zabeau, President.
Address: P.O. Box 195, Clarksburg, West Virginia 26302-0195.
Telephone: (304) 624-4464.

Belgian Tourist Office.
Founded in 1947, it promotes travel and tourism to Belgium. It also provides information services and maintains a speakers bureau and publishes *Belgium Newsbreaks* five times yearly.

Address: 745 Fifth Avenue, New York, New York 10151.
Telephone: (212) 758-8130.

MUSEUMS AND RESEARCH CENTERS

The Belgian Researchers.
Provides books, periodicals, and other materials for genealogical research. Principal objective: "Keep our Belgian heritage alive in our hearts and in the hearts of our posterity." Publishes *Belgian Laces*, the official quarterly newsletter.

Contact: Pierre L. Inghels, President and Editor.
Address: Fruitland Lane, LaGrande, Oregon 97850.
Telephone: (503) 963-6697.

Center for Belgian Culture of West Illinois.
Promotes Flemish history and culture, and provides leadership in perpetuating Belgian heritage and teaching the values of Belgian culture.

Contact: Mary Morrissey, Archivist.
Address: 712 Eighteenth Avenue, Moline, Illinois 61265.
Telephone: (309) 762-0167.

Genealogical Society of Flemish Americans.

Provides information and library materials pertaining to Flemish genealogical research. Publishes *Flemish American Heritage*.

Address: 18740 Thirteen Mile Road, Roseville, Michigan 48066.

University of Wisconsin—Green Bay Special Collections Library/Belgian American Ethnic Resource Center.

The center is a cooperative project of the State Historical Society of Wisconsin and the University of Wisconsin—Green Bay. Of special interest in the Center's holdings are materials on persons of Belgian descent, whose families originally settled in Brown, Kewaunee, and Door counties. These materials include family papers, church records, photographs, oral history interviews, and records of school districts and towns.

Contact: Debra L. Anderson, Special Collections Librarian.

Address: 2420 Nicolet Drive, Green Bay, Wisconsin, 54311-7001.

Telephone: (414) 465-2539.

SOURCES FOR ADDITIONAL STUDY

Amato, Joseph. *Servants of the Land: God, Family and Farm, the Trinity of Belgian Economic Folkways in Southwestern Minnesota.* Marshall, Minnesota: Crossings Press, c. 1990.

Bayer, Henry C. *The Belgians, First Settlers in New York and in the Middle States.* New York: Devin-Adair Company, 1925.

Belgians in the United States. Brussels, Belgium: Ministry of Foreign Affairs, 1976.

Bernardo, Stephanie. *The Ethnic Almanac.* Garden City, New York: Dolphin Books, Doubleday & Company, 1981.

Holand, Hjalmer Rued. *Wisconsin's Belgian Community; An Account of the Early Events in the Belgian Settlement in Northeastern Wisconsin with Particular Reference to the Belgians in Door County.* Sturgeon Bay, Wisconsin: Door County Historical Society, 1933.

Sabbe, Philemon D., and Leon Buyse. *Belgians in America.* Belgium: Lannoo, Tielt, 1960.

Santiago, Chiori. "Carillons: Making Heavy-Metal Music with Staying Power," *Smithsonian,* November 1994; pp. 113-124.

BULGARIAN AMERICANS

by
Eleanor Yu

Aside from the rare adventurer, few Bulgarians settled in the United States before the great immigration wave of the early twentieth century, in which thousands of southern and eastern Europeans altered the country's ethnic cast.

OVERVIEW

Bulgaria is a small country on the east coast of the Balkan Peninsula in southeastern Europe. Its land area is approximately 42,823 square miles, or 110,550 square kilometers, making it slightly larger than the state of Tennessee. It boasts a varied topography, with flatlands in the north (the Danubian Plateau) and center (the Thracian Plain) and two large mountain ranges spanning the country from west to east—the Balkans across the center and the Rhodopes across the south. The Danube River separates Bulgaria from Romania and forms the country's northern border. Bulgaria shares its western border with Serbia and Macedonia and its southern border with Greece and Turkey. The Black Sea coastline bounds the country to the east.

Bulgaria's population numbered about 8.9 million in 1990. Two-thirds of the populace is urban, with over one million people living in the capital city, Sofia. In 1991, ethnic Bulgarians accounted for 85.3 percent of the population, ethnic Turks represented 8.5 percent, Gypsies 2.6 percent, Macedonians 2.5 percent, and Armenians, Russians, and Greeks each accounted for less than one percent. About 85 percent of the population belongs to the Bulgarian Orthodox Church. Smaller numbers are Muslim (13 percent), Jewish (0.8 percent), Roman Catholic (0.5

percent), and Protestant. Since the country cast off Soviet-sponsored Communism in late 1989, Bulgarians have increasingly turned to public worship, and religious observance has been on the upswing.

The official state language is Bulgarian. Turkish has survived several waves of repression during Communist rule and is the primary language of about eight percent of citizens. The Bulgarian flag is composed of three horizontal stripes, white, green, and red in color.

The country's main agricultural regions—the Danubian and Maritsa plains—grow large quantities of corn, tomatoes, tobacco, wheat, barley, grapes, sugar beets, oil-seeds, potatoes, and soybeans. The famous crop of the dry and dusty Tundzha Valley, or the "Valley of the Roses," makes Bulgaria the world's largest exporter of attar, or extract, of roses.

HISTORY

The ancient Thracians were one of the original civilizations of the eastern Balkans. For much of the first millennium B.C., they inhabited large parts of modern Bulgaria, northern Greece, and European Turkey. Over the centuries, however, Thrace's lack of a strong, central leadership made it an attractive target for various conquering armies, from the Persians in the sixth century B.C., to the Macedonians, who settled the region under Alexander the Great, to the Romans, who overpowered the Thracians in 50 A.D. When the attenuated Roman Empire divided itself into two parts, Thrace fell under the administration of the eastern, or Byzantine, empire.

By the sixth century A.D., migrant Slavic tribes, encountering little opposition from Byzantine troops, had established themselves south of the Danube and absorbed the smaller Thracian population. Almost two centuries later, the Bulgars, a Turkic tribe from central Asia, began their conquest of the region. They, too, assimilated into the larger Slavic population; over time the culture of the warlike, nomadic Bulgar conquerors fused with the ways of the Christianized, agricultural Slav. What evolved was a unified kingdom whose cultural and military achievement, at its height, rivalled that of Byzantium.

The First Bulgarian Kingdom arose in the early ninth century. Aggressive warfare against Byzantium had pushed the borders of Bulgaria to the Carpathian Mountains in the north and to the Aegean Sea in the south. In 865, Bulgarian czar Boris I, perhaps seeking to stabilize relations with Byzantium, made Eastern Orthodox Christianity the official state religion. Shortly after, Bulgaria established its own patriarchate, independent of the Eastern Orthodox Church in Constantinople. Not only did this mean the Bulgarian Orthodox Church could conduct its services in the Slavic language, but it also kept ecclesiastical authority within the country's borders. The close identification of the Bulgarian Orthodox religion with the nation was a thread that wove through much of the country's history, as the Church repeatedly found itself shouldering the burden of nation-building and acting as sanctuary to Bulgarian culture.

Under the reign of Boris I's son, Czar Simeon (893-927), the First Bulgarian Empire reached its maximum size and its golden age of art, literature, and commerce. A handful of monasteries still bear frescoes dating from this period. After Simeon's reign, the empire began to decline. It was plagued by constant warfare against the Byzantines, the Magyars, and the Kievan Russians and by internal disarray. In 1014, the Bulgarian czar Samuel lost a decisive battle to the Byzantine Emperor Basil II, who ordered the mass blinding of 14,000 Bulgarian prisoners. By 1018, the whole of Bulgaria had fallen once more under the sway of Byzantine rule.

The Second Bulgarian Empire began in 1185, when the brothers Asen and Peter forced the weakening Byzantine Empire to recognize an independent Bulgarian state. The brothers made Turnovo their capital. With the ascension of Asen II (1218-41), medieval Bulgaria reached its zenith in cultural development and in territorial growth. The kingdom extended from the Adriatic to the Black Sea, touching the Aegean at its southern frontier and enveloping Belgrade in the north. Trade flourished, as did learning, religion, and the arts. Bulgaria entered a second and more brilliant "golden age," and Turnovo was the seat of Slavic culture.

This period of relative tranquility ended around 1240, when Tartar invaders were cutting a swath through Europe. Bulgaria, torn by internal dissension and unable to repel the Tartars' frequent raiding parties, was forced to pay tribute to the invaders. The Tartars were driven out in 1300, and there followed another period of expansion and prosperity. But as the fourteenth century neared its end, a new threat stood poised at the southern frontier of the Bulgarian kingdom—the armies of the Ottoman Empire, which had already gained a foothold on the European shores of the Aegean.

In 1385 Sofia became the first major Bulgarian city to fall to the Ottoman Empire. The turning point in the half-century-long Ottoman offensive in the Balkans was the defeat of the powerful Serbian army at the battle of Kosovo Polje in 1389. With this victory, the Turks were able to gain control of the Balkan Peninsula. They wasted no time in crushing what remained of Bulgarian resistance and imposed a five-century-long rule over Bulgaria.

Turkish colonization had profound short- and long-term effects on the development of the Bulgarian nation. While looting Orthodox monasteries, Turkish troops destroyed great masterpieces of Bulgarian culture, including scores of paintings, frescoes, and manuscripts from the golden ages. Stripped of its independence as well as its riches, the Bulgarian Orthodox Church was made a sub-patriarchate of the Greek Orthodox Church for four centuries. Many Bulgarians were enslaved, forced to convert to Islam, or exiled to other parts of the Ottoman Empire. The Turks replaced the existing social structure with a more oppressive form of feudalism, rewarding Turkish landlords and converts to Islam with the most fertile land, while burdening Bulgarian peasants with heavy local and state taxes.

However, Turkish subjugation was not absolute. Bulgarians were permitted a limited form of local self-government. They spoke their native tongue among themselves without restriction. The Bulgarian artisan and merchant classes prospered as they sold food and cloth to the rest of the Ottoman Empire. The empire's centralized government left remote mountain villages and monasteries untouched. As a result, the villages were able to preserve Bulgarian culture, while the monasteries served as a refuge for literature and religious learning.

From the monasteries, a wave of nationalist feeling fanned out to the rest of the country in the 1760's. At the same time the Ottoman Empire, increasingly plagued by corruption and misrule, was sliding ever closer to its eventual disintegration. One monk in particular, Father Paisii of Hilendar, is credited with stoking the flames of the Bulgarian "National Revival. " His history of the Bulgarian people encouraged his compatriots to agitate for Bulgarian-language schools and ecclesiastical independence from the Greek Orthodox Church.

In 1870, worn down by revolts and European enemies, the Ottoman sultan conceded the autonomy of the Bulgarian church and mandated the creation of the Bulgarian Exarchate. Meanwhile, Bulgarian expatriates in Serbia and Romania, dissatisfied by the slow pace of Turkish reform, were forming armed, revolutionary groups that sought the violent overthrow of the Turks. In 1876, the Bucharest-based Bulgarian Revolutionary Central Committee organized the "April Uprising" against the Turks. Although that revolt failed, the brutal Ottoman reprisals, which killed 30,000 Bulgarians, drew Europe's attention to what had previously been considered an Ottoman backwater.

INDEPENDENCE AND THE MODERN ERA

Outraged on behalf of its little "Slavic brother" and backed by international public opinion, Russia led the clamor for Bulgarian autonomy. The major European powers tried to secure reforms from the sultan through diplomacy. Negotiations foundered, however, on the question of autonomous Bulgarian provinces, and Czar Alexander II of Russia declared war on Turkey in April 1877.

The eight-month War of Liberation ended in Turkish defeat. In March of 1878, Russia imposed upon the Turks the Treaty of San Stefano, which created a Russian-protected "Big Bulgaria" that encompassed Bulgaria proper and most of Macedonia and Thrace. Fearing Russia's growing influence in the Balkans, the western European powers dismantled the treaty within months. In July 1878, the Congress of Berlin reduced the size of Bulgaria by two-thirds and confined the new nation to the area between the Danube River and the Balkan Mountains. Although they were largely populated by ethnic Bulgarians, Macedonia, Thrace, and Southern Bulgaria (called Eastern Rumelia) were returned to Turkey. The new treaty also gave the Ottoman state the right to invade Bulgaria in times of civil unrest.

Pro-Bulgarian sentiment simmered in the Turkish provinces of Macedonia, Thrace, and Eastern Rumelia. Uprisings persisted in Macedonia, in particular, where a large portion of the populace spoke a Bulgarian dialect and adhered to the Bulgarian Orthodox faith.

Formed in 1893, the Internal Macedonian Revolutionary Organization (IMRO) dedicated itself to armed rebellion. The IMRO's most memorable revolt, the Ilinden, or St. Ilya's Day uprising, on August 2, 1903, ended in the deaths of thousands of Macedonians and the destruction of entire villages at the hands of the Turkish army.

Bulgaria's territorial ambitions led it into the successive Balkan Wars of 1912 and 1913. Covetous of its lost territories, Bulgaria joined Serbia and Greece in 1912 in a successful offensive against Turkey. Then, when Greece and Serbia each claimed large portions of Macedonia, Bulgaria turned on its erstwhile allies, only to lose to them in 1913. Although forced to yield some land, Bulgaria finished the wars with a net gain in territory.

In World War I, the promise of Serbian Macedonia enticed Bulgaria into an alliance with the losing Central Powers (Germany, Austria-Hungary, and Ottoman Turkey). In the 1930's, the authoritarian King Boris III cemented Bulgaria's relationship with fascist Germany and Italy. Hoping to recover Thrace and Macedonia, Bulgaria again allied itself to the losing side in World War II. It declared war on the United States, Great Britain, and France on December 13, 1941. However, Boris successfully resisted sending Bulgarian troops to bolster Germany's eastern front, arguing that the troops were needed at home as a deterrent to attack. Nor did the Bulgarian people support Nazi Germany's anti-Jewish policies; although Boris acquiesced to a number of repressive measures against Jews, he staved off the Nazi-ordered deportation of 50,000 Bulgarian Jews.

The Soviet army invaded Bulgaria in September 1944, only hours after the Soviet Union declared war on the Balkan country. Shortly afterward, a coalition of Bulgarian resistance groups, dominated by the Communists, seized control of the government. Under the eye of the occupying Soviet army, the Bulgarian Communists abolished the monarchy and established the People's Republic in September 1946. A new constitution, modelled on the Soviet constitution, was drafted in 1947. Soviet troops withdrew from Bulgarian soil that same year.

The Communists consolidated their power over the next four decades, earning Bulgaria a reputation as Moscow's most loyal Warsaw Pact ally. Under the leadership of Vulko Chervenkov (1949-1956) and Todor Zhivkov (1956-1989), Bulgarian foreign and domestic policy rarely strayed from the Soviet Union's. Evidence indicates that the Bulgarian state security police, the Durzhavna Sigurnost, often acted in lieu of the KGB, accepting assignments from which Moscow wanted to distance itself.

As the 1980's drew to a close, the shock waves of Soviet *perestroika* reverberated across eastern Europe. Bulgarians articulated their unhappiness with the regime through public protests and increasingly visible dissident activity. On November 10, 1989, one day after the fall of the Berlin Wall, reformers within the Communist party forced the resignation of Zhivkov.

Post-Communist politics in Bulgaria is dominated by two major parties—the Bulgarian Socialist Party, as the Communist party renamed itself, and the Union of Democratic Forces, which won the new government's first election, only to lose power 11 months later. The country's transition to capitalism has been uncertain, with the privatization of state-run enterprises proceeding slowly. A soaring crime rate and economic crisis have led some to call for the restoration of the monarchy and others to call for a return to Communism.

THE FIRST BULGARIANS IN AMERICA

Aside from the rare adventurer, few Bulgarians settled in the United States before the great immigration wave of the early twentieth century, in which thousands of southern and eastern Europeans altered the country's ethnic cast. The earliest documented Bulgarian immigrants were converts to Protestantism, who arrived around the middle of the nineteenth century to pursue higher education in America, as Nikolay G. Altankov notes in *The Bulgarian-Americans*, published by Ragusan Press in 1979. Their passages were funded by American Protestant groups intent on grooming talented natives for missionary work back in Bulgaria. Although some Bulgarian students did return home to spread the gospel, others chose to remain in the States, settling in their adopted country with their families.

Early Bulgarian Americans included Ilya S. Iovchev, who arrived in 1870 and became a journalist, and Hristo Balabanov, who came to the States in 1876, earned an M.D., then established a medical practice in Tacoma, Washington, in 1890.

SIGNIFICANT IMMIGRATION WAVES

Bulgarians have a long tradition, dating to the Byzantine period, of migrating to flee political turmoil. Every unsuccessful revolt against the Turks in the eighteenth and nineteenth centuries was accompanied by mass migrations of Bulgarians to Russia, the Ukraine, Moldavia, Hungary, Romania, Serbia, and other Balkan nations. Expatriate Bulgarian communities formed and thrived in some of those countries. Today, an estimated two million ethnic Bulgarians live beyond the country's borders, with the vast majority residing in Russia and Romania.

Bulgarians first started immigrating to the United States in large numbers between 1903 and 1910. During this period, approximately 50,000 Bulgarians from Turkish-occupied Macedonia and from Bulgaria proper, or "the kingdom," arrived in the United States. Economic opportunity was the primary attraction for Bulgarians from "the kingdom," who were escaping overpopulation and unemployment in their native regions. Macedonian-Bulgarians had an additional impetus to emigrate; the unsuccessful St. Ilya's Day revolt of 1903 drew brutal reprisals from the Turkish army, which laid waste to three Macedonian provinces and killed 5,000 revolutionaries and villagers. Some 30,000 homeless Macedonians fled to Bulgaria. Within months, the largest wave of Bulgarian and Macedonian Bulgarian emigration had begun.

After 1910, political developments continued to influence the ebb and flow of emigration from Bulgaria. Territorial loss following the Balkan Wars and the First World War drove between 400,000 and 700,000 ethnic Bulgarians from Aegean Thrace, Macedonia, and Dobrudzha into Bulgaria proper. Their arrival strained the already limited economic resources of the country and led many Bulgarians, in turn, to seek work abroad.

For the typical Bulgarian immigrant of the early twentieth century, passage to the United States was not obstacle-free. With little of value to his name, a peasant would sell his land and livestock, mortgage his farm, or take a high-interest loan from a steamship agent in order to fund his transatlantic trip. Such a costly outlay meant there was no turning back. Some immigrants began their journeys at Danube River ports, traveling to Vienna and continuing overland by train to any number of European port cities (Hamburg, Le Havre, Trieste), where they spent up to a week or more in detention camps before boarding a ship to New York. Others embarked from the Greek ports of Piraeus or Salonika. Although their points of departure varied, most immigrants spent the month-long ocean voyage in steerage, in the hold of the ship, where crowded, unsanitary conditions and poor food encouraged the spread of disease. Many Bulgarians sought to avoid stringent entrance exams at Ellis Island, the immigration station in New York City, by entering the country illegally, through Canada or Mexico.

Bulgarian immigration never boomed the way immigration from other southern or eastern European countries did, and in 1924, the National Origins Immigration Act limited the number of Bulgarians who could enter the United States to a mere 100 a year. From 1924 until the lifting of the national origins quota restrictions in 1965, only 7,660 Bulgarians were officially admitted to the United States. Historians believe thousands more made America their home during this period, entering illegally via Canada or Mexico or with non-Bulgarian passports issued by the country of their last residence rather than the country of their birth. Many Bulgarians, it is believed, have been recorded as Turks, Greeks, Serbs, Romanians, Russians, or Yugoslavs. At one point, U.S. immigrations statistics did not distinguish Bulgarians from Serbs and Montenegrins. For these reasons, the actual number of people of Bulgarian ancestry living in the United States is believed to be significantly higher than the 1990 U. S. Census figure—slightly over 70,000 as opposed to the official 20,894.

"While I am not a whole American, neither am I what I was when I first landed here; that is, a Bulgarian.... I have outwardly and inwardly deviated so much from a Bulgarian that when recently visiting in that country I felt like a foreigner.... In Bulgaria I am not wholly a Bulgarian; in the United States not wholly an American."

Stoyan Christowe in 1919, cited in *Ellis Island: An Illustrated History of the Immigrant Experience,* edited by Ivan Chemayeff et al. (New York: Macmillan, 1991).

The 1924 quota restrictions affected not only the dimension of Bulgarian immigration but its character as well. Most of the immigrants of the interwar years (1919-1939) were women and children joining husbands and fathers who had already established themselves in America. Otherwise, immigration from Bulgaria during these years had dwindled to a trickle.

The rise of the Communist state in 1945 precipitated a new wave of immigration. In contrast to the earlier immigrants, the postwar emigres were primarily political refugees and professionals who left Bulgaria with no expectation of returning. Thousands fled in the wake of the Soviet invasion of Bulgaria in 1944. Following retreating German troops to Germany or Austria, some Bulgarians settled in western European countries; others entered the United States under the Displaced Persons Act of 1947. A handful became Americans under the auspices of a 1944 congressional act that granted citizenship to refugees who were accepted into U. S. military service overseas. Until the Bulgarian borders were sealed in 1949, refugees continued to leave by the thousands. The route to America was often circuitous, with refugees typically spending several years in non-Communist European countries—Greece, Turkey, Italy, Austria, Germany—or even in South America before finally making their way to the United States. After 1956, the flow of postwar refugees slowed to a mere 100 to 300 a year, but periodic relaxations on travel or border regulations continued to give the determined occasion to flee.

In 1989, the demise of single-party rule in Bulgaria brought an end to Communist restraints on travel and opened the country's borders. Many Bulgarians, fleeing economic instability under the new government, are once again leaving for western European countries or America. Since 1990, they have been immigrating to the United States at a rate of about 1,000 a year. Like those who emigrated during the Cold War, these immigrants are predominantly skilled workers and professionals.

SETTLEMENT PATTERNS

The early immigrants tended to settle in Slavic or Balkan enclaves in the Midwest and the Northeast, where unskilled laborers could find work in factories, mills, and mines. The earliest recorded Bulgarian communities arose shortly after the turn of the century in the cities of Steelton and Philadelphia, Pennsylvania; Cleveland and Dayton, Ohio; Chicago, Illinois; St. Louis, Missouri; and New York City. Smaller numbers of Bulgarians settled in the American West or Northwest as farmers or railroad workers. Between 1910 and 1914, a group of ethnic Bulgarians from Bessarabia established a farming community in North Dakota. Another group established itself in Yakima, Washington, as fruit growers.

Nevertheless, the most popular destination for new arrivals was the Midwest, where, for instance, the twin cities of Granite City and Madison, Illinois counted over 6,000 Bulgarian inhabitants in 1907. As the automobile industry grew, Detroit became home to the largest concentration of Bulgarians in this country—there were 7,000 in the city alone in 1910, with an additional 1,500 scattered in nearby Michigan cities. An estimated 10,000 Bulgarian Americans continue to live in Michigan today. In contrast, only about three to four thousand Bulgarians reside in the New York metropolitan area. Other cities hosting large numbers of Bulgarian Americans include Gary, Fort Wayne, and Indianapolis, Indiana; Lorain, Toledo, Cleveland, Youngstown, and Akron, Ohio; and Los Angeles, California. Pittsburgh, once a hub for Bulgarian immigrants, has declined in importance in recent years, while the greater New York and Los Angeles areas have attracted growing numbers of recent immigrants.

ACCULTURATION
AND ASSIMILATION

As an ethnic group, Bulgarian Americans do not have a conspicuous or clearly defined image in the United States. Scholars have attributed the group's low profile to a number of factors. Bulgarian immigration, even at its height (1907-1910), never approached the magnitude of immigration by other comparable southern or eastern European nationalities. Practically nonexistent before 1900, Bulgarian immigration also occurred later. Those who did come led largely nomadic lives or were dispersed around the country and tended not to form distinct ethnic communities. There were no "little Bulgarias" from which the American public could draw its stereotypes.

According to Nikolay Altankov, the first scholar to make an extensive study of Bulgarian Americans, the group's own attitudes may have encouraged the indifference of the general public. Far from being vocal or visible, Bulgarians tend to shy away from involvement in public life. With some exceptions, they prefer to devote their energies to friends and families rather than to politics or ethnic activities.

When the early immigrants did attract notice, their "Bulgarian-ness" was often obscured by their identification with other Slavs. During the heyday of Bulgarian immigration, outsiders might have recognized Granite City's "Hungary Hollow" as an eastern European enclave, but few bothered to distinguish Bulgarians from their Magyar or Slavic neighbors. Insofar as Bulgarians were confused with larger Slavic groups, they encountered the same prejudices as those immigrants. Their opportunities for employment were limited, and they took the low-paying, unskilled, and often dangerous work that the native-born refused. They faced the inevitable derogatory epithets. Established Americans looked down on the newcomers, whose unfamiliar customs and lack of English skills alienated them from the mainstream and whose poverty forced them to live in crowded, unsanitary conditions.

By contrast, immigrants who arrived during the Cold War as political refugees received a more welcome reception. Their strong anti-Communist stance inspired sympathy. They were better educated, more cosmopolitan, and more highly skilled than the earlier immigrants. As academics, doctors, engineers, and small business owners, they had stronger financial prospects in their adopted country. However, because their numbers were small and they were even less likely to settle in specifically Bulgarian neighborhoods, they failed to raise the profile of Bulgarian Americans.

The descendants of the early immigrants, the second generation, often chose to live in non-Bulgarian neighborhoods and marry out of their ethnicity. Educated in American schools and steeped in American culture, they were eager to cast aside the "differentness" that marked their parents. Increasingly, they spoke only English. Observance of Bulgarian customs went the way of regular attendance at a Bulgarian church. In short, second-generation Bulgarian Americans assimilated into American life, frequently at the expense of ethnic heritage. And yet, from the relatively comfortable vantage point as third-generation Americans, their children are feeling the draw of their past. Many Americans of Bulgarian descent are rediscovering their ethnic roots. Bulgarian folk dance and music, in particular, are enjoying a new popularity among Bulgarians and non-Bulgarians alike.

TRADITIONS, CUSTOMS, AND BELIEFS

In Bulgaria, practice of traditions varies from region to region. A city dweller, for instance, might not adhere as strictly to tradition as a villager does. And the customs the urbanite follows differ from those practiced by the farmer, whose life is shaped by close ties to the land and a greater dependency on the vagaries of nature. Historical circumstance has exacted its tolls, somewhat estranging the postwar generations of Bulgarians, educated under Communism, from the beliefs of their ancestors. These tendencies are preserved among immigrants to the United States. Although immigrants bring their traditions to their adopted country, their American-born children, in their haste to assimilate, may be eager to shed long-held customs. Nonetheless, certain traditions marking rites of passage, such as baptisms, weddings, and funerals, have had tremendous staying power.

PROVERBS

Bulgarian proverbs usually rhyme in the original language. Even in translation, however, they convey common Bulgarian values such as hard work and respect for friends: God gives, but doesn't put it in the cowshed; A group that gets along together will be able to raise a mountain; A clear account makes a good friend; Study brings success; Nothing is impossible to a Bulgarian.

CUISINE

Like the cuisines of its Balkan neighbors, Bulgarian cooking has assimilated many elements of Turkish cuisine. There is an emphasis on dairy products, mainly yogurt and cheese; on nuts, especially the walnuts and sunflower seeds of the Tundzha Valley; and on fresh, seasonal fruits and vegetables. Traditional meat dishes—stews, sausages, kebabs (grilled meats)—are most often made of lamb, veal, or pork. Also popular are chicken, beef, brains, kidney, and liver. Bulgarian dishes are generally spicier than those of neighboring countries, and cooks are liberal in their use of herbs and strongly flavored condiments such as garlic and chili peppers.

Because many of the ingredients in Bulgarian cuisine are available in the United States, first- and second-generation Bulgarian Americans have continued cooking and consuming the dishes they enjoyed in Bulgaria. However, family meals often become more elaborate and meat more frequent if the family prospers in its adopted country. Conversely, the diets of poor, early immigrant laborers tended to match their humble living conditions.

Traditional breakfasts are simple, eaten at home before the work day begins. The breakfast usually consists of bread, fruit, and cheese—the most familiar being *sirene*, a salty, feta-like cheese, and *kashkaval*, a hard cheese similar to Cheddar—which are washed down with a glass of yogurt (*kiselo mlyako*) or *boza*, a millet drink. Mid-day meals tend to be soups or fried dishes, cooked in butter or oil, while grilled meat or spicy stews, preceded by a salad tossed in yogurt or in oil, are the mainstay of evening meals. Bulgarians have traditionally relied on numerous light snacks (fruit, cheese, bread, and other baked goods), eaten throughout the day, to sustain them as they labored in the fields or pastures or, later, in the factories and mines.

The classic Bulgarian dishes are simple and hearty. The "national soup," *tarator*, is a cold cucumber and yogurt soup seasoned with dill and garlic and topped with chopped walnuts. Another popular starter, the *salata shopska*, is a mixed salad of tomatoes, cucumbers, cabbage, peppers, and onions tossed in vinegar and sunflower oil and sprinkled with a light layer of crumbled cheese. Bulgarian meals are invariably accompanied by the oven-baked bread known as *pitka*, which is served with *ciubritsa*, an aromatic condiment with a native herb resembling tarragon at its base.

Of the traditional Bulgarian main dishes, *gyuvech* is the best known. Baked in an earthenware dish, it is a rich, spicy stew of various vegetables—usually some combination of peppers, chilies, onions, tomatoes, eggplant, and beans—cooked with meaty chunks of veal, pork, lamb, or beef, then slathered with a yogurt-egg sauce which bakes into a crust. Also popular, *sarmi* is made by stuffing cabbage leaves with minced meat and rice. Other common meat dishes are

kebabche, a grilled patty of minced pork, lamb, and veal flavored with garlic, and *kyufte*, a meatball of the same ingredients, as well as the more universal chops and filets of veal and pork.

Desserts, too, reflect Bulgaria's history and its unique geopolitical position: the middle Eastern pastry *baklava*, a layered pastry of chopped nuts drenched in honey, is as common as *garash*, a chocolate layer cake with central European antecedents. Local fruits make another post-dinner favorite, the dessert varying with the season—strawberries, raspberries, plums, cherries, peaches, apples, and grapes. Coffee, or *kafe*, is consumed Turkish-style or as European *espresso*.

DANCE AND MUSIC

Music and dance are central to Bulgarian culture. Music has bound together the community in times of oppression and in celebration. Significantly, there are few strictly solo performances of folk dance or music. Songs are used to commemorate religious occasions, traditional holidays, past wars, and historical events, births, marriages, deaths, departures, and harvests. Even religious services are chanted in song-like fashion rather than read. Song and dance are very much a part of the fabric of daily life, as well. Shepherds can still be heard in the Rhodope Mountains playing plaintive songs to their flocks, using the traditional goatskin bagpipe. In villages and cities alike, a Bulgarian youth will announce romantic intentions by challenging the object of his or her interests to a dance contest. And any given performance of the popular line dance, the *horo*, will include participants of all ages in its circle.

Because Bulgarian music and dance are communal in nature, they are preserved among immigrants only to the extent that there is a close-knit community. Early Bulgarian immigrants often held evening parties, or *vecherinka*, at Bulgarian-owned saloons or coffee houses, where workers sought release from their long, difficult days in song, dance, and drink. Saint's days and holidays were greeted with the greatest festivity, as men performed variations on the basic *horo*, or circular line dance. The immigrants could briefly forget their hardships in lively dances like the *ruchenitsa*, which allowed them to showcase their agility in leaps and squats, or the *kopenitsa*, with its tricky, rhythmically complex steps. Increasingly isolated from Bulgarian American daily life, however, traditional music and dance is relegated today to weddings and other special events or to the occasional performance at ethnic festivals.

Although its role in Bulgarian American life has perhaps declined, Bulgarian folk music has inspired a new generation of Western artists, from the American pop singers David Byrne and Paul Simon to the English singer-songwriter Kate Bush, to the ranks of non-Bulgarian Americans who have formed traditional Bulgarian folk dance and music groups in the United States. New York City alone boasts the women's singing group, Zhenska Pesen, and the Bosilek Bulgarian Dance Troupe. Contemporary music from Bulgaria is also enjoying an unprecedented popularity in the West, and many recordings are available on Western labels. The best known of these is *Le Mystere des Voix Bulgares*, performed by the Bulgarian State Radio and Television Female Vocal Choir.

Bulgarian music is distinguished by its rhythmic complexity, heavy ornamentation, and the stirring and slightly nasal sound of the "open-throated" singing style. Most traditional folk songs are ornately decorated solos performed by a woman against the steady drone of a bagpipe or another voice. (Songs for dancing, categorized as "useful" and, therefore, less artistic music, were simpler and less decorated.) In some villages, a polyphonic style arose in which the women sing in two- or three-part harmony and decorate their songs with whoops, vibrati, and slides. The female singers are sometimes accompanied by men playing traditional Bulgarian instruments; these include, most commonly, the *ghaida*, or goatskin bagpipe; the *kaval*, a sheperd's flute made of three wooden tubes; the *gadulka*, a stringed instrument with no frets or fingerboard on its neck; the *tambura*, a lute-like stringed instrument with a long, fretted neck; and the *tapan*, a large, two-sided drum.

HOLIDAYS CELEBRATED BY BULGARIAN AMERICANS

Bulgarian Americans celebrate Christmas (Koleda), New Year's Day (Surva), and Easter (Velikden) and, to a greater or lesser degree, a smattering of prominent saints' days. These include St. Cyril and St. Methodius Day on May 11, St. Constantine and St. Elena Day on May 21, St. Elijah's Day (Ilinden) on July 20, the Birth of the Virgin on September 8, St. John of Rila's Day (Ivan Rilski) on October 19, St. Demetrius's Day (Dimitrovden) on October 26, the Day of the Archangels Michael and Gabriel (Arhangelovden) on November 8, and St. Nicholas's Day (Nikulden) on December 6. Arguably the most important secular holiday, March 3rd marks the liberation of Bulgaria from the Turks. Immigrant families also observe the standard American holidays, such as Thanksgiving and the Fourth of July.

Most saint's days are recognized simply by feasting or attendance at special church services, where candles are lit before the appropriate icon. Other saint's days coincide with seasonal celebrations of pagan origins and incorporate pre-Christian customs into a Christian framework. On New Year's or Saint Basil's Day, for instance, groups of young children carrying *survaknitsa*, bundles of twigs draped with colored thread and dried fruit, supposedly bring luck and prosperity to their neighbors by visiting their homes and lightly slapping them with the fruit-laden twigs. *Kukerov den* welcomes the start of the agricultural year. On the first Sunday before Lent, young men ensure fertility by parading and dancing in huge masks, or *kuker*, made of animal skins and fur. On March 1st, or *Baba Marta*, people celebrate the first day of spring by wearing or giving away *martenitsa*, a good luck charm made of two woolen balls, one red, symbolizing red cheeks, and the other white, for white skin. A second springtime fertility rite, in which unmarried women perform dances and songs, coincides with St. Lazar's Day, eight days before Easter. Summer begins on the day of St. Constantine and St. Elena, while St. Demetrius's Day, October 26, is a harvest holiday marking the end of the agricultural year. The extent to which Bulgarian American families observe these holidays is often determined by the presence or absence of ties to a larger Bulgarian American community.

LANGUAGE

Bulgarian is a south Slavic language, closely related to Serbo-Croatian and Slovenian and more distantly to Russian. It is one of the oldest written languages in Europe. Like Russian, Bulgarian uses the 29-character Cyrillic alphabet, which was adapted from the Greek alphabet in the ninth century A.D. to accommodate the sounds of the Old Slavonic tongue. The Orthodox missionaries

Cyril and Methodius created this alphabet for the spoken Slavic language, and their disciples Kliment and Naum translated religious texts into Old Church Slavonic using the script, which they named Cyrillic after its creator. The alphabet spread from early medieval Bulgaria to other Slavic civilizations. With substantial justification, Bulgarians consider their native tongue the ur-Slavic language that influenced all the other Slavic languages.

Bulgarian has gained by its contact with other civilizations. It retains over 2,000 words from the pre-Cyrillic Old Slavonic tongue. Four centuries of Greek Orthodox supervision over the Bulgarian church has added Greek religious terms, as well as some Greek words used in daily life, to the Bulgarian language. The Turks, then the Russians, donated vocabulary relating to political, economic, and day-to-day life. The postwar era introduced to Bulgarian a number of western European words, especially in the fields of technology and science.

Bulgarians in the United States have likewise incorporated many American English words into their daily speech. However, only the immigrant generation uses this mongrelized Bulgarian; their American-educated children are more likely to consider English their primary language.

GREETINGS AND OTHER POPULAR EXPRESSIONS

Zdravei—Hello; *Kak ste?*—How are you?; *Blagodarya*—Thank you; *Nyama zashto*—You're welcome; *Molya*—Please; *Izvinete*—Excuse me; *Dobro utro*—Good morning; *Dobar den*—Good day; *Dobar vecher*—Good evening; *Leka nosht*—Good night; *Dovizhdane*—Goodbye; *Chestito*—Congratulations; *Chestit rozhden den*—Happy birthday; *Chestita nova godina*—Happy new year; *Nazdrava*—To your health.

FAMILY AND COMMUNITY DYNAMICS

Bulgarian American communities took root slowly in the decades preceding the First World War. The unmarried men who first came to the United States believed their stay would be temporary. That perception, coupled with the mobile nature of their work, initially inhibited the creation of permanent communities. Nevertheless, immigrant social life came to organize itself around two types of institutions during the early part of this century: the *boort*, or boardinghouse, and the *kafene*, or cafe.

The *boort* was a Bulgarian-owned boardinghouse that allowed groups of immigrant men to save money by living together and pooling their household duties and expenses. It was usually run by a Bulgarian who had met with enough success in America to buy a house. Confining his private quarters to a single room or two, he would rent out the remaining room or rooms. The boardinghouse owner often held a factory job as well. If he was married, his wife and family might provide meals or other housekeeping services to the boarders for an additional fee. More often, the boarders chose to do their own chores. The typical *boort* was overcrowded and sparsely furnished. Boarders slept and ate in shifts, six or more to a single room. They often worked different rotations at the same factory or mine. Although conditions ran to the squalid, many immigrants preferred saving their earnings to living in comfort.

The *kafene* (cafe or coffeehouse) offered an escape from the rigors of work and crowded households. In addition to serving familiar food and drinks, it functioned as a center for recreation and socializing. The proprietor of a *kafene* was usually more educated and better established in his new country than was the boardinghouse owner. He had a better command of the English language than his customers and was often called upon to act as translator, attorney, travel agent, or in any number of other capacities. As a natural outgrowth of his multiple roles, he sometimes ran another business—a newsstand, a grocery store, a rooming house, an employment agency, a bank—on the side.

FAMILY ROLES

Among the first generation, family relations adhered rather closely to the traditional Bulgarian model. The close-knit family was headed by a patriarch who made all pivotal decisions. The father's parents often lived in his household, caring for the children while the father and mother worked. Social life revolved around the extended family to a far greater degree than in western European societies. Marriages were arranged by family members or professional marriage brokers.

With assimilation, however, came the disintegration of this model. Because women were relatively scarce, they were more highly valued in the immigrant community than they were in Bulgaria. Bulgarian wives, realizing how essential their labor was to their families' survival in the new country, became more independent-minded. Immigrant women were forming their own organizations and clubs as early as 1913. Bulgarian men, lacking both fluency in English and status in American society, found their patriarchal roles somewhat diminished. Their children assumed an ambassadorial role, explaining and interpreting the society and language of America to their parents. And increasingly, second-generation children left home to attend college or go to work. In contrast, grown-up children in Bulgaria left their parents' homes only to marry, settling nearby even then. As families assimilated, the traditional hierarchies flattened, giving women and children a greater voice in their households.

TRADITIONS OF EARLY LIFE

According to Orthodox tradition, a child born on the day of an important saint must take that saint's name, or face an unhappy life unprotected by the saint.

Baptism is considered an important rite that establishes individual identity before the eyes of God. The godparents bring the child, dressed in new clothes for the occasion, to church. Relatives and friends are invited to attend. If either godparent has not been baptized, he or she must be baptized at that time in order to be permitted to be godparent. The priest blesses the child and then bathes the child in a tub of warm water. Then he sprinkles with holy water a fragrant plant symbolic of good health, called the *zdravets*. After the baptism, there may be a celebratory dinner at the parents' home, to which guests typically bring gifts of money. Each year thereafter, the godmother goes to church and lights a candle on the child's baptism day.

Proshtupulnik is a non-religious tradition that celebrates a child's first step. Family and friends are invited to bring objects symbolic of various professions. These objects—a paint brush to symbolize art, scissors for the tailor, a pen for the writer, money for the banker, a globe for the world traveler, and so on—are arranged on a small table. The parents then roll a rounded loaf of bread toward the table and urge the newly

ambulatory child to chase it. Once the bread falls at the foot of the table, the child is instructed to choose one of the objects on top. According to tradition, the child will choose the tool of his or her future profession.

WEDDINGS

Typically a month in duration, the Bulgarian engagement period seems short to most Americans. Once a couple announces their intention to marry, the parents of the groom visit the bride's home. Bringing gifts and money for her parents, they formally invite the prospective bride to join their family. An engagement party takes place at the bride's home after she and her parents have agreed to the marriage. This practice has been modified in the United States, where it may be difficult to arrange wedding festivities in one month's time and where Bulgarians marry non-Bulgarians.

Shortly after the engagement, a maid of honor and a best man are chosen. Their roles are more than ceremonial; they are expected to aid the couple in the wedding preparations and to help them throughout their married life. Among other responsibilities, they are expected to be godparents to the couple's children. It is also understood that the maid of honor should buy or otherwise provide the bride's bouquet and wedding dress.

On the last night of the engagement—the night before the wedding—the bride's house resounds with sad songs of leavetaking. Far from celebrating the joys of marriage, these songs mourn the bride's imminent departure from her parents' home. Each subsequent part of the wedding is also characterized by appropriate music; folk songs mark the arrival of the groom's party at the bride's house, the emergence of the bride to join them, and the procession to the church. A traditional wedding band plays lively dance music throughout the festivities following the ceremony.

The wedding ceremony, which usually takes place early in the day, is similar to other Eastern Orthodox wedding services. The priest leads the service; he asks the couple if they wish to marry, blesses them, then declares them married. Husband and wife exchange rings, after which the priest places crowns on their heads to signify their future together as the joint rulers of their family. The couple then drinks wine or champagne from a common glass, thus ensuring their future prosperity. As the ceremony draws to a close, the guests line up to offer the bride fresh flowers. The couple might now engage in a folk custom that supposedly foretells which spouse will rule over the other in married life: each tries to be the first to step on the other's foot. Many modern couples, preferring to regard each other as equal partners, choose to forego this custom.

In cities, newlyweds visit and lay flowers at various monuments while the guests make their way to the reception. The purpose of this custom is to allow the bride and groom to be the last to arrive at the reception, which is usually held in a restaurant, hotel, or private home. Once they arrive, the couple finds, placed on a table, a round, home-baked loaf of bread and a bowl of honey. Before the assembled guests, the bride dips a chunk of bread in honey and puts it in the mouth of the best man while the groom follows suit with the maid of honor. Then the bride and groom feed each other pieces of honey-dipped bread, each trying to outdo the other with larger and more unmanageable chunks. A second loaf of bread is provided for another custom, in which the husband and wife each grip the bread and pull. Whoever breaks the larger piece will, according to tradition, be the dominant partner in the marriage.

At the reception, a feast of lavish dishes and wine is punctuated by live folk music. Guests of all ages join in the *horo*, a circular line dance, whose leader leaps and performs difficult steps while waving a long flagpole. Traditionally, the wedding band was composed of folk instruments; today it may be a union of Bulgarian folk and modern Western instruments. The band's playlist may also be divided between modern pop songs and folk music.

FUNERALS

In Bulgaria today, a family announces a relative's death by issuing cards or fliers to acquaintances and posting notices in offices or on building walls. Funeral services are usually held inside a sermon hall at the cemetery rather than at the graveside. There, a priest or employee of the cemetery leads prayers for the dead and reads a short sermon. A band plays solemn music as the coffin is led to the grave. Guests bring flowers, making sure that each bouquet includes an even number of flowers, since odd-numbered bouquets are reserved for festive occasions. Close family members dress in black for the first 40 days following the funeral, and sometimes longer. Mirrors in the home of the deceased are covered with black cloth.

Forty days after the funeral, the family of the deceased holds another service to celebrate the soul's flight from the body. Followers of the Bulgarian Orthodox faith believe that the spirit leaves the body forty days after death; some say there is scientific proof the body becomes perceptibly lighter on that day. More fliers, bearing a photo of the deceased, are posted announcing the occasion. Guests congregate at the grave or at church, where they light candles for the deceased and are fed ceremonial foods. The most common dish eaten on this day is *zhito*, or boiled whole wheat topped with sugar and nuts.

RELIGION

Most Bulgarian Americans belong, at least nominally, to the Bulgarian Orthodox Church, an independent national branch of Eastern Orthodoxy. The first Bulgarian Church in America was established in 1909 in Granite City, Illinois. Shortly after the founding of Granite City's St. Kyril and St. Methody, the Holy Synod, the church's Sofia-based ruling body, authorized the dedication of a second church, Holy Annunciation, in Steelton, Pennsylvania. In the succeeding decades, 30 additional Bulgarian churches were founded, all under the jurisdiction of the Holy Synod. (Many of these no longer exist.) Administratively, the churches belonged to the Bulgarian Eastern Orthodox Mission for the United States and Canada. In 1938, the mother church elevated the mission to the level of a diocese and installed Bishop Andrei Velichki (d. 1972) as its titular head. However, the rise of Communism in Bulgaria contributed to a growing friction between the American churches and the authorities in Sofia until nine churches finally broke relations with the Holy Synod in 1963. They established an independent diocese headed by Bishop Kyril Yoncheff.

In subsequent years, the Bulgarian American churchgoing community became increasingly polarized, as some continued to attend churches that recognized the authority of the Holy Synod in Bulgaria and others refused to go to churches which they believed were compromised by ties to the Communist regime. Even after the collapse of Communism a bitter divide still separates churches of the independent diocese from those of the loyalist diocese.

The church has nonetheless remained at the heart of community life. After attending services conducted entirely in Bulgarian, immigrants can attend social events organized by church groups or simply exchange gossip and argue politics. New immigrants may take advantage of English lessons or job counseling services.

EMPLOYMENT AND ECONOMIC TRADITIONS

In the nineteenth century, it had become commonplace for Bulgarian peasants from poor, mountainous regions to leave their homes and seek temporary work abroad, usually in neighboring countries. These migrant workers, called *burchevii*, wandered to such countries as Turkey and Egypt, but always with the intention of returning home with their earnings. Most of the early immigrants in America were *burchevii*. They tended to be single men, usually uneducated peasants and laborers who found work in the industrial centers of America, in railroad construction, or in the steel mills, mines, and automobile factories of the Midwest and Northeast.

Between 1910 and 1929, the number of Bulgarians who returned to their native country outstripped the number who immigrated to the United States. Some returnees left to marry and buy plots of land with their savings. Others went back to serve in the Bulgarian army during the Balkan Wars and the First World War. Those who stayed continued working in factories and mines in order to save enough to money to enable second- and third-generation Bulgarian Americans to receive an education and enter the professional ranks of American society.

POLITICS AND GOVERNMENT

The earliest Bulgarian American political organizations grew out of social need. Groups of immigrants who hailed from the same village formed mutual benefit societies in which members pledged to support each other in times of financial hardship. Patterned after similar organizations in the home country, the first-known Bulgarian organizations, founded by Macedonian Bulgarians, arose in the United States around 1902. They reflected the predominance of Macedonian Bulgarians among the early immigrant pool. In 1906, Iliia Iovchev, a Bulgarian-born employee of the Immigration Bureau at Ellis Island, started the Bulgarian and Macedonian Immigrant Society *Prishlets* (newcomer). Its purpose was to help immigrants through the admission procedures at Ellis Island and settle in the New World. A women's charitable organization called *Bulgarkata v Amerika* devoted itself to performing charity work on behalf of both the local community and the women's native villages in 1913. That same year, the Bulgarian People's Union, the first group with a national profile, emerged. By that time, nearly 30 mutual benefit societies had been organized around the country. Their numbers continued to mount, and by 1933 there were over 200 such organizations with a total of 10,000 members.

One of the longest-lived national organizations was the Macedonian Political Organization (MPO), founded in Fort Wayne, Indiana, in 1922. With branches in many cities, it supported the claim that Macedonians are ethnically Bulgarian and promoted the creation of an independent Macedonia. From 1926 onward, the MPO published a Bulgarian-language weekly called the *Makedonska Tribuna*. The group changed its name to the Macedonian Patriotic Organization in 1952.

Some immigrants were also involved in the national political scene. Before World War II, many Bulgarian American workers were active in leftist or labor causes; some belonged to the Bulgarian Socialist Labor Federation, a group founded in 1910 that later merged with the American Socialist Labor Party. Postwar immigrants, on the other hand, tended to belong to strongly anti-Communist organizations, such as the Bulgarian National Committee, set up in 1949 by former Bulgarian politician Georgi M. Dimitrov. Competing right-wing groups organized the royalist Bulgarian National Front in New York in 1958. In an attempt to unite a number of splinter groups, an anti-Communist umbrella organization calling itself the American Bulgarian League arose in 1944. Its goal was to promote understanding between Bulgaria and America.

The fall of communism in Bulgaria has led to a revival in organizational activity in America. As new groups arise to support specific political agendas in Bulgaria, existing groups have refocused their activities to help newly arrived immigrants or to bridge cultural gaps between the United States and Bulgaria.

Individual and Group Contributions

Although Bulgarian Americans are comparatively few in number, their contributions to American society have been significant. The list below provides a small sample of notable Bulgarian Americans.

ART

The artist Christo Javacheff (1935-), or "Christo," fled Bulgaria in 1956, and settled in New York several years later with his French-born wife and son. Before gaining admission to the United States, he studied and created art in Vienna, Geneva, and Paris. It was in Paris that Christo's signature style began to emerge, as he experimented with wrapping objects in lengths of cloth or string. Later, Christo focused on the design of monumental, non-permanent installations for public spaces. His art interacted with existing buildings, structures, or geographical features. For example, an early project marked the first anniversary of the construction of the Berlin Wall by blocking off a busy Parisian street for three hours with an "iron curtain" constructed of 204 oil drums. Later projects continued to provide oblique, but highly visible, social commentary.

Other accomplished Bulgarian American artists include Atanas Kachamakov, a sculptor who founded an art school in Los Angeles; Constantine Vichey, a Columbia-educated architect and the designer of the Varig and Aeroflot offices in New York City; and Nevdon Koumrouyan, a jewelry designer whose work has been exhibited at the Smithsonian Institution.

BUSINESS

Arguably the most influential Bulgarian American businessman today, Frank Popoff has headed the chemical giant, The Dow Chemical Company, since he was named its Chief Executive Officer in December 1987 and its Chairman in December 1992. Born in Bulgaria, Popoff immigrated to the United States as a small child. He joined Dow Chemical in 1959, immediately after earning his M.B.A. from Indiana University, and rose quickly through the ranks. Popoff serves on the boards of several corporate and philanthropic organizations.

The banker Henry Karandjeff came from an earlier generation of immigrants and had a more local profile. Born in a Macedonian village in 1893, he arrived in the United States at the age of 13. He graduated from the St. Louis University in 1919 and later founded two savings and loans banks in Granite City, Illinois. When he retired, he left a successful business to his son.

LITERATURE AND JOURNALISM

Peter Dimitrov Yankoff (1885-?) drew upon his immigrant experience to pen the 1928 novel, *Peter Menikoff: The Story of a Bulgarian Boy in the Great American Melting Pot*. Another Bulgarian immigrant, Boris George Petroff, wrote *Son of Danube* (1940).

The journalist Christ Anastasoff authored scores of articles, many of them about Bulgarian and Macedonian immigrants. His book *A Visit to Yugoslavia and Macedonia* was published in 1957. Boyan Choukanov catered to a primarily Bulgarian American audience as editor of the *American Bulgarian Review* and as host of the weekly cable television show "Balkan Echo" in New York City. Stephane Groueff, a New York-based reporter, published *Manhattan Project*, a book about the history of the development of the atomic bomb. On CNN International, the face and voice of Ralitsa Vassileva (1964-) is beamed around the world by satellite as she anchors the news network's "Headline News" and "World Report" shows.

MEDICINE

The psychiatrist George Kamen (1942-) was still living in Bulgaria when he pioneered the idea of group therapy in the late 1960s. The revolutionary new treatment brought him both professional acclaim and political troubles. Because Kamen worked with groups of patients who discussed with each other their deepest thoughts and emotions, he inevitably attracted official scrutiny. Kamen soon became the target of a campaign of harassment, and decided to flee Bulgaria. After several unsuccessful attempts, he escaped to Vienna, and from there, to political asylum in West Germany. Kamen and his wife Katia, also Bulgarian, arrived in the United States in 1980. Today he has a private practice in New York City.

POLITICS

A colorful and energetic writer and politician, Stoyan Christowe (1898-) emigrated from his native Macedonia in 1911. The teenager first settled in St. Louis with a group of older men from his village. Christowe taught himself English and was admitted to Valparaiso University in Indiana. He became a reporter after graduating and, in 1928, was sent to the Balkans as a foreign correspondent for the *Chicago Daily News*. During the Second World War, Christowe served in Military Intelligence in the Pentagon. In 1961 he was elected a Vermont state representative, a post he held until his election to the State Senate in 1965. Running as a Republican, Christowe was re-elected to four more terms. He retired in 1972. Christowe's eventful life provided excellent material for his books, which include memoirs, novels, and a volume about Macedonia.

MEDIA

PRINT

Good Luck Bulgarian Newspaper.
This Bulgarian-language monthly was first conceived as a newsletter in 1991. Its founders, two immigrants who had been journalists in their native Bulgaria, changed to a broadsheet format in 1993. Combining material from their native country and their adopted one, the editors dedicate the first three pages of each issue to Bulgarian news and the two succeeding pages to practical advice about living in the United States, such as the fundamentals of starting a business. The remaining three pages contain advertising and articles focusing on American news and culture.

Contact: Orlin Krumov or Sam Todorov, Editors.

Address: 338 West Miner Street, Apartment 3-B, Arlington Heights, Illinois 60005.

Telephone: (708) 632-1542.

Makedonska Tribuna (Macedonian Tribune).
Biweekly general interest newspaper in Bulgarian and English.

Contact: A. A. Virginia N. Surso.

Address: Macedonian Patriotic Organization, 124 West Wayne, Fort Wayne, Indiana 46802.

Telephone: (219) 422-5900.

Fax: (219) 422-4379.

ORGANIZATIONS AND ASSOCIATIONS

Bulgarian American Chamber of Commerce.
Founded in 1993, the Chamber of Commerce is a non-profit organization that promotes cooperation among Bulgarian-owned businesses in the English-speaking world. Its annual directory contains listings of businesses, services, churches, and social organizations located in the United States, Canada, and Australia. The Chamber also sponsors cultural events and visits from famous Bulgarians. Its guests have included the opera soprano Ghena Dimtrova, the Bulgarian President Zhelyu Zhelev, and the exiled Bulgarian king, Simeon.

Contact: Ogden Page, President.

Address: 6464 Sunset Boulevard, Suite 850, Hollywood, California 90028.

Telephone: (213) 962-2414.

Bulgarian American Enterprise Fund.
Created in 1989 under the aegis of the Bush administration, this private investment fund is interested in developing the Bulgarian economy. The Fund's activities are two-fold: it invests in Bulgarian businesses in Bulgaria and it encourages American companies to do business in Bulgaria.

Contact: Frank Bauer, President.

Address: 333 West Wacker Drive, Suite 2080, Chicago, Illinois 60606.

Telephone: 312-629-2500.

Bulgarian National Front (BNF).
Works to promote and defend the democratization of Bulgaria and the return to free market economy and Western values, and to make known in America the culture and history of Bulgaria.

Contact: Dr. Ivan Docheff, President.

Address: P.O. Box 46250, Chicago, Illinois 60646.

Telephone: (609) 597-4605.

SOURCES FOR ADDITIONAL STUDY

Altankov, Nikolay. *The Bulgarian-Americans*. Palo Alto, California: Ragusan Press, 1979.

Carlson, Claudia, and David Allen. *The Bulgarian Americans*. New York: Chelsea House Publishers, 1990.

Christowe, Stoyan. *The Eagle and the Stork, an American Memoir*. New York: Harper's Magazine Press, 1976.

CARPATHO-RUSYN AMERICANS

by
Paul Robert
Magocsi

After being cut off from the European homeland for nearly half a century, Rusyn American contacts with the homeland were renewed following the Revolution of 1989, the fall of communism, and the collapse of the Soviet Union.

OVERVIEW

Carpatho-Rusyns (also known in English as Ruthenians) come from an area in the geographical center of the European continent. Their homeland, known as Carpathian Rus' (Ruthenia), is located on the southern and northern slopes of the Carpathian Mountains where the borders of Ukraine, Slovakia, and Poland meet. Carpatho-Rusyns have never had their own state and have lived since the sixth and seventh centuries as a national minority, first in the kingdoms of Hungary and Poland, then from the late eighteenth century to 1918 in the Austro-Hungarian Empire. Since the end of World War I, borders have changed frequently, and Carpatho-Rusyns have found themselves living in several different countries: from 1919 to 1939 in Czechoslovakia and Poland; during World War II in Hungary, Slovakia, and Nazi Germany; and from 1945 to 1989 in the Soviet Ukraine, Czechoslovakia, and Poland. Since the Revolution of 1989 in East Central Europe and the fall of the Soviet Union two years later, the Carpatho-Rusyns have lived, for the most part, in three countries: Ukraine, Slovakia, and Poland. There are also smaller numbers in neighboring Romania, Hungary, the Czech Republic, in the Vojvodina region of Yugoslavia, and in nearby eastern Croatia.

As a people without their own state, Carpatho-Rusyns have had to struggle to be recognized as a distinct group and to be accorded rights such as education in their own language and preservation of their culture. At various times in the twentieth century, they have also tried to attain autonomy or self-rule. These efforts have met with varying degrees of success depending on the general political situation in the countries where they have lived. For example, during the interwar years (1919-1938) in Czechoslovakia, Carpatho-Rusyns did have their own province called Subcarpathian Rus', in which they enjoyed state support for education and culture as well as a degree of political autonomy. On the other hand, during the four decades of communist rule following World War II, Carpatho-Rusyns were not even recognized as a distinct people but were simply considered a branch of Ukrainians. Since the Revolution of 1989, they are recognized in Slovakia, Poland, Hungary, the Czech Republic, and Yugoslavia, but not in Ukraine.

Related to their status as a national minority is the problem of numbers. Since they are not recognized in countries like Ukraine, or have not been recorded in Poland, it is impossible to know with certainty how many Carpatho-Rusyns there are in the European homeland today. Informed estimates place their number possibly at 800,000 to one million. This includes 600,000 to 800,000 in Ukraine; 100,000 in Slovakia; 40,000 in Poland; 30,000 in Yugoslavia; 20,000 in Romania; and the rest in Hungary, Croatia, and the Czech Republic.

Minority status has also contributed indirectly to confusion regarding the very name used to describe the group. Traditionally, they have called themselves *Rusyns* or *Rusnaks*, but the states who have ruled them, and their own leaders, have used many other names, including *Carpatho-Russian*, *Carpatho-Ukrainian*, and *Uhro-Rusyn*. In Poland, Carpatho-Rusyns adopted the name Lemko at the outset of the twentieth century. In the United States, the group has also identified itself by many names: aside from Carpatho-Rusyn, the most popular have been *Carpatho-Russian, Lemko, Ruthenian,* or the vague and ethnically meaningless *Byzantine* or *Slavish*.

Carpatho-Rusyns began immigrating to the United States in the late 1870s and in the 1880s. By the outbreak of World War I in 1914, approximately 225,000 had arrived. This was to be the largest number of Carpatho-Rusyns ever to reach America. When emigration resumed after World War I, only about 20,000 came in the second wave during the interwar years. From World War II to

the present, the numbers have been smaller still—at the most, 10,000. Upon arrival in the United States, the vast majority of Carpatho-Rusyns identified with the state that they had left. It is, therefore, impossible to know their exact number. Based on immigration statistics and membership records in religious and secular organizations, it is reasonable to assume that there are about 620,000 Americans who have at least one ancestor of Carpatho-Rusyn background.

At the time of the first and largest wave of immigration (1880s to 1914), the Carpatho-Rusyn homeland was located entirely within the Austro-Hungarian Empire. That empire was itself divided into two parts: about three-quarters of Carpatho-Rusyns lived in the northeastern corner of the Hungarian Kingdom, with the remainder in the Austrian province of Galicia. In both parts of Austria-Hungary, the economic situation for Carpatho-Rusyns was the same. Their approximately 1,000 villages were all located in hilly or mountainous terrain from which the inhabitants eked out a subsistence-level existence based on small-scale agriculture, livestock grazing (especially sheep), and seasonal labor on the richer plains of lowland Hungary. Their livelihood was always precarious, however, and following a growth in the population and shortage of land, many felt they had no choice but to emigrate to the United States.

Most of the earliest immigrants in the 1870s and 1880s were young males who hoped to work a year or so and then return home. Some engaged in seasonal labor and may have migrated back and forth several times between Europe and America in the decades before 1914. Others eventually brought their families and stayed permanently. Whereas before World War I, movement between Europe and America was relatively easy for enthusiastic young laborers, after World War II, communist rule in the European homeland put an effective end to virtually all cross-border emigration and seasonal migration.

Since earning money was the main goal of the immigrants, they settled primarily in the northeast and north central states, in particular the coal mining region around Scranton and Wilkes-Barre in eastern Pennsylvania, and in Pittsburgh and its suburbs in the western part of that state. Other cities and metropolitan areas that attracted Carpatho-Rusyns were New York City and northeastern New Jersey; southern Connecticut; the Binghamton-Endicott-Johnson City triangle in south central New York; Cleveland and Youngstown, Ohio; Gary and Whiting, Indiana; Detroit and Flint, Michigan; and Minneapolis, Minnesota.

By 1920, nearly 80 percent of all Carpatho-Rusyns lived in only three states: Pennsylvania (54 percent), New York (13 percent), and New Jersey (12 percent). This settlement pattern has been in large part retained by the second-, third-, and fourth-generation descendants of Carpatho-Rusyns, although most have left the inner cities for the surrounding suburbs. Since the 1970s, there has also been migration out of the northeast, in particular to the sunbelt states of Florida, Arizona, and California.

Like other eastern and southern Europeans, Carpatho-Rusyns were not discriminated against because of their color, although they were effectively segregated from the rest of American society because of their low economic status and lack of knowledge of English. They were never singled out as a group, but rather lumped together with other Slavic and Hungarian laborers and called by the opprobrious epithet, *Hunkies*. This was, however, a relatively short-term phase, since the American-born sons and daughters of the original immigrants had, by the late 1930s and 1940s, adapted to the host society and become absorbed into the American middle class. Effectively, Americans of Carpatho-Rusyn descent are an invisible minority within the white middle class majority.

ACCULTURATION AND ASSIMILATION

The relationship of Carpatho-Rusyns toward American society has changed several times during the more than 100 years since they began to arrive in significant numbers in the United States. There are basically three phases, or periods, during which the attitudes of Carpatho-Rusyns toward American society have ranged from minimal adaptation to total assimilation and acceptance of the American norm.

During the first period, from the 1880s to about 1925, Carpatho-Rusyns felt estranged both linguistically and culturally from the American world surrounding them. Not only did they speak a foreign language, they were also members of a distinct Eastern Christian church that initially did not exist in the United States. Upon arrival, Carpatho-Rusyns were all Byzantine Rite Catholics, or Greek Catholics; that is, adherents of a

church that followed Orthodox ritual but was jurisdictionally united with the Roman Catholic church. The American Roman Catholic hierarchy, however, did not accept-and in some cases did not even recognize-Greek Catholic priests. Since religion was a very important factor in their daily lives in Europe, where Greek Catholicism had become virtually synonymous with Carpatho-Rusyn culture and identity, the immigrants, after finding jobs to support themselves materially, sought ways to assure for themselves spiritual fulfillment.

Not finding their own church and being rejected by the American Roman Catholics, Carpatho-Rusyns built their own churches, invited priests from the European homeland, and created fraternal and mutual-benefit organizations to provide insurance and worker's compensation in times of sickness or accident as well as to support the new churches. The oldest and still the largest of these fraternal societies was the Greek Catholic Union, founded in 1892 in Wilkes-Barre, Pennsylvania and then transferred to the suburbs of Pittsburgh in 1906. The churches and fraternals each had their services and publications in the Carpatho-Rusyn language, as well as schools in which children were taught the language of their parents. In short, during this first period, the immigrants felt that they could not be accepted fully into American society, and so they created various kinds of religious and secular organizations that would preserve their old world culture and language.

The second period in Rusyn American life lasted from about 1925 to 1975. For nearly a half-century, the children of immigrants born in the United States increasingly rejected the old world heritage of their parents and tried to assimilate fully into American life. New youth organizations were founded that used only English, while the most popular sports clubs, even within the pre-World War I organizations, were devoted to baseball, basketball, bowling, and golf. By the 1950s, the formerly vibrant Rusyn-language press had switched almost entirely to English. Even the Byzantine Rite Catholic church, which in the intervening years developed into a recognized religious body, began in the 1950s to do away with traditions that were different from those in the Roman Catholic church. In short, Carpatho-Rusyns seemed to want to do everything possible—even at the expense of forgetting their ethnic and religious heritage—to be like "other" Americans. Even the international situation was helpful in this regard, since throughout virtually this entire period, Carpatho-Rusyn Americans were cut off from the European homeland by the economic hardships of the 1930s, World War II, and finally the imposition of communist rule and the creation of the Iron Curtain after 1945.

The third phase in Rusyn American life began about 1975 and has lasted to the present. Like many other "assimilated" Americans, the third-generation descendants of Carpatho-Rusyn immigrants have wanted to know what their grandparents knew so well but what their parents tried desperately to forget. The stimulus for this quest at ethnic rediscovery was the "roots fever" that surrounded the nationwide telecast of the African American saga *Roots* and the celebrations surrounding the bicentennial of the United States in 1976.

New organizations such as the Carpatho-Rusyn Research Center and several Rusyn folk ensembles were founded in the late 1970s, and several new publications began to appear that dealt with all aspects of Carpatho-Rusyn culture. Finally, the Revolution of 1989 and the fall of communism opened up the European homeland and provided new incentives for travel and opportunities for firsthand rediscovery of one's roots and ancestral family ties. Thus, since the 1970s, an increasing number of Americans of Carpatho-Rusyn background have begun to learn about and maintain, at the very least, nostalgic ties with an ancestral culture that they otherwise never really knew. Moreover, in contrast to earlier times, American society as a whole no longer stigmatized such interest in the old world, but actually encouraged the search for one's roots.

LANGUAGE

Carpatho-Rusyns are by origin Slavs. They speak a series of dialects that are classified as East Slavic and that are most closely related to Ukrainian. However, because their homeland is located within a political and linguistic borderland, Carpatho-Rusyn speech has been heavily influenced by neighboring West Slavic languages like Slovak and Polish, as well as by Hungarian. Several attempts have been undertaken in the European homeland and in the United States to codify this unique speech pattern into a distinct Carpatho-Rusyn literary language. The most successful results have been in the Vojvodina region of Yugoslavia, where a local Rusyn literary language has existed since the early 1920s, as well as in present-day Slovakia where a Rusyn literary language was formally codified in 1995.

The early immigrants to the United States used Rusyn for both spoken and written communication. As early as 1892, the *Amerikansky russky viestnik* (American Rusyn Bulletin) began to appear in Mahanoy City and eventually Homestead, Pennsylvania as the weekly and, at times, three-times-weekly newspaper of the Greek Catholic Union. It was published entirely in Rusyn until 1952, after which it switched gradually and then completely into English. That newspaper was one of 50 weekly and monthly Rusyn-language publications that have appeared in the United States, including the daily newspaper *Den'* (*The Day;* New York, 1922-1926). Traditionally, the Rusyn language uses the Cyrillic alphabet. Cyrillic was initially also used in the United States, although by the 1920s a Roman-based alphabet became more and more widespread. Today only one newspaper survives, the bilingual weekly *Karpats'ka Rus'/Carpatho-Rus'* (Yonkers, New York, 1939-), half of which is published in Rusyn using the Cyrillic alphabet.

First-generation immigrants, in particular, wanted to pass on the native language to their American-born offspring. Hence, church-sponsored parochial and weekend schools were set up, especially from 1900 to 1930. To preserve the native language, several Rusyn American grammars, readers, catechisms, and other texts were published. The language was also used on a few radio programs during the 1940s and 1950s in New York City, Pittsburgh, Cleveland, and other cities with large Rusyn concentrations. At present there are no radio programs, and the language is taught formally only to students attending the Byzantine Catholic Seminary in Pittsburgh and the Carpatho-Russian Orthodox Diocesan Seminary in Johnstown, Pennsylvania.

FAMILY AND COMMUNITY DYNAMICS

In the Carpatho-Rusyn homeland, where there was a need for agricultural laborers, families were often large, with an average of six to ten children. Family homesteads might also house grandparents as well as a newly wedded son or daughter and spouse waiting to earn enough to establish their own home. Many villages comprised three or four extended families interrelated through blood or through relationships such as godparents.

The immigrants who came to the United States were initially males who lived in boarding houses. Those who remained eventually married in America or brought their families from Europe. The extended family structure typical of the European village was replaced by nuclear families living in individual houses or apartments that included parents and on average, three to four children.

Coming to the United States primarily before World War I, Carpatho-Rusyns entered a society in which there were little or no welfare programs or other forms of public assistance. The ideal was to take care of oneself, depending perhaps only on a fraternal insurance organization to which dues were paid. There was never any expectation that the government would assist individuals or families in what were considered their private lives. Such attitudes of self-reliance were passed on to the second and third generations, most of whom shunned public assistance even when it became available beginning in the 1930s. Only since the 1970s, with the widespread closing of steel mills and related industries in western Pennsylvania, where thousands suddenly found themselves out of work, have attitudes toward public assistance changed. This means that today third-, fourth-, and fifth-generation Carpatho-Rusyns are likely to accept unemployment insurance whenever their livelihood is threatened.

The traditional old world pattern of marriages arranged by parents, sometimes with the help of a matchmaker, was, with rare exceptions, not followed among Carpatho-Rusyn immigrants. Instead, individuals have courted and found their own partners. At least until the 1950s, parents did not urge their daughters to continue their education after high school, but instead to get married and serve as the homemaker for a family. Boys, too, were often encouraged to go to technical schools or to begin work as an apprentice in a trade. Since the 1960s, however, an increasing number of both young men and women are encouraged to attend colleges and universities, after which they work in fields such as communications, service industries, and medicine (especially nursing).

Whereas before the 1950s women were encouraged to become homemakers, they were always welcome to take an active part in community activity. At least since the 1930s, women have served on the governing boards of Rusyn American fraternals, have had their own sports clubs, and have been particularly effective in establishing ladies' guilds which, through social events, have been able to raise extensive funds to help local church parishes. To this day, many ladies' guilds operate catering and small food services from the basements of churches, cooking traditional Rusyn dishes like *holubky* (stuffed cabbage) and *pirohy* (three-cornered cheese- or potato-filled ravioli) and selling them to the community at large. The profits go to the church.

Carpatho-Rusyns had a vibrant community life during the first three decades of this century. Fraternal organizations, social clubs, political groups, and churches sponsored publications, theatrical and musical performances, public lectures, parades, and picnics, all of which were in part or wholly related to the preservation and promotion of a Carpatho-Rusyn culture and identity. Such activity virtually ceased or lost any specific Carpatho-Rusyn content in the decades immediately following World War II.

There has been a marked revival of activity, however, since the 1970s. Several new song and dance ensembles, the largest of which is Slavjane in Pittsburgh, were founded by third-, fourth-, and fifth-generation descendants of the pre-World War I immigrants. A scholarly organization, the Carpatho-Rusyn Research Center, was founded in 1978; it has distributed thousands of books about Rusyn culture and history, and publishes a quarterly, the *Carpatho-Rusyn American* (Fairview, New Jersey; Pittsburgh, Pennsylvania, 1978-). Several other local cultural and social organizations were established or renewed in cities and towns where Rusyns have traditionally lived, such as Minneapolis (The Rusin Association), Yonkers, New York (Carpatho-Russian American Center), and Pittsburgh (Carpatho-Rusyn Society). This trend toward cultural renewal and the rediscovery of one's heritage has been enhanced by the political changes that have taken place in East Central Europe after 1989. As a result, visits to families and friends that were effectively cut off by the Iron Curtain are now becoming a common occurrence.

RELIGION

Carpatho-Rusyns are Christians and, for the most part, they belong to various Eastern Christian churches. They trace their Christian origins back to the second half of the ninth century, when the Byzantine Greek monks Cyril and Methodius and their disciples brought Christianity from the East

Roman or Byzantine Empire to Carpathian Rus'. After 1054, when the Christian world was divided into Roman Catholic and Eastern Orthodox spheres, the Carpatho-Rusyns remained part of the eastern tradition. This meant that in Carptho-Rusyn churches, Church Slavonic (written in the Cyrillic alphabet) was used instead of Latin as the liturgical language, priests could marry, and after the sixteenth century the "old calendar" was maintained, so that nonmovable feasts like Christmas were celebrated about two weeks after they were celebrated according to the western calendar. Eastern Christians also recognized as the head of their church the ecumenical patriarch, who resided in Constantinople, the capital of the former Byzantine Empire.

The question of church jurisdiction changed in the mid-seventeenth century, when some Carpatho-Rusyn bishops and priests united with the Catholic church based in Rome. These Uniates, as they were first called, were at first allowed to keep all their eastern Orthodox traditions, but they were required to accept the authority of the Pope in Rome instead of the Orthodox ecumenical patriarch. Because the Uniates continued to use the eastern liturgy and follow eastern church practices, they were eventually called Greek Catholics, and today Byzantine Rite Catholics. Since the seventeenth century, Carpatho-Rusyns have been divided into two branches of Eastern Christianity—Orthodoxy and Byzantine Rite Catholicism.

Regardless of whether Carpatho-Rusyns were Orthodox or Byzantine Rite Catholic, the church remained a central feature of their life-cycle in the European homeland. Until well into the twentieth century, all rites of passage (birth/baptisms, weddings, funerals) and public events in Rusyn villages and towns were determined by the church calendar. In many ways, Carpatho-Rusyn culture and identity were synonymous with either the Byzantine Rite Catholic or Orthodox churches. Virtually all the early Carpatho-Rusyn cultural leaders, including the nineteenth-century "national awakener" Aleksander Dukhnovych, were priests.

Because religion was so important, it is not surprising that Carpatho-Rusyns tried to recreate aspects of their church-directed life after immigrating to the United States. From the very outset, however, the Byzantine Rite Catholics met with resistance from American Catholic bishops, who before World War I were intolerant toward all traditions that were not in accord with American

Roman Catholic norms (especially those that used "foreign" languages and followed practices like a married priesthood). As a result, thousands of Byzantine Rite Catholics left the church and joined the Orthodox church. This "return to the ancient faith" began as early as 1892 and was led by a priest who at the time was based in Minneapolis, Father Alexis Toth.

Aside from losing members to Orthodoxy, the Byzantine Rite Catholic church was also having difficulty maintaining traditional practices. After 1929, Byzantine Rite Catholics were forced by Rome to accept the practice of celibacy for priests and to turn over all church property, which until then was generally held by laypersons who had built and paid for the buildings. This so-called "celibacy controversy" caused great dissatisfaction, and led to the defection of thousands more Byzantine Rite Catholics, who created a new American Carpatho-Russian Orthodox church. The Byzantine Rite Catholics also gave up other traditional practices, and by the 1950s and 1960s changed to the western calendar and used primarily English in their services.

The division between Orthodoxy and Byzantine Rite Catholicism in the European homeland has continued among Carpatho-Rusyns and their descendants in the United States. Today the Byzantine Rite Catholic church has four dioceses located in Pittsburgh, Pennsylvania; Passaic, New Jersey; Parma, Ohio; and Van Nuys, California. The American Carpatho-Russian Orthodox church has one diocese based in Johnstown, Pennsylvania. The Orthodox Church in America, with its seat in New York City, has 12 dioceses across the country. The approximate Carpatho-Rusyn membership in these churches is as follows: Byzantine Rite Catholics—195,000; Carpatho-Russian Orthodox—18,000; Orthodox Church in America—250,000.

In the early years of the immigration, when Carpatho-Rusyns did not yet have their own churches, many Byzantine Rite Catholics attended, and eventually joined, Roman Catholic churches. Subsequently, intermarriage increased the number of Carpatho-Rusyn Roman Catholics, who today may number as high as 80,000 to 100,000. The community's internal religious controversies and the proselytizing efforts of American Protestant churches, especially in the early decades of the twentieth century, have also resulted in the growth of several evangelical sects among Carpatho-Rusyns and conversions, especially to various Baptist churches.

EMPLOYMENT AND ECONOMIC TRADITIONS

Although the vast majority of Carpatho-Rusyns who came to the United States during the major wave of immigration before World War I left small villages where they worked as small-scale subsistence-level farmers or as livestock herders, only a handful found jobs in agriculture in the United States. As one priest and community activist quipped earlier in the century: "Our people do not live in America, they live *under* America!" This remark reflects the fact that many of the earliest Carpatho-Rusyn immigrants found employment in the coal-mining belt in eastern Pennsylvania. Since they lacked industrial and mining skills upon arrival, they were given the most menial tasks, such as coal splitting and carting. Carpatho-Rusyns were also attracted to the iron mines in upstate Minnesota; the lead mines of south central Missouri; the coal mines of southern Oklahoma and Washington state; the gold, silver, and lead mines of Colorado; and the marble quarries of Vermont. Even more important than mining for Carpatho-Rusyns was the growing steel industry of Pittsburgh and its neighboring towns. The steel mills and associated industries employed most Carpatho-Rusyns who lived in western Pennsylvania and neighboring Ohio.

Already during the pre-World War I decades, women were obliged to work outside the home in order to supplement the family income. With limited English-language and work skills, at first they were only able to find work as cleaning women in offices or as servants and nannies in well-to-do households. The second-generation American-born were more likely to find work as retail salespersons, waitresses, and workers in light industries such as shoe, soap, and cigar factories.

Like women, the second-generation American-born men had moved slightly up the employment ladder to work as skilled and semi-skilled workers, foremen, or clerical workers. By the third and fourth generation, there was a marked increase in managerial and semi-professional occupations. In general, however, Carpatho-Rusyns and their descendants have preferred working in factories, mills, mines, and other industries, rather than trying to establish their own businesses.

A dependence on the existing American industrial and corporate structure has, in recent decades, had a negative effect on thousands of Rusyn Americans who thought the jobs or industries that they and their fathers and grandfathers worked in would always be there for themselves and their children. The widespread closing of coal mines in eastern Pennylvania and the collapse of America's steel industry put thousands of Rusyn Americans out of work. As a result, Carpatho-Rusyns, like other middle-class working Americans in the past two decades, have had to lower their expectations about economic advancement and to retrain themselves for, and especially to encourage their children to prepare for, jobs that are no longer in coal and steel, but in electronics, computers, and service-related industries.

POLITICS AND GOVERNMENT

At least until World War I, Carpatho-Rusyns in the European homeland did not have any experience in politics. They were used to being ruled and not to participating in the governing process. The result was skepticism and a deep-seated mistrust toward politics which was to continue after immigration to the United States. Not surprisingly, first-generation Carpatho-Rusyns, and even their American-born descendants, have rarely become elected officials in the United States. It was not until the 1970s that the first individuals of Carpatho-Rusyn background were to be found in elected offices beyond the local level, such as Mark Singel, the lieutenant governor of Pennsylvania, and Joseph M. Gaydos, Democratic congressman from Pennsylvania. As for the majority of Carpatho-Rusyns, their relation to political life was limited to participation in strikes, especially in the coal fields and in steel and related industries during the decades of the 1890s to 1930s. While there were some Carpatho-Rusyn political clubs established during the 1930s and 1940s to support Democratic party candidates, these were generally few in number and short-lived.

On the other hand, Carpatho-Rusyn Americans have in the past played an active and, at times, a decisive role in homeland politics. This was particularly so during the closing months of World War I, when Carpatho-Rusyn Americans, like other immigrant groups from east central and southern Europe, proposed various options for the future of their homelands following what proved to be the imminent collapse of the Russian, Austro-Hungarian, and Ottoman Empires.

In the spring and summer of 1918, both Byzantine Rite Catholic and Orthodox religious and lay leaders formed political action committees, the most important of which was the American Council of Uhro-Rusyns in Homestead, Pennsylvania. The Homestead-based council chose a young, American-trained Carpatho-Rusyn lawyer, Gregory Zatkovich, to represent them. Under his leadership, the American Rusyns joined with other groups in the Mid-European Union in Philadelphia, lobbied the American government, and followed President Woodrow Wilson's suggestion that the Carpatho-Rusyn homeland might become part of the new state of Czechoslovakia. An agreement to join Czechoslovakia was reached in Philadelphia in November 1918, after which Zatkovich led a Rusyn American delegation to convince leaders in the homeland of the desirability of joining Czechoslovakia.

The "American solution" was indeed accepted in 1919 at the Paris Peace Conference. Only the Lemko Rusyns north of the mountains were left out; eventually they were incorporated into the new state of Poland. In recognition of his role, Zatkovich, while still an American citizen, was appointed by the president of Czechoslovakia to be the first governor of its eastern province called Subcarpathian Rus'.

During the 1920s and 1930s, the Rusyn American community closely followed political events in the homeland, and frequently sent protests to the League of Nations, calling on the Czechoslovak government to implement the political autonomy that had been promised, but not fully implemented, in the province of Subcarpathian Rus'. The United States government was now less interested in faraway East Central Europe, so that Rusyn American political influence on the homeland declined and eventually ended entirely, in particular after Subcarpathian Rus' was annexed to the Soviet Union in 1945 and the rest of East Central Europe came under Soviet-inspired communist rule.

After being cut off from the European homeland for nearly half a century, Rusyn American contacts with the homeland were renewed following the Revolution of 1989, the fall of communism, and the collapse of the Soviet Union. Both secular and church bodies began once again to provide moral and financial assistance to Rusyn organizations in the homeland. Rusyn Americans also became active in the World Congress of Rusyns, established in eastern Slovakia in March 1991.

Often related to contacts with the European homeland has been the question of national identity. Throughout their entire history in the United States, politics for most Carpatho-Rusyns has meant trying to decide and reach a consensus on the question: "Who are we?" At least until about 1920, most Carpatho-Rusyns in the United States considered themselves to form a distinct Slavic nationality called Rusyn or Uhro-Rusyn (that is, Hungarian Rusyn). By the 1920s, there was a strong tendency, encouraged especially by the Orthodox church, to consider Rusyns as little more than a branch of the Russian nationality. Hence, the term *Carpatho-Russian* became a popular term to describe the group. By the 1950s and 1960s, two more possible identities were added, Slovak and Ukrainian.

Since the 1970s, however, there has been a pronounced return to the original Rusyn identity, that is, the idea that Carpatho-Rusyns are neither Russian, nor Slovak, nor Ukrainian, but rather a distinct nationality. Several of the older religious and lay organizations have reasserted the Rusyn orientation, and it has been fully embraced from the outset by all the new cultural and scholarly institutions established in the United States since the 1970s. The Rusyn orientation in America has been encouraged further by the Rusyn national revival that has been occurring in all the European homeland countries (Slovakia, Ukraine, Poland, Hungary, Yugoslavia) since the Revolution of 1989.

INDIVIDUAL AND GROUP CONTRIBUTIONS

ART

Undoubtedly, the most famous American of Carpatho-Rusyn descent was Andy Warhol (born Andrew Warhola, 1928-1987), the pop artist, photographer, and experimental filmmaker. At the height of his career in the 1960s and 1970s, he had become as famous as the celebrities he was immortalizing. Recalling the idealized saintly images (icons) that surrounded him when he was growing up and attending the Byzantine Rite Catholic Church in Pittsburgh's Rusyn Valley (Ruska dolina) district, Warhol created on canvas and in photographs new "American icons" that epitomized the second half of the twentieth century. Since his untimely death in 1987, his older brothers, John and Paul Warhola, have become instrumental in perpetuating the Carpatho-Rusyn heritage of Andy and his family. That heritage figures prominently in the new Andy Warhol Museum in Pittsburgh. The Warhol Foundation, which funded the Pittsburgh museum, has also donated paintings and provided financial support for the Warhola Family Museum of Modern Art, founded in 1992 in Medzilaborce, Slovakia, just a few miles away from the Carpatho-Rusyn village where both Andy Warhol's parents were born.

ENTERTAINMENT AND COMMUNICATIONS

In the 1940s and 1950s, Lizabeth Scott (born Emma Matzo, 1922) played the role of a sultry leading lady in several Hollywood films, while Sandra Dee (born Alexandra Zuk, 1942) was cast in roles that depicted the typical American teenage girl of the 1950s and 1960s. Her very name was later used as a nostalgic symbol of that era in the musical *Grease*. In more recent years, other Americans of Carpatho-Rusyn descent have been active in television, including the actor Robert Urich (1946-) and the FOX Television newscaster, Cora-Ann Mihalik (1955-).

RELIGION

It is in the area of religion where Carpatho-Rusyns have made a particularly significant contribution to American life. Three individuals stand out for their work not only on behalf of Eastern Christianity, the traditional faith of Carpatho-Rusyns, but also of Roman Catholicism and American evangelical Protestantism.

The Russian Orthodox Church of America, today the Orthodox Church in America, is one of the oldest in the United States. It was founded as early as 1792, when Alaska was a colony of the Russian Empire. The real growth of that church was connected not to the Alaskan mission, however, but to its influence over thousands of immigrants from East Central Europe who settled in the northeastern United States during the decades before World War I. The expansion of Russian Orthodoxy during those years is attributable largely to Father Alexis Toth (1853-1909), a former Byzantine Rite Catholic priest who joined the Orthodox Church in 1891. Not only did he bring his own Minneapolis parish with him, he also set out on missionary activity in several northeastern states, converting nearly 25,000 Carpatho-Rusyns

and other East Slavic immigrants to Orthodoxy. The church grew so rapidly that it moved its headquarters from San Francisco to New York City. For his services, Toth was hailed as the "father of Orthodoxy in America," and in 1994 he was made a saint of the Orthodox Church of America.

The two other influential religious activists were both born in the United States of Carpatho-Rusyn parents. Miriam Teresa Demjanovich (1901-1927) converted to Roman Catholicism as a child, became a member of the Sisters of Charity, and devoted the rest of her years to a life of pure spirituality. A year after her death, a collection of her "spiritual conferences" was published, *Greater Perfection* (1928), which became so popular that they were translated into several languages, including Chinese. Her followers have established a Sister Miriam Teresa League in New Jersey, which is working to have her made a saint in the Roman Catholic church.

Perhaps the best known religious activist of Carpatho-Rusyn descent in American society as a whole is Joseph W. Tkach (b. 1927), since 1986 Pastor General of the Worldwide Church of God. Tkach is editor of the popular religious magazine *Plain Truth*, and he is the guiding force behind the church's syndicated news-oriented television series, "The World Tomorrow," rated as one of the top religious programs in the United States.

MEDIA

PRINT

Carpatho-Rusyn American.
A forum on Carpatho-Rusyn ethnic heritage.

Contact: Patricia Krafcik, Editor.
Address: Carpatho-Rusyn American, P.O. Box 192, Fairfax, Virginia 22030.
Telephone: (703) 691-8585.
Fax: (703) 691-0513.

Karpatska Rus'/Carpatho-Rus'.
A Carpatho-Russian newspaper of the Lemko Association.

Contact: Alexander Herenchak, Editor.
Address: 556 Yonkers Avenue, Yonkers, New York 10704.

The New Rusyn Times.
A cultural-organizational publication of the Carpatho-Rusyn Society.

Address: 125 Westland Drive, Pittsburgh, Pennsylvania 15217.

Telephone: (412) 682-2869; or (216) 561-9418.

Trembita.

The newsletter of the Rusin Association.

Contact: Lawrence Goga, Editor.

Address: 1115 Pineview Lane North, Minneapolis, Minnesota 55441.

Telephone: (612) 595-9188.

ORGANIZATIONS AND ASSOCIATIONS

Carpatho-Russian American Center.
A social and cultural center that caters primarily to Lemkos and their descendants.

Contact: John Ryzyk, President.

Address: 556 Yonkers Avenue, Yonkers, New York 10704.

Telephone: (914) 969-3954.

Carpatho-Rusyn Research Center.
The main publishing house for materials on Carptho-Rusyns worldwide, it also supports research projects.

Address: Box 131-B-Main Street, Orwell, Vermont 05760.

Carpatho-Rusyn Society.
Promotes Carpatho-Rusyn cultural activity in western Pennsylvania/eastern Ohio.

Address: 125 Westland Road, Pittsburgh, Pennsylvania 15217.

Telephone: (412) 682-2869.

Lemko Association of the United States and Canada.
The oldest Rusyn American cultural/social organization concerned primarily with immigrants and their descendants from the Lemko Region in Poland.

Contact: Alexander Herenchak, President.

Address: 555 Province Lane Road, Box 156, Allentown, New Jersey 08501.

Telephone: (609) 758-1115.

SOURCES FOR ADDITIONAL STUDY

Barriger, Lawrence. *Good Victory: Metropolitan Orestes Chornock and the American Carpatho-Russian Orthodox Greek Catholic Diocese.* Brookline, Massachusetts: Holy Cross Orthodox Press, 1985.

Dyrud, Keith. *The Quest for the Rusyn Soul: The Politics of Religion and Culture in Eastern Europe and America, 1890-World War I.* Philadelphia, London, and Toronto: Associated University Presses for the Balch Institute Press, 1992.

Gulovich, Stephen C. "The Rusin Exarchate in the United States," *Eastern Churches Quarterly* VI, 1946, pp. 459-485.

Magocsi, Paul Robert. *The Carpatho-Rusyn Americans.* New York and Philadelphia: Chelsea House Publishers, 1989.

———. *Opportunity Realized: The Greek Catholic Union's First One Hundred Years.* Beaver, Pennsylvania: Greek Catholic Union of the U.S.A., 1994.

———. *Our People: Carpatho-Rusyns and Their Descendants in North America,* third revised edition. Toronto: Multicultural History Society of Ontario, 1994.

Orthodox America, 1794-1976: Development of the Orthodox Church in America, edited by Constance J. Tarasar and John H. Erickson. [Syosset, New York], 1975.

Pekar, Athanasius B. *Our Past and Present: Historical Outlines of the Byzantine Ruthenian Metropolitan Province.* Pittsburgh, Pennsylvania: Byzantine Seminary Press, 1974.

Simirenko, Alex. *Pilgrims, Colonists, and Frontiersmen: An Ethnic Community in Transition.* New York: Free Press of Glencoe, 1964.

Warzeski, Walter C. *Byzantine Rite Rusyns in Carpatho-Ruthenia and America.* Pittsburgh, Pennsylvania: Byzantine Seminary Press, 1971.

CREOLES

by
Helen Bush Caver
and Mary T. Williams

The identification of a Creole was, and is, largely one of self-choice.

OVERVIEW

Unlike many other minority groups in the United States, Creoles did not migrate from a native country. The term Creole was first used in the sixteenth century to identify descendants of French, Spanish, or Portuguese settlers living in the West Indies, Latin America, and the southern part of what is now the United States. A single definition sufficed in the early days of European colonial expansion, but as Creole populations established divergent social, political, and economic identities, the term acquired different meanings. In the West Indies, Creole refers to a descendant of any European settler. In Louisiana, it identifies French-speaking populations of French or Spanish descent. These populations are variously defined as pure white or a mixture of Spanish or French with some African ancestry. The latter were generally products of miscegenation in a seignorial society.

Opinions differ about the derivation of the term Creole. Some scholars hold that Creole comes from the Spanish verb *crear*, which means to create or to be born. Others point to the Portuguese *crioulo*, which means a slave born in the master's household.

HISTORY

The era of French domination in the United States began in the late seventeenth century, as

French explorers and settlers moved into the New World with their customs, language, and government. Their control continued until 1768 when France ceded Louisiana to Spain. Even with Spanish control, French language and customs continued to prevail.

The majority of Creoles, however, are descendants of French colonials who fled Saint-Dominque (Haiti) for North America's Gulf Coast when a slave insurrection (1791) challenged French authority. According to Thomas Fiehrer's essay "From La Tortue to La Louisiane: An Unfathomed Legacy," Saint-Dominque had more than 450,000 black slaves, 40,000 to 45,000 whites, and 32,000 *gens-de-couleur libres,* who were neither white nor black. As Fiehrer explained, "Money doubtless bleached some pedigrees." By 1815, over 11,000 refugees had settled in New Orleans. These people, somewhat vaguely known as Creoles, owed their existence to the overseas expansion of France and, during the seventeenth and eighteenth centuries, had developed a loose ethno-cultural identity.

Saint-Dominque's Pierre Dominique Toussaint L'Ouverture (1743-1803), a self-educated slave, established a formal government in 1801, sending more refugees to the Gulf Coast. Some exiles went directly to present-day Louisiana; others went to Cuba. Of those who went to Cuba, many came to New Orleans in the early 1800s after the Louisiana territory had been purchased by the United States (1803). This influx from Saint-Dominque and Cuba doubled New Orleans' 1791 population. Some refugees moved on to St. Martinville, Napoleonville, and Henderson, rural areas outside New Orleans. Others traveled further north along the Mississippi waterway.

In Louisiana, the term Creole came to represent children of black or racially mixed parents as well as children of French and Spanish descent with no racial mixing. Persons of French and Spanish descent in New Orleans and St. Louis began referring to themselves as Creoles after the Louisiana Purchase to set themselves apart from the Anglo-Americans who moved into the area. Today, the term Creole can be defined in a number of ways. Louisiana historian Fred B. Kniffin, in *Louisiana: Its Land and People,* has asserted that the term Creole "has been loosely extended to include people of mixed blood, a dialect of French, a breed of ponies, a distinctive way of cooking, a type of house, and many other things. It is therefore no precise term and should not be defined as such."

Louisiana Creoles of color were different and separate from other populations, both black and white. These Creoles of color became part of an elite society; in the nineteenth century they were leaders in business, agriculture, politics, and the arts, as well as slaveholders. Nonetheless, as early as 1724 their legal status had been defined by the *Code Noir* (Black Code). According to Violet Harrington Bryan in *The Myth of New Orleans in Literature, Dialogues of Race and Gender,* they could own slaves, hold real estate, and be recognized in the courts, but they could not vote, marry white persons, have contact with slaves, and had to designate themselves as *f.m.c.* or *f.w.c.* (free man or color or free woman of color) on all legal documents.

FIRST CREOLES IN AMERICA

According to Virginia A. Dominguez in *White By Definition,* much of the written record of Creoles comes from descriptions of individuals in the baptismal, marriage, and death registers of Catholic churches of Mobile, (Alabama) and New Orleans, two major French outposts on the Gulf Coast. The earliest entry is a death record in 1745 wherein a man was described as the first Creole in the colony. The use of Creole in reference to colored individuals appears in local Louisiana documents as early as 1779.

ACCULTURATION AND ASSIMILATION

Misconceptions about Creoles persist. The greatest controversy stems from the presence or absence of African ancestry. In an 1886 lecture at Tulane University, Charles Gayarre ("Creoles of History and Creoles of Romance," New Orleans: C. E. Hopkins, c. 1886) and F. P. Poche (in a speech at the American Exposition in New Orleans, *New Orleans Daily Picayune,* February 8, 1886) both stated that Louisiana Creoles had "not a particle of African blood in their veins." In "A Few Words About the Creoles of Louisiana" (Baton Rouge: Truth Books, 1892), Alcee Fortier repeated the same defense. These three men were probably the most prominent Creole intellectuals of the nineteenth century. Lyle Saxon, Robert Tallant, and Edward Dreyer continued this argument in 1945 by saying, "No true Creole ever had colored blood."

Sister Dorothea Olga McCants, translator of Rodolphe Lucien Desdunes' *Our People and Our*

History (Baton Rouge: Louisiana State University Press, 1973), gives attention to the term Creole. She says that the free mixed-blood, French speaking descendants from Haiti living in New Orleans came to use the word to describe themselves. The phrase "Creole of color" was used by these proud part-Latin people to set themselves apart from American blacks. These Haitian descendants were cultured, educated, and economically prosperous as musicians, artists, teachers, writers, and doctors. In "Louisiana's 'Creoles of Color'," James H. Dorman has stated that the group was clearly recognized as special, productive, and worthy by the white community, citing an editorial in the *New Orleans Times Picayune* in 1859 that referred to them as "Creole colored people." Prior to the Civil War, a three-caste system existed: white, black, and Creoles of color. After the Civil War, however, the Creoles of color—who had been part of the free black population before the war—were merged into a two-caste system, black and white.

The arrival of Anglo-Americans in the northern areas of the Louisiana territory changed the civilization of the many Creoles already residing in present-day Missouri, particularly in architecture; the horizontal log cabin of the American frontiersman superseded the French cabin built of vertical logs. French geographical names were likewise displaced, and the festive Gallic Sunday was frowned upon by the incoming Protestant settlers. By the time Missouri became a state, much of the French culture had been erased and the Creoles were quickly assimilated into the dominant European culture. However, some traces of French culture survive to the present day.

Acadians (Cajuns) are another ethnic population in Louisiana who are sometimes confused with Creoles. Both groups are French Catholics; yet there the similarity ends. The Cajuns have a distinct identity derived from their common French background, their frontier experience, and their relocation from Canada to Louisiana. During their intracontinental sojourn, Cajuns had to cope with diverse Native American groups and immigrants from various national areas to maintain their separate status. Cajuns settled west of the Mississippi and pursued occupations close to the land, like farming and fishing. Creole identity was manifested in New Orleans or small cities where the people engaged in occupations not involving manual labor. Creoles, including Creoles of color, have tended to self-isolation, even in cities, by educating their children in private schools and keeping to themselves.

Some Creole and Cajun groups have long been in contact. Cajuns have historically been a white ethnic population and have interacted with Creoles of color according to racial dictates of the era in which they lived. In the 1970s Cajuns underwent a revitalizing movement, which sometimes included Creoles. To counter such inclusion and to revitalize group identity, an organization called Creole, Inc., has been formed to specifically recognize the black French/Creole minority in southern Louisiana. Other indications of a renewed interest in Creole group identity are the popularization of Zydeco music, the Festival Internationale in Lafayette, Louisiana, and the publication, since 1990, of *Creole Magazine*.

The identification of a Creole was, and is, largely one of self-choice. Important criteria for Creole identity are French language and social customs, especially cuisine, regardless of racial makeup. Many young Creoles of color today live under pressure to identify themselves as African Americans. Several young white Creoles want to avoid being considered of mixed race. Therefore, both young black and white Creoles often choose an identity other than Creole.

TRADITIONS, CUSTOMS, AND BELIEFS

With imported furniture, wines, books, and clothes, Creoles once existed in a total French atmosphere. Part of Creole social life has traditionally centered on the French Opera House; from 1859 to 1919, it was the place for sumptuous gatherings and glittering receptions. The interior, graced by curved balconies and open boxes of architectural beauty, seated 805 people. Creoles loved the music and delighted in attendance as the operas were great social and cultural affairs.

Sometime after First Communion, girls made their initial appearance in society at the French Opera House in a gown imported from Paris. However, no Creole girl's picture was ever to be published in the newspapers, and nothing was ever to be printed in the newspapers about her.

INTERACTION WITH OTHER ETHNIC MINORITIES

Creoles clung to their individualistic way of life, frowned upon intermarriage with Anglo-Americans, refused to learn English, and were resentful and contemptuous of Protestants, whom they considered irreligious and wicked. Creoles generally succeeded in remaining separate in the rural sections but they steadily lost ground in New Orleans. In 1803, there were seven Creoles to every Anglo-American in New Orleans but these figures dwindled to two to one by 1830.

Anglo-Americans reacted by disliking the Creoles with equal enthusiasm. Gradually, New Orleans became not one city, but two. Canal Street split them apart, dividing the old Creole city from the "uptown" section where the other Americans quickly settled. To cross Canal Street in either direction was to enter another world. These differences are still noticeable today.

CUISINE

Creole cooking is the distinguishing feature of Creole homes. It can be as subtle as Oysters Rockefeller, as fragrantly explicit as a jambalaya, or as down to earth as a dish of red beans and rice. A Creole meal is a celebration, not just a means of addressing hunger pangs.

New Orleans was Spanish before it was French, and French before it was American. The Europeans who settled there found not only the American Indians, whose filé (the ground powder of the sassafras leaf) is the key ingredient of Creole gumbos, but also immense areas of inland waterways and estuaries alive with crayfish, shrimp, crab, and fish of many different varieties. Also, the swampland was full of game. The settlers seized what they found and produced a cuisine based on good taste, experimentation, and spices. On the experimental side, it was in New Orleans that raw, hard liquor was transformed into the more sophisticated cocktail, and where the simple cup of coffee became café Brulot, a concoction spiced with cinnamon, cloves, and lemon peel and flambéed with cognac. The seasonings used are distinctive, but there is yet another essential ingredient—a heavy black iron skillet.

Such dexterity produced the many faceted family of gumbos. Gumbo is a soup or a stew, yet too unique to be classified as one or the other. It starts with a base of highly seasoned roux, scallions, and herbs, which serves as a vehicle for oysters, crabs, shrimp, chicken, ham, various game, or combinations thereof. Oysters may be consumed raw (on the half-shell), sautéed and packed into hollowed-out French bread, or baked on the half-shell and served with various garnishes. Shrimp, crayfish, and crab are similarly starting points for the Creole cook who might have croquettes in mind, or a pie, or an omelette, or a stew.

CREOLE DANCES AND SONGS

Creoles are a festive people who enjoy music and dancing. In New Orleans, public balls were held twice weekly under Spanish rule, and when the French took over, they continued the practice. Cotillions presented by numerous academies provided young ladies and gentlemen with the opportunity to display their skills in dancing quadrilles, *valses á un temps*, *valses á deux temps*, *valses á trois temps*, polkas, and *polazurkas*. Saturday night balls and dances were a universal institution in Creole country. The community knew about the dances by means of a flagpole denoting the site of the dance. Families arrived on horseback or in a variety of wheeled carriages. The older adults played *vingt-et-un* (Twenty-one) or other card games while the young danced and engaged in flirtations until the party dispersed near daybreak. During the special festive season, between New Year's and Mardi Gras, many brilliant balls were scheduled. Only the most respected families were asked to attend with lists scrutinized by older members of the families to keep less prominent people away.

Creole songs lacked religious elements and were often short. They contained elements of satire, ridicule, or mockery, sometimes a suggestive vulgarity, and frequently mentioned food. Some typical songs include "*Mo l'aime toi, chere;*" "*Fais do-do, fais do-do;*" and "*Youn, tou tou.*" The "*Fais do-do*" accompanies a dance similar to the Virginia Reel.

PROVERBS

A rich collection of Creole proverbs can be found in several references. One of the best is from Lafcadio Hearn's *Gombo Zhebes, Little Dictionary of Creole Proverbs* (New Orleans: deBrun, n.d.): the monkey smothers its young one by hugging it too much; wait till the hare's in the pot before you talk; today drunk with fun, tomorrow the paddle; if you see your neighbor's beard on fire, water your own; shingles cover everything; when the oxen lift their tails in the air, look out for bad weather; fair words buy horses on credit; a good cock crows in any henhouse; what you lose in the fire, you will find in the ashes; when one sleeps, one doesn't think about eating; he who takes a partner takes a master; the coward lives a long time; conversation is the food of ears; it's only the shoes that know if the stockings have holes; the dog that yelps doesn't bite; threatened war doesn't kill many soldiers; a burnt cat dreads fire; an empty sack cannot stand up; good coffee and the Protestant religion were seldom if ever seen together; it takes four to prepare the perfect salad dressing—a miser to pour the vinegar, a spendthrift to add the olive oil, a wise man to sprinkle the salt and pepper, and a madcap to mix and stir the ingredients.

HEALTH AND MENTAL HEALTH ISSUES

Health conditions among Creoles during the early history of America was deplorable. Many of the diseases that plagued the European colonies were prevalent. Pleurisy, pneumonia, skin diseases, dental problems, children's diseases, epilepsy, dysentery, diseases of the stomach, and malaria were the most common. Due to better housing and dietary conditions, these diseases and the ravages of tuberculosis, declined in the twentieth century. Today, Creoles have Catholic hospitals, general hospitals, private doctors, and medical insurance benefits.

LANGUAGE

French has always been the language of the Creole; it should not be confused with the language known as Louisiana Negro Creole. Morphologically and lexically Louisiana Negro Creole resembles Haitian Creole; it is usually thought to have been derived from the language spoken by the slaves of the refugees from Saint-Dominque who came to Louisiana at the beginning of the nineteenth century. For many years, Louisiana Negro Creole was predominantly a language of rural blacks in southern Louisiana.

French continues to be the language of Creoles but is not as widespread as it once was. As Americans from other states began to settle in Louisiana in large numbers after 1880, they refused to learn French. Yet because many Anglo-American children taunted Creole children, they soon wished to speak English rather than French. Most Creole families, white and black, send their children to private schools or to schools within the Creole district. The curriculum at these schools usually includes instruction in the French language. French is also frequently the language spoken in homes, at family gatherings, and at fes-

tivals. The state of Louisiana supports this bilingual heritage by supplying teachers of French for most schools. Differences can be noted in the pronunciation of certain words depending upon the locality from which the speaker comes.

Older Creoles complain that many young Creoles today do not adhere to the basic rules of language propriety in speaking to others, especially to older adults. They claim that children walk past homes of people they know without greeting an acquaintance sitting on the porch or working on the lawn. Young males are particularly criticized for greeting others quickly in an incomprehensible and inarticulate manner.

GREETINGS AND OTHER POPULAR EXPRESSIONS

Creoles have some unusual sayings. According to Leonard V. Huber in "Reflections on the Colorful Customs of Latter-Day New Orleans Creoles," an ugly man who has a protruding jaw and lower lip had *une gueule de benitier* (a mouth like a holy water font), and his face was *une figure de pomme cuite* (a face like a baked apple). A man who stayed around the house constantly was referred to as *un encadrement* (doorframe). The expression *pauvres diables* (poor devils) was applied to poor individuals. Anyone who bragged too much was called *un bableur* (a hot air shooter). A person with thin legs had *des jambes de manches-á-balais* (broomstick legs). An amusing expression for a person who avoided work was that he had *les cotes en long* (vertical ribs). Additional Creole colloquialisms are: *un tonnerre a la voile* (an unruly person); *menterie* (lie or story); *frou-frou* (giddy); *homme de paille, pistolet de bois* (a man who is a bluff).

FAMILY AND COMMUNITY DYNAMICS

Traditionally, the father in a Creole family was the absolute head of his household. His word was final in all matters. He was also generous, devoted, and kind unless a family member did something to invite scandal; then his wrath knew no bounds. Providing for a household of people was not the least of his problems. There were limitations to the kind of employment open to him. Manual work was for common people. He had to have a job requiring a coat and tie. Most Creoles worked for banks, cotton firms, and sugar and coffee importers, or sought governmental positions in the courts, city hall, or mortgage offices. They were also professionals, doctors, notaries, and lawyers. A Creole man was judged by his appearance and he maintained it regardless of conditions at home.

Creole women were concerned with their appearance and their families. They loved fine clothes and would never leave home unless they were completely attired, including gloves and veil. For evening, the more affluent wore imported gowns from Paris, which were usually enhanced with jewelry. The young wife was usually a beauty but age and increasing numbers of children altered her appearance. Creole mothers dedicated their lives to home and family. They were excellent housekeepers, hostesses, and conversationalists. They also took the lead in prodding the family toward the church. In the nineteenth century the Creole wife remained loyal to her husband despite his mistresses and other absences from home, and she rarely remarried after the death of her husband. Widowers did remarry, and relatively soon, to provide a mother for their children. Often the new mother was a spinster sister of the deceased wife.

The Creoles also felt it a duty to take widowed cousins and orphaned children of kinspeople into their families. Unmarried women relatives (*tantes*) lived in many households. They provided a much-needed extra pair of hands in running the household and rearing the children. Children sometimes loved them as much as they did their mothers. Creoles today are still closely knit and tend to marry within the group. However, many are also moving into the greater community and losing their Creole ways.

WEDDINGS

In the old days, Creoles married within their own class. The young man faced the scrutiny of old aunts and cousins, who were the guardians and authorities of old family trees. The suitor had to ask a woman's father for his daughter's hand. The gift of a ring allowed them to be formally engaged. All meetings of young people were strictly chaperoned, even after the engagement. Weddings, usually held at the St. Louis Cathedral in New Orleans, were opulent affairs with Swiss Guards meeting the wedding guests and preceding them up the aisle. Behind the guests came the bride, accompanied by her father, and then the groom, escorting the bride's mother. The groom's parents

followed, and then all the relatives of both bride and groom. A relative's absence was interpreted as a silent protest against the wedding. The bride's gown was handed down through generations or purchased in Paris to become an heirloom. Unlike today's weddings, there were no ring bearers, bridesmaids, or matrons of honor, or any floral decorations in the church. Ceremonies were held in the evenings. Some things do remain the same. St. Louis Cathedral is still the place for New Orleans' Creole weddings, and many relatives still attend, though in fewer numbers.

Plantation weddings in the nineteenth century were even more elaborate. Everything came from New Orleans and was shipped by boat to the plantation. Five hundred guests at a wedding were not unusual, nor was chartering a steamboat to bring guests to the plantation.

BAPTISMS

Baptisms usually took place when the child was about a month old. The godfather (*parrain*) and the godmother (*marraine*) were always relatives, usually from each side of the family. It was a decided honor to be asked to serve as a godparent. The *marraine* gave the infant a gift of a gold cross and chain, and the *parrain* offered either a silver cup or a silver knife and fork. The godfather also gave a gift to the godmother and paid for the celebration that followed the baptism. It was an expensive honor to be chosen *parrain*.

FUNERALS

Upon someone's death each post in the Creole section of town bore a black-bordered announcement informing the public of the death and the time and place of the funeral. Usually the notices were put in the neighborhood where the dead person had lived, but if the deceased had wealth, notices would be placed all over the Vieux Carré. These notices were also placed at St. Louis Cathedral on a death notice blackboard. Invitations were issued for the funeral, and funeral services were held in the home.

The wearing of mourning was a rigorous requirement. The deceased's immediate family put on *grand deuil* (full mourning). During the six months of full mourning it was improper to wear jewelry or anything white or with colors. Men wore a black tie, a black crepe band on the hat, and sometimes a black band on the arm. After six months, the widow could wear black clothes edged with a white collar and cuffs. Slave or black Creole funeral processions often lasted an hour and covered a distance of less than six squares or one-third mile. News of the deaths were received through the underground route by a system of telegraph chanting. In New Orleans today, there are great processions with bands playing when black Creoles die.

Cemeteries held an important place in Creole life. A family tomb received almost as much attention as a church. To not visit the family tomb on All Saints' Day (November 1) was unforgivable. Some outstanding cemeteries are St. Louis Number One, the oldest in Louisiana, and St. Louis Number Two. St. Roch Cemetery, which is noted for its shrine, was built by Father Thevis in fulfillment of a vow to Saint Roch for protection for the congregation of Holy Trinity Church from the yellow fever epidemic of 1868. Cypress Grove, Greenwood, and Metairie cemeteries are among the most beautiful burial grounds in Louisiana. Large structures resembling churches with niches for life-like marble statues of the saints may be found in Metairie Cemetery.

EDUCATION

Creole children receive a thorough French education. Traditionally, the selection of a school brought in many unwritten laws of caste. Where the children were sent reflected the social standing of the family. During antebellum days, the boys frequently went to school in Paris while girls attended convents under the watchful eyes of French nuns. Some girls were sent to boarding schools, particularly to the Ursuline Convent or to one of the Sacred Heart Academies located at Grand Coteau, the St. Michael's Academy at Convent, or in New Orleans to the Holy Angels Academy or St. Mary's Academy of the Dominicans. French thought, literature, and art comprised the major part of the curriculum.

Most Creoles, black or white, sent their children to parochial schools. The Ursuline Order and the Sacred Heard Order educated girls and Jesuits provided education for boys. Although schools segregated by color are no longer present, most Catholic schools attended by Creoles are still separated by gender.

RELIGION

Roman Catholicism is strongly associated with Creoles. French and Spanish cultures from which Creoles originate are so closely associated with Catholicism that some people assume that all Louisianians are Catholic and that all people in Louisiana are of French and/or Spanish ancestry. Records from churches in Mobile, New Orleans, and other parts of the area indicate the presence of both black and white Creoles in church congregations very early in the eighteenth century.

After segregation of the Catholic church in 1895, certain churches became identified with Creoles of color. In 1916 Corpus Christi Church opened in the seventh ward, within walking distance of many Creoles of color. St. Peter Claver, Epiphany, and Holy Redeemer are also associated with black populations. Each church has a parish school run by the Blessed Sacrament Sisters. St. Louis Cathedral and St. Augustine's Church are prominent in the larger Creole society, with women predominating in attendance. Today, only about half of the people in Louisiana are Catholics but the early dominance of Catholicism has left its mark on people of other denominations. In the southern part of the state, especially in New Orleans, place and street names are often associated with particular saints.

Almost all of the material written about Creoles describes a devotion to the Virgin Mary, All Saint's Day (November 1), and the many activities associated with the observance of Lent and Holy Week, especially Mardi Gras. Other important religious figures are St. Jude (the patron saint of impossible cases), St. Peter (who opens the gates of Heaven), and St. Anthony (who helps locate lost articles).

Holy Week is closely observed by Creoles, both as a religious celebration and as a time of customs and superstition. On Holy Thursday morning, housewives, when they heard the ringing of church bells, used to take pots from the stove and place them on the floor, making the sign of the cross. Also, nine varieties of greens were cooked—a concoction known as *gumbo shebes*. On Good Friday Creoles visited churches on foot and in silence to bring good fortune.

Few Protestants and no known Jews are found in the white Creole community, which seems unusual given the frequency of intermarriage in the eight or ten generations of Creole life in the area. Today, many Creoles are nonpracticing Catholics with some agnostics, some atheists, and a very few professing a non-Catholic faith.

EMPLOYMENT AND ECONOMIC TRADITIONS

The Creoles' image of economic independence is rooted in the socioeconomic conditions of free people of color before the Civil War. Creoles of color were slave owners, land owners, and skilled laborers. Of the 1,834 free Negro heads of households in New Orleans in 1830, 752 owned at least one slave. New Orleans persons of color were far wealthier, more secure, and more established than blacks elsewhere in Louisiana.

Creole occupations vary widely. In general, they require a strong educational background. Creole people of color and their descendants have carved out their own occupational niche over time. Carpentry, cabinet making, cigar manufacturing, masonry, housepainting, and plastering are all tasks that have been traditionally dominated by Creoles of color. More recently, Creoles of color have been pursuing careers that require more schooling.

Economic independence is highly valued in the colored Creole community. Being on welfare is a source of embarrassment, and many of those who receive government aid eventually drop out of the community. African Americans with steady jobs, respectable professions, or financial independence frequently marry into the community and become Creole, at least by association.

The Creoles have been quick to adapt strategies that maintain their elite status throughout changing economic conditions. Most significant is the push to acquire higher education. Accelerated education has allowed Creoles to move into New Orleans' more prestigious neighborhoods, first to Gentilly, then to Pontchartrain Park, and more recently to New Orleans East.

POLITICS AND GOVERNMENT

When the Constitutional Convention of 1811 met at New Orleans, 26 of its 43 members were Creoles. During the first few years of statehood, native Creoles were not particularly interested in national politics and the newly arrived Americans were far too busy securing an economic basis to seriously care much about political problems. Many Creoles were still suspicious of the American system and were prejudiced against it.

Until the election of 1834, the paramount issue in state elections was whether the candidate was Creole or Anglo-American. Throughout this period, many English-speaking Americans believed that Creoles were opposed to development and progress, while the Creoles considered other Americans radical in their political ideas. Since then, Creoles have actively participated in American politics; they have learned English to ease this process.

MILITARY

During the War of 1812, many Creoles did not support the state militia. However, during the first session of Louisiana's first legislature in 1812, the legislature approved the formation of a corps of volunteers manned by Louisiana's free men of color. The Act of Incorporation specified that the colored militiamen were to be chosen from among the Creoles who had paid a state tax. Some slaves participated at the Battle of New Orleans, under General Andrew Jackson, and he awarded them their freedom for their valor. Many became known as "Free Jacks" because only the word "Free" and the first five letters of Jackson's signature, "Jacks," were legible.

INDIVIDUAL AND GROUP CONTRIBUTIONS

CHESS

In 1858 and 1859 Paul Morphy (1837-1884) was the unofficial but universally acknowledged chess champion of the world. While he is little known outside chess circles, more than 18 books have been written about Morphy and his chess strategies.

LITERATURE

Kate O'Flaherty Chopin (1851-1904) was born in St. Louis; her father was an Irish immigrant and her mother was descended from an old French Creole family in Missouri. In 1870 she married Oscar Chopin, a native of Louisiana, and moved there; after her husband's death, she began to write. Chopin's best-known works deal with Creoles; she also wrote short stories for children in *The Youth's Companion*. *Bayou Folk* (1894) and *The Awakening* (1899) are her most popular works. Armand Lanusse (1812-1867) was perhaps the earliest Creole of color to write and publish poetry. Born in New Orleans to French Creole parents, he was a conscripted Confederate soldier during the Civil War. After the war, he was principal of the Catholic School for Indigent Orphans of Color. There he, along with 17 others, produced an anthology of Negro poetry, *Les Cenelles*.

MILITARY

Pierre Gustave Toutant Beauregard (1818-1893), is perhaps the best known Louisiana Creole. He was born in New Orleans, educated in New York (unusual for the time), graduated from West Point Military Academy, and served with General Scott in the War with Mexico (1846). Beauregard was twice wounded in that conflict. He served as chief engineer in the draining of the site of New Orleans from 1858 to 1861. He was also a Confederate General in the Civil War and led the siege of Ft. Sumter in 1861. After the Civil War, Beauregard returned to New Orleans where he later wrote three books on the Civil War. He was elected Superintendent of West Point in 1869.

MUSIC

Louis Moreau Gottschalk (1829-1869), was a pianist and composer born in New Orleans. His mother, Aimée Marie de Brusle, was a Creole whose family had come from Saint-Dominique. Moreau went to Paris at age 13 to study music. He became a great success in Europe at an early age and spent most of his time performing in concerts to support members of his family. His best known compositions are "Last Hope," "Tremolo Etudes," and "Bamboula." Gottschalk is remembered as a true Creole, thinking and composing in French. An important figure in the history and development of American jazz, "Jelly Roll" Ferdinand Joseph Lementhe Morton (1885-1941), was a jazz musician and composer born in New Orleans to Creole parents. As a child, he was greatly influenced by performances at the French Opera House. Morton later played piano in Storyville's brothels; these, too, provided material for his compositions. His most popular works are "New Orleans Blues," "King Porter Stomp," and "Jelly Roll Blues."

MEDIA

PRINT

The Alexandria News Weekly.
Founded in 1975, this general newspaper for the African American community contains frequent articles about Creoles.

Contact: Rev. C. J. Bell, Editor.
Address: 1746 Wilson, Alexandria, Louisiana 71301.
Telephone: (318) 443-7664.

Bayou Talk.
A Cajun creole newspaper.

Address: Jo-Val, Inc., Box 1344, West Covina, California 91793-1344.

Creole Magazine.
Published since December 1990 by Creole, Inc., it contains articles about African American Creoles in southwestern Louisiana and includes advertisements, a calendar of events, and organizations.

Contact: Ruth Foote, Editor.
Address: P.O. Box 91496, Lafayette, Louisiana 70590.
Telephone: (318) 269-1956.
Fax: (318) 332-4775.

Louisiana Weekly.
Black community newspaper published since 1925, which contains frequent articles about Creoles.

Contact: C. C. Dejoie, Jr., Publisher.
Address: 616 Barone Street, New Orleans, Louisiana 70150.
Telephone: (504) 524-5563.

The Times of Acadiana.
A weekly newspaper with Acadian/Creole emphasis.

Address: P.O. Box 3528, Lafayette, Louisiana 70502.
Telephone: (318) 237-3560.

RADIO

KAOK-AM.
Ethnic programs featuring Cajun and Zydeco music.

Contact: Ed Prendergast.
Address: 801 Columbia Southern Road, Westlake, Louisiana 70669.
Telephone: (318) 882-0243.

KVOL-AM/FM.
Features a weekly Creole broadcast with African American programming, news, and Zydeco music.

Contact: Roger Canvaness.
Address: 123 East Main Street, Alexandria, Louisiana 70501.
Telephone: (318) 233-1330.

ORGANIZATIONS AND ASSOCIATIONS

Creole American Genealogical Society (CAGS).
Formerly Creole Ethnic Association. Founded in 1983, CAGS is a Creole organization which promotes Creole American genealogical research. It provides family trees and makes available to its members books and archival material. Holds an annual convention.

Contact: P. Fontaine, Executive Director.
Address: P.O. Box 3215, Church Street Station, New York, New York 10008.

MUSEUMS AND RESEARCH CENTERS

Beau Fort Plantation Home.
Collects Louisiana Creole period furnishings, furniture, and ornaments for display in a 1790 Creole house.

Contact: Jack O. Brittain, David Hooper, or Janet LaCour.
Address: P.O. Box 2300, Natchitoches, Louisiana 71457.
Telephone: (318) 352-9580.

Bayou Folk Museum.
Collects furniture, furnishings, and artifacts relating to the educational, religious, social, and economic life of Creoles. Contains agricultural tools, doctor's office with instruments, and a blacksmith shop. Guided tours, lectures for study groups, and permanent exhibits.

Contact: Marion Nelson or Maxine Southerland.
Address: P.O. Box 2248, Natchitoches, Louisiana 71457.
Telephone: (318) 352-2994.

Louisiana State University.
Contains local history and exhibits, tools for various trades, and historic buildings. Conducts guided tours, provides lectures, and has an organized education program.

Contact: John E. Dutton.
Address: 6200 Burden Lane, Baton Rouge, Louisiana 70808.
Telephone: (504) 765-2437.

Melrose Plantation.
Collects furnishings dating from 1796 to the early 1900s. Contains plantation gardens with the African and Yucca Houses. Museum sponsors an annual historic tour of Natchitoches and the Can River Country in October.

Contact: Maxine Southerland.
Address: Box 2248, Natchitoches, Louisiana 71457.
Telephone: (318) 379-0055.

SOURCES FOR ADDITIONAL STUDY

Ancelet, Barry Jane, Jay D. Edwards, and Glen Pitre. *Cajun Country*. Jackson: University Press of Mississippi, 1991.

Bryan, Violet Harrington. *The Myth of New Orleans in Literature: Dialogues of Race and Gender*. Knoxville: University of Tennessee Press, 1993.

Davis, Edwin Adams. *Louisiana: A Narrative History*. Baton Rouge: Claitor's Book Store, 1965.

Dominguez, Virginia R. *White by Definition: Social Classification in Creole Louisiana*. New Brunswick: Rutgers University Press, 1986.

Dorman, James H. "Louisiana's 'Creoles of Color': Ethnicity, Marginality, and Identity," *Social Science Quarterly* 73, No. 3, 1992: 615-623.

Eaton, Clement. A *History of the Old South: The Emergence of a Reluctant Nation*, third edition. New York: Macmillan, 1975.

Ebeyer, Pierre Paul. *Paramours of the Creoles*. New Orleans: Molenaar Printing, 1944.

Fiehrer, Thomas. "From La Tortue to La Louisiane: An Unfathomed Legacy," in *The Road to Louisiana: The Saint-Dominique Refugees, 1792-*

1809, edited by Carl A. Brasseaux and Glenn R. Conrad. Lafayette, Louisiana: Center for Louisiana Studies, University of Southwestern Louisiana, 1992; 1-30.

Huber, Leonard V. "Reflections on the Colorful Customs of Latter-day New Orleans Creoles," *Louisiana History*, 21, No. 2, 1980; 223-235.

Kniffin, Fred B. *Louisiana: Its Land and People*. Baton Rouge: Louisiana State University Press, 1968.

Saxon, Lyle, Robert Tallant, and Edward Dreyer. *Gumbo Ya-Ya: A Collection of Louisiana Folktales*. Boston: Houghton Mifflin, 1945.

Despite their small, low-profile population, Croatian Americans have made distinguished individual contributions to American literature, music, science, and business.

CROATIAN AMERICANS

by
Edward Ifkovic

OVERVIEW

The newly independent republic of Croatia is located on the Balkan peninsula in southeastern Europe. Throughout much of the twentieth century, Croatia was one of five republics within Yugoslavia, an amalgam of ethnicities and religions tenuously held together by dictatorship and economic feasibility.

Croatia, which runs along the Adriatic to Montenegro, has a distinctive elongated geography that is largely the result of demarcations imposed upon it throughout this century. Occupying 21,829 square miles, Croatia is bordered by Bosnia-Hercegovina on the south, by Italy on the west, by Slovenia to the north and northwest, by Hungary to the north and northeast, and by Vojvodina, an autonomous Serbian province, to the east.

According to a 1981 census, Croatia has a population of more than 4.6 million people, 75 percent of whom are ethnic Croatian. Ethnic Serbians comprise another 11.5 percent of the population, and the remaining 13.5 percent includes Slovenians, Hungarians, Italians, and Czechs. Among Croatians, the predominant religion is Roman Catholicism, although some practice Islam.

HISTORY

Croatia's long, turbulent history has been affected

by the control of empires that have included the Ottoman, Hapsburg, and Venetian empires. During the fifth century B.C., nomadic Slavic tribes from beyond the Carpathian Mountains of Poland and Russia drifted down into the Balkans, pushing out the Romans. Among the migrating South Slavic people, new religious ethnic identities evolved. The Croatians and Slovenians were strongly influenced by the Roman Catholic Church, and the Serbians, Montenegrins, and Macedonians by the Eastern Orthodox Church. The small independent countries of Slovenia and Croatia did not survive the Middle Ages. After a period of self-rule under King Tomislav and King Peter Kresimir IV, Croatia fell under the governance of Hungary in 1102.

During the fourteenth century, the Ottoman Turks began invading the Balkans. A powerful people, the Ottomans had gradually taken the region of Asia Minor now known as Turkey from the Byzantines, who had controlled a great empire there since before the fall of Rome. By 1350 the Ottomans had begun their invasion of the Balkan Peninsula. After the legendary battle of Kosovo in 1389, Serbia fell under Turkish rule.

With the defeat of the Serbians, the Turks began to make inroads into Croatian territory. The Croatians turned to the Austrians for military support, but with the rise of the Austro-Hungarian Empire, the Croatians found themselves in a slave-like condition. For generations, the Croatians were used as a military buffer between Europe and the Turks. In 1573 Matija Gubec led an inspiring if disastrous rebellion against the Austrian nobles, but Austro-Hungarian control of the Croatians continued until 1918.

During the nineteenth century, Slavic nationalism grew in proportion to the decline of the Austro-Hungarian Empire. World War I erupted as a result of conflict between independent Serbia and the Austro-Hungarian Empire, and with the 1918 defeat of Austria-Hungary and its German allies, European geography was restructured.

U.S. President Woodrow Wilson advocated independence for various nationalities, and South Slavs seized the opportunity for freedom. Based on the "Yugoslav Idea," a Serbo-Croatian Coalition issued a Declaration of Yugoslav Independence and the Kingdom of Serbs, Croats, and Slovenes was formed on July 20, 1917, under the rule of Serbian Prince Alexander. Eight years later, Alexander changed the country's name to Yugoslavia.

MODERN ERA

Internal dissension and ethnic rivalries persisted in the new Yugoslavia. Serbians conceived of the country as a Greater Serbia with a centralist government, while Federalist Croatians and Slovenians demanded that each republic have a strong voice in the government. When Stejpan Radic, the respected head of the Croat Peasant Party, was assassinated in Parliament in 1928, the king dissolved Parliament and made himself dictator. The king was himself assassinated by right-wing Croatian sympathizers in Marseilles, France, in 1934 and his cousin, Prince Paul, assumed control of the country.

On March 27, 1941, Yugoslavia (under fascist dictator Ante Pavic) signed a pact allying itself with Germany. When the Yugoslavian people revolted against this government action with chants of "Better war than pact, better grave than slave," the military assumed control of the country and proclaimed young Peter II king. In retaliation, Adolf Hitler ordered an attack on Belgrade on April 6, 1941. After a bloody battle, the Nazis conquered Yugoslavia and set up a puppet government in Croatia. The fascist Ustashe eliminated thousands of Jews, Serbians, and unsympathetic Croatians. Underground resistance to the Germans included the Partisans, under the command of Croatian Communist Marshal Tito, and the Chetniks, who supported the monarchy in exile and, some believe, later collaborated with the Germans.

The Partisans viewed the war as an opportunity to create a Communist government in postwar Yugoslavia. Tito's forces wrested large sections of the country from German control, ultimately winning the support of Communists and non-Communists, including the Allies. When the war ended, the Socialist Party assumed control of the government and abolished the monarchy.

The 1945 Partisan massacre of thousands of Croatians alarmed the many Croatian Americans who wanted to support the new Titoist government. Despite such tactics, Tito used his personality and power to help placate ethnic and religious rivalries within Yugoslavia. Refusing to allow Yugoslavia to become a puppet of the Soviet Union, Tito asserted Yugoslav independence from Russian control in 1948, thus establishing Yugoslavia as one of the most liberal and progressive Socialist countries of Eastern Europe. Upon Tito's death in 1980, Yugoslavia was ruled by a collective state presidency and party presidium, which immediately suffered severe economic difficulties and saw the resurgence of nascent rivalries.

The breakdown of Communism in Eastern Europe, most dramatically illustrated by the 1989 dismantling of the Berlin Wall, toppled a number of Communist governments and affected still others, including Yugoslavia-where old rivalries and long-buried aspirations for independence resurfaced. Following the lead of Slovenia, Croatia challenged growing Serbian hegemony. In Yugoslavia's first postwar free elections, held in 1990, the Croatian Democratic Union (HDZ) ran on an anti-Communist platform and won 205 of 356 seats in Parliament.

Despite Croatia's first real independence in 1,000 years, many feared a rise in nationalistic fascism under the leadership of Franjo Tudjman, who viewed Greater Croatia as a means of countering Greater Serbia. Government corruption and censorship added to these fears and overall dissatisfaction. On June 25, 1991, Croatia and Slovenia issued declarations of independence.

Although Croatia was recognized by the international community, including the EC, its secession from Yugoslavia was not smooth. Serbian forces attacked Croatia, with long sieges of Dubrovnik, Vukovar, and other Croatian cities. The 1991 and 1992 seven-month war against the combined forces of the Yugoslav army and Serbian paramilitaries left thousands dead and many villages destroyed. The Serbians instituted policies of "ethnic cleansing" in Croatian villages and throughout Bosnia. With control of one-third of Croatian territory, the Serbians attacked ethnic Croatians in Bosnia and Croatia proper.

Independent Croatia is now recognized by 53 nations, including the United States; however, the war in the Balkan Peninsula continues to spread despite United Nations peace efforts. The future stability of Croatia can only be addressed within the greater context of peace in the Balkans.

THE FIRST CROATIANS IN AMERICA

During the Middle Ages, the Adriatic ports of Croatia's "Dalmatian Coast" were thriving centers of commerce and trade. The Italian ports of Venice and Genoa fought for control of the high seas, as did the small but powerful independent Republic of Ragusa, a city-state in Croatia now known as Dubrovnik.

Skilled Ragusan navigators and seaman were in great demand, as well as crew members on most European ships. Many scholars believe Dalmatian sailors were on Columbus' ships to the New World. An often-repeated Croatian legend has it that one of Columbus' sailors amassed considerable wealth in gold and returned to his native Ragusa to build a beautiful palace at Bonda.

In 1494 Ragusa signed a treaty with Spain, which allowed Ragusan ships to trade with Spanish colonies. Because Ragusa's government had banned slavery in 1416, the Ragusan ships were not allowed to transport slaves from Africa to the colonies. Many Ragusan sailors remained in the colonies, married English women, and changed their names. It is documented, for example, that brothers Mato and Dominko Kondjevic sailed to America in 1520 and remained for 30 years before returning home with substantial wealth.

Legend and early American history unite in the story of John White, who in 1587 established an English colony on Roanoke Island off the coast of North Carolina. When poverty and disease threatened the survival of the settlement, White returned to England to seek aid. The colonists had agreed to leave a sign on a tree if trouble developed or they were forced to leave. Upon his return to the island, White found the houses in ruins and no sign of life, but discovered the word Croatan deeply etched into the bark of a tree. It has been theorized that the Ragusan ship Croatian, believed to have left for America in the 1580s, touched the shore at Roanoke, picked up the surviving English colonists, and was later lost at sea. Another story tells of survivors of a sunken Ragusan ship who were helped by friendly Native Americans who later became known as the Croatians. Years later, a visitor noted that some of the Croatian Indians had light skin, fair hair, and blue eyes—characteristic of Ragusans.

These stories remain undocumented legend; however, a letter sent by the government of Dubrovnik to its diplomatic representative in Madrid, states that by 1600, "many Ragusans" were already living in America.

THE MISSIONARIES

The work of Croatian and Slovene missionaries in America is well documented. Priests and members of religious orders ventured into the American wilderness. One of the first was Baron Ivan Ratkay (Ratkaj), a wealthy Croatian nobleman, who early in life rejected the comfortable existence into which he was born to commit himself to doing God's work. After joining the Jesuit Order, he underwent rigorous training in Rome and Madrid and was named a missionary to the uncharted regions of New Spain.

Ratkay arrived in America in 1673 and began teaching and baptizing the Taramuhara Indians of the Southwest. A scholar, he also pursued interests that included the study of the area's physical geography. Detailed records of his travels through the New Mexican region proved valuable to many of the pioneers who followed him. In 1683 Ratkay died at age 36 at the hands of Native Americans—supposedly poisoned for forbidding drinking and dancing.

Another missionary, Father Ferdinand Konscak, worked in the unsettled regions of California and Mexico under the name Padre Consago Gonzales. The son of an army officer, Father Konscak was born in 1703 in Verazdin, Croatia, and attended the Jesuit College in Budapest, Hungary. For more than 22 years he remained in California at the San Ignacio Mission. A traveler, Father Konscak also discovered that Lower (Baja) California was a peninsula rather than an island and constructed an accurate, detailed map of the region. In 1770 J. Baegert copied the map in his pioneer guidebook *Nachrichten von Kalifornien*. Father Konscak also founded the village of San Antonio Real.

Croatian missionary Josip Kundak worked in the Midwest with Native Americans and growing German and Swiss immigrant populations. In 1854 he established the Benedictine Abbey in St. Meinhard, Indiana. He also founded a mission in Jasper, Indiana, and the town of Ferdinand. Honoring the centennial of his death, the governor of Indiana proclaimed December 8, 1957 "Father Kundak Day" to show, in his words, "tribute to a great missionary, pioneer, and citizen who left Croatia, the land he loved, to come and colonize the wilderness of this great state, for which we owe him a huge debt of gratitude."

DALMATIANS IN THE SOUTH AND WEST

When the Civil War began, Dalmatian colonies (Dalmatia is a region in Croatia) had spread into Mississippi and Alabama. U.S. Census records of the 1850s and 1860s reveal hundreds of Dalmatian saloonkeepers, grocers, tugboat operators, and restaurant owners. By 1880 an estimated 20,000 Croatians lived in the United States, primarily in the South and the West. Not surprisingly, many fought on the side of the Confederacy during the Civil War, forming the Austrian Guards and two Slavonian rifle units.

Throughout the nineteenth century, Dalmatian sailors jumped ship at major American ports, especially at favored locations such as New Orleans. The former seamen found the oyster business a natural transition. Some, like Luka Jurisich, who arrived in Bayou Creek, Louisiana, from Duba, in 1855, are credited with building the trade in the region. Dalmatians also became early developers of oyster fisheries in Biloxi, Mississippi. Today, the huge fishing industry in these regions is heavily populated by descendants of the early Dalmatian settlers.

Many Dalmatians moved from New Orleans to ports in the Far West, establishing large colonies such as the one that grew in and around San Francisco. Some arrived as early as 1835, predating settlers from the Eastern states. Although gold enticed many Croatians to move west, those who settled in California were captivated by the climate, which they likened to that of their sunny Adriatic homeland. Most made their living, not from gold, but by operating businesses. According to one study, more than 50 Dalmatian businesses occupied a single San Francisco street in the 1850s and 1860s.

In 1857 the Slavonic Illyrian Mutual and Benevolent Society was formed in San Francisco as the first Slavic charitable society of its kind in America. In 1861 the Society purchased land for the first Croatian-Serbian cemetery in the United States. Vincent Gelcich, president of the Society in 1860, was a physician who served as a surgeon and colonel in the Union Army during the Civil War. This society, which helped immigrants survive in the new land, is still in existence today.

Perhaps the most important Dalmatian contribution to America was made in agriculture. Mateo Arnerich, a sailor from Brac, arrived in San Francisco in 1849, the year after gold was discovered at Sutter's Mill. One of the first Dalmatians to settle in the Santa Clara Valley, Arnerich bought land and established the vineyards that made his wealth. His two sons became lawyers and one, a member of the State Legislature, was the first Croatian to hold public office in the United States. In the 1870s, Mark Rabasa introduced the apple industry to northern California. Another Dalmatian, Steve Mitrovich, imported the Dalmatian fig to Fresno and displayed the "Adriatic fig" at the Columbian Exposition in Chicago in 1893, winning first prize.

Because of Dalmatian success at growing and developing a superior quality of grapes, figs, plums, apples, and apricots in Pajaro Valley, the region was called New Dalmatia. Although the novelist Jack London feared "alien" control, he described the flourishing 12,000-acre apple paradise of the Dalmatians in his 1913 novel *Valley of the Moon:* "Do you know what they call Pajaro Valley? New Dalmatia. We're being squeezed out. We Yankees thought we were smart. Well, the Dalmatians came along and showed they were smarter.... First, they worked at day labor in the fruit harvest. Next, they began, in a small way, buying the apples on the trees. The more money they made, the bigger became their deals. Pretty soon they were renting the orchards on long leases; and now they own the whole valley, and the last American will be gone."

The discovery of silver in the Nevada Territory in the late 1850s inspired the influx of Croatian settlers into towns like Virginia City, Carson City, Austin, and Reno. These Slavs were commonly referred to as "Sclavonians" or "Slavonians." The successful Slavonian Gold and Silver Mining Company at Resse River, Nevada, was organized in 1863, but most settlers made their living in businesses that served miners. The largest food provision house in Nevada in the 1860s was owned by Dalmatians, and Marco Medin, one of the first men to arrive in Nevada during the silver fever, grew rich in the fruit and saloon businesses.

The lives of Antonio Mazzanovich, Antonio Milatovich, and Captain John Dominus illustrate a more colorful side of Croatian history. Mazzanovich enlisted as a bugler in the U.S. 6th Cavalry when he was 11 years old and helped pursue the famous Apache Geronimo through the Southwest, which he recalled in his memoirs, *Trailing Geronimo* (1931). Milatovich sued the Republic of Mexico when a revolutionary change of government deprived him of more than one million acres of Mexican land he had acquired. He lost his fortune when the new government refused his claim on the basis of his Austrian citizenship. The Croatian Captain John Dominus, who sailed to America in his own ship, subsequently settled in Hawaii, where he built a lavish mansion that was later used as the official residence of the Governor. Captain Dominus disappeared at sea while attempting to reach China. His son, John Owen Dominus, married the Hawaiian princess Lydia Kamekaha Kapaaka in 1862. She became Queen Liliuokalani, the last reigning queen of Hawaii, and Dominus served as her Prince Consort until his death in 1891.

THE GREAT MIGRATION: AFTER 1880

From 1880 through 1914, Croatians and other Eastern European peasants immigrated to the United States in large numbers. Fleeing from poverty brought on by changes in land inheritance laws, blight, and deteriorating farming soil quality, and a decreasing infant mortality rate that increased the population, a young generation looked to America *trbuhom za kruhum* ("with belly after bread").

Because statistics were so poorly kept in general, and Slavs were so often lumped together or confused with other groups, it is not known how many Croatians entered the United States during the Great Migration. In the 1930s Croatian historian Ivan Mladineo estimated that approximately half a million Croatians were living in America at that time.

The first wave of immigrants consisted of primarily illiterate, unskilled male laborers who came to the United States to make their fortunes and then return home. Many made frequent trips between the United States and Eastern Europe, and became known as "birds of passage." These men sent money to their villages, markedly improving the economic conditions of the Croatians who remained at home. In 1938 the *South Slav Herald* reported that two thirds of the new homes built in Croatia during the previous 30 years had been built with American money.

According to the 1907 Immigration Commission survey, about 66 percent of Croatians who came to America returned home. Between 1899 and 1924, the rate was nearly half. The thousands who returned to Croatia took new ideas with them, including ideas about democracy. In 1906 Croatian writer Antun Matos wrote "America is presently the most important factor in the creation of Croatian democracy."

Following World War II, millions were left homeless, and the rise to power of Communist regimes in Yugoslavia and other parts of Eastern Europe meant that others could not return home. Of the 400,000 Displaced People initially admitted into the United States, 18,000 were "Yugoslavs."

Laws like the Refugee Relief Act of 1953 and the Refugee Escape Act of 1960, and the demise of the quota system in 1965, facilitated more Croatian emigration. This new wave included many educated professionals. In "A Clash of Two Immigrant Generations," Bogdan Raditsa discussed the sharp contrast between the earlier, unskilled Croatian immigrants and their later counterparts, revealing the "bitterness that divides the Croatians who came here as displaced persons after 1945 from the Croatian American families established in this country for four or five decades." According to the 1990 U.S. Census, there are an estimated 544,000 Croatian Americans living in the United States.

SETTLEMENT PATTERNS

Today, Pennsylvania's Croatian population of nearly a quarter million is the largest in the country. During the Great Migration, most Croatians settled in the industrial cities of the Midwest in already established immigrant communities. In places like Ohio, Pennsylvania, Illinois, Michigan, Minnesota, Wisconsin, and Indiana, they worked in coal mines, and in the iron and steel mills. California also supports a sizable Croatian population. There settlers found employment in fishing and mining. In San Francisco Croatian Americans introduced new methods of drying fruits, packaging, and shipping.

The traditional patriarchal Croatian family structure, which emphasized control and rigid discipline, remained a part of the early immigrant lifestyle and contributed to the Slavs reputation as a dependable hard worker. Aside from arrests for drunkenness, there was little crime among the Croatians in America. Industrialists struggling against labor unions often exploited the new immigrants, making them scabs during worker strikes.

ACCULTURATION AND ASSIMILATION

Although events since the breakup of Yugoslavia in the early 1990s have made Croatia more visi-
ble internationally, Croatians are still mislabeled and subsumed into larger classifications such as Austrian-Hungarian or Yugoslavian. Croatians have also been the object of discrimination.

During the period of the Great Migration, Croatians and other Slavs were often lumped together and assessed as an uninspired, stolid, sluggish people who were only useful as drudges and unskilled grunts. They were called derogatory names like "Hunkies," "modgies," and "strams" and labeled "Bo hunks" or "dumb Polacks."

The unskilled, often illiterate early immigrants gave little thought to assimilation. They clustered together, often in cooperative boarding-houses called *drustvo*, and worked at unskilled labor 12 to 16 hours a day, and in the process, resisted acculturation. One Slavic commentator wrote, "My people do not live in America; they live underneath America. America goes on over their heads."

During and after World War I, when many Croatians who had planned to return to Europe could not, the number who became American citizens increased sharply. By 1919 a study showed that 60 to 65 percent of the immigrants had taken out naturalization papers. The Jugoslav Central organization—formed in Detroit in 1932 to promote unity among Slovenians, Serbians, and Croatians—had as one of its chief goals the encouragement of U.S. citizenship.

THE ROLE OF THE NEWSPAPER

Even though many Croatian immigrants were illiterate, newspapers assumed an importance in the "Little Croatias" of America. They reported changes in American immigration law, carried employment opportunities, and kept up with major European events.

The most popular newspaper among early immigrants was *Narodni List* (1898), published in New York by Frank Zotti, a colorful and controversial Croatian figure of the time. Zotti's tabloid featured gutsy topical reporting, melodramatic fiction and popular peasant poetry. The Croatian Fraternal Union's *Zajednicar* (Unity) began in 1905 in Pittsburgh, and is still published today with a circulation of 70,000.

TRADITIONAL MUSIC AND FOLK DANCE

The popular *kolo* or circle dance is performed to the accompaniment of the tamburitsa, a traditional mandolin-like stringed instrument. The tamburitsa is a modern version of the one-stringed *gusle* used for centuries by the village poets. A tamburitsa band performed at the White House during Theodore Roosevelt's presidency and in concert at Carnegie Hall in 1900. Today, Duquesne University supports tamburitsa orchestras and festivals and runs the Tamburitsa School of Music-the only one of its kind in America.

Singing societies, which have also been popular, are patterned after an early group called "Zora" (Dawn), which was founded in Chicago in 1903 to keep old folk songs and past experiences alive.

TRADITIONS, CUISINE, AND FOLK CULTURE

For Croatians, food, tradition, and folk culture are interconnected, especially as a part of holiday celebrations. In many Croatian households, the Christmas celebration begins on Christmas Eve with a meal of (cod fish). On Christmas Day, *sarma* (cabbage and sauerkraut) and *orehnjaca* (nut cake) are traditional favorites.

St. Nicholas Day and Easter are also important holidays to Croatians. St. Nicholas Day, December 6, is a children's holiday for giving presents. Lamb and ham are central to celebrating Easter, a celebration of eating following a meatless Lent. *Pogaca* is an Easter bread that is braided and decorated with painted eggs. Food is blessed in the church and sometimes broken egg shells are scattered throughout the household.

In Croatia, name days paid homage to the saint for whom you were named. As immigrants and later generations gradually adopted the American custom of celebrating birthdays, this traditional celebration disappeared.

TRADITIONAL COSTUMES

Traditional Croatian dress is distinguishable by its fine embroidery. Women wear long linen dresses, often white, covered by a colored apron and a shawl over the shoulders. They usually cover their heads with a kerchief. Croatian men wear white shirts topped with a colored vest or jacket. Their pants are often dark linen or wool, worn with high leather boots or knee-socks. The outer garments are embroidered in red or gold with geometric designs or images such as birds or flowers. Today, such costumes are only worn on holidays or during special occasions.

HEALTH AND MENTAL HEALTH ISSUES

In the early days of settlement Croatians relied on home health care. The local midwife, a Croatian woman, most often handled childbirth in the home. Because there were no labor compensation laws then, men injured on the job had no benefits for hospitalization. Folk remedies, the use of practiced "bonesetters," and superstitions often were used in place of English-speaking doctors (dropping hot coals in water to dispel headaches from evil eyes, for example), but there was little involvement with the American medical establishment. Those involved with settlement houses in cities—as with Jane Addams' in Chicago—became conversant with doctors and health care—matters of ventilation and cleanliness, for example. Croatians were hesitant to accept welfare. In New York before World War I one charity group reported that it had never had one application from a Croatian. There have been no studies done of mental health conditions among Croatian immigrants, and little on their health care. Successive generations, of course, have adopted American ways for dealing with the medical community.

LANGUAGE

The Croatian language spoken by early immigrants was largely dialect, identifiable by the region from which the immigrant came. The three primary dialects of Croatian are *cakavski*, from Dalmatia, *kajkavski* from the far northwest near Zagreb, and two varieties of *stokavski* (*stokavski ijekavski* is the literary variant for Croatians). These dialects are often so various that Croatians in America sometimes have difficulty understanding each other.

Writers like Louis Adamic and Clement Mihanovich have pointed out the manner in which Croatians have added familiar endings to English words. Some linguists distinguish this as a "new" dialect. For example, the Croatian word for automobile is *kola* and the Americanized-Croatian word is *kara* (car); *novine* (paper) has become *papir*; *Soba* (room) is now *rum*. This bastardization of the language has alarmed many purists.

Croatian and Serbian are, for the most part, the same language. Serbian, however, uses a Cryilic alphabet, while Croatian uses a Latin alphabet. Until the breakup of Yugoslavia, the official language was Serbo-Croatian (*Srpsko-hrvatski*) or Croato-Serbian (*Hrvasko-srpski*). In America, many Croatians refuse to use the term "Serbo-Croatian," an issue which became less significant when Croatia gained independence in 1990. Several American colleges and universities teach Serbo-Croatian, including Stanford University, Yale University, and Northwestern University.

GREETINGS AND OTHER POPULAR EXPRESSIONS

Common Croatian expressions include: *Dobro jutro* ("dobro yootro")—Good morning; *Dobar dan* ("dobahr dahn")—Good afternoon; *Dobro vece* ("dobro vehcheh")—Good evening; *Laku noc* ("lahkoo noch")—Good night; *Zbogom* ("zbogom")—Good-bye; *Kako stje* ("kahko steh")—How are you?; *Hvala* ("fahlah")—thank you; *sretan bozic* ("srehtan bozich")—Merry Christmas.

FAMILY AND COMMUNITY DYNAMICS

Because most of the early immigrants were single men, the saloon became their most important social institution. More than a place to drink, the Croatian saloon provided a place to exchange news about the Old Country, translate letters, and do banking.

Immigrants also organized benevolent fraternal associations for protection in the event of on-the-job injury or unemployment. These included the Slavonian Mutual and Benevolent Society, organized by Croatians and Serbians in San Francisco in 1857; the United Slavonian Benevolent Association, founded in New Orleans in 1874; and the Austrian Benevolent Society (later the First Croatian Benefit Society), established in New York in 1880, among others.

As more and more men decided to settle in America, they sent for their wives and marriageable women. Coming from a pre-industrial, Roman Catholic peasant culture, these women were occupied with housekeeping and child rearing. The rural concept of the godmother and godfather (*kum* and *kuma*) survived for some time in America The parents of a newborn child selected family members, or friends considered part of the extended family (*zadruga*) to care for the child in the event that something happened to the parent and to take charge of the child's spiritual well-being, a responsibility that was taken seriously.

"In Croatia I enjoyed my godparents as really my real parents. They never talked about my mother and father in America. So, in other words, I didn't know that there was somebody in America. I didn't even know where America was or heard of America. Nothing."

Louis Zauneker in 1923, cited in *Ellis Island: An Illustrated History of the Immigrant Experience,* edited by Ivan Chermayeff et al. (New York: Macmillan, 1991).

Communal Croatian life and the tradition of taking in as many boarders as possible to earn money had socialized women to serve large numbers of people. Men went into the workplace and, thus, the larger American society, and children went to American schools where they learned the language and mores, but women remained isolated in the home. Divorce was uncommon, but did occur. Although both partners were ostracized by the larger community, the woman was more harshly treated.

Over time, however, the woman's subservient position in America changed, largely because women ran most of the boarding houses and achieved some measure of economic security from doing so. As Croatian American women became more "Americanized," some men argued that once "a Croatian woman becomes Americanized and accepts the liberalization policy of American women ... permissiveness with the children develop." Some Croatian women countered that because they bore fewer children and were free of the patriarchal restraints and demands of the Old Country, successive generations of mothers maintained better relationships with their children.

As the educational and economic lives of second- and third-generation Croatians improved, most left the Little Croatia ghettoes and the parochial schools where Croatian nuns taught in Croatian, and these communities began to die.

INTERACTION WITH OTHER ETHNIC GROUPS

Croatian interaction with Serbians and Slovenians grew out of a similarity of language and the fact that they often settled near one another. Croatians also interacted with other Slavic peoples who emigrated from Austria-Hungary, as well as with Germans, Italians, and Hungarians, with whom they shared the common bond of Roman Catholicism. Although immigrant men attend Catholic Mass with their Irish foremen, they had little social contact.

Alliances with Serbians were temporary and topical as old enmity persisted. There is a saying that "There is no putting history behind one's self in the Balkans; the battles one's ancestors fought are today's battles as well." Fights and flare-ups still erupt today.

RELIGION

Devout Roman Catholics, the Croatians organized the first U.S. Croatian parish in 1895 in Allegheny City, Pennsylvania. Despite California's large Croatian population in the nineteenth century, a Croatian parish was not organized there until 1903. As late as 1912, there were still only 12 Croatian parishes and four parochial schools in America. The number doubled within the next decade. By the 1970s only 30 Croatian parishes and two dozen parochial schools remained for a declining Catholic Croatian population. Today's Croatians are heavily disaffected with religion, and with the clergy in particular.

Most of the small number of Protestant Croatians came from Slovakia and Slovenia. Croatian Muslims who emigrating to America largely from the Croatian section of Bosnia arrived after World War II and settled in Cleveland and Chicago.

EMPLOYMENT AND ECONOMIC TRADITIONS

Many companies paid immigrants' passage to America in return for a guaranteed period of servitude. Although this practice was outlawed in 1885, industrialists found ways around the law and Croatians were sent to coke foundries, iron mines, lumber camps, and factories across America.

A 1910 study revealed that Croatians in Pennsylvania were the lowest paid of the immigrant groups, and their unemployment rates the highest, with only 34 percent full-time, full-year employees. When Croatians arrived in industrialized American cities, manufacturers coerced them into replacing striking workers. Uneducated and often unaware of the dynamics of American labor-management politics, the immigrants were happy to have jobs. Manufacturers were adept at pitting one ethnic group against another. Railroad magnate Jay Gould once declared: "I can hire one half of the working class to kill the other half."

By 1900 when labor unions were gaining power, Croatians and other Slavs played a role in establishing the viability of the United Mine Workers of America, which helped break the cycle of using immigrants as scabs and strikebreakers. In 1909 Anton Pavisic was a leader in a coal miners' strike at McKees Rocks, Pennsylvania, where more than 2,000 fellow Croatians followed him. The first miners' compensation law introduced into the Michigan legislature was introduced by Anthony Lucas, a Croatian.

POLITICS AND GOVERNMENT

Politically, Croatian Americans have been torn between concern for Croatia and involvement in American democracy. Early immigrants were more preoccupied with the former, and this concern persisted for many generations. Croatian organizations formed in America campaigned for political goals abroad. These organizations ranged from conservative to radical.

During the years of the Great Migration, groups like the National Croatian Society (NCS) and the Croatian League combated the tyrannical Austria-Hungary rule. In 1912 the Reverend Nikola Grskovic founded the Croatian Alliance, calling for complete Croatian independence from the Hapsburgs and advocating an alliance with the other South Slavs.

Influential South Slavic Americans, like Serbian American Michael Pupin, worked on committees dedicated to the formation of the new nation of Yugoslavia after World War I. Michael Pupin and other high-profile South Slavs were joined by Reverend Grskovic, Joseph Marohnic, and other leaders to create the South Slavic National Council of Chicago, with its main goal being the formation of Yugoslavia. When the Kingdom of Serbs, Croats, and Slovenes was realized in 1918, Croatian Americans were dissatisfied with the pan-Serbian centralist Yugoslav government and appealed in vain to the League of Nations for more encompassing ethnic representation.

During World War II, the Yugoslav Relief Committee was created to aid those living under a Nazi-installed puppet government in Croatia. After the war, American South Slavs—often under the guidance of high profile leaders like Slovenian American Louis Adamic—compelled the American government to lend its support to the Partisan cause in Yugoslavia. Increasingly, Americans were supporting Tito and his partisan forces. At a 1943 meeting, the Congress of American Croatians advocated support of Tito, a momentous decision called for by the more than 700 affiliates of the Congress.

With the installation of Communism in Yugoslavia by Tito after 1945, and rumors of mass killings of Croatians by Tito's command, many Croatians withdrew their support. The émigrés who came to America at that time included many radicals expelled from Yugoslavia. They organized in America and perpetrated terrorist acts to advance the cause of an independent Croatian state. The majority of Croatians in America condemn such extremists.

Although interest in the homeland and its politics continues, the intensity of this interest has gradually diminished. Represented prominently in the Democratic Party, Croatian Americans have won local legislative seats, governorships, and positions in Congress. Active as voters and local campaigners, Croatians have become an integral part of American life.

RELATIONS WITH INDEPENDENT CROATIA

The majority of American Croatians have supported the newly independent Republic of Croatia. In fact, as the old Yugoslav federation began to crumble, American Croatians mounted letter campaigns and fund raising events to support the creation of a new government. In particular, when Germany recognized the new Republic in 1990, many Croatian Americans wrote to the American government to do likewise. Since independence, there has been the on-going war with old guard Serbian nationalists, both in Croatia proper and from without. Croatian Americans have worked to raise funds for war relief, health care, and for political action groups. The casualties in human life have alarmed many here, as has the wanton destruction of venerable old landmarks, like those in Dubrovnik. Some organizations, like the Croatian New Yorker Club, a group of business and professional people, organized a traveling exhibit of art work done by Croatian and Bosnian children in refugee camps in Croatia—to heighten awareness of the war in Croatia and Bosnia and to raise money to aid some displaced children, many orphaned by the war.

INDIVIDUAL AND GROUP CONTRIBUTIONS

Despite their small, low-profile population, Croatian Americans have made distinguished individual contributions to American literature, music, science, and business.

ACADEMIA AND JOURNALISM

Dr. Henry (Zucalo) Suzzallo (1873-1933) was born in San Jose, California, and earned degrees from Stanford, Columbia, and the University of California. During World War I, he advised President Wilson, and was appointed to the War Labor Policy Board in 1918. Suzzallo assumed the presidency of the University of Washington in 1915, a position he held until 1926. During his tenure at Washington, Suzzallo helped increase enrollment, raise academic standards, and create new programs. In 1927 he became chair of the Carnegie Foundation for the Advancement of Teaching and served as president of the foundation until his death. His books (such as *Our Faith in Education*) are examples of the commitment he always felt to the children of America. Other notable Croatian Americans include: historian

Francis Preveden who did comprehensive studies of Croatians; Ivo Banac, a professor of comparative literature at Yale University; and Clement S. Mihanovich, St. Louis University sociologist. George Prpic has done extensive writing on Croatian culture in both America and Croatia. Vlaho S. Vlahovic, a Dalmatian, edited the *Slavonic Monthly*. Bogdan Raditsa was a columnist and journalist for years.

FILM, TELEVISION, AND THEATER

Actor Peter Coe (Knego) left a football career with the Detroit Lions to play "touch-guy" roles in numerous motion pictures. Silent screen star Laura La Plante reached her peak during the 1920s. Walter Kray was one of the stars of the television series "The Roaring Twenties." Slavko Vorkapic (1884-?) acted throughout the 1920s and later became a director who worked with film montage and special effects. John Miljan was in more than four hundred movies, playing lead opposite such actresses as Joan Crawford and Virginia Bruce. Gene Rayburn is a television emcee. Michael Lah brought a new sensitivity and artistry to the animated cartoon.

INDUSTRY AND AGRICULTURE

Hugo Tomich was a metal manufacturer and Marcus Nalley (Marko Narancic) a food-processing manufacturer. Samuel Zorovich, who came from Dalmatia in 1923, built an empire manufacturing cement. Nick Bez (Nikola Bezmalinovic) emigrated from the island of Brac in 1910 and eventually owned a fleet of salmon vessels, ultimately controlling much of the industry in Alaska. Paul Marinis, entrepreneur, was called "The King of Salmon" in the 1950s. John Slavich was owner of Del Monte Fruit Company, one of the largest in America. Nikola Sulentic was the inventor of the first valve-spring lifter.

In 1901 Anthony Lucas (Lucic) became the first man to discover oil in Texas. In 1936 the American Institute of Mining and Metallurgical Engineering established the Anthony F. Lucas Medal, an award for "distinguished achievement and practice in finding and producing petroleum."

LITERATURE

Works like Ivan Mladineo's *Zetva* (*Harvest*) remain inaccessible to the English-reading audience. The popular almanac (*kalendar*), filled with popular poetry, written in the ever-present decameter, was the wellspring for the start of a Croatian American literature. Zdravko Muzina, an influential journalist, issued *Hrvastko-Amerikanska Danica za Godinu 1895*. Josip Marohnic, "the founder of popular Croatian literature in America," published the first book of Croatian poetry in America, *Amerikanke*.

In 1937 Gabro Karabin published the autobiographical "Honorable Escape" in *Scribner's*. The tale of his psychological journey from the steel mills that were his home, the story promised a literary career that never materialized. Victor Vecki wrote *Threatening Shadows* (1931), the story of a Croatian American doctor in California. Antun Nizeteo's *Bez Povratka* (*Without Return*, 1957). and Nada Kestercanek-Vujica's *Short Stories*, 1959, were written in Croatian. The poet Boris Maruna, who lived in America, also wrote in Croatian. Joseph Hitrec, a Croatian whose works do not deal with Croatian experience, came to America after years of travel, mostly in India. In 1946 he published *Ruler's Morning and Other Stories*, tales set in India. Other works by Hitrec include *Son of the Moon* (1948) and *Angel of Gaiety* (1951). George Vukelich wrote short stories and a novel. Edward Ifkovic wrote *Anna Marinkovich* (1980), the story of a Croatian immigrant family living on a farm in Connecticut during the Depression.

MUSIC

Milka Ternina (1863-1920), an operatic soprano, sang for nine seasons with the Metropolitan Opera Company in New York. She premiered in the United States in the opera *Tosca* with Enrico Caruso. Hailed by Italian conductor Toscanini as the "world's greatest artist," Ternina returned to Zagreb in 1906, where she discovered the young Zinka Milanov. Ternina coached Milanov for three years. Milanov made her Met debut in *Il Trovatore* and for three decades remained as the Metropolitan's in-house coloratura. Violinist Louis Svecenski (1862-?) studied in Zagreb and Vienna, and in 1885 accepted a bid to become first violinist for the Boston Symphony Orchestra. He performed in the United States for 33 years Guy Mitchell was a popular recording artist in the 1950s and had his own television series in 1957. His recordings include "The Roving Kind," "Singing the Blues," and "My Heart Cries for You." Tony Butala was one of The Lettermen, whose most famous recording was "Can't Take My Eyes Off of You."

POLITICS

Rudolph G. Perpich, a dentist who began a career in politics in 1956, served two terms in the Minnesota state senate. Elected lieutenant governor in 1970, he became governor of Minnesota in 1976 when Governor Wendell Anderson resigned. Perpich was elected to two more terms in 1982 and 1986.

Mike Stepovich, the first governor of the state of Alaska, had earlier helped establish a colony in Alaska. Nick Begich, of Alaska, was elected to the House of Representatives in 1970. Michael A. Bilandic was elected mayor of Chicago in 1977 after the death of Richard Daley. Dennis J. Kucinich served as mayor of Cleveland in the 1970s.

SPORTS

Teodor Beg, a wrestler from Croatia, won eight gold medals for wrestling. Baseball players of Croatian descent include Walt Dropo of the Baltimore Orioles, Joseph Beggs of the Cincinnati Reds, and Roger Maras and Mickey Lolich, stars of the 1968 World Series. Joseph L. Kuharich coached the Washington Redskins football team from 1954 to 1958 and in 1955 was named coach of the year. "Pistol" Pete Marovich had a nationally publicized career with the New Orleans Jazz. Eleanor Laich was one of Olson's All-American Redheads. Mike Karakas played hockey for the Chicago Black Hawks, and Johnny Polich for the New York Rangers. Helen Crienkovich won world diving championships. Fritzie Zivich was the world welterweight boxing champ in 1941.

VISUAL ARTS

Ivan Mestrovic (1883-1962) showed his marble sculptures in one-man shows in Belgrade, Zagreb, and London, before establishing a studio in Paris in 1907. After World War I, he joined the art faculty of Syracuse University in New York, and then taught at Notre Dame University, where he lived until his death. Mestrovic's work demonstrated a consciousness of the suffering of people in Austria-Hungary. His work also shows the influence of Michelangelo, whose art he studied for four years in Rome. The first artist to hold a one-man exhibit at the Metropolitan Museum of Art in New York, Mestrovic has left a legacy of works that can be found throughout the United States in churches, parks, and institutions that include Grant Park in Chicago and the Mayo Clinic in Minnesota.

The painter Vlaho Bukovac (1865-1963) studied art in Paris and worked in San Francisco. His home in his native Cavtat is now a museum. Another painter, Maksimiljan (Makso) Vanka, studied painting in Zabreb and Brussels. He came to the United States in 1934 with his American wife and attracted fame when he painted the towering frescoes for St. Nicholas' Catholic Church in Millvale, Pennsylvania. Louis Adamic's novel *Cradle of Life* (1936) is based on Bukovac's life.

MEDIA

PRINT

American Croat/Americki Hrvati.

Contact: Peter Radielovic, Editor and Publisher.

Address: P.O. Box 3025, Arcadia, California 91006.

Telephone: (213) 795-3495.

Croatian Almanac.

Published by the Croatian Franciscan Press.

Address: Croatian Ethnic Institute, 4851 Drexel Boulevard, Chicago, Illinois 60615.

Telephone: (312) 268-2819.

The Croatian Voice.

Contact: Steven Varga, Publisher.

Address: P.O. Box 14278, Cleveland, Ohio 44114.

Telephone: (216) 431-0811.

Ragusan Press.

Contact: Adam Eterovich, Publisher.

Address: 2527 San Carlos Avenue, San Carlos, California 94070.

Telephone: (415) 592-1190.

The Trumpeter.

Published quarterly by the Croatian Philatelic Society (CPS).

Contact: Ekrem Spahich, Editor.

Address: 1512 Lancelot Road, Borger, Texas 79007.

Zajednicar (CFU Junior Magazine).

Weekly magazine published by the Croatian Fraternal Union.

Contact: Bernard M. Luketich, President.

Address: 100 Delaney Drive, Pittsburgh, Pennsylvania 15235.

Telephone: (412) 351-3909.

RADIO

WKBN-AM (57).

Youngstown, Ohio. "The Croatian Radio Hour," a two-hour weekly show, is hosted by Milan Brozovic.

WKTX-AM (830).

"Croatian Cultural Radio Program," airs weekly for two hours, with host Zvonimir Dzeba.

Address: P.O. Box 1432, Akron, Ohio 44309

WNWK-FM (105) and WNYE-AM (91.5).
"Croatian Radio Club."

Address: 37-18 Astoria Boulevard, Astoria, New York 11103.

Telephone: (201) 947-9754.

ORGANIZATIONS AND ASSOCIATIONS

Croatian Academy of America (CAA).
Sponsors lectures for members and the public on Croatian literature, history, and culture.

Contact: Diane Gal, Executive Secretary.

Address: P.O. Box 1767, Grand Central Station, New York, New York 10163-1767.

Croatian American Association.

Address: 818 18th Street, N.W., Suite 950, Washington, D.C. 20006.

Telephone: (202) 429-5543.

Croatian American Society.

Contact: Dr. Slobodan Lang, President.

Address: Odranska 6, 41000, Zagreb, Croatia.

Telephone: 011 385 41/538-006.

Croatian Genealogical Society (CGS).
Encourages Croatia genealogical and heraldic research.

Contact: Adam S. Eterovich, Director.

Address: 2527 San Carlos Avenue, San Carlos, California 94070.

Telephone: (415) 592-1190.

Croatian New Yorker Club.

Contact: Anton Angelich.

Address: 4705 Henry Hudson Parkway, Apartment 7J, Riverdale, New York 10471.

National Federation of Croatian Americans.

Address: P.O. Box 11538, Washington, D.C. 20008.

Telephone: (412) 343-4534

MUSEUMS AND RESEARCH CENTERS

Croatian Heritage Museum and Library.

Address: Lakeshore Blvd. and Route 91, Eastlake, Ohio 44094.

Immigrant Archives.
Managed by Hrvatska Matica Iseljenika (Croatian Homeland Association).

Contact: Ivo Smoljan, Director.

Address: Trnjaska bb. 41000 Zagreb, Croatia.

Telephone: 011 385 41/530-002.

Museum of the Croatian Fraternal Union.

Address: 100 Delaney Drive, Pittsburgh, Pennsylvania 15245.

SOURCES FOR ADDITIONAL STUDY

Balch, Emily Greene. *Our Slavic Fellow Citizens*. New York: Charities, 1910.

Croatia: Land, People, and Culture, edited by Francis H. Eterovich and Christopher Spalatin. Toronto: University of Toronto Press, 1964.

Gorvorchin, Gerald G. *Americans from Yugoslavia*. Gainesville: University of Florida, 1961.

Preveden, Francis. *A History of the Croatian People*. New York: Philosophic, 1962.

Prpic, George. *The Croatian Immigrants in America*. New York: Philosophic, 1971.

Raditsa, Bogdan. "Clash of Two Immigrant Cultures," *Commentary*, January 1958, pp. 8-15.

Shapiro, Ellen. *The Croatian Americans*. New York: Chelsea House, 1989.

"South Slavic American Literature," in *Ethnic Perspectives in American Literature*, edited by Robert Di Pietro and Edward Ifkovic. New York: MLA, 1983.

Community festivals
such as polka
celebrations and
houby (mushroom)
hunting contests
continue to play a
prominent role in
Czech American
culture.

CZECH

by
Christine Molinari

AMERICANS

OVERVIEW

Under Communist rule until 1989, the Czech Republic (Ceská Republika), which shared a common federal government with Slovakia until 1992, is now an independent state with democratic, multiparty institutions. Located in central Europe and occupying a territory of 78,864 square kilometers, it is bordered on the northwest and southwest by the Federal Republic of Germany, on the south by Austria, on the southeast by Slovakia, and on the north by Poland.

The Czech Republic has a population of 10,339,000. Of that number, 81.3 percent claim to be of Czech ethnic origin; 13.2 percent are Moravian; and the remaining 4.5 percent belong to other groups, notably Slovak, Polish, German, Silesian, Romany (Gypsy), Hungarian, or Ukrainian. The majority of Czechs (39.2 percent) are Roman Catholic, with a smaller number (4.1 percent) adhering to Protestant denominations. Czech is the official language. The capital city, Prague, preserves one of the oldest and richest architectural traditions in Europe, with many buildings, such as the Romanesque Church of St. George and the Gothic St. Vitus Cathedral, dating back to the Middle Ages. The flag of the Czech Republic, designed and first flown in New York to honor the visit of the World War I patriot Tomas G. Masaryk, consists of a blue triangle on a rectilinear background of white and red.

HISTORY

The Czechs are a Slavic people, closely related to the Slovaks in speech and custom, but with a distinct history and national identity. The term "Czech" denotes the inhabitants of historic Bohemia, Moravia, and Silesia, while "Slovak" is reserved for those people who settled on the southern slopes of the Carpathian Mountains and who historically were dominated by the Hungarians.

Between the fifth and seventh centuries, the Slavic ancestors of the Czechs swept across the region that subsequently became known as Bohemia. Although for a time assimilated into the neighboring Moravian Empire, Bohemia emerged as the stronger power and absorbed Moravia in the eleventh century. Under its ruling dynasty, the Přemsylides, Bohemia became Christian in the ninth century and a member of the Holy Roman Empire in the eleventh century, led by the German kings but retaining its own monarchy. Two prominent rulers of the House of Přemsyl were Wenceslas the Holy (c. 907-929) and Otaker II (1253-78), who extended Bohemia's territorial borders to the Adriatic. After the decline of the Přemsylides, Bohemia was ruled for a time by the House of Luxembourg. The union of King John of Luxembourg with the Czech princess Elizabeth produced a son, Charles IV (1346-1378), who, as emperor of the Holy Roman Empire, established Bohemia as the center of the empire and made Prague its cultural center. He founded the University of Prague in 1348. In the fifteenth century the university became the center of a church reform movement led by Jan Hus (1369-1415), who was burned as a heretic in 1415. Divided between the followers of Hus—the Hussites—and the Catholics, the country was attacked by crusaders and plunged into turmoil.

Through a dynastic union with the Jagiello family in Poland, the kings of Bohemia eventually became linked to the House of the Austrian Habsburgs, which ruled there from 1526 to 1918. Favoring monarchical control over the Protestant Reformation, the Habsburgs opposed the Bohemian estates, a struggle that resulted in the defeat of the Bohemian Protestant insurgents at the Battle of the White Mountain in 1620. Many thousands of noblemen were expelled from the country, and Bohemia was completely absorbed into the Habsburg empire, with German becoming the primary language of instruction in the schools. However, a national awakening in the nineteenth century, culminating in the political protest movement of 1848, reestablished a sense of Czech identity. After the Austrian declaration of war on Serbia and Russia in 1914, the Czechs and Slovaks, in a struggle to establish a common republic, joined the side of the Allies. Under the leadership of Masaryk, Eduard Beneš (1884-1948), and Milan Rastislav Stefánik, they were able to persuade the Allied governments to dissolve the Habsburg Empire. With the surrender of Austria on October 28, 1918, a revolutionary committee in Prague declared the establishment of the Czechoslovak Republic.

MODERN ERA

The Czechoslovak Republic, a parliamentary democracy, was governed from 1918 to 1935 by Masaryk, who was succeeded by his pupil Benes. But after occupation by the invading forces of Adolph Hitler in 1939, the republic never completely regained autonomy. In the aftermath of World War II, the Soviet Union began to tighten its control over central Europe, and in February 1948 it staged a governmental crisis in Czechoslovakia that solidified Communist control over the Czech government. A trend toward democratic liberalization in the 1960s culminated in the events of the Prague Spring in 1968, when a cultural revolution headed by the reformer Alexander Dubĉek was suppressed by the military intervention of the Soviet Union. Under Soviet leader Mikhail Gorbachev, a further period of liberalization began in the 1980s that led to the downfall of Communism in 1989, when largely peaceful strikes and demonstrations in Prague swept aside the old regime and elevated dissident playwright Vaclav Havel to the presidency. After a brief coexistence in a federation with Slovakia, the Czech Republic became fully independent in 1992.

THE FIRST CZECHS IN AMERICA

Prior to the nineteenth century, few Czechs had immigrated to the United States, and evidence of their presence during the colonial and revolutionary periods is sketchy. Hermann Augustine (1605-1686), one of the founders of the Virginia tobacco trade and compiler of the first map of Maryland and Virginia, is thought to be the first Czech immigrant. In 1638 Czech Protestant exiles, who had set sail for America in the service of the Swedish army, assisted in the building of Fort Christina on a tributary of the Delaware River.

The first major immigration wave occurred in 1848 when the Czech "Forty Eighters" fled to

These Czech emigrants are waving from the S.S. *President Harding,* which landed in New York City on May 25, 1935. They later joined relatives in Ohio.

the United States to escape political persecution by the Habsburgs. This year also saw the arrival of Vojta Náprstek, a radical free thinker and a vocal opponent of the Austrian government who, as part of a general amnesty extended to political refugees, returned in 1857 to his native land where he opened an American museum to acquaint European Czechs with America.

By the late 1850s there were an estimated 10,000 Czechs living in the United States. Chicago, tied to the West by rail and more readily accessible to the immigrants, became the most populous Czech settlement. By 1870, other cities with Czech concentrations included St. Louis, Cleveland, New York, and Milwaukee.

At the turn of the century, Czech immigrants were more likely to make the journey to the United States with their families. This marks a contrast with the immigration patterns of other ethnic groups, such as the Germans, English, Poles, and Slovaks, who tended to come over individually, as exhibited by the high ratio of

male to female immigrants in the U.S. demographic statistics of the period. Moreover, it was not uncommon in large families for the head of the household to make more than one trip to the United States, bringing along one or more children each time. In addition, many of those who immigrated in the late nineteenth century were of Moravian ancestry. One important characteristic of this group was their staunch adherence to the Catholic faith at a time when membership among Czech Americans was declining and a distinct anti-Catholic spirit prevailed.

RECENT IMMIGRATION

By the turn of the century, a widening gap between the first and second generations was already in evidence. In 1900 there were 199,939 American-born Czechs as opposed to 156,640 Czechs who had been born in Europe. The number of Czechs entering the country was further reduced by the temporary Emergency Quota Act, legislated by Congress in 1921, and the National Origins Act of 1924. Settlement patterns were also changing. Perhaps as a reflection of the growing trend toward urbanization in the United States, two-thirds of Czech Americans now lived in urban areas.

The next major immigration to the United States occurred during the dismemberment of Czechoslovakia, when approximately 20,000 fled to escape Nazi persecution. About one-quarter of these were professionals, including scholars and artists.

Between 1946 and 1975, 27,048 Czechs immigrated to the United States. With the Communist takeover in 1948, a large number of refugees, many of them students, teachers, journalists, and professional people, began pouring into the United States. Financial support for these refugees was provided by the American Fund for Czechoslovakia, established with the assistance of Eleanor Roosevelt. Subsequent immigration of refugees was supported by the Displaced Persons Act of 1948, which permitted the admission of refugees of Communist countries.

In 1968 the relaxed atmosphere in Czechoslovakia under the Dubĉek regime was conducive to the immigration of hundreds of refugees to the United States. Many of them were middle-aged, skilled, and educated; consequently, they had little difficulty finding employment. Although they made significant contributions to American society, this recent community of immigrants has been characterized more by its capacity for assimilation than by its ability to stimulate a resurgence in Czech American culture.

According to the 1990 U.S. Census, 1,296,000 Americans reported themselves to be of Czech ancestry, with 52 percent residing in the Midwest, 22 percent in the South, 16 percent in the West, and ten percent in the Northeast. The number of foreign-born Czechs in the United States has been steadily decreasing, and with the collapse of Communism in Eastern Europe, Czech immigration to the United States has significantly slowed.

SETTLEMENT PATTERNS

The oldest significant Czech colony in the United States is in New York, which by 1854 had about 40 families. In Texas, the first Czech settlement was established at Catspring in 1847. In 1848 the Czechs settled alongside Germans, Irish, and Norwegians in Wisconsin, mainly in the counties of Adams, Kewaunee, Manitowok, Marathon, and Oconto, with the first major Czech farming town established at Caledonia, north of Racine. Other settlements followed in Iowa, Kansas, and Nebraska. The first Czech settlers to arrive in Chicago in 1852 settled in what is today the Lincoln Park area, assisting in local building by cutting trees and loading lumber. Minnesota Territory was populated by the first Czechs in 1855, while the Dakota Territory saw its first Czech settlements in 1870. Czech Americans also lent names to several U.S. towns and cities in which they settled, including New Prague and Litomysl in Minnesota, and Pilsens, Iowa, to name a few.

ACCULTURATION AND ASSIMILATION

The Czechs were uniquely suited to assimilate into American society. Although they lacked direct experience with democratic institutions, the first generation—many of whom left their homeland to escape the oppression of the Austrian Habsburgs—nevertheless brought with them a love of liberty and social equality. A relatively large proportion of nineteenth-century Czech immigrants were literate, a result of the educational policies of the Austrian regime that made education compulsory to age fourteen throughout Bohemia and Moravia.

On arrival, many Czechs Americanized their last names. Some last names were translated into English (e.g., Jablečník became Appleton or Krejči became Taylor), while others were changed to American-sounding equivalents (e.g., Červeny became Sweeney, and Vlk became Wolf).

The years between 1914 and 1941 marked a turning point for the Czech community in two important ways. First, as a result of World War I, the Czech community had become less isolated. A growing trend toward Americanization could be seen in the second and third generations, which were already moving out of the Czech communities and marrying into families with ethnic backgrounds that differed from their own. Second, perhaps partially in response to this trend, the Czech American community was becoming more protective of its traditions, emphasizing the study of Czech language and culture.

As relatively recent arrivals in the United States, the Czechs were forced to deal with prejudice as they established their homes in the midst of other immigrant communities. The self-sufficiency of Czech urban settlements, with their assemblage of Czech-owned banks, theaters, amusement halls, and shops, may have contributed to a perception of Czechs as "clannish." Despite the Czechs' insistence that they be referred to as "Czechs," many Americans persisted in calling them by the pejorative "Bohunks" or by the less pejorative, but equally unacceptable "Bohemians." When the Czechs began moving out of urban neighborhoods into the suburbs after World War II, their search for new homes was not always greeted with enthusiasm. Some efforts at community expansion were met with strong prejudice, as when a Czech real-estate developer attempting to purchase land in a Chicago suburb returned home to find a burning cross on his land.

To many early twentieth-century observers, the Czechs were a relatively "successful" immigrant community. They were perceived as law-abiding and family- and community-oriented, and because they were dedicated to becoming fully Americanized, their assimilation into American culture was relatively smooth and complete.

TRADITIONS, CUSTOMS, AND BELIEFS

Community festivals such as polka celebrations and *houby* (mushroom) hunting contests continue to play a prominent role in Czech American culture. Some traditions celebrated in the early days of immigration were centered around the church. At box-supper church fund raisers, women baked their fanciest dinners and put them into boxes decorated with crepe paper, hearts, and ribbons to be auctioned off to the highest bidder.

Customs frequently were derived from old pagan traditions. On Palm Sunday, children created an effigy of *Smrt* ("death"), a lifesize straw doll that might be dressed in rags and have a necklace of eggs. The straw woman, who symbolized the end of winter, was then cast into a river as the children sang a welcome to the beginning of spring. On New Year's Eve, young men would gather in circles and fire their rifles into the air three times, a practice known as "shooting the witches."

Czech superstitions include the belief that a bird that flies into a house is an omen of death. A dream about a body of water could also mean that a death would occur. Pebbles were placed inside eggshell rattles made for children, to drive away evil spirits. A garnet that dimmed while worn on the body was thought be a sign of melancholy.

PROVERBS

Czech proverbs express popular wisdom on themes such as the family, labor, fortune, and benevolence. Common proverbs among Czech Americans in the United States include: Father and mother have taught us how to speak, and the world how to keep quiet; Too much wisdom does not produce courage; A pocketful of right needs a pocketful of gold; The poor are heaven's messengers; He who has daughters has a family, and he who has sons has strangers; If there were no children, there would be no tears; All the rivers do what they can for the sea; Better a lie that heals than a truth that wounds; As long as the language lives, the nation is not dead.

CUISINE

Czech American cooking boasts a range of savory meat dishes and rich, flavorful desserts that can be prepared with simple ingredients. Potatoes, mushrooms, and cabbage are the staples of Czech cooking. Czech cooks in Minnesota prepared a potato strudel; flour was added to mashed potatoes to form a stiff dough, which was then sprinkled with cinnamon and melted goat's milk butter and baked in the oven. Mushrooms picked during autumn field trips were brought home in bushels and set out in neat rows to dry. They were then turned into a sour mushroom soup which contained sauerkraut juice and fried onions. Sauerkraut, made from boiled cabbage, could also be mixed with pork and rice to make a cabbage roll.

The best-known Czech dessert is *koláče*, a sweet, squared-shaped dough bread filled with cheese; stewed prunes, apricots, or other fruit; or a mixture of poppy seed, custard pudding, and honey. Traditional at Christmas time was *vánočka*, a Christmas twist loaf flavored with mace, anise, and lemon and sprinkled with almonds and seedless raisins.

TRADITIONAL COSTUMES

Czech American traditional costumes were worn as everyday apparel in some parts of the country until the twentieth century, when they were worn only on ceremonial occasions. Women's billowy skirts, multicolored or solid, were topped by gold-trimmed black vests and blouses with full puffed sleeves that might be trimmed in gold or lace and embroidered with a floral geometric motif. Women's bright caps were worn flat on the head and had flaps on either side. Men's trousers were

of a solid hue but often decorated according to individual taste. Men wore a black vest over a full embroidered shirt.

Bridal costumes were particularly ornate. The bride wore a crown covered with rosemary wreaths made by the groom; this crown might also be strewn with long, flowing ribbons. Her white vest was covered with light sea beads or with red, yellow, or green streamers. The groom wore a close-fitting blue or red vest and a plumed hat.

CZECH DANCES AND SONGS

Most Americans are familiar with the *polka,* but few of them know that it is a Czech courtship dance. The polka originated in Prague in 1837. Derived from the Czech word for "half," it is danced with a half step to music written in two-quarter time, with the accent on the first three eighth notes. Another popular Czech dance is the *beseda,* a collection of mazurkas, polkas, and waltzes arranged according to local tradition and performed at festivals.

Czech melodies, strongly Western European in character, were usually composed to accompany dances. The *koledy*—ritual carols that were sung at Christmas, the New Year, and Easter—date back to the fourteenth and fifteenth centuries. A typical rustic band included a clarinet, violins, and the *dudy,* a shepherd's bagpipe that had a goat's head on top. Another traditional Czech instru-

ment played in the United States is the *tamburash,* a stringed instrument similar to the lute.

HOLIDAYS CELEBRATED BY CZECH AMERICANS

For Czech Americans, Christmas began on December 24 with a Christmas dinner that was served as soon as the first stars came out. Before dining, it was customary to eat consecrated bread dipped in honey; extra place settings were made for deceased members of the family, who were said to be present in spirit. Christmas Day, December 25, was celebrated at church in an extended ceremony where the women and girls stood in front of the altar for the duration of the service. New Year's Eve (sometimes called St. Sylvester's) was celebrated in the streets, with revelers spending all night in song and dance. Also commemorated were Epiphany (January 6), to honor the journey of the Magi; St. Valentine's Day; and Whitsunday, in remembrance of the Ascension. On Sprinkling Day, the first Monday of Easter week, boys would go through the town spraying the girls with little homemade "spritzers" or, if lucky enough to abduct one of them, would throw her into the river; the girl was required to show her gratitude for this treatment by baking the boy a homecooked meal. Czechs also observe St. Joseph's Day (March 19), a day honoring their national heritage.

Mother's Day was more than just the promotional holiday it is today. It was celebrated either at church, if it fell on a Sunday, or at a separate festival, and was marked by the wearing of red and white carnations grown especially for the occasion, a red carnation signifying that one's mother was living, the white carnation that she was no longer living.

A festival celebrated by Czech Americans in Iowa and Minnesota is the Rogation Days—the Monday, Tuesday, and Wednesday before the Feast of the Ascension. After the mass, the congregation would follow the priest through the fields, reciting the Litany of the Saints and praying for a good harvest.

HEALTH AND MENTAL HEALTH ISSUES

Czech immigrants sometimes turned to home remedies to cure common ailments. A wedding ring tied around the neck of a child was believed to cure fever. Poultices made of bread and milk were used to heal cuts. Concern about scoliosis prompted Czech women to ensure that their babies had adequate calcium, and at one time it was mandatory for newborns to have their hips examined to see whether they would develop the disease. Czech Americans have always been very diet conscious. When fruits were in scarce supply in the winter, they served rosehip tea as well as sauerkraut, a rich source of vitamin C.

Czech Americans believe that there is a strong connection between mental and physical well-being. Their commitment to physical fitness led to the establishment of the Sokol (Falcon) gymnastic organization, which strives to develop a person "perfect physically, spiritually, and morally, of a firm and noble character, whose word is irrevocable, like the law."

LANGUAGE

Czech is a Slavic language with a declension system based on seven cases. The present orthographic system was introduced in the fourteenth century by the religious reformer Jan Hus, who instituted a system of diacritical markings to eliminate consonant clusters. Thus, the consonants "š," "č," "ř," "ž," "ň," "ť'" and "ď'" stand for "sh," "ch," "rzh," "zh," "ny," "ty," and "dy," respectively. Czech is a phonetic language; every sound is pronounced exactly as it is written, with the accent always on the first syllable.

Because of the differences between Czech and English—Czech is a Slavic language, while English is Germanic—the acquisition of English as a second language presents a unique challenge to Czech Americans. The U.S. public school system and Czech American benevolent organizations have provided systematic English-language instruction to assist Czech American immigrants in learning English. Numerous American colleges and universities also teach the Czech language, including Stanford University, Yale University, the University of Chicago, the University of Michigan, and Harvard University.

GREETINGS AND OTHER POPULAR EXPRESSIONS

Greetings and expressions include *dobré jitro*—good morning; *dobrý den*—good afternoon; *dobrou noc*—good night; *nazdar*— hello; *s Bohem*—goodbye; *na shle-da-nou*—till we meet again; *prosím*—please; and *děkuji pěkne*—thank you very much. Other polite expressions are *Jak se máte?*—a polite form of "How are you?"), and *Jak se más* (the familiar form); *Jak se jmenujetě?*— What's your name? (polite form), and *Jak se jmenujes* (familiar form); *Těšsí mne*—Nice to meet you; and *Dobré chutnání*—Enjoy your meal.

FAMILY AND COMMUNITY DYNAMICS

The lifestyle of the nineteenth-century Czech immigrants was determined by the region and community in which they settled. Those who came to New York in the 1860s lived in sparsely furnished rented quarters, and it was not uncommon to find two families sharing the same small apartment. Immigrants who came to Chicago in the early 1850s had trouble settling permanently there: driven from place to place, they resided in makeshift housing until they could find permanent lodging. While the men loaded lumber to assist in the new building in the area, the women and children did the chores and went to the slaughterhouse where they could obtain the poorer cuts of meat, often purchased on a cooperative plan.

Hardships also were endured in rural communities. Dwellings in Nebraska, Kansas, and Iowa were simple sod houses—no more than underground burrows. Immigrants to rural Wisconsin built log cabins and lived off meager provisions, in some cases subsisting on cornbread and on the "coffee" that they made from ground roasted corn.

The accumulation of wealth by first-generation families made it easier for the second generation to purchase property. They began by building wood-frame homes and eventually saved enough money to build with brick. In the early twentieth century, an estimated 64 percent of Czech families living in Chicago owned their own dwellings, a high proportion for an immigrant community at that time. Children were sent to college and frequently went on to pursue professional vocations, such as law, education, or medicine.

Historically, the Czechs have been markedly active in community groups that have assisted immigrants and have promoted greater familiarity with Czech culture. In 1854 Czechs in Ripon, Wisconsin, formed the Czech-Slavonic Benevolent Society, the oldest continuous benevolent society in the United States, to provide insurance and aid to immigrants, as well as social services to the young, the elderly, and the poor. The Sokol (Falcon) gymnastic organization, established in St. Louis in 1865, continues to attract people of all ethnic backgrounds to its sponsored gymnastic meets.

Czech American women have played an exceptionally important role in community life, forming a number of active social and political organizations. By 1930 approximately one-third of the membership of Czech American benevolent societies consisted of women. The National Council of Women in Exile, convened in 1948, provided assistance to Czech refugees. Although Czech women were prominent in their communities, the women's suffrage movement in the early twentieth century was viewed with either polite tolerance or outright scorn and had difficulty winning acceptance among Czech Americans.

WEDDINGS

Traditional Czech weddings were announced by the groom's attendants, who would go from house to house extending the invitations. Food and drink were prepared days in advance. On the day of the wedding, the couple, their parents, and the bridal party would gather for the wedding breakfast. The groom was not allowed to see the bride in her gown until 2:00 in the afternoon, when the sponsor would present the bride and the parents to the groom, admonishing him to be kind, gentle, and worthy, and telling the bride to be moral, obedient, and submissive. After the wedding ceremony, as the guests proceeded to the feast, friends of the couple would stand along the path and tie a ribbon from one side to the other, requesting a donation. This gift was later presented to the couple or was sometimes given to the musicians as a gratuity. At the wedding feast, the bridesmaids would present the guests with sprigs of rosemary, a symbol of fidelity, and a collection would be taken up for the birth of the first child.

BAPTISMS

Preparation for the birth of a child began even before the wedding, when the bride-to-be would knit a set of white bonnets, boots, jackets, and shawls—sometimes enough for a family of six children—which were then carefully arranged in neat, ribbon-tied bundles and set aside until the arrival of the firstborn. Baptisms occurred a week after birth. They were followed by baptismal parties, where the godfather recited a customary toast and the godmother presented the gifts. Godparents adhered to their pledge to safeguard the child in the event of the parents' death. Six weeks after the baptism, the baby was taken to the church, where the religious officiant joined with the parents at the altar to say prayers of thanksgiving for the baby's arrival and health.

FUNERALS

In the nineteenth and early twentieth centuries, vigils were still kept in the home, a custom brought over from Europe. The casket might be brought to the home by the undertaker, if the village were prosperous enough to have one; in some villages, the caskets were kept in the general store. Family members would take turns sitting by the side of the deceased, who was waked in the home for a period of days.

On the day of the funeral, the religious officiant came to pray over the coffin with the family. In some rural areas, as in central Texas, businesses might be closed one hour before a funeral. The town bells summoned the townsfolk to the service. After the procession to the cemetery, the family would gather around the grave and sing hymns while the earth was shoveled into the grave. In *My Ántonia*, a novel about the life of a Czech immigrant family on the Nebraska plain, Willa Cather related the superstition that a suicide could not be buried in the cemetery, but only at a crossroads. In populous areas, the Czechs sometimes established their own national cemeteries; Bohemian National Cemetery in Chicago is one example.

After the funeral, not just the surviving husband or wife, but the entire family would observe a period of mourning, usually for several months. Widows observed the custom of wearing black; other family members, children included, were expected to preserve an atmosphere of deep solemnity, neither laughing nor indulging in games or amusement.

INTERACTIONS WITH OTHER ETHNIC MINORITIES

The earliest immigrants settled in proximity to ethnic groups for whom they had a strong affinity. In an important early study on Czech immigration, Thomas Čapek noted that many Czech settlements were located near German settlements (e.g., in St. Louis and Milwaukee) and observed that "the Čechs were drawn to the Germans by a similarity, if not identity, in customs and mode of life." By 1900, intermarriages with other nationalities were more common, most of them occurring with Germans, but also with Austrians, Hungarians, and Poles.

During World War II, Czech Americans participated in the national American Slav Congress, which convened in Detroit in 1940 and 1942. The war effort brought them closer to other Slavic ethnic groups, particularly to the Poles, an alliance that had its international parallel in a European concord of November 1940, when Czech and Polish refugees living in Europe agreed to establish friendly relations after the conclusion of the war.

RELIGION

Many of the Czechs who immigrated to the United States were Roman Catholic when they arrived. But the Czech immigration movement is unique in that as many as 50 percent of the Czechs immigrants broke their religious ties when they arrived to the United States. Their arrival in this country gave many Czechs an opportunity to sever with the Roman Catholic Church, an institution that was closely associated with the oppressive Habsburg regime that they had left behind. Some of them were also influenced by movements that questioned all forms of religious dogma.

The first Roman Catholic church was established in St. Louis. In 1920, *Katolik*, the official almanac of the Czech Benedictines, listed as many as 338 Roman Catholic parishes and relat-

ed organizations (Kenneth D. Miller, *The Czech-Slovaks in America* [New York: George H. Doran Company, 1922] p. 127). Traditionally, the Roman Catholic Church was strong in Texas, Wisconsin, Nebraska, and Minnesota and had a greater following in rural than urban areas. Among urban centers, Chicago and St. Louis had the strongest Czech Roman Catholic following. The Roman Catholic Church maintained its following by establishing churches or mission stations, founding benevolent chapters, publishing Catholic periodicals, and opening schools, which included a Czech college and seminary: Illinois Benedictine College (formerly St. Procopius), located in Lisle, Illinois.

In the early part of the twentieth century, approximately two percent of the Czechs living in the United States were Protestant. Unlike the Slovaks, who tended to adhere to the old-world Calvinist and Lutheran denominations, Czech Protestants tended to affiliate with American denominations. Common affiliations were Presbyterian, Methodist, the Bohemian Moravian Brethren, and Congregational. The predominantly high number of Presbyterian adherents was due both to the perceived similarities between the Presbyterian Church and the old-world Reformed Church and to early missionary efforts.

The Moravian Brethren, who settled in Bethlehem, Pennsylvania, were descendants of the followers of Jan Hus, the initiator of the reform movement. During the persecution of Protestants by the Habsburg dynasty in the seventeenth century, the Moravians, who had converted many German Waldensians living in Moravia, emigrated to Saxony. In time, members of this group, the majority of whom were German, made their way to Pennsylvania, where they purchased a large tract of land from William Penn. The Brethren established a number of schools; in keeping with the precepts of the educator Comenius, who believed in equal education for women, they founded the first American preparatory school for girls in 1742.

EMPLOYMENT AND ECONOMIC TRADITIONS

Many of the Czechs who immigrated to the United States in the late 1850s were farmers or laborers. Of the three classes of Czech peasants who lived in Europe—the *sedlák*, or upper-class farmer, who owned 25-100 acres and a farmhouse; the _chalupník_, or cottager, who owned 5-25 acres and a small cottage; and the _nadeníci_, or day laborer, who dwelt on the nobleman's estate or on the farm of the _sedlák_ and owned no property—Czech immigrants to the United States most frequently derived from the middle, or cottager, class. This was probably because the _sedlák_ had little to gain by leaving behind his rich farmland, while the nadeníci did not have the means to emigrate.

Settlers who came to the Midwest lived in log cabins; those on the plains resided in dugouts and sod houses. With no tools at their disposal, farmers were constrained to hard manual labor. In the off-season they focused on survival, migrating to the cities or to the lumber and mining camps to find what work they could.

Occasionally, Czechs specializing in a certain industry—such as the cigar-making industry in New York—had emigrated from a particular region, in this case, Kutna Horá, which was preeminent in the cigar trade. In the 1870s, 95 percent of the Czechs in New York were employed in the cigar-making industry. Working conditions were harsh, and wages poor. Joseph Chada has noted that it took the average Czech industrial laborer ten years to attain the economic status of the average American laborer. Many women and children were also employed in these factories.

Urban-dwellers were eager to purchase property. Community-minded and thrifty, the Czechs created the building and loan association, an institution which became one of their most significant contributions to U.S. economic life. The building and loan association, introduced in Chicago in 1873, was a small cooperative agency to which shareholders made minimal weekly contributions with an aim toward eventually purchasing a home. So successful were these agencies that during the Great Depression, when other banks were failing, Czech building and loan associations posted a total of $32,000,000 in deposits, a substantial figure for that period.

By the first half of the twentieth century, Czech businesses were flourishing. Czech breweries (Pilsen and Budweiser are both derived from Czech place names) kept pace with the best German establishments. The Bulova watch company, a Czech enterprise, is an example of a successful, well-established Czech American business. And the character of the Czech labor force was changing as well. By the second generation, among Czech laborers, there was a greater preponderance of salesmen, machinists, and white-collar laborers.

POLITICS AND GOVERNMENT

The Czechs were relatively slow to take part in U.S. political life. By the 1880s, however, Czechs were playing an increasingly active role in government, both at the state and local levels. Most Czechs voted the democratic ticket, in part because of the perception that the democrats favored labor. Some Czechs ran successfully for high public office. Charles Jonás served as senator of Wisconsin in 1883 and as governor of Wisconsin in 1890.

By the 1880s support had grown among Czech American labor for the socialist movement. But in the aftermath of the Haymarket Riot of 1886—a violent confrontation between labor protesters and police in Haymarket Square in Chicago, initially triggered by the crusade for the eight-hour work day—the movement was forced underground. With the emergence of the American Socialist Party, Czech Americans renewed their membership, many of them recruited by appeals in the ethnic press. By 1910, Czech American socialists numbered approximately 10,000. They reduced their activities during World War I, however, as the concerns of nationalism began to loom over those of internationalism. And as the lifestyle of second- and third-generation Czech Americans improved, they became less concerned with the labor situation. By the 1920s the movement had all but come to a standstill.

"The factories in the regions of Seventieth street, New York, are filled with Bohemian women and girls employed in the making of cigars. ... [They] dread going into the cigar factories. The hygiene is bad, the moral influences are not often the best, and the work is exhausting."

Jane E. Robbins, "The Bohemian Women in New York," cited in _The Czechs in America, 1633-1977_, edited by Vera Laska, (Dobbs Ferry, New York: Oceana Publications, 1978; p. 111).

The prospect of establishing Czech independence from Austria led Czech Americans fervently to support the Allied cause during World War I. Prior to the outbreak of the war, Czech Americans openly demonstrated their support for the Serbs and rallied for the establishment of an independent Czech homeland. The Czech National Alliance was established in Chicago to provide political and financial support to the Czech cause in Europe. Also characteristic of this period was the willingness of the Czech American community to band together with the Slovak American community to establish a common political framework that would unite Bohemia, Moravia, and Slovakia under a single government. On October 25, 1915, the Czechs and Slovaks met in Cleveland to agree on such a program. In April 1917, the Czechs succeeded in gaining the introduction of resolutions in Congress supporting the establishment of an independent European homeland.

Czech Americans also played an active role in supporting the cause of Czechoslovakia during World War II. During the Munich Crisis, Czechs organized a protest rally of 65,000 at Chicago Stadium. The war efforts of Czech Americans were coordinated primarily by the Czechoslovak National Council. In addition to publishing *News Flashes from Czechoslovakia*, with a circulation of 5,000-105,000, the council aided soldiers and refugees who participated in the Allied campaign. Czech Americans effectively used propaganda to direct world attention to the Nazi massacre of the village of Lidice.

After the Soviet takeover of Czechoslovakia, Czechs were admitted to the United States under the American Displaced Persons Act. The Czechoslovak National Council assisted these individuals in their struggle to regain their homeland, primarily through the publication of anti-Communist propaganda. In addition to requesting members of the Czech American community to sign affidavits that would assist refugees in obtaining shelter and employment, on June 3, 1949, the Council presented a memorandum to President Harry Truman, requesting that the United States push for United Nations-sponsored free elections in Czechoslovakia.

MILITARY

Czech Americans on the whole were opposed to slavery and therefore supported the North during the U.S. Civil War, serving at Chancellorsville, Fredericksburg, and Bull Run. Many of those living in the Confederacy (primarily in Texas) avoided conscription into the Southern army at enormous cost to their lives, hiding in the woods or swamps or serving as drivers on perilous journeys to Mexico.

Czech Americans in the First World War either served in the Czechoslovak Army on the Western Front (if they were immigrants) or enlisted as draftees in the U.S. Army. Approximately 2,300 Czech immigrants served in European Czech contingents. During World War II Czech American loyalties were divided between providing active military service to their country and providing moral support to the Czech community in Europe, both duties which they admirably fulfilled. They also made a financial contribution to the war effort by investing substantially in war loans.

INDIVIDUAL AND GROUP CONTRIBUTIONS

ACADEMIA

Aleš Hrdlička (1869-1943), curator of the physical anthropology division at the Smithsonian Institution, developed the theory that Native Americans migrated to North America from Asia across the Bering land bridge and did extensive research on Neanderthal man. Jaroslav Pelikan (1923-) is the author of the five-volume *The Christian Tradition*, an authoritative work on the history of Christian doctrine. Francis Dvorník (1893-1975) was a noted Byzantine scholar affiliated with the Dumbarton Oaks Center for Byzantine Studies. Managed by Harvard University, the center is located in Washington, D.C.

FILM, TELEVISION, AND THEATER

Milos Forman (1932-), who immigrated to the United States in 1969, won Academy Awards for best direction for *One Flew over the Cuckoo's Nest* (1975) and *Amadeus* (1984). Actress Kim Novak (1933), who made her screen debut in 1954, starred in such films as *Pal Joey* and *Boys Night Out*. Television and screen actor Tom Selleck (1945-) is best known for his role in the television series "Magnum P.I." (1980-1988). John Kriza (1919-1975) was a ballet dancer who performed with the American Ballet Theater and the Chicago Opera Ballet.

JOURNALISM

Charles Jonáš (1840-1896), who served in the Wisconsin state legislature, founded *Pokrok* (Progress), an anticlerical weekly. In 1869 Frank Kořízek (1820-1899) established the weekly

Slowan Amerikánsky in Iowa City. Lev J. Palda (1847-1912), the founder of Czech American socialism, established the first Czech social-democratic or socialist newspaper, *Národní noviny* (*National Newspaper*), in St. Louis, Missouri. Josephine Humpal-Zeman (1870-1906), an important figure in the women's suffrage movement, founded the *Ženské Listy* (*Woman's Gazette*).

LITERATURE

René Wellek (1903-), a member of the Prague Linguistic Circle, settled in the United States in 1939, where he established the field of comparative literature at Yale University. Bartos Bittner (1861-1912) was an essayist and political satirist. Paul Albieri (1861-1901) wrote stories of military life.

MUSIC

The composer Antonin Dvořák (1842-1904) lived in the United States from 1892 to 1895, where he wrote the *New World Symphony*, a piece inspired by American folk motifs, particularly Native American rhythms and African-American melodies. Rafael Kubelík (1914-), son of the violinist Jan Kubelík, studied music at the Prague Conservatory and conducted the Czech Philharmonic (1936-39, 1942-48) and the Chicago Symphony Orchestra (1950-53). In 1973-74 he was musical director of the Metropolitan Opera. Bohuslav Martinu (1890-1950), a contemporary composer whose music exhibits French and Czech influences, wrote the *Double Concerto* (1940), an expression of grief at the partition of Czechoslovakia. Jarmila Novotna Dauberk (1907-1993) was an opera singer with the Metropolitan Opera Company who studied under the renowned Czech opera singer Emmy Destinn; she also performed at the Salzburg Festival and the National Theater in Prague. Ardis Krainik (1929-) is general director of the Lyric Opera in Chicago. The pianist Rudolf Firkusny (1912-1993) made his first appearance with the Czech Philharmonic in 1922 and played with numerous orchestras in the United States, including those in New York, Philadelphia, Boston, Chicago, and Detroit.

PUBLIC LIFE

Ray Kroc (1902-1984), founder of McDonald's restaurants, was a pioneer in the establishment of the fast-food industry. Francis Korbel (1830-1920), who entered the United States in cognito to avoid an arrest warrant, purchased redwood forest in northern California and established the Korbel winery. Louis D. Brandeis (1856-1941), descended from a Bohemian Jewish family that immigrated to the United States in 1849, became the first Jewish Supreme Court Justice (1916-39). He helped to draft the Czechoslovak Declaration of Independence, issued in 1918. Anton Joseph Cermak (1873-1933), a mayor of Chicago who established Illinois as a stronghold of support for Franklin D. Roosevelt, was killed in Miami by an assassin intending to kill President Roosevelt. Eugene A. Cernan (1934-) was copilot on the Gemini 9 mission, lunar module pilot of the Apollo 10 mission, and spacecraft commander of Apollo 17. James Lovell (1928-) served on the Apollo 8 mission, the first manned flight around the moon.

SCIENCE AND TECHNOLOGY

Biochemists Gerty Cori (1896-1957) and Carl Cori (1896-1984) won the 1946 Nobel Prize for physiology or medicine, for their studies on sugar metabolism. The physician Joseph Goldberger (1874-1929) discovered a cure for pellagra, which he correctly attributed to diet deficiency, against the prevailing view that it was due to infection. Frederick George Novy (1864-1957) made important contributions to the field of microbiology. Joseph Murgas (1864-1930) was a pioneer in wireless technology who, although never able to amass sufficient resources to carry out his research, shared research with Guglielmo Marconi that contributed to the invention and patenting of the device.

SPORTS

George Halas (1895-1983) was founder and owner of the Chicago Bears football team. As head coach he led his team to seven championship seasons. Jack Root (1876-1963) was the first world champion lightweight boxer in 1903. Stan Musial (1920-) was an outstanding baseball hitter and outfielder with the St. Louis Cardinals who won seven batting championships. Martina Navratilova (1956-) has dominated women's tennis since the 1970s, winning the U.S. Open and Wimbledon numerous times and becoming only the fifth person in history to win the Grand Slam. Ivan Lendl (1960-) has likewise dominated men's tennis, winning the U.S. Open in 1985 and the Australian Open in 1989. Stan Mikita

(1940-) was an outstanding hockey center with the Chicago Blackhawks, with 541 career goals.

VISUAL ARTS

Andy Warhol (1927-87) was an artist and filmmaker whose name is particularly associated with the Pop art movement. He is perhaps most famous for his paintings of mass-produced images of consumer goods, such as the Campbell's soup can. Alphonse Mucha (1860-1939) was an Art Nouveau decorative artist, recognized for his posters promoting the actress Sarah Bernhardt.

MEDIA

PRINT

Hlas Národa (Voice of the Nation).
Publishes items related to religious and political topics and events in both the United States and the Czech Republic.

Contact: Vojtech Vit, Editor.
Address: 2340 South 61st Avenue, Cicero, Illinois 60650-2608.
Telephone: (708) 656-1050.

Hlasatel.
Publishes general news items in both Czech and English.

Contact: Milo R. Tuma, Editor.
Address: 1545 West 18th Street, Chicago, Illinois 60608.
Telephone: (312) 226-3315.

Hospodar.
Prints general news, letters, and features on farm topics.

Contact: Jerome Kopecky, Editor.
Address: 214 West Oak, West, Texas 76691.
Telephone: (817) 826-5282.

RADIO

KMIL-AM (1330).
Broadcasts eight hours weekly in Czech.

Contact: Joe Smitherman.
Address: Drawer 832, Cameron, Texas 76520.
Telephone: (817) 697-6633.

WCEV-AM (1450).
"Czechoslovak Sunday Radio Hour" in Chicago is a weekly one-hour broadcast in Czech.

Contact: Diana Migala.
Address: 5356 West Belmont Avenue, Chicago, Illinois 60641-4103.
Telephone: (312) 282-6700.

WRMR-AM (850).
"Czech Voice of Cleveland" broadcasts in Czech on Sunday, 11:00 to 12:00 p.m.

Contact: Jim Davis.
Address: 1 Radio Lane, Cleveland, Ohio 44114.
Telephone: (216) 696-0123.

ORGANIZATIONS AND ASSOCIATIONS

American Sokol Educational and Physical Culture Organization (ASEPCO).
Founded in 1865, ASEPCO is a physical fitness organization for children and adults of all ages, with 8,500 adult members and 8,000 gymnasts. It sponsors gymnastic meets and competitions, clinics, workshops, and schools; conducts educational activities; and offers lectures and films.

Contact: Nancy Pajeau, Secretary.
Address: 6424 South Cermak Road, Berwyn, Illinois 60402.
Telephone: (312) 795-6671.

Czech Catholic Union (CCU).
Founded in 1879, the CSU is a Catholic fraternal benefit life insurance society that makes an annual donation to the Holy Family Cancer Home, bestows awards, participates in local civic and cultural events, and provides services for children.

Contact: Mary Ann Mahoney, Secretary-Treasurer.
Address: 5349 Dolloff Road, Cleveland, Ohio 44127.
Telephone: (216) 341-0444.

Czechoslovak Genealogical Society (CGS).
Founded in 1988, CGS supports research in Czechoslovakian culture and genealogy, hosts workshops, and maintains a research library.

Contact: Mark Bigaouette, President.
Address: P.O. Box 16225, St. Paul, Minnesota 55116.
Telephone: (612) 426-1222.

Czechoslovak Society of America Fraternal Life (CSA).
Founded in 1854, CSA is a fraternal benefit life insurance society that hosts contests, including a Miss National CSA competition; bestows awards;

and coordinates scholarship programs. The CSA also maintains a museum, biographical archives, and a library of Czech books and periodicals.

Contact: Vera A. Wilt, President.
Address: 2701 South Harlem Avenue, Berwyn, Illinois 60402.
Telephone: (708) 795-5800.

Czechoslovak Society of the Arts and Sciences (CSAS).
Founded in 1958, CSAS sponsors lectures, concerts, and exhibitions. It promotes the activities of professors, writers, artists, and scientists interested in Czech or Slovak concerns.

Contact: F. Marlow.
Address: 4064 Woodcliff Road, Sherman Oaks, California 91403.
Telephone: (818) 784-0970.

MUSEUMS AND RESEARCH CENTERS

Czechoslovak Heritage Museum and Library.
Founded in 1854, the museum houses a large collection of books, periodicals, and historic documents, as well as costumes, dolls, and antiques.

Contact: Dagmar Bradac.
Address: 2701 South Harlem Avenue, Berwyn, Illinois 60402.
Telephone: (708) 795-5800.

Moravian Historical Society.
Hosts guided tours through its collection of art and artifacts on the history of the Moravian Church. The museum also exhibits paintings by John Valentine Haidt, as well as early musical instruments.

Contact: Rev. Charles Zichman, President.
Address: 214 East Center Street, Nazareth, Pennsylvania 18064.
Telephone: (215) 754-5070.

National Czech and Slovak Museum and Library.
Located in the restored home of a Czech immigrant, this museum preserves national costumes, as well as porcelain ethnic dolls, handwork, wood-carved items, paintings, prints, maps, and farm tools. There is also a library with reference materials and oral history videotapes.

Contact: Patty Hikiji, Executive Director.
Address: 10-16th Avenue, S.W., Cedar Rapids, Iowa 52404.
Telephone: (319) 362-7173.

The Western Fraternal Life Association.
Houses a library and archives and sponsors educational lectures on Czech language and culture.

Contact: Charles H. Vyskocil.
Address: 1900 First Avenue, N.E., Cedar Rapids, Iowa 52402.

Wilber Czech Museum.
Maintains a collection of dolls, dishes, murals, pictures, laces, costumes, and replicas of early homes and businesses.

Contact: Irma Ourecky.
Address: 102 West Third Street, Wilber, Nebraska 68465.
Telephone: (402) 821-2485.

SOURCES FOR ADDITIONAL STUDY

Čapek, Thomas. The Čechs (Bohemians) in America. Boston and New York: Houghton Mifflin, 1920.

Cather, Willa. My Ántonia. Boston: Houghton Mifflin, 1918.

Chada, Joseph. The Czechs in the United States. Chicago: SVU Press, 1981.

Dvornik, Francis. Czech Contributions to the Growth of the United States. Washington, D.C., 1961.

Laska, Vera. The Czechs in America, 1633-1977. Dobbs Ferry, New York: Oceana Publications, 1978.

Miller, Kenneth D. The Czech-Slovaks in America. New York: George H. Doran Company, 1922.

Writers' Program of the Work Projects Administration in the State of Minnesota. The Bohemian Flats. St. Paul, Minnesota: Minnesota Historical Society Press, 1986.

The majority of the Danes who immigrated to the United States looked to agriculture for a livelihood.

DANISH AMERICANS

by
John Mark Nielsen
and Peter L. Petersen

OVERVIEW

Denmark is geographically the southernmost of the Nordic nations, which also include Finland, Iceland, Norway, and Sweden. Its land mass includes Jutland, a peninsula extending north from Germany, and more than 480 islands. Denmark consists of 16,630 square miles (43,094 sq. km.). With the exception of its 42-mile southern border with Germany, Denmark is surrounded by water. Sweden lies to the east across the Oresund, a narrow body of water that links the North and Baltic Seas; Norway lies to the north; and the North Sea to the west. Denmark has nearly 4,500 miles of coastline, and no part of the nation is more than 30 miles from the sea. Denmark also possesses Greenland, the world's largest island, and the Faeroe Islands, both of which are semiautonomous. Denmark means "field of the Danes." The Danish national flag, the oldest national banner in the world, is a white cross on a red field. Legend has it that the banner, called *Dannebrog*, descended from the heavens in the midst of a battle between the Danes and the Estonians on June 15, 1219.

Although the smallest of the Nordic countries in terms of land mass, Denmark, with 5.2 million people, is second in population after Sweden. The Danish people are among the most homogeneous in the world. Almost all Danes are of Nordic stock, and most are members of the Lutheran church. In 1990 foreigners made up less than 2.5 percent of the population. Because of the ancient practice called patronymics, whereby Peter, the son of Jens, became Peter Jensen, many Danes have the same surname. Although a government decree in 1856 ended patronymics, some 60 percent of all present day Danish names end in "sen" with Jensen and Nielsen being the most common. Approximately one out of every four Danes lives in the capital of Copenhagen (*København*) and its suburbs on the eastern island of Sealand. Other major cities include Århus, Odense, and Ålborg. The country's official language is Danish, but many Danes, especially the young, also speak English and German.

HISTORY

It was not until the Viking Era of the ninth and tenth centuries that Danes, along with Swedes and Norwegians—collectively known as Norsemen or Vikings—had a significant impact upon world history. Sailing in their magnificent ships, Vikings traveled west to North America, south to the Mediterranean, and east to the Caspian Sea. They plundered, conquered, traded, and colonized. For a brief period in the eleventh century, a Danish king ruled England and Norway.

While Vikings roamed far and wide, those Danes who stayed at home cleared fields, built villages, and gradually created a nation. After a king with the colorful name of Harald Bluetooth (d. 985) was baptized in circa 965, Christianity began to spread across Denmark. Many Vikings encountered the religion on their voyages and were receptive to it. The current Queen of Denmark, Margrethe II (1940-), traces her sovereignty back to Harald's father, Gorm the Old (d. 950), thus making Denmark one of the oldest monarchies in the world. Slowly the forces of Crown and Church helped make Denmark a major power in northern Europe. Under the leadership of Margrethe I (1353-1412), Denmark, Norway, and Sweden were joined in 1397 in the Kalmar Union. Eventually, the growth of nationalism led Sweden to abandon the union in 1523, but Norway and Denmark remained allied until 1814. Like much of Europe in the early sixteenth century, Denmark struggled with the religious and political issues set in motion by the Protestant Reformation. In 1536 King Christian III defeated the forces of Roman Catholicism, and Denmark embraced Lutheranism.

Growing rivalry with Sweden and various rulers along the north German coast created new problems for Denmark, but the greatest international disaster to befall the country came during the Napoleonic Wars (1804-1814) when an ill-fated alliance with France left the nation bankrupt and Norway lost to Sweden. New threats to Danish territory soon followed from the south. After decades of intrigue and diplomatic maneuvering, Denmark and Prussia went to war in 1864 over the status of the Danish-ruled Duchies of Schleswig and Holstein. The Prussians quickly gained the upper hand and Denmark was forced to surrender both Duchies. This meant a loss of about 40 percent of its territory and more than 30 percent of its population. This defeat reduced Denmark to the smallest size in its history and dashed any remaining dreams of international power.

The nineteenth century was also a time of great domestic change for Denmark. A liberal constitution, which took effect June 5, 1849, brought to an end centuries of absolute monarchy. Danes could now form political parties, elect representatives to a parliament, and were guaranteed freedom of religion, assembly, and speech. The country also underwent an economic revolution. Danish farmers found it difficult to compete with the low-priced grains offered in European markets by American and Russian exports and increasingly turned to dairy and pork production. The growth of industry attracted many job-hungry Danes to developing urban centers. But agricultural change and the rise of industrialism were not enough to stop rising discontent and eventually one out of every ten Danes felt compelled to emigrate; most traveled to the United States.

MODERN ERA

Throughout the first half of the twentieth century Denmark pursued a policy of neutrality in international affairs. While this policy enabled the country to remain a non-belligerent in World War I (1914-1918), it did not prevent a German occupation during much of World War II (1939-1945). It was during this occupation that the Danish people won the admiration of much of the world by rescuing 7,200 of some 7,800 Danish Jews from Nazi forces in 1943. After World War II, Denmark moved away from neutrality, and in 1949, it joined with the United States, Canada, and nine other European nations to form the North Atlantic Treaty Organization (NATO), a pact aimed at containing the expansion of the

Soviet Union. In 1973 Denmark became the first and thus far the only Scandinavian country to join the European Economic Community (EEC).

The twentieth century also witnessed great economic and social change. Danish agriculture became more specialized and moved toward increased exports while industrial development transformed most urban areas. Denmark gradually became a prosperous nation, and with the development of a welfare system which provides education, health care, and social security from cradle to grave, its citizens now enjoy one of the highest living standards in the world. Since 1972, Queen Margrethe II has presided over this small, peaceful, and civilized land whose character is best symbolized by its most famous author, Hans Christian Andersen (1805-1875), a writer of fairy tales with profound psychological depths, and by one of its modern exports—the small, colorful plastic bricks called Lego.

THE FIRST DANES IN AMERICA

Although it is clear that Vikings reached the coast of Newfoundland early in the eleventh century, it is impossible to determine if there were any Danes among these early voyagers. Jens Munk (1579-1628), a Danish explorer, reached North America in 1619, 12 years after the English first settled at Jamestown. The Danish king, Christian IV (1577-1648), had sent Munk to find a trade route to the Orient via the Northwest Passage. With two ships and 65 men, Munk reached Hudson Bay before winter halted his exploration. Near the mouth of the Churchill River, members of the expedition celebrated a traditional Danish Christmas—the first Lutheran Christmas service in North America. Another Danish explorer, Vitus Jonassen Bering (1681-1741), discovered in 1728 that a narrow body of water separated the North American and Asian continents. Today this strait is named the Bering Sea in his honor. Bering also was the first European to find Alaska in 1741.

Other Danes sought warmer climes. In 1666 the Danish West Indies Company took possession of the island of St. Thomas in the Caribbean. Eventually, Danes took control of nearby St. John (1717) and St. Croix (1733). Danish planters imported slaves from Africa; raised cotton, tobacco, and sugar on the islands; and engaged in a lively commerce with England's North American colonies and, later, the United States. In 1792, Denmark became the first country to abolish the slave trade in overseas possessions. Denmark sold the islands, today called the Virgin Islands, to the United States in 1917 for $25 million.

Individual Danish immigrants reached North America early in the seventeenth century. By the 1640s approximately 50 percent of the 1,000 people living in the Dutch colony of New Netherlands (later New York) were Danes. It has long been believed that Jonas Bronck—for whom the borough of the Bronx was named—was a Dane, but recent research suggests that he may have been a Swede. After 1750 several Danish families who were members of a religious denomination called the Moravian Brethren immigrated to Pennsylvania where they settled among German Moravians in the Bethlehem area.

Most Danish immigrants to North America from colonial times until 1850 were single men, and quickly blended into the general population. Rarely, with few exceptions, does the name of a Danish immigrant appear in the historical annals of this period. Hans Christian Febiger or Fibiger (1749-1796), often called "Old Denmark," was one of George Washington's most trusted officers during the American Revolution. Charles Zanco (1808-1836) gained a degree of immortality by dying at the Alamo in March 1836 during the struggle for Texan independence. A Danish flag stands today in one corner of the Alamo Chapel as a reminder of Zanco's sacrifice. Peter Lassen (1800-1859), a blacksmith from Copenhagen, led a group of adventurers from Missouri to California in 1839, establishing a trail soon to be followed by "forty-niners." Lassen is considered one of the most important of California's early settlers. Today a volcano in northern California, a California county, and a national park bear his name.

SIGNIFICANT IMMIGRATION WAVES

Between 1820 and 1850, the number of Danes entering the United States averaged only about 60 each year. But soon this trickle became a steady stream. From 1820 to 1990, more than 375,000 Danes came to the United States, the vast majority arriving between 1860 and 1930. The peak year was 1882, when 11,618 Danes entered the country. Converts to the Church of Jesus Christ of Latter Day Saints (Mormons) represent the first significant wave of Danish immigrants to America. Mormon missionaries from Utah arrived in Denmark in 1850, only months after the Constitution of 1849 granted the Danish people religious freedom. Between 1849 and 1904, when Mormons stopped recruiting immigrants, some 17,000 Dan-

ish converts and their children made the hazardous journey to the Mormon Zion in Utah, making Danes second only to British in number of foreigners recruited by the church to the state. Many of these Danes settled in the small farming communities of Sanpete and Sevier counties, south of Salt Lake City; today these counties rank second and fifth respectively among all the counties in the United States in terms of percent of Danish ancestry in their population.

Another source of sizable Danish emigration was the Schleswig area of Jutland. As noted earlier, Denmark had been forced to surrender Schleswig to Prussia in 1864. Some 150,000 residents of North Slesvig were thoroughly Danish and many bitterly resented their area's new status. After Wilhelm I, King of Prussia, became Emperor of Germany in 1871, the policy of Prussia in Schleswig was essentially that of Germany. This meant the abolition of the Danish language in the schools and the conscription of young Danish men for the German military. Between 1864 and 1920, when North Schleswig was returned to Denmark as a result of a plebiscite following Germany's defeat in World War I, some 50,000 North immigrated to the United States. Ironically, most of these Danes appear in census statistics as immigrants from Germany rather than Denmark.

Most Danes who immigrated to the United States after 1865 were motivated more by economic than religious or political motives. Like

much of nineteenth-century Europe, Denmark experienced a steep rise in population. Better nutrition and medical care had produced a sharp decline in infant mortality, and Denmark's population rose from approximately 900,000 in 1800 to over 2,500,000 by 1910. Denmark's economy was unable to absorb much of this increase, and the result was the rise of restless and dissatisfied elements within the population. For these people, migration to a nearby city or to America appeared to offer the only chance for a better life. Many used the Homestead Act or other generous land policies to become farmers in the United States. The work of emigration agents, often employed by steamship companies and American railroads with land to sell, and a steady stream of American letters (some containing pre-paid tickets) from earlier immigrants, stimulated the exodus. During the 1870s almost half of all Danish immigrants to the United States traveled in family groups, but by the 1890s family immigration made up only 25 percent of the total. Perhaps more than ten percent of these later immigrants, largely single and male, would eventually return to Denmark.

SETTLEMENT

By 1900 a Danish belt of settlement had spread from Wisconsin across northern Illinois and southern Minnesota and into Iowa, Nebraska, and South Dakota. The largest concentration of these settlers was in western Iowa where today the adjacent counties of Audubon and Shelby rank first and third respectively in the United States in percentage of population with Danish ancestry. Communities with Danish names—Viborg and Thisted in South Dakota; Dannebrog and Nysted, Nebraska; and Ringsted, Iowa—attest to the role of Danes in settling the Midwest.

As the midwestern and eastern Great Plains began to fill with settlers, a variety of immigrant leaders and organizations sought to establish Danish agricultural colonies elsewhere by arranging for land companies to restrict sales in specific tracts to Danes. The *Dansk Folkesamfund* (Danish Folk Society) sponsored several of these colonies, including settlements at Tyler, Minnesota, in 1886; Danevang, Texas, 1894; Askov, Minnesota, 1905; Dagmar, Montana, 1906; and Solvang, California, 1911. Similar colonies were established in Mississippi, North Dakota, Oregon, Washington, and Alberta, Canada. Most of these colonies were quite small and eventually blended into the surrounding community. An exception is Solvang, 45 miles north of Santa Barbara, which has become a major tourist attraction and bills itself today as "A Quaint Danish Village."

Not all Danish emigrants sought land; a significant minority settled in American cities. Chicago led the way in 1900 with over 11,000 Danish-born residents while New York counted 5,621. Omaha, Nebraska, and its neighboring city of Council Bluffs, Iowa, also had sizable Danish populations. Smaller concentrations of Danes could be found in Racine, Wisconsin (the city with the highest percentage of Danes among its population), the Twin Cities of Minneapolis and St. Paul, and in San Francisco. By 1930 political and economic reform in Denmark, along with the closing of the American farming frontier, brought this wave of immigration to an end.

The latest wave of immigrants came during the 1950s and the 1960s when some 25,000 Danes, mostly highly educated young professionals, moved to the United States where they settled in major cities, particularly New York, Chicago, Los Angeles, and San Francisco.

ACCULTURATION AND ASSIMILATION

Historians agree that the Danes were among the most easily acculturated and assimilated of all American ethnic groups. A variety of studies indicate that in comparison to other immigrants Danes were more likely to speak English, become naturalized citizens, and marry outside their nationality. Several factors explain the relative ease of Danish assimilation. In comparison to people from many other countries, the number of Danish immigrants to the United States was quite small. In the census of 1990, 1,634,669 Americans listed Danish as their ancestry group. This represents only 0.7 percent of the total population of 248,709,873. Even in Iowa, which had more Danish American residents than any other state from 1890 to 1920, people born in Denmark made up little more than two percent of the total population. Danes were generally literate and understood the democratic process, were Protestant in their religion, and easily blended with the northern and western European majority. Because Danes offered little challenge to the more established Americans, they seldom encountered resistance.

TRADITIONS, CUSTOMS, AND BELIEFS

Danes have a variety of traditions and customs that have been adapted or preserved in Danish American society. Everyday life customs include men and women shaking hands with everyone when entering or leaving a group. Danes and Danish Americans take great pleasure in setting a proper table and following a proper etiquette. This often means using fine Danish porcelain from one of the two famous Danish porcelain makers, Royal Copenhagen or Bing and Grøndahl. Being a guest requires that one bring flowers for the hostess. When a guest meets the host or hostess shortly after being entertained, the proper greeting is *Tak for sidst* ("tuck for seest")—Thanks for the last time.

Entertaining and tradition merge in the many customs surrounding Christmas. Because of the dark Scandinavian winter nights, Christmas, with its message of hope, light, and love, is especially welcomed and celebrated in Denmark. Danish Christmas customs are also celebrated by Danish Americans. December begins with baking. No home is without at least seven different kinds of Christmas cookies. These treats are shared with guests, and it is customary to take decorated plates of cookies to friends and relatives. This custom is the origin of the well known porcelain Danish Christmas plates that can be found in many homes.

These Danish Americans are sampling the food at a 1995 ethnic festival.

The celebration of Christmas culminates on Christmas Eve, a holiday traditionally shared with close family. Usually the family attends church in the late afternoon and then returns to a feast of roast goose and all the trimmings. A special dessert is prepared: *risengrød* ("reesingroidth"), a rice pudding in which one whole almond is placed. The person who discovers the almond will have good luck throughout the coming year. After dinner, the family sees the decorated Christmas tree for the first time. It is lit with candles and decorated with paper cuttings of angels, woven straw ornaments, heart-shaped baskets, and strings of Danish flags. In Danish American homes, the tree is decorated earlier and lit with electric lights. The family joins hands and dances around the tree, singing favorite carols. Gifts are exchanged, and the family enjoys coffee and cookies. To assure happiness and good fortune, before the family goes to bed it is important to take a bowl of porridge to the *nisse* ("nisa")— the mythical little people of Denmark who inhabit the lofts and attics of homes.

CUISINE

Danes love to eat, and often do so six times a day. This includes morning and afternoon coffee and cookies and *natmad* ("nat-madth"), a snack eaten before going to bed. Many Danish Americans continue this routine. A Danish breakfast consists of an array of breads, cheeses, jellies and plenty of butter. This is often topped off with pastry that in no way resembles what has come to be known in America as a "Danish." This pastry is baked fresh, with flaky, golden brown crust, and rich fillings.

Lunch often includes open-faced sandwiches, or *smørrebrød* ("smoorbroidth"). These are artfully created to be both a feast for eye and palate. Combinations include: sliced, smoked beef, fried onions and a mayonnaise topping; carrots and peas mixed with mayonnaise topped with mushrooms; parboiled egg slices topped with anchovies or smoked eel; and a children's favorite, liverpaste and slices of pickled red beets, which is eaten like peanut butter and jelly sandwiches in the United

States. Beer, *sodavand* ("soda-van")—soda, and coffee are popular beverages.

The most important and time-consuming meal of the day is *middag* ("mid-da")—midday, though it is eaten in the evening. Danes linger for at least an hour over this meal. *Middag* might include stuffed pork, fish (often plaice or cod) or *frikadeller* ("fre-ka-della")—Danish meatballs of pork, beef, flour, and egg. The meal would also include *brunede kartofler* ("bru'-na-the-car-tof-ler")—potatoes browned in butter and sugar; *rødkål* ("roidth-coal")—red cabbage; marinated fresh cucumbers; beer or a glass of red wine; and a dessert of cookies and fruit pudding, *rød grød med fløde*.

Other popular Danish dishes served in Danish American communities are: *rullepølse* ("rol'-la-poolsa")—spiced, pressed veal; *medisterpølse* ("ma-dis'-ta-poolsa")—pork sausage; *sød suppe* ("sooth soopa")—sweet soup made with fruit; *æbleskiver* ("able skeever")—Danish pancake balls; and *kringler* ("cringla")—almond filled pastry.

Danes and Danish Americans welcome any excuse for gathering together and eating. Formal dinners are held at Christmas, confirmations, wedding anniversaries and "round" birthdays—birthdays that can be divided by ten. Formal dinners normally last at least four to five hours and include toasts, light-hearted speeches, singing, and much conversation.

TRADITIONAL COSTUMES

Danish peasant costumes were colorful, yet practical. A woman's costume consisted of headdress, scarf, outer bodice, knitted jacket, apron, shift, and leather shoes with clasps of silver or pewter. The scarf was often embroidered in bright colors of red and yellow on one side and with more somber, mourning colors on the other so that it could be reversed depending on the occasion. The cut and design of headdress, scarf, and apron reflected regional identities. Men wore hats or caps, a kirtle or knee-length coat, shirt, waistcoat, trousers, woolen stockings, and shoes or high boots. By the 1840s, these folk costumes of rural Denmark became a thing of the past. On special occasions in the Danish American community, some will dress in "traditional" costumes, but these often reflect a nostalgic recreation of the past rather than a true authenticity.

DANISH DANCES AND SONGS

Danish folk dancing mirrors other northern European countries with both spirited and courtly dances. On the Faeroe Islands, a stately line dance dates back to the time of the Vikings. Singing is a part of many Danish and Danish American gatherings. Popular are songs from the period of Danish Romanticism (1814-1850), which celebrate former national greatness or the gently rolling Danish countryside. The two Danish national anthems capture these important themes: *"Kong Christian stod ved højen mast"* (King Christian Stood by Lofty Mast) by Johannes Ewald (1743-1781) and *"Der er et yndigt land"* (There is a Lovely Land) by Adam Oehlenschlager (1779-1850).

INTERACTIONS WITH OTHER ETHNIC MINORITIES

Danish immigrants often interacted first with other Scandinavians and with the German American community. Because they shared beliefs, attitudes, and general customs similar to the dominant culture in America, they made the transition to life in the United States without having to change many of their traditions.

LANGUAGE

Danish is a North Germanic language closely related to Norwegian and Swedish, and is also related to the West Germanic languages, including German and English. Contemporary Danish has adopted many English and American words such as weekend, handicap, film, and hamburger. Danish, however, has also had an influence on English. When Danish Vikings settled in England in the ninth century and established the Danelaw, many of their words became a part of English. Examples are: by, fellow, hit, law, sister, take, thrive, and want. The English town of Rugby is Danish for "rye town," and the word "bylaw" means "town law." Modern Danish has three vowels not found in English: "æ" (pronounced as a drawn-out "ei" in eight); "ø" (pronounced as "oi" in coil or as "oo" in cool), and "å," formerly spelled "aa" (pronounced as "o" in or).

There is a popular saying among Danes that "Danish is not a language at all; it's a throat disease." Unlike the other Scandinavian languages, Danish makes use of the guttural "r" and the glottal stop, a sound produced by a momentary closure of the back of the throat followed by a quick release. The language is not as melodic as Norwegian or Swedish. Danes or Danish Americans challenge people who do not speak the language to say the name of a popular dessert, a fruit pudding made from raspberries or currants called, *rød grød med fløde* ("roidth groidth meth floodthe")—literally: red gruel with cream. The guttural "r"s and the "ø" sound, made deep in the back of the throat, make this phrase virtually impossible to say for someone who does not speak Danish.

Because the Danish language is similar to English in syntax and the use of regular and irregular verbs, Danish immigrants did not have as much difficulty learning English as many other immigrants did. Almost all Danish immigrants were literate when they arrived which also contributed to rapid linguistic assimilation.

GREETINGS AND OTHER POPULAR EXPRESSIONS

Though Danes quickly acquired English, many phrases and expressions remain popular and are understood within the Danish American community. Common greetings and other expressions include: *goddag* ("go'-day")—good day; *godmorgen* ("go'-mo'-ren")—good morning; *godaften* ("go'-af-ten")—good evening; *farvel* ("fa'-vel")—goodbye; *på gensyn* ("po gen-soon")—see you later; *værsgo* ("vairs-go")—please; or, would you be so kind?; *til lykke* ("til looka")—congratulations; *tak* ("tuck")—thanks; *mange tak* ("monga tuck")—many thanks; *velkommen* ("vel-komin")—welcome; *glædelig jul* ("gla-le yool")—Merry Christmas; *godt nytår* ("got newt'-or")—Happy New Year. When toasting each other, the Danes, like other Scandinavians, use the word *skål* ("skoal") which literally means "bowl." One popular tradition suggests that the expression was used when Vikings celebrated victory by drinking from the skulls of their enemy. A more civilized Danish word for which there is no exact English equivalent is *hyggelig* ("hoo'-ga-le"). *Hyggelig* describes a warm, cozy environment in which friends eat, drink and converse.

FAMILY AND COMMUNITY DYNAMICS

EDUCATION

Education has played an important role in the Danish American community. A significant early influence were folk high schools. Inspired by the writings of Bishop Nicolai Frederik Severin Grundtvig (1783-1872)—a Danish poet, pastor and educator—these schools offered an education that sought to instill a love of learning in its students, though they offered no diplomas and no tests or grades were given. Folk schools were established in Elk Horn, Iowa (1878-1899); Ashland, Michigan (1882-1888); West Denmark, Wisconsin (1884); Nysted, Nebraska (1887-1934); Tyler, Minnesota (1888-1935); Kenmare, North Dakota (1902-1916); and Solvang, California (1910-1931). Because the educational philosophy differed from many American institutions, folk high schools eventually ceased to exist. Grundtvig's philosophy lives on in adult education programs and in the work of the Highlander Research and Education Center in Tennessee which played an important role in the civil rights movement of the 1950s and 1960s. Elderhostel, a popular program offering one-week educational experiences on college and university campuses for senior citizens, has roots in the folk high school experience and the thoughts of Grundtvig. Two liberal arts colleges founded by Danish Americans are Dana College in Blair, Nebraska, and Grand View College, in Des Moines, Iowa.

HOLIDAYS CELEBRATED BY DANISH AMERICANS

In addition to Christmas, many Danish Americans celebrate *Grundlovsdag*, or Constitution Day on June 5, marking the date in 1849 when the modern Danish state was born. An unusual celebration held on the fourth of July in Denmark and attended by many Danish Americans is *Rebildfest*. It was begun by Danish Americans in 1912 and is billed as the largest celebration of American independence held outside the United States.

RELIGION

With the exception of the Mormons in Utah and small numbers of Methodists, Baptists, and Seventh Day Adventists, most Danish immigrants were Lutheran and at least nominal members of the *Folkekirke*, the Danish National Church. After the adoption of the liberal constitution of 1849, the Church of Denmark was no longer a state church; however, it has always been state-supported. For many years there was no established Danish Lutheran organization in the United States, and those immigrants who were religiously inclined frequently worshiped with

Norwegian or Swedish Lutherans. Eventually two clergymen from Denmark and some laymen met in Neenah, Wisconsin, in 1872 and organized what became the Danish Evangelical Lutheran Church. The church faced many difficulties, including slow growth. By one estimate, only about one out of every ten Danish immigrants joined a Danish Lutheran church.

A second problem involved the development within the Danish National Church of a factionalism which immigrants carried to the United States. On one side were the followers of the aforementioned Grundtvig, the Danish educator and church leader, who emphasized the Apostle's Creed and the sacraments. These people were called Grundtvigians. Their opponents were identified as members of the Inner Mission. They stressed Biblical authority, repentance, and the development of a personal faith. Eventually the theological disputes within the Danish Church in the United States grew so serious that in 1892 it was forced to close its seminary at West Denmark, Wisconsin. Two years later many of the Inner Mission members left the church and formed their own organization. In 1896 they joined with another Inner Mission group that had started a small Danish Lutheran church headquartered at Blair, Nebraska, in 1884. This new body called itself the United Danish Evangelical Lutheran Church. The divisions among Danish Lutherans in the United States weakened the church's role as a rallying point, thus contributing to the immigrant's rapid assimilation.

> "He who can do a little of everything gets along best. He must not shirk hard work, and he must not shirk being treated like a dog. He must be willing to be anyone's servant, just like any other newcomer here."
>
> Peter Sørensen, in a letter dated April 14, 1885.

The Danish Church (*Grundtvigian*) was more inclined than the United Danish Church to stress its immigrant heritage. It opened Grand View Seminary in Des Moines, Iowa. The seminary also offered non-theological courses and in 1938 it became an accredited junior college. Its seminary function ceased in 1959 and Grand View continues today as a four-year liberal arts college. The Danish Church and its 24,000 members joined with three non-Danish Lutheran bodies in 1962 to form the Lutheran Church in America.

The United Church (Inner Mission) operated Trinity Seminary (founded 1884) and Dana College on the same campus at Blair, Nebraska. In 1956 Trinity moved to Dubuque, Iowa, where four years later it merged with Wartburg Seminary. In 1976 Queen Margrethe II of Denmark came to Dana and gave the spring commencement address in recognition of the American Bicentennial. The 60,000-member United Church joined with German and Norwegian churches to form the American Lutheran Church in 1960.

In 1988, when the Lutheran Church in America and the American Lutheran Church merged to create the Evangelical Lutheran Church in America, the century-long organizational division among Danish Lutherans in the United States came to an end.

EMPLOYMENT AND ECONOMIC TRADITIONS

The majority of the Danes who immigrated to the United States looked to agriculture for a livelihood. Many who were farm laborers in Denmark soon became landowners in the United States. Danish immigrants contributed to American agriculture, particularly dairying, in a variety of ways. Danes had experience with farmers' cooperatives and helped spread that concept in the United States. The first centrifugal cream separator in the United States was brought to Iowa by a Dane in 1882. Danes worked as buttermakers, served as government inspectors, and taught dairy courses at agricultural colleges.

Young, single women often took jobs as domestic servants, but few remained single very long as they were in demand as spouses. Men who sought non-farm work found it in construction, manufacturing, and various business enterprises. Other than small concentrations in a Danish owned *terra cotta* factory in Perth Amboy, New Jersey, and in several farm equipment manufacturing companies in Racine, Wisconsin, urban Danes were rarely identified with a specific occupation.

POLITICS AND GOVERNMENT

Given their small numbers and widespread distribution across the United States, Danes have seldom been able to form any kind of voting bloc beyond local elections in a few rural areas. Nevertheless, politicians of Danish descent have served as governors of Iowa, Minnesota, Nebraska, and California. Several others have served in the United States Congress. In every election these Danish American politicians have had to depend upon non-Danish voters for a majority of their support. Danes have not displayed any collective allegiance to a particular political party.

Two events in the twentieth century involving Denmark have attracted significant political interest among Danish Americans. The first of these was the status of Schleswig after World War I. Danish Americans organized to lobby the administration of President Woodrow Wilson to ensure that a provision granting Schleswigers the right to vote on their status be included in any peace treaty with Germany. Accordingly, in February 1920, residents of North Schleswig voted to return to Denmark after 56 years of foreign rule. Danish Americans expressed considerable concern about the German occupation of Denmark during World War II. After the war many Americans sent relief parcels to their Danish relatives.

MILITARY

By one estimate nearly 30,000 Danish Americans served in the armed forces of the United States during World War I. During World War II, 195 members of the United Danish Evangelical Lutheran Church died in the service of their country—a sizable number for a church that had less than 20,000 adult members and only 192 congregations. Generally, it appears that Danish Americans were no more or less willing to serve in the military than other Americans.

RELATIONS WITH DENMARK

Relations between Denmark and the United States have been unusually cordial. In 1791 Denmark became the eighth nation to recognize the independence of the United States, and it has maintained uninterrupted diplomatic relations since 1801, longer than any other country. In 1916, by a margin of nearly two to one, Danes voted to approve sale of the Danish West Indies (the U.S. Virgin Islands) to the United States. During World War II the United States and Denmark signed a treaty authorizing the United States to build two air bases in Greenland. After the war the United States provided Denmark with $271 million in Marshall Plan aid. In 1949 both nations joined the North Atlantic Treaty Organization (NATO) and thereafter jointly operated several military installations in Greenland.

INDIVIDUAL AND GROUP CONTRIBUTIONS

ACADEMIA

Peter Sørensen "P.S." Vig (1854-1929), church leader and teacher, wrote six books on the Danish immigrant experience and contributed to and edited the two-volume *Danske i Amerika* (*Danes in America*), published circa 1908. Marcus Lee Hansen (1892-1938), who studied under the renowned American historian Frederick Jackson Turner, is acclaimed as a scholar who early understood the importance of the immigrant experience in American life; his book, *The Atlantic Migration*, was awarded the Pulitzer Prize for history in 1941. The preeminent historian, Henry Steele Commager (1902-) has written of the influence his maternal grandfather, the Danish born Adam Dan, had on him as a child; Dan was one of the founders of the Danish Lutheran Church in America and an important writer in the immigrant community. Alvin Harvey Hansen (1887-1975), a Harvard economist influenced by the economic theories of John Maynard Keynes, played a role in the formation of the Social Security System in 1935 and the Full Employment Act of 1946 that established the Council of Economic Advisors.

FILM, TELEVISION, AND THEATER

The most famous Danish American entertainer is Victor Borge (1909-). Fleeing Copenhagen after the Nazi occupation of Denmark in 1940, Borge came to New York; in 1941, a successful guest appearance on Bing Crosby's Kraft Music Hall radio program launched his career. Known as "The Clown Prince of the Piano," Borge has since entertained audiences with a unique blend of music and humor. Jean Hersholt (1886-1956) appeared in over 200 films between 1914 and 1955; he is best remembered for his creation in the 1930s of the popular radio character, "Dr. Christian." Another well-known actor of Danish descent is Buddy Ebsen (1908-), who starred in three long-running television series, "Davy Crockett," "The Beverly Hillbillies," and "Barnaby Jones." More recently, Leslie Nielsen (1926-), a descendant of Danish immigrants to Canada, has gained wide popularity in the *Naked Gun* films.

JOURNALISM

Jacob A. Riis (1849-1914), the most important Danish American journalist, fought for the rights of the poor; his work, *How the Other Half Lives* (1890), described the impoverished conditions of laborers in New York City. Riis had a powerful ally in the person of President Teddy Roosevelt. Two important newspaper men in the Danish American community were Christian Rasmussen (1852-1926) and Sophus Neble (1862-1931). Rasmussen, a Republican, founded or purchased a number of papers in Minnesota, Wisconsin, and Illinois, and his printing company, headquartered in Minneapolis, published magazines and books as well. Neble's newspaper, *Den Danske Pioneer* (*The Danish Pioneer*), published in Omaha, championed the Democratic Party and had the largest circulation of any Danish American newspaper, reaching an estimated readership of 100,000.

LITERATURE

A number of writers have described the Danish immigrant experience. Most, however, have written in Danish. Kristian Østergaard (1855-1931) wrote both poetry and fiction; his five novels combine fantastic tales of Indians, horse thieves, and bank robbers with accounts of Danish immigrants struggling to create Danish communities on the prairies. The poet, Anton Kvist (1878-1965), found audiences through the Danish American press; many of his poems were set to music and sung within Danish immigrant circles. Enok Mortensen (1902-1984) published several collections of stories, novels, and an important history, *The Danish Lutheran Church in America* (1967); his novel, *Den lange plovfure* (*The Long Plow Furrow*), published in Denmark in 1984, is the last novel by an immigrant who participated in the major wave of Danish immigration. The most important Danish American novelist writing in English was Sophus Keith Winther (1893-1983); three of his novels, *Take All to Nebraska* (1936), *Mortgage Your Heart* (1937), and *This Passion Never Dies* (1937), portray the struggles of the Grimsen family who arrives in Nebraska in the 1890s; the novels illustrate the darker side of the rural experience as fluctuating grain prices drive the family into bankruptcy. Julie Jensen McDonald's novel, *Amalie's Story* (1970), recounts the story of an immigrant

woman whose poor parents are forced to give her up for adoption. Later she finds success as an immigrant in the Danish American community in Iowa.

MUSIC AND DANCE

Lauritz Melchior (1890-1973), the great heroic tenor, won world-wide acclaim on European and American stages for his roles in the operas of Richard Wagner. Born in Copenhagen, Melchior began his career with the Metropolitan Opera in 1926; shortly before World War II, he immigrated to the United States with his German-born wife, settling in California where he starred in a number of films; he continued to perform with the Metropolitan Opera until his retirement in 1950. Peter Martin (1946-) first appeared as a guest artist with the New York City Ballet; he became the company's principal dancer in 1970, and in 1983 he was named ballet master and co-director of the company. Libby Larsen (1950-), an award-winning composer and the granddaughter of Danish immigrants, was named composer-in-residence with the Minnesota Orchestra in 1983.

POLITICS AND GOVERNMENT

Several Danish Americans have served multiple terms in the United States Congress. For example, Ben Jensen (1892-1970) represented Iowa's Seventh District from 1938 to 1964 while voters in Minnesota's Second District sent Ancher Nelsen (1904-) to Congress for eight terms between 1958 and 1974. Lloyd Bentsen (1921-), the grandson of a Danish immigrant to South Dakota, was elected to the House of Representatives from Texas in 1948; at the age of 27 he was then the youngest member of Congress. In 1970 Bentsen won election to the Senate, and in 1988, he was the vice-presidential candidate on the Democratic ticket headed by Michael Dukakis. President Bill Clinton appointed Bentsen as Secretary of the Treasury in 1992. Another high-profile member of the Clinton Cabinet, Attorney General Janet Reno (1938-), is also of Danish descent; her father, Henry Reno, was an immigrant who changed his surname from Rasmussen to Reno after his arrival in the United States; prior to her appointment, Reno had served as State Attorney in Dade County, Florida. Although she never reached full Cabinet rank, Esther (Eggertsen) Peterson (1906-), has held a variety of important governmental posts. An outspoken consumer advocate, Peterson was named by President John F. Kennedy as assistant Secretary of Labor and director of the Women's Bureau in the United States Department of Labor; in 1977 President Jimmy Carter appointed her as Special Assistant to the President for Consumer Affairs.

SCIENCE AND TECHNOLOGY

Max Henius (1859-1935), a chemist, specialized in fermentation processes; proud of his Danish heritage, he was the prime mover in founding the Danes Worldwide Archives in Ålborg, Denmark, and establishing the Rebild Celebration of the Fourth of July in Denmark. Niels Ebbesen Hansen (1866-1950), a horticulturist, did pioneering work in the development of drought resistant strains of alfalfa. Peter L. Jensen (1886?-1961) and an American partner invented the loudspeaker system and founded the Magnavox Company; later, he established the Jensen Radio Manufacturing Company, which makes Jensen Speakers. A Danish born blacksmith who settled in Nebraska, William Petersen (1882-1962) invented and registered the name VISE-GRIP which is manufactured by the Petersen Manufacturing Company. William S. Knudsen (1879-1947), who was born in Copenhagen, became president of General Motors in 1937 and was chosen by President Franklin D. Roosevelt to lead the development of defense production programs during World War II.

SPORTS

While there have been a number of Danish Americans of later generations who have played in professional sports, the most famous recent Danish American immigrant to play professionally is Morten Andersen (1960-), the kicker for the New Orleans Saints. Born in Denmark, Andersen came to the United States at the age of 17 as a high school exchange student; before coming to this country, he had never kicked a football. After the 1993 NFL season, Andersen was already fifteenth among the NFL's all-time leading scorers.

VISUAL ARTS

One of the most important monuments in the United States is Mount Rushmore National Memorial in South Dakota. The heads of presidents Washington, Jefferson, Lincoln and Theodore Roosevelt were sculpted by Gutzon Borglum (1867-1941), the son of Danish immigrants. Christian Guldager (1759-1826), the earliest of Danish American artists, painted George Washington's portrait in 1789. A Danish Mormon, Carl Christian Anton Christensen (1831-1912), created a panorama of works depicting important events in the history of the Mormon trek to Utah. Benedicte Wrensted (1859-1949), born in Hjørring, Denmark, photographed many Native Americans at her studio in Pocatello, Idaho. More recently, two artists, Olaf Seltzer (1877-1957) and Olaf Wieghorst (1899-1988) have been recognized for their depictions of the Old West. Marshall Fredericks (1908-) is a contemporary, award-winning sculptor of Danish descent who has exhibited in the United States and Europe.

MEDIA

PRINT

A comprehensive study of the role of the press in Danish immigrant life is Marion Marzolf's book, *The Danish-Language Press in America*, published by the Arno Press of New York in 1979. Marzolf explores the history of the two existing Danish language newspapers *Bien* and *Den Danske Pioneer* as well as a number of others which have ceased publication, illustrating how stories and readership reflected an assimilating ethnic group.

Bien (The Bee).

The only weekly Danish newspaper printed in the United States. Founded in 1882 in California, it continues to print stories in Danish and English on international news and news of Denmark and the United States. A special focus is on Danish American lodges and organizations on the west coast.

Contact: Poul Dalby Andersen, Editor.

Address: 1527 West Magnolia Boulevard, Burbank, California 91506.

Telephone: (818) 845-7300.

Church and Life (originally Kirke og Folk).

A monthly publication by the Danish Interest Conference of the Evangelical Lutheran Church in America. Articles often reflect the influence of the Danish church reformer, N.F.S. Grundtvig, and are published in both English and Danish.

Contact: Thorvald Hansen, Editor.

Address: 1529 Milton, Des Moines, Iowa 540316.

Telephone: (515) 262-5274.

Den Danske Pioneer (The Danish Pioneer).
The oldest Danish newspaper published in the United States, it was founded in Omaha, Nebraska, in 1872. Because of its liberal agenda it was banned in Denmark between 1887 and 1898. In 1958, the paper was sold and moved to Illinois where today it is published bi-weekly and carries news of the Danish American community and stories of interest from contemporary Denmark in both Danish and English.

Contact: Chris Steffensen, Editor.

Address: Bertlesen Publishing Company, Glen Lake Road, Hoffman Estates, Illinois 60195.

Telephone: (708) 882-2552.

RADIO AND TELEVISION

While there has been no radio or television program devoted specifically to a Danish speaking audience, individuals of Danish descent have made important contributions to American media. The A. C. Nielsen Company, founded in 1923 by Arthur C. Nielsen, Sr., pioneered media market listener surveys for radio and television. The Nielsen Ratings have become an integral part of programming decisions both by the networks and cable companies. Bill and Scott Rasmussen, a father and son team with roots in Chicago's Danish American community, founded the Entertainment and Sports Programming Network (ESPN) in 1979.

ORGANIZATIONS AND ASSOCIATIONS

Danish American Chamber of Commerce and Danish American Society (DACC and DAS).
The DACC is an organization of over 200 business leaders, firms, and institutions that promotes commercial relations between the United States and Denmark and seeks to avoid duplication of governmental activities. The DAS is an affiliated society sponsoring cultural events. Separate organizations of the Chamber of Commerce exist in Chicago and Los Angeles.

Contact: Werner Valeur-Jensen, DACC Board Chairman; or Mrs. Neel Halpern, DAS President.

Address: 1 Dag Hammarskjold Plaza, 885 Second Avenue, 18th Floor, New York, New York 10017.

Telephone: (212) 980-6240.

Danish American Heritage Society (DAHS).
Founded in 1977, the DAHS has a membership of 650 individuals across the United States. Its purpose is to promote an interest in Danish culture, heritage, and language and to encourage research in the life, culture, and history of Danish Americans. The society publishes a journal, *The Bridge*, and a newsletter.

Contact: Gerald Rasmussen, President.

Address: 29681 Dane Lane, Junction City, Oregon 97448.

Telephone: (503) 998-8562.

Danish Brotherhood in America (DBA).
Founded in 1882 in Omaha, Nebraska, the DBA is a fraternal association of 8,000 members, featuring social activities celebrating the Danish American heritage and offering life and health insurance to members. In 1995 the DBA is proposing a merger of its insurance functions with a larger fraternal benefit society while retaining its name and independent lodge structure.

Contact: Jerome Christensen.

Address: 1323 Wright Street, Blair, Nebraska 68008.

Telephone: (402) 426-5894.

Danish Interest Conference of the Evangelical Lutheran Church of America (DIC).
Founded in 1962 when the Danish Evangelical Lutheran in America merged with several other Lutheran synods, the DIC seeks to preserve Danish contributions to the Lutheran heritage. A meeting is held annually at the Danebod Folk High School in Tyler, Minnesota.

Contact: Roland Jespersen, President.

Address: 116 North Seventh Street, Box 376, Eldridge, Iowa 52748.

Telephone: (319) 285-4693.

Danish Sisterhood in America (DSA).
Founded in 1883 at a time when the Danish Brotherhood did not accept women as members, the DSA continues as an active social organization of 3,200 members, celebrating Danish heritage and supporting education through scholarships.

Contact: Karen Favero, National Secretary.

Address: 3002 192nd Street, N.E., Seattle, Washington 98155.

Telephone: (206) 364-0994.

Rebild National Park Society, Inc.

Founded in 1912, this society of over 1,000 members supports what is acclaimed as the largest observation of American independence outside the United States. The festival is held annually on the Fourth of July in Rebild National Park, just outside the city of Ålborg, Denmark.

Contact: Erik Meyer, Corporate Secretary.

Address: 1788 North Fern Street, Orange, California 92667.

Telephone: (714) 637-8407.

Society for the Advancement of Scandinavian Studies.

With more than 600 members in the academic communities in the United States and Scandinavia, it publishes the respected journal, *Scandinavian Studies*.

Contact: Dr. Terje Leiren.

Address: Department of Scandinavian Studies, DL-20, University of Washington, Seattle, Washington 98195.

Telephone: (206) 543-1510.

MUSEUMS AND RESEARCH CENTERS

Danes Worldwide Archives.

Founded by Danish Americans in 1932 to record the history of Danes who immigrated to other countries, the archives contain letters, manuscripts, diaries, biographies, photographs, tape-recorded interviews, and over 10,000 titles related to Danish emigration. Also available are the emigration lists compiled by the Copenhagen police between 1860 and 1940 and microfilms of church records from most Danish parishes. There is a charge of $25 (U.S.) for requests received by mail or telephone.

Contact: Birgit Flemming Larsen.

Address: Ved Vor Frue Kirke, P.O. Box 1731, DK-9100 Ålborg, Denmark.

Telephone: 45 98 12 57 93.

Danish Immigrant Archives-Dana College.

Contains an extensive collection of books in Danish published in the United States, as well as periodicals, newspapers, journals, and letters relating to Danish immigration. The religious emphasis is on Danish Lutherans influenced by the more pietistic Inner Mission movement. Special holdings include the Lauritz Melchior, Sophus Keith Winther, and Hansen-Mengers Collections. Genealogy is not a focus of the archives.

Contact: Sharon Jensen.

Address: 2848 College Drive, Blair, Nebraska 68008-1099.

Telephone: (402) 426-7300.

Danish Immigrant Archives-Grand View College.

A repository for books, periodicals, letters, documents, and memoirs relating to Danish immigration. The archives' religious emphasis is on those Danish Lutherans influenced by N.F.S. Grundtvig, and the archives include a special N.F.S. Grundtvig Studies Collection. Genealogy is not a focus of the archives.

Contact: Rudolph Jensen.

Address: 1351 Grandview Avenue, Des Moines, Iowa 50316-1599.

Telephone: (515) 263-2800.

Danish Immigrant Museum.

Tells the story of the life and culture of Danish immigrants with displays of house furnishings, costumes, tools, church furniture, photographs, and many other items. The collection contains over 8,000 artifacts and includes a family history room for researching genealogy. Situated in Elk Horn, Iowa, the museum is located in an area settled by Danish immigrants during the late nineteenth century.

Contact: Director.

Address: Box 178, Elk Horn, Iowa 51531.

Telephone: (712) 764-7001.

SOURCES FOR ADDITIONAL STUDY

Danish Emigration to the U.S.A., edited by Birgit Flemming Larsen and Henning Bender. Ålborg, Denmark: Danes Worldwide Archives, 1992.

Hale, Frederick Hale. *Danes in North America.* Seattle: University of Washington Press, 1984.

Hvidt, Kristian. *Flight to America.* New York: Academic Press, 1975.

———. *Danes Go West.* Skørping, Denmark: Rebild National Park Society, Inc., 1976.

MacHaffie, Ingeborg, and Margaret Nielsen. *Of Danish Ways*. Minneapolis: Dillon Press, Inc., 1976.

Mussari, Mark. *The Danish Americans*. New York: Chelsea House Publishers, 1988.

Nielsen, George. *The Danish Americans*. Boston: G. K. Hall & Co., 1981.

Petersen, Peter L. *The Danes in America*. Minneapolis: Lerner Publication Company, 1987.

Riis, Jacob A. *The Making of an American*. New York: Grosset & Dunlap, 1901.

Stilling, Niels Peter, and Anne Lisbeth Olsen. *A New Life*. Ålborg, Denmark: Danes Worldwide Archives, 1994.

DUTCH AMERICANS

by
Herbert J. Brinks

Mainstream culture has either attracted Dutch ethnics out of their enclaves or the surrounding culture has so altered the ethnic communities that they can no longer flourish on ethnic exclusivity.

OVERVIEW

Located in northwestern Europe, the Netherlands is bounded to the east by Germany, to the south by Belgium, and to the north and west by the North Sea. The Netherlands has about 16,000 square miles of landmass, making the country roughly equal in size to New Jersey and Maryland combined. The nation supports a population density of about 1,000 people per square mile. A coastal region, incorporating two major harbors (Rotterdam and the Hudson Bay), the Netherlands' economy is heavily dependent upon shipping.

During the New Stone Age (c. 8000-3500 B.C.), the Netherlands' landmass roughly equaled its current 16,000 square miles, but by 55 B.C., when Rome's legions gained hegemony in the area, rising sea levels and erosion from winds, tides, and rivers reduced the coastal areas by at least 30 percent. Since then, the Dutch have employed various strategies to regain the land lost to the sea. Simple earthen hills (village sites) linked by dikes long preceded the complex drainage systems that drain the enclosed lowlands today with electrically powered pumps.

Windmills, preserved currently as historic monuments, pushed water up and out of the Netherlands for some five centuries (1400-1900) because viable habitation of the western provinces (South Holland, Zeeland, and North Holland) required flood control along the Rhine River delta and along the North Sea's shifting shoreline. The massive Delta Works, stretching across the islands of South Holland and Zeeland, was constructed following disastrous floods in 1953 to protect the Netherlands from storms and high water. Because the most productive farm land together with the most populous commercial and industrial districts lie as much as 20 feet below sea level, hydrological science has become a hallmark of Dutch achievement.

HISTORY

While historians believe that nomadic peoples hunted and fished in the Netherlands as early as 16,000 B.C., the area was not settled until about 4000 B.C. Around 60 B.C., Roman armies under Julius Caesar conquered the Saxon, Celtic, and Frisian groups occupying the Netherlands at that time. The Romans built roads and made improvements to existing dikes in the lowlands. In the A.D. 400s, as Rome weakened, the Germanic Franks conquered the area and later introduced the Dutch to Christianity.

From the 700s to the 1100s, the Dutch were subjected to violent raids by Viking sailors from Scandinavia. During this unstable period, power passed to local nobles, whose arms and castles offered protection in return for rent, labor, and taxes. This system gradually declined when, beginning in the 1300s, much of the Netherlands was taken by the dukes of Burgundy, a powerful French feudal dynasty. In the early 1500s, Charles V, Duke of Burgundy, inherited the thrones of both Spain and the Holy Roman Empire. While he was well-liked by the Dutch, his successors were not. In 1568 the Dutch prince, William the Silent (1533-1584), led a rebellion against the Spanish Habsburgs (Phillip II, 1527-1621), initiating the Eighty Years' War (1568-1648). Although William was assassinated in 1584, his efforts eventually resulted in Dutch independence. For this reason, he is often regarded as the Father of the Netherlands.

Resistance to the Spanish united the lowlanders, who previously had local (rather than national) loyalties. In 1579 the Union of Utrecht unified the seven northern lowland provinces. (Their 1580 agreement, essentially a defensive alliance, served as a national constitution until 1795.) Two years later (1581), those provinces declared the Netherlands an independent country. Meanwhile, Dutch exploration and trade had flourished and by the 1620s, the Dutch shipping fleet was the world's largest. This "Golden Age" lasted until the 1700s, after which the Netherlands underwent a gradual decline as the balance of colonial power shifted in favor of England. The beginning of this change can be traced to the 1664 sale of New Netherland (New York) to England.

MODERN ERA

The Netherlands was occupied by the French during the Napoleonic Era (1795-1813). Afterwards, in 1814, descendants of the House of Orange established a monarchy, which was reformed successively in 1848, 1896, and 1919 to create a broadly based democracy. Today, the Netherlands has a constitutional monarchy with a bicameral, multi-party system administered by a premier and a coalition cabinet of ministers. Queen Beatrix (1938-), the titular head of state, performs largely ceremonial duties.

THE FIRST DUTCH SETTLERS IN AMERICA

Following English explorer Henry Hudson's 1609 exploration of the Hudson River, a new joint stock company, the Dutch West India Company (1621), gained colonization rights in the Hudson River area and founded New Netherland (New York). The Dutch West India Company was chartered specifically to trade in the New World, where the Dutch had acquired colonies in Brazil, the Caribbean, and the east coast of North America. Pursuing its commercial interest in New Netherland, the company established Fort Orange (Albany), Breuckelen (Brooklyn), Vlissingen (Flushing), and in Delaware, Swanendael (Lewes). In 1624 the company also established the Dutch Reformed Church (the Reformed Church in America) which has exercised a significant influence in the Dutch American community.

In New Amsterdam (New York City) Governor Peter Stuyvesant (1592-1672) attempted to eliminate all worship apart from that of the Dutch Reformed Church, but his governing board in Amsterdam opposed the policy as detrimental to commerce. Like Amsterdam itself, New Amsterdam did not enforce rules which prohibited worship to Jews, Catholics, and others. Thus, New Amsterdam flourished and, as New York City, it continues to host a diverse populace with widely varying religious expressions.

After the British captured New Netherland in 1664, Dutch immigration virtually ceased but England imposed no severe restraints on the

In this 1921 photograph a
Dutch woman and her
children prepare to depart
from the S.S. *Vedic* in
New York City.

Dutch and the vast majority remained in New York. By 1790 they numbered about 100,000 and, in addition to New York City, they clustered in towns and villages scattered along the Hudson and Mohawk Rivers. In New Jersey they established towns beside the Hackensack, Passaic, and Raritan Rivers. In such places they dominated the local culture, spoke Dutch, and established both Reformed churches and day schools. After the American Revolution, the Dutch more rapidly assimilated into the dominant Anglo-American culture by adopting English for worship, by attending public schools, and by attaining social status within the general culture. Consequently, when a new wave of Dutch immigrants came to the United States in the 1840s, they found few in New York or elsewhere who spoke Dutch.

SIGNIFICANT IMMIGRATION WAVES

Nineteenth-century Dutch immigration, numbering about 200 people annually before 1845, increased that year to 800 and averaged 1,150 annually over the next decade. That movement, which stemmed from religious and economic discontent in the Netherlands; a potato famine (1845-1846) and high unemployment combined with a division in the Reformed Church that pitted conservative Calvinists against the increasingly liberal State Church, forced many Dutch to emigrate. At the same time, three clergymen organized colonies on the Midwestern frontier. In 1848 Father Theodore J. Van den Broek (1783-1851) established a Catholic community in Little Chute, near Green Bay, Wisconsin. Two conservative Reformed pastors, Albertus Van Raalte (1811-1876) and Hendrik P. Scholte (1805-1868) founded respectively, Holland, Michigan (1847) and Pella, Iowa (1847). Once these communities were established, printed brochures and private correspondence triggered a persistent flow of newcomers until 1930, when immigration quotas and the Great Depression closed out that 85-year period of migration. During that era, Dutch immigration followed typical northern European patterns, increasing or decreasing in response to economic prospects at home or in the United States. With peaks in the mid-1870s, the early 1880s and 1890s, and again from 1904 to 1914, a total of about 400,000 Netherlanders immigrated to the United States between 1845 and 1930.

Seventy-five to 80 percent of these immigrants originated from rural provinces surrounding the Netherlands' urban core. They settled mainly in the Midwest, clustering where the original colonies had been established in Wisconsin, Michigan, and Iowa. They also settled in and around Chicago, in Paterson, New Jersey and in Grand Rapids, Michigan. Those with hopes of becoming independent farmers moved West and gained land under the Homestead Act, which encouraged settlement in northwestern Iowa, South Dakota, Minnesota, Montana, Washington, and California. In nearly every settlement,

they organized and had prominent roles in local towns where they established churches, private schools, and farm-related businesses of all sorts. After 1900, when the best homestead lands were occupied, the Dutch selected urban industrial locations and formed solid ethnic enclaves in Grand Rapids, Chicago, and Paterson. By 1930 Dutch immigrant communities stretched from coast to coast across the northern tier of states, but they concentrated most heavily around the southern half of Lake Michigan, from Muskegon, Michigan, through Chicago and north to Green Bay, Wisconsin.

After World War II, when a war-ravaged economy and a severe housing shortage caused a third of the Dutch populace to seriously consider emigration, a new wave of 80,000 immigrants came to the United States. The Dutch government encouraged emigration and sought to increase the annual U.S. immigration quota of 3,131. Consequently, under special provisions of the Walter-Pastori Refugee Relief Acts (1950-1956), about 18,000 Dutch Indonesians were admitted to the United States. These Dutch Colonials, who had immigrated to the Netherlands after 1949 when Indonesia became independent, settled primarily in California, the destination of many other postwar Dutch immigrants. The 1970 U.S. Census recorded the highest number (28,000) of foreign-born Dutch in California, while seven other states—Michigan, New York, New Jersey, Illinois, Washington, Florida, and Iowa—hosted nearly the whole 50,000 balance. Apart from Florida, these states had been traditional strongholds for Dutch Americans.

ACCULTURATION AND ASSIMILATION

During the chief era of Dutch immigration, 1621-1970, religious and ideological viewpoints structured the character of public institutions in the Netherlands. In the Dutch Republic (1580-1795), Reformed Protestants controlled the government, schools, public charities, and most aspects of social behavior. Although both Catholics and Jews practiced their faith without hindrance, they could not hold public offices. Then, beginning in the 1850s, when the national constitution permitted a multi-party system, political parties grew from constituencies identified with specific churches or ideologies. The Reformed, the Catholic, and the

Socialist groups each organized one or more parties. In addition, each group established separate schools, labor unions, newspapers, recreational clubs, and even a schedule of television programs to serve constituencies. Dutch Americans recreated parts of that structure wherever they clustered in sufficient numbers to sustain ethnic churches, schools, and other institutions. Since the 1960s, these enclaved groups have begun to embrace mainstream American institutions more rapidly and they have altered the goals of their private organizations to attract and serve a multicultural constituency.

Religious and cultural separation flourished primarily in the ethnically dense population centers of Reformed Protestants. Dutch Catholics, apart from those in the Green Bay area, were not concentrated in large numbers. Instead they joined other Catholic parishes in Cincinnati, St. Louis, New York City, and elsewhere. Even around Green Bay, Dutch Catholics intermarried readily with Catholics of other ethnicities. Lacking large and cohesive enclaves, Dutch Catholics were neither able nor inclined to re-establish ethnic institutions in America. Similarly, Dutch Jews settled mainly in cities such as New York, Philadelphia, and Boston, where they assimilated the social and religious patterns of much larger Jewish groups from Germany, Russia, and Poland. One prominent Dutch rabbi in New York, Samuel Myer Isaacs (1804-1878), attempted to maintain a Dutch identity by founding a synagogue, a school, and the orthodox periodical *The Messenger*, but these institutions faltered after his death.

Currently, the major strongholds of Dutch American separatism are fragmenting rapidly. Reformed churches, schools, colleges, theological schools and even retirement facilities for the aged are campaigning to gain a full spectrum of non-Dutch clients. Marriage outside of the ethnic group has become common and media-driven popular culture has altered traditional behavior among all age groups. In short, mainstream culture has either attracted Dutch ethnics out of their enclaves or the surrounding culture has so altered the ethnic communities that they can no longer flourish on ethnic exclusivity.

There are no aggressively mean-spirited or demeaning stereotypes of Dutch Americans. They are correctly perceived as valuing property, inclined to small business ventures, and culturally conservative with enduring loyalties to their churches, colleges, and other institutions. The perception that they are exceptionally clannish is also accurate, but that characteristic is demonstrated primarily among Reformed Protestants. Other ethnic stereotypes—financial penury, a proclivity for liquor and tobacco, and a general humorlessness—reflect individual rather than group features.

CUISINE

The earlier immigrants' plain diets (potatoes, cabbage and pea soup with little meat beyond sausage and bacon) could not compete with America's meat-oriented menu. In general, Dutch foods are not rich or exotic. Potatoes and vegetables combined with meat in a Dutch oven, fish, and soups are typical. The Indonesian rice table, now widely popular in Dutch American kitchens, came from Dutch colonials. Holiday pastries flavored with almond paste are a major component of Dutch baked goods. Social gatherings thrive on coffee and cookies with brandy-soaked raisins during the Christmas season.

TRADITIONAL COSTUMES

In the Netherlands traditional costumes vary by region, demonstrating local loyalties, once paramount, that still flavor Dutch life. Men often dressed in baggy black pants and colorful, wide-brimmed hats, while women wore voluminous black dresses, colorfully embroidered bodices, and lace bonnets. Such costumes have been replaced by modern clothes in the Netherlands. In the United States, traditional dress is reserved for special occasions.

HOLIDAYS CELEBRATED BY DUTCH AMERICANS

Dutch Jews and Christians generally celebrate the holidays associated with their particular religious affiliation. However, many postwar immigrants have preserved a distinctive pattern of Christmas observance which separates gift exchanges on St. Nicholas Day (December 6) from the religious celebrations of December 25.

HEALTH AND MENTAL HEALTH ISSUES

There are no specifically Dutch related medical problems or conditions. Health and life insurance, either private or from institutional sources, has long ago replaced the need for immigrant aid cooperatives which once provided modest death benefits. Reformed churches regularly assisted widows, orphans, and chronically dependent people prior to the Social Security system. In isolated cases, church funds are still used to supplement the incomes of especially needy persons or to assist those with catastrophic needs. For mental diseases, a cluster of Reformed denominations established the Pine Rest Psychiatric Hospital in 1910, but that institution now serves the general public. Other institutions, the Bethany Christian Home adoption agency and the Bethesda tuberculosis sanitorium, have also been transformed to serve a multicultural clientele.

LANGUAGE

In general, the Dutch language is no longer used by Dutch Americans. The vast majority of postwar immigrants have adopted English and the small number of immigrants who have arrived since the 1960s are bilingual because English is virtually a second language in the Netherlands. Still, some Dutch words and expressions have survived: *vies* ("fees") denotes filth and moral degradation; *benauwd* ("benout") refers to feelings of anxiety, both physical and emotional; *flauw* ("flou") describes tasteless foods, dull persons, and faint feeling; and *gezellig* ("gezelik") is a comfortable social gathering. Typical Dutch greetings, *dag* ("dag"), which means "good day" and *hoe gaat het* ("who gat het") for "how are you doing," are no longer in common usage in the United States.

There are small groups of Dutch Americans—descendants of nineteenth century immigrants—who have maintained provincial Dutch dialects (including dialects from Overijssel, Drenthe, and Zeeland) that have all but disappeared in the modern-day Netherlands. Consequently, some Dutch linguists have traveled to western Michigan and other Dutch American strongholds to record these antiquated dialects.

Formal Dutch remained vital among the immigrants until the 1930s, due partly to its use for worship services, but World War I patriotism, which prohibited the use of German, Dutch and other languages, signaled the demise of Dutch usage in Reformed churches. Long before World War I, however, Dutch Americans, and especially their American-born children, began to reject the ancestral language. It was well understood and frequently asserted among them that economic opportunities were greater for those who spoke English. Consequently, daily wage earners, business people, and even farm hands adopted English as quickly as possible. Formal Dutch is currently used only in commemorative worship services, and in the language departments of several colleges founded by Dutch Americans. Among these, only Calvin College in Grand Rapids, Michigan, offers a major in Dutch language and literature.

FAMILY AND COMMUNITY DYNAMICS

Colonial New Netherland (New York), like Jamestown and other trading post colonies, attracted single men, few women, and even fewer families. Every account of New Amsterdam (New York City) refers to its rough and raucous social character—the products of an astonishing mixture of people, languages, and behavior which severely tested polite standards of social order. By the time of the British conquest in 1664, however, the arrival of immigrant women and the high colonial birth rate provided a population base for marriages and family life.

When the British took formal control of the colony, the Dutch populace, about 8,000 people, struggled to retain their cultural identity. Until about 1720, Dutch ethnics married within the group, worshiped together, and joined hands for economic and political objectives. Family cohesion was at the core of this ethnic vitality, but by 1800, Dutch ethnicity had weakened because economic and cultural bonds were established outside of the ethnic subculture. These bonds eventually led to marriages across ethnic lines.

Apart from New York City, in the many towns founded by the Dutch (such as Albany and Kinderhoek, New York, and Hackensack and New Brunswick, New Jersey) ethnic solidarity persisted well into the nineteenth century. In such places Dutch families adhered to the values instilled by Reformed churches and their day schools. Men dominated all the public institutions, while women managed typically large households with six or seven children. Domestic life, including the education of girls, depended largely on Dutch homemakers. Girls and boys gained basic skills from part-time teachers who were also expected to indoctrinate their students for church membership. Formal education continued for boys, who excelled academically, usually in the form of an apprentice relationship with lawyers, pastors, and business firms. Women received the bulk of their training from mothers

and older female relatives. By 1800 most of the parochial schools were replaced by public instruction, which led to an increase in the level of formal education for girls.

In the nineteenth century, most Dutch immigrants to America had family members who had preceded them. The newcomers (80 percent) came largely from rural areas and resettled in rural America where extended families were frequently reconstituted. Siblings, parents, and even grandparents regularly joined the first settlers, contributing to the family-oriented character of that ethnic subculture. The original colonies in Michigan, Iowa, Illinois, and Wisconsin spawned more than one hundred similarly rural towns and villages which attracted successive waves of farmers, farm hands, and craftspeople. When Dutch immigration shifted from rural to urban destinations (1890-1930), the newcomers clustered in enclaves that grew once again when extended families reunited in places like Paterson, New Jersey; Grand Rapids, Michigan; and the Chicago area. These Dutch American communities still exist, but the urban enclaves have regrouped in suburban areas, while many farmers have moved either to ethnic towns or suburban neighborhoods. Throughout its history, the Dutch subculture has been sustained by a complex institutional structure of churches, schools, homes for the aged, recreational organizations, and small businesses.

Private schools, which were especially attractive to devoted traditionalists, provided educational opportunities without a notable gender bias, but most women became housewives and supported the male-dominated institutions which served the ethnic subculture. Since the 1960s, Dutch American women have moved beyond the teaching, secretarial, nursing, and homemaking professions into medicine, law, business, and ecclesiastical positions.

The new infusion of 80,000 Dutch immigrants, who arrived after World War II (1946-1956), reinvigorated Dutch ethnicity across the continent. It is more from them than their nineteenth-century predecessors that ethnic foods and customs have been introduced to the Dutch American community.

RELIGION

Neither Dutch Catholics nor Jews have retained discernible ethnic practices in their religious exercises. Both groups are part of international organizations which, because they used either Latin or Hebrew in formal rituals, were not drawn into major controversies regarding vernacular language usage in worship. Furthermore, due to their general dispersion, Dutch Catholics and Jews have had few opportunities to dominate either a parish or a synagogue. Instead they have worshiped and intermarried readily within multi-ethnic religious communities. Furthermore, Dutch Jews and Catholics have not acted in concert to support particular branches of Judaism or specific viewpoints within the Roman Catholic Church. Even the Dutch Catholic stronghold around Green Bay, Wisconsin, has become ethnically diverse, including French, German, and Flemish Catholics. One village, Little Chute, however, does continue to promote its Dutch ethnicity with a mid-September celebration (*kermis*), featuring a Dutch-costume parade, games, and craft exhibits. And Holland, Michigan, hosts its annual tulip festival in the spring.

By contrast, Dutch Protestants, most of whom affiliated with a cluster of Reformed churches, have spawned a long history of controversy regarding language usage, doctrinal interpretations, and liturgical expressions—all issues that were intimately related to cultural adaptation. In the Colonial Era the Dutch Reformed Church experienced crippling divisions (1737-1771) due to conflicting views of ordination and theological education. One group favored continued interdependence with church authorities in the Netherlands (the Classis of Amsterdam), that the American party, led by Theodore Frelinghuysen (1692-1742), promoted education and clerical ordination at "home" in the colonies. Then, in 1792, the Dutch Reformed Church became an independent denomination known as the Reformed Protestant Dutch Church (RCA). With that the RCA moved toward mainline status by adopting English, cooperating with other major church groups (Presbyterian, Methodist, and Episcopal), and participating in interdenominational campaigns to establish churches on the Midwestern frontier.

In the late 1840s about 3,000 Dutch Protestant immigrants settled in Michigan, Illinois, and Wisconsin, and by 1850 a large majority of these newcomers became affiliated with the New York-based RCA. The immigrants' spiritual patriarch, Albertus Van Raalte, had contacted the RCA's leaders before immigrating, and because he found them both helpful and doctrinally compatible, he and his followers united with the RCA. Some Midwestern immigrants, however, objected to this fusion; they initiated a separatist movement in 1857 which became the Christian Reformed Church (CRC).

Throughout the next hundred years, the two denominations pursued different strategies for cultural adaptation. The RCA acquired American church programs, including the revival, the Sunday school movement, and ecumenical cooperation, while neglecting its Netherlandic connec-

tions and traditions. The CRC, however, remained loyal to its religious cohorts in the Netherlands. That posture was marked by its general use of Dutch until the 1920s, and by the CRC's efforts to recreate Calvinistic schools and other institutions on the Dutch model. In this practice they followed the views of Dr. Abraham Kuyper (1837-1920), the most prominent Reformed leader in the Netherlands. Consequently, the CRC attracted a majority of the Reformed immigrants who arrived between 1880 and 1920.

Since the 1960s and especially during the period from 1985 to 1995, the RCA and CRC have become increasingly similar. Netherlandic theology and culture no longer influence the CRC significantly and the denomination increasingly emulates the liturgical and theological ethos of conservative evangelical groups affiliated with the National Association of Evangelicals. Although the RCA, with membership in the World Council of Churches, is more broadly ecumenical than the CRC, the two denominations have appointed a joint committee to encourage cooperation. At the same time, the growing tide of congregationalism has diminished denominational cohesion among them so that, like American political parties, the two denominations contain a wide spectrum of viewpoints. Neither denomination, then, can be labeled exclusively liberal or conservative.

The prospect for an eventual reunification of the RCA and CRC is good. At present their respective clergymen, theological professors, and parishioners move freely across denominational boundaries, and their parishioners have a long history of acting jointly to establish nursing homes, retirement facilities, and mental health institutions. The two denominations proclaim identical confessions of faith and no barriers restrict their mutual participation in sacramental rites. They are divided primarily by traditions, which are becoming increasingly irrelevant due to a rapid assimilation of America's mainstream religious attitudes and values.

EMPLOYMENT AND ECONOMIC TRADITIONS

Free enterprise capitalism was introduced to the United States by the joint stock companies that colonized the eastern seaboard. The New Netherland Colony (New York) exemplified that phenomenon just as obviously as Jamestown and the

New England Company. Understandably, then, Dutch immigrants have never been seriously disoriented by economic procedures in the United States. Virtually the whole populace of New Amsterdam and its surrounding areas was defined by its relationship to the joint stock company. Early Dutch immigrants were stockholders, officers, and employees, or traders operating illegally on the fringes of the company's jurisdiction. In all these cases, including the farmers who provisioned the trading posts, small and large businesses dominated daily life in New Amsterdam.

Like others with roots in the Colonial Era, Dutch merchants, farmers, and land speculators benefited from being among the first to invest in the New World. Families such as the Van Rensselaers, Schuylers, and Roosevelts quickly joined the ranks of prominent Americans. By contrast, Cornelius Vanderbilt left a small farm to become a captain of great wealth 150 years after his ancestors immigrated to America in 1644. In fact, for all of the early Dutch Americans, as well as nineteenth-century immigrants, self-employment and economic security were major objectives.

Throughout most of the nineteenth century, Dutch immigrants preferred agriculture as the means to economic independence. Because 80 percent of them were farm hands, day laborers, small farmers, and village craftsmen, they readily became self-employed farmers either on inexpensive government land or, after 1862, on free homestead land until about 1900.

Dutch immigrants arriving in the twentieth century were frequently employed in factories, the construction trades, and garden farming. But during the prosperous 1950s, many if not most Dutch Americans developed small family businesses—construction, trucking, repair shops, and retailing. They ranged from door-to-door vendors of eggs and garden farm produce to developers of supermarket chains. Few were unionized shop workers. Supported by the G.I. Bill of Rights (1944), many Dutch American veterans acquired college and professional training to enter law, medicine, dentistry, and teaching so that today nearly every Dutch American family has post graduate professionals among its children and grandchildren. Those who remain in agriculture (less than ten percent) cultivate large farms. For non-professionals, incomes average about $30,000 and for the 50 percent who have attended college and professional schools, incomes are between $30,000 and $100,000. Home ownership, usually in suburbs or small towns, is a common feature of the Dutch American community.

POLITICS AND GOVERNMENT

The vast majority of Dutch Americans are Republicans but they are usually not political activists. During the Anglo-Boer War (1899-1902), Dutch Americans organized to influence U.S. foreign policy in favor of the South African Boers. Because they distrusted Great Britain, the Dutch resisted Woodrow Wilson's pro-British policies prior to World War I. But when war broke out, they did not resist the draft. Instead, to demonstrate their loyalty, they enlisted, bought war bonds, and adopted English. During that era, religious and educational leaders promoted patriotism, which has remained vibrant to the present.

In places where the Dutch are concentrated, especially in western Michigan and northwestern Iowa, they have elected Dutch Americans to local, state and national offices. With few exceptions, Republican loyalty has not been breached by ethnic cohesion.

"We all have our pet notions as to the particular evil which is `the curse of America,' but I always think that Theodore Roosevelt came closest to the real curse when he classed it as a lack of thoroughness."

Dutch immigrant Edward Bok, from his Pulitzer Prize-winning account of his editorial career, *The Americanization of Edward Bok*, 1920.

INDIVIDUAL AND GROUP CONTRIBUTIONS

BUSINESS

Major business leaders stretching from the railroad builder, Cornelius Vanderbilt (1794-1877), to Wayne Huizenga (1938-), co-founder of Waste Management Inc. and the Blockbuster Video chain, demonstrate that Dutch Americans have reached the highest levels of commercial success. But again, apart from its early engagement in establishing world-wide capitalism, Netherlandic culture has had little to do with the specific endeavors of its most prominent Dutch American entrepreneurs. Others in this category—Walter Chrysler (1875-1940) of auto fame, retail innovator Hendrik Meijer (1883-1964), and the Amway Corporation's cofounders—Jay Van Andel (1924-) and Richard De Vos (1926-)—have created uniquely American institutions.

Among less prominent entrepreneurs, the Hekman brothers and several book publishers have adapted ethnic business ventures to gain national markets. John Hekman (1866-1951), his brother Jelle (1888-1957), and Jan Vander Heide (1905-1988) both inherited and purchased small-scale bakeries which currently market nationally under the Keebler and Dutch Twin labels. A third Hekman brother, Henry (1890-1962), developed his furniture company with an upscale inventory of office and home furniture. In this he joined several other Dutch-owned furniture companies in western Michigan—such as Bergsma Brothers, Hollis Baker, and especially Walter D. Idema, who with others founded the metal office furniture giant, Steelcase Inc. Doubtless the area's large number of Dutch immigrants with woodworking skills has contributed to Grand Rapids' long-standing identity as the furniture city.

ENTERTAINMENT

Pop culture icons like film producer Cecil B. de Mille (1881-1951) and rock star Bruce Springsteen (1949-) are Dutch American.

LITERATURE

Americans of Dutch descent have contributed significantly to American literature but, while firmly embedded in the literary canon, the works of Walt Whitman (1819-1892), Herman Melville (1819-1891) and Van Wyck Brooks (1885-1963) demonstrate little or nothing that reflects a Dutch American ethos. Well-known authors whose Dutch ethnicity shaped and informed their works include Peter De Vries (1910-1993), David (1901-1967) and Meindert De Jong (1906-1991), along with Frederick Manfred (1912-), and Arnold Mulder (1885-1959). Both De Vries' *The Blood of the Lamb* and Manfred's *The Green Earth* draw deeply from the wells of ethnic experience. Unlike Arnold Mulder's characters, who trade ethnic culture for that of the American mainstream, Manfred's *Englekings* and De Vries' *Don Wanderhope* incorporate their ethnicity and struggle with its meaning. David De Jong's *With a Dutch Accent* highlights conflicts between settled and newly arriving immigrants within Dutch enclaves, while Meindert De Jong crafted his widely acclaimed children's literature from recollections of his Netherlandic (Frisian) boyhood.

POLITICS

Dutch American political activists who achieved national prominence—Martin Van Buren (1782-1862), Theodore Roosevelt (1858-1919), Anna Eleanor Roosevelt (1906-1975), and Franklin Delano Roosevelt (1882-1945)—achieved nothing of significance that can be ascribed to their Netherlandic backgrounds. In contrast, Senator Arthur Vandenberg (1884-1951) and current U.S. Representatives Peter Hoekstra (1954-) and Vern Ehlers (1934-) owe much of their political success to the large percentage of Dutch ethnic support they attract in their districts. Similar correlations are evident in northwestern Iowa or in Whatcom County, Washington where the executive director, Shirley Van Zanten, receives crucial support from ethnic cohorts. The Dutch, wherever they cluster together—in western Michigan, in the Chicago area, in Washington State, and in Iowa—are pervasively conservative and Republican. Of 41 Dutch Americans holding national, state, and local offices, 35 are Republican. Thus, socialist Daniel de Leon (1852-1914) and pacifist A. J. Muste (1885-1967) are clearly atypical among their ethnic cohorts.

PUBLISHING

Grand Rapids, Michigan, has also become a center for the publication of religious books, led by the William B. Eerdmans Publishing Company. Eerdmans (1882-1966) and Louis Kregel (1890-1939) began by printing and reprinting Dutch and English books, catechisms, and pamphlets for the Reformed community. Since then, the Kregel firm has continued to feature the republication of standard religious works, while Eerdmans issues an inventory of new studies in theology, literature, and history aimed at a wide spectrum of religious interest groups. The Baker Book House, founded by Louis Kregel's son-in-law, Herman Baker (1912-1991), publishes primarily for traditional religious groups. Peter J. Zondervan (1909-1993) left Eerdmans in 1931 to organize the Zondervan Corporation which, with a chain of Midwestern book stores, has created a market among Christian fundamentalists. Edward Bok

(1863-1930) came to America from Holland as a small child; he became editor of *Ladies' Home Journal* and addressed it to America's homemakers—a revolution in publishing.

THEOLOGY, PHILOSOPHY, MEDICINE, AND HISTORY

Due largely to their abiding interest in Reformed religious perspectives, Dutch Americans are prominent in theology, philosophy and in some facets of history. They have founded theological schools in Grand Rapids, Michigan (Calvin Theological Seminary, 1876), in New Jersey (New Brunswick Theological Seminary, 1784), and in Holland, Michigan (Western Theological Seminary, 1866). Graduates Lewis B. Smedes (1921-) and Richard Mouw (1941-), both currently at Pasadena's Fuller Theological Seminary, have gained national acclaim from their publications and lectures. Robert Schuller (1926-) is the most widely known preacher with a Dutch Reformed heritage. Among theological school professors, Ira John Hesselink (1928-) at Western, Cornelius Plantinga (1946-) at Calvin, James Muilenburg (1896-?) at Union, and Simon De Vries (1921-) at the Methodist Theological School in Delaware, Ohio, have gained wide acclaim due to their classroom teaching and many publications. In philosophy, Yale's Nicholas Wolterstorff (1932-) and Alvin Plantinga (1932-) from Notre Dame have reinvigorated religious discussions throughout the international community of philosophers. Both William Bousma (1923-), in his re-examination of John Calvin (1509-1564), and Dale Van Kley (1941-), with revisionist studies of the French Revolution, have rekindled and directed an interest in the historical significance of religion in Western history. Famed pediatrician Benjamin Spock (1903-) guided millions of young parents with his baby books.

MEDIA

Dutch-language journalism, vibrant between 1870 and 1920, included over 50 periodicals, but none have survived without adopting English. *De Wachter* (*Watchman*) persisted from 1868 to 1985 with subsidies from the Christian Reformed Church. Two bilingual periodicals, *D.I.S.*—published by the Dutch International Society—and the *Windmill Herald*, retain an audience from among the postwar immigrants, but with the passing of that generation, even bilingual periodicals will probably cease to exist.

The Windmill Herald.
Bi-weekly newspaper for Dutch and Flemish communities; first published in 1958.

Contact: A. A. Van der Heide, Editor.
Address: Vanderheide Publishing Co. Ltd., P.O. Box Bag 9033, Surrey, British Columbia, Canada V3T 4X3.
Telephone: (604) 597-2144.

ORGANIZATIONS AND ASSOCIATIONS

The American Association for Netherlandic Studies.
Sponsors biennial interdisciplinary conferences on the study of the Dutch language and of Netherlandic culture around the world. It publishes the biennial journal *PAANS* and biannual *Newsletter*.

Contact: Margriet Lacy, President.
Address: Butler University, Dean's Office, LAS, 4600 Sunset Avenue, Indianapolis, Indiana 46208.
Telephone: (317) 283-9678.

Association for the Advancement of Dutch American Studies (AADAS).
Sponsors biennial conferences on nineteenth and twentieth century Dutch ethnic history in North America.

Contact: Larry J. Wagenaar, President.
Address: Joint Archives of Holland, Hope College Campus, Holland, Michigan 49423.
Telephone: (616) 394-7798.

The Dutch American Historical Commission.
Composed of representatives from Calvin College, Calvin Theological Seminary, Hope College, the Netherlands Museum, and the Western Theological Seminary, the commission publishes significant studies of nineteenth- and twentieth-century Dutch American history and coordinates the preservation of historical source materials.

Contact: John Huisken, President.
Address: Hope College, Holland, Michigan 49423.

Dutch Family Heritage Society (DFHS).
Gathers and disseminates information on Dutch history, culture, and genealogy in the United States, Canada, and Netherlands.

Contact: Mary Lynn Spijkerman Parker, President.
Address: 2463 Ledgewood Drive, West Jordan, Utah 84084.
Telephone: (801) 967-8400.

The Dutch International Society.

With a North American and Netherlandic membership, the society maintains international relationships by travel tours, the quarterly *D.I.S. Magazine,* and sponsoring cultural programs and events.

Contact: Peter Wobbema, President.
Address: 5370 Eastern Avenue, S.E., Grand Rapids, Michigan 49508.
Telephone: (616) 531-2298.

The Holland Society of New York.

Organized to collect and preserve information about the history of Colonial New Netherlands, membership consists primarily of Colonial Era descendants.

Contact: Peter Van Dyke, President.
Address: 122 East 58th Street, New York, New York 10022.
Telephone: (212) 758-1675.

Netherland-America Foundation (NAF).

Works to advance educational, literary, artistic, scientific, historical, and cultural relationships between the United States and the Netherlands.

Contact: Wanda Fleck, Administrator.
Address: 1 Rockefeller Plaza, 11th Floor, New York, New York 10020.
Telephone: (212) 767-1616.

MUSEUMS AND RESEARCH CENTERS

Calvin College and Theological Seminary Library Archives.

Contains manuscripts, books, microfilm, and periodicals for the study of nineteenth- and twentieth-century Dutch American history, religion, and culture in the United States, Canada, and the Netherlands. Its publications include: *Origins,* a biannual historical journal; the annual *Newsletter;* and *Heritage Hall Publication Series.*

Contact: Zwanet Janssens, Archivist.
Address: 3207 Burton Street, S.E., Grand Rapids, Michigan 49546.
Telephone: (616) 957-6313.

Dutch Heritage Center.

Contains books, manuscripts, microfilm, and periodicals for the study of Dutch American history and culture in the greater Chicago area.

Contact: Hendrik Sliekers, Curator.
Address: Trinity Christian College, 6601 West College Drive, Palos Heights, Illinois 6463.
Telephone: (708) 597-3000.

Holland Society of New York.

Included in its collection are books, manuscripts, films, and paintings related to Dutch American culture, history, and genealogy. The society publishes *De Halve Maen,* a quarterly journal.

Contact: Margaret Hutchinson, Librarian.
Address: 122 East 58th Street, New York, New York 10022.
Telephone: (212) 758-1878.

The Joint Archives of Holland.

Contains the combined archival resources of Hope College, the Western Theological Seminary, and the Holland, Michigan, community, and centers on the general history of Dutch Americans in the nineteenth and twentieth centuries.

Contact: Larry J. Wagenaar, Director.
Address: Hope College Campus, Holland, Michigan 49423.
Telephone: (616) 394-7798.

Northwestern College Library Archives.

Provides manuscripts, books, microfilm, and periodicals for the study of nineteenth- and twentieth-century Dutch American history in northwestern Iowa, Orange City, and Northwestern College.

Contact: Nella Kennedy, Archivist.
Address: Orange City, Iowa 51041.
Telephone: (712) 737-7000.

SOURCES FOR ADDITIONAL STUDY

Balmer, Randall, H. *A Perfect Babel of Confusion: Dutch Religion and English Culture in the Middle Colonies.* New York: Oxford University Press, 1989.

Bratt, James H. *Dutch Calvinism in Modern America: A History of a Conservative Subculture.* Grand

Rapids, Michigan: Eerdmans Publishing Co., 1984.

Brinks, Herbert J. *Dutch Immigrant Voices, 1850-1930: Correspondence from the USA.* Ithaca, New York: Cornell University Press, 1995.

De Jong, Gerald F. *The Dutch in America, 1609-1974.* Boston: Twayne Publishers, 1975.

Fabend, Firth H. *A Dutch Family in the Middle Colonies, 1660-1800.* New Brunswick, New Jersey: Rutgers University Press, 1991.

Goodfriend, Joyce D. *Before the Melting Pot: Society and Culture in Colonial New York City, 1664-1730.* Princeton, New Jersey: Princeton University Press, 1992.

Kroes, Rob. *The Persistence of Ethnicity: Dutch Calvinist Pioneers in Amsterdam, Montana.* Chicago: University of Illinois Press, 1992.

Lambert, Audrey M. *The Making of the Dutch Landscape: An Historical Geography of The Netherlands.* London: Academic Press, 1985.

Lucas, Henry. *Netherlanders in America: Dutch Immigrants to the United States.* Ann Arbor: University of Michigan Press, 1955.

Swierenga, Robert P. *The Dutch in America: Immigration Settlement and Cultural Change.* New Brunswick, New Jersey: Rutgers University Press, 1985.

Van Hinte, Jacob. *Netherlanders in America: A Study of Emigration and Settlement in the Nineteenth and Twentieth Centuries of the United States of America.* Grand Rapids: Baker Book House, 1985.

The descendants of English expatriates are so numerous and so well integrated in American life that it is impossible to identify all of them.

ENGLISH
AMERICANS

by
Sheldon Hanft

OVERVIEW

England, a country slightly larger than New York State, occupies 50,363 square miles (130,439 square kilometers) of the southern end of the largest island off the Atlantic coast of Europe. A land of rolling hills, moderate climate, abundant rainfall, fertile plains, many navigable rivers, and nearly 2,000 miles of ocean coastline, it is mineral rich and very arable. From the southwestern plateau of Cornwall and southeastern marshy downs through the gentle plains, the Pennine uplands, and the lake country, to the Cambrian mountains and Cheviot Hills, which shapes its western and northern borders with Wales and Scotland, no point is more than 75 miles from the seas that brought commerce, migrations, and invasion throughout much of England's early history.

While 80 percent of its 50 million people are native born, England has large communities of Scots (nearly ten percent), Irish, and Welsh in its border counties and about two million Asian Indians, Pakistani, West Indians, and other non-white peoples in its large cities. These Asian and Caribbean groups settled in England during and after the collapse of the British empire in the last half century. London, with a population approaching seven million, is the capital of England and the United Kingdom. The government is a constitutional monarchy with a Parliament and a cabinet system dominated by the Conservative and Labour parties. Seventy-eight percent of the English population belong to the Church of England (the Anglican Church, or the COE), which is legally established (tax supported) and officially governed by the monarch and the Archbishop of Canterbury. There are also sizable groups of Methodists, Evangelicals, Roman Catholics, Muslims, Jews, and Quakers in England. The national flag, commonly called the "union jack," has a broad red English cross (of St. George) with white borders imposed over the Scottish cross (of St. Stephen), shown as thinner red diagonals with thin white borders traversing from corner to corner on a field of royal blue.

HISTORY

The English descend from the Celtic tribes who brought iron age technology and Druid ceremonies, reflected in such monumental megaliths as Stonehenge, to the British isles in the first millennium. Their language and heritage are reflected in Welsh and Gaelic more strongly than in the English language. Roman conquests, begun by Emperor Claudius, brought England and Wales under Roman control by the end of the first century. During the next three centuries, England developed as a typical Roman colony, protected by the 73-mile-long Hadrian's Wall in the north and policed by the legions, who also constructed roads. During their occupation, Romans promoted commerce, established their institutions, and introduced Christianity in England.

The collapse of Roman rule in the early fifth century ended urban life, as groups of Germanic Angles, Jutes, and Saxons carved the country into tribal enclaves and later created the heptarchy. This diverse group of seven Anglo-Saxon kingdoms vied among themselves for control of the island and later resisted the waves of Viking invaders from the eighth to the eleventh centuries. The most famous Anglo-Saxon ruler was Alfred the Great, who defeated the Danish Vikings, began the English navy, and made Roman Catholicism dominant.

In 1066 William of Normandy conquered England, ending a century of instability, and imposed systemic feudalism by constructing hundreds of castes. During the next three centuries, the institutions of Common Law and Parliamentary government developed, Henry II created a large Angevin empire, Richard the Lionhearted won fame on the Crusade of Kings, and his brother John provoked a baronial revolt that led to the signing of the Magna Carta—the first serious limitation on monarch's power in England. Royal power was further weakened by England's defeat in the Hundred Years' War (1337-1453), depopulation caused by the Black Death, and the baronial War of the Roses, which brought the Tudor dynasty to the throne in 1485.

Henry VII's victory at Bosworth restored strong central government, began transatlantic exploration, developed fiscal reform, and reasserted strong kingship. Henry VIII patronized the Renaissance, separated the Church of England from papal control, and furthered the Tudor revolution in government administration. After "Bloody" Mary's brief effort to return to Catholicism during the middle of the sixteenth century, her younger sister, Queen Elizabeth, restored Henry's church and defended it from the Spanish Armada of 1588. Her prosperous reign supported explorers like Sir Francis Drake and Sir Walter Raleigh, a cultural revival led by William Shakespeare and Francis Bacon, and let merchant adventurers settle England's first permanent American colony.

Between 1603 and 1714 a succession of Stuart rulers encountered Parliamentary opposition to their religious, tax, social, and constitutional policies, which resulted in massive emigration, three civil wars between 1642 and 1649, the public execution of Charles I, and Oliver Cromwell's republican Commonwealth. While Charles II was restored in 1660, the Glorious Revolution ensued in 1688-1689, establishing a Bill of Rights and making England the chief opponent of Louis XIV's wars during the reigns of William and Mary and Queen Anne.

In 1715, eight years after England united with Scotland, the present dynasty, the Hanoverian Windsors, ascended to the throne. During the eighteenth century, England compiled a vast empire, defeated the French in the Seven Years' War (1756-1763), and dominated international trade, notwithstanding having lost the 13 American colonies. Led by such English writers as John Locke and Sir Isaac Newton, the Enlightenment constituted the century's main cultural movement. The English organized the alliance that eventually defeated Napoleon in 1815.

Strengthened by electoral reforms, the Industrial Revolution, and imperialistic expansion in Africa and Asia, Britain remained a dominant world power throughout most of the nineteenth century. Although troubled by the Potato Famine, which began in Ireland, the reign of Queen Victoria (1837-1901) has become synonymous with the expansion of imperialism and the cosmopolitan culture of the age. While creating an empire on which the sun never set, as it was said, England adopted social and economic reforms that made the government more democratic despite challenges to England's economic and political leadership.

The burden of fighting two world wars, the loss of much of its empire, and the demands of its new "welfare state" policies diminished England's political importance in the second half of the twentieth century. To accommodate these changes, Britain strongly allied itself with the United States and reluctantly increased its involvement in the European Common Market, a policy reflected in the difficult struggle to complete the channel tunnel connecting England with France in 1994. Yet the policy continues to meet strong resistance in Parliament and among the peoples of the British Isles. The challenges of surrendering their historical independence and cooperating with the policies and obligations of Common Market membership remain among the most difficult problems facing England and Great Britain at the end of the twentieth century.

CONTEMPORARY ENGLAND

Contemporary England is at the center of the United Kingdom of Great Britain and Northern Ireland, which also includes Scotland, Wales, the Sea Islands, and the Channel Islands. Presently, the United Kingdom is composed of several distinctive areas that maintain their national churches and ethnic traditions and harbor a reluctance to be absorbed into a "greater England." In the 1960s the desire for greater independence led to national referenda in Wales and Scotland and erupted into sustained violence in Northern Ireland. These movements have declined considerably in recent decades. Less than ten percent of the people of the United Kingdom live in Scotland, while 5.5 percent inhabit Wales and under three percent live in Northern Ireland. The Channel Islands, mainly Jersey and Guernsey (off the French coast) and the Isle of Man (in the Irish Sea), historically considered part of England, have received self-government and dependency status in the last half century.

Scotland, directly north of England, has nearly five million inhabitants who occupy the northern 37 percent of the main island. It is a diverse area of over 30,414 square miles of land (78,772 square kilometers) that includes the Inner and Outer Hebrides and other islands in the Irish Sea and the Orkney and Shetland Islands in the North Sea. Edinburgh is its capital and three-quarters of its population live in its southern lowlands. This region makes use of inexpensive hydroelectric power and North Sea oil, which sustain an industrial complex and the textile, fishing, herding, and whiskey industries traditional in this region. The English language is spoken throughout Scotland, but Scottish accents are strongly divergent from those in England. Nearly 100,000 Scots speak Gaelic in addition to English.

The principality of Wales is 8,018 square miles (20,768 square kilometers) of generally mountainous terrain and nearly 2.8 million residents. While English is the official language, about 12 percent of its residents are bilingual in Welsh and English and about two percent speak only Welsh. Although the Church of England is established, it never won the loyalty of the general populace. During the nineteenth-century Industrial Revolution, Welsh "Calvinistic Methodists" gained the support of most of the working class and added a religious dimension to the social and economic issues separating working-class Welsh from the wealthier social groups who accepted the established Church. Administratively, Wales remains part of England, and, while Welsh nationalism has declined as a political force, it remains an important cultural and social expression of the Welsh character.

While England occupied parts of Ireland since the Middle Ages and conquered the whole island in the sixteenth century, deep religious loyalties, punitive economic legislation, and cultural differences left native Irish Catholics resentful of the transplanted Protestant minority who enjoyed great privilege. This division fueled periodic rebellions and led, in 1920, to a division of the island into a predominantly Catholic republic in the south and a predominantly Protestant Northern Ireland, which stayed part of the United Kingdom. These six Ulster counties with an area of 5,452 square miles (14,121 square kilometers) and over 1.5 million people were given semiautonomous local government centered in Belfast under the supervision of a royal governor and a Parliamentary committee. The eruption of sectarian violence in 1969 prompted London to resume direct control of local government. Negotiations in the 1990s provided hope for a solution to "the troubles."

Elizabeth II, of the House of Hanover-Windsor is the reigning sovereign. She married a Greek prince, Philip Mountbatten, and succeeded her father, George VI, to the throne in February 1952 and was crowned on June 2, 1953 in a ceremony televised worldwide. Her husband was made Duke of Edinburgh in 1947 and added the title of Prince of the United Kingdom and Northern Ireland a decade later. Prince Charles Philip Arthur George, born November 14, 1948, was created Prince of Wales and is the heir apparent. His son, William Philip Arthur Lewis, born June 21, 1982, is next in the line of succession.

The Sovereign is the titular head of government and summons the meeting of Parliament—the national legislature, the members of which sit for five years or less. The House of Lords, empowered only to delay legislation, is composed of the two archbishops and 24 bishops of the Church of England, 763 hereditary nobles, and 314 life peers who are nominated by the government and created by the monarch. The House of Commons has 650 members directly elected by universal suffrage from 516 districts in England, 71 in Scotland, 36 in Wales, and 12 in Northern Ireland. Scottish, Welsh, and Irish nationalist parties elect some members to Parliament, and a Social Democratic Party has emerged to weakly challenge the Conservative and Labour parties. Asian and West Indian members of Parliament were returned from urban constituencies in every election since 1987.

Executive power is exercised by the Prime Minister and his or her cabinet, who are appointed by the monarch from among the members of the party receiving a majority in the House of Commons. Cabinet members must sit in Parliament, and they, individually and collectively, are responsible to the Crown and the Parliament whose support they must have in order to frame legislation, tax, and determine domestic and foreign policy.

While no longer an economic superpower, England remains a major manufacturing, food-producing, and commercial nation that has regained a favorable balance of trade. London remains one of the premier financial markets in the world, and its universities, museums, scientific establishment, and tourist attractions draw millions of people to England, especially from former colonies that remain affiliated through the British Commonwealth of Nations.

IMMIGRATION, SETTLEMENT, AND EMPLOYMENT

The English were the first non-Native Americans to settle the area that became the United States of America. From the first permanent colonies established at Jamestown, Virginia, in 1607 and at Plymouth and Massachusetts Bay in 1620-1622 to James Oglethorpe's settlement in Savannah, Georgia, in 1732, English joint-stock companies, proprietors, and Crown officials sought to create a modified version of their native society in their American colonies. While many Englishmen came to America to exercise their own religion, and others sought liberation from the religious intolerance on both sides of the Atlantic—as did Roger Williams, fonder of Rhode Island—most English settlers were drawn by the economic opportunities and cheap land. Despite their diverse origins, the majority of colonies came under royal control, established the Church of England Episcopal Church after 1776, and created laws that adapted and imposed the English systems of law, governmental administration, education, commercial and financial management, and agriculture, as well as the arts and popular entertainment.

The group of single men sent by the Virginia company in 1607 to find gold and create a profitable trade failed, and the survival of the colony was doubtful, even under royal proprietorship, for two decades. It was not until the late 1620s, when stability agriculture and a profitable tobacco export began attracting an annual English immigration of several thousand men and women, that the success of Jamestown was assured. This rate of English immigration to the Chesapeake area was maintained until the early part of the next century, when it expanded as England suffered economic difficulties. After Maryland and Delaware were founded, the latter by Catholics, indentured Englishmen and working-class families constituted a majority of the new English settlers.

In addition to the small number of gentry, clergy, lawyers, officials, and minor aristocratic families who settled in the Chesapeake basin to develop plantations, over 30,000 male and female prisoners convicted of serious felonies were transported to Virginia, Maryland, and southern Pennsylvania between 1717 and 1776. Most of the prisoners and indentured servants, as well those as those who paid their passage to the Chesapeake, were young men with some training, possessions, and vocational skills. Although all colonies from Virginia to Georgia received a stream of English prisoners and indentured servants, many were successful in attracting the younger sons and poorer cousins of gentry and merchant families. In the late-seventeenth and eighteenth centuries sizable numbers of Scots, Germans, French, Irish, and Scotch-Irish settled in the South, and they accepted the culture and institutions already established.

Pilgrim and Puritan settlement in Massachusetts Bay attracted over 20,000 settlers from East Anglia and the counties west of London between 1620 and 1642. During these decades English settlements were planted in New Hampshire and Maine, and several English communities were established in Rhode Island and Connecticut by religious reformers who were not tolerated in Massachusetts. Unlike the southern colonies, most of the New England settlers were older and came to America with their family, friends, and assorted relatives. In some instances whole congregations immigrated to New England in this period. The influences of the clergy and the government was strong throughout the region, and successful efforts were made to convert Indians to Christianity.

English settlers from Virginia migrated into North Carolina in the seventeenth century, and English immigrants settled in all of the colonies between Connecticut and Maryland in the middle decades of the century. When an English fleet captured New Amsterdam in 1664 renaming it New York, their countrymen already comprised a majority of the city's population and were well established in New Jersey. While Pennsylvania, founded by English Quakers, attracted large numbers of German, French, Welsh, Scottish, and Scotch-Irish settlers, the colony retained its English character throughout the colonial period.

In the late seventeenth century most English immigrants were younger men who came from the rural areas of southern and south central England. Unlike the New England farming families, most who settled in the region from the Chesapeake to Charleston came as indentured servants and had training as farmers, skilled tradesmen, laborers, or craftsmen. By the last decade of the century, when the English and their descendants comprised 90 percent of the European settlers, Southern planters began importing slaves and the number of new indentured servants decreased. In the eighteenth century, many of those who indentured themselves to get to America were older than those who came before them and were accompanied by their family or related to the families in whose employ they remained.

In the eighteenth century, people from London and the northern counties comprised the majority of English immigrants. The percentage of women increased slightly, from about 15 percent to nearly 25 percent of the English settlers. English Americans began to intermarry more frequently than any other European group. This was partly due to the increased numbers of mobile tradesmen, craftsmen, and merchants among the new English Americans. After the government began transporting felons to the colonies after 1717, the number of unskilled settlers increased in the New England and middle colonies that were willing to accept them. Economic and political troubles brought new spurts of English immigration in the 1720s and in the decades preceding the American Revolution. Americans cited the writings of John Locke, the defender of England's Glorious Revolution, to condemn George III for abusing their "rights as Englishmen."

While English settlers and their descendants constituted only about 60 percent of the European settlers and half of the four million residents living from Maine to Georgia, according to the 1790 census, they had ensured the dominance of English institutions and culture throughout the new republic. This was reflected in the leaders of the national and state governments as well as in the movement to add an English-style Bill of Rights to the new Constitution. While Massachusetts had the largest number of English Americans, only in Pennsylvania, New Jersey, and the Northwest Territory were they a plurality. A cadre of English-trained officials, educated clergymen, wealthy merchants, landlords, and professionals dominated the governments and social structure in all of the colonies, despite the growing influx of immigrants from other parts of Great Britain and Europe.

English immigration to America sharply decreased between 1780 and 1815, as a consequence of English involvement in India and Latin America, events surrounding the French Revolution and Napoleonic conquest, and a "second war of independence" with the United States. During the War of 1812 British aliens were forced to register with local marshals; many English merchants were kept from their trade and forced to relocate; and for the duration of the war English aliens were treated with suspicion, and their freedom of movement was severely restricted.

In the decades preceding the war, London prevented English craftsmen from immigrating to America and restricted the number of settlers each ship could transport. Despite the general decline in immigration to America, several short spurts of English immigration to America occurred. One such increase developed at the end of the Revolutionary War, and another resulted from the monarchy's suppression of English radicals in 1793.

Although German, Irish, Scandinavian, Mediterranean, and Slavic peoples dominated the new waves of immigration after 1815, English settlers provided a steady and substantial influx throughout the nineteenth century. The first wave of increasing English immigration began in the late 1820s and was sustained by unrest in England until it peaked in 1842 and declined slightly for nearly a decade. Most of these were small farmers and tenant farmers from depressed areas in rural counties in southern and western England and urban laborers who fled from the depressions and from the social and industrial changes of the late 1820s-1840s. While some English immigrants were drawn by dreams of creating model utopian societies in America, most others were attracted by the lure of new lands, textile factories, railroads, and the expansion of mining.

The Chartist movement in the late 1840s, with its massive urban protests, spurred another period of English immigration, which peaked in 1854 and coincided with the waves of Germans and central Europeans who fled to America after the failed revolutions of 1848. With this new influx, as with the previous one, there was a preponderance of English people traveling with one or more family members, and the number of industrial workers, tradesmen, and craftsmen outnumbered farmers more than three to one. Along with its economic appeal, America attracted English settlers because of its similar language and customs and the popular admiration for "things English," especially in its large cities and in the South. A number of English labor unions, Poor Law authorities, charitable organizations, and utopian colonization schemes also encouraged English resettlement in America.

During the last years of 1860s, annual English immigration increased to over 60,000 and continued to rise to over 75,000 per year in 1872, before experiencing a decline. The final and most sustained wave of immigration began in 1879 and lasted until the depression of 1893. During this period English annual immigration averaged more than 80,000, with peaks in 1882 and 1888. The building of America's transcontinental railroads, the settlement of the great plains, and industrialization attracted skilled and professional emigrants from England. Also, cheaper steamship fares enabled unskilled urban workers to come to America, and unskilled and semiskilled laborers, miners, and building trades workers made up the majority of these new English immigrants. While most settled in America, a number of skilled craftsmen remained itinerant, returning to England after a season of two of work. Groups of English immigrants came to America as missionaries for the Salvation Army and to work with the activities of the Evangelical and Mormon Churches. The depression of 1893 sharply decreased English immigration, and it stayed low for much of the twentieth century.

"We were put on a barge, jammed in so tight that I couldn't turn 'round, there were so many of us, you see, and the stench was terrible."
Eleanor Kenderdine Lenhart in 1921, cited in *Ellis Island: An Illustrated History of the Immigrant Experience*, edited by Ivan Chermayeff et al. (New York: Maxmillan, 1991).

Throughout the nineteenth century, England was the largest investor in American land development, railroads, mining, cattle ranching, and heavy industry. Perhaps because English settlers gained easy acceptance, they founded few organizations dedicated to preserving the traditions of their homeland. While the English comprised only 15 percent of the great nineteenth-century European migration to American, those going to America from England made up less than ten percent of the people leaving England between 1820 and 1920. These migrations in the late nineteenth century were important in that they altered the distribution of English settlers in America. By the end of the century the middle-Atlantic states had the largeest number of English Americans, followed by the north-central states and New England. The growing number of English settling in the West and Pacific Coast regions left the South with the smallest percentage of English Americans by the end of the century.

In the twentieth century, English immigration to America decreased, a product of Canada and Australia having better economic opportunities and favorable immigration policies. English immigration remained low in the first four decades of the century, averaging about six percent of the total number of people from Europe.

English culture, literature, and family connections became widely coveted in the early decades of the twentieth century, due to a number of well-publicized marriages of wealthy Americans to children of English aristocrats and to the introduction of Western history and literature courses stressing America's English heritage in colleges and in the public school curriculum after World War I. During the decade of the Great Depression of the 1930s more English returned home than immigrated to the United States. For the first time, more English women than men immigrated.

This decline reversed itself in the decade of World War II when over 100,000 English (18 percent of all European immigrants) came from England. In this group was a large contingent of war brides who came between 1945 and 1948. In these years four women emigrated from England for every man. Although total English immigration increased to over 150,000 (the level maintained in the 1920s) it was less than 12 percent of the European influx during the 1950s. In the 1960s English immigration rose by 20,000 (15.5 percent of all Europeans migrating) and continued in the next decade because of the so-called brain drain of English engineers, technicians, medical professionals, and other specialists being lured to America by multinational corporations. In the three decades since 1970, English immigrants, who were about 12 percent of the total arriving from Europe, were usually unmarried, professionally trained men and women. While the average age of immigrants rose in the last decades of the twentieth century, the number of married people and children continued to decline, and immigrants continued to merge almost imperceptibly into American society.

The periods of increased English immigration in this century are notable because they involved more people from middle and upper-class groups whose migrations raised political issues in England, not because the level of immigration was significant. For most of the period between 1921 and 1969, when immigration quotas were based on the country of origin, England did not fill the generous quotas granted to it. Despite the slight decline in English immigration under the current immigration structure adopted in the 1970s, 33 million Americans identify themselves as being of English descent in the 1990 census. They constitute the third largest ethnic group in the United States, and despite the fact that the Southeast is the region of the nation with the largest number of Americans of English descent, the states currently having the largest number of English Americans are California, Texas, Florida, New York, and Ohio.

ACCULTURATION AND ASSIMILATION

Since all but two of the original colonies were founded by Englishmen, were administered by English officials, were protected by England's army and navy, and were led by English-trained clergy, lawyers, and educators, they adapted English models in their laws, constitutions, educational system, social structure, and cultural pursuits. From the colonial period it remained fashionable for wealthy Americans to send their sons to England for a year of college, and English styles in literature, poetry, music, architecture, industry, and clothing were the models to emulate until the twentieth century. Throughout the colonial period Americans supported England's wars enthusiastically, and when resentment and resistance to English policies developed in America in the 1760s and 1770s, Americans looked to Parliament for redress of their grievances, which they perceived as emanating from a tyrannical King and his corrupt ministers. Numerous colonial towns created in this period were named in honor of William Pitt and John Wilkes, two popular English Parliamentarians who opposed George III.

While differences developed, it is not surprising that English immigrants had little difficulty in assimilating to American life. Although some loyalists left the United States for England and other colonies after the revolution, the American resentment against the policies of the English government was rarely transferred to English settlers who came to American in the first decades of the nineteenth century. This separation is seen in the sharp rise in English imports in the two decades after the American Revolution. As British naval policies and practices, adopted in their long struggle against Napoleonic France, kindled new conflicts with America, which culminated in the War of 1812, popular resentment against English immigrants intensified. In such states with large German, French, and Celtic communities as Maryland, Pennsylvania, New York, and the Carolinas, broadsides and pamphlets such as *Niles' Weekly Register,* rebuked English immigrants for their "assumed superiority," their poverty, and their provincialism. During the War of 1812, English merchants, primarily in Charleston, Baltimore, and New York, were relocated and prevented from conducting their business, and recent English immigrants were required to register with local government agencies.

In 1820, English immigration again increased and the new settlers found an easy acceptance, though some resentment remained in the Northeast and in the cities of the Atlantic seaboard with large Irish and Scotch-Irish communities. Faced with few language barriers and a familiar legal and political system at the local level and American variants of nearly every English religious denomination, they had little inclination to establish their own churches, newspapers, or political organizations. While the immigrants often confined their socializing to friends and relatives from their own county (shire) or region of England, their children found easy acceptance, resettled comfortably, and merged into the general population virtually unnoticed by all but their parents.

The only English social organizations to endure for several generations were the assorted groups of Odd Fellows, English fraternal societies for the working class recreated in America by Thomas Wildey and John Welch in Baltimore in 1819 and James B. Barnes in Boston the following year. These lodges appealed to the more skilled immigrant tradesmen and craftsmen because they provided the companionship of English pubs, employment connections, and shelter from critics of English immigrants. Despite difficulties in the 1830s and 1860s, the fraternity survived by accepting immigrants from other parts of Britain and Americans of mixed lineage. Its appeal to waves of English immigrants from 1870 to 1893 was limited, and at the turn of the century there were fewer than three dozen chapters, mostly in New England and the northern states. The organization survived to the present by opening its membership to all Americans and by devoting its activities to civil affairs.

While a few social organizations and newspapers were established for English immigrants in the early nineteenth century, they all failed to gain significant support and did not last long. New York was the home of the first newspaper published in 1827 for English American readers. Named *Albion; or, the British and Colonial Foreign Gazette*, it survived until 1863 and outlasted its rivals, the *Old Countryman* (1830-1835), the *Emigrant* (1835-1838), and the *Anglo-American* (1843-1847). Inexpensive editions of English newspapers became available in the 1840s and undermined the three efforts made in the 1870s and 1880s to publish dailies for the expanding communities of English residents in Massachusetts and New York.

In comparison with other new immigrants, the English immigrants in the decades preceding

This English American is holding a selection of traditional foods in front of his Salisbury, Connecticut, pub and inn.

the Civil War were more prone to separate from the community of their fellow immigrants, more willing to intermarry, and more enthusiastic in embracing the culture of their new land. For most groups of English immigrants throughout the century their ethnic identity was expressed by their participation in the Episcopal Churches in most states and in the Methodist and Baptist Churches in the rural South. Throughout the century, such groups as the Domestic and Foreign Missionary Society of the Episcopal Church of England, the Society for the Propagation of the Gospel, and the Salvation Army sent ministers and missionaries to English congregations in America. With funds raised in England and in English immigrant communities along the Atlantic seaboard, Kenyon College and Jubilee College were established in Ohio and Illinois, respectively, to train Episcopal ministers for service in towns in the middle and far western states where numerous English immigrant communities of miners, craftsmen, and farmers had settled. In many of these states, English immigrants avoided political office beyond the local level and were more reluctant than members of other ethnic groups to apply for American citizenship.

The tendency to adapt and integrate increased in the second half of the century. One study concluded that less than 20 percent of children from the turn of the century's largest community of English immigrants eventually married someone of English descent. While a number of

English immigrant groups in the second half of the nineteenth century, like the textile workers in Lowell, Massachusetts, the cutlery workers in Connecticut, and English miners in West Virginia, may have lived close together and established distinctly English denominational congregations, they were absorbed into the mainstream of American life within a generation. While some communities of English miners, mill workers, and agricultural settlers in the Midwest established libraries, social clubs, and musical societies to provide English culture, most, including the chapters of the St. George's Society in Madison, Wisconsin, and in Clinton, Iowa, rarely survived for more than a decade.

While English immigrants unsuccessfully tried to establish local labor unions, labor exchanges, and political pressure groups in this period, small groups of English skilled workers in industrial and mining communities in the East and Midwest were able to maintain some social cohesion and community identity in the periods of heightened immigration. These groups were able to maintain, for as long as two decades, the self-help associations, buying cooperatives, fraternal lodges, and sporting associations common in English communities in the late Victorian era.

The English immigrants in the last three decades established their own groups of working-class fraternal, social, political, and literary organizations. The Sons of St. George was one of the most durable of these groups and survived until the Great Depression. Originally excluding all but native born English and their descendants, the lodges developed insurance services, secret rituals, and special social functions that were characteristic of other groups. The organization declined as English immigration decreased and America became more isolationist in the two decades following World War I.

A major stimulus for English immigrants to organize was the emergence of the Irish as a major constituency in American politics. In order to increase their political influence, English American groups encouraged the reluctant English immigrants to become citizens in the last decades of the century. While a smaller percentage of English renounced their loyalty to their homeland than did immigrants from other parts of Europe, the census of 1900 showed a significant increase in the percentage of English Americans becoming citizens of the United States. This trend continued and grew in the twentieth century until the rate of English immigrant assimilation matched that of other European settlers.

One result of this trend was the organization of English American and British American political clubs in Philadelphia, Boston, and New York, as well as in smaller industrial towns including Elizabeth, New Jersey, and Stanford, Maine; and in Ohio, Iowa, and California, where communities of English miners, artisans, and industrial workers asserted their political muscle, predominantly on behalf of the Republican party. These activities escalated after an 1887 banquet celebration of Queen Victoria's Golden Jubilee in Boston's Faneuil Hall was disrupted by thousands of angry Irish protesters, who tried to prevent the entry of the 400 ticket holders. When only a few British politicians condemned the protest, English American and Scottish American leaders organized a federation of more than 60 political action clubs and launched a number of periodicals. Massachusetts, New York, Pennsylvania, and Illinois each had a dozen or more English communities that organized politically, and New Hampshire, Connecticut, New Jersey, Ohio, Michigan, Iowa, and California each had several chapters. These clubs had little impact on the elections of 1888 and 1892, and most were absorbed into a broader anti-Catholic confederation, the American Protective Association, an offshoot of the nativism and populist movements of the 1890s.

Three publications launched in the late 1880s—the *British-American Citizen*, published in Boston between 1887 and 1913; the *Western British American*, published in Chicago between 1888 and 1922; and the *British-American*, published in New York and Philadelphia between 1887 and 1919—attained a limited degree of success by appealing to immigrants from all parts of Britain. They were not successful in uniting Americans of Scottish, English, Irish, and Welsh descent into a single effective political action group, but they did serve to sharpen the ethnic identity of their readers and underscore the importance of the British contribution to American society. The survival of these periodicals after the collapse of the political clubs was due in part to improved diplomatic relations between the United States and Britain after 1895, which led to an alliance in World War I.

The Anglo-American partnership begun in World War I has endured to the present. Britain's actions and policies throughout the century, represented in the American consciousness by the Tommies in the trenches of World War I, Prime

Minister Winston Churchill's resistance to Hitler, and Prime Minister Margaret Thatcher's support of America in the Persian Gulf War, has increased the popularity and general acceptance of English immigrants.

COMMON STEREOTYPES AND MISCONCEPTIONS

Derived from stage plays, BBC television shows, and novels, many of which have been made into Hollywood movies, a number of overdrawn stereotypes abound that exaggerate class distinctions and distort the social attitudes of English Americans. The long-lasting series, "Masterpiece Theater," and the many movies made from Noel Coward plays and Agatha Christie mysteries have reinforced the cartoonish view of the English aristocracy as a rather stuffy, humorless, reserved, and insensitive group of social relics living hollow lives and wasting their remaining resources on trivial pursuits. They survive the traumas of modern life only with the assistance of their ever-dependable gentlemen's gentleman. English rulers and political leaders are unrealistically portrayed as charismatic, cosmopolitan, and solely responsible for all of the grand achievements in English history. From the craftiness of Henry VIII and Queen Elizabeth to the architects of the British Empire and such gifted orators like Pitt and Churchill, English leaders emerge as incorruptible patriots with unerring policies and a love of their citizens not matched in the history books. Despite its inaccuracy, this image is the one with which American presidents from John Fitzgerald Kennedy to Bill Clinton have tried to associate themselves in the course of their relations with England.

The stereotypes of middle-class English Americans keep alive an unreal idealization of the Victorian era. This depiction of the irascible and hardworking English detective, lawyer, professor, or businessman with an idiosyncratic personality has become a stock figure on both sides of the Atlantic. They are the more respectable versions of such working-class bounders as the comic strip character Andy Capp, lazy sports zealots inclined to violence, alcoholism, and womanizing. Working-class women, typified by the cheerful movie heroine Mary Poppins, are just the opposite; English nannies, secretaries, and junior executives are perceived as extremely hardworking and efficient and are in great demand in the homes of elite families and in the offices of American corporations.

HEALTH AND MENTAL HEALTH ISSUES

There are no particular health problems or psychological conditions that are specifically associated with British Americans. A number of descendants of British Americans were among the founders of medical societies and others have been prominent in the health insurance industry. England expatriates brought the cooperative movement to America in the early nineteenth century and were early supporters of group health insurance. The success of the National Health system in Britain created benefits for employers, making British multinational corporations advocates of national health insurance in the United States.

LANGUAGE

The popularity in America of English music—both classical and contemporary—movies, television, and theater, and of English performers might suggest that the only distinction between the speech of England and America is in the accents. Pronunciation in England, however, is an important indicator of social class and region of origin, as it is in America. Yet Americans make little distinction between the working-class cockney staccato of the east end of London and the slower, precise articulation of well-educated professional. After living in the United States for several decades, most English immigrants are not identifiable by their accents, and their descendants are indistinguishable from other native born Americans.

The sharper distinction between English of the immigrant generation and those born in the United States is a vocabulary of several hundred words and phrases. While some newer English words, especially slang words, are popularized in America by English musicians and actors, the names of ordinary items distinguish the immigrant English from other Americans. While an American might guess that petrol powers an automobile, he might be hesitant to open the car's bonnet (hood) or eat some crisps (potato chips) or ring off (hang up) the telephone. The English refer to sausages as bangers and call the toilet the "loo" or the "W.C." (for water closet).

FAMILY AND COMMUNITY DYNAMICS

As in other areas of American society, it was the English pattern of the nuclear family—focused on

English Morris Dancers perform at the Red Lion Inn in Stockbridge, Massachusetts.

the husband, wife, and children with an occasional relative family living in close proximity—that set the pattern of early life in the colonial era. While women were in short supply in the early decades of the colonial era, the majority of Puritan settlers came to New England with their families, as whole congregations and sizable groups of religious dissidents transferred their hopes of a "Godly commonwealth" to America. They set the pattern for establishing Sunday "blue laws," to sanctify the Sabbath by prohibiting public drinking, dancing, and work-related activities and encouraging prayer and charitable and missionary activities, especially among family members. Outside New England the pastimes described in King James' *Book of Sports* (1681) were more prevalent; and modest displays of entertainment, especially dancing, singing, and athletic competitions among family groups were common and often held under the auspices of the local Episcopal congregation. As noted above, English immigrants, especially those who were part of the larger waves of migration in the nineteenth century,

usually settled in small towns with other English miners, metal workers, farmers, and skilled textile specialists and recreated English-style pubs, choral groups, sporting clubs, self-help societies, unions, and fraternal organization, few of which endured for very long beyond the lifetime of the founders.

In all social classes, to differing degrees, English American women dominated the domestic and social life of family as well as its relations with friends and extended family as completely as men dominated the public aspects of family life and business. As in the land of their birth, family celebrations and the maintenance of connections with the prominent relatives or members of "cadet" branches of the family were left to women, especially in more affluent and socially prominent families. Among middle- and upper-class families, care was taken to educate and discipline the older children and to encourage them to continue family businesses and social obligations. Their greater reliance on family, kinsmen, and contacts from their native regions of England and the ease with which they blended into American society, may help explain why English immigrants were last among the new settlers to embrace American citizenship.

This may partially explain the greater proclivity of their children to eventually marry spouses who were not of English ancestry and their willingness to leave the communities in which they were reared. They found that they could be "at home" anywhere in America and that their heritage was not an obstacle, but rather an asset, in finding a mate who could improve their social and economic status.

For most groups of English immigrants throughout the century, the church was central to ethnic identity. The literature and scriptures of the Episcopal, Methodist, and Baptist churches across the country were nearly the same as those in the communities of their birth. Many of these congregations maintained and supported projects of the Episcopal Church of England, the Society for the Propagation of the Gospel, and the Salvation Army, making it easy for descendants of English immigrants to transfer their loyalties from their parents' congregation to one in the community to which they had moved to create their own family. This pattern may change in the future, as the acceptance of the ordination of women and negotiations for a reconciliation with the Vatican and the Church of England proceed and as the Episcopal Church worships with its own "modern" Prayer Book.

From the colonial era, English Americans were concerned about higher education and the need for a trained ministry. A large percentage of the early colleges in America were founded and supported by English immigrants and their descendants especially in New England and the southeast. A number of traditional English sports such as sculling (team rowing) and rugby are still supported at colleges founded by English Americans, but the three English aristocratic pastimes that enjoy the greatest popularity in America, and have shed their English identity, are "lawn" tennis, horse racing, and sailing. In a scattering of communities in America, rugby, cricket, and English football (soccer) fields—where teams wearing traditional outfits of long socks, short pants, and shirts with broad horizontal stripes—keep alive a uniquely English sports heritage.

While many groups, including the New England Puritans and the English Quakers in Pennsylvania, were among the earliest advocates of free public education at all levels, the wealthy and professional classes of English settlers favored private schools and colleges, often affiliated with their particular denomination. When they could, they provided their older sons with a junior year abroad at a British university, as a substitute for the "grand tour" of the continent provided by their own parents. Many endowments were provided to subsidize the education of the children of expatriates in England, the most famous of which is the Rhodes scholarship program, named for the English financier and colonial official Cecil Rhodes. Throughout the United States, English immigrants and their descendants were among the leading philanthropists, supporting museums, colleges, and cultural organizations and many donated facilities in England to enable American colleges to conduct exchange and study-abroad programs. After World War II, Americans of English descent raised millions of dollars for the restoration of churches, schools, and other public buildings in England and that they had visited or attended.

Few particularly English holidays are celebrated by English Americans. In some communities small Guy Fawkes Day commemorations are held on November 5 to remember the deliverance of the King and Parliament from a plot in 1605 to destroy them by gunpowder. The English equivalent of July 4, it is celebrated in a similar fashion, with games, fireworks, and a large meal. Among some royalist families, St. Charles Day, marking the martyrdom of King Charles I on January 29, 1649 is celebrated with a somber ritual resembling a wake but featuring the imbibing of spirits, flag waving, and the reading of Charles's final speech from the gallows.

Because of their shared heritage, the family structure and community dynamics of English Americans have differed little from the rest of mainstream American. The mass media have continued to shape the culture of English and American societies in similar ways in the late twentieth century.

RELIGION

Beginning in the colonial era, the Church of England was active in every colony, despite the fact that many groups of English immigrants came to America to escape that institution and enjoy the freedom to practice other forms of Christianity. In the federalist period, as the Church of England became the Episcopal Church of America, other evangelical denominations including Quaker and Methodist ended their affiliation with their English counterparts and joined the American religious establishment. Throughout the history of the United States, there was little need for English expatriates to found separate churches, as virtually all English denominations found support in the American religious establishment. The exceptions to this situation were the groups of mill workers, miners, and tradesmen who settled in distinct enclaves in small towns in the 1870s and 1880s. A half dozen of these communities formed small congregations affiliated with less prominent English evangelical sects but were absorbed by other mainstream denominations within a decade. The Episcopal and Methodist-Episcopal churches remained an important segment of American Protestantism, and English immigrants and their descendants make up a significant and influential part of their membership.

POLITICS AND GOVERNMENT

The histories of England and America were inseparable during the colonial period, and English settlers dominated all aspects of colonial government and society. The American colonies successfully fought a war of rebellion against Britain from 1776 to 1783, after which several thousand English loyalists migrated to other Crown colonies, while others returned home. Several diplomatic problems, American aspirations to annex Canada, and the impressment of American sailors by the British navy led to the War of 1812. After America defeated Britain in 1815, a nationalist spirit swept the victorious nation, resulting in harsh public criticism of England, a brief period during English immigration was discouraged, and a number of conflicts renewed tension between the two countries.

Diplomatic relations began to improve as Britain promised naval support for the Monroe Doctrine, sealing off the American continent from colonial settlements by European powers, and as disputes over the Canadian border were settled. While new problems arose during the American Civil War and the period of Western expansion, cordial relations developed in the last part of the nineteenth century as the interests of Britain and America were challenged by other imperialist nations. Throughout the twentieth century a special relationship has endured, through alliances in two world wars and the Cold War. Britain was America's strongest supporter the Persian Gulf War, and the United States supported Britain in its war against Argentina to retain the Falkland Islands.

INDIVIDUAL AND GROUP CONTRIBUTIONS

During all of American history English immigrants and their descendants were prominent on every level of government and in every aspect of American life. Eight of the first ten American presidents and more than that proportion of the 42 presidents, as well as the majority of sitting congressmen and congresswomen, are descended from English ancestors. The acronym WASP, for white Anglo-Saxon Protestant, is used to describe the dominant political and cultural demographic segment in America.

The descendants of English expatriates are so numerous and so well integrated in American life that it is impossible to identify all of them. While they are the third largest ethnic nationality identified in the 1990 census, they retain such a pervasive representation at every level of national and state government that, on any list of American senators, Supreme Court judges, governors, or legislators, they would constitute a plurality if not an outright majority.

MEDIA

PRINT

Albion.

An interdisciplinary quarterly journal that features scholarly articles and reviews of books dealing with English history and culture. It is published by the North American Conference on British Studies and Appalachian State University.

Contact: Michael J. Moore, Editor.

Address: Department of History, Boone, North Carolina 28608-3906.

Telephone: (704) 262-6004.

British-American Trade News.

Monthly publication that provides a variety of information, statistics, and projections for the purpose of fostering trade between the two countries. It is published by the British-American Chamber of Commerce.

Address: 10 East 40th Street, New York, New York 10016.

Telephone: (212) 889-0680.

British Record.

A free bimonthly newsletter published by the British Information Services that provides a brief listing of British news items, cultural events, and short feature articles on people and places of general interest.

Address: 845 Third Avenue, New York, New York 10022.

Telephone: (212) 752-8400.

In Britain.

Monthly magazine published by the British Tourist Authority that includes an abundance of pictures and special features of tourists attractions, festivals, and historical and architectural monuments.

Address: 680 Fifth Avenue, New York, New York 10019.

Telephone: (212) 581-4708.

Manchester Guardian Weekly.

North American edition of *The Guardian*. It summarizes the news of the week in England and contains a variety of features, book reviews, international news, advertisements aimed at expatriates, and selections extracted from the Parisian *Le Monde* and the *Washington Post*. It has the largest circulation of any English newspaper in America.

Address: 19 West 44th Street, Suite 1613, New York, New York 10036-6101.

Telephone: (212) 944-1179.

Union Jack.

Brings news of Britain to the British community in the United States.

Contact: Ronald Choularton, Editor.

Address: Box 1823, La Mesa, California 91944-1823.

Telephone: (619) 466-3129.

RADIO AND TELEVISION

British Broadcasting Corporation (BBC).

Publishes *London Calling*, a program guide for several shortwave radio programs broadcast by the BBC to the United States and other countries.

Also distributes such BBC television series such as "The East-Enders," "Mystery Theatre," and "Are You Being Served," which are featured on America's Public Broadcasting System.

Address: 630 Fifth Avenue, New York, New York 10017.

Telephone: (212) 507-1500; or, (212) 507-0033.

ORGANIZATIONS AND ASSOCIATIONS

British Social and Athletic Club.

Founded in 1966 and centered in California, it has a dozen branches in the state and abroad. It provides a range of social and recreational activities and teaches and promotes cricket and soccer. It sponsors group flights to important matches around the world and has branches in Australia and New Zealand.

Address: 13429 Tiara Street, Van Nuys, California 91401.

Telephone: (213) 787-9985.

Daughters of the British Empire in the United States of America National Society.

Founded during World War I, this charitable society maintains facilities for aged British men and women.

Address: 4703 Ivanhoe Road, Houston, Texas 77027.

Telephone: (713) 626-7221.

English Speaking Union of the United States.

Founded in 1920 to promote British American friendship and understanding it sponsors debates, lectures, and speakers. It provides scholarships and travel grants and has over 70 branches throughout the United States. It publishes a quarterly newsletter.

Address: 16 East 69th Street, New York, New York 10021.

Telephone: (212) 879-6800.

International Society for British Genealogy and Family History (ISBGFH).

Strives to foster interest in the genealogy and family history of persons of British descent, improve U.S.-British relations, increase the educational opportunities and knowledge of members and the public, and encourage preservation of historical records and access to records.

Contact: Hazel M. Tibbitts, Corresponding Secretary.

Address: P.O. Box 3115, Salt Lake City, Utah 84110-3115.

Telephone: (801) 240-4314.

North American Conference on British Studies.

Founded in 1951, it is a national scholarly group that promotes scholarly research and discussion of British history and culture. It has seven regional branches, publishes *Albion* and the *Journal of British Studies*, and awards several prizes for the best new works in British Studies.

Contact: Reba Soffer, President.

Address: History Department, California State University, Northridge, California 91330.

St. George's Society of New York.

Founded in 1770, it is a charitable organization whose membership is limited to British citizens, their descendants, and members of Commonwealth nations. It provides assistance for needy British expatriates in the New York area.

Contact: John A. Ford, President.

Address: 15 East 26th Street New York New York 10010.

Telephone: (212) 532-2816.

MUSEUMS AND RESEARCH CENTERS

The Folger Shakespeare Library.

Maintains a collection of over 300,000 volumes and rare manuscripts on Shakespeare, drama, history, and government in Tudor and Stuart England. Founded in 1932, it provides scholarships, seminars, and evening colloquia for scholars and students of Renaissance Britain. It supports a diverse publication program, research projects, and traveling exhibits.

Contact: O. B. Hardison, Jr., Director.

Address: 201 East Capital Street, Washington, D.C. 20003.

Telephone: (202) 546-4800.

Paul Mellon Center for British Art and British Studies.

Founded in 1968, the center is part of Yale University. It includes the Mellon collection of British art and rare books, and it features a gallery, lecture, and seminar rooms and a library of over 100,000 volumes. It is affiliated with the undergraduate and graduate programs at the University and provides scholarships for research projects.

Address: Box 2120, Yale Station, New Haven, Connecticut 06520.

Telephone: (203) 432-4594.

SOURCES FOR ADDITIONAL STUDY

Berthoff, Roland T. *British Immigrants in Industrial America, 1790-1950*. New York: Russell and Russell, 1968.

Bridenbaugh, Carl. *Vexed and Troubled Englishmen, 1590-1642*. London: Oxford University Press, 1976.

The British in America: 1578-1970, edited by Howard B. Furer. Dobbs Ferry, New York: Oceana Publications, 1972.

Bryson, Bill. *The Mother Tongue: English and How It Got to Be That Way*. New York: Morrow, 1990.

Cohen, Robin. *Frontiers of Identity: The British and the Others*. London: Longmans, 1994.

Erickson, Charlotte. *Invisible Immigrants: the Adaptation of English and Scottish Immigrants in Nineteenth Century America*. Coral Gables, Florida: University of Miami Press, 1972.

To Build a New Land: Ethnic Landscapes in North America, edited by Allen G. Noble. Baltimore: Johns Hopkins University Press, 1992.

ESTONIAN AMERICANS

by
Mark A.
Granquist

Estonian Americans
have created a large
network of social
and cultural
organizations,
schools, churches,
and clubs to keep
alive the language
and culture of their
homeland.

OVERVIEW

Located on the east coast of the Baltic Sea, the Republic of Estonia is the northernmost of the three Baltic Republics. The country measures 17,413 square miles (45,100 sq. km.), including some 1,500 islands in the Baltic Sea. The population is approximately 72 percent urban in character, and the capital city is Tallinn. Estonia is bordered on the north by the Gulf of Finland, on the east by Lake Peipus and Russia, on the south by Latvia, and on the west by the Baltic Sea.

The 1992 census estimated the population of Estonia at 1,607,000. Of these inhabitants 65 percent are Estonian, while 30 percent are Russian, and the rest are Ukrainian and Byelorussian. The ethnic Russian immigration intensified during the Soviet period (1940-1991) and is concentrated in the east, especially around Narva. Lutherans constitute the largest religious group, although there are other Protestant denominations (principally Baptist) and a significant number of Eastern Orthodox Christians. The official language is Estonian, with Russian also widely spoken. The Estonian flag consists of three evenly spaced horizontal bands—blue on the top, black in the middle, and white on the bottom.

HISTORY

The Estonians are a Baltic-Finnish group related

187

to the Finno-Ugric peoples. Their first significant historical contact was with the Vikings, who in the ninth and tenth centuries conquered the Estonian homeland, bringing trade and cultural exchange. In the Middle Ages the Swedes, Danes, and Russians all attempted to conquer the land and to introduce Christianity, but it was not until the thirteenth century that the Germans prevailed and introduced Christianity by force. The Teutonic Order, a German order of crusading knights and priests, won control of Estonia by 1346, subjugating the native population and establishing a tradition of German rule that would extend into the twentieth century. As the power of the Teutonic Knights began to wane in the fifteenth century, Poland, Lithuania, and Russia all laid claim to Estonian territory, but it was Sweden who won control after the dissolution of the Teutonic Order in 1561. With Russia's defeat of Sweden in the Great Northern War, Estonia was transferred to Russian rule in 1721. Although some Estonians looked favorably to Russian rule as a way to free their country from German and Swedish domination, Russian government proved to be a mixed blessing. During the eighteenth century rural Estonians lost many of their traditional liberties. Serfdom was finally eliminated by 1819, and other social reforms followed. Imperial attempts at the "Russification" of Estonian life in the late nineteenth century broke the grip of the Baltic-Germans over the country, but these efforts came

into conflict with an ascendant wave of Estonian nationalism.

The January 1905 Revolution in Russia spread to Estonia, with Estonian leaders demanding national autonomy. When the revolution was crushed by imperial forces, many Estonian revolutionary leaders fled abroad. With the collapse of imperial government in 1917, Estonia won first autonomy and then independence. This was opposed by the Communists, who backed down only with the advance of German troops into the Baltic States in 1918. From 1917 to 1920, with British and Finnish aid, Estonians fought for independence from Russia. By 1920 Estonian troops had forced all remaining Soviet troops out of Estonia, and the country was finally independent. Between the World Wars, the newly emerging state had to contend externally with continued pressure and intrigue from the Soviets and internally with economic and political instability. In 1940, with the secret compliance of the Germans, Soviet troops took over Estonia and incorporated it into the Soviet Union. From 1941 to 1944, Estonia was occupied by the Nazis, and when Soviet troops reentered Estonia in 1944, large numbers of Estonians (perhaps ten percent of the total population) fled the country. Estonia continued as a Soviet Republic until 1991, undergoing another wave of Russification in the 1950s and 1960s. With the breakup of the Soviet Union, Estonia declared its independence in 1991, and a new Estonian government was elected in 1992.

SIGNIFICANT IMMIGRATION WAVES

During the period of Swedish rule over Estonia in the seventeenth century, a few Estonians assisted the Swedes in establishing the colony of New Sweden on the Delaware River. Estonian immigration to the United States was nevertheless quite limited until the late nineteenth century. The first Estonian immigrants were fortune hunters or seamen who jumped Russian sailing vessels. Immigration records do not identify them as Estonians, referring to them instead as "Russians," a practice that continued until 1922. In 1894, one group settled near Fort Pierre, South Dakota, while others settled in New York and San Francisco.

The first significant wave of immigration came after the failure in Estonia of the 1905 Revolution. This wave brought a strong Socialist contingent to the United States that led to the formation of many Estonian American Socialist and Communist organizations. Population estimates of the Estonian American community during this period vary widely and are difficult to reconcile. By 1930, official immigration and census records reveal that there were only about 3,550 Estonian Americans in the United States. Other sources, however, including government estimates, suggest that this number was much larger, recording 5,100 Estonian Americans in 1890, 44,100 in 1910, and 69,200 in 1920. The establishment of an independent Estonia in 1920, combined with the tightening of American immigration laws in the 1920s, dramatically slowed Estonian immigration to the United States. After World War II, there was a tremendous exodus of Estonians from Soviet rule; most Estonians made their way to Sweden or Germany, although about 15,000 of them came to the United States. Unlike the group that arrived in 1905, this group was strongly anti-Socialist and nationalistic; it spanned a larger exile community and was connected by a web of international organizations. The U.S. Census of 1990 lists 26,762 Americans claiming Estonian as a first or second ancestry.

SETTLEMENT PATTERNS

Early settlements arose on both coasts, in New York City and around San Francisco and Astoria, Oregon. In the late nineteenth century, there were rural, agricultural colonies of Estonian Americans in Fort Pierre, South Dakota; Bloomville, Wisconsin; Dickenson, North Dako-ta; and Chester, Montana, among other places. But these rural Midwestern settlements did not represent the bulk of Estonian immigrants. Rather, the two major waves of Estonian immigration in the twentieth century were mainly urban in nature. Major Estonian American settlements were located in the northeastern United States (Boston, Connecticut, New York City, New Jersey, Baltimore, and Washington), in the Midwest (Detroit and Cleveland), and on the West Coast (San Francisco and Los Angeles). More than half of Estonian Americans lived in the Northeast, with 20 percent concentrated in California and 15 percent in the Midwest. There was limited reverse migration back to Estonia in the 1920s, but this never became a significant trend. During the period of German and Russian occupation from 1940 to 1991, there was virtually no reemigration.

RELATIONS WITH SETTLED AMERICANS

Estonian immigrants have not stirred much reaction from the dominant culture in America, as the group is rather small in number. Because they share many characteristics with their white, middle-class urban neighbors, they quickly assimilate into their surroundings and have become part of their local communities. These immigrants tend to be literate, skilled, and hardworking and have made successful lives in the United States. One possible source of tension was the emergence of a radical socialist and communist movement among Estonians from 1905 to 1920. Instigated by refugees who took flight from Estonia during the 1905 Russian Revolution, this radicalizing movement captured and transformed many Estonian American institutions, causing great turmoil within the immigrant community. Coming at a time when Estonians were considered Russian in the popular mind, and when fear of communism was rampant, this did not go far to create a positive image of the Estonian immigrant. Nevertheless, the events of World War II, the Russian invasion of Estonia, and the flood of refugees out of the country created a swell of popular recognition for all the Baltic countries, including Estonia.

ACCULTURATION AND ASSIMILATION

Estonian immigrants in the United States have generally assimilated well into the mainstream of American society, especially after 1945. Before World War II, the Estonians did not push hard to become American citizens; in 1930 only 42 percent of immigrants had citizenship (a pace behind Finnish and other Baltic immigrants). In the late twentieth century, however, Estonian Americans have rapidly climbed the social and economic ladder, specializing in areas of technical expertise. A number of factors have contributed to a high degree of assimilation among Estonian Americans: the size of the community, its rapid educational and social success, and the wide geographical dispersion of the immigrants.

Estonian Americans have created a large network of social and cultural organizations, schools, churches, and clubs to keep alive the language and culture of their homeland. This network is coordinated by the Estonian American National Council, headquartered in New York City. A major goal of these institutions is to retain and transmit the Estonian heritage to succeeding generations. A network of 14 Estonian schools in the United States teaches Estonian language, history, and culture to the children of the community. Estonian American scouting is a national program with sponsored activities. Local Estonian American groups include women's and veterans' organizations and literary and cultural circles. Before 1992 and the establishment of the independent Republic of Estonia, many groups were dedicated to the opposition of communism and the eventual freedom of the Baltic states.

The tensions inherent in acculturation and assimilation are best displayed in the lives of the refugees who fled Estonia after World War II. On the one hand, they were glad to be in the United States and emphasized success within the American culture. On the other hand, as with many political refugees from Soviet communism, they held a strong passion for the overthrow of communism in Estonia and maintained hope that they would someday return to their native land. This refugee status created internal turmoil for some Estonian Americans, as they tried to balance the demands of their homeland and heritage with feelings of patriotism for the United States and a desire to assimilate into American society. Today, much of the active Estonian American community is composed of these first- and second-generation immigrants.

INTERACTION WITH OTHER ETHNIC GROUPS

Estonian Americans are closely affiliated with immigrants from other Baltic countries (Latvia, Lithuania, and Finland). Not only did these groups arrive in the United States at roughly the same time, they share a common history in Europe. Since the Soviet takeover of the Baltic Republics in 1940, Americans of Baltic descent have joined in common action toward securing independence for their ancestral homelands. A number of groups were formed around this issue, including the Joint Baltic American National Committee (1961) and the Baltic World Council (1972). There are also joint cultural and educational efforts and celebrations, and a Baltic Women's Council (1947).

CUISINE

Estonian cooking combines the culinary influences of Scandinavia, Germany, and Russia with native traditions. The raw ingredients come from the forests, farms, and coastal waters of Estonia: berries, pork, cabbage, sour cream, and seafood (salmon, herring, eel, sprat) are staples. From Scandinavia and Finland come the traditional foods of the smorgasbord; from Germany come sauerkraut and various cold potato salads. Russian influences also abound. *Rossolye* is a cold mixed salad of potatoes, vegetables, diced meat, and herring, with a sour cream-vinegar dressing. *Mulgikapsad* is a pork and sauerkraut dish that takes its name from an Estonian province. Other salads, common to the Baltic region, include a preserved mixed fruit salad and a sour cream-cucumber salad.

TRADITIONAL COSTUMES

Estonian Americans do not wear a distinctive everyday garment that would set them apart as being Estonian. As with many other European groups, Estonians have colorful regional costumes that immigrants sometimes brought with them, but these are worn only on special occasions, such as ethnic celebrations or festivals.

Traditional costumes for women include a tunic shirt, a full colorful skirt, and an embroidered apron. The headdresses worn by women vary according to region and village. In southern Estonia, the traditional headdress for a married woman is a long, linen, embroidered kerchief worn around the head and down the back. In northern Estonia, small, intricately designed *coifs* (hats) adorn women's folk costumes. Heavy necklaces are also common. Men's costumes generally consist of wide-legged pants gathered at the knee and loose-fitting shirts. The principal headdress for men is a high, stiff felt hat or fur cap with earflaps, the latter of which is worn during the winter months. Both men's and women's traditional costumes include a decorative broach used to fasten shirts and blouses. During the winter, traditional Estonian costumes included high felt boots called *valenka* to protect them from the cold.

HOLIDAYS CELEBRATED BY ESTONIAN AMERICANS

Along with the traditional Christian and American holidays, there are certain festival days that are of special significance to the Estonian American community. February 24 is celebrated as Estonian Independence Day, marking the formal declaration of Estonian independence in 1918. A two-day holiday in June combines two separate celebrations, St. John's Eve (Midsummer) on June 23, and Victory Day on June 24. Reaching far back into history, Midsummer is a common festival in the Scandinavian and Baltic countries. Victory Day commemorates the defeat of the Soviet Armies in the Estonian War of Independence (1918-1920). In their celebration of Christmas, Estonians extend the holiday a day or two after December 25; the first few days after Christmas are devoted to visiting friends and family.

A feature of resurgent Estonian nationalism during the nineteenth and twentieth centuries has been national song festivals, celebrated for a period of days during the summer. Estonians in Europe and North America continue to celebrate these festivals, organizing mass gatherings to honor Estonia and to maintain national identity. In North America Estonians from Canada and the United States gathered in such celebrations from 1957 to 1968, twice in New York and twice in Canada. The Estonian World Festivals, a series of worldwide Estonian gatherings, began in 1972. The first such event was in Toronto, followed by Baltimore, Maryland, and Stockholm.

HEALTH AND MENTAL HEALTH ISSUES

Estonian Americans have embraced medicine as it is practiced in the United States and have been eager to become medical practitioners. A 1975 survey by the *Väliseestlasea kalendar* (*Almanac for the Estonian Abroad*) listed over 100 Estonian American doctors or dentists, of whom 25 percent were women.

LANGUAGE

The Estonian language is a branch of the Baltic-Finnish group of the Finno-Ugric family, related to Finnish. Most ethnic Estonians speak Estonian, but ethnic Russians and others in Estonia continue to speak Russian because Estonian is considered to be a difficult language to learn. Historically, there have been a number of dialects, but the one spoken around the capital of Tallinn has come to dominate literary expression, thus ruling the development of modern Estonian. Another form of Estonian is spoken by Estonian war refugees in Sweden and has absorbed some Swedish influences. The written language uses the Roman alphabet and consists of 14 consonants and nine vowels ("a, ä, e, i, o, ö, õ, u," and "ü"). The consonants ("c, f, q, w, x, y," and "z") are generally used only in names and words of foreign origin. The language has a musical quality and employs a great number of diphthongs and other vowel combinations.

The Estonian American community has made strong attempts to maintain the language, with mixed success. A number of schools, publications, congregations, and learned societies within the community still use Estonian as a means of discourse. This is somewhat problematic within the larger community because new generations and the non-Estonian spouses of mixed marriages have a hard time understanding Estonian. Still, Estonian is taught at Indiana University, Kent State University, and Ohio State University, and a number of public libraries throughout the United States offer Estonian language collections, including the Boston Public Library, the New York Public Library, and the Cleveland Public Library.

GREETINGS AND OTHER POPULAR EXPRESSIONS

Common Estonian greetings and other expressions include: *Tere hommikut* ("tere hommikoot")—Good morning; *Tere õhtut* ("tere erhtut")—Good evening; Jumalaga ("yoomahlah-gah")—Good-bye; *Kuidas käsi käib* ("kooydahs kasi kayb")—How are you?; *Tänan hästi* ("tanahn haysti")—Fine, thanks; *Palun* ("pahloon")—Please; *Tänan* ("tanahn")—Thanks; *Vabandage* ("vahbahndahge")—Excuse me; *Jah* ("yah")—Yes; *Ei* ("ey")—No; and *Nägemieseni* ("nagesmiseni")—See you later.

FAMILY AND COMMUNITY DYNAMICS

Before 1920 the Estonian American community tended to be dominated by young single men and women who came either to look for work or to escape the religious and political repression of tsarist Russia. Because the vast majority lived in cities on the East or West Coast, a stable immigrant community, with a predominance of families and other social and cultural institutions, was slow to develop. But the 1920s and 1930s saw the appearance of a strong immigrant community that was augmented after 1945 by the arrival of war refugee families. A significant degree of educational and economic advancement, a high rate of intermarriage, and the dispersal of this relatively small community have moved the Estonians well into the mainstream of American life. In addition, research has shown a considerable degree of ethnic consciousness among the contemporary Estonian Americans that will help hold the community together.

"After I got my citizenship, I sponsored two Estonian immigrant families. And a few years ago, I married a man from one of those families. So I have a new life. I feel that I have been blessed, really. This country has given me many things: a home, friendship, a chance to live again."

Leida Sorro in 1951, cited in *American Mosaic: The Immigrant Experience in the Words of Those Who Lived It,* edited by Joan Morrison and Charlotte Fox Zabusky (New York: E.P. Dutton, 1980).

EDUCATION

Education has played an important role in shaping the Estonian American community and in moving these immigrants into mainstream American life. Because Estonia in the nineteenth century was more advanced in literacy than many other parts of the Russian Empire, many of the early immigrants were literate. Likewise, a significant number of the political refugees who fled Estonia after the abortive 1905 Revolution were educated, and the Socialist ferment within the community produced journals, newspapers, and reading rooms. However, the emphasis on education was nowhere more apparent than in the refugees who arrived in the United States after 1945. Many of them were members of the educational and political elite of Estonia, and in the United States they pushed for their children to get a good education. Studies of the second generation of these Estonian Americans have shown that a large majority have at least some college education, a modest majority have completed college, and a sizable number have graduate degrees. Also among this last group of immigrants were a number of Estonian intellectuals and academics who took positions in the American educational system. Estonian Americans have tended to specialize in science and technology, moving into fields such as engineering and architecture.

The Estonian American community has established a number of institutions to promote advancement in scholarship and education. These include Estonian academic fraternities and sororities, as well as an Estonian Students Association in the United States that promotes students' knowledge of Estonian language and culture and Estonian study abroad (especially in Finland). Learned societies, such as the Estonian Educational Society and the Estonian Learned Society in America, sponsor publications and conferences. A number of other specialized educational groups have a broader membership that extends throughout North America and Europe.

Estonian schools, located in major centers of the Estonian American community, are designed to supplement the education of Estonian youth by teaching them Estonian language, geography, history, and culture. These schools are interlinked in a regional and national network.

THE ROLE OF WOMEN

Since the advent of the Estonian American community, women have traditionally worked outside the home, pursuing education and careers. In 1932 an anonymous Estonian American writer commenting in his journal *Meie Tee* (quoted in *The Estonians in America, 1627-1975: A Chronology and Factbook,* p. 83) remarked about his community: "Estonian women here have always worked, even though the husband might have a well-paying job. Perhaps this is ... an established tradition." A 1968 survey of young Estonian American women showed that only 14 percent had ended their education at the high school level, whereas 61 percent were college graduates. The advanced level of women's education and work outside the home partly explains the swift rise in socioeconomic status of the Estonian American community. Estonian American women have also formed numerous local, national, and international women's organizations centered on educational, cultural, and social concerns and have banded with other Baltic-American women's groups to achieve common goals.

RELIGION

In Estonia the dominant form of Christianity is Lutheranism, with smaller numbers of Baptist and Orthodox adherents. In Estonian American communities Lutheranism continues to be the dominant religious force. Headquartered in Stockholm, the Estonian Evangelical Lutheran Church is easily the largest organized religious group within the Estonian American community, with 38 congregations and 12,032 members across North America. The Estonian American Baptists came to the United States before World War I to escape persecution in Estonia and have maintained a number of congregations. The Baptist congregation in New York City, one of the first congregations formed, was an important early institution within the immigrant community. Estonian Orthodox parishes are active in Los Angeles, San Francisco, Chicago, and New York City. There are also several Estonian Pentecostal congregations.

This is not to say, however, that religious belief and affiliation have been universally important for Estonian immigrants in America; indeed, many Estonians were ambivalent or even hostile toward religious belief, especially early in this century. There are a number of reasons for these negative feelings, which spring from religious faith and practice in Estonia. The Lutheran Church in Estonia had traditionally been dominated by the Baltic-Germans, who monopolized many aspects of Estonian national life; not until 1860 did ethnic Estonians serve as Lutheran pastors. Thus, to many nineteenth-century Estonians Lutheranism represented a "foreign" presence. Another factor in the ambivalence of early Estonian immigrants toward religion was their adherence to socialist and communist ideologies that opposed organized religion. These dynamics proved to be very difficult for early Estonian American pastors to overcome, as they clashed with anticlerical and socialist immigrant groups.

The first religious leader in the Estonian American community was the Reverend Hans Rebane, who arrived in New York in 1896. Rebane had been invited by the American denomination, the German Missouri Lutheran Synod, to establish a mission for Estonian and Latvian Lutheran immigrants. Rebane established a small congregation in New York City and visited other Estonian settlements in the East and Midwest. Rebane also established a newspaper, *Eesti Amerika Postimees* (*Estonian American Courier*), the first Estonian publication in the United States. Rebane used this newspaper to push his religious views and feuded with Estonian socialist groups until his death in 1911. Though the congregation in New York survived, and the Missouri Synod continued mission work among Estonian immigrants, this work was not particularly successful. During the period before World War II only two other Estonian American congregations took hold: a Baptist congregation formed in 1919, and a Pentecostal congregation formed in 1928, both in New York City.

After 1945 the influx of Estonian war refugees resulted in the construction of a number new Lutheran congregations, all linked with the Estonian Evangelical Lutheran Church (EELC). Established in 1954, the EELC has Lutheran congregations in most major Estonian settlements in North America. The other religious force to appear after 1945 was Estonian Orthodox Christianity, establishing several regional parishes. Orthodoxy took root in Estonia during the nineteenth century, winning Estonian converts who were discontent with German-dominated Lutheranism and Russian inducements. The first Estonian Orthodox parish was formed in New York City in 1949.

Especially since 1945 religion has come to play an important role in the life of the Estonian American community and has helped maintain a sense of group identity and cultural cohesion.

EMPLOYMENT AND ECONOMIC TRADITIONS

The large majority of early immigrants settled in cities on the East and West Coasts, seeking jobs in labor and industry. Many Estonian men worked in the construction trades, and some rose to the level of independent contractors. Many women worked as domestics or in small retail or industrial operations. In the 1920s and 1930s numbers of Estonians were employed as building attendants and superintendents in apartments and office buildings, especially in New York. Other Estonians started small businesses, some of which were fairly successful.

An early conflict within the Estonian American community was over socialism and communism. Many of the refugees from the failed 1905 Revolution were socialists who were influential in establishing a strong socialist-oriented urban worker's movement among the Estonian Americans. Workers' societies were formed in centers of Estonian settlement, and in 1908 a central committee was organized to coordinate their activities. These organizations were often the only collective Estonian bodies in the community and thus came to be influential. However, the leadership of these organizations proved to be more radical than the American socialists and the majority of Estonian American workers. Between 1917 and 1920 the Estonian workers' movement was split over the issue of whether to support the Soviet military takeover of the newly independent Republic of Estonia. Many of the movement's leaders adopted a communist platform that supported inclusion of Estonia within the Soviet Union, whereas the majority of the rank and file opposed the move. The split shattered the effectiveness of the immigrant institutions and the Estonian American workers' movement as a whole. The communists were eventually absorbed into the American Communist Party, losing any particular ethnic identity.

After 1945 the employment and economic status of the community shifted in response to the new wave of political refugees, many of whom were well-educated professionals. A strong emphasis on education, professionalism, and the two-income family brought prosperity and socioeconomic mobility to the Estonian American community, which became predominantly middle class. Education, engineering and applied technology, medicine, science, and music and the arts were the leading professions. In 1962 a study of young Estonian American professionals found that 43 percent worked in the fields of engineering and technology; 18 percent in the sciences; 16 percent in the humanities and social sciences, respectively; and seven percent in medicine. Some Estonians have gone into business, often starting small- to medium-sized businesses within the Estonian American community.

POLITICS AND GOVERNMENT

Political activity within the Estonian American community has been responsive to events within Estonia itself. Fluctuations in Estonia's status as an independent country have had a significant impact on this activity.

Because of Estonia's dependent status in the nineteenth century, many Estonian immigrants had not formed a clear consciousness of their national identity. But the rise of Estonian nationalism, coupled with the socialist struggle against the tsarist government, prompted the Estonian American community toward greater involvement in the affairs of the homeland. As political refugees began streaming into the country after the 1905 Revolution, the leadership of the immigrant community and many of its institutions passed into socialist hands. The communist revolution and the struggle to free Estonia (1917-1920) split the Estonian American community between those who supported a free Estonia and those who supported its inclusion into the Soviet Union. The Estonian nationalists prevailed because of a growing sense of national pride and because of the arrival (after 1920) of many veterans of the Estonian struggle for independence. In the wider sphere of American politics, the immigrant community was not particularly active unless the Republic of Estonia's affairs were directly involved. The number of immigrants seeking citizenship during this period was lower than for other Baltic nationalities.

The Soviet invasion of Estonia in 1940, along with the arrival of the war refugees after 1945, dramatically changed the face of the Estonian American community and its political efforts. The major concern now was Estonian independence from Soviet control. Many Estonian and Baltic-American groups formed to support their Estonian homeland in achieving this goal. Their initial activities centered on lobbying both the U.S. government and the United Nations to prevent the legal recognition of the Soviet conquest of Estonia. Because of their efforts (in concert with Latvian and Lithuanian Americans), the U.S. government never formally recognized the annexation of the three Baltic countries by the Soviet Union in 1940 and again in 1944 until 1991 when these countries regained their independence. Consequently, in the post World War II years, all three Baltic nations maintained consulates in the United States. Estonian Americans, as well as other Eastern European immigrant groups, were particularly outraged by the 1945 U.S.-Soviet agreement at Yalta, which they viewed as a sellout of the nations under communist domination.

After 1945 most Estonian Americans supported the Republican Party, faulting the Democrats for the Yalta agreement and viewing the Republicans as more sympathetic to their concerns. This trend of support for the Republican Party has continued. In 1970 the Estonian Amer-

ican National Republic Committee was formed, with a network of Estonian American Republican clubs established in geographic centers of the immigrant community. Socialist influence in the community has diminished.

UNION ACTIVITY

Estonian American involvement in organized labor grew with the rise of the workers' movement in the early twentieth century. Support for this movement saw the rise many local workers' and socialist organizations and a number of newspapers and periodicals. Many of the activities of the workers' movement went beyond economic and union concerns to include social and cultural activities as well as political mobilization. However, the socialist leaders of the movement tended to be more radical than either the rank and file or the American labor movement, and this was the cause of much friction. With the drift toward communism and agitation over Estonian independence, the worker's movement became divided and lost much of its vitality.

ARMED FORCES

Estonian Americans have served in the U.S. armed forces in every significant military conflict in the twentieth century. There was a small Estonian American presence during the two World Wars, while a larger group fought in the Korean and Vietnam Wars. In 1951 an Estonian American, Kalju Suitsev, was awarded a Silver Star and Purple Heart for bravery in Korea. In Vietnam many Estonian youth participated, including a number who were killed or decorated for bravery. Given the fervent patriotic and anti-communist stance of the Estonian American community during this period, support for military service was strong.

RELATIONS WITH ESTONIA

The intense support given to the Republic of Estonia during the 1920s and 1930s, and the agitation for a free Estonia after 1940, galvanized the immigrant community and created a course of common action. The drive toward nationalism has not always won universal support, however, the most notable example being the Estonian American communists who favored Soviet rule over Estonia. It remains to be seen how Estonian independence, achieved in 1991, will shape the activities of the Estonian American community.

INDIVIDUAL AND GROUP CONTRIBUTIONS

Although small in number, Estonian Americans have played a significant part in their communities and in the United States. Their most striking accomplishments have been in the fields of education, engineering and technology, architecture and applied arts, and music.

ARCHITECTURE

The most prominent of all Estonian Americans is probably the architect Anton Hanson, who was born in Estonia in 1879 and immigrated to the United States in 1906. Hanson was one of the designing architects of the Seattle World's Fair, for which he was awarded the grand prize.

EDUCATION

Herrman Eduard von Holst (1841-1904) studied in Estonia and received his doctorate from the University of Heidelberg in Germany. He became the first chair of the history department at the University of Chicago and wrote a number of important works on American and European history. He also held academic positions in Germany and France. Theodore Alexis Wiel was born in Estonia in 1893 but attended college in America. After being decorated for service in France in World War I, Wiel earned a doctorate in international relations and taught at American International College, where he also served as dean. Ragnar Nurske (1907-1959) studied in Estonia and England before coming to the United States, where he taught Economics at Columbia University. Nurske authored a number of works on international economics and also served on the League of Nations prior to World War II. Ants Oras was an English professor at the University of Tartu, Estonia. He came to America via England after World War II and taught at the University of Florida. Arthur Vööbus (1909-1990) obtained his doctorate in Estonia in 1943 and came to the United States after the war. A biblical scholar and expert on early Syrian Christianity, Vööbus taught at the Lutheran School of Theology in Chicago.

FILM AND THEATER

Miliza Korjus was born in Estonia to Estonian and Polish parents. A soprano, Korjus performed the leading role in the film *The Great Waltz* (1938), a biography of the waltz king, Johann Strauss. Korjus later settled in California to continue her singing career. Ivan (John) Triesault, born in Estonia, was a film actor who made over 25 films, from *Mission to Moscow* (1942) to *Von Ryan's Express* (1965). He specialized in playing character roles, including German military officers.

GOVERNMENT

William Leiserson (1883-1957), born in Estonia, received his Ph.D. from Columbia University in 1911. A specialist in labor affairs, he was employed by the U.S. Department of Labor and was appointed by President Franklin Roosevelt to the Labor Arbitration Commission in 1939.

INDUSTRY

Carl Sundbach, born in Estonia in 1888, invented a freezer that greatly reduced the time required to bulk freeze fish. William Zimdin (1881-1951) was an international businessman and millionaire. Zimdin began his career in the United States in 1920 by arranging transactions between the United States and the Soviet Union; he eventually settled in California. Otto Lellep, born in Estonia in 1884, was a metallurgical engineer who came to the United States in 1917. Working in the United States and Germany, he developed a cement baking oven and made advancements in the processing of steel, iron ore, and nickel. Lellep went into business manufacturing his ovens in the United States after World War II. John Kusik, born in Estonia in 1898, rose to become director and senior vice president of the Baltimore and Ohio Railroad and served on a number of other corporate boards.

JOURNALISM

Edmund Valtman (1914-) came to the United States in 1949. A political cartoonist with the *Hartford Times*, Valtman received the Pulitzer Prize for his drawings in 1961.

MUSIC

Ludvig Juht (1894-1957), an Estonian-born musician, specialized in the contrabass. Juht had an international career in Estonia, Finland, and Germany until he was brought to America in 1934 by Serge Koussevitzky to be principle contrabass with the Boston Symphony Orchestra. In addition, Juht taught at both the New England Conservatory of Music and Boston University, and worked as a composer. Evi Liivak was born in Estonia in 1925 and studied the violin. In 1951 she joined her American husband in the United States and has enjoyed an international career.

SCIENCE AND TECHNOLOGY

Elmar Leppik, a biologist educated in Estonia and Europe, came to America in 1950. He taught at a number of American universities and then worked as a research scientist with the U.S. Department of Agriculture in Maryland. Igor Taum, born in Estonia in 1922, came to the United States in 1945 and has served as a research physician at Rockefeller University, New York City, where he specializes in the study of viruses. Richard Härm, born in 1909, was educated in Estonia and Germany prior to coming to the United States after World War II. He taught mathematics at Princeton University. Rein Kilkson (1927-) was born in Estonia, and received his doctorate at Yale University in 1949. A physicist, he did research in the areas of biophysics and virology and taught at the University of Arizona. Lauri Vaska (1925-), a chemist, discovered a new chemical compound, which was eventually named the "Vaska compound." Vaska taught at Clarkson College of Technology, Potsdam, New York. Harald Oliver, Jyri Kork, and Rein Ise have participated as scientists in the U.S. space program on the Apollo moon project and the Skylab space station.

VISUAL ARTS

Voldemar Rannus (1880-1944) came to the United States in 1905. A sculptor, Rannus studied at the National Academy of Design in New York, and later in Europe. He molded a bas-relief of Albert Beach (the designer of the New York City subway) for the subway station near the New York City Hall. Andrew Winter (1893-1958) painted realistic winter scenes and seascapes. Born in Estonia, he came to the United States and studied here, eventually settling in Maine.

MEDIA

PRINT

Journal of Baltic Studies.
Published by the Association for the Advancement of Baltic Studies (AABS), this quarterly provides a forum for scholarly discussion on topics regarding the Baltic Republics and their peoples.

Contact: William Urban or Roger Noel, Editors.

Address: 111 Knob Hill Road, Hacketstown, New Jersey 07844.

Meie Elu.
Estonian weekly newspaper in Canada, established in 1950.

Contact: Tony Parming, Editor.
Address: Estonian Publishing Co., 958 Broadview Avenue, Toronto, Ontario, Canada M4K 2R6.
Telephone: (416) 466-0951.
Fax: (416) 461-0448.

Meie Tee (Our Path).
Estonian American monthly journal, established in 1931, with general information about the American and worldwide Estonian community. Published by the World Association of Estonians.

Address: 243 East 34th Street, New York, New York 10016.
Telephone: (212) 684-9281.

Vaba Eesti Sõna (Free Estonian Word).
Estonian American weekly newspaper, established in 1949. Known for its staunch anticommunist and nationalist views.

Contact: Harald Raudsepp, Editor.
Address: Nordic Press, Inc., 243 East 34th Street, New York, New York 10016.
Telephone: (212) 686-3356.

Väliseestlase Kalendar (Calendar for Estonians Abroad).
Annual publication for the immigrant community, established in 1953.

Address: The Nordic Press, P.O. Box 123, New York, New York 10156.
Telephone: (212) 686-3356.

Yearbook of the Estonian Learned Society in America.
Published by the Estonian Learned Society in America to advance and disseminate scholarly knowledge for and about Estonia and Estonians.

Address: 243 East 34th Street, New York, New York 10016.

ORGANIZATIONS AND ASSOCIATIONS

Estonian American National Council (EANC).
Founded in 1952, this umbrella organization represents all Estonian Americans and major Eston-

ian American organizations. Coordinates the efforts of the member groups; supports political, cultural, and social activities; provides grants for study; and maintains a library and archives at its headquarters in New York City.

Contact: John J. Tiivel, Secretary General.
Address: 243 East 34th Street, New York, New York 10016.
Telephone: (212) 685-0776.

Estonian Evangelical Lutheran Church (EELC).

Founded in 1954. Ecclesiastical structure for all Estonian Lutherans outside of Estonia, headquartered in Sweden. Promotes religious education and outreach in the immigrant communities, conducts religious services, and maintains congregations. The North American branch of the EELC consists of 38 congregations in the United States and Canada.

Contact: Rev. Udo Petersoo, Archbishop for North America.

Address: 383 Jarvis Street, Toronto, Ontario, Canada M5B 2C7.
Telephone: (416) 925-5465.

Estonian Heritage Society (EHS).

Promotes and seeks to preserve Estonian cultural heritage.

Contact: Mart Aru, Chair.
Address: P.O. Box 3141, 200090 Tallinn, Estonia.
Telephone: (142) 449216.

Estonian Learned Society in America.

Founded in 1950, this scholarly organization represents Estonian Americans with graduate degrees; it seeks to encourage Estonian studies, especially in English and supports translation of Estonian literary works. Publishes a yearbook every three to four years.

Contact: Viktor Koressaar, President.
Address: 243 East 34th Street, New York, New York 10016.

Estonian Relief Committee, Inc.

Founded in 1941, this committee assists Estonians with settlement and employment in the United States. It also supports Estonian American activities and groups, especially Estonian American scouting programs.

Contact: Alfred Anderson, Secretary-General.
Address: 243 East 34th Street, New York, New York 10016.
Telephone: (212) 685-7467.

Federated Estonian Women's Clubs.

Founded in 1966, this club coordinates and encourages ties between Estonian women's organizations throughout the world. It also sponsors scholarship and cultural activities, such as folk art, language training, Estonian handicrafts, and camping.

Contact: Juta Kurman, President.
Address: 243 East 34th Street, New York, New York 10016.

United Baltic Appeal (BATUN).

Serves as an information center dealing with events and circumstances pertinent to Estonia, Latvia, and Lithuania.

Contact: Baiba J. Rudzifis-Pinnis, President.
Address: 115 West 183rd Street, Bronx, New York 10453.
Telephone: (718) 367-8802.

MUSEUMS AND RESEARCH CENTERS

Estonian Archives in the United States.

The main archives for documents on the immigrant settlements and their development. Located in the Estonian American community of Lakewood, New Jersey, this institution is particularly valuable to the study of Estonian Americans.

Address: 607 East Seventh Street, Lakewood, New Jersey 08701.

Estonian Educational Society (EHS).

Maintains school of Estonian language and history and library of 3,000 volumes in Estonian.

Contact: Rudolf Hamar, Manager.
Address: Estonian House, 243 East 34th Street, New York, New York 10016.
Telephone: (212) 684-0336.

Estonian Society of San Francisco.

A cultural, educational, and social foundation for Estonian Americans on the West Coast. It sponsors ethnic scouting, dancing, and scholarship and maintains a library and reading room.

Contact: August Kollom, President.

Address: 537 Brannan Street, San Francisco, California 94107.

Telephone: (415) 797-7892.

Immigration History Research Center.

Located at the University of Minnesota, this is a valuable archival resource for many of the immigrant groups from Eastern and Southern Europe, including the Estonians. In addition to newspapers and serials, the center also has a collection of books and monographs, along with the records of Estonian American groups in Minnesota and Chicago.

Contact: Dr. Rudolph Vecoli, Director.

Address: 826 Berry Street, St. Paul, Minnesota 55114.

Telephone: (612) 627-4208.

Office of the Estonian Consulate General.

Representing the Republic of Estonia in the United States, it is a valuable resource for general information on Estonia and the Estonian American community.

Address: 9 Rockefeller Plaza, New York, New York 10020.

SOURCES FOR ADDITIONAL STUDY

Balys, J., and Uno Teemant. "Estonian Bibliographies: A Selected List," *Lituanus: The Lithuanian Quarterly*, 19, No. 3, 1973; 54-72.

Brown, Francis, and Joseph Slabey Roucek. *One America: The History, Contributions, and Present Problems of Our Racial and National Minorities*, revised edition. New York: Prentice-Hall, 1945.

The Estonians in America, 1627-1975: A Chronology and Factbook, edited by Jaan Pennar, et al. Ethnic Chronology Series, No. 17. Dobbs Ferry, New York: Oceana Publications, Inc., 1975.

Parming, Marju, and Tönu Parming. *A Bibliography of English-Language Sources on Estonia*. New York: Estonian Learned Society in America, 1974.

Raun, Toivo. *Estonia and Estonians* (Studies in Nationalities of the U.S.S.R.). Stanford, California: Hoover Institution Press, 1987.

Tannberg, Kersti, and Tönu Parming. *Aspects of Cultural Life: Sources for the Study of Estonians in America*. New York: Estonian Learned Society in America, 1979.

Walko, M. Ann. *Rejecting the Second Generation Hypothesis: Maintaining Estonian Ethnicity in Lakewood, New Jersey*. New York: AMS Press, 1989.

By the end of the twentieth century, Finnish Americans had essentially become invisible. They worked hard to be indistinguishable from other Euroamericans and, as descendants of white Europeans, fit easily into the mass culture.

FINNISH

by

Marianne

Wargelin

AMERICANS

OVERVIEW

Finland, a nation-state created in the closing days of World War I, is located in the far northern reaches of Europe. It is bounded by Sweden to the west, Russia to the east, Norway to the north, and the Gulf of Finland to the south. About 90 percent of Finns are Lutheran; the Russian Orthodox church (two percent) is the second largest in the nation. Finnish people continue to maintain a unique language spoken today by only about 23 million people worldwide.

The nearly five million people of contemporary Finland reflect the traditional groups who settled in the nation centuries ago. The largest group consists of Finns who speak Finnish; the second largest group, some six percent, are Finland-Swedes (also known as Swede Finns) who speak Swedish; the most visible minority groups are the Sami (about 4,400), who speak Sami (or Lappish) and live in the North, and the Gypsies (about 5,500), who live in the South.

HISTORY

The ancestors of these peoples came under the domination of the Swedes in the twelfth century, when Finland became a province of Sweden. While the Swedish provinces operated quite independently for a time, efforts to centralize power in the kingdom in the sixteenth century made Finns citizens of Sweden. Sweden was the primary power in the Baltic region for more than a hundred years, until challenged by Russia in the eighteenth century. By 1809 Sweden was so weakened that she was forced to cede her entire Baltic holdings, including Finland, to Russia.

Russia gave Finland a special status as a "Grand Duchy," with the right to maintain the Lutheran religion, the Finnish language, and Finnish constitutional laws. This new status encouraged its leaders to promote a sense of Finnish spirit. Historically a farming nation, Finland did not begin to industrialize until the 1860s, later than their Nordic neighbors; textile mills, forestry, and metal work became the mainstays of the economy. Then, in the final days of the nineteenth century, Russia started a policy of "Russification" in the region, and a period of oppression began.

Political unrest dominated the opening years of the twentieth century. Finland conducted a General Strike in 1906, and the Russian czar was forced to make various concessions, including universal suffrage—making Finland the first European nation to grant women the right to vote—and the right to maintain Finland's own parliament. The oppressive conditions returned two years later, but Finland remained a part of Russia until declaring its own independence in the midst of the Russian Revolution of 1917. A bitter civil war broke out in Finland as the newly independent nation struggled between the philosophies of the bourgeois conservatives and the working class Social Democrats. In 1919 the nation began to govern itself under its own constitution and bill of rights.

MODERN ERA

With basic democratic rights and privileges established, the 1920s and 1930s emerged as a period of political conservatism and right wing nationalism. Then, in 1939, the Soviet Union invaded Finland. War between the two nations ensued—first in a war known as the Winter War, then in the so-called Continuation War. When it ended, Finland made major concessions to the Soviets, including the loss of a considerable portion of its eastern territory.

In the 1950s Finland continued its transformation from a predominantly agricultural economy into a modern industrial economy. By the 1960s it had established itself as a major design center in Europe, and by the end of the 1970s it maintained a post-industrial age culture with a stable economy that continued to produce premier quality work in the arts. Throughout the rest of the twentieth century, Finland maintained a strict policy of neutrality toward its neighbors to the east and west.

THE FIRST FINNS IN AMERICA

The first Finns in North America came as colonists to New Sweden, a colony founded along the Delaware River in 1638. The colony was abandoned to the Dutch in 1664, but the Finns remained, working the forest in a slash-and-burn-style settlement pattern. By the end of the eighteenth century, their descendants had disappeared into a blur amidst the dominant English and Dutch colonist groups. However, many Finnish Americans believe that a descendant of those Finnish pioneers, John Morton, was a signer of the Declaration of Independence. Few material signs—other than their distinctive log cabin design and place names—remain to mark their early presence.

A second colonial effort involved Finns in the Russian fur trading industry. In Sitka, Alaska, Finns mixed with Russian settlers in the 1840s and 1850s, working primarily as carpenters and other skilled craftsmen. Two of Alaska's governors were Finnish: Arvid Adolph Etholen (1799-1876) served from 1840 to 1845, and Johan H. Furuhjelm (1821-1909) served from 1859 to 1864. A Finnish pastor, Uno Cygnaeus (1810-1888), who later returned to Finland to establish the Finnish public school system, also served the Finnish American community. Today, this Finnish presence is represented in the Sitka Lutheran church, which dates from that period. After 1867, when Alaska was transferred to the United States, some of the Sitka Finns moved down to communities developing along the northwest coastline—places like Seattle and San Francisco.

Colonial settlers were small in number. Similarly, according to Reino Kero in *Migration from Finland to North America in the Years Between the United States Civil War and the First World War*, the Finnish sailors and sea captains who left their ships to enter the California Gold Rush or to establish new lives in American harbor cities like Baltimore, Galveston, San Francisco, and New York, numbered only several hundred. One sailor, Charles Linn (Carl Sjodahl; 1814-1883), became a wealthy southern merchant who ran a large wholesale business in New Orleans and later established Alabama's National Bank of Birmingham and the Linn Iron Works. He is credited with opening the immigration from southern Finland to the United States when, in 1869, he brought 53 immigrants from Helsinki and Uusimaa to work for his company.

SIGNIFICANT IMMIGRATION WAVES

Finnish immigration is considered to have occurred primarily between 1864 and 1924. Early Finnish immigrants to the United States were familiar with agricultural work and unskilled labor and were therefore new to industrial work and urban life. Later, skilled workers like carpenters, painters, tailors, and jewelers journeyed to the States, but the number of professionals who immigrated remained small until after 1965. Most scholars have estimated that, at the most, some 300,000 Finnish immigrants remained to become permanent residents and citizens of the United States of America. Of these, about 35,000 were Finland Swedes and about 15,000 Sami.

The first immigrants arrived in 1864, when Finns from northern Finland and Norway settled on homestead prairie lands in south central Minnesota. The next year 30 Finnish miners living in Norway went to work in the copper mines in Hancock, Michigan. These Finns, originally from northern Finland, developed the first permanent Finnish American communities in the American Midwest. Continued economic depression in Finland encouraged others to leave their homeland; the number of immigrants grew to 21,000 before 1887.

Those from northern Norway and Finland who traveled as family groups were part of the Great Laestadian Migration of 1864-1895, a migration that began shortly after the death of founder Lars Levi Laestadius (1800-1861). Looking for ways to maintain a separatist lifestyle as well as to improve their economic standing, Laestadian families began a migration that has continued in some form to the present day. Finnish American Laestadian communities formed in the mining region of Michigan and in the homestead lands of western Minnesota, South Dakota, Oregon, and Washington. These Laestadians provided a sense of community stability to the additional immigrants, single men who had left their families in Finland and who migrated from job to job in America. Some of these men returned to Finland; others eventually sent for their families.

After 1892 migration shifted from northern to southern Finland. Most emigrants from this phase were single and under the age of 30; women made up as much as 41.5 percent of the total. A very large increase in the birthrate after 1875 added to the pool of laborers who left home to work in Finland's growing industrial communities. This wave of internal migration to the city foreshadowed an exodus from Finland. "Russification" and a conscription for the draft added even further to the numbers after 1898.

Twentieth-century emigration from Finland is divided into three periods: before the General Strike; after the General Strike and before World War I; and between World War I and the passage of the Immigration Restriction Act. Before the General Strike, the immigrants who settled in the States were more likely to be influenced by the concepts of Social Democracy. After the General Strike, the immigrants were largely influenced by the use of direct force rather than political action to resolve social problems. Immigrants after World War I—now radicalized and disenchanted from the experience of the bloody civil war—brought a new sense of urgency about the progress of socialism.

Two immigration periods have occurred since the 1940s. After World War II, a new wave of immigration, smaller but more intense, revitalized many Finnish American communities. These Finns were far more nationalistic and politically conservative than earlier immigrants. A more recent wave of immigration occurred in the 1970s and 1980s, as young English-speaking professionals came from Finland to work in high-tech American corporations.

SETTLEMENT

Finnish American communities cluster in three regions across the northern tier of the United States: the East, Midwest, and West. Within these regions, Finland Swedes settled in concentrations in Massachusetts, New York City, Michigan, Wisconsin, Minnesota, Oregon, Washington, and California. Sami peoples settled predominantly in Michigan, Minnesota, the Dakotas, Oregon, and Washington.

The 1990 U.S. Census Bureau report confirms that these regions still exist for the 658,870 Americans who claim Finnish ancestry. The five states with the largest populations are Michigan, with 109,357 (1.2 percent of the total state population); Minnesota, with 103,602 (2.4 percent);

California, with 64,302 (.02 percent); Washington, with 44,110 (0.9 percent); and Massachusetts (0.5 percent). Half of all Finnish Americans—310,855—live in the Midwest, while 178,846 live in the West. Three further regions—the southeastern United States (Florida and Georgia), Texas, and the Southwest (New Mexico and Arizona)—have developed as retirement communities and as bases for Finnish businesses selling their products to an American market.

Reverse immigration occurred both in the nineteenth and twentieth centuries. In the nineteenth century, many men came without families and worked for a while in mining (especially copper and iron ore mining) and lumber, in fishing and canning, in stone quarries and textile mills, and on railroads and docks; they then returned to the homeland. Others came and worked as domestics, returning to Finland to retire. The most significant reverse immigration occurred in the late 1920s and early 1930s, when 10,000 Finnish American immigrant radicals and their families sold all their belongings and left to settle in the Finnish areas of the Soviet Union. They took their dreams of creating a workers' paradise with them, as well as solid American currency, American tools, and technical skills. Today, reverse migration occurs primarily among the Laestadians who may marry and move to Finland.

Like the Swedes and Norwegians, Finns in America were tolerated and accepted into the communities of "established" Americans during the first wave of mass immigration. Their early competitors for work in the mines were the Irish and the Cornish, two groups with whom they had ongoing strained relations.

Finnish Americans soon developed a reputation for clannishness and hard work. Work crews of strictly Finnish laborers were formed. As documented in *Women Who Dared*, Finnish domestics were always sought after because they worked so hard and excelled at cooking and homemaking. Reputations for good and hard work were tarnished, however, when the second wave of immigrants began to organize themselves and others to fight poor wages and working conditions. Finns became known as troublemakers for organizing strikes and leading protests. They were blacklisted and efforts were made to deport them. Racist slurs—epithets like "Finn-LAND-er" and "dumb Finn"—developed, and some Finns became victims of violent vigilantism. Specific efforts to single them out from other working-class immigrants as anti-American put them on the front pages of local, regional, and national newspapers.

By the end of the twentieth century, Finnish Americans had essentially become invisible. They worked hard to be indistinguishable from other Euroamericans and, as descendants of white Europeans, fit easily into the mass culture. Many do not visibly identify with any part of their heritage.

Key issues facing Finnish Americans in the future relate to their position as a culture on the margin. Recent generations seem to be drawn more strongly to America's hegemonic culture and therefore continue to move away from their unique heritage.

ACCULTURATION AND ASSIMILATION

Finnish Americans themselves are a multicultural society. Being a part of the Laestadian, Finland-Swede, or Sami minorities is different than being part of the Finnish American hegemony. Early Finnish Americans had a reputation for being clannish. Reported by sociologists studying Finns in the 1920s and 1930s, this impression was echoed by those citizens who lived beside them. Reenforcing this belief was their unusual language, spoken by few others anywhere. Finnish immigrant children, who spoke their native language in the grade schools of America, were marked as different; Finnish was difficult for English speakers to learn to use, a fact that encouraged American employers to organize teams of "Finnish-only" workers. And the "sauna ritual," an unheard of activity for Anglo-Americans, further promoted a sense that Finns were both exotic and separatist.

Once in the United States, Finnish immigrants recreated Finnish institutions, including churches, temperance societies, workers' halls, benefit societies, and cooperatives. Within those institutions, they organized a broad spectrum of activities for themselves: weekly and festival programs, dances, worship services, theater productions, concerts, sports competitions, and summer festivals. They created lending libraries, bands, choirs, self-education study groups, and drama groups. Furthermore, they kept in touch with each other through the newspapers that they published—over 120 different papers since the first, *Amerikan Suomalainen Lehti*, which appeared for 14 issues in 1876.

Finnish immigrants used these recreated Finnish institutions to confront and ease their entrance into American culture. The activities helped them assimilate. For example, Finnish American socialists created their own Socialist Federation that functioned to organize Finns; then, the federation itself joined the Socialist Party of America's foreign-language section, which then connected them with the struggle for socialist ideas and actions being promoted by "established" Americans. In a similar manner, the Finnish Evangelical Lutheran Church in America wrote their Sunday school readers in Finnish, yet used the reader to teach American citizenship and history, including stories of American role models like Abraham Lincoln, together with Finnish cultural heroes.

To help maintain their own identities in America, early Finnish immigrants also developed at least two institutions that had no counterpart in Finland. The first was a masonic-type lodge called the Knights of Kaleva, founded in 1898, with secret rituals based on the ancient Finnish epic *The Kalevala*. (A women's section called the Ladies of Kaleva followed in 1904.) Local chapters, called a *tupa* for the knights and a *maja* for the ladies, provided education in Finnish culture, both for the immigrants and for the larger "established" American community. The second institution, directed toward the immigrants' children, was based on the American Sunday school movement. Both the Church Finns and the Hall Finns

published materials specifically for use in Sunday schools. They taught their children the ways of Finnish politics and religion in Finnish-language (and later in English-language) Sunday schools and summer camps.

Finnish American businesses and professional services were developed to serve Finnish communities. In big cities like Minneapolis, Detroit, and Chicago, immigrants created Finntowns, while in small cities like Worcester and Fitchburg, Massachusetts, or Astoria, Oregon, they created separate institutions. In some cities—like those on the Iron Range in Minnesota—Finns became the largest foreign-born population group. Finns actually made up more than 75 percent of the population of small towns like Wakefield, Michigan, and Fairport Harbor, Ohio.

The immigrants were quick to adopt American ways. Almost off the boat, young women would discard the triangular cotton scarf (*huivi*) worn over their hair or the heavy woolen shawl wrapped around their bodies and begin to wear the big wide hats and fancy puffed sleeve bodices so popular in the States at the end of the nineteenth century. Men donned bowler hats and stiff starched collars above their suit coats. Those Finnish immigrant women who began their lives in America working as domestics quickly learned to make American style pies and cakes. And the Finns' log cabins, erected on barely cleared cutover lands, were covered with white clapboard siding as soon as finances permitted.

Recent emigrants from Finland have been quick to adopt the latest in American suburban living, becoming models of post-modern American culture. Privately, however, many Finnish Americans maintain the conventions of the homeland: their houses contain the traditional sauna, they eat Finnish foods, they take frequent trips to Finland and instruct their children in the Finnish language, and their social calendar includes Finnish American events. In the process, they bring new blood into Finnish American culture, providing role models for Finnishness and reenergizing Finnish language usage among the third and fourth generations.

MISCONCEPTIONS AND STEREOTYPES

Finnish Americans became the victims of ethnic slurs after socialist-leaning Finnish immigrants began to settle in the United States at the turn of the twentieth century. Finnish immigrant promoters of labor activism prompted racist responses directed at all Finnish Americans. The racist response reached its apex in 1908, when "established" Americans turned to the power of federal law, bringing to federal district court the deportation trial of one John Swan, a Finnish immigrant worker. According to Carl Ross in *The Finn Factor*, the unusual argument that Finns were actually of Mongolian descent—and therefore subject to the Asian Exclusion Act—hit many Finnish Americans hard and polarized the community into two camps, one conservative, identifying itself as "True Finns," and the other socialist, promoting American citizenship to its membership. In spite of efforts on both sides, various vigilante activities continued against Finnish Americans even into the late 1930s, as the 1939 wrecking of the Finn Hall in Aberdeen, Washington, attests. Being called a "Finn-LAND-er" became "fighting words" to both first and second generation Finnish Americans.

Stereotyping hastened Finnish assimilation into the American mainstream. As white Europeans, they could do just that. Some Finnish Americans anglicized their names and joined American churches and clubs. Others, identifying themselves as indelibly connected to America's racial minorities, entered into marriages with Native Americans, creating a group of people known in Minnesota and Michigan as "Finndians."

TRADITIONS, CUSTOMS, AND BELIEFS

In this drive to assimilate, Finnish customs that could remain invisible to the outside world were maintained in the States. Such diverse activities as berry picking, hunting, trapping, woodworking, knitting, and weaving can all be traced to the homeland. And many Finns in America have not lost their love for the sauna.

Today, the institutions of the immigrants are, for the most part, gone. For example, except for the Laestadians, few Finnish Lutheran churches offer a glimpse into the rituals of the Church of Finland. Yet an identifiable Finnish American culture remains. Beginning in the 1950s, older institutions began to be replaced by a Finnish American club movement, which includes such organizations as the Finlandia Foundation, the Finnish American Club, and the Finnish American Historical Society. Some organizations from the former days, like the Saima Society of Fitchburg and the Knights of Kaleva in Red Lodge, Montana, have been recycled to serve a new generation's club needs. Meanwhile, large Finnish American populations like the one in greater Detroit have created a new Finn Hall tradition that unifies all the various political and religious traditions.

FinnFest USA and Salolampi Language Village further strengthen Finnish traditions and customs in the States. An annual national summer festival, FinnFest USA, founded in 1983, brings Finnish Americans from all political and religious camps together for three days of seminars, lectures, concerts, sports events, dances, and demonstrations. The festival's location revolves each year to a different region of the Finnish American geography. Salolampi, founded in 1978, offers a summer educational program that allows young people to immerse themselves in Finnish language and culture. Part of the Concordia College Language Villages Program in northern Minnesota, the school serves children from throughout the United States.

A Finnish American renaissance has also blossomed. The movement began in the 1960s, when third and fourth generation Finnish Americans looked to their own past for models that could help solve the social crises in America. It expanded to include efforts to define and express themselves as members of a culture of difference. The renaissance, which includes cultural revival and maintenance as well as new culture creativity, has nurtured new networks between Finland and the United States.

Within the new social history movement, the renaissance gave rise to a new generation of scholars and creative writers who focused on Finnish American history. By the 1970s, in response to the folk music movement of a decade earlier, musicians also turned to their Finnish American heritage for inspiration. The renaissance includes the visual arts as well.

While this collective renaissance activity can be found throughout the various regions of Finnish America, its center is in Minnesota, most specifically the Twin Cities, where the University of Minnesota has provided a home at the Immigration History Research Center (IHRC) and Finnish Department. The IHRC helped to direct the "Reunion of Sisters Project: 1984-1987," a unique cultural exchange program that brought women and men together from Finland and the United States to consider their common cultural heritage. Then, in 1991, the IHRC co-sponsored the first conference organized to examine this renaissance, a conference entitled "The Making of Finnish America: A Culture in Transition."

CUISINE

The Finnish diet is rich in root vegetables (carrots, beets, potatoes, rutabagas, and turnips) and in fresh berries (blueberries, strawberries, and raspberries in season). Rye breads (*ruisleipa* and *reiska*) and cardamom seed flavored coffee bread (*pulla* or *nisu*) are absolute necessities. Dairy products—cheeses, creams, and butters—make the cakes, cookies, pancakes and stews quite rich. Pork roasts, hams, meat stews, and fish—especially salmon, whitefish, herring, and trout, served marinated, smoked, cooked in soups, or baked in the oven—complete the cuisine. At Christmas, many Finnish Americans eat *lutefisk* (lye-soaked dried cod) and prune-filled tarts. The traditional, meatless Shrove Tuesday meal (the day before Lent) centers on pea soup and rye bread or pancakes. Plainness, simplicity, and an emphasis on natural flavors continue to dominate Finnish and Finnish American cooking even today. Spices, if used, include cinnamon, allspice, cardamom, and ginger. One beverage dominates: coffee (morning coffee, afternoon coffee, evening coffee). "Coffee tables," as the events are called, served with the right assortment of baked goods, are central to both daily life and entertaining.

More recent Finnish immigrants favor foods that gained popularity after World War II—foods often associated with Karelia, the province lost to the Soviets in the Winter War. Among these are *karjalan piirakka* (an open-faced rye tart filled with potato or rice); *uunijuusto* (an oven-baked cheese, often called "squeaky cheese"); and *pasties*, (meat, potato, and carrot or rutabaga pies).

TRADITIONAL CLOTHING

Finnish immigrants who landed on American soil in the nineteenth and early twentieth centuries as workers wore heavy woolen stockings, shirts, and skirts. Women wore a triangular scarf, called a *huivi*, over their heads. However, no traditional clothing was worn for special events and ceremonies. By the 1930s, as Finnish Americans became more affluent, the popularity of Finnish national folk costumes increased. (By this time, members of the middle-class were in a position to travel to Finland to purchase costumes.)

HOLIDAYS CELEBRATED BY FINNISH AMERICANS

Finnish Americans observe a number of holidays celebrated in Finland. On December 6, many communities commemorate Finnish Independence Day. Christmas parties known as *Pikku Joulut* are central to the holiday season, just as *Laskiainen* (sliding down the hill) is celebrated on Shrove Tuesday. Some communities also hold programs in honor of the Finnish epic *The Kalevala* on Kalevala Day each February 28. Festive midsummer celebrations, featuring a *kokko* or large bonfire, occur every year.

Finns in the United States invented St. Urho's Day, a humorous takeoff on St. Patrick's Day, a traditional Irish holiday celebrated on March 17. St. Urho's Day, observed in Finnish American communities each March 16, purportedly commemorates the saint's success in driving the grasshoppers out of Finland.

HEALTH AND MENTAL HEALTH ISSUES

According to some commentators, Finnish Americans are people with a high propensity for heart disease, high cholesterol, strokes, alcoholism, mental depression, and lactose intolerance.

Many Finnish people believe in natural health care. Immigrants in both the nineteenth and early twentieth centuries used such traditional healing methods as massage and cupping (or bloodletting). The sauna is a historic part of healing rituals. When Finns are sick, they take a sauna. Even childbirth was handled by midwives in the sauna. A Finnish proverb, *Jos ei sauna ja viina ja terva auta niin se tauti on kuolemaksi*, states that if a sauna, whiskey, and tar salve do not make you well, death is imminent. Saunas treat respiratory and circulatory problems, relax stiff muscles, and cure aches and pains. Modern Finnish Americans often turn to chiropractors and acupuncturists for relief of some ailments, but the family sauna remains the place to go whenever a cold hits.

LANGUAGE

As late nineteenth- and early twentieth-century immigrants, Finns spoke either Finnish or Swedish. Those who spoke Swedish used a form known as Finland-Swedish; those who spoke Finnish used a non-Indo-European language, part of a small language group known as Finno-Ugric. Immigrants to America most likely spoke a regional form of Finnish: most nineteenth-century Finns spoke a northern rural Finnish, while later immigrants spoke a southern rural Finnish. An entirely new language was born in the United States—dubbed "Finglish." Finns arriving in America at the close of the twentieth century tend to speak in a Helsinki dialect.

Assimilation issues often revolved around the maintenance of language. John Wargelin (1881-1970), past president of Suomi College, lost his presidency in 1928 largely because he advocated using English at the college. The Finnish Socialist Federation exploded over orders that they "Americanize" their cultural practices, including their use of Finnish. Various churches vacillated on the language question, most of them finally giving in to using English after World War II. The Laestadians, however, have moved more slowly. Some groups still do all their preaching in Finnish; others use simultaneous translation.

GREETINGS AND OTHER POPULAR EXPRESSIONS

Typical greetings in Finnish include the following: *Hyvä paivä* ("huv-vaeh pa-e-vaeh")—Good day; *Hyvä ilta* ("huv-vaeh ill-tah")—Good evening; *Tervetuloa* ("terr-veh-too-loh-ah")—to welcome someone; *Tervesiä* ("terr-veh-see-ah")—a general response to a greeting; *Näkemiin* ("nah-keh-mean")—Good-bye, until we meet again; *Kiitos* ("key-tohs")—Thank you; *Hauska Joulua* ("how-skah yo-lu-ah")—Merry Christmas; *Onnellista*

Uutta Vuotta ("own-nell-ee-stah oo-tah vu-oh-tah")—Happy New Year; *Mitä kuuluu* ("mi-taah koo-loo")—How are you?; *Kyllä* ("kyl-lah")—Yes; *Hyvä huomenta* ("huv-vaeh who-ow-men-tah")—Good morning; *Olkaa hyva* ("ol-kah huv-vaeh")—please; *Oma tupa, oma lupa*—Your own cottage, your own independence. All Finnish words are pronounced with the accent on the first syllable.

FAMILY AND COMMUNITY DYNAMICS

Typical family structure among Finnish immigrants was patriarchal. Rural Finnish families were usually large, but in the urban areas, where both husband and wife worked, families often had only one child. Today only the Laestadians continue the tradition of large families.

Since immigrants were separated from their parents and extended families, Finnish American communities developed among immigrants from the same village or region. The 1920 U.S. Census Bureau records indicate that Finnish Americans mostly married other Finnish Americans, both in the first and second generations. By the 1990s, however, Finnish Americans of the third and fourth generations were marrying outside their ethnic group. One exception is the American Laestadian community, whose members prefer courtships within the community and who travel to Finland to meet suitable members of their faith.

EDUCATION

Education is highly valued by Finnish Americans. Even early immigrants were largely literate, and they supported a rich immigrant publishing industry of newspapers, periodicals, and books. Self-education was central. Thus, immigrant institutions developed libraries and debate clubs, and immigrant summer festivals included seminars, concerts, and plays. That tradition continues today in the three-day FinnFest USA festival, which maintains the lecture, seminar, and concert tradition.

In spite of economic hardship, many immigrant children achieved high school and college educations. Two schools were founded by the Finns: the *Työväenopisto*, or Work Peoples College, in Minnesota (1904-1941), where young people learned trades and politics in an educational environment that duplicated the folk school tradition in Finland; and *Suomiopisto*, Suomi College, in Hancock, Michigan (1895), which began by duplicating the lyceum tradition of Finland. The only higher education institution founded by Finnish Americans, Suomi provides a Lutheran-centered general liberal arts curriculum to its students. The college continues to honor its Finnish origins by maintaining a Finnish Heritage Center and Finnish American Historical Archives. Suomi started as an academy and added a junior college in 1923 and a four-year college in 1994. The Finnish Evangelical Lutheran Church in America (Suomi Synod) established and maintained a seminary there from 1904 to 1958.

Although parochial education never was part of the Finnish tradition, Finnish Americans did develop a program of summer schools and camps where young people learned religion, Finnish culture, politics, and cooperative philosophies. Camps teaching the ideals and practice of cooperativism ran until the late 1950s.

THE ROLE OF WOMEN

Finnish women have played leading roles in family affairs and community life. In the old country, they ran and organized the household. In addition, immigrant women oversaw the farms while the men found work in the cities, mines, and lumber camps. The women also found daytime employment outside the home, working in laundries and textile manufacturing. In the evenings, they were active in choirs, theaters, politics, and the organization of religious events.

PHILANTHROPY

Finnish Americans practice group-organized philanthropy. Together, they raise barns, build community halls and churches, and do the ritual spring cleaning. Finnish Americans have also supported famine relief in Finland, assisted the Help Finland Movement during the Winter War, and even held a fund-raising drive for microfilming Finnish language newspapers in 1983.

RELIGION

Over 90 percent of Finnish American immigrants are Lutherans—some more devout than others. Baptized into the church so that their births were recorded, they were also confirmed so that they could marry and be buried—all with official state records.

During the nineteenth century, within the State Church of Finland, four different religious revivals occurred: the Awakenists, the Evangelicals, the Laestadians, and the Prayers movement. These movements operated within the church itself. In addition, socialism—a secular movement with all the fervor of a religion—also developed. During the immigration process, many Finns left the church entirely and participated only in socialist activities. Those who remained religious fell into three separate groups: Laestadians, Lutherans, and free church Protestants.

The Laestadians, who came first, called themselves "Apostolic Lutherans" and began to operate separately in the heady atmosphere of America's free religious environment. However, they could not stay unified and have since divided into five separate church groups. These congregations are led by lay people; ordained ministers trained in seminaries are not common to any of the groups.

In 1898 the Finnish National Evangelical Lutheran church was formed as an expression of the Evangelical movement. The Finland Swedes, excluded from these efforts, gradually formed churches that entered the Augustana Lutheran Synod (a Swedish American church group). In recent years, the Suomi Synod became part of an effort to create a unified Lutheran church in the United States. They were part of a merger that created first the Lutheran Church in America in 1963, and then the Evangelical Lutheran Church in America in 1984.

The Suomi Synod maintained the Church of Finland "divine worship" service tradition and continued the practice of a clergy-led church. However, a new sense of power resting in the hands of the congregation developed, and the church evolved into a highly democratic decision-making institution. Although women were not yet granted the right to be ordained, they were given the right to vote in the affairs of the church in 1909. In addition, they were elected to high leadership positions on local, regional, and national boards. Pastors' wives were known to preach sermons and conduct services whenever the pastor was serving another church within his multiple-congregation assignment. The rather democratic National Synod also granted women the right to vote in the affairs of the congregation. This became an issue when the National

Synod merged with the Lutheran Church-Missouri Synod, which did not allow women to vote.

In addition to Lutherans, Finnish immigrants also organized a variety of free Protestant churches: the Finnish Congregational church (active mainly in New England, the Pacific Northwest, and California), the Finnish Methodist church, the Unitarian church, and the Pentecostal churches.

EMPLOYMENT AND ECONOMIC TRADITIONS

In the Midwest and the West, early Finnish immigrant men worked as miners, timber workers, railroad workers, fishers, and dock hands. In New England, they worked in quarries, fisheries, and in textile and shoe factories. When single women began to settle in the United States, they went into domestic work as maids, cooks, and housekeepers. In the cutover lands across northern Michigan, Wisconsin, and Minnesota, and in the farmlands of upstate New York and New England, immigrant families left work in industry to raise grain crops and potatoes and run dairy and chicken farms. In the cities, Finnish American immigrants worked in several crafts—as carpenters, painters, tailors, and jewelers.

Later generations who have had the advantage of an American education have chosen professions that expand on the worklife of the immigrants. Men frequently specialize in agriculture-related subjects, such as natural resources management, mining engineering, and geology. A large percentage of women study nursing and home economics, working as both researchers in industry and as public managers in county extension agencies. The fields of education, medical research, the arts, music, and law have also attracted Finnish American students.

POLITICS AND GOVERNMENT

Finnish Americans are a politically active people. As voters in American politics, they overwhelmingly supported the Republican party until the 1930s. After Franklin Delano Roosevelt became president in 1933, Finnish Americans became known as Democratic voters.

Early immigrants emphasized Temperance Societies as a political action force. In 1888 they organized the *Suomalainen Kansallis Raittius Veljeysseura* (the Finnish National Temperance Brotherhood), which later had as many as 10,000 members. Many immigrants after 1892 had socialist leanings, and itinerant Finnish agitators found many converts in the States. In 1906 the *Amerikan Suomalaisten Sosialistiosastojen Järjestö* (the Finnish American Socialist Federation) was formed; two years later, the organization became the first foreign-language affiliate within the Socialist Party of America. (Over the next decade, however, the federation began to lose members because of its increasing alignment with the Communist party.)

At the turn of the twentieth century, Finnish Americans worked to change U.S. national policy toward Finland. In 1899 a Finnish American delegation presented a petition to President William McKinley asking for aid to Finland in its fight against czarist Russia. They also lobbied for early recognition of the Finnish Republic and for relief support to the homeland.

Finnish American immigrant women organized feminist-based groups as early as 1895 for the purpose of self-education and the improvement of conditions for women. After 1906—when women in Finland were granted the right to vote—Finnish Americans became heavily involved in American suffrage politics, passing petitions throughout the Finnish American community, participating in suffrage parades, and appearing at rallies. They organized into two wings: one aligned with the temperance movement, which promoted suffrage per se; the other aligned with the socialist movement, which promoted working women's issues. Each published a newspaper, the *Naisten Lehti* (*Women's Newspaper*), and the *Toveritar* (*The Working Woman*). Both worked to improve conditions for all American women through political action.

Finns have been very active in union organizing, working often as leaders of strikes that developed in the mining and timber industries. Their workers' halls were centers of union activity and headquarters for strikes, notably in the Copper Country Strike of 1913-1914 and the two Mesabi Range strikes of 1907 and 1916. After World War II, Finnish Americans were central to the organizing of iron miners into the Steelworkers Union on the Marquette Range in Michigan. In addition, Detroit auto workers used the Wilson Avenue Finn Hall to develop their union organizing.

Finnish American proponents of socialism pose with their families outside their Glassport, Pennsylvania, meeting hall.

Finns have been elected to political positions, mainly on local and regional levels, serving as postmasters, clerks, sheriffs, and mayors. As of 1995, no Finn had been elected state governor, and only one Finn, O. J. Larson, had been a member of the U.S. Congress. (He was elected to the House in 1920 and again in 1922.) However, Finnish Americans have served in state Houses in Michigan, Minnesota, Wisconsin, and Alaska. Barbara Hannien Linton, who represents a northern Wisconsin district, is one of the most prominent and progressive members of the Democratic Party in the Wisconsin state legislature. The first woman elected to the office of mayor of Ohio— Amy Kaukkonen—was a Finnish American medical doctor. She beat her opponent on a prohibition platform in 1922.

During the effort to win support for U.S. entry into World War I, the administration of President Woodrow Wilson orchestrated a loyalty movement among the Finns. In spite of their anti-draft stance in World War I, Finns have readily served in the U.S. armed forces, beginning with the Civil War, when former Finnish sailors and recent immigrants signed on. Finns served in the Spanish-American War, World Wars I and II, and the Spanish Civil War. Finnish American nurses—mostly female—also contributed to the American war effort over the years.

RELATIONS WITH FINLAND

Finnish Americans have long been involved in the political issues of Finland. The American Finnish Aid Committee gathered considerable funds for famine relief in 1902. After the General Strike occurred in 1906, a number of Finnish agitators sought a safe haven in the Finnish American community. After Finland declared itself a republic, Finnish Americans worked with Herbert Hoover to provide food to famine-stricken Finland. Later, they lobbied effectively in Washington, D.C., to get official recognition from the

American government for the new nation-state. Their most concerted effort on behalf of the Finns, however, occurred in 1939 and 1940, after the Winter War broke out. They mobilized efforts at such a level, again with Hoover's assistance, that they were able to send $4 million in aid to the war-torn country. Individual family efforts to collect food and clothing for relatives continued well into the end of the decade. In the 1990s Finnish Americans worked actively as volunteers and fund-raisers, promoting religion in the Finnish sections of the former Soviet Union.

INDIVIDUAL AND GROUP CONTRIBUTIONS

Finnish Americans as a group tend not to promote the concept of individual merit. (*Oma kehu haisee*—a Finnish proverb often quoted by Finnish Americans—means "self-praise smells putrid.") The following sections list contributions made by Finnish Americans:

ARTS AND ARCHITECTURE

The father and son architectural team of Eliel (1897-1950) and Eero (1910-1961) Saarinen is closely associated with Michigan's Cranbrook Institute, where Finnish design theory and practice were taught to several generations of Americans. Eero Saarinen designed a number of buildings, including the Gateway Arch in St. Louis; the General Motors Technical Center in Warren, Michigan; the TWA terminal at New York's Kennedy International Airport; and Dulles International Airport near Washington, D.C.

Painters include Elmer Forsberg (1883-1950), longtime professor at the Chicago Institute of Arts and a significant painter in his own right. Religious painter Warner Sallman (1897-1968), a Finland Swede, is most famous for his "Head of Christ," the mass-produced portrait of a Nordic-looking Jesus that became an icon of American Protestantism.

Photojournalist Kosti Ruohomaa, a second generation Finnish American from Maine, created a portfolio of photographs after working more than 20 years for *Life* and other national magazines. Rudy Autio (1926-), also a second generation Finnish American, is a fellow of the American Crafts Council whose work is in the permanent collections of major museums. Minnesota-born sculptor Dale Eldred (1934-1993) became head of the Kansas City Institute of Arts and creator of monumental environmental sculptures that are displayed throughout the world.

BUSINESS AND INDUSTRY

The earliest successful Finnish American businessman was Carl Sjodahl (Charles Linn; 1814-1883) who began as a sailor and became a wealthy wholesaler, banker, and industrialist in New Orleans and Birmingham, Alabama. Another early Finnish seaman, Captain Gustave Niebaum (1842-1908), established the Inglenook winery in California.

Vaino Hoover, former president and chief executive officer of Hoover Electric Company, designed and manufactured electric actuators and power flight control system components for aircraft and deep sea equipment. An important figure in the American defense industry of the 1950s and 1960s, he was a member of President Dwight D. Eisenhower's National Defense Advisory Committee. Yrjö Paloheimo (1899-1991) was a philanthropist as well as a rancher in New Mexico and southern California. He organized Help Finland activities in the 1940s, founded a farm and garden school for orphans in Finland in 1947, and established the Finlandia Foundation in 1952. In addition, he and his wife organized the Old Cienaga Village, a living history museum of early Hispanic life in New Mexico. Finnish American Armas Christian Markkula, co-founder of the Apple Computer Co., is listed as one of the 500 richest men in America.

EDUCATION

Finnish Americans in education include Margaret Preska (1938-). One of the first women in the United States to head an institution of higher learning, she was president of Mankato State University from 1979 to 1992. Robert Ranta (1943-) is dean of the College of Communication and Fine Arts at the University of Memphis and also serves as a freelance producer of such television specials as the Grammy Awards.

GOVERNMENT

Among the best-known Finnish Americans in government is Emil Hurja (1892-1953), the genius political pollster who orchestrated Franklin Delano Roosevelt's victorious presidential elections. Hurja became a member of the Democratic National Committee during the 1930s. O. J. Larson was a U.S. representative from Minnesota in the early 1920s. Maggie Walz (1861-1927), publisher of the *Naisten Lehti* (*Women's Newspaper*), represented the Finnish American suffragists in the American suffrage and temperance movements. Viena Pasanen Johnson, co-founder of the Minnesota Farmer Labor Party, was the first woman member of the Minnesota State Teachers' College board of directors. She later became a national leader in the Women's International League for Peace and Freedom. Gus Hall (1911-) remains president of the Communist Party of America.

LITERATURE

Jean Auel (1936-), author of *Clan of the Cave Bear* and other bestselling novels dealing with prehistoric peoples, is a third generation Finnish American. Less well known but still significant to American letters is Shirley (Waisanen) Schoonover (1936-), whose *Mountain of Winter* (1965) has been translated into eighteen languages. Anselm Hollo (1934-), the renowned translator and writer with more than 19 volumes of verse to her credit, teaches at the Naroba Institute. Pierre DeLattre, author of two novels, *Tales of a Dalai Lama*, 1971, and *Walking on Air*, 1980, has been published in some 50 magazines. Recent writers emerging from the small press movement include poet Judy Minty, fiction writer and poet Jane Piirto, and fiction writers Lauri Anderson, Rebecca Cummings, and Timo Koskinen.

MUSIC

Composer Charles Wuorinen (1938-)—the youngest composer to win a Pulitzer Prize—was named a MacArthur fellow in 1986. His music is performed by major symphony orchestras throughout the United States. Tauno Hannikainen was the permanent director of the Duluth Symphony and associate conductor of the Chicago Symphony Orchestra. Heimo Haitto was a concert violinist who performed as soloist with major philharmonics in Europe and the United States. Legendary virtuoso accordionist Viola Turpinen (1909-1958) became a recording artist and professional musician. Jorma Kaukonen (1942-) played lead guitar for Jefferson Airplane. Elisa Kokkonen, a young emerging solo violinist, performs with major orchestras in the United States and Europe.

RELIGION

Finnish America's major contributor to American Lutheran theology was renowned professor of theology Taisto Kantonen (1900-1993) of Wittenburg University. Melvin Johnson (1939-), an administrator at the Evangelical Lutheran Church in America headquarters in Chicago, and retired theologian Raymond W. Wargelin are among the most prominent living church leaders of Finnish descent in America.

SCIENCE AND TECHNOLOGY

Olga Lakela, a former professor of biology at the Duluth campus of the University of Minnesota and the author of numerous scientific papers on plant and bird life in Minnesota, had her name inscribed on the Wall of Fame at the 1940 New York World's Fair as one of 630 Americans of foreign birth who contributed to the American way of life. Ilmari Salminen, a research chemist with Eastman Kodak, specialized in color photography. Vernen Suomi, now an emeritus professor at the University of Wisconsin-Madison, was responsible for several inventions currently used in the exploration of outer space. A younger generation of scientists includes Donald Saari (1940-), a Northwestern University mathematician in astronomy and economics; Markin Makinen (1939-), a biophysicist at the University of Chicago; and Dennis Maki (1940-), a medical doctor who serves as an infectious disease specialist in the Medical School at the University of Wisconsin-Madison.

SPORTS

Finnish American sports figures have achieved recognition in track, cross country skiing, ski jumping, and ice hockey. The Finnish American Athletic Club was one of the strongest organizations in U.S. track and field competition. U.S. Olympic hockey and ski jumping teams have included Finnish Americans. Midwestern American sports teams in the 1930s were often called "Flying Finns," after legendary Finnish runner Paavo Nurmi, whose tour of the United States during the 1920s caused a sensation among American track and field enthusiasts. Waino Ketonen was world champion middleweight wrestler from 1918 to 1927. Rick Tapani, pitcher for the Minnesota Twins, and sportscaster Dick Engberg are both third generation Finnish Americans.

THEATER AND FILM

Stage actor Alfred Lunt (1892-1977), who teamed with his actress-wife Lynn Fontanne from the 1920s through the 1950s was a second generation Finnish American from Wisconsin; he showed his Finnish pride when he chose Robert Sherwood's poignant *There Shall Be No Night* as a touring vehicle and a significant way for the duo to present the plight of Finns fighting in the Winter War in Finland. Bruno Maine was scenic art director for Radio City Music Hall, and Sointu Syrjälä was theater designer for several Broadway shows. Movie actor Albert Salmi (1928-1990) began his career in the New York City Finnish immigrant theater, and Maila Nurmi, who once used the stage name Vampira, hosted horror movies on television in the late 1950s in Los Angeles. She also starred in Ed Wood's immortal alien flick *Plan 9 from Outer Space*, considered by many critics to be the worst movie of all time. Other Finnish American actresses include Jessica Lange (1949-) and Christine Lahti (1950-), granddaughter of early Finnish American feminist Augusta Lahti.

MEDIA

PRINT

Amerikan Uutiset.

A weekly newspaper in Finnish with some English; it has a long tradition of providing a national forum for nonpartisan political and general news from Finnish American communities across the country. Founded in 1932, the paper was later bought by Finland-born entrepreneurs interested in creating a more contemporary Finland news emphasis. It has the largest Finnish American readership in the nation.

Contact: Sakri Viklund, Editor.

Address: P.O. Box 8147, Lantana, Florida 33462.

Telephone: (407) 588-9770.

Fax: (407) 588-3229.

Baiki: The North American Sami Journal.

A quarterly journal published since 1991 by descendants of Sami peoples. It explores their own unique heritage.

Contact: Faith Fjeld, Editor.

Address: 3548 14th Avenue South, Minneapolis, Minnesota 55407.

Telephone: (612) 722-0040.

Fax: (612) 722-3844.

Christian Monthly.

Published by and for the members of the national organization serving Finnish Apostolic church congregations, this periodical features religious articles and information about upcoming religious services both for regional and national audiences.

Contact: Alvar Helmes, Editor.

Address: Apostolic Lutheran Book Concern, P.O. Box 2126, Battle Ground, Washington 98604-2126.

Finnish Americana.

founded in 1978, this English-language annual journal features creative writing as well as scholarly articles. The journal reflects the growth of a new group of Finnish Americans interested in Finnish American history and culture. *Finnish Americana* is the major forum for the new generation of Finnish American intellectuals.

Contact: Michael G. Karni, Editor.

Address: P.O. Box 120804, New Brighton, Minnesota 55112.

Telephone: (612) 636-6348.

Fax: (612) 636-0773.

Finnish American Reporter.

A newsprint journal featuring personal essays, Finnish American community news, and brief news articles reprinted from and about Finland. Founded in 1986, this monthly has gradually built itself into the leading publication for readers seeking an American-oriented presentation of Finnish American cultural life. It is published by the Työmies Society, the left-wing political movement of Finnish America.

Contact: Lisbeth Boutang, Editor.

Address: P.O. Box 549, Superior, Wisconsin 54880.

Telephone: (715) 394-4961.

Fax: (715) 392-5029.

New Yorkin Uutiset.

A weekly independent newspaper featuring news from Finland and Finnish American communities. Founded in 1906 as a daily, the paper—written primarily in Finnish with some English articles—is now a weekly. *New Yorkin Uutiset* takes a nationalistic and politically conservative position on issues.

Contact: Leena Isbom, Editor.

Address: The Finnish Newspaper Co., 4422 Eighth Avenue, Brooklyn, New York 11220.

Telephone: (718) 435-0800.

Fax: (718) 871-7230.

Norden News.

A weekly newspaper featuring news from Finland and Finland-Swede American communities. This Swedish-language paper provides the only current information on the Finnland-Swede community in the United States.

Contact: Erik R. Hermans, Editor.

Address: P.O. Box 2143, New York, New York 10185-0018.

Telephone: (212) 944-0775.

Fax: (212) 944-0763.

Raivaaja (Pioneer).

A weekly newspaper featuring news from Finland and Finnish American communities. Founded in 1905 as a daily, the newspaper provides a voice for Social Democratic Finnish Americans.

Contact: Marita Cauthen, Editor.

Address: P.O. Box 600, Fitchburg, Massachusetts 01420-0600.

Telephone: (508) 343-3822.

Työmies/Eteenpäin.

A weekly newspaper of the Finnish American left wing. Published since 1903, it continues to present Finnish American communist views. Readership remains small and largely Finnish-language directed. The newspaper features both news from Finland and news about the United States, written from a politically radical perspective.

Address: P.O. Box 549, Superior, Wisconsin 54880.

Telephone: (715) 394-4961.

Fax: (715) 394-7655.

Voice of Zion.

A monthly periodical published by the Association of American Laestadian Congregations. This bilingual publication provides devotional articles as well as news articles about religious events occurring in the United States, Canada, Finland, and Sweden.

Contact: Jon Bloomquist, Editor.

Address: 10911 Highway 55, Suite 203, Plymouth, Minnesota 55441.

Telephone: (612) 544-8118.

Fax: (612) 544-8229.

RADIO

KAXE-FM, Northern Minnesota.

"Finnish Americana and Heritage Show," In Bemidji, 94.7 FM; in Brainerd, 89.5 FM; in Grand Rapids, 91.7 FM. This English-language program—presented the first Sunday of each month—includes Finnish folk and popular music as well as information about Finnish music events in Minnesota.

KUSF-FM (90.3), San Francisco, California.

"Voice of Finland," a weekly one-hour program in the Finnish language provides music, news, interviews, and information about Finnish activities occurring in the region.

WCAR-AM (1900), Detroit, Michigan.

"Finn Focus," a light entertainment program in Finnish provides music, news, notice of local activities and interviews.

WLVS-AM (1380), Palm Beach County, Florida.

"Hyvät Uutiset" (Good News), sponsored by the Lake Worth Finnish Pentecostal Congregation, is a weekly half hour broadcast in Finnish featuring religious music and talk. "American Finnish Evening Hour" provides light entertainment, music, and information about happenings in the listening area and in Finland. "Halls of Finland," a program broadcast in Finnish, includes news reports about local events and activities occurring in the United States and in Finland. "Religious Hour" is sponsored by the Apostolic Lutheran church.

WYMS-FM (88.9), Milwaukee, Wisconsin.

"Scandinavian Hour," broadcast once a month, this program provides news from Finland and the local region, interviews, and Finnish music. Broadcast in two languages. "Scenes from the Northern Lights" originates in Bloomington, Indiana, and is offered through syndication on National Public Radio (NPR). It features a wide variety of Finnish music (rock, pop, classical, folk, opera).

TELEVISION

WLUC, Marquette, Michigan.

"Suomi-Kutsu" (Finland Calling) is telecast weekly on Sundays from 10:00 to 11:00 a.m. The first half hour is a newsmagazine about Finland and Finnish America, featuring interviews, music, news, and video essays. The second half hour is a Finnish language devotional worship service led by area Lutheran clergy.

ORGANIZATIONS AND ASSOCIATIONS

Finlandia Foundation.
Founded in 1952, this national philanthropic organization's mission is to cultivate and strengthen cultural relations between the United States and the Republic of Finland. Finlandia Foundation distributes over $70,000 annually for cultural programs, grants, and scholarships.

Contact: Carl W. Jarvie, President.

Address: 607 Third Avenue, Suite 610, Seattle, Washington 98104.

Telephone: (206) 285-4703.

Fax: (206) 781-2721.

Finnish American League for Democracy (FALD).
Promotes the study of Finnish American history and culture.

Contact: Marita Cauthen, Executive Officer.

Address: P.O. Box 600, 147 Elm Street, Fitchburg, Massachusetts 01420.

Telephone: (508) 343-3822.

MUSEUMS AND RESEARCH CENTERS

Finnish American Historical Archives of the Finnish American Heritage Center, Suomi College.
Features the best collection of materials that predate the twentieth century, as well as modern materials, including records of the Help Finland Movement, the Finnish Evangelical Lutheran Church in America (Suomi Synod), and the celebration of the 300th anniversary of the Delaware Colony. A small uncataloged and unsystematic collection of material objects has accumulated; parts of this collection are usually on display. A large photograph collection, an oral history collection, and microfilm archives of newspapers and records stored in Finland round out the resources.

Address: 601 Quincy Street, Hancock, Michigan.

Telephone: (906) 487-7347.

Fax: (906) 487-7366.

Immigration History Research Center of the University of Minnesota.
This collection—one of the largest available anywhere—is part of a larger collection of 24 late immigration groups. The Finnish section includes materials from the Finnish American radical and cooperative movements, Finnish American theater, and music.

Address: 826 Berry Street, St. Paul, Minnesota 55114-1076.

Telephone: (612) 627-4208.

Fax: (612) 627-4190.

Other archival collections of Finnish American materials are more regional. For example, the Iron Range Research Center in Chisholm, Minnesota, has a rich northern Minnesota collection, and the Finnish Cultural Center at Fitchburg State College in Fitchburg, Massachusetts, has been trying to reconstitute materials from the New England region.

Finnish Americans have not developed any major museums. The most systematically catalogued collection of Finnish American materials can be found at the Michigan State University Museum in East Lansing, Michigan; the Nordic Heritage Museum in Seattle, Washington, includes an interesting display of Finnish culture, collected and organized by the local Finnish American community.

Finnish Americans have preserved their cultural landscape history at two significant sites listed on the National Register of Historic Places. The Hanka Homestead in Arnheim, Michigan, provides an example of a small backwoods farmstead, while the town of Embarrass, Minnesota, is an excellent example of an entire Finnish American farming community.

SOURCES FOR ADDITIONAL STUDY

Finnish Diasporaii: United States, edited by Michael G. Karni. Toronto: The Multicultural History Society of Ontario, 1981.

The Finnish Experience in the Western Great Lakes Region, edited by Michael G. Karni, Matti E. Kaups, and Doublas J. Ollila, Jr. Vammala, Finland: Institute for Migration, Turku, 1972.

The Finns in North America: A Social Symposium, edited by Ralph Jalkanen. East Lansing: Michigan State University Press, 1969.

Hoglund, A. William. *Finnish Immigrants in America, 1880-1920.* Madison: University of Wisconsin Press, 1960.

Jalkanen, Ralph. *The Faith of the Finns: Historical Perspectives on the Finnish Lutheran Church in America.* East Lansing: Michigan State University Press, 1972.

Jutikkala, Eino, and Kauko Pirinen. *A History of Finland.* New York: Dorset Press, 1988.

Ojakangas, Beatrice A. *The Finnish Cookbook.* New York: Crown, 1964.

Ross, Carl. *The Finn Factor in American Labor, Culture, and Society.* New York Mills, Minnesota: Parta Publishing, 1977.

Sampo: The Magic Mill—A Collection of Finnish American Writing, edited by Aili Jarvenpa and Michael G. Karni. Minneapolis: New Rivers Press, 1989.

Women Who Dared: The History of Finnish American Women, edited by Carl Ross and K. Marianne Wargelin Brown. St. Paul: Immigration History Research Center, University of Minnesota, 1986.

Wuorinen, John. *The Finns on the Delaware, 1638-1655: An Essay in American Colonial History.* New York: Columbia University Press, 1938.

———. *A History of Finland.* New York: Columbia University Press, 1965.

FRENCH

by
**Laurie Collier
Hillstrom**

AMERICANS

Despite their

relatively small

numbers, French

immigrants have

tended to be more

successful and

influential than

other groups in

America.

OVERVIEW

The French Republic (République Française)—more commonly known as France—occupies 212,918 square miles, making it the largest country in Western Europe and slightly smaller than the state of Texas. It is hexagonal in shape, with half its borders, or 1,920 miles, made up of coastline. It borders on the Atlantic Ocean to the west, the English Channel to the northwest, Belgium and Luxembourg to the north, Germany to the northeast, Switzerland to the east, Italy to the southeast, the Mediterranean Sea to the south, and Spain to the southwest. The topography of France includes the Pyrenees mountains along the southern border and the Alps along the southwest border. The remaining terrain varies from mountain ranges to plains to forests, and includes four major river systems.

The population of France was approximately 55.5 million in 1987, and it has remained relatively stable over time. The capital and major cultural center is Paris, where about one-fifth of the total population resides. France has held a prestigious position in Western culture since the Middle Ages, showing particular influence in art, architecture, philosophy, and literature. The country became a leading member of the European Economic Community (EEC) and later the European Community (EC) and is one of the five permanent members of the United Nations Security Council. The French national flag consists of three wide vertical stripes of blue, white, and red.

About 80 percent of French people consider themselves Roman Catholic, though only 20 percent of French Catholics attend church regularly. According to Jonathan Harris in *The Land and People of France*, French discord with the Catholic church dates back to the eighteenth century, when the church reached the height of its wealth and power. Since then, anticlericalism has been a pervasive attitude in French society. France is also home to about 800,000 Protestants, who, despite their minority status, enjoy a strong influence in business and the government. In addition, with 700,000 Jewish residents, France has the largest Jewish community in Europe besides Russia. About 1.5 million Muslims—mostly emigrants from the former French colonies of Algeria, Morocco, and Tunisia—comprise another sizable religious minority in France.

Since conditions in France historically have been considered humane and prosperous, relatively few French citizens have decided to emigrate. On the contrary, an estimated four million people from other lands have chosen to immigrate to France in the past 150 years. The most prevalent sources of immigrants to France in modern times include Portugal, Spain, Italy, eastern Europe, northern Africa, and Asia. The foreign population in France grew by 4.5 percent annually throughout the 1970s. Although this rate slowed to 0.7 percent during the 1980s, immigrants comprised seven percent of the population of France by the early 1990s. One estimate suggested that up to 500,000 of these immigrants had remained in the country illegally. While France has faced some problems in assimilating such large numbers of immigrants from different cultures, some experts claim that the French have largely succeeded in forging a sense of national identity.

HISTORY

The history of France dates back to about 1000 B.C., when Celtic tribes moved into large areas of northern Europe. The Celts who remained in the area that eventually became France were known as Gauls. Around 600 B.C., Greek colonists settled in the Mediterranean area of Marseilles, and their civilized ways had a strong influence on the Gauls. In 59 B.C., however, Julius Caesar led Roman forces in conquest of the area, which the Romans ruled for the next 500 years. During this time they built the foundation of many modern French roads and cities and ensured that Latin would form the basis of the French language. After the fall of the Roman Empire in 476 A.D., France was ruled as an absolute monarchy by four successive dynasties. By the time King Henry IV established the Bourbon dynasty in 1589, France had developed a strict system of social hierarchy known as feudalism. Wealthy aristocrats owned the land and participated in government, while the poorer people worked the land and had few rights.

The stage was set for French immigration to North America in the early 1500s, during a religious movement known as the Reformation. At this time, many citizens of France and other European nations protested against some of the doctrines and corrupt practices then prevailing in the Roman Catholic church. The Reformation caused conflict throughout Europe, eventually dividing the church into two separate factions, Catholics and Protestants. John Calvin, a French priest, was instrumental in the spread of Protestantism. His followers, called Huguenots, built 2,000 churches in France by the mid-1500s, though they also became the targets of persecution by French Catholics during 30 years of civil war. King Henry IV, who was born a Protestant but converted to Catholicism, stopped the conflict temporarily in 1594 by enacting the Edict of Nantes, which granted political rights and freedom of religion to French Protestants. After spending several years unsuccessfully pressuring Protestants to convert, however, King Louis XIV revoked the Edict of Nantes in 1685. This sudden loss of rights and status caused thousands of Huguenots to leave France for North America. The majority of Huguenot immigrants were skilled, well-educated, and prosperous.

Another important event in French history that affected immigration to North America occurred in 1763, with the conclusion of the Seven Years' War (also known as the French and Indian War) between France and England. These traditional enemies had clashed repeatedly over expansionist policies and colonization in Europe, North America, and India. After losing this conflict, France relinquished to England control of its colonies, through the Treaty of Paris. According to Jean-Baptiste Duroselle in *France and the U.S.: From Beginnings to Present* (1976), French Americans "nursed the knowledge that they had been abandoned by a country that was no longer their homeland, and of which they today retain nothing but the language." Duroselle goes on to state that

In 1989 French Americans celebrated the bicentennial of the French Revolution.

this event marked the end of French political power in the land that would become the United States. The American Revolution began just 12 years later, however, and France was persuaded to provide invaluable military aid to the American side. In fact, many historians claim that the French support enabled the United States to form.

France became embroiled in its own revolution in 1789. As the French middle class, or bourgeoisie, became more prosperous and powerful, they began to resent the feudal system and demanded equal rights and tax reform. King Louis XVI accepted some of the people's demands, but later brought troops into Paris to try to crush the rebellion. On July 14, crowds of armed protesters destroyed the Bastille, a fortress that was used to hold political prisoners and that gradually had become a symbol of oppression. This event marked the end of the old regime and the beginning of the French Republic, and it has been celebrated ever since as a national holiday—Bastille Day. France soon adopted a constitution that ensured equal rights for all citizens and limited the powers of the monarchy and the church. The French Revolution continued, however, as conservative and radical forces vied for control of the new government. These factions staged reciprocal campaigns of violence against one another that came to be known as the Reign of Terror.

In the meantime, France entered into war with a coalition of European nations determined to halt the revolution and its radical ideas.

Napoleon Bonaparte gained prominence as a French military leader and then overthrew the government of France in 1799, granting himself dictatorial powers as Emperor Napoleon I. Although Napoleon scored many popular military victories and initiated lasting reforms to the French educational and legal systems, he also severely limited individual rights. His rules made it virtually impossible for French citizens to emigrate, for example, so only a few immigrants came to the United States until the end of his reign in 1815.

Public opinion in the United States, which had been generally positive toward France since the American Revolution, gradually became negative during the Reign of Terror. The United States ended up claiming neutrality during the French Revolution and refused to provide assistance during the resulting war in Europe. Relations with France became the subject of intense debate among the leaders of the U.S. Congress and in the newly influential American press. Negative attitudes toward France peaked in 1797 with the XYZ Affair, when three unnamed French diplomats demanded a huge bribe before they would agree to speak with American delegates about a new treaty. This perceived insult caused the United States to begin preparing for a war with France.

During this time, French Americans—especially those who had come to the United States as refugees from the French Revolution—were viewed by some American leaders as a potential threat to national security. In 1798 the U.S. government passed the controversial Alien and Sedition Acts, which were intended to monitor and limit the power of immigrant groups. For example, the Acts increased the residency requirement from five to 14 years before immigrants were allowed to vote, forced ships to compile dossiers on immigrant passengers, and granted the government the power to deport anyone it considered "dangerous." The Acts became the subject of considerable public outrage and were allowed to expire two years later. Shortly thereafter, the 1803 purchase of the Louisiana Territory from Napoleon helped relax the tension over immigration. This vast tract of land doubled the size of the United States and provided a new frontier for a large wave of new immigrants.

After Napoleon was defeated at Waterloo in 1815, France was ruled first as a constitutional monarchy and then as a republic. In 1848, Napoleon's nephew Louis Napoleon Bonaparte was elected president of the republic, but he soon overthrew the government and proclaimed himself Emperor Napoleon III. He was soundly defeated in the Franco-Prussian War in 1870, however, which resulted in the loss of the French provinces Alsace and Lorraine to the German Empire. Thousands of Alsatians chose to immigrate to the United States at this time rather than live under German rule. France approved the democratic constitution of the Third Republic in 1875.

World War I helped improve relations between France and the United States when French and American soldiers fought together. In the period between the World Wars, France endured a weak government and low birth rates. These conditions contributed to the fall of France in 1940, shortly after the beginning of World War II, and to its occupation by German troops for the next four years. The Fourth Republic was established in 1946, but the government was unstable and faced constant conflict with French colonies seeking independence. Charles de Gaulle was elected president of the Fifth Republic in 1958 and managed to bring peace and economic recovery to France.

PARADOXES OF FRENCH IMMIGRATION

The history of French immigration to the United States involves a number of paradoxes. In only a few cases did groups of French citizens make a collective decision to leave France for the United States. Instead, typical French immigrants came as individuals or families seeking change or economic opportunity. Some analysts attribute this lack of group movement to the humane climate of France, while others claim that in general the French are reluctant to organize into groups. As a result, the number of immigrants to the United States from France has always been smaller than from other European countries.

According to the *Statistical Abstract of the United States,* for example, immigrants from France accounted for only 0.46 percent of total American immigrants over the 30-year period from 1961 to 1991—or 78,300 out of a total 16.98 million. In addition, only 18,000 people came to the United States from France between 1980 and 1988, compared to 112,000 from England and 56,000 from Germany ("French American Relations: Rapprochement," *Economist,* March 16, 1991). In total, approximately 740,000 immigrants from France have settled in the United States since 1820, and between 30,000 and 40,000 came earlier. In 1990, 119,233 people living in the United States told the U.S. Census Bureau that they had been born in France. The flow of French immigrants to the United States also has been very stable in comparison to other countries, ranging from a high of 77,000 during the decade of the 1840s to a low of 18,000 during the 1970s.

While these figures provide useful information about the trends of French immigration, demographers admit that counting French Americans has been problematic since U.S. colonial times. For many years U.S. officials tended to overestimate the number of French immigrants because they equated immigrants' nationality with their last place of domicile before arrival. This policy meant that many people who actually hailed from Germany or Eastern Europe and had settled in France temporarily in order to facilitate their eventual passage to the United States were regarded as French Americans. Another problem in the U.S. immigration figures involves inconsistent treatment of the French speaking people who came to America from Canada or the Caribbean. French Canadian Americans, Acadians (or Cajuns), and Creoles form distinct U.S. ethnic groups but are not always distinguished from French Americans in census figures. Compounding the problems with U.S. immigration figures, for many years French officials tended to underestimate the number of emigrants because they wished to downplay any outflow of French citizens. However, most sources agree that French immigration to the United States has been small and steady over time.

Despite their relatively small numbers, French immigrants have tended to be more successful and influential than other groups in America. French immigrants are generally urban, middle-class, skilled, and progressive, and they are most likely to be employed as artisans or merchants. The U.S. Census of 1910 showed that French Americans were more literate, more concentrated in liberal professions, and had fewer children and larger living spaces than other immigrant groups. In the 1930s, moreover, French Americans accounted for ten percent of the entries in *Appleton's Encyclopedia of American Biography*, although they made up only two percent of the overall population. In typically paradoxical style, however, many French immigrants returned to France despite their high rate of success in the United States. In fact, a 1980 estimate showed that only one-third of registered French immigrants ultimately decided to seek U.S. citizenship.

THE FIRST FRENCH AMERICANS

Many of the earliest French settlements in North America were mainly intended as trading outposts. Jean Ribaut, a French Huguenot sailor, established two of the first French colonies near Beaufort, South Carolina, and Jacksonville, Florida, in the 1550s. He settled in these locations in order to compete with the Spanish for control of trade in the Caribbean region. In 1534, French explorer Jacques Cartier became the first to travel the length of the St. Lawrence River. Although he failed to find the gold he was seeking, by 1542 he did reach the area that would become Quebec, including Montreal, in Canada. After forming an alliance with the powerful Algonquin Indians, Samuel de Champlain founded the first permanent French settlement in Quebec in 1608.

Originally, French colonial policy allowed only Catholics to emigrate, but most French Catholics were reluctant to leave their homes. As a result, the few people who came to North America from France were mostly explorers, traders, or Jesuit missionaries seeking to convert the Indians. These individuals tended to spread out and travel far into the wilderness. In fact, by the time the Pilgrims arrived in New England in 1620, the French had already discovered three of the Great Lakes. This migration to the Midwest later led to French bases in Detroit and St. Louis.

Robert Cavelier de La Salle traveled the length of the Mississippi River to the Gulf of Mexico in 1682, and upon completion of his journey founded Louisiana by claiming the entire Mississippi Basin in the name of King Louis XIV of France. Jean-Baptiste Bienville followed by forming a successful French colony in New Orleans in 1717.

SIGNIFICANT IMMIGRATION WAVES

There have been several notable waves of French immigrants to the United States based upon economic, religious, or political factors. For the most part, however, French immigration has been a result of individual decisions rather than a mass movement. The earliest flow of French immigrants began around 1538 and consisted of Huguenots who felt alienated from mainstream French society due to their Protestant faith. The Huguenots' emigration peaked after King Louis XIV revoked the Edict of Nantes in 1685, outlawing the Protestant religion and forcing the Huguenots to either convert to Catholicism or face death. According to Albert Robbins in *Coming to America: Immigrants from Northern Europe*, the king's official decree gave orders to "kill the greatest part of the Protestants that can be overtaken, without sparing the women, to the end that this may intimidate them and prevent others from falling into a similar fault."

Many Huguenots decided to flee from France, but it was still illegal for Protestants to emigrate. Those who managed to leave often had to pay bribes or use connections to acquire false passports. As a result, the majority of the 15,000 Huguenots who arrived in North America were wealthy and skilled, and they eventually gained prominence as craftsmen and merchants. The Huguenots established a strong presence in New York with settlements in Harlem, Staten Island, New Rochelle, and New Paltz. In fact, the first child born in New York City was Jean Vigné, the son of a Huguenot immigrant. Pennsylvania, Virginia, South Carolina, and Massachusetts also became the sites of successful Huguenot settlements. Since the Huguenots could not settle among French Catholics and felt alienated from France, most accepted North America as their new homeland and changed their names to sound more English.

With the beginning of the French Revolution, a wave of Roman Catholic refugees emigrated from France to the United States. Many of these immigrants were either wealthy aristocrats or working-class people, such as chefs and hairdressers, who depended upon the aristocrats for their livelihood. Another important group of refugees to arrive at this time included 100 French priests. Since there were only 25 priests in the American colonies prior to their arrival, these immigrants had a strong influence on the development of the American Catholic church. Missionary work carried the Roman Catholic refugees to far-ranging French colonial areas, such as Michigan, St. Louis, and Louisiana.

About 10,000 political refugees managed to leave France during the French Revolution, and many of these immigrants traveled through French colonies in the Caribbean to reach the United States. This group included about 3,000 people of mixed black and French ancestry who settled in Philadelphia. Following Napoleon's defeat in 1815, a large wave of French immigration began, which lasted through the start of the American Civil War. Napoleon's brother Jérome came to the United States at this time with several hundred former soldiers and tried unsuccessfully to establish settlements in Texas, Alabama, and Ohio.

The California Gold Rush, which began in 1848, convinced a record number of French immigrants to make their way to the United States. About 30,000 people arrived between 1849 and 1851, with an all-time high of 20,000 coming in 1851 alone. Unfortunately, few of these immigrants ever found the riches they were seeking. According to Abraham P. Nasatir in *French Activities in California*, the following letter written by Montes Jean—one of the French immigrant "forty-niners"—describes the conditions immigrants encountered in San Francisco in December 1849: "It is twenty-four days since we arrived in California, but in what condition.... We have been very fortunate being in a country where a great deal is earned and where work is not lacking. I say 'work'; that is to say, go to the dock of San Francisco, become a working man, carry bales of merchandise to various stores and you will be quite well paid. For carrying a trunk weighing about a hundred livres for a distance of fifty meters or more one is paid three dollars (about sixteen francs); and in this way we have lived up to now, when I am writing you. But at present, since people are arriving in large numbers, prices are diminishing greatly. One cannot go to the mines at this time on account of the rising waters and because the routes are miry and submerged.... Food is very expensive in this country. Bread, for example, costs a half-dollar a livre, and meat twenty-six sous de France. Work is not progressing very much at present, although there are two hundred vessels in the harbor."

In 1871 a group of Alsatian Jews settled in Los Angeles, after the Franco-Prussian War put the French provinces Alsace and Lorraine under German rule. Immigration slowed significantly during the American Civil War, and the years immediately following saw a larger percentage of unskilled workers from France moving to the United States. A number of French Jews immigrated after the fall of France to the Germans in 1940. From the end of World War II onward, a strong cultural and economic recovery in France caused the flow of French immigrants to slow considerably. Most French immigrants in the second half of the twentieth century came to the United States because they married an American citizen or simply wanted to try something different, rather than out of religious, economic, or political necessity.

SETTLEMENT PATTERNS

French American settlement patterns reflect the fact that French immigrants typically came to the United States as individuals or families seeking economic opportunity. Rather than joining groups of previous French settlers or establishing French American communities, these immigrants most often scattered to the areas where new opportunities seemed likely to be found. For example, the number of ethnic French living in Louisiana dropped from 15,000 in 1860 to half that number by 1930 as the prosperity of the South declined. In the meantime, the French population of California rose from 8,000 in 1860 to 22,000 by 1970 as immigrants pursued new opportunities in the West. According to *We the People: An Atlas of America's Ethnic Diversity*, in 1980 more immigrants directly from France lived in California, New York, New Jersey, and Pennsylvania than in any other states. Many of these French immigrants possessed professional skills that were most valuable in urban environments. Less than 40 percent of French Americans immigrated directly from France, however, as the majority came from French speaking parts of Canada. In general, these groups came from different French social classes and tended to avoid contact with each other despite their shared language.

According to the U.S. Census of 1980, the counties with the largest number of people of French ancestry—including those whose ancestors immigrated to the United States directly from France as well as those whose ancestors immigrated from Canada or the Caribbean—were Worcester, Massachusetts, with 90,332; Providence, Rhode Island, with 72,461; Middlesex, Massachusetts, with 66,911; Los Angeles, California, with 65,263; and Hillsborough, New Hampshire, with 58,278. The counties (parishes) with the highest percentage of their population claiming French ancestry were all in Louisiana: Vermillion, with 43.13 percent French ancestry; St. Martin, with 37.67 percent; Evangeline, with 36.22 percent; Lafourche, with 36.2 percent; and Avoyelles, with 33.48 percent.

ACCULTURATION AND ASSIMILATION

Historically, the people who immigrated to the United States from northern Europe—including France—were more readily accepted than some other immigrant groups. For example, when the U.S. Congress passed a law restricting immigration in the 1920s, northern European groups received the most liberal quotas. This favored status allowed northern European immigrants to assimilate more easily into American culture. The type of individual who was most likely to leave France for the United States, moreover, had a particularly strong propensity toward assimilation. For instance, a high percentage of French immigrants were professionals or merchants who earned their livings among the greater population and within an urban environment. At the same time, very few French farmers—who would have lived in rural areas and been more isolated from the dominant culture—decided to emigrate. Typical French immigrants were also modernists who felt estranged from mainstream French culture and viewed the United States as a progressive, classless, secular, and innovative society. "Given this background of alienation and yearning," Patrice Louis René Higonnet explains in the *Harvard Encyclopedia of American Ethnic Groups*, "it is hardly surprising that French immigrants, self-selecting and at odds with the national ethos, should have been assimilationists."

Higonnet also attributes the absence of group spirit among French Americans to their geographic dispersion, a general French distaste for group interaction, and the fact that French immigrants came to the United States seeking new forms of society and culture. One early example of assimilation among French immigrants was when the Huguenots chose to join the less-extreme Anglican Church in North America. In the modern era, despite the strong cultural nationalism found in France, French Americans have shown a higher rate of intermarriage than any other non-English-speaking immigrant group. In fact, French Americans tend to assimilate so quickly and completely that most sources can only cite their overall impact on American culture. As James S. Pula confirmed in *The French in America*, "Place names and linguistic quirks remain as a lasting testimony to the influence of France on American culture, but the people have all but disappeared into an abyss of assimilation. Unlike many other national groups, the French generally held no special reluctance toward Anglicizing their names and their speech."

TRADITIONAL BELIEFS, ATTITUDES, AND CUSTOMS

The rapid assimilation of French immigrants into American society ensured that few traditional customs were carried over and practiced by French Americans. Instead, Americans studied and emulated French culture, manners, cuisine, fashion, art, and literature. French Americans mainly disseminated information and acted as role models. French culture first gained widespread popularity in the United States in the early nineteenth century—shortly after the Revolutionary War—when Americans followed the events and supported the principles of the French Revolution. French chefs and restaurants bolstered the popularity of French cuisine, while the influence of French impressionists on American art became apparent. Several U.S. presidents also ordered French furniture and silverware for use at the White House.

CUISINE

French immigrants introduced a wide range of interesting foods to America. For example, French Americans made the first yeast breads in North America and brought technical farming skills that vastly improved American rice and wines. Huguenots grew and prepared the first okra, artichokes, and tomatoes. The popularity of French cuisine took off in the 1780s, following the alliance between France and the United States during the American Revolution. Many respected French chefs, such as Arthur Goussé in Los Angeles, immigrated to the United States and established restaurants. Even non-French Americans began to prepare buns and rolls, omelettes, and delicate soups. A number of French culinary terms remain prominent in modern times, including *bouillon*, *purée*, *fricassée*, *mayonnaise*, *pâté*, *hors d'oeuvres*, *bisque*, *fillet*, *sauté*, *casserole*, *au gratin*, and *à la mode*.

FASHION

Imported French attire gained popularity in the early nineteenth century as well, particularly items such as gloves and lace. Around 1850, the French custom of wearing beards swept across the United States. In 1908, several women wearing imported French skirts and fishnet stockings were arrested for indecent exposure. France has maintained its position on the leading edge of world fashion through the present day.

HOLIDAYS CELEBRATED BY FRENCH AMERICANS

The French national holiday of Bastille Day—which commemorates the uprising that destroyed a major symbol of oppression in Paris and led to the formation of the First Republic in 1789—is celebrated in some communities throughout the United States on July 14. In addition, the New Orleans tradition of Mardi Gras—a week-long series of parades and parties usually held in February—was first organized in 1827 by French American students.

HEALTH AND MENTAL HEALTH ISSUES

The average life expectancy in France is exactly the same as in the United States—70 years for men, and 78 years for women. Although there are no known congenital diseases specific to French Americans, the French have shown a higher than average susceptibility to lung and throat cancers, mainly because they tend to smoke and drink heavily. In fact, with four million alcoholics in its population, France has one of the highest rates of alcoholism in the world.

LANGUAGE

French is a Romance language derived from Latin. It has enjoyed a prestigious position in world culture for over three centuries. French was the official language of diplomatic negotiations, and the preferred language among the upper class-

es of Western civilization, beginning around 1650. By about 1920, however, English began to gain popularity, and it eventually surpassed French in terms of international status. In 1975 the French National Assembly, reacting to what it viewed as an encroachment of English slang upon the French language (commonly called "franglais"), passed a law restricting the use of untranslated English words in advertising materials. They also hoped to discourage the French public from using English words when an equivalent French term existed.

As of 1990, an estimated 1.93 million people in the United States spoke the French language at home. The influence of French is also apparent in American English. For example, since French explorers often served as guides for other settlers after the United States purchased the Louisiana Territory, French words were used to describe many aspects of the frontier experience, such as *portage*, *rapids*, *bayou*, *butte*, *peak*, *gopher*, *prairie*, *pass*, and *cache*. French explorers also left a legacy of American place names, including Baton Rouge, Sault Ste. Marie, Detroit, Couer d'Alene, Marquette, Joliet, Lake Champlain, Lake Pontchartrain, Des Moines, Eau Claire, Fon du Lac, Charlevoix, and Terre Haute. Finally, numerous French words occur in everyday American usage, such as *croquet*, *poker*, *roulette*, *automobile*, *garage*, *lingerie*, *restaurant*, *crayon*, *bouquet*, and *boutique*.

GREETINGS AND POPULAR EXPRESSIONS

Common French greetings and other expressions include: *Bonjour*—Hello, Good morning, Good afternoon; *Comment allez-vous*—How do you do; *Au revoir*—Good-bye; *Très bien*—Very good; *Oui, c'est ça*—Yes, that's right; *Merci beaucoup*—Thank you very much; *À votre service*—You're welcome; or, Don't mention it.

FAMILY AND COMMUNITY DYNAMICS

EDUCATION

The French educational system, which was initiated during Napoleon's rule, has had a marked influence on schooling in the United States since the early 1800s. The French system features innovative nursery and primary schools, followed by *collèges*, the equivalent of American junior high schools. Students then must decide whether to complete their secondary education at an academic or a vocational *lycée*—a three-year preparatory school similar to American high schools. Admission to French universities is based upon a rigorous, competitive examination in a specific subject area. Only top students may attend the *grandes écoles*, or elite schools, that serve as a prerequisite for top jobs in business and government. Educators in the United States emulated the French system of progressive schooling culminating in admission to a private or municipal university. In France, however, the entire educational system is administered by the Ministry of National Education, while in the United States education is controlled by states or local communities. Proponents of the French system claim that it is superior, in that it demands students' best efforts and rewards exceptional performance. On the other hand, some detractors claim that the system works to maintain a social class system in France, since the vast majority of students at the *grandes écoles* hail from upper-class backgrounds.

RELIGION

The majority of French immigrants to the United States have been Roman Catholic. This fact is so partly because Catholics form a majority in France, and partly because during colonial times only Catholics were allowed to emigrate. Descendants of the 15,000 French Huguenots who came to the United States tend to be Anglican. More recently, the United States became a refuge for French Jews during and after World War II.

EMPLOYMENT AND ECONOMIC TRADITIONS

On the whole, French immigrants have been highly successful and have made a lasting impact in the United States. According to *We the People*, the French immigrants who remained in the United Stated tended to be "less traditional and more enterprising, ambitious, and forward-looking" individuals who typically "adjusted without much apparent stress to American ways." In contrast to other immigrant groups, only 12 percent of French Americans were farmers. Instead, French immigrants most often worked as professionals, clerical workers, cooks, waiters, artists, and managers.

Specific French immigration waves contributed different labor practices to American society. For example, the Huguenots introduced a number of skilled crafts to the United States, including sophisticated techniques of weaving, leather dressing, lace making, and felt manufacture. Some historians claim that the Huguenots' stylish ways helped transform crude frontier settlements into civilized cities and towns. Refugees from the French Revolution and the fall of Napoleon who came to the United States tended to be former army officers or aristocrats. These educated individuals often taught the French language or such elite activities as fencing and dancing. A number of French chefs, hairdressers, dress designers, and perfumers accompanied the wave of aristocrats and introduced French cuisine and fashion to America.

POLITICS AND GOVERNMENT

Americans of French ancestry began to influence politics in the United States during colonial times. Most French immigrants rapidly became "Americanized," however, and participated in government as individuals rather than as a group. Four U.S. presidents—John Tyler, James B. Garfield, Theodore Roosevelt, and Franklin D. Roosevelt—were of French Huguenot descent.

MILITARY SERVICE

Many descendants of French Huguenots, including Paul Revere, were distinguished patriots during the American Revolution. In addition, the French government provided invaluable support to the American cause. One French army captain in particular, Marquis de Lafayette, had an important influence on the events at this time. Lafayette fought brilliantly as a major general in George Washington's army, and later returned to France to convince King Louis XVI to formally recognize the independence of the United States and to provide military aid against the British. French immigrants fought passionately on both sides of the American Civil War. For example, Brigadier General Benjamin Buisson, a veteran of the Napoleonic Wars, formed troops out of French volunteers to defend New Orleans for the Confederacy. A number of all-French American groups, known as Zouave units, fought for both the North and the South, wearing uniforms in the French colonial tradition.

INDIVIDUAL AND GROUP CONTRIBUTIONS

ARTS AND LEISURE

Pierre Charles L'Enfant (1754-1825), a civil engineer by training, fought with Lafayette during the American Revolution. He later became the architect of the United States capital city in Washington, D.C. His designs of majestic buildings and tree-lined squares were considered visionary. French artist Régis François Gignoux came to the United States in 1844. He served as the first president of the Brooklyn Art Academy and had a vast influence on American landscape painting. In 1876, John La Farge painted the first mural in America to decorate Trinity Church in Boston. He later went on to develop techniques that allowed stained glass to be used on a large scale for decorative purposes. Marcel Duchamp, the French Dadaist painter and conceptual artist, lived in New York from 1942 until his death in 1968.

Celebrated poet Henry Wadsworth Longfellow (1807-1882), of French descent, was perhaps best known for his epic *Song of Hiawatha*, published in 1855. John Greenleaf Whittier (1807-1892) became a prominent abolitionist as well as poet. French American author and naturalist Henry David Thoreau (1817-1862) gained renown with the 1854 publication of *Walden*, a diary of his two years in the wilderness near Concord, Massachusetts. Two other respected French American writers were Edna St. Vincent Millay (1892-1950), who won the Pulitzer Prize in 1923 for *The Harp Weaver, and Other Poems*, and Stephen Vincent Benét (1898-1943), who won the 1929 Pulitzer Prize for his epic poem "John Brown's Body."

Among the French American actors to gain prominence in the United States were Leslie Caron (1931-), Charles Boyer (1899-1978), and Claudette Colbert (1905-). After making her American debut in 1924, Colbert won an Academy Award as best actress for her role in *It Happened One Night* in 1934. Actor Robert Goulet made his debut in the Broadway production of *Camelot* in 1960, and went on to appear in many feature films and receive both Tony and Emmy Awards. Composer Maurice Jarée won several Academy Awards for the musical scores he wrote for such classic American films as *Lawrence of Arabia*, *Dr. Zhivago*, *Grand Prix*, and *The Longest Day* in the 1960s. In sports, French American jockey Ron Turcotte rode the most famous American racehorse of all time, Secretariat, to victory in the Triple Crown of horse racing.

EDUCATION

Thomas Gallaudet (1787-1851) founded the first American school for the deaf in Hartford, Connecticut, in 1817. He also established teachers' training schools and promoted advanced education for women. Gallaudet College, a national institute for the deaf, was established in Washington, D.C. in 1855. French American Edouard Seguin (1812-1880) was responsible for significant developments in the education of mentally retarded individuals. In 1842, Father Edward Sorin, a French priest, founded a seminary which later became the University of Notre Dame. Finally, James Bowdoin served as governor of Massachusetts and first president of the American Academy of Arts and Letters. He also founded Bowdoin College and established the Massachusetts Humane Society.

GOVERNMENT

One of the most influential French Americans in the history of U.S. government was John Jay (1745-1829). Among his many contributions, Jay acted as president of the Continental Congress, negotiated the treaty with England that ensured American independence, and served as the first Chief Justice of U.S. Supreme Court.

INDUSTRY

One of the most famous French Americans, partly due to the variety of his contributions, was Paul Revere (1735-1818). The son of Huguenot Apollos Revoire de Romagnieu, Revere led several protests against British rule of the American colonies, including the Boston Tea Party. He also made the legendary "midnight ride" to warn Massachusetts residents that British soldiers were approaching at the start the American Revolution. In his time, however, Revere was also known as a talented silversmith who developed a distinctly American style. He designed and engraved the plates for the first paper money in Massachusetts and established the first mill for rolling copper sheets. Pierre Faneuil, who belonged to a wealthy and influential family of merchants, donated to the city of Boston the public market and meeting place known as Faneuil Hall.

Eleuthère Irénée Dupont de Nemours (1772-1834), who was considered a radical in France, came to the United States after losing his publishing business during the French Revolution. He opened a gunpowder mill in 1799, which grew rapidly during the War of 1812. Eventually, under the management of his heirs, his holdings grew into the Dupont Chemical-General Motors complex, one of the largest industrial concerns in the world. In 1851, French American John Gorrie invented an ice machine and received the first U.S. patent for mechanical refrigeration. Philip Danforth Armour, whose Armour brand meats are still sold in the United States, first entered the meat-packing business in 1863. His contributions to the industry included the development of advanced slaughtering and modern refrigeration techniques.

SCIENCE AND MEDICINE

Civil engineer Octave Chanute came to the United States from France at the age of six. He conducted numerous experiments in aeronautics and created the wing design that became the basis for the Wright Brothers' successful airplane. John J. Audubon (1785-1851), the son of a French immigrant who fought in the American Revolution, is remembered as America's premier naturalist. His comprehensive study *Birds in America,* which included over 1,000 illustrations drawn or painted by Audubon, appeared beginning in 1827. Matthew Fontaine Maury is credited as the founder of the modern science of hydrography. He was the first person to chart the flow of the Gulf Stream, to conduct deep-sea soundings, and to imagine the potential of a transoceanic cable. His best-known work, *The Physical Geography of the Sea,* was published in 1856. Marine explorer Jacques Cousteau (1910-) contributed to the invention of the aqualung in 1943 and won an Academy Award in 1957 for his documentary film feature *The Silent World.*

In medicine, surgeon François Marie Provost performed the first successful cesarean sections in Louisiana in 1809. Alexis Carrel (1873-1944) became famous during his tenure at the Rockefeller Institute as the first doctor to sew blood vessels together, transplant animal organs, and keep human tissue alive in jars. He wrote the seminal work *Man, the Unknown,* and won the Nobel Prize for Medicine in 1912.

MEDIA

PRINT

France-Amérique.
Published by Trocadero Publishing, Inc., this weekly periodical is a French language tabloid established in 1943 by prominent refugees. It covers news from France and Franco-American life in the United States.

Address: 330 West 42nd Street, Suite 2600, New York, New York, 10036.
Telephone: (212) 629-4460.

France Today.
Published ten times annually by France Press, Inc., *France Today* covers contemporary issues, events, trends, and travel in France.

Address: 1051 Divisadero, San Francisco, California, 94115.
Telephone: (415) 921-5100.

Journal Français d'Amérique.
Published bi-weekly by France Press, Inc., this periodical covers French history, politics, culture, and travel.

Contact: Anne Prah Perochon, Editor.
Address: 1051 Divisadero, San Francisco, California, 94115.
Telephone: (415) 921-5100.

ORGANIZATIONS AND ASSOCIATIONS

Federation of French American Women (FFFA).
Also known as Federation Feminine Franco-Americaine. Founded in 1951, the 8,000-member FFFA promotes French culture; conducts an oral history program; sponsors French speaking contests, youth festivals, ethnic vacations, and an annual scholarship for outstanding students of French; compiles statistics; and maintains an archive and a hall of fame.

Contact: Marthe W. Whalon, President.
Address: 240 Highland Avenue, Fall River, Massachusetts, 02720.
Telephone: (508) 678-1800.

French American Foundation (FAF).
Founded in 1976, FAF works to strengthen relations between the United States and France by cre-

ating opportunities for French and American professionals to discuss problems of concern to both societies. FAF sponsors exchanges of specialists, internships, study tours, conferences, and fellowships, including the Tocqueville Grant Program for U.S. doctoral candidates and a continuing Chair in American Civilization at a university in Paris.

Contact: Diantha D. Schull, Executive Director.
Address: 41 East 72nd Street, New York, New York, 10021.
Telephone: (212) 288-4400.

French Institute/Alliance Française (FIAF).

Formed in 1971 through the merger of Alliance Française de New York (founded 1898) and French Institute in the United States (founded 1911), FIAF encourages study of French language and culture among its 8,600 members and fosters friendly relations between French and American peoples. FIAF also offers a program of French lectures, films, concerts, theater, and art; operates a school of French for adults; and maintains a library of 40,000 volumes in French.

Contact: Jean Vallier, Director.
Address: 22 East 60th Street, New York, New York, 10022-1077.
Telephone: (212) 355-6100.

National Association of Franco-Americans (AFA).

Also known as Assemblée Nationale des Franco-Americains. Founded in 1977, AFA works to provide a cultural identity and create a forum for the exchange of ideas among its 7,000 members, who share a French linguistic heritage or belong to a French speaking population in the United States. AFA also represents Franco-Americans in legislative matters, conducts research on Franco-American history and culture, and publishes a bimonthly newsletter.

Contact: Real Gilbert, President.
Address: 83 Amherst Street, P.O. Box 2000, Manchester, New Hampshire, 03105.
Telephone: (603) 627-0505.

Societé Historique Franco-Americaine (SHFA).

Founded in 1899, SHFA studies and honors the role played by people of French ancestry in the evolution of the United States. SHFA also compiles documents, statistics, and archives; presents historical lectures; and sponsors research.

Contact: Marthe Biron Peloquin, President.

Address: 1 Leyland Road, Westford, Massachusetts, 01886.
Telephone: (508) 692-6370.

MUSEUMS AND RESEARCH CENTERS

The American and French Research on the Treasury of the French Language (ARTFL) Project.

Cooperative effort of the University of Chicago and the Centre National de la Recherche Scientifique that is involved in the development of an online database covering French language and literature from the Middle Ages to the present, including more than 150 million words of major literary, technical, and philosophical texts.

Contact: Dr. Robert Morrissey, Director.

Address: Department of Romance Languages and Literature, 1050 East 59th Street, Chicago, Illinois, 60637.

Telephone: (312) 702-8488.

The Center for French and Francophone Studies.

Located at Louisiana State University, the center conducts research into French and francophone culture of the southern United States and the Caribbean, including studies of mores and customs, work, law and commerce, role of women, Creole languages, and literature.

Contact: Professor Edouard Glissant, Director.

Address: Department of French and Italian, Louisiana State University, 225 Prescott Hall, Baton Rouge, Louisiana, 70803.

Telephone: (504) 388-6589.

The Centre for Research on French Canadian Culture.

An integral unit of the University of Ottawa, the center conducts research into all aspects of French culture in Canada and North America, including history, literature, fine arts, social sciences, and education. It also maintains a reference library of 5,200 books and an archive containing manuscripts, photographs, audio- and videotapes, and periodicals that is open to the public.

Contact: Yolande Grise, Director.

Address: Lamoureux Hall, Room 274, 145 Jean-Jacques Lussier Street, Ottawa, Ontario, Canada, K1N 6N5.

Telephone: (613) 564-6847.

The Centre for the Study of the Language, Art, and Culture of Francophones in North America.

An integral unit of Laval University, the center maintains a folklore archive center containing 10,000 iconographic records and 200,000 documents of songs, legends, and memoirs concerning French culture and identity in North America.

Contact: Jocelyn Letourneau, Director.

Address: Pavillon Charles De Koninck, Cite universitaire, Quebec, Canada, G1K 7P4.

Telephone: (418) 656-5510.

The Henri Peyre Institute for the Humanities.

An integral unit of the graduate school of the City University of New York, the institute conducts research into French literature, philosophy, politics, film, and the arts with the support of the French government.

Contact: Dr. John W. Kneller, Co-director.

Address: 33 West 42nd Street, New York, New York, 10036.

Telephone: (212) 790-4481.

SOURCES FOR ADDITIONAL STUDY

Bernstein, Richard. "The Myth of the Anti-American," *Fragile Glory: A Portrait of France and the French*. New York, Knopf, 1990.

Brasseaux, Carl A. *The "Foreign French": Nineteenth-Century French Immigration into Louisiana*. Lafayette: University of Southwestern Louisiana, Center for Louisiana Studies, (n.d.).

Duroselle, Jean-Baptiste. "The Hereditary Enemy," *France and the United States: From Beginnings to Present*, translated by Derek Cotton. Chicago: University of Chicago Press, 1976.

Harris, Jonathan. *The Land and People of France*. New York: Lippincott, 1989.

Maisel, Albert Q. "The French," *They All Chose America*. New York: Thomas Nelson, 1955.

Nasatir, Abraham P. *French Activities in California*. Stanford: Stanford University Press, 1945.

Pula, James S. *The French in America, 1488-1974: A Chronology and Fact Book*. Dobbs Ferry, New York: Oceana, 1975.

Robbins, Albert. *Coming to America: Immigrants from Northern Europe*. New York: Delacorte Press, 1981.

The family is at the center of the French-Canadian American's world.

FRENCH-CANADIAN AMERICANS

by

Marianne
Fedunkiw

OVERVIEW

Canada, with an area encompassing just over six million square miles, is the largest country in the world. This American neighbor to the north is bordered on the other three sides by oceans: the Pacific to the west, the Atlantic to the east, and the Arctic to the north. At 5,525 miles, the border with the United States is the longest undefended border in the world.

More than half of the 26.9 million people in Canada are concentrated in the corridor between Windsor, Ontario, and Québec City, Québec. Much of the remaining population live in the southern areas of each of the nation's ten provinces and two territories. The country's largest cities are Toronto, with 3.8 million residents, Montréal with 3.1 million, and Vancouver with 1.6 million. Although there are French Canadians in each of the provinces, by far the greatest number can be found in the province of Québec. In 1991, 81 percent of the population of Québec cited French as their "mother tongue" (the first language spoken as a child and still understood), compared to about nine percent for English. The next-highest concentration of French-speaking Canadians is in New Brunswick (33 percent). All of the remaining provinces reported figures of less than five percent, ranging from 0.4 to 4.6 percent. Overall, 6.5 million

Canadians, or 24 percent of the population in 1991, reported French as their "mother tongue." English-speaking Canadians numbered 16.5 million, or almost 61 percent of the total population.

There is also a strong and growing trend of bilingualism in Canada. According to the 1986 census, 16 percent of the population spoke both English and French, again with the province of Québec leading the way. In Québec almost 60 percent of anglophones, more than 30 percent of francophones, and close to half of all allophones (those whose mother tongue is neither English nor French) were bilingual. For comparison, outside Québec only about five percent of anglophones and 80 percent of francophones were bilingual.

Québec was by far the leading point of departure for French-Canadian immigration to the United States, although there were those who travelled south from Nova Scotia, New Brunswick, Manitoba, and Ontario. Québec is the largest province, making up almost 16 percent of Canada's total area and over one-fourth of its population. The provincial motto is *Je me souviens* (I remember), and the flower is the fleur-de-lis. Both motto and flower are featured prominently on the provincial coat of arms.

HISTORY

The man who is credited with discovering the Canadian mainland was French explorer Jacques Cartier (1491-1557). He was seeking gold and riches via the famed Northwest Passage to the East, but reached Newfoundland instead in May 1534. He made another journey to Canada in 1535 and, unlike earlier explorers, continued west along the St. Lawrence River as far as modern-day Québec City, and then pressed on even farther to the future site of Montréal. This first foray into the interior was difficult—particularly because of the harsh winter conditions in Québec City and the rampant scurvy that killed many men. The remainder were said to be saved by a native tea made from the bark of the white spruce tree.

Cartier's third voyage to Canada was a failure in terms of establishing a settlement. Permanent settlement would have to wait until the fur trade gave reason to send more than the occasional fishing vessel. Samuel de Champlain (1567-1635) finally established the first trading post on the site of Québec City in 1608. Champlain, too, had sought the Northwest Passage, but he soon realized that beaver pelts would be responsible for the survival of any settlements. He set up a system of company monopolies to systematically hunt and sell pelts and, in exchange for 300 settlers coming to the new land annually, to serve as the area's government from 1627 until 1642.

Unfortunately, Champlain's early settlement was attacked by English and Iroquois Confederacy rivals. The Catholic church, an integral part of French settlement, also suffered during the mid-seventeenth century at the hands of those opposed to French colonization. Groups such as the Jesuit missionaries, who were sent to convert the natives, were often attacked, and many missionaries and their followers were tortured and killed.

In addition to founding Québec, Champlain ventured into northern New York (he discovered the lake named for him in 1609), and explored the Atlantic coast as far as Massachusetts, including many of the larger rivers in Maine. However, Champlain's efforts to establish a successful French colony were thwarted by weather, battles with the English and certain native groups, and limited support from France. He died in Québec in 1635, at the age of 68.

NEW FRANCE

For all of the hardships, the King of France, Louis XIV, did not give up. In 1665 he sent two ships to Québec containing the first regular troops to be sent to Canada, in addition to Alexandre de Prouville, the Marquis de Tracy (1596-1670), who was made lieutenant-general for all French possessions in North America. The government changed from Champlain's company monopolies to a Sovereign Council composed of the governor of New France, a bishop, and an intendant—the latter being the chief representative of royal power in a French colony. France shipped boatloads of *demoiselles bien choisies* (women of good health and upbringing), or *filles du roi* (king's girls), to raise the numbers and help settle New France. Jean Talon (1626-1694), the first intendant of New France, was instrumental in doubling the population between 1666 and 1678, to 7,605 settlers. He was joined in his efforts by the first bishop, François de Montmorency-Laval (1623-1708), who established a seminary that would become the University of Laval, and the governor of New France, Louis de Buade, Comte de Frontenac (1622-1698).

Talon also successfully implemented the seignorial system, in which feudal land tenures were granted to settlers free of charge in exchange for clearing the land and pledging loyalty to the King of France. The seigneur would, in turn, subdivide his acreage to tenants who paid a nominal rent, cleared, and farmed the land. These *habitants* were the first French Canadians. Soon the settlements had, at their center, a parish church and an established *curé* (priest) to meet their religious needs. In addition to the *habitants*, there were the *coureurs de bois*, traders who negotiated for furs with the Indians in the upper reaches of the Ottawa River and in the Great Lakes.

SETTLEMENTS OUTSIDE QUÉBEC

The French settled in other parts of North America as well. By the Treaty of Utrecht (1713), France ceded Hudson Bay, Newfoundland, and Acadia to England. The French, however, retained control of present-day Cape Breton Island on the east coast of Nova Scotia where they built the fortress of Louisburg (1720-1740) to defend its remaining territory. In addition to Acadia, or the Maritime provinces of Canada, the French could be found in the coastal region of northern Maine. The first Acadian settlement was established in 1604 by Pierre du Gua, Sieur de Monts at St. Croix Island in the Bay of Fundy. In 1755, 6,500 Acadians were deported to the American colonies of the Atlantic Seaboard for having refused to take an oath to the king of England. Many of them would later find their way to Louisiana where they became known as Cajuns, a derivation of the word Acadian. Other early French towns in the United States included Detroit, Michigan, founded by Antoine de Lamothe Cadillac (1658-1730) in 1701. Cadillac also served as colonial governor of the Louisiana territory.

Finally, outside of Québec, the major concentration of French settlers was in what are now Louisiana, Mississippi, Missouri, and Illinois. The Louisiana Territory was claimed for France in 1682 and named by explorer Robert Cavelier, Sieur de la Salle (1643-1687), after King Louis XIV. French forts along the Mississippi River spread northward from New Orleans. A pair of French Canadians founded and helped to colonize this southern French territory. Pierre le Moyne d'Iberville (1661-1706) established the city of Biloxi, Mississippi, in 1699, and Jean-Baptiste le Moyne de Bienville, established New Orleans in 1718. In 1803 the United States bought the land, which spread from the Mississippi River to the Rocky Mountains, from France for $15 million in the Louisiana Purchase.

There are many other place names in the United States that tell the tale of French influence and settlement. The state of Maine is said to have been named for the province of Mayne in France, and Vermont comes from the French words *vert mont*, which mean "green mountain." Duluth, Minnesota, is named for Daniel Greysolon, Sieur Du Lhut (1636-1710), who won the Lake Superior and upper Mississippi region for France. Likewise, Dubuque, Iowa, is named for Julien Dubuque (1762-1810), a pioneer settler of Iowa. Vestiges of the French connection remain in Minnesota's motto, *L'Étoile du Nord* (The star of the north).

WAR WITH THE ENGLISH

The English, French, and Spanish all wanted to claim North America for their own. After a series of smaller skirmishes, the French and Indian Wars of 1689-1763 (between the French and the English) finally led to the fall of the French colonies. These battles, offshoots of various European wars, culminating in the Seven Years' War, saw the French and native peoples aligned against the British and their American colonists. In 1745 English forces captured the fort at Louisburg. (It was returned to France in 1748.) The most renowned battle, however, took place on the Plains of Abraham in modern-day Québec City in 1759. By the time the assault was over, both the French General, Louis-Joseph de Montcalm (1712-1759), and the British commander, Brigadier General James Wolfe (1727-1759), lay dead on the battlefield. The Treaty of Paris was signed in 1763 and France ceded her Canadian and American territories east of the Mississippi to England, as well as much of French Louisiana to Spain as compensation for Florida, which Spain yielded to Great Britain. This temporarily ended immigration from France to the Canadian colonies—the French numbered around 60,000 in 1763. During the American Revolution, some French Canadians moved to the United States to escape British rule, while many American Loyalists (who were British sympathizers) were granted land in Québec and the Maritime Provinces.

In recognition of the differing interests of English and French Canadians, what are now the provinces of Ontario and Québec became Upper Canada and Lower Canada, respectively, in 1791. Lower Canada had its own legislature, and French Canadians were allowed to practice their Roman Catholic religion. Nevertheless, tensions culminated in a revolt in 1837, when Britain tried to unite the two Canadas. After the rebellion was quelled, the two halves were successfully joined in 1840. Many of the French rebels fled to the United States, particularly to New England. Finally, the Dominion of Canada was established in 1867.

THE RIEL REBELLION

The battle to maintain French Canadian culture and language in a land under British rule also surfaced outside of Québec. Resentful of the encroaching power of the English from the East, Louis Riel led a group of French Canadian Métis (individuals who are part French and part American Indian) settlers in an attack on Upper Fort Garry, the main camp of the Hudson Bay Company, in 1869. Riel was one-eighth native Canadian and seven-eighths French Canadian, and his Métis followers were of similarly mixed native and French ancestry. They captured the fort and used it as leverage to bargain for special rights for the French and the Métis in Manitoba.

Riel's actions—including the execution of Thomas Scott, a Protestant who fought the French Canadians and Métis—led to a growing hatred on the part of the English in the East. Although Manitoba entered the Canadian confederation in 1870, Riel was banished from Canada in 1875. He settled in Montana temporarily, but returned to Canada in 1884 to participate in the fight for French Canadian and Métis independence. He was charged with treason and later executed for his part in the Saskatchewan Rebellion of 1885.

MODERN-DAY FRENCH CANADA

French Canadians continued to resent having to subordinate themselves to British rule throughout the twentieth century. When World War I broke out in 1914, French Canadians fought against conscription to fight in what they perceived to be Britain's war. French-speakers also fought to have their culture and language recognized and maintained. The 1960s saw a resurgence in the "Quiet Revolution" to preserve "Québec for the French Canadians." In 1976, the Parti Québecois (PQ), a group of militant separatists, was elected to national office for the first time. Their leader was René Lévesque (1922-1987). The year after gaining power, the PQ declared French to be the official language of the province of Québec, but this was overturned by the Supreme Court of Canada in 1979.

A number of referenda have been taken in Québec to gauge popular support for the idea of separating from Canada. In 1980 the vote was against separating, but just a year later the province refused to acknowledge the new Canadian constitution. To address this issue, the premiers of the provinces met in 1987 and drew up the Meech Lake Accord (named for the site of the meetings). The Accord recognized Québec as a "distinct society," but changes to the constitution were not forthcoming, since many English Canadians were opposed to special treatment for Québec. The Accord failed to be ratified by all the provinces. In 1994 Québec once again voted in favor of the PQ, which has renewed its call for independence. Separatism, therefore, remains by far the most significant issue facing French Canadians in Québec during the later decades of the twentieth century.

EARLY SETTLEMENT IN THE UNITED STATES

Exploration by the French was not limited to Canada. Jesuit missionaries travelled south along the Mississippi River, and in 1673 Louis Joliet (1648-1700) and Jesuit Priest Jacques Marquette (1637-1675) explored the Mississippi River. Robert Cavelier, Sieur de la Salle (1643-1687), discovered the mouth of the Mississippi in 1682.

MAJOR IMMIGRATION WAVES: 1830-1870

Small groups or individuals of French Canadian descent have decided to settle in the United States since the major periods of exploration in the seventeenth century. Some fled the aftermath of the Patriote Rebellion of 1837, when hostility toward the French was high. The large number who crossed the border in the nineteenth century, particularly to the New England states, made their choice to seek a better life. These were predominantly young adults, some with families and others who were single. Traditionally, French-Canadian Americans had large families, and these numbers, coupled with dismal economic conditions, drove them south. Some estimates put the extent of the migration at 600,000, which had the effect of draining Canada of a generation.

Work in textile mills and the logging industry—anything besides the backbreaking farm work in Québec—was what drew them. For example, six mills opened in the Lewiston area of the state of Maine alone between 1819 and 1869. When they did settle, French-Canadian Americans sought to build a sense of community much like what they were used to "back home"—centered about a parish church and school, thus combining both the nuclear family and the extended family of the ethnic community. By 1850 about 20,000 French Canadians had settled in the New England area, with the majority living in Vermont. By 1860 there were another 18,000, including clusters in Massachusetts, Rhode Island, and New Hampshire.

THE WAVE CONTINUES: 1865-1920

The influx of French Canadians in the years following the American Civil War resulted from the initiative of American businessmen to expand the textile and shoe industries. Although the French Canadian population was largest in Vermont throughout the 1850s and 1860s, since 1870 Massachusetts has claimed the majority. In his book *The French-Canadian Heritage in New England*, Gerard J. Brault notes that the French Canadians "have the distinction of being the only major ethnic group to have immigrated to the United States in any significant number by train." Most French Canadians settled in a circular pattern around Boston—in towns such as Lewiston, Maine, Manchester, New Hampshire, and Lowell, Massachusetts, to the north; Worcester and Holyoke, Massachusetts, to the west; and Woonsocket, Rhode Island, and Fall River, Massachusetts, to the south. New York State also attracted some settlers as did the Midwestern states of Michigan, Illinois, and Minnesota. The majority of Franco-American settlements were established from the 1860s to the 1880s, though some areas of Vermont had high numbers of French-Canadian Americans as early as 1815.

Québec did not enjoy losing its youth. Starting in 1875, the Canadian government made fairly successful efforts to bring them back by offering either free or cheap land. In fact, up to half of those who had travelled south returned to Canada by 1900. In the first two decades of the twentieth century, recessions in the United States and relative prosperity meant that immigration to the United States fell off from previous years and some French Canadians returned home.

French Canadian settlers in the United States maintained a high level of concentration and a low level of mobility. By 1900 towns such as Woonsocket, Rhode Island (60 percent French-Canadian American), and Biddeford, Maine (also at 60 percent), were very much French Canadian. The most outstanding example is the area in Maine, along the Canadian frontier, known as the St. John Valley, which was almost entirely Franco-American. This level of concentration heightened the sense of community for the new immigrants and facilitated getting French Canadian priests to serve the thriving parishes. Spiritual guidance and a sense of community became all the more important because, for those who toiled in tedium at the mills, "home" was no longer fresh air and open land but crowded, dingy tenement houses.

1920 TO 1960: EDUCATION KEEPS THINGS ALIVE

According to *The Canadian Born in the United States,* a book published in 1943 using American census data, 47 percent of those reporting themselves as "French Canadian born" immigrated to the United States earlier than 1900. Almost 16 percent of those in the United States through the year 1930 came from 1901 to 1910, while about ten percent came between 1920 and 1930.

The 1920s and 1930s were decades of strength for French-Canadian Americans—organizations had been established, French-language newspapers were thriving, and there were successful battles against attempts to abolish teaching in French. Mount Saint Charles Academy, a Franco-American diocesan high school in Woonsocket, Rhode Island, was established in 1924 and hailed as a strong academic school. Assumption College in Worcester, Massachusetts, continues to offer Franco-American studies as well as French-language instruction. Founded in 1904, it was built upon the model of the French Canadian *collège classique*, in which liberal arts were taught with traditional values and Catholic doctrine.

Elementary schools were set up in great numbers in the 1920s and 1930s. These were parochial schools, supported by the parishes, and they offered a half-day of exposure to the French language and culture. By the 1960s, however, these schools, faced with the increased cost of having to pay lay teachers, were forced to close.

Maintaining French identity became more of a challenge after World War II. The initial immigrants had established a vibrant community of

French-language parishes, schools, press, and fraternal organizations, but the group was slowly assimilating and there was no large wave of immigration to keep up the enthusiasm. Immigration to the United States dropped off after the Great Depression of the 1930s. At the same time, many French-Canadian Americans took advantage of the proximity of their home country and lived where the economic conditions or political situation was better for them.

The French were also regarded differently in Canada than in the United States—in Canada they represented one of the two founding nations, while in the United States they were just one of many ethnic groups to arrive in America after much of the country had been settled. After World War II, the original incentives to remain a tight community faded away. More French-Canadian Americans had the opportunity to get an education, for example, and their economic situations improved so that they no longer had to huddle in tenement houses while working long, hard hours in the textile and shoe mills. As a result, many began to drift outside of traditional Franco-American enclaves. For example, most of the once-numerous French-speaking parochial schools near Albany, New York, had ceased to exist by the 1960s, having been demolished for urban renewal or sold to other denominations.

This trend reversed in the 1970s and 1980s, however, with a move toward reviving French Canadian traditions and language. Many books have been written, in both English and French, on the Franco-American experience, and a number of historical centers, such as the French Institute at Assumption College in Worcester, Massachusetts, support Franco-American studies.

SETTLEMENT PATTERNS IN 1990

Historically, most of the French Canadian immigrants settled in the New England states, geographically closest to the province of Québec. Some, however, travelled further to settle in Illinois, Minnesota, New York, Wisconsin, Michigan, and even California. By 1990, the state with the highest number of French-Canadian Americans was Massachusetts, with 310,636, followed by Michigan with 174,138, California with 156,625, New York with 155,531, New Hampshire with 118,857, Connecticut with 110,426, Florida with 110,221, and Maine with 110,209. All other states have less than 100,000.

Although California ranks third, the Northeast predominates as home to French-Canadian Americans—that region alone makes up 45 percent of the total of 2.16 million who cited French Canadian ancestry in the 1990 census. This total is a small percentage of the American population—just under one percent of the total 248.7 million—but it ranks French-Canadian Americans at sixteenth on a tally of the most frequently reported ancestry groups. Franco-American New England is often divided into three regions: central and southeastern New England, which includes southern Maine; western Vermont and upper New York State; and northern Maine, particularly the area known as the St. John Valley.

It is interesting to note that the number of individuals citing French Canadian as their ancestry for the 1990 census was substantially larger than for the census a decade earlier. One possible explanation cited by census takers was that French Canadian was listed among sample response categories—intended to help those who were uncertain of their ethnic origin—in 1990, but not in 1980.

ACCULTURATION AND ASSIMILATION

TRADITIONS, CUSTOMS, AND BELIEFS

French Canadian life, in Canada and in the United States, centered around the community—first that of the family (which tended to be large), and then that of the larger French-speaking community. One thing French-Canadian Americans had in common with their French Canadian ancestors was resistance to other ethnic influences. In Canada, French-speakers long opposed all things British, and in the United States, Irish or English Americans often viewed the newest immigrants as interlopers. This lack of acceptance helped to draw Franco-Americans closer together and resulted in maintaining traditions, customs, and language through the generations. Many of the traditions and beliefs are also tied to a strong sense of religion. To be a Franco-American immigrant was to be a strict Catholic, especially for the early settlers.

PROVERBS

Many French Canadian proverbs can be interpreted as similar to those found today in English, although several are French Canadians in origin. Some well-known examples include: Each to their own taste; God dictates and women decide; Better to prevent than to heal; If the young knew and if the old could...; To leave is to die a little; Speech is silver, but silence is golden; Better late than never; Slow but sure; After the storm comes good weather; Tell me with whom you associate, and I will tell you who you are; and, One you have is worth more than two you think you may get.

CUISINE

French Canadian farmers ate hearty, simple meals. Breads and other carbohydrates were popular and readily available. Breakfast items included pancakes, fried eggs, salt pork spread on slices of bread, coffee, and tea. Soup, made from peas, cabbage, or barley, was a staple for lunch and dinner meals; also on the daily menu might be potatoes, bread and butter covered in maple syrup, pork, and seasonal vegetables. In the Roman Catholic tradition, no meat was served on Fridays.

More elaborate meals were prepared for special religious holidays and celebrations. *Tourtière* (pork and spice pie), *cretons* (pork terrine), *ragoût boulettes* (a stew of chicken, beef, or veal), *boudin* (blood sausage) and sugar pies are some of the dishes associated with French Canadians. In fact, one French Canadian dish, *poutine* (french fries covered with gravy and cheese curds) is now being served in North American fast-food restaurants.

TRADITIONAL COSTUMES

Traditional French Canadian costumes harken back to the days when the *coureurs de bois* hunted for beaver pelts and the *voyageurs* explored Canada. Most recognizable were the brightly colored, woven sashes, or *ceintures fléchées*.

As Brault explains, more common were the clothes worn by the farmers. They wore flannel shirts over loose-fitting pants fashioned of *droguet*, or drugget, a durable and coarse woolen fabric. The pants would be held up by suspenders or a broad leather belt. On his feet, a man would wear stockings and moccasin-style boots. To combat the cold, the French Canadian farmer would add a vest or sweater, a *tuque* (woollen cap), and an overcoat made of wool or animal skins fastened about his waist with a *ceinture flechee*.

Women made many of their materials, such as the drugget. They, too, would wear woolen stock-

ings and moccasins in addition to a flannel skirt over a heavy slip or *jupon*, as well as a long-sleeved bodice and sturdy apron. In the winter, women would wear heavier blouses and skirts, shawls, and a cotton or woollen *capuche* on their heads to keep warm. Since most French-Canadian Americans today live in towns or cities rather than on farms, these clothes are worn only on festive cultural occasions. Part of the assimilation process was to adopt clothing that was "American."

FRANCO-AMERICAN SONGS AND DANCES

Rounds were a popular form of song for French Canadians. Round dances, in which the participants, often children, danced in a circle making certain actions as they sang, were also popular.

Among the most popular traditional folk songs were those that told stories of settlers, voyageurs, or kings, and courtships between maidens and young men. For example, "À Saint Malo" told the tale of ladies and sailors who argued over the price of grain until the women eventually won and got the grain for nothing. Perhaps the best-known song is "Alouette," which came from France but is identified with Québec. It can be sung as a round and tells the tale of a lark.

Traditional French Canadian dances include the *quadrille* and the *gigue* (or jig). Square dances, with many of the calls in French, also became popular in the twentieth century. All of these involved musical accompaniment, with fiddles, harmonicas, and later accordions. As part of the tight family and community structures in French Canadian life, music and dancing was featured at any celebration.

HOLIDAYS CELEBRATED BY FRENCH-CANADIAN AMERICANS

Some of the major holidays are part of the Christmas season, from Advent (a time of fasting and prayer) to Christmas and its midnight mass followed by a *réveillm* (a repast designed to "wake you up"). There is also the feast on New Year's Day (a holy day of Obligation for Catholics that includes family visits and the *bénédiction paternelle* in which the father blesses all of his children and grandchildren) and finally Epiphany (called *la Fête des Rois*) on January 6. For the evening meal on January 6 it was a French Canadian tradition to serve the Twelfth Night Cake (*le gâteau des Rois*—"the cake of kings"). Inside the cake were a pea and a bean; whoever got the slice with the bean was deemed king and whoever found the pea was named queen. *La Chandeleur* or Candlemas, another winter holiday held on February 2, included a candlelit mass and pancake parties in the evening.

In addition to the religious liturgies and worship of Holy Week and Easter, there is Saint-Jean-Baptiste day on June 24. John the Baptist was declared the patron saint of French Canadians by the Pope in 1908. A society was established in the saint's name in 1834 to promote patriotic celebrations. November featured both All Saints' Day and Saint Catherine's Day, during which it was a French Canadian custom to pull taffy.

HEALTH AND MENTAL HEALTH ISSUES

There are no ailments specific to French Canadians in the United States, with the exception of occupational maladies related to the fact that many of the newly arrived immigrants worked in dusty, grimy mills or quarries. Dr. Paul Dufault (1894-1969) and Dr. Gabriel Nadeau (b. 1900), both French Canadian immigrants, were leaders in the treatment of tuberculosis, spending the better part of their careers at the Rutland, Massachusetts State Hospital, the first State Hospital for tuberculosis patients in the United States.

LANGUAGE

French belongs to the Latin and Romance group of Indo-European languages. In *The French Canadian Heritage in New England*, Brault notes that "correct" speech was a sign of status, but that did not stop the evolution of syntactical and phonological differences. One French Canadian "dialect," called *joual*, is synonymous with the lower classes, or at least with loose pronunciation. Brault goes on to summarize some of the most obvious phonetic differences in the French spoken by French Canadians in Canada and the United States compared to France. A computerized dictionary called *Trésor de la langue française au Québec* (*The Treasures of the French Language in Québec*) documents Canadian French.

GREETINGS AND OTHER POPULAR EXPRESSIONS

Some of the most common French Canadian sayings are similar to those of France. Greetings and popular expressions include: *Bonjour*, or *Salut*— each of which can be translated as "hello" depending on what degree of formality is intended; *Au revoir*— Good bye; *Bonne chance*—Good luck; *Merci*—Thank you; *De rien* or *Il n'ya pas de quoi*—You're welcome, or (literally in the first case), It was nothing; *Félicitations*—Congratulations; *Bonne Fête* or *Joyeux Anniversaire*—Happy Birthday; *Bonne Année*—Happy New Year; *Joyeux Noël*—Merry Christmas; and À *votre šanté*—To your health.

FAMILY AND COMMUNITY DYNAMICS

The family is at the center of the French-Canadian American's world. In previous decades this meant not only the nuclear family but the extended clan who would come together to eat, play card games, sing, drink, and dance.

INTERACTIONS WITH OTHER ETHNIC MINORITIES

Some tension has existed historically between French immigrants and French Canadians because, while French immigrants tended to be well-educated, most of the first French Canadian immigrants were farmers and received little if any formal education.

Although the French-Canadian Americans worked with Irish Americans in the mills and had a common religion in Catholicism, the language barrier and the sense that the Irish were established immigrants, having come a generation earlier, led to tension. In his 1943 account of New England immigrants, *The Shadows of the Trees*, Jacques Ducharme writes that "many were to feel the *caillou celtique*, or 'Kelly Biscuit,' for in the early days the Irish were not averse to violence by way of showing their distaste for the newcomers." There was opposition to French teaching in schools, and it spilled over into the workplace, where there was favoritism based upon background, and the church, where it took years before American bishops brought French-speaking priests to Franco-American parishes.

There was also rampant prejudice against Catholics and Jews in New England in the 1920s. By 1925 the Ku Klux Klan numbered more than half a million. It supported the Protestants in the area and their efforts to "take back what was their own." This resulted in cross burnings and hooded Klansmen fighting with French-Canadian Americans throughout New England. Many French Canadian immigrants hid in their houses while the Klan stormed through the streets.

WEDDINGS

The tradition for immigrants at the turn of the century was a conservative courtship where a potential suitor might visit a young girl's home on Sunday evenings to spend time with the entire family. After a series of visits that became more private—although always in public pursuits, such as buggy rides or swinging on the porch—the young man, or *cavalier*, would ask the father for the hand of his *blonde* in marriage. Often the young man was at least 21, although his fiancée could be as young as 16.

The wedding itself was a festive affair marked by feasting and dancing. In parishes, the bans would be read for three consecutive Sundays, naming the intention of that particular couple to marry. With all parishioners being so informed, if any impediments to the upcoming marriage existed, they could be announced then. Brault notes that in rural Québec, the bans might only be read once, because this procedure was viewed as embarrassing to the couple.

Much like today, the groom was given a stag party in his honor. In this case it was called the *enterrement de la vie de garçon*, or "burial of the bachelor life," and was symbolized by a mock funeral in which the groom lay on planks while a eulogy, sincere or in fun, was read over him. The bride, in turn, might be honored with a shower.

Wedding attire was influenced by the fashion of the time. The elaborateness of the ceremony was dictated by the wealth of the participants. The church bells pealed for the morning nuptial mass and a reception followed. Honeymoons often meant a few days' stay at a relative's home. Brault says that after marriage, French Canadian women were often expected to dress more conservatively and in darker colors, while men displayed their marital status by growing a mustache or wearing a gold watch and chain. Today, many of the marriage practices reflect a greater assimilation into American culture as well as a move away from a predominantly rural way of life.

BAPTISMS

Until recently, French-Canadian Americans tended to have large families, often with ten or more children. Baptisms, as a religious rite, were an integral part of life. As Brault describes, if there was any risk that the newborn might not survive, the priest was called immediately to baptize the baby. Otherwise the ceremony was performed within the first week. Traditionally, boys were given, as part of their name, Joseph, and girls given the name Marie, in addition to being named by the parents. Often one of the other given names was that of a godparent.

The role of godparent, as in other cultures, is filled by close relatives or friends. They are responsible for bringing up the child if the parents die, part of which includes ensuring that the child is brought up in the Catholic faith. After the baptismal ceremony, the parents, godparents, child, and guests returned to a family home for a celebratory meal. Godparents would bring gifts for the child, and, in the past, for the mother and the church sexton, who would ring the church bells to mark the occasion.

FUNERALS

Brault states that French Canadians feared sudden death or *la mort subité* most because it meant there would be no time to prepare for death, particularly for the administering of the last rites by a priest. When a person died, the church sexton signalled the death by ringing the church bells. This, Brault says, not only told all those in the town that there had been a death, but also revealed who had died: one stroke signalled a child, two a woman, and three a man.

The wake took three days, during which visitors greeted the family in their home. Until it became the practice to carry out wakes in "funeral parlours," the dead were laid out in the family home. Flowers were not part of the setting, although it was customary to shroud the room in white sheets so it resembled a chapel and to hang a cross between a pair of candles at the person's head. The visitors came to pray with the family and gathered once an hour to recite the rosary.

After the wake, a morning funeral was held, complete with a mass in church, and then the body was taken to the cemetery for burial. The priest accompanied the family and other mourners and said a prayer as the casket was lowered into the burial plot. Everyone then returned to the family's home for a meal in honor of the dead person.

RELIGION

Religion is at the heart of French Canadian life. While in Canada, French Canadians were staunch Roman Catholics; this did not change when they immigrated to the United States. In fact, as was true in Canada, the church was an integral part of the early settlements—often the priest acted as counselor in secular matters, in addition to spiritual leader. Some of the earliest parishes were established in the 1830s and 1840s in rural northern Maine. By the turn of the century, there were 89 Franco-American parishes.

In his book *Ethnic Diversity in Catholic America*, Harold J. Abramson states that the completeness with which French-Canadian Americans transplanted their religion, especially to the New England area, was partly due to being close to Canada. Basically, the immigrants set up the same sort of parish-centered social organization that had existed in the home country. In his book about Franco-American life in New England, *The Shadows in the Trees*, Jacques Ducharme wrote: "The Franco-Americans are profoundly attached to their parish church, and there one may see them every Sunday.... From Maine to Connecticut these churches stand, forming a forest of steeples where men, women and children come to pray in French and listen to sermons in French. When the tabernacle bell rings, know that it proclaims the presence of *le bon dieu*."

Despite their proximity to Canada, French Canadians in New England experienced many of the trials typical to new immigrants, including discrimination by religion and language. The church offered them a place where their language could be freely spoken and celebrated. But in the early days, mass was often conducted by priests who spoke little or no French. Because of this, many attendees could not understand sermons, risked getting their meatless days wrong, and gave little for special collections because they did not understand what they were for.

The fight for French masses began in earnest in the late nineteenth century. For example, in October of 1884 parishioners at the Notre-Dame-de-Lourdes Church in Fall River, Massachusetts, began a two-year struggle against the Irish American Bishop of Providence, Rhode Island, to gain a French-speaking priest after the death of their French Canadian pastor. Their battle successfully ended what became known as "the Flint Affair."

Often it was the Irish Americans who opposed French-language services. In May 1897, for example, French-Canadian Americans in North Brookfield, Massachusetts, wrote to the Papal Delegate to tell him that their Irish American priest would not allow religious services or teaching in French. It was not until 1903 that a French priest and French services were permitted. Such fights also went on in Rhode Island, Connecticut, and Maine communities. It was also a matter of some time before French Canadians assumed positions of power within the Catholic church. The first Franco-American bishop was Georges-Albert Guertin (1869-1931), named Bishop of Manchester in 1906. He was followed by, among others, Ernest J. Primeau (1960-1974) and Odore J. Gendreau (1975-).

These battles with the Irish Americans over religious issues continued into the 1920s. One of the most notable was the "Sentinelle Affair" of 1924-1929. A group of French-Canadian Americans, most from Woonsocket, Rhode Island, had been concerned about their religion, language, and culture surviving in the United States. They resented the hierarchy of the Catholic church in the United States, which was mostly Irish, and militantly defended the Franco-American parochial schools and the fragile autonomy of the French-language parishes.

Religion played another role in Franco-American communities through religiously affiliated fraternal organizations. Like other ethnic groups, the French-Canadian Americans set these up to offer insurance as well as language and cultural activities to new and recent immigrants. The oldest of the two most prominent mutual benefit and advocacy organizations is the Association Canado-Américaine, founded in 1896, followed by the Union St. Jean Baptiste in 1900. Both still exist today, although the Union has since become affiliated with Catholic Family Life Insurance.

EMPLOYMENT AND ECONOMIC TRADITIONS

Immigration to the United States in the late nineteenth and early twentieth centuries effectively drained Québec of a large number of its young adults. Economic times were tough in Canada, and the newly opened mills in New England offered employment for both women and men—although this was hard, back-breaking, and often unhealthy work. Many children joined the labor force in the mills as well. Women also earned money by taking in boarders. Another group of French Canadians settled near the forest of northern Maine to work in the logging industry.

Although the first major wave of immigrants was made up predominantly of farmers, mill workers, and lumbermen with little education, there was also a select group of educated individuals, such as priests, doctors, and lawyers who came to serve the needs of their people. Of course, as Franco-Americans became more established, the numbers of professionals grew. There is a rich history of French-language journalism, particularly in the nineteenth and early twentieth centuries. For example, in the early 1870s, Hugo Dubuque (1854-1928) of Fall River, Massachusetts, led the way in refuting Labor Commissioner Carroll D. Wright's description of French-Canadian Americans as "the Chinese of the Eastern States;" Dubuque became a Massachusetts Superior Court Justice after serving for ten years (1888-1898) in the Massachusetts House of Representatives. Another judge, Alfred J. Chretien, (b. 1900), who was born in Fall River, Massachusetts, attended Harvard University after spending his adolescence in Québec. After graduating, he established a law practice in Manchester, New Hampshire, and went on to be named Chief Justice of the Manchester Municipal Court in 1940. He played an active role in the formation of the Legal Aid Society of New Hampshire and was a member of the National Council of Juvenile Court Judges.

A number of French-Canadian Americans have distinguished themselves in labor unions and syndicates. J. William Belanger (1902-c.1992), born in Newmarket, New Hampshire, began his working career at the age of 14 in the Hamlet Mills. As an employee of the Hope Knitting Company in Central Falls, Rhode Island, he founded a union affiliated with the American Federation of Labour (AFL) during the Great Depression, and later became director of the Textile Union of Massachusetts, affiliated with the Congress of Industrial Organizations (CIO). In 1948 he was elected president of the Massachusetts CIO.

The first financial institution controlled by French Canadians in New England, the Banque Coopérative Lafayette, was set up in 1894 in Fall River, Massachusetts. Not long afterwards, the first Franco-American Credit Union in the United States, La Caisse Populaire Sainte-Marie, opened in Manchester, New Hampshire on November 24, 1908. Credit Unions were founded in most of the important Franco-American centers of New England. Initially parish-based, they later became independent entities that did much to support small businesses and to encourage home ownership.

POLITICS AND GOVERNMENT

In his study of Franco-American life in New England, Gerard J. Brault states Franco-Americans have supported the Democratic presidential candidate since the election of 1928 when the Catholic Al Smith was defeated by Herbert Hoover. Franco-Americans also voted for Franklin Delano Roosevelt, but by 1952 and 1956 most voted for the Republican Dwight D. Eisenhower. There are also regional trends: most today are Democrats, with the exception French-Canadian Americans in New Hampshire and Vermont, where many are "dyed-in-the-wool Republicans." The Franco-American elite has also supported Republican candidates in the past. Even the working class has voted the Republican ticket, as in Rhode Island, to elect one of their own, Aram Pothien, as governor or to distinguish themselves from the Irish who usually voted the Democratic ticket, as in Worcester, Massachusetts. Brault adds, however, that no recent comprehensive study has addressed the issue of historical voting patterns for the group at large. Patterns usually take into account religious and economic considerations, with French-Canadian Americans choosing the candidate who, on these two counts, is most supportive of their views.

In addition to being involved in local politics—Maine alone boasts of more than 500 Franco-American mayors and state legislators in a single century. According to Brault, there have been a number of Franco-Americans in state and federal politics as well. Aram J. Pothier (1854-1928), a Republican, was chosen governor of Rhode Island in 1908 and served two terms, from 1909 to 1915 and from 1925 to 1928. Subsequent Franco-American governors also served in Rhode Island, including Democrats Emery J. Sansoucy (1857-1936) from 1921 to 1923 and Philip W. Noël (1931-) from 1973 to 1977.

On a federal level, Franco-American senator Félix Hébert (1874-1969), a Republican, was elected in 1928 and served until 1934. Jean-Claude Boucher (1894-1960) was also a senator. Born in Rivière-Ouelle, Québec, his family moved to Lewiston, Maine, around the turn of the century, and he was elected a senator from Maine in 1935. Journalist Antonio Prince (1894-1973) made a run for the senate in 1935 as a Democratic candidate, but was not successful. Georgette Berube of Lewiston, Maine, a member of the state legislature, also made a run in the Democratic primary of June 1982, but was defeated.

Among those who have been elected U.S. representatives, there have been three French-Canadian Americans from Rhode Island (Louis Monast from 1927-1929; Aime J. Forand with two terms, 1937-1939 and 1941-1961; and Fernand J. St. Germain from 1961-82) and two from New Hampshire (Alphonse Roy from 1938-1939 and Norman E. D'Amours from 1975-1984). Internationally, editor Elie Vézina (1869-1942) was named a special ambassador to Haiti by President Herbet Hoover as a member of a Commission of Inquiry in 1930. Vézina, born in Québec, founded the newspaper *Le Devoir* in Michigan. Franco-Americans were also named to consular posts in France; Alphonse Gaulin, Jr., (b. 1874) of Woonsocket, Rhode Island, was Consul to LeHavre in 1905 and to Marseilles in 1909, and Eugene-L.Belisle was named Consul to Limoges in 1906.

MILITARY SERVICE

Franco-Americans have served in all of the major wars, including the American Revolution; some 800 French-Canadian Americans are believed to have fought for American independence. Rémi Tremblay (1847-1926) fought in the Civil War and wrote about his experiences in a novel entitled *Un Revenant* (1884). There are also many tales of French Canadians being tricked into enlisting in the Union Army. After being offered jobs in the United States and given gifts of money, many signed a document they could not read and travelled south only to find themselves put in uniform and bullied into taking part in the Civil War. For many who survived, it was a natural decision to stay in the United States, and if they were married, they sent for their families as soon as they were able.

One of the most famous images of World War II features a Franco-American, Private René A.

Gagnon (1924-1979) of Manchester, New Hampshire, one of three raising the American flag on Mount Suribachi during the battle for Iwo Jima on February 19, 1945. It was captured on film by Associated Press photographer Joe Rosenthal. Gagnon survived the battle and returned from the war to settle in Hooksett, New Hampshire.

RELATIONS WITH FRENCH CANADA

Because of the proximity of Canada—at least to the large pockets of French-Canadian Americans in New England—many French Canadians in the United States still have strong ties to their home country. However, family ties seem to diminish with each passing generation: many third- and fourth-generation French-Canadian Americans have lost touch with relatives who stayed in Canada. French-language newspapers and Franco-American studies programs help French-Canadian Americans keep abreast of what is going on in Québec.

INDIVIDUAL AND GROUP CONTRIBUTIONS

ACADEMIA

Will Durant (1885-1981), raised in Massachusetts and New Jersey, received his Ph.D. from Columbia University at the age of 32. He published the first installment of *Story of Civilization* in 1935, and the tenth volume, entitled *Rousseau and Revolution* (co-written with his wife Ariel), won the 1968 Pulitzer Prize for general nonfiction.

Maximilienne Tétrault (1884-1959) of Southbridge, Massachusetts, studied at the University of Boston and at the Sorbonne in Paris, after which she taught French at the University of Baltimore, at Notre-Dame in Indiana, and from 1936 to 1944 in Detroit. Her doctoral thesis dealt with the role of the press in the evolution of the Franco-Americans of New England.

Professor Joseph Medard Carrière (1902-1970), whose specific interest was in folklore, published, in 1937, *Tales from the Folklore of Missouri*. He was awarded the Chevalier de la Legion d'honneur by the French government in 1950.

Professor Gérard J. Brault (1929-) was born in Chicopee Falls, Massachusetts. A specialist in the Middle Ages, he is also interested in the language and culture of Franco-Americans. In 1986 he published *The French-Canadian Heritage in New England,* an important English-language work on Franco-American life in the United States.

Armand Chartier (1938-), born in New Bedford, Massachusetts, is a professor of French at the University of Rhode Island. He published *Historie des Franco-Américains de la Nouvelle-Augleteure* in 1991, a thorough compendium of facts and figures on Franco-Americans from 1775 to 1990.

Claire Quintal (1930-) is a professor of French at Assumption College in Worcester, Massachusetts, as well as the founding director of its French Institute. A native of Central Falls, Rhode Island, she is a scholar of Franco-American, French, and French-Canadian culture. Under her direction, the Institute has organized 11 colloquia, publishing the proceedings of these between 1980 and 1995.

Eloise Brière, born in Northhampton, Massachusetts, in 1946, has taught at Rutgers University and the State University of New York in Albany. Among her published work is *The North American French Language in New York State* (1982) and *Franco-American Profiles* (1984).

FILM, TELEVISION, AND THEATER

Hubert Prior "Rudy" Vallée (1901-1988) earned a doctorate from Yale but is best known for his film and stage career as a bandleader. In 1927 he created the Connecticut Yankees orchestra and later opened the New York cabaret club Villa Vallee. He starred in *The Vagabond Lover* (1939) and later on television. Born in Island Pond, Vermont, he was brought up in Westbrook, Maine, where he is buried in St. Hyacinthe cemetery.

Eva Tanguay (1878-1947), born in Marbletin, Québec, was brought up in Holyoke, Massachusetts. She starred for many years in the *Ziegfeld Follies.* Paul Bunyan (who had a blue bull named "Babe") was a French Canadian made famous by the loggers of Michigan. The "strong man" tradition was once very current throughout French North America. The best known of these were Joe Montferrand and Louis Cyr, who both performed in New England. The name Montferrand became synonymous with strength among Franco-Americans.

JOURNALISM

Many Franco-Americans have had distinguished careers in journalism, particularly in the early years of immigration to the New England states, when many started up French-language publications. One such individual was Ferdinand Gagnon (1849-1886), often referred to as "the father of Franco-American journalism." Gagnon was born in Saint-Hyacinthe, Québec, and after studying at the seminary there, moved to Manchester, New Hampshire before settling in Worcester, Massachusetts. There he published *Le Travailleur,* the foremost newspaper of its day.

Born in Wottonville, Québec, Philippe-Armand Lajoie (1887-1964) moved to New England with his family in 1889. Lajoie became editor of Fall River's *L'Indépendant* in 1926, which later became one of the four best French-language dailies in New England. In addition to his writings, he was a noted composer of religious music.

Marthe Biron-Péloquin (1919-) came from a family of journalists. Her father, Louis-Alphonse Biron (1861-1947), was born in Saint-Louis-de-Lotbiniere, Québec, but after moving to Lowell, Massachusetts, he founded *L'Impartial* in 1898 and later acquired *L'Étoile* (1939-1957), a local daily. Marthe wrote for *L'Étoile,* and served as an editor for *Bulletin de la Fédération féminine franco-américaine* (*Bulletin of the Federation of Franco-American Women*) from 1973 to 1986.

Alexandre Bélisle (1856-1923) founded *L'Opinion publique* (*Public Opinion*), in Worcester, Massachusetts, in 1893. Bélisle also published a history of the French-language press in 1911, called *Histoire de la presse franco-américaine.*

Born in L'Epiphanie, Québec, Élie Vézina (1869-1942) immigrated to Michigan in 1890 where he founded the weekly *Le Devoir* in Muskegon. Vézina then worked in Chicago for the *Courrier de l'Illinois.* In 1930 President Herbert Hoover named him to a special commission in Haiti.

Wilford Beaulieu (1900-1978) founded of *Le Travailleur* in Worchester, Massachusetts in 1931. The second newspaper in New England by that name, it honored the memory of Ferdinand Gagnon. A literary and cultural affairs weekly, the paper was an ardent voice in the cause of French *survivance* in New England. It ceased to be published after the death of its owner/publisher.

LITERATURE

Among the best-known Franco-American authors is "Beat Generation" novelist Jean-Louis "Jack" Kerouac (1922-1969). In addition to *On the Road*, he profiles his youth spent in the French-speaking community of Lowell, Massachusetts, in books such as *Doctor Sax* (1959), *Visions of Gerard* (1963), and *Vanity of Duluoz* (1968). Another famous author is Grace (DeRepentigny) Metalious (1924-1964) of Manchester, New Hampshire, who wrote *Peyton Place* in 1956. The fiction best-seller was made into a film in 1957 and a long-running television series in the 1960s. Two of Metalious' other novels, *The Tight White Collar* (1960) and *No Adam in Eden* (1963), deal with working-class French Canadians in New England.

Josaphat Benôit (1900-1976), in addition to being editor of *L'Avenir national*, a paper in Manchester, New Hampshire, and co-founder of the paper *L'Action* in 1949, wrote a number of books dealing with Franco-Americans, such as *L'Âme franco-américaine* (1935), *Rois ou esclaves de la machine?* (1935), and *Catéchisme d'historie franco-américaine* (1939).

Georges-Alphonse Boucher was born in 1865 at Rivière-Bois-Clair, Québec. Trained as a physician, he settled in Brockton, Massachusetts, in 1890. His first work of poetry was titled *Ode à Québec*, which was followed by three editions of *Je me souviens* and then *Sonnets de guerre* (1943), inspired by World War II. Other works include *Chants du nouveau monde* and his memoirs, *Vie abrégée*, published after his death in 1956.

Rémi Tremblay (1847-1926) was author of *Un Revenant*, one of the earliest novels published by a Franco-American, which dealt with the Civil War battle of Cold Harbor. Rosaire Dion-Lévesque (1900-1974), another Franco-American poet, translated Walt Whitman's *Leaves of Grass*. Novelist and journalist Camile Lessard-Bissonette (b. 1883) was the author of *Canuck* (1936). Poet, novelist, and critic Louis Dantin (1865-1945), who was born Eugene Seers in Québec but later lived in Boston, wrote *Les Enfances de Fanny*.

Novelist Gérard Robichault, who spent his childhood and youth in Maine, writes such autobiographical novels as *Papa Martel* and *The Apple of His Eye*. Annie Prouex won the National Book Award (1993) and the Pulitzer (1994) for *The Shipping News*. The novel also received the Heartland Prize from the *Chicago Tribune* and the *Irish Times International* Fiction Prize. Prouex was awarded a Pen/Faulkner Award in 1993 for her first novel *Postcards*. Annie David Plante (1940-), who was born in Providence, Rhode Island, is a prolific writer with nine novels to his credit. Robert B. Perreault, the only Franco-American to publish a French-language novel since 1938, wrote *L'Heritage* (1983). Playwright Grégoire Chabot and poets Paul P. Chassé and Normand C. Dubé are also worthy of mention.

MUSIC

Composer Calixa Lavallée (1842-1891), born in Verchères, Québec, left for the United States at age 15, in 1857, to participate in the Civil War as part of the Fourth Rhode Island Regiment. After that he studied in Paris and, in 1879, became organist of the cathedral in Boston. Among his compositions are operas, marches, waltzes, and the music for the Canadian national anthem, "O Canada."

Opera singer Albaninée Emma Lajeunesse (1847-1930) moved to Plattsburgh, New York, from Chambly, Québec, in 1852, then back to Montréal before settling in Albany, New York, in 1864. She was a soloist, at age 18, at the cathedral in Albany and went on to sing at Covent Garden in London as well as touring Europe, Russia, Ireland, and the United States in various operatic roles. At the request of Edward VII, she sang at the funeral of Queen Victoria.

The Champagne brothers—Octave (1859-1941), Eusebe (1865-1929), and Philias (1871-1957)—played various instruments in local bands and orchestras in Lowell, Massachusetts where the family had settled. Masterful performers of French Canadian folk music, they also played their own compositions. Octave published and distributed the songs written by the other two.

Violinist Joseph-Émile Chambord Giguère (1877-c. 1957) was the son of French-Canadian musicians who moved to the United States around 1874. Giguère, who was born in Woonsocket, Rhode Island, studied in both Canada and the United States as well as at the Royal Conservatory in Brussels, Belgium. After returning from Europe, he toured North America extensively.

Montréal-born composer and musician Pierre-Amedee Tremblay (1876-c.1949) served as organist at cathedrals in Salt Lake City and Los Angeles. He composed the operetta *L'Intransigeant* and also published, in 1902, a collection of French Canadian folksongs, *Dix-huit chansons populaires du Canada*.

C. Alexander Peloquin (1918-), born in Northbridge, Massachusetts, is a noted organist and composer of sacred music. He began his career in Woonsocket, Rhode Island, and has for more than 40 years been organist at the Catholic Cathedral in Providence, Rhode Island. Named Director of Choral Activities at Boston College in 1955, he also founded the Peloquin Chorale in Rhode Island after World War II.

SCIENCE AND TECHNOLOGY

Inventor Victor Bélanger (1856-1918), the founder of the Worcester, Massachusetts, newspaper *Le Courrier de Worcester* is credited for developing a rotating coil for spinning cotton. Another inventor was John C. Garand (1888-1974). Born in St. Remi, Québec, Garand moved to Jewett City, Connecticut. He is credited with the design of the .30 caliber Springfield rifle, which was used by American troops during World War I. His M1 rifle, which eliminated manual operation of the bolt mechanism, was adopted as standard equipment by the Army, Navy, and Marines in 1936 and was a staple weapon during World War II and the Korean War.

SPORTS

Napoléan ("Larry" or "The Big Frenchman") Lajoie (1875-1959), a member of the Cleveland Indians baseball team, was a contemporary of Ty Cobb. Lajoie still ranks as the player with the seventh-highest batting average in major league history, averaging .339 in his 21 years in the major leagues, which ended in 1919. He was elected to the Baseball Hall of Fame in 1937. Another Cleveland Indian was Louis Boudreau, born in Harvey, Illinois, in 1917. He was with the Cleveland team from 1938 to 1950, as both player and manager, during which time he was the youngest manager in the major leagues. Boudreau went on to play for and manage the Boston Red Sox (1950-1955) and then moved on to the Kansas City Athletics (1955-1957). He was nominated to the Hall of Fame in 1970. A third famous Franco-American in baseball is Leo Durocher (1905-1982), born in Springfield, Massachusetts. Durocher spent 41 years in the major leagues, first as a player and later as a manager. He led the Brooklyn Dodgers and then the New York Giants to three National League pennants in the years 1941, 1951, and 1954, and the Giants to a World Series victory in 1954.

Other Franco-American athletes include marathon runner and Olympic gold medalist Joan Benoit (1957-); boxer George "Kid" Lavigne (1869-1936); and Henri Renaud, the first Franco-American to win the Boston Marathon on April 19, 1909.

VISUAL ARTS

Sculptor Lucien Gosselin (1883-1940) was born in Whitefield, New Hampshire. The nephew of French-Canadian sculptor Louis-Philippe Hébert, he studied in Paris from 1911 to 1916 and is known for his statues, monuments, and designs for commemorative medals. Another artist of the period was Lorenzo de Nevers (1877-1967), born in Bai-du-Febure, Québec. He spent ten years in Paris (1902-1912) at the Ecole des Beaux-Arts and upon his return, he established his studio in Central Falls, Rhode Island, where his family had prospered in the furniture business. He is known for his religious paintings, portraits, and landscapes.

Born in Old Town, Maine, Bernard Langlais (1921-1977) is known for his large and somewhat whimsical carvings of animals. The Ogunquit Museum of American Art has three of his sculptures—"Seated Bear," "Horse in Field," and "Lion"—in its permanent collection. Another Franco-American sculptor, Armand Lammtague (c. 1940-), who was born in Central Falls, Rhode Island, is known for his life-size statues of sports figures, especially Larry Bird, the basketball star, and Bobbie Orr of hockey fame.

Woodcarving is a celebrated art in Franco-American culture. One of the most famous wood-carvers was Adelard Côté (1889-1974), originally from St. Sophie, Québec. Côte moved to Biddeford, Maine, in his early twenties. Although a blacksmith by trade, he began whittling in his fifties and was a prolific artist, creating elaborate primitive carvings, many with moving parts.

Photographer Ulric Bourgeois (1874-1963) received his first camera at age 11. This artist, born in Fulford, Québec, moved to Manchester, New Hampshire, soon after he married in 1899, and opened up a studio. His work documents Franco-American life in New England and Québec, which he visited often. His life provided inspiration for the Québec film *J.A. Martin, photographe.*

Media

PRINT

The first French Canadian newspaper published in the United States was *Le Patriote Canadien*, the first issue of which was printed in Burlington, Vermont, on August 7, 1839. The Franco-American press served not only to disseminate news, but also as a forum for ideas. French-language and bilingual papers flourished in the United States until the 1930s, when many were abandoned by readers in favor of English-language dailies. Some of those available today follow.

Le F.A.R.O.G. Forum.

A bilingual quarterly, first printed in 1972, it comes out of the University of Maine's Center for Franco-American Studies with a circulation of more than 4,500. The Center also publishes the bilingual quarterly newspaper *Le Forum*, which offers articles on the activities of prominent Franco-Americans, book reviews, genealogy information, and scholarly pieces on Franco-American studies.

Contact: Rhea Côté-Robbins.

Address: Center Franco-Américain, University of Maine, 126 College Avenue, Orono, Maine 04469.

Telephone: (207) 581-3775.

Femmes D'Action.

Magazine addressing the social, educational, and health issues of French-Canadian women.

Contact: Marie-Lyne Renaud, Marketing Director.

Address: Federation Nationale des Femmes Canadiennes-Françaises, 325, rue Dalhouse, piece 525, Ottawa, Ontario, Canada K1N 7G2.

Telephone: (613) 232-5791.

Fax: (613) 232-6679.

Le Journal de Lowell.

Founded in 1975, the journal has a circulation of about 4,200, mostly in Massachusetts. This French-language monthly features news on the New England region as well as news from Québec and France.

Contact: Albert V. Côté.

Address: P.O. Box 1241, Lowell, Maine 01853.

Telephone: (508) 453-1780.

La Revue Canado-Américaine.

Published by the Association Canado-Américaine.

Contact: Paul Paré.

Telephone: (603) 622-2883.

Le Soleil de la Floride.

This monthly, founded in 1983 with a circulation of 65,000, reaches French-speaking readers throughout Florida, Québec, and parts of the Caribbean, especially French-Canadian "snowbirds" who spend winter in warmer climates.

Contact: Jean Leurac.

Address: 2020 Scott Street, Hollywood, Florida 33020.

Telephone: (305) 923-4510.

L'Union.

This bilingual quarterly newspaper, which is free to its members, is sent to some 16,000 households. It is published by the Union Saint-Jean-Baptiste (USJB), a fraternal life insurance organization for French-Canadian Americans with 44,000 members.

Contact: Joseph Gadbois (English); or, Bernard Theroux (French).

Address: 68 Cumberland Street, P.O. Box F, Woonsocket, Rhode Island 02895-9987.

Telephone: (401) 769-0520.

RADIO

WCUW-FM (91.3).

"L'Heure Française" Airs every Saturday from noon to 1:30 p.m.

Contact: Marcel Raymond.

Address: 297 Pleasant Street, Worcester, Massachusetts 01609.

Telephone: (508) 753-0711.

WFAU-AM (1340).

"La Boite à Chansons" airs every Sunday from 10:00 a.m. to noon.

Contact: Jean-Paul Poulain.

Address: 160 Bangor Street, Augusta, Maine 04330.

Telephone: (207) 623-5044.

WFEA-AM.

"Franco-American Hour" broadcasts music and information from 9:00 a.m. to 11:00 a.m. on Sundays.

Contact: Joe Maltais.

Address: 500 Commercial Street, Manchester, New Hampshire 03101.

Telephone: (603) 669-5777.

WHTB-AM (1400).
Broadcasts every Sunday from 5:00 to 6:00 p.m.

Contact: Bernard Theroux.

Address: Fall River, Massachusetts.

Telephone: (508) 678-9727.

WKRI-AM (1400).
"The French Program," airs on Sundays from noon to 1:00 p.m.

Contact: Roger Laliberte.

Address: 1585 Centerville Road, Warwick, Rhode Island 02893.

Telephone: (401) 821-6200.

WLAM-AM (1740).
"L'Heure Farnçaise," broadcast on Sundays from 8:00 to 10:00 a.m.

Contact: Constance Cote.

Address: P.O. Box 929, Lewiston, Maine 04240.

Telephone: (207) 784-5401.

WMHB-FM (90.5).
"Mondo Franco."

Contact: Paul Gregorie.

Address: Bates College, Lewiston, Maine 04240.

Telephone: (207) 784-5044.

WMOU-AM (1230).
"Le Programme Canadien-Français," broadcast every Sunday from 7:00 a.m. to noon.

Contact: Robert Barbin.

Address: 38 Glen Avenue, Berlin, New Hampshire 03570.

Telephone: (603) 752-1230.

WNRI-AM (1380).
Broadcast on Saturdays and Sundays from 10:00 a.m. to noon.

Contact: Roger Laliberte.

Address: 786 Diamond Hill Road, Woonsocket, Rhode Island 02895.

Telephone: (401) 769-0600.

WSMN-AM (1590).
"The French Program," broadcast every Sunday from 9:00 a.m. to noon.

Contact: Maurice Parent.

Address: 502 West Hollis Street, P.O. Box 548, Nashua, New Hampshire.

WWON-AM (1240).
Airs every Sunday from 9:00 a.m. to 10:00 a.m.

Contact: Normand Vaillancourt.

Address: 187 Madeline Avenue, Woonsocket, Rhode Island 02895.

Telephone: (401) 762-1240.

TELEVISION

"Bonjour."
This half-hour program is produced in Manchester, New Hampshire on the Cable Network and re-broadcast on the public broadcasting system in Maine, is repeated a number of times each week. It includes interviews of French-Canadian Americans on topics from music to cooking. Broadcast in French, it serves local audiences in New England and New York. It is also broadcast in the Canadian provinces of New Brunswick, Nova Scotia, Ontario, and Québec.

Contact: Paul Paré.

Address: Association Canado-Americaine, 52 Concord Street, P.O. Box 989, Manchester, New Hampshire 03105-0989.

Telephone: (603) 625-8577.

ORGANIZATIONS AND ASSOCIATIONS

In addition to the organizations listed below, there are many local historical societies and genealogical societies for Franco-Americans throughout the United States. See Le Répertoire de la vie française en Amérique, a sourcebook of French Canadian organizations in the United States and Canada, for more information.

Action for Franco-Americans in the Northeast.
Contact: Yvon A. Labbé.

Telephone: (207) 581-3775.

Association Canado-Américaine.
Supports 45,000 members and local branches in many states, including Connecticut, Maine, Massachusetts, New Hampshire, and Rhode Island, as well as in Canada. Its interests include life insurance, cultural excursions, a summer camp, and a French-language cable television program for the New England region.

Contact: Eugene Lemieux.
Address: 52 Concord Street, P.O. Box 989, Manchester, New Hampshire 03105-0989.
Telephone: (603) 625-8577.

Conseil de la Vie Francaise en Amerique/The Council for French Life in America (CVFA).
Founded in 1937 to promote the interests of French Canadians throughout North America. Among its membership is the Société Canadienne-Française du Minnesota and other such local groups for French-Canadian Americans, as well as groups that more generally promote French language and culture. They publish the annual reference guide to French-language organizations in North America and sponsor various awards, such as the Bourse Archibald Lemieux for Franco-Americans. The head office for this North American council is in Canada.

Contact: Paul Paré, President.
Address: 56 Saint-Pierre Street, 1st Floor, Québec City, Québec, Canada G1K 4A1.
Telephone: (418) 692-1150.

Fédération Féminine Franco-Américaine de la Nouvelle-Angleterre.
Consists of some 5,000 women in 49 local associations who organize conferences, projects for seniors, cultural exchanges, and aid for students in French programs in a bid to promote French cultural interests in the New England region. Among the local associations are branches in Bristol, Connecticut; Lowell, Massachusetts; Manchester, New Hampshire; Woonsocket, Rhode Island; and New Bedford, Massachusetts.

Contact: Claire Quintal, President.
Address: Assumption College, 500 Salisbury Street, Worcester, Maine 01615-0005.
Telephone: (508) 767-7415.

Société Historique Franco-Américaine (SHFA).
Founded in 1899. This institution holds regular lecture meetings and publishes a bulletin that contains the texts of the lectures and articles on its notable members.

Contact: Marthe B. Peloquin.
Telephone: (508) 692-6370.

Union St. Jean Baptiste.
This organization, which serves over 40,000 members, has local branches throughout New England.

Contact: Joe Gadbois.
Telephone: (401) 769-0520.

MUSEUMS AND RESEARCH CENTERS

Center Franco-Américain.
Established in 1991, the Center is loosely affiliated with the fraternal organization Association Canado-Américaine. This resource center has an art gallery with featured exhibitions, a library, and offers French-language classes. The Center is also affiliated with the Federation Americaine Franco-American des Aînés/Francophone American Federation of the Elderly (FAFA), founded in 1981 to promote the interests of Franco-American seniors in both local affairs, as well as on a state and national scale.

Contact: Adele Baker, Director.
Address: 52 Concord Street, P.O. Box 989, Manchester, New Hampshire 03105-0989.
Telephone: (603) 669-4045.

Center Franco-Américain de l'Université du Maine.
Part of the University of Maine since 1972. Resources here include library and video materials on Franco-Americans and their publications, *F.A.R.O.G. Forum* and *Maine Mosaic*.

Contact: Yvon A. Labbé, Director.
Address: 126 College Avenue, University of Maine, Orono, Maine 04469.
Telephone: (207) 581-3775.

Conseil International d'Etudes Francophones.
Founded in 1981, this research center conducts studies of Franco-American literature, history, culture and language. Although its headquarters are at Montclair State University in New Jersey, it

includes in its membership 300 individuals and 25 organizations.

Contact: Maurice Cagnon, President.

Address: French Department, Montclair State University, Upper Montclair, New Jersey 07043.

Telephone: (201) 655-4000.

Fédération Franco-Américaine du New York.

Sponsors lectures on the French in America, Québec films, language courses, the *Fête du Roi* (Twelfth Night) a winter cultural celebration, and exchanges with Québec. These activities, mostly in English, are for the public as well as members. Founded in Cohoes, New York in 1980, this organization, with about 140 members, also publishes a bulletin, *Franco-Nouvelles*, at least nine times a year.

Contact: Bernard Ouimet.

Address: Box 12-942, Albany, New York 12212.

Telephone: (518) 692-2690.

Institut Français.

Founded in 1979, the institute is associated with Assumption College. It has organized 11 colloquia and published 12 books dealing with the French experience in New England. These include *The Little Canadas of New England*, as well as books on schools, religion, literature, the press, women, and folklore. The center collects documents on Franco-Americans and its holdings contain such archival materials as manuscripts, newspapers, and books.

Contact: Claire Quintal, Director.

Address: Assumption College, 500 Salisbury Street, Worcester, Massachusetts 01615-0005.

Telephone: (508) 752-5615.

SOURCES FOR ADDITIONAL STUDY

Brault, Gerard J. *The French-Canadian Heritage in New England.* Hanover: University Press of New England, 1986.

Doty, C. Stewart. *The First Franco-Americans: New England Life Histories from the Federal Writers' Project, 1938-1939.* Orono: University of Maine at Orono Press, 1985.

Ducharme, Jacques. *The Shadows of the Trees: The Story of French-Canadians in New England.* New York: Harper & Brothers, 1943.

French America: Mobility, Identity, and Minority Experience across the Continent, edited by Dean R. Louder and Eric Waddell, translated by Franklin Philip. Baton Rouge: Louisiana State University Press, 1993.

Parker, James Hill. *Ethnic Identity: The Case of the French Americans.* Washington: University Press of America, Inc., 1983.

GERMAN AMERICANS

by
La Vern J. Rippley

German immigrants to the United States have distinguished themselves in virtually every field of endeavor.

OVERVIEW

Situated in the heart of Europe, Germany today adjoins nine neighbors: Denmark to the north; Poland and the Czech Republic to the east; Austria and Switzerland to the south; and the Netherlands, Belgium, Luxembourg, and France to the west. With a population of nearly 80 million, Germany follows Russia as the most populous nation in Europe. In size, however, Germany is smaller than either France or Spain and equates roughly with the combined area of Minnesota and Wisconsin. With an average of 222 people per square kilometer, Germany has one of the highest population densities in Europe.

HISTORY

Recorded German history begins with the battle between the Roman legions and Arminus, a prince of the Germanic Cherusci tribe, recounted in the chronicles of Tacitus. *Deutschland,* the Germans' name for their country, came into use in the eighth century when Charlemagne incorporated German and French speakers into a common nation. As cohesion among the population of the eastern realm increased, the term *Deutschland* applied to all German speakers. Once confined west of the Elbe River, Germans gradually penetrated father east into former Slavic territory, often peacefully, but sometimes by force.

Almost from the time of Charlemagne, Germany bore versions of the name Holy Roman Empire of the German Nation, beginning with the Salian dynasty and proceeding with the rule of the Hohenstaufens, the Habsburgs, and the Hohenzollerns. Germany suffered religious schism when Martin Luther proposed reforms in 1517, which led to the pillaging of the country by those who profited from the weakened central political, religious, and social ruling structures. The religiously motivated Thirty Years' War (1618-1648), which erupted a century after Luther's death, devastated Germany's territory and its moral fiber until the age of French absolutism. During this period, also known as the Enlightenment, Prussian king Frederick the Great (1740-1786) became a patron of the American Revolution. Frederick sent Baron von Steuben, Johannes DeKalb, and others to train American military novices at Valley Forge and elsewhere.

During the Napoleonic period, the Holy Roman Empire dissolved in favor of the *Deutscher Bund* (German Confederation), a loose confederation of individual sovereign states that functioned with a single participatory government unit, the *Bundestag*, a delegated parliament in Frankfurt. The *Bundestag* often behaved like a monarchical oligarchy, suppressing freedom, enforcing censorship, and controlling the universities and political activity.

Arguments arose among the liberals over whether to establish a "greater Germany," along the lines of Great Britain, or a "smaller Germany," which would include only the more traditionally German principalities without Austria. Because Austria wanted to bring into the union its more than a dozen ethnic groups, the National Assembly opted for a smaller Germany, for which they offered a constitution to King Friedrich Wilhelm IV of Prussia. The king's rejection of the constitution triggered popular uprisings in the German states, which were in turn met by military suppression. A large group of German intellectual liberals, known as the Forty-eighters, immigrated to the United States during this period to escape persecution. The contemporary flag of Germany with its black, red, and gold stripes derives from the flag of the Forty-eighter parliament.

Following three short wars in 1864, 1866, and 1870, the new Prussian chancellor Bismarck united the remaining German states into the smaller German Reich, which lasted until World War I. German industry grew during the late nineteenth century. Domestic unrest erupted when Kaiser Wilhelm I attempted to suppress the domestic socialist working class. In the early twentieth century, Germany struck up alliances with Austria and the age-old Ottoman Turkey, triggering fear abroad. Ultimately, the entente between France, England, and Russia led to Germany's defeat in World War I in November 1918.

MODERN ERA

With the framers of the Versailles Treaty, German Social Democrats and the Catholic Center Party succeeded in writing a constitution dubbed the Weimar Republic. The Republic was doomed from the outset by its struggles with burdensome war reparations, inflation, foreign military occupation west of the Rhine, a war guilt clause in the Versailles Treaty, and heavy losses of territory. In 1925 Field Marshal von Hindenburg, a hero on the Eastern Front in World War I, was elected president. Stricken by the political-economic disaster of 1929, Hindenburg in 1933 appointed to the chancellorship Adolf Hitler. Hitler promptly banned parties, expelled Communists from the government, and restructured the military. Hitler's goals were to purify Germany by removing people with all but the purest Teutonic blood and to expand German territory throughout Europe. In 1940 Germans occupied France, Czechoslovakia, Poland, Austria, and Hungary, and acted on the policy of extermination of unwanted peoples that nearly resulted in destroying the Jews and Gypsies of Europe.

Hitler's troops rounded up Jews in Germany and in other countries, forcing them to give up their lands and property. Systematically, Jews and political prisoners in Western Europe were shipped from Belgium, France, Germany, Greece, Italy, and Holland to forced-labor camps and to prisons. Concentration camps, which held Jews captive without regard for the accepted norms of arrest, appeared in France, Germany, and Austria, as well as Poland and Czechoslovakia. There were camps built to exterminate the Jews; most were gassed, and some were shot, drowned, or starved to death. Nearly six million people were killed by Nazi command, although there was some national resistance. When Germany was defeated in World War II, the country was divided into several parts governed by the various countries of the opposing armies. Eventually the Western countries that had opposed the Germans combined their sections into a European-influenced West Germany. This part of Germany was established as a democratic republic in 1949. The territory of Germans in the east was formed into a Russian satellite, and East Germany became a communist people's republic. For nearly 40 years distrust among Germans was encouraged by the Soviet Union on the one hand and by the West on the other. Both feared a united Germany. Finally in 1990 a revolution in East Germany deposed the communist regime there and the leaders sought reunification with West Germany. The two German states agreed to reunite under a two-house parliament and the pattern of free elections that had been developed by West Germany. Germany has worked to balance the economies of an agriculturally entrenched east and a west with a long-standing industrial sector.

THE FIRST GERMANS IN AMERICA

With their arrival at Jamestown in 1607 and for nearly four centuries afterward, Germans have been one of the three largest population components of American society. When Columbus arrived in America in 1492, he did so in the name of Ferdinand and Isabella of Spain, that is, with the entitlement of the Habsburgs who also ruled Germany as part of the Holy Roman Empire. It was a German cosmographer, Martin Waldseemüller, who suggested that the New World be designated "America."

German immigration began in the seventeenth century and continued throughout the postcolonial period at a rate that exceeded the immigration rate of any other country; however, German immigration was the first to diminish, dropping considerably during the 1890s. Contrary to myth, the first German immigrants did not originate solely in the state of Pfalz. Although emigrants from Pfalz were numerous from 1700 to 1770, equally high percentages came from Baden, Württemberg, Hesse, Nassau, and the bishoprics of Cologne, Osnabrück, Münster, and Mainz. During the American pre-Revolutionary War period, immigrants came primarily from the Rhine valley, an artery that gives access to the sea. German emigration during this period was almost exclusively via French or Dutch ports like LeHavre or Rotterdam.

SIGNIFICANT IMMIGRATION WAVES

Between 1671 and 1677 William Penn made trips to Germany on behalf of the Quaker faith, result-

ing in a German settlement that was symbolic in two ways: it was a specifically German-speaking ward, and it comprised religious dissenters. Pennsylvania has remained the heartland for various branches of Anabaptists: Old Order Mennonites, Ephrata Cloisters, Brethren, and Amish. Pennsylvania also became home for many Lutheran refugees from Catholic provinces (e.g., Salzburg), as well as for German Catholics who also had been discriminated against in their home country.

By 1790, when the first census of Americans was taken, more than 8.6 percent of the overall population of the United States was German, although in Pennsylvania more than 33 percent was German. During the Revolutionary War, these German Americans were numerically strengthened by the arrival of about 30,000 Hessian mercenaries who fought for England during the hostilities, of whom some 5,000 chose to remain in the New World after the war ceased.

In addition to those who had arrived for political and religious reasons until about 1815, Americans and some foreign shippers brought many Germans to America under the redemptioner system. The scheme was that a German peasant traveled on a sailing vessel without charge and on arrival at an Atlantic port was sold to an American businessman to work from four to seven years to redeem his passage and win his freedom. Some of the early sectarians—Baptist Dunkers, Schwenkfelders, Moravian Brethren, and others—were only able to reach America in this way.

Populous as German immigrants to America were by the end of the eighteenth century, the major waves of immigration came after the conclusion of the Napoleonic Wars in 1815. Germany's economy suffered in several ways. Too many goods were imported, especially cloth from industrialized England. Antiquated inheritance laws in southwestern Germany caused land holdings continuously to be divided, rendering farms too minuscule for assistance. A failing cottage industry collapsed when faced by a flood of foreign products. Finally, the population had grown artificially large because of growing dependence on the potato. Like Ireland, rural Germany in the 1840s was suddenly hit by famine precipitated by the potato blight.

Because the 1848 revolutions in Europe failed to bring democracy to Germany, several thousand fugitives left for America in addition to the nearly 750,000 other Germans who immigrated to America in the following years. While a

In this 1949 photograph, a two-year-old girl waits for her parents to complete their customs inspection in New York City following the family's arrival from Germany.

mere 6,000 Germans had entered the United States in the 1820s, nearly one million did so in the 1850s, the first great influx from Germany. Despite annual fluctuations, especially during the Civil War period when the figure dropped to 723,000, the tide again swelled to 751,000 in the 1870s and peaked at 1,445,000 in the 1880s.

During the nineteenth century religious and political refugees were numerous. During the

1820s, for example, Prussia forced a union of the Reformed and Lutheran congregations, which by the late 1830s caused many Old Lutherans to emigrate. Saxon followers of Martin Stephan came in 1839 to escape the "wickedness" of the Old World. Other refugees were the Pietists, who founded communal societies in America (including Harmony and Economy Pennsylvania—established by the Rappists—as well as Zoar in Ohio, St. Nazianz in Wisconsin, and Amana in Iowa).

Societies sponsored by German princes sought to use emigration as a solution to social problems at home. For example, the Central Society for German Emigrants at Berlin (1844), the National Emigration Society at Darmstadt (1847), the Giessener Emigration Society (1833), and the Texas Braunfels Adelsverein (1843) operated on the principle that a one-way ticket for the downtrodden was cheaper than a long-term subsidy. Also influential in unleashing a tidal wave of German emigration were writers like Gottfried Duden whose book (1829) about Missouri became a best-seller.

During the 1850s small farmers and their families dominated the first major wave of immigrants, who often came from southwest Germany. Soon after artisans and household manufacturers were the main arrivals from the more central states of Germany, while day laborers and agricultural workers from the rural northeast estates characterized subsequent waves of German immigrants. Not until German industrialization caught up with the English in the late nineteenth century did German emigrants no longer have to leave the country to improve their lives. Beginning in the late 1880s and for several decades thereafter, migrants from depressed German agricultural regions were destined less for America than for the manufacturing districts of Berlin, the Ruhr, and the Rhine in Germany itself.

Interspersed among these waves of economic emigrants were fugitives from oppression, including thousands of German Jews who left because of economic and social discrimination. Young men sometimes fled to avoid serving in the Prussian military. Organized industrial laborers also fled the antisocialist laws enacted when a would-be assassin threatened the life of Germany's Kaiser Wilhelm I, who blamed socialist labor leaders for the attempt. Catholics, too, were oppressed by Bismarck's infamous May Laws during the 1870s, which suppressed the influence of the Catholic Center Party and its drive for greater democracy during the first decade of the new emperor's reign.

Also during the latter half the nineteenth century, a host of agents fanned out across Germany to drum up emigration. Some were outright recruiters who were technically outlawed. More often these agencies took the form of aid societies working to better the lot of the emigres in Germany, such as the Catholic Raphael Society, the Bavarian *Ludwigsmissionsverein*, the Leopoldinen *Stiftung* in Vienna, the Pietist society of Herrnhut in Saxony, and the Lutheran support groups at Neuendettelsau of Franconia in northern Bavaria. Frankenmuth, Michigan, for example, traces its roots to the latter organization. Aiding the immigrants on this side of the Atlantic were such agencies as the Catholic Leo House in New York and the Central-Verein in St. Louis. Much better funded promoters were those established by the north-central states (most prominently, Michigan, Wisconsin, and Minnesota) as they joined the Union, many of which had ample support from their legislatures for their Immigration Commissioners. Even more influential were transcontinental railroads that sent agents to the ports of debarkation along the Atlantic and Germany to recruit immigrants to either take up their land grants or supply freight activity for their lines. Especially active was the Northern Pacific during the time when German immigrant Henry Villard headed the corporation and sought to populate his land grant with industrious German farmers.

In the latter phases of German immigration, newcomers joined established settlers in a phenomenon called "chain migration." Chain migration is defined as the movement of families or individuals to join friends and family members already established in a given place. Chain migration strengthened the already existing German regions of the United States. One such concentrated settlement pattern gave rise to the phrase "German triangle," that is, St. Paul, St. Louis, and Cincinnati, with lines stretching between them so that the triangle incorporates Chicago, Milwaukee, Indianapolis, Fort Wayne, Davenport, and other strongly German cities. Other descriptors include the more accurate "German parallelogram," which stretches from Albany westward along the Erie Canal to Buffalo and farther westward through Detroit to St. Paul and the Dakotas, then south to Nebraska and Kansas, back to Missouri, and eastward along the Ohio River to Baltimore. Except for large settlements in Texas, San Francisco, and Florida, German American settlement is still largely contained within the German belt.

The number of German Americans has remained constant. From 1850 to 1970 German was the most widely used language in the United States after English. In the 1990 U.S. census, 58 million Americans claimed sole German or part-German descent, demonstrating the persistence of the German heritage in the United States.

"We were stationed in Hamburg in a tremendous big place. It was sort of an assembly building where you got processed. There was an exodus from Europe at that time, and they had all races in this place. You could see people from Russia, Poland, Lithuania, you name it. I can't describe the way I felt—it was part fear, it was exciting. It's something I'll never forget."
Ludwig Hofmeister in 1925, cited in *Ellis Island: An Illustrated History of the Immigrant Experience*, edited by Ivan Chermayeff et al. (New York: Macmillan, 1991).

SETTLEMENT

Germans settled in different locations depending upon when they arrived and where the best locations for economic opportunity were situated. When France, which had attempted to colonize Louisiana in the early eighteenth century with the help of Germans, assumed an important role in the cotton trade, German immigrants arrived in New Orleans and made their way up the Mississippi, Ohio, and Missouri rivers. Others arrived in New York and travelled the Erie Canal and the Great Lakes to the Midwest. The primary port of arrival for early immigrants was Philadelphia and many Germans chose to settle in Pennsylvania. The German American population of 58 million breaks down demographically as follows: 39 percent live in the Midwest, 25 percent in the South, 19 percent in the West, and 17 percent in the Northeast. With regard to specific states, Americans reporting German ancestry are the most numerous in California, followed by Pennsylvania, Ohio, Illinois, and Texas. In terms of absolute numbers, the Germans have always been at their largest in New York City. The German Americans are nowhere more densely settled than in Wisconsin, Minnesota, North Dakota, South Dakota, Nebraska, and Iowa—in the traditional German belt.

ACCULTURATION AND ASSIMILATION

In many respects, the Germans were slower to assimilate than their fellow immigrants from other countries. This was due in part to their size and in part to their overall percentage of the population. When a cross-section of basic needs can be supplied within an ethnic community, the need to assimilate in order to survive is less urgent. Germans had their own professionals, businesses, clergy, churches, and especially schools. However, second generation German immigrants were drawn more quickly into the mainstream and the survival of German communities depended upon immigration.

TRADITIONS, CUSTOMS, AND BELIEFS

The true picture of German culture differs substantially from that presented in the popular media where Germans are presented as either brutal or as jolly, overweight, and beer-guzzling. Equally enigmatic is post-World War II German Americans' perception of their heritage as inseparable from certain icons and costumes, notably, beer mugs, fast high-quality cars, sausage and sauerkraut—enlivened by the spirit of Bavarian folk music. In the United States Bavarian culture is regarded as synonymous with all German culture, even though Bavarian customs and language are confined to the regional state of Bavaria and its capital, Munich. German Day festivals almost always feature Bavarian dance and clothing such as the *lederhosen* (men's shorts with suspenders) and the *dirndl* (women's full skirt). Replicas of German cities—such as Leavenworth, Washington, or Frankenmuth, Michigan—invariably assume an air of Alpine Bavaria.

HOLIDAYS

In addition to traditional American holidays, Catholic communities celebrate the feast of Corpus Christi in which there are outdoor processions to altars decorated with flowers. At the Epiphany, neighbors visited from house-to-house and young men adorned with paper crowns would sing in exchange for treats. The German Christmas served as the basis for the American celebrations; it emphasizes the family and the exchange of gifts; often, the Christmas tree is not illuminated until Christmas eve. December 6 was the traditional time of St. Nicholas' visit. Another tradition that has survived from German American communities is the greeting of the New Year by gunfire—young men would ride horses through the neighborhood and fire their shotguns when midnight arrived.

This German American Tricentennial Multicycle from Philadelphia, Pennsylvania, is traveling along Fifth Avenue in New York City during the 1988 Steuben Day Parade.

LANGUAGE

The German language is related to Danish, Norwegian, Swedish, Dutch, and Icelandic, as well as to English. High German, the dialect spoken in the east-west central geographic elevation, differs linguistically from the language spoken in the lower-lying geographic regions of northern Germany, where once Low German was in everyday usage. It is also radically different from Bavarian and Swiss German which typically is voiced in the southern, more Alpine regions. Spoken natively by 100 million people, German is the mother tongue of thousands of people who live beyond all of Germany's current borders. Ten percent of all books published in the world are in German.

FAMILY AND COMMUNITY DYNAMICS

There was a low rate of tenancy among early German immigrants, who purchased homes as early as possible. German Americans have traditionally placed a high value upon home ownership and prefer those made of brick. The traditional German American family was essentially patriarchal with women assuming subservient roles. Because many German immigrants were from agricultural areas, they brought with them a traditional concept of the family. Farm families were, of necessity, large and family members worked together for the good of all. Wives and daughters worked together with husbands and sons to manage the harvests. In families whose work was not farm-centered, though, wives worked with their husbands in small family operated businesses. Children frequently left school early with the boys entering family businesses and the girls entering domestic service. According to 1880 census figures, though, a smaller proportion of German American women were part of the work force than other immigrant groups. Those who were employed outside the home did not work in factories or in jobs in which a knowledge of English was necessary; instead, they labored in janitorial work or the service industry.

To emphasize the importance of their language in the transmission of cultural values, German Americans strove to maintain their own German-language schools, first by establishing private institutions and later, after 1849, by pressuring school districts to offer German or bilingual education where parents requested it. In addition to the German-language instruction offered in the public schools, there was the instruction in the parochial schools operated especially by Catholics and Lutherans, which enrolled thousands of the children of German immigrants.

Parochial schools started in colonial times and continued through the nineteenth century, sometimes sponsored by nonreligious organizations such as a local German school society which functioned as legal owner of the school. Some of these schools operated according to new pedagogical principles and had a lasting impact on the American school system. For example, they introduced kindergarten. At all school levels sports programs, which had their origin in the German socialist *Turner* societies, became an integral aspect of American training for physical fitness. A few German American leaders dreamed of having their own university with German as the language instruction, but in spite of *Kultur* enthusiasm, it never came to fruition.

At the lower levels Germans achieved success in the political arena. When the question of teaching subjects in German drew the attention of truancy alarmists in Wisconsin and Illinois around 1890, the Wisconsin legislature passed the infamous Bennett Law, which required that children attend school more faithfully and which added the stipulation that at least some of the subjects be taught in English. In Illinois a similar measure was called the Edwards Law. As a result, the Lutheran and Catholic constituents of these states campaigned to defeat Wisconsin's governor William Dempster Hoard and to free the German language schools of state intervention. Over time, however, German faded in favor of English.

To supply teachers for these many schools, German Americans maintained a teachers' college while the *Turner* gymnastic societies developed their own teacher preparation institute for the production of scholars who would educate pupils. After the turn of the twentieth century, a special three-million-strong organization, the German American Alliance, actively promoted the cause of German. They did so in part to preserve their culture and in part to maintain a clientele for German products like newspapers, books, and beer. In 1903 the Alliance urged in its *German-American Annals*, "Only through the preservation of the German language can our race in this land be preserved from entire disappearance. The principal aim should be the founding of independent parochial schools in which the language of instruction would be German, with English as a foreign language."

Elementary German language school enrollments reached their zenith between 1880 and 1900. In 1881 more than 160,000 pupils were attending German Catholic schools and about 50,000 were in Missouri Synod Lutheran schools. Of the roughly one-half million people attending school with a curriculum partly or all in German, as counted by the German American Teachers Association around the turn of the century, 42 percent were attending public schools, more than a third were in Catholic schools, and 16 percent were in Lutheran private schools.

However, when World War I broke out, the German element was so discredited in the United States that when Congress declared war in April 1917, within six months legal action was brought not only to dampen considerably German cultural activities but also to eliminate the German language from American schools. The flagship case was the Mockett Law in Nebraska, which anti-German enthusiasts repealed. Eventually, 26 other states followed suit, banning instruction *in* German and *of* German. When the Missouri Synod Lutherans of Nebraska brought the test case, *Meyer v. Nebraska*, the ban on German was reconfirmed by all the courts until it reached the U.S. Supreme Court. On June 4, 1923, the Supreme Court held that a mere knowledge of German could not be regarded as harmful to the state, and the majority opinion added that the right of parents to have their children taught in a language other than English was within the liberties guaranteed by the Fourteenth Amendment. Nevertheless, as a language of instruction in schools, during church service, and at home, German gradually drifted into oblivion as assimilation accelerated.

RELIGION

Religious differences have characterized the German people. Most of the population is Protestant and practice a form of Lutheranism—the Protestant Reformation church created by the German religious leader Martin Luther. Religion was important to German immigrants and the lack of ministers attracted Moravian missionaries in the early eighteenth century. The success of these churches strengthened the established Reformed churches, which rejected the ecumenical stance of the Moravians. In the eighteenth century the language, doctrine, and rituals of some of the established synods of the Reformed church had become Americanized and they were unable to attract new immigrants. The conservative synods, such as the Missouri Synod, were more successful, however.

Many German immigrants were Catholic; but because the Catholic church was controlled essentially by the Irish there was much friction between the two groups. Many parishes were established by lay people, which resulted in frequent friction between the pastors and trustees in pioneer churches. The German American churches, which used the German language exclusively, featured a liturgy rich with ritual and music and offered its parishioners a variety of associations and societies. They also addressed numerous social needs by supporting and operating orphanages and hospitals. By the twentieth century, however, many of the German American Catholic parishes underwent severe attrition when many of its members moved to suburban mixed parishes.

POLITICS AND GOVERNMENT

On the whole, Germans in America have been reluctant to participate in politics. They arrived without the necessary language skills, even if they had *not* lacked a tradition that conditioned them for political participation. Thus, at the national level, the first and most prominent German figure in American politics was Carl Schurz, who was influential in the election of Abraham Lincoln, served as ambassador to Spain, became a general in the Civil War, later was elected U.S. senator from Missouri, and finally was appointed Secretary of the Interior under Rutherford Hayes. At the state level, too, the Germans seem to have avoided public office. Except for John P. Altgeld, the German-born governor of Illinois from 1893 to 1897, no German was ever elected to head an American state. Even in the U.S. Senate, few German-born and a surprisingly small number of German Americans have ever entered that upper house.

Not until Dwight D. Eisenhower was there an American president with a German surname.

Eisenhower's ancestors were colonial Pennsylvania Germans who had moved to Texas and then Kansas, but certainly this president was no friend of Germans. Political scientists have shown how strongly the Germans came to resent Franklin Roosevelt and General Eisenhower for their defeat of Germany during World War II. This resulted in a fading from Democratic Party support until the candidacy of President Harry Truman in 1948. During that campaign the German American electorate returned in droves to their traditional Democratic Party, handing Truman a surprise victory over Republican Thomas E. Dewey. Apparently, Truman's strong stand against Stalin at Potsdam, his subsequent anti-Communist actions in Greece, and his May 1948 decision to save Berlin by airlift aided his November reelection chances with German Americans. There was no similar outpouring for Eisenhower in 1952, who won in spite of only mild German support.

LABOR UNIONS

Occupationally, the Germans were skilled in such trades as baking, carpentry, and brewing. They were also laborers, farmers, musicians, and merchants. According to the 1870 census figures, 27 percent of German Americans were employed in agriculture, 23 percent in the professions, and 13 percent in trades and transportation. By 1890, however, some 45 percent reportedly were laborers or servants, perhaps as a result of industrial workers' migration rather than a farmers' migration. This may explain why the labor movement in the United States gained considerable impetus from its German component.

The mid-nineteenth century witnessed the introduction of the communist ideologies of Wilhelm Weitling (1808-1871) and Joseph Weydemeyer (1818-1866), which gave impetus to early struggles for social and economic reform. The International Workingmen's Association in America was founded in 1869 as the first of the communist and socialist groups in America; and its membership was predominantly German American. And in 1886, German American anarchists were also instrumental in the forming of the labor movement implicated in the infamous Chicago Haymarket bombing during the labor strikes of that period. Had it not been for the greater need for workers to unite against their employers and join the American Federation of Labor (AFL), German trade unions might have been consolidated in the late 1880s. In future years many leaders of American labor were German American, including Walter

Reuther, who fought on the picket lines during the 1930s before becoming president of the AFL-CIO following World War II. For German immigrants, labor union membership enabled them to not only improve working conditions, it helped them to form a solidarity with workers from other ethnic backgrounds.

RELATIONS WITH GERMANY

During the period from 1945 to 1990, the United States, with allies Great Britain and France, officially occupied West Germany, each in a special zone. The Americans occupied Bavaria, the Rhine-Main Frankfurt, and Palatinate areas. Each country was also allocated a sector in the capital of Berlin. During the Cold War, dramatic confrontations focused on Berlin because it lay 110 miles from the Iron Curtain. For 11 months in 1948 and 1949, the Soviets noosed a land blockade around the city, only to have the Allies supply the needs of two million inhabitants by air. For example, when the city's electrical power supply was severed, West Berliners lived in darkness until an entire generating plant could be flown in and assembled on site.

After Khrushchev met John F. Kennedy at a June summit in Vienna, East German border police erected the Berlin Wall on August 13, 1961. Throughout the Cold War, the wall was an important political symbol. It figured in the political phraseology of each U.S. president, most prominently in Kennedy's "Ich bein ein Berliner" speech at the City Hall, which endeared him to Berliners for all time. After the collapse of Communism the wall was dismantled in 1990. Today a small portion of the wall stands as a museum. Before unification of the two Germanies on October 3, 1990, the four World War II Allied victors' flags were lowered from the *Komandatura* palace in Berlin. Thus ended four centuries of control, returning Germany to full international autonomy, which further restored the confidence of Americans in their German descent. With its strong economy and continuous universal military conscription, Germany remains the linchpin of NATO and the core member in the European Community.

INDIVIDUAL AND GROUP CONTRIBUTIONS

German immigrants to the United States have distinguished themselves in virtually every field of endeavor. John Roebling (1806-1869) is still known from his prowess with bridges, although the once famous empire builder, John Jacob Astor (1763-1848), is little remembered for his American Fur Company. Baron Friedrich von Steuben (1730-1794) commands respect as a military hero, but cartoonist Thomas Nast (1840-1902) is all but forgotten, although his elephant and donkey mascots for the Republicans and Democrats and his Santa Claus are not. With the arrival of the computer screen, Ottmar Mergenthaler's (1854-1899) famous Linotype printing system has met oblivion. Even Wernher von Braun's (1912-1977) pioneer rocketry, which still carries Americans and their satellites into outer space, is fading from consciousness.

BUSINESS

In business John August Sutter (1803-1880) is remembered less for his Pacific trading prowess than for the fact that gold was found on his California land holdings in 1848. Claus Spreckels developed sugar refining in California and Hawaii, while Frederick Weyerhaeuser masterminded the Northwest timber industry. Henry Villard, born Heinrich Hilgard, completed the Northern Pacific Railroad. Prominent brewers include Philip Best, Valentin Blatz, Frederick Miller, Joseph Schlitz, and the Coors and the Anhaeuser-Busch families.

MUSIC

In music there were the father and son Walter Damrosch (1862-1950) and Leopold Damrosch, Erich Leinsdorf (1912-), and Bruno Walter Schlesinger, all conductors in New York; opera singers Ernestine Schumann-Heink (1861-1936) and Lotte Lehmann (1888-1976); and the composers Paul Hindemith (1895-1963), Kurt Weill (1900-1950), and Arnold Schoenberg (1874-1951).

SCIENCE AND TECHNOLOGY

In atomic energy Albert Einstein (1879-1955) is the most prominent scientist. In the laboratories it was his German-born colleagues, Nobel laureates James Franck (1882-1964), Otto Loewi (1873-1961), Victor Hess (1883-1964), Felix Bloch (1905-1983), Otto Stern (1888-1969), and Hans Bethe (1906-) who mattered. On the Manhattan Project they worked with two German-educated

Hungarians, Edward Teller (1908-) and Leo Szilard (1898-1964), all under the command of Julius Robert Oppenheimer (1904-1967), the American-born son of Forty-eighter immigrants, who had taken his Ph.D. at the University of Goettingen before engineering the bomb. Szilard and the German-born scientists Erwin Schrödinger (1887-1961) and Max Delbrück (1906-1981) later worked closely with colleagues to develop the Crick-Watson model of DNA. George Westinghouse (1846-1914) invented, among many other things, the air brakes to stop trains. For his electric motors, Charles Steinmetz (1865-1923) became known as the wizard of Schenectady.

SPORTS

George Herman Erhardt Ruth (1895-1948), better known as the Babe, and Lou Gehrig, both the sons of German immigrants, continue to enjoy sports fame.

VISUAL ARTS

In architecture there was the famous Bauhaus School headed by Walter Gropius (1883-1969) at Harvard and Ludwig Mies van der Rohe (1886-1969) in Chicago. Marcel Breuer and Josef Albers (1888-1976) created the designation "modern design," overshadowed now by the so-called post-modern style.

MEDIA

PRINT

Amerika Woche.
Newspaper with text in English and German.

Contact: Werner Baroni, Editor.
Address: 4732 North Lincoln Avenue, Chicago, Illinois 60625.
Telephone: (312) 275-5054.

Der Deutsch-Amerikaner/German American Journal.
Newspaper published by the German American National Congress; promotes the organization's efforts to maintain German culture, art, and customs.

Contact: Ernst Ott, Editor.
Address: 4740 North Western Avenue, Second Floor, Chicago, Illinois 60625.

Telephone: (312) 275-1100.
Fax: (312) 274-4010.

IGAR News.
Monthly publication of the Institute for German American Relations; promotes friendly German American relations through education.

Contact: Dr. Bruce D. Martin, Editor.
Address: 9380 McKnight Road, Suite 102, Pittsburgh, Pennsylvania 15237-5951.
Telephone: (412) 364-6554.

Nordamerikanische Wochen-Post.
Published in Troy, Michigan, this weekly carries a front page directly from Germany, reports on many German American organizations, and includes coverage of business activity in Germany. It is currently the best-edited and most widely distributed such publication in America.

Contact: Regina Bell, Editor.
Address: Detroit Abend-Post Publishing Co., 1120 East Long Lake Road, Troy, Michigan 48098.
Telephone: (313) 528-2810.
Fax: (313) 528-2741.

Society for German-American Studies— Newsletter.
Quarterly publication of the Society; focuses on German immigration and settlements in the United States and on German American history and culture.

Contact: LaVern J. Rippley, Editor.
Address: St. Olaf College, Northfie, Minnesota 55057.
Telephone: (507) 663-3233.

New Yorker Staats-Herold is the oldest and among the best North American German-language publications. America Woche, Wächter und Anzeiger, California Staats-Zeitung, and similar publications typify efforts of regional German-language newspapers to continue their noble traditions. Such organizations as the Deutsch-Amerikanische Nationalkongress, headquartered in Chicago, publishes its own monthly, as do a number of its chapters.

RADIO

German-language programs on radio stations abound. There are at minimum one-hour radio programs on perhaps a dozen radio stations in Chicago, and several radio programs in Milwaukee; Pittsburgh; Detroit; Saginaw; St. Paul;

Cleveland; Toledo; Cincinnati; Denver; Seminola, Florida; New Braunfels, Texas; and on the West Coast.

ORGANIZATIONS AND ASSOCIATIONS

Throughout the German belt there continue to exist hundreds of German societies. In Michigan alone where the *Wochen-Post* carries a listing, there are 28 ranging from the Arion singers and the *Berlin Verein* to *Schwäbischer Männerchor* and the *Verein der Plattdeutschen* (Low German speakers). In other states there are dozens more, some representing Germans from beyond the borders of the nation, such as the German-Bohemian Society of New Ulm, the Germans from Russia Heritage Society in Bismarck, and the Transylvanian Saxons in Cleveland. New York City alone has perhaps 100 German clubs, listed periodically in the local German newspaper. So, too, hundreds of once German-language churches offer services routinely but not regularly, sometimes weekly, more often monthly for a persistent but waning German-language clientele.

German American Information and Education Association (GIEA).

Patriotic conservative organization seeking to improve the public image of "Germanity" and to publicize contributions to American culture made by German Americans.

Contact: Stanley Rittenhouse, President.

Address: P.O. Box 10888, Burke, Virginia 22015.

Telephone: (703) 425-0707.

German American National Political Action Committee (GANPAC).

Seeks to represent what the committee considers to be the interests of German Americans.

Contact: Hans Schmidt, Chair.

Address: P.O. Box 1137, Santa Monica, California 90406.

MUSEUMS AND RESEARCH CENTERS

The Society for German American Studies, headquartered at the University of Cincinnati, functions as a scholarly umbrella for many others that have a more social or genealogical orientation. The Pennsylvania German Society in Philadelphia has a major library, while research centers with the name Max Kade Institutes recently have sprung up on university campuses, notably, at Madison, Wisconsin; Lawrence, Kansas; Indianapolis; and Penn State. There is no semblance of a German American museum, although local historical societies in the "German" states have much material.

SOURCES FOR ADDITIONAL STUDY

Allen, James Paul, and Eugene James Turner. *We the People: An Atlas of America's Ethnic Diversity.* New York: Macmillan, 1988.

America and the Germans: An Assessment of a Three-Hundred-Year History, two volumes, edited by Frank Trommler and Joseph McVeigh. Philadelphia: University of Pennsylvania Press, 1985.

Conzen, Kathleen Neils. "Germans," *Harvard Encyclopedia of American Ethnic Groups,* edited by Stephan Thernstrom. Cambridge, Massachusetts: Belknap Press of Harvard University Press, 1980.

Kloss, Heinz. *Atlas of German-American Settlements.* Marburg: Elwert, 1974.

News from the Land of Freedom: German Immigrants Write Home, edited by Walter D. Kamphoefner, Wolfgang Helbich, and Ulrike Sommer, translated by Susan Carter Vogel. Ithaca, New York: Cornell University Press, 1991.

O'Connor, Richard. *The German-Americans.* Boston: Little, Brown, 1968.

Piltz, Thomas. *The Americans and the Germans.* Munich: Heinz Moos, 1977.

Pond, Elizabeth. *Beyond the Wall: Germany's Road to Unification.* Washington, D.C.: Brookings Institution, 1993.

Rippley, La Vern J., and Eberhard Reichmann. *The German-Americans: An Ethnic Experience*, translated by Willi Paul Adams. Indianapolis: Max Kade German-American Center, 1993.

Totten, Christine M. *Roots in the Rhineland: America's German Heritage in Three Hundred Years of Immigration, 1683-1983*. New York: German Information Center, 1988.

Walker, Mack. *Germany and the Emigration, 1816-1885*. Cambridge: Harvard University Press, 1964.

Wittke, Carl. *Refugees of Revolution: The German Forty-eighters in America*. Philadelphia: University of Pennsylvania Press, 1952.

Wust, Klaus. *Three Hundred Years of German Immigrants in North America, 1683-1983: A Pictorial History*. Baltimore and Munich: Heinz Moos, 1983.

GREEK AMERICANS

by
Jane Jurgens

OVERVIEW

Officially known as the Hellenic Republic, Greece is a mountainous peninsula located in southeastern Europe, between the Aegean and Mediterranean Seas. With a landmass of 51,000 square miles (132,100 square kilometers), Greece is bordered to the north by Bulgaria and Macedonia. Nearly 2,000 islands surround its eastern, southern, and western borders. The nine major land areas that constitute Greece include Central Pindus, Thessaly, the Salonika Plain, Macedonia/Thrace, Peloponnesus, the Southeastern Uplands, the Ionian Islands, the Aegean Islands, and Crete.

The capital city, Athens, and the cities of Thessaloniki (Salonika), Patras, Volos, and Larissa have the largest populations in Greece, which has a total population of approximately ten million. Ninety-seven percent of the ethnically and linguistically homogeneous nation speaks Greek, and one percent, Turkish. The Eastern Orthodox church is the dominant religion; only about 1.5 percent of the population is Muslim, and a small percentage is Roman Catholic, Greek Catholic, or Jewish.

Traditionally, Greeks referred to themselves as "Hellenes" and to the country of Greece as "Hellas." The word "Greek" comes from the Latin

Graeci, a name given to the people of this region by the Romans.

The Greek flag features a small white cross in the upper left corner flanked to the right and bottom by alternating white and blue stripes. The white cross symbolizes the Greek Orthodox religion, while the blue stripes stand for the sea and sky, and the white stripes for the purity of the Greek struggle for independence. The national anthem is "The Hymn to Freedom" ("*Imnos pros teen elefteeriahn*"). The basic monetary unit is the drachma.

HISTORY

Greece is an ancient country that was continuously occupied from 6000 B.C., the beginning of its Neolithic period, until the nineteenth century. The Bronze Age, traditionally divided into early, middle, and late phases, dated from 2800 B.C. to 1000 B.C. It was during this period that Minoan civilization of Crete and the Mycenean civilization of mainland Greece flourished. These civilizations were destroyed around 1000 B.C. just as the individual city-state or "polis" was beginning to experience rapid growth. In 479 B.C. the city-states united to defeat Persia, a common enemy, but national unity proved to be short-lived. The power struggle between Athens and Sparta, the principal city-states, dominated the period.

Athens reached its zenith during the fifth century B.C., a period known as its Golden Age. At this time Athens experimented with a form of internal democracy unique in the ancient world, achieved a singular culture, and left enduring literary and architectural legacies. Socrates, Plato, Xenophon, Herodotus, Sophocles, Euripides, and Aeschylus came into prominence, and in 432 B.C. the Parthenon on the Acropolis was completed. The Peloponnesian War fought between Athens and Sparta from 431 to 404 B.C. and a plague that raged through Athens in 430 contributed to bring the Golden Age to an end. For a time Sparta dominated the Greek world, but war and severe economic decline hastened the decline of all of the city-states.

Greece came under Macedonian domination between 338 and 200 B.C. The Macedonian king, Alexander the Great, conquered Greece, Persia, and Egypt to create an empire, and he carried the idea of Hellenism to places as far away as India. The Hellenistic Age that followed Alexander's rule lasted until 146 B.C., As a Roman state from 127 B.C. to A.D. 330, Greece and its city-states

had no political or military power. When the Roman Empire was divided in A.D. 395, Greece became part of the Eastern Empire, which continued as the Byzantine Empire until 1453. That year the Turks captured Constantinople, the capital of Byzantium, and Greece became part of the Ottoman Empire.

MODERN PERIOD

Greece's declaration of independence from the Ottoman Empire on March 25, 1821, resulted in the Greek War of Independence, which lasted until 1829, and began the history of independent modern Greece. Great Britain, France, and Russia assisted Greece in its struggle for independence, and Greece came under the protection of these powers by the London Protocol of 1830. In 1832 the Bavarian Otto I became the first king of Greece, and in 1844 a conservative revolutionary force established a constitutional monarchy. George I, who succeeded Otto I, created a more democratic form of government with a new constitution in 1864.

During the 1880s and 1890s, transportation, education, and social services rapidly improved. Then in 1897 a revolt against the Turks in Crete led to war between Greece and the Ottoman Empire and to eventual self-governance for Crete. A revolt by the Military League in 1909 prompted the appointment of Eleuthérios Venizélos as Prime Minister of Greece. Between 1910 and 1933 Venizélos enacted major financial reforms.

During World War I Greece joined the Allied forces in opposing Germany. After the war Greece regained much of the territory it had lost to the Ottoman Empire. But in 1921 Greece began a war against the Turks in Asia Minor and suffered a crushing defeat in 1922. In 1923, under the Treaty of Lausanne, more than 1.25 million Greeks moved from Turkey to Greece, and more than 400,000 Turks in Greece moved to Turkey.

Between the World Wars, the Greek population vacillated between the establishment of a republican form of government and the restoration of monarchy. In 1936 Greece became a military dictatorship under General Ioannis Metaxas, who remained in power until 1944. The Germans occupied Greece during World War II, and the country did not recover until the 1950s, when it began slowly to regain economic and political stability. In 1952 Greece joined the North Atlantic Treaty Organization and also granted women the right to vote and to hold political office. During

1952 to 1963 Alexander Papagos and Konstantinos Karamanlis each held the office of prime minister.

On April 27, 1967, Colonel George Papadopoulos led a military coup, resulting in the suspension of constitutionally guaranteed rights and the imposition of harsh social controls. Papadopoulos declared Greece a republic in 1973 and put an end to the monarchy before his government was overthrown. In November 1974 Greece held its first free elections in more than a decade. Parliament adopted a new constitution in 1975, and a civilian government was established.

The first Socialist government in Greece gained control in 1981, the year Andreas Papandreou—the son of George Papandreou and a member of the Panhellenic Socialist movement— succeeded conservative Georgios Rallis as prime minister. In 1989 a conservative-communist coalition formed a new government, and pledging that Greece would be an active participant in the greater European community, Papandreou was reelected.

THE FIRST GREEKS IN AMERICA

According to official records, the Greek sailor Don Teodoro or Theodoros, who sailed to America with the Spanish explorer Panfilio de Narvaez in 1528, was the first Greek to land in America. The names of other Greek sailors who may have come to America during this period are John Griego and Petros the Cretan. There is some speculation that Juan De Fuca, who discovered the straits south of Vancouver Island, may have been a Greek named Ionnis Phocas.

One of the first Greek colonies was at New Smyrna near Saint Augustine, Florida. Andrew Turnball and his wife Maria Rubini, daughter of a wealthy Greek merchant, persuaded approximately 450 colonists to journey to America and settle. With the promise of land, Greek colonists primarily from Mani in the south of Greece, as well as Italians, Minorcans, and Corsicans, began arriving in Florida on June 26, 1768. The colony was an overwhelming failure and was officially disbanded on July 17, 1777, but many of the colonists had already moved to neighboring Saint Augustine, where they were becoming successful as merchants and small businessmen. A small community of Greeks also built a chapel and school there.

SIGNIFICANT IMMIGRATION WAVES

The first wave of Greek immigrants included about 40 orphans who had survived the Greek Revolution of 1821 and who were brought to the United States by American missionaries; survivors of the 1822 massacre of Chios by the Turks; and merchant sailors who settled in the Americas. Most of these Greeks were from islands such as

Chios, and others came from Asia Minor, Epirus, and Macedonia. By 1860 about 328 Greeks were living in the United States, with the majority residing in California, Arkansas, New York, and Massachusetts.

The U.S. Greek population remained small until the 1880s, when poor economic conditions in Greece prompted many Greeks to immigrate to the United States. During the 1880s most who came were from Laconia (notably, from the city of Sparta), a province of the Peloponnesus in southern Greece. Beginning in the 1890s, Greeks began arriving from other parts of Greece, principally from Arcadia, another province in the Peloponnesus. The largest numbers arrived during 1900-1910 (686) and 1911-1920 (385). Most were young single males who came to the United States to seek their fortunes and wished to return to Greece as soon as possible. About 30 percent of those who came before 1930 did return, some of whom went to fight in the Balkan Wars of 1912-1913.

The Immigration Acts of 1921 and 1924 reversed the open-door policy of immigration and established quotas. The Act of 1921 limited the number of Greek admittants to 3,063, while the Act of 1924 limited the number to 100. Legal petition increased the quota, and during 1925-1929 about 10,883 Greeks were admitted. Another 17,000 Greeks were admitted under the Refugee Relief Act of 1953, and 1,504 were accepted as a result of further legislation in 1957.

The Immigration Act of 1965 abandoned the quota system and gave preference to immigrants with families already established in the United States. The new Greek arrivals usually were better educated than their predecessors and included men and women in equal numbers, as well as family groups.

From 1820 to 1982 a total of 673,360 Greeks immigrated to the United States. After 1982, the number of Greeks entering the United States is as follows: 1983 (3,020); 1984 (2,865); 1985 (2,579); 1986 (2,512); 1987 (2,653); 1988 (2,458); 1989 (2,157); 1990 (2,742); 1991 (1,760); 1992 (1,790). The 1990 Census reports the number of people claiming at least one ancestry as Greek at 1,110,373.

SETTLEMENT

During the 1890s Greeks began settling in major urban areas, including the industrial cities of the Northeast and Midwest. The first immigrants settled in Massachusetts and southern New Hampshire. The city of Lowell, Massachusetts, attracted the majority of Greeks, and by 1920 it had the third largest Greek community in the United States. Greeks also settled in the New England towns of Haverhill, Lynn, Boston, Peabody, and Manchester. The largest Greek settlement in the twentieth century was in New York. Greeks also settled in western Pennsylvania, particularly Pittsburgh, and in the Midwestern cities of Detroit, Milwaukee, Cleveland, Youngstown, and Chicago.

Small Greek communities existed in Galveston, Texas, and Atlanta, Georgia, but the largest concentration of Greeks in the South was at Tarpon Springs, Florida. In the first half of the twentieth century, this unique settlement of Greeks made its living by sponge diving.

Attracted to mining and railroad work, large numbers of Greeks settled in Salt Lake City, with smaller numbers inhabiting Colorado, Wyoming, Idaho, and Nevada. The heaviest early concentration on the Pacific Coast was in San Francisco. Today, Greeks live primarily in urban areas and are increasingly moving to the South and West. The 1990 Census reveals that New York State still has the largest population of Greeks, with the highest concentration in the Astoria section of the borough of Queens. The next largest populations are in California, Illinois, Massachusetts, and Florida.

ACCULTURATION AND ASSIMILATION

Few negative Greek stereotypes persist. Greeks share the American work ethic and desire for success and are largely perceived as hardworking and family-oriented. They are also said to possess a "Zorba"-like spirit and love of life. However, many Greek Americans perceive the recent Greek immigrants as "foreign" and often as a source of embarrassment.

TRADITIONS, CUSTOMS, AND BELIEFS

Greeks have an assortment of traditional customs, beliefs, and superstitions to ensure success and ward off evil and misfortune. Old beliefs persist in some communities in the United States. For example, belief in the "evil eye" is still strong and is supported by the Greek Orthodox church as a generalized concept of evil. Precautions against the evil eye (*not* endorsed by the church) include wearing garlic; making the sign of the cross behind the ear of a child with dirt or soot; placing an image of an eye over the lintel; wearing the *mati*, a blue amulet with an eye in the center; and recitation of a ritual prayer, the *ksematiasma*. Greeks may also respond to a compliment with the expression *ptou, ptou*, to keep the evil eye from harming the person receiving the compliment. Greeks also "knock wood" to guard against misfortune, and reading one's fortunes in the patterns of coffee dregs remains popular.

PROVERBS

The Greeks "have a saying for it": In wine there is truth; You make my liver swell (You make me sick); God ascends stairs and descends stairs (Everything is possible for God); An old hen makes the tastiest broth (Quality improves with age); He won't give her any chestnuts (He wouldn't cut her any slack); I tell it to my dog, and he tells it to his tail (To pass the buck); I went for wool, and I came out shorn (To lose the shirt off one's back); Faith is the power of life.

CUISINE

Greek food is extremely popular in the United States, where Greek American restaurants flourish. In Greek restaurants and in the home, many of the traditional recipes have been adapted (and sometimes improved on) to suit American tastes. In Greece meals are great social occasions where friends and family come together and the quantity of food is often impressive. Olive oil is a key ingredient in Greek cooking and is used in quantity. Traditional herbs include parsley, mint, dill, oregano (especially the wild oregano *rigani*), and garlic. You will find on most Greek tables olives, sliced cheese (such as feta, *kaseri*, and *kefalotiri*), tomato, and lemon wedges, along with bread. Fish, chicken, lamb, beef, and vegetables are all found on the Greek menu and are prepared in a variety of ways. Soup, salad, and yogurt are served as side dishes. Sheets of dough called *phillo* are layered and filled with spinach, cheese, eggs, and nuts. Greeks create such masterpieces as *moussaka*, a layered dish of eggplant, meat, cheese, and bread crumbs sometimes served with a white sauce. Other popular Greek dishes in the United States include *souvlakia*, a shish kabob of lamb, vegetables, and onions; *keftides*, Greek meatballs; *sagana-ki*, a mixture of fried cheese, milk, egg, and flour; *dolmathes yalantzi*, grape leaves stuffed with rice, pine nuts, onions, and spices; and gyros, slices of beef, pork, and lamb prepared on a skewer, served with tomatoes, onions, and cucumber yogurt sauces on pita bread.

Soups include *psarosoupa me avgolemono*, a rich fish soup made with egg and lemon sauce; *spanaki soupa*, spinach soup; *mayreritsa*, an Easter soup made with tripe and/or lamb parts and rice; and *fasolatha*, a white bean Lenten soup made with tomatoes, garlic, and spices. Salads always accompany a meal. The traditional Greek salad (*salata a la greque*) is made with lettuce or spinach, feta cheese, tomatoes, onions, cucumbers, olives, oregano, and olive oil.

The national drink of Greece is *ouzo* ("oozoh"), an anise-flavored liquor that tastes like licorice and that remains popular with Greek Americans. Traditionally, it is served with appetizers (*mezethes*) such as olives, cheese, tomato, and lemon wedges. A popular Greek wine, *retsina*, is produced only in Greece and is imported to the United States.

TRADITIONAL COSTUMES

Greek traditional costumes come in a variety of styles, some dating back to ancient times. Women's clothing is heavy, with many layers and accessories, designed to cover the entire body. The undergarments include the floor-length *poukamiso* (shirt) made of linen or cotton and the *misofioni* (underskirt) and *vraka* (panties), usually of muslin. The outer garments consist of the *forema-palto*, a coatdress of embroidered linen; the *fousta* (shirt) of wool or silk; the *sigouni*, a sleeveless jacket of embroidered wool worn outside the *forema-palto*; the *kontogourni* or *zipouni*, a short vest worn over the *fousta*; the *apodia*, an apron of embroidered wool or linen; and finally the *zonari*, a long belt wrapped many times around the waist. Buckles on these belts can be very ornate.

Traditionally, men's costumes are less colorful than women's costumes. Men's urban and rural clothing styles vary by region. The *anteria* is a long dress coat with wide sleeves once worn in the city. In rural areas, men wore the *panovraki* (or its variation, the *vraka*), white or dark woolen pants, narrow at the bottom and wide at the waist, with the *poukamiso*, a short pleated dress. The *foustanela* is a variation on the old style and soon became the national costume of Greece. The *foustanela* is a short white skirt of cotton or muslin with many folds that is worn above the knee. It is worn with the *fermizi*, a jacket of velvet or serge with long sleeves that is thrown over the back; waist-high white stockings; and a shirt with wide sleeves made of cotton, muslin, or silk. The *foustanela* is a common sight on Greek Independence Day.

HOLIDAYS AND CELEBRATIONS

Greeks celebrate many Greek Orthodox holy days throughout the year, in addition to Christmas Day, Easter Day, and New Year's Day. Greeks in the United States also celebrate Greek Independence Day on March 25, commemorating their independence from the Ottoman Empire in 1821. In Chicago and New York, cities with a sizable Greek population, people dress in traditional costumes and sing the national anthem. The program of events also includes a parade, public address, folk dance, song, and poetry recitation.

MUSIC AND DANCE

Greek music and dance are an expression of the national character and are appreciated by people of all ethnic backgrounds. As Marilyn Rouvelas stated in *A Guide to Greek Traditions and Customs in America:* "To the uninitiated, the music invites images of intriguing places, food and people. For the Greeks, the sounds and rhythms express their very essence: their dreams, sorrows and joys. Add dancing and nothing more need be said."

Varieties of Greek popular music include *dimotika* (*thimotika*), *laika,* and *evropaika. Dimotika* are traditional rural folk songs often accompanied by a clarinet, lute, violin dulcimer, and drum. *Laika* is an urban style of song, developed at the turn of the century, which may feature the bouzouki, a long-necked stringed instrument. *Evropaika* is Eurostyle music set to Greek words that is popular with the older generation.

Traditional Greek dances may be danced in a circle, in a straight line, or between couples. The *kalamatianos* is an ancient dance with many variations in which both men and women participate. It has 12 basic steps and is danced in a semicircle to 7/8 time. All variations are performed by the leader who stands facing the semicircle. The *sirtos,* perhaps the most ancient dance, is similar to the *kalamatianos,* but it is more controlled, performed to 2/4 time. First danced in the mountainous region of Epirus in northwestern Greece, the *tsamiko,* traditionally danced by men, is today performed by both men and women. It was danced by the fighters and rebels in the Greek Revolution of 1821. The *hasapiko* is a popular folk dance for both men and women that is danced in a straight line, with one dancer holding the shoulder of the other. The *sirtaki,* a variation of the *hasapiko,* culminates with the "Zorba" dance popularized in the movie *Zorba the Greek.* Although the Zorba has no roots in Greek dance history, it does capture the mood and temperament of the Greek spirit. Originating in the Middle East, the *tsifteteli* is a seductive dance performed by one or two people. The *zeibekiko* is a personal dance traditionally danced only by men, either singly or as a couple. It is a serious, completely self-absorbed dance in which the dancer freely improvises the steps.

LANGUAGE

Greek is a conservative language that has retained much of its original integrity. Modern Greek is derived from the Attic Koine of the first century A.D. During Byzantine times, the language underwent modifications and has incorporated many French, Turkish, and Italian words. Modern Greek retained the ancient alphabet and orthography of the more ancient language, but many changes have taken place in the phonetic value of letters and in the spelling. Although about 75 percent of the old words remain from the ancient language, words often have taken on new meanings. Modern Greek also retains from the ancient language a system of three pitch accents (acute, circumflex, grave). In 1982, a monotonic accent (one-stress accent) was officially adopted by the Greek government.

Greeks are fiercely proud of the continuity and relative stability of their language and much confusion and debate persists about "correct Greek." Two separate languages were once widely written and spoken in Greece: demotic Greek (*Demotiki*), the more popular language of the people, and *Katharevousa,* the "pure" archaic language of administration, religion, education, and literature. In 1967 demotic Greek was recognized as the official spoken and written language of Greece and is the language adopted for liturgical services by the Greek Orthodox church in the United States.

Modern Greek contains 24 characters with five vowels and four vowel sounds. It is traditionally written in Attic characters; the letters, their names, transliterations, and pronounciations are: "Aα"—alpha/a ("ah"); "Ββ"—beta/v ("v"); "Γγ"—gamma/g ("gh," "y"); "Δδ"—delta/d, dh ("th"); "Eϵ"—epsilon/e ("eh"); "Zζ"—zeta/z ("z"); "Hη"—eta/e ("ee"); "Θθ"—theta/th ("th"); "Iι"—yiota/i ("ee"); "Kκ"—kappa/k, c ("k"); "Λλ"—lambda/l("l"); "Mμ"—mu/m ("m"); "Nν"—nee/n ("n"); "Θξ"—kse/x ("ks"); "Oo"—omicron/o ("oh"); "Ππ"—pee/p ("p"); "Pρ"—rho/r ("r"); "Σσ"—sigma/s ("s"); "Tτ"—taf/t ("t"); "Υυ"—ypsilon/y ("ee"); "Φφ"—fee/ph ("f"); "Xχ"—khee/h ("ch" [as in "ach"]); "Ψψ"—psee/ps ("ps" [as in "lapse"]); "Ωω"—omega/o ("oh").

Today Greek language schools continue to encourage the study of Greek, and new generations are discovering its rich rewards.

GREETINGS AND OTHER POPULAR EXPRESSIONS

Some of the more common expressions in the Greek language include: Οχι ("ohchi")—No; Ναι ("neh")—Yes; Ευχαρσμετω (efcharisto)—Thank you; Καλημερα ("kahleemera")—Good morning; Καλησπερα ("kahleespehrah")—Good afternoon/night; Γειασου/σαζ ("yah soo/sahs")—Hello/Good-bye (informal); Χαιρετε ("chehrehteh")—Greetings/Hello (formal); Οπα! ("ohpah")—Hooray! Toasts may include Για χαρα ("yah chahrah")—For joy; Καλη τυχη ("kahlee teechee")—Good luck. Other popular expressions are Χρονια πολλα ("chrohnyah pohllah")—Many years/Happy birthday; Καλη χρονια ("kahlee chrohnyah")—Good year; Καλη Σαρακοστι ("kahlee sahrahkohstee")—Good Lent; Καλα Χριστουγεννα ("kahlah christooghehnna")—Merry Christmas. Expressions used at Easter are Καλο Πασχα ("kahloh pahschah")—Happy Easter (used before Easter); Καλη Ανασταση ("kahlee ahnahstahsee")—Good Resurrection (said after the Good Friday service); Χριστο ανεστι ("christohs ahnehstee")—Christ has risen (said after the Good Friday service) and its response, Αγηθω ανεστι ("ahleethohs ahnehstee")—Truly he has risen.

FAMILY AND COMMUNITY DYNAMICS

If there is one self-defining concept among Greeks, it is the concept of *philotomo*, which may be translated as "love of honor." *Philotomo* is a highly developed sense of right and wrong involving personal pride and honor and obligation to family and community. It shapes and regulates an individual's relationships as a member of both a family and the community. Because the acts of each individual affect the entire family and community, each person must work to maintain both personal and family honor. It is *philotomo* that "laid the foundation for Greek success in America," wrote G. Kunkelman in *The Religion of Ethnicity*.

The idea of family and attachment to the Greek Orthodox church remains strong among Greek Americans. In many communities, the ideal family is still a patriarchy where the man, as husband and father, is a central authority figure and the woman a wife and mother. Children are highly valued, and frequently parents will sacrifice a great deal to see that their children accomplish their goals. Elderly parents may still move in with their children, but "Americanization," with accompanying affluence, assimilation, and mobilization, has rendered this arrangement less practicable.

Another change from traditional Greek custom is the rising number of marriages between Orthodox and non-Orthodox Greeks. The 1994 *Yearbook* of the Greek Orthodox Archdiocese of North and South America reports that between 1976 and 1992, the number of marriages between Orthodox Greeks was 35,767, while the number between Orthodox and non-Orthodox Greeks was 53,790; the divorce rate is 6,629 and 5,552, respectively.

WEDDINGS

The wedding service conducted by a Greek Orthodox priest may be said in both Greek and in English, but the traditional elements of the Greek wedding remain unchanged. The hour-long ceremony is conducted around a small table on which two wedding crowns, the book of the Gospels, the wedding rings, a cup of wine, and two white candles are placed. The two-part Greek Orthodox wedding includes the betrothal and the wedding proper. During the betrothal the rings are blessed to signify that the couple is betrothed by the church. The priest first blesses the rings and then, with the rings, blesses the couple, touching their foreheads with the sign of the cross. The rings are placed on the bride's and groom's right hands, and the official wedding sponsors (*koumbari*) exchange the rings three times. During the wedding ceremony the bride and groom each hold a lighted white candle and join right hands while the priest prays over them. Crowns (*stephana*) joined with a ribbon are placed on their heads, and the *koumbaros* (male) or *koumbara* (female) is responsible for exchanging the wedding crowns three times above the heads of the couple during the service. Traditionally read are the Epistle of Saint Paul to the Ephesians and the second chapter of the Gospel of Saint John, which stress the mutual respect and love the couple now owe each other and the sanctity of the married state. After the couple shares a common cup of wine, they are led around the table by the priest in the Dance of Isaiah, which symbolizes the joy of the church in the new marriage. The *koumbaros* follows, holding the ribbon that joins the crowns. With the blessing of the priest, the couple is proclaimed married, and the crowns are removed.

The wedding reception reflects the influence of both Greek and American tradition and is notable for its abundance of food, dancing, and singing. The wedding cake is served along with an assortment of Greek sweets that may include baklava and *kalamatianos*, and *koufeta*—traditional wedding candy—is often distributed in candy dishes or in *bonbonieries* (small favors given to guests after the wedding).

BAPTISM/CHRISMATION

The *koumbari* who act as wedding sponsors usually act as godparents for a couple's first child. The baptism begins at the narthex of the church, where the godparents speak for the child, renouncing Satan, blowing three times in the air, and spitting three times on the floor. They then recite the Nicene Creed. The priest uses the child's baptismal name for the first time and asks God to cleanse away sin. The priest, the godparents, and the child go to the baptismal font at the front of the church, where the priest consecrates the water, adding olive oil to it as a symbol of reconciliation. The child is undressed, and the priest makes the sign of the cross on various parts of the child's body. The godparents rub olive oil over the child's body, and the priest thrice immerses the child in the water of the baptismal font to symbolize the three days Christ spent in the tomb. The godparents then receive the child and wrap it in a new white sheet. During chrismation, immediately following baptism, the child is anointed with a special oil (*miron*), which has been blessed by the Ecumenical Patriarch of Constantinople. The child is dressed in new clothing, and a cross is placed around its neck. After the baptismal candle is lighted, the priest and godparents hold the child, and a few children walk around the font in a dance of joy. Finally, scriptures are read, and communion is given to the child.

FUNERALS

The funeral service in the Greek Orthodox church is called *kithia*. Traditionally, the *trisayion* (the three holies) is recited at the time of death or at any time during a 40-day mourning period. In the United States the *trisayion* is repeated at the funeral service. At the beginning of the service, the priest greets the mourners at the entrance of the church. An open casket is arranged so that the deceased faces the altar. During the service mourners recite scriptures, prayers, and hymns, and they are invited by the priest to pay their last respects to the deceased by filing past the casket and kissing the icon that has been placed within. The family gathers around the casket for a last farewell, and the priest sprinkles oil on the body in the form of the cross and says a concluding prayer. After the priest, friends, or family members deliver a brief eulogy, the body is taken immediately for burial (*endaphiasmos*). At the cemetery the priest recites the *trisayion* for the last time and sprinkles dirt on the casket while reciting a prayer. After the funeral guests and family share a funeral meal (*makaria*), which traditionally consists of brandy, coffee, and *paximathia* (hard, dry toast). A full meal may also be served, with fish as the main course.

THE ROLE OF WOMEN

As stated in the introduction to *American Aphrodite*, "Greek-American women have been without a voice since the first Greek immigrants arrived here as wives, mothers, sisters and daughters, usually, but not always, some months behind the menfolk, making no sound, proclaiming no existence." Traditionally, the lives of Greek women have centered on the home, the family, and the Greek Orthodox church. Since the earliest period of settlement in the United States, the burden of preserving Greek culture and tradition has been the responsibility of women. Women among the first and second generations of immigrants became the traditional keepers of songs, dances, and other folk customs and often cut themselves off from the *xeni*, the foreigners, who were essentially anyone outside the Greek community.

Today many Greek women are seriously challenged in their efforts to accommodate the values of two different worlds. The pressure to remain part of the community, obey parents' rules, and be "good Greek girls" who marry "well" and bear children is still strong. The conflict arises between family loyalty and self-realization, between duty to parents and community and the pursuit of the "American way of life." Many Greek American girls are given less freedom than their male counterparts and tend to remain close to their mothers even after marriage. The pursuit of education and a career is secondary and may even be perceived as "un-Greek" or unwomanly.

Although Greeks tend to be a highly educated ethnic group, the pursuit of higher education remains the province of men. The 1990 Census reports that twice as many Greek men as women received university degrees, with a significantly higher proportion of men going on to receive advanced degrees.

"I felt grateful the Statue of Liberty was a woman. I felt she would understand a woman's heart." Stella Petrakis in 1916, cited in *Ellis Island: An Illustrated History of the Immigrant Experience,* edited by Ivan Chermayeff et al. (New York: Macmillan, 1991).

RELIGION

Theodore Salutos in *The Greeks in the United States* wrote: "Hellenism and Greek Orthodoxy—the one intertwined with the other—served as the cord that kept the immigrant attached to the mother country, nourished his patriotic appetites and helped him preserve the faith and language of his parents." The Greek Orthodox church helped to meet the emotional and spiritual needs of the immigrant. The early churches grew out of the *kinotitos* (community) where a *symvoulion* (board of directors) raised the money to build the church. The first Greek Orthodox church in the United States was founded in New Orleans in 1864. As Greek communities grew, other churches were established in New York (1892); Chicago (1893); Lowell, Massachusetts (1903); and Boston (1903). By 1923, there were 140 Greek churches in the United States.

Today, the liturgy and spirit of the Greek Orthodox church help to keep alive Greek ethnic cultural traditions in the United States. According to Kunkelman, to a Greek American, "ethnicity is synonymous with the church. One is a Greek not because he is a Hellene by birth; indeed many of Greek parentage have abandoned their identities and disappeared into the American mainstream. Rather one is Greek because he elects to remain part of the Greek community and an individual is a member of the Greek community by virtue of his attachment to the Greek Orthodox church, the framework on which the community rests."

For many, the Greek Orthodox church is the center of community life. In the United States all dioceses, parishes, and churches are under the ecclesiastical jurisdiction of the Archdiocese of North and South America, an autonomous self-governing church within the sphere of influence of the Ecumenical Patriarch of Constantinople and New Rome. The Ecumenical Patriarch has the power to elect the archbishop and the bishops, directs all church matters outside the American church, and remains the guiding force in all matters of faith. Founded in 1922, the Archdiocese is located in New York City. It supports 62 parishes in the Archdiocesan District of New York, as well as the parishes in ten dioceses across the Americas.

"Orthodox" comes from the Greek *orthos* (correct) and *doxa* (teaching or worship). The Greek Orthodox share a common liturgy, worship, and tradition. In its fundamental beliefs, the church is conservative, resistant to change, and allows little flexibility. The Orthodox tradition is an Eastern tradition with the official center of Orthodoxy at Constantinople. After the tenth century Eastern and Western traditions grew apart on matters of faith, dogma, customs, and politics. East and West finally divided on the issue of papal authority.

The basic beliefs of the Orthodox are summarized in the Nicene Creed dating back to the fourth century. The Orthodox believe that one can achieve complete identification with God (*theosis*). All activities and services in the church are to assist the individual in achieving that end. The most important service is the Divine Liturgy in which there are four distinct liturgies: St. John Chrysostom (the one most frequently followed), St. Basil (followed ten times a year), St. James (October 23), and the Liturgy of the Presanctified Gifts (Wednesdays and Fridays of Lent and the first three days of Easter Holy Week). The church uses Greek Koine, the language of New Testament

Greek, as its liturgical language. The seven sacraments in the church are Baptism, Chrismation, Confession, Communion, Marriage, Holy Unction (Anointing of the Sick), and Holy Orders. The Greek Orthodox calendar has many feast days, fast days, and name days. The most important feast day ("the feast of feasts") is Holy Pascha (Easter Sunday). In addition to Easter, the "twelve great feasts" are the Nativity of the Mother of God, the Exaltation of the Holy Cross, the Presentation of the Mother of God in the Temple, Christmas, Epiphany, the Presentation of Jesus Christ in the Temple, Palm Sunday, Ascension of Jesus Christ, Pentecost, the Transfiguration of Jesus Christ, and the Dormition (death) of the Mother of God.

The Greek Orthodox church also follows the Byzantine tradition in its architecture. The church is divided into the vestibule (the front of the church representing the world), the nave (the main area where people assemble), and the sanctuary. The sanctuary is separated from the nave by an iconostasis, a screenlike partition. Only the priests enter the sanctuary. Icons (images of saints) decorate the iconostasis in prescribed tiers. The service takes place in the sanctuary, which contains an altar table and an oblation (preparation) table. The Greek Orthodox church is filled with symbols, including crosses and icons, which create an aura of heaven on earth.

The church today continues to face the process of Americanization. The American Orthodox church has many American elements: an American-trained clergy, the introduction of English into the service, modern music written for organ, modern architecture and architectural features (pews, choir lofts, separate social halls). The limited role of women in the church is being questioned. Until the second century, women fully participated in the church as teachers, preachers, and deacons. After that period, however, their roles were limited by official decree. Today women are taking more active leadership roles; however, the question of ordaining women to the priesthood has not been seriously considered.

EMPLOYMENT AND ECONOMIC TRADITIONS

The first immigrants were for the most part young single men who had no intention of remaining permanently in the United States. They came to work in the large industrial cities of the Northeast

and Midwest as factory laborers, peddlers, busboys, and bootblacks. Those who went to the mill towns of New England worked in textile and shoe factories, while the Greeks who went West worked in mines and on the railroads. These Greeks often were subject to the *pardone* system, a form of exploitative indentured servitude employed in many of the larger industrial cities of the North and in the large mining corporations of the West.

Greeks in America have stressed individual efforts and talent and have had a long tradition of entrepreneurship in the United States, and many who were peddlers and street merchants in the United States became owners of small businesses. First-generation Greeks who were fruit and vegetable peddlers became owners of grocery stores; flower vendors opened florist shops. Greeks in Lowell, Massachusetts, became successful in numerous businesses. By 1912, according to a publication of the National Park Service, *Lowell: The Story of an Industrial City*, they owned "seven restaurants, twenty coffee houses, twelve barber shops, two drug stores, six fruit stores, eight shoeshine parlors, one dry-goods store, four ticket agencies, seven bakeries, four candy stores [and] twenty-two grocery stores."

In the 1920s Greeks owned thousands of confectionery stores across the country and usually owned the candy-manufacturing businesses that supplied the stores. When the candy businesses collapsed, Greeks became restaurant owners. By the late 1920s several thousand Greek restaurants were scattered across the country. Many immigrants of the 1950s and 1960s went into the fast-food restaurant business.

The Greek professional class remained small until the 1940s. During the first quarter of the twentieth century, most Greek professionals were doctors. The next largest group comprised lawyers, dentists, pharmacists, and chemists. A few became professors of literature, philosophy, and the classics. Although the Greeks were slow to develop an academic tradition in this country in part because of low economic incentive, a new professional class began to emerge after World War I. Today Greek Americans engage in many professional academic endeavors. Instead of remaining in family-held businesses, third- and fourth-generation Greek Americans increasingly are pursuing professional careers.

Currently, Greeks are found in almost every occupation and enterprise and constitute one of the wealthier economic groups in the United States. The average per capita income of all persons with Greek ancestry according to the 1990 Census is $18,361.

POLITICS AND GOVERNMENT

Numerous Greek American political and social organizations have existed since the 1880s. These organizations often were made up of Greeks who had come from the same region in Greece. They had a shared sense of Hellenism and a common religion and language and often aligned themselves with native Greek concerns. The *kinotitos* (community) was an organization similar to the village government in Greece. Although the *kinotitos* helped to preserve Greek traditions, it sometimes hindered assimilation.

In 1907 the Pan-Hellenic Union was founded to coordinate and incorporate local organizations; to provide a means of helping Greece obtain more territory from the Ottoman Empire; and to support the return of Constantinople to Greece and the consolidation of all Greek colonies in the Eastern Mediterranean under Greek authority. It also helped Greeks to adapt to their new home in the United States. Many Greek immigrants were slowly beginning to accept the fact that they would not be returning to Greece and that the United States was their permanent home. In 1922 the American Hellenic Educational Progressive Association (AHEPA) was founded. Although the AHEPA supported the assimilation of Greeks to the American way of life, it did not relinquish its strong attachments to Greece. During World War II, the AHEPA was a major contributor to the Greek War Relief Association.

The one issue that mobilized the Greek American community to political action was the Turkish invasion of Cyprus on July 15, 1974. The efforts of well-organized lobby groups to effect an arms embargo against Turkey were impressive. The AHEPA played a leading role in these activities, along with other lobby groups—the American Hellenic Institute and its public affairs committee, the influential United Hellenic American Congress, and the Hellenic Council of America. The Greek Orthodox church and local community organizations also assisted. Primarily because of the successful lobbying of these groups, the United States imposed an arms embargo on Turkey on February 5, 1975.

Greek political figures are almost overwhelmingly Democratic. They include Michael Dukakis, Paul Tsongas, John Brademas, Paul Spyro Sarbanes, and George Stephanopoulos. Although Greek Americans traditionally have voted Democratic, their increasing wealth and status have led to an even division within the Greek American community between Republicans and Democrats.

MILITARY

Greek Americans have participated in large numbers in all major wars fought by the United States. Greek American men with veteran status number 90,530; women number 2,635.

INDIVIDUAL AND GROUP CONTRIBUTIONS

Greek Americans have made significant contributions in virtually all of the arts, sciences, and humanities, as well as in politics and business. Following is a sample of their achievements.

ACADEMIA

Aristides Phoutridis, a distinguished professor at Yale University, established Helikon, the first

Greek student organization, in 1911 in Boston. George Mylonas (1898-1988) had a distinguished career in the fields of Classical and Bronze Age art and archaeology. His numerous books include *Mycenae, the Capital City of Agamemnon* (1956), *Aghios Kosmas* (1959), *Eleusis and the Eleusinian Mysteries* (1961), *Mycenae and the Mycenean Age* (1966), *Mycenae's Last Century of Greatness* (1968), *Grave Circle B of Mycenae* (1972), *The Cult Center of Mycenae* (1972), and *The West Cemetery of Eleusis* (1975). Theodore Salutos (1910-1980) was a professor of history at the University of California, Los Angeles, who is well known for his studies of the Greek immigration experience. His most important work, *Greeks in the United States* (1964), became a model for other works on this topic.

EDUCATION

John Celivergos Zachos (1820-1898), one of 40 orphans who came to the United States during the Greek Revolution of 1821, was associate principal of the Cooper Female Seminary in Dayton, Ohio (1851-1854), principal and teacher of literature in the grammar school of Antioch College in Yellow Springs, Ohio (1854-1857), a surgeon during the Civil War, a teacher at Meadville Theological School (1866-1867), and a teacher and curator at Cooper Union in New York until 1898. Michael Anagnos (1837-1906) became the director of the famous Perkins Institute for the Blind in Boston where he promoted vocational training and self-help.

FILM, TELEVISION, AND THEATER

Olympia Dukakis (1931-), a well-known film actress and the cousin of politician Michael Dukakis, has appeared in a number of roles since the 1960s. Selected films include *Lilith* (1964), *Twice a Man* (1964), *John and Mary* (1969), *Made for Each Other* (1971), and *The Idolmaker* (1980). Her most recent films are *Steel Magnolias* (1989) and *Moonstruck* (1987), for which she won an Academy Award for Best Supporting Actress. John Cassavetes (1929-1989) was a well-known stage, screen, and television actor, director, playwright, and screenwriter. His many film appearances include *Fourteen* (1951), *Affair in Havana* (1957), *The Killers* (1964), *The Dirty Dozen* (1967), and *Rosemary's Baby* (1968). He directed and produced many films including *Too Late Blues* (1962), *A Child Is Waiting* (1963), *A Woman under the Influence* (1974), and *Big Trouble* (1986). George Tsakiris

(1933-), a singer, dancer, and actor, has been in films since the 1940s. He starred in roles in *Gentlemen Prefer Blondes* (1953); *White Christmas* (1954); *West Side Story* (1961), for which he won a Golden Globe Award and an Academy Award for Best Supporting Actor; *Diamond Head* (1962); and *Is Paris Burning?* (1963). Elia Kazan (1909-) was born Elia Kazanjoglou in Constantinople. He is well known as a director, producer, actor, and writer. His best-known productions include *A Streetcar Named Desire* (1951), *A Face in the Crowd* (1957), *Splendor in the Grass* (1961), *America, America* (1963), and *The Arrangement* (1969). He directed such films as *A Tree Grows in Brooklyn* (1945), *Gentlemen's Agreement* (1947), *On the Waterfront* (1953), and *East of Eden* (1954). His writings include *America, America* (1962), *The Arrangement* (1969), *The Assassins* (1972), *The Understudy* (1974), *Acts of Love* (1978), and *The Anatolian* (1982). Katina Paxinou (1900-1973), born Katina Constantopoulos, was a popular actress who starred in many films, including *For Whom the Bell Tolls* (1943), *Confidential Agent* (1945), *Mourning Becomes Electra* (1947), *The Inheritance* (1947), and *Prince of Foxes* (1945). Telly Savalas (1923-1994), a popular film and television actor, is best known for his role as Theo Kojack in the National Broadcasting Corporation's television series "Kojack" (1973). Born in Garden City, New York, Savalas starred in several films including *The Young Savages* (1961), *Birdman of Alcatraz* (1962), *The Greatest Story Ever Told* (1965), and *The Dirty Dozen* (1967).

JOURNALISM

Constantine Phasoularides published the first Greek American newspaper in New York in 1892, the *Neos Kosmas* (*New World*). Nicholas Gage (1939-), born in Lia, is a journalist and writer, associated with the *Worcester Telegram and Evening Gazette*, *Boston Herald Traveler*, Associated Press, *Wall Street Journal*, and the *New York Times*. He left the *New York Times* in 1980 to write *Eleni*, a work detailing the events surrounding the execution of his mother by Communist guerrillas in Greece in the 1940s.

LITERATURE

In 1906 Mary Vardoulakis wrote *Gold in the Streets*, the first Greek American novel. Olga Broumas (1949-), born in Syros, is a feminist poet who writes a poetry of the "body" with distinct lesbian-erotic motifs. Many of her poems capture the spirit of the Greek homeland. Her works include *Beginning with O* (1977), *Sole Savage* (1980), *Pastoral Jazz* (1983), and *Perpetua* (1985). Kostantinos Lardas (1927-) writes both poetry and fiction. His major works are *The Devil Child* (1961) and *And In Him Too; In Us*, which was nominated for a Pulitzer Prize in 1964. Henry Mark Petrakis (1923-) is a major figure in Greek American fiction. His novels include *Lion of My Heart* (1959), *The Odyssey of Kostas Volakis* (1963), *The Dream of Kings* (1966), *In the Land of Morning* (1973), and *Hour of the Bell* (1976). Petrakis writes of the immigrant experience of the conflict between the old and new generations.

MILITARY

Captain George Partridge Colvocoresses (1816-1872) distinguished himself as commander of the *Saratoga* in the Civil War. His son Rear Admiral George P. Colvocoresses fought in the Spanish-American War was appointed the commandant of midshipmen at the U.S. Naval Academy.

MUSIC

Dimitri Mitropoulos (1896-1960), a well-known composer-conductor, conducted the Minneapolis Symphony (1937-1949) and the New York Philharmonic. Maria Callas (1923-1977), born Mary Kalogeropoulou, was a noted operatic soprano. Callas made her film debut in *Tosca* (1941). She is remembered as a true artist for her original interpretations of Bellini, Donizetti, and Cherubini and in her roles as Norma, Medea, Violetta, and Lucia, as well as Tosca.

POLITICS

The first Greek American to be elected to the U.S. Congress was Lucas Miltiades Miller (1824-1902). Miller, a Democrat from Wisconsin, served in Congress from March 4, 1891, to March 3, 1893. Spiro Agnew (1918-), a Republican who served as governor of Maryland in 1966, became vice president of the United States under Richard Nixon on November 5, 1968, and was reelected as vice president on November 7, 1972. John Brademas (1927-), a Democrat from Indiana, served in Congress from 1959 to 1981. He became president of New York State University in 1981 until his retirement in 1992. Michael Dukakis (1933-) was governor of Massachusetts in 1975-1979 and 1983-1991 and was Democratic candidate for president in 1988. Paul Efthemios

Tsongas (1941-), congressman from Massachusetts, served in the House of Representatives during 1974-1979 and in the U.S. Senate during 1979-1985. Paul Spyro Sabannes (1933-) was a Democratic congressman from Maryland who was reelected to the Senate in 1982. Gus Yatron (1927-), Democratic congressman from Pennsylvania, served in the U.S. House of Representatives during 1969-1989. George Stephanopoulos (1961-) was director of communications for President Bill Clinton's administration during 1992-1993 before becoming senior advisor to the president for policy and strategy.

SCIENCE AND TECHNOLOGY

George Papnicolaou (1883-1961) was professor emeritus of anatomy at Cornell Medical College. His research led him to develop the "pap smear," a test designed to detect cervical cancer. Polyvios Koryllos was a professor of medicine at the University of Athens and Yale University. He is well known for his work in diagnosing tuberculosis. John Kotzias was a neurologist who discovered the drug L-dopa for the treatment of Parkinson's disease.

SPORTS

Alex Karras (1935-) was a well-known football player (a two-time All-American) for the Detroit Lions from 1958 to 1971. He hosted the National Football League's Monday Night Football and has made numerous television appearances. Alex Grammas (1926-) was a professional baseball player between 1954 and 1963 who played with the St. Louis Cardinals, Cincinnati Reds, and the Chicago Cubs. He was a baseball manager in 1969 and 1976-1977. Harry Agganis (1930-1955) distinguished himself in baseball, football, and basketball. Although he was drafted by the Cleveland Browns football team on graduation from Boston University in 1953, he signed with the Boston Red Sox. Jimmy Londos (c. 1895-1975), born Christopher Theophilus, won the world heavyweight wrestling championship on June 25, 1934.

MEDIA

PRINT

Historically, the Greek ethnic press in the United States has kept pace with the needs of Greek

Americans, and its presence has contributed to a strong ethnic cohesion in the Greek community. The first Greek American newspaper in the country was *Neos Kosmos* (*New World*), first published in New York by Constantine Phasoularides in September 1897. It was followed by the *Thermopylae*, published by John Booras in 1900. The *Ethnikos Keryx* (*National Herald*), which began publication in New York on April 2, 1915, was one of the few newspapers to have a significant influence on the Greek reading public. Its serious competitors in New York are *Proini* (*Morning News*), which publishes only in Greek, and the *Greek American*, which publishes only in English. In Chicago the *Greek Star* (*Hellenikos Aster*) and the *Greek Press* (*Hellenikos Typos*), both published in Greek and English, still hold a sizable readership.

Currently, there are 27 Greek American newspapers in the United States; seven are published in either Greek or English, respectively, and 14 are published in both languages. The majority focus on community events and church news, as well as on news from Greece and the lobbying activities of Greek American politicians.

Campana.

Founded in 1917, *Campana* is published semi-monthly in Greek and English and features the news from Greece, with information about Greeks abroad. Covers local and community events.

Contact: Costas Athansasiades, Editor.

Address: 30-96 42nd Street, Long Island City (Astoria), New York 11101.

Telephone: (718) 278-3014.

Ethnikos Keryx (The National Herald).

Begun in 1915, the *Herald* is the oldest daily newspaper in the Greek language in the United States. Features international, national, and local news and items about Greece of interest to the community.

Contact: Anthony Diamataris, Editor.

Address: 41-17 Crescent Street, Long Island City, New York 11101.

Telephone: (718) 784-5255.

The Greek American.

Widely read English-language publication that focuses on the political events in Greece and in the United States. Publishes a national calendar of events that lists activities taking place in the larger Greek community.

Contact: Tina Maurikos, Editor.

Address: 25-50 Crescent Street, Astoria, New York 11102.

Telephone: (718) 626-7676.

Fax: (718) 956-8076.

Greek Press (Hellenikos Typos).

Founded in 1929 and published bi-weekly in English and Greek, *Greek Press* covers political, educational, and social events, as well as local and international news of interest to the Greek community.

Contact: Helen Angelopoulos, Editor.

Address: 808 West Jackson Boulevard, Chicago, Illinois 60607.

Telephone: (708) 766-2955.

Fax: (708) 766-3069.

Greek Star (Hellenikos-Aster).

Founded in 1904, *Greek Star* is the oldest continuously published Greek newspaper in the United States. A bi-weekly publication of the United Hellenic American Congregation, it appears in Greek and English and features local and international news of interest to the Greek community in Chicago. Covers news from Cyprus and Greece.

Contact: Nicholas Philippidis, Editor.

Address: 4715 North Lincoln, Chicago, Illinois 60625.

Telephone: (312) 878-7331.

The Hellenic Chronicle.

A weekly English-language publication dedicated to the promulgation of American, Hellenic, and Orthodox ideals. Features political, national, international, and local news of interest to the Greek community. Contains an Entertainment Arts and Social section.

Contact: Nancy Agris Savage, Editor.

Address: 324 Newbury Street, Boston, Massachusetts 02115.

Telephone: (617) 262-4500.

Proini.

Competing with *The National Herald*, this daily publishes community news and news from Greece and Cyprus, sporting events, artistic and cultural events, and editorials.

Contact: Fanny Holliday Petallides, Publisher.

Address: 25-50 Crescent Street, Astoria, New York 11102.

Telephone: (718) 626-7676.

RADIO

WEDC-AM.

"Hellenic American Radio Hour" airs every Saturday, 7:00 to 8:00 p.m. One of the oldest Greek radio shows in the Chicago area (75 years). Features community events, discussion of family problems, religious issues, music, and news from Greece.

Contact: Tom Chiampas and Katina Chiampas.

Address: 5413 North Nagle Avenue, Chicago, Illinois 60630.

Telephone: (312) 775-6577.

WEEF-AM.

"Greek Orthodox Hours of the Chicago Diocese" airs every Tuesday and Wednesday, 11:00 p.m. to 12:00 a.m. Discusses topics related to the Greek Orthodox church.

Contact: Paula Rekoumis and Sotirios Rekoumis.

Address: 7902 Maple Street, Morton Grove, Illinois.

Telephone: (708) 967-8798.

WLYN-AM.

"Soul of Greece" programs are scheduled daily Monday through Friday (3:00 p.m. to 7:00 p.m.), Saturday (2:00 p.m. to 6:00 p.m.), Sunday (8:00 a.m. to 12:00 p.m.; and 1:00 p.m. to 2:00 p.m. Features local, community, and international news; cultural events; sports; and music. Broadcasts about 95 percent in Greek (with the news in English).

Contact: Oscar Papanastasiou or Pauline Papanastasiou.

Address: 427 Union Street, Lynn, Massachusetts 01910.

Telephone: (617) 592-3002.

WNTN-AM.

"Greek Cultural Radio Program of Boston," a noncommercial, one-hour program that broadcasts twice a week. Features topics relating to Greek heritage, customs, and history. In Greek and English.

Contact: Athanasios Vulgaropoulos.

Address: 26 Tudor Street, Waltham, Massachusetts 02154.

Telephone: (617) 894-7666.

WUNR.

"The Other Program," a talk show where people can call in with questions; "The Athenian Hour," featuring cultural and news events; "Hellenic Voice of Massachusetts"; "Let Us Sing," playing selections of Greek music.

Address: 160 North Washington, Boston, Massachusetts 02114.

Telephone: (617) 367-9003.

TELEVISION

Cable Television Network (CTN) of New Jersey, Inc.

A 24-hour cable network service available to more than 1.7 million homes in New Jersey. The cable service currently airs "Greek Orthodox," produced by Greek Orthodox Communications, Inc.

Contact: James DeBold, Information Manager.

Address: 128 West State Street, Trenton, New Jersey 08608.

Telephone: (609) 392-8682.

"Grecian Spotlight," Channel 26, Chicago.

A weekly show that highlights community events in the Chicago area, sports, news, and music of Greece.

Contact: Ernest Panos, Producer.

Address: 168 North Michigan Avenue, Chicago, Illinois 60601.

Telephone: (312) 906-8888.

"The Greek Spirit," WYBE, Channel 35, Philadelphia.

The program broadcasts on Sundays, 10:00 p.m. to 11:00 p.m. About 80 percent of the program is in the Greek language. It features dance, local and community events, news from Greece (through ERT-1, Channel 1, from Athens). Through cable services, the program is seen in New York and New Jersey. Channel 35 also broadcasts "Hellenic World" (in English), on Sundays, 4:30 p.m. to 5:00 p.m. It features items on the history, historical personalities, and antiquities of Greece and Greek life.

Contact: George Burlotos.

Address: Cooper Landing, Suite 4E, Cherry Hill, New Jersey 08002.

Telephone: (609) 482-5681.

"Hellenic Television Program," Channel 47, New York.

The program broadcasts one and one-half hours every week, on Sundays. It includes documentaries, sports, dances, news from Greece, and local and community events. It can be seen in the tristate area of New York, Connecticut, and New Jersey.

Contact: Takis Paralikas.

Address: 32-09 31st Avenue, Astoria, New York 11106.

Telephone: (718) 956-3434.

"National Greek TV Show," Channel 26, Chicago, and Channel 47, New York.
A weekly variety show (one hour in Chicago; one and one-half hours in New York) that features local events, national and international news, sports, interviews, and music. The show is part of the *Greek Channel* distributed by Time Warner Cable (serving Queens, New York, and West Brooklyn), which broadcasts Greek programming for 19 hours a day.

Contact: Demitrios Kastanas, Producer.

Address: 30-97 Steinway Street, No. 206, Astoria, New York 11103.

Telephone: (718)726-0900.

ORGANIZATIONS AND ASSOCIATIONS

Greek Orthodox Ladies Philoptochos Society.
Founded in 1931. The Society promotes the values of the family and the Greek Orthodox faith and engages in many charitable, educational, and religious activities on behalf of the church. Its membership of more than 400,000 includes women 18 years and older.

Contact: Terry Kokas, Director.

Address: 345 East 74th Street, New York, New York 10021.

Telephone: (212) 744-4390.

Greek Orthodox Youth Adult League.
Conducts workshops on religious education for Greek youth. Assists the church both nationally and locally, with 6,000 to 10,000 members.

Contact: Tom Kanelos.

Address: 80 East 79th Street, New York, New York 10021.

Telephone: (708) 295-7924

Order of American Hellenic Educational Progressive Association (AHEPA).
Founded in 1922. The AHEPA is dedicated to the preservation of the Greek national identity in the United States. The oldest Greek fraternal organization in the United States has a membership of more than 500,000 members, with many chapters across the county. It engages in numerous charitable, publishing, and educational activities. It includes the Daughters of Penelope, a women's auxiliary; the Maids of Athens, a girls' organization; and the Sons of Pericles, a boys' organization. Publishes *AHEPAN*, a bimonthly.

Contact: Constantine Gekas, Executive Director.

Address: 1909 Q Street, N.W., Suite 500, Washington, D.C. 20009.

Telephone: (202) 232-6300.

United Hellenic American Congress (UHAC).
Founded in 1974. The UHAC was established to preserve the cultural traditions of Greece. It coordinates many of the cultural activities of the Greek community in the Chicago area. Every year the UHAC issues a Greek Heritage Calendar of Events and is active in promoting the Greek Independence Day parade. The UHAC was a prominent lobbyist in the Greek American protest against the Turkish invasion of Cyprus.

Contact: Andrew Athens.

Address: 40 North Franklin, Suite 215, Chicago, Illinois 60610.

Telephone: (312) 822-9888.

MUSEUMS AND RESEARCH CENTERS

Greek-American Folklore Society.
Founded 1983. Society members conduct classes and workshops on traditional dances and songs from every region of Greece. The Society presents hundreds of performances throughout the year and offers exhibits of and lectures on traditional Greek costumes. It coordinates the *Panegyri*, an annual conference of Greek folklore societies, as well as the Hellenic Folk Music Festival. The Society has 50 to 60 members.

Contact: Paul Ginis.

Address: 29-04 Ditmars Boulevard, Astoria, New York 11105.

Telephone: (718) 728-8048.

Hellenic Cultural Museum at Holy Trinity Cathedral.

Opened on May 3, 1992. The museum is considered to be the first Greek cultural museum in the United States. This "people's museum" contains important collections of scrapbooks, diaries, letters, artifacts, newspapers, and photographs documenting the lives of the Greeks who settled in Utah from 1905 to the present. The museum contains a unique display of mining operations.

Contact: Chris Metos.

Address: 279 South 300 West, Salt Lake City, Utah 84101.

Telephone: (801) 328-9681.

Hellenic Museum and Cultural Center.

Opened 1992. The center preserves original documents, artifacts, and other archival source materials relating to the Greek American immigrant experience. It also collects the artistic works (crafts, embroideries, furniture) of Greek Americans.

Contact: Elaine Kollintzas, Executive Director.

Address: 400 North Franklin Street, Chicago, Illinois 60610.

Telephone: (312) 467-4622.

Immigration History Research Center.

Located at the University of Minnesota, this center contains important primary source materials on many aspects of the life of Greek immigrants in the United States. The collection includes the papers of the immigrant historian Theodore Salutos.

Contact: Joe Whorl.

Address: 826 Berry Street, St. Paul, Minnesota 55114.

Telephone: (612) 627-4208.

Saint Photios Foundation.

Founded in 1981. A Greek fraternal organization dedicated to preserving a shrine in Saint Augustine, Florida, commemorating the Greeks of New Smyrna, the first Greeks immigrants to arrive in America in 1768. The museum has a small library and cultural exhibit.

Contact: Father Dimitrios Couchell.

Address: 41 Saint George Street, Post Office Box 1960, Saint Augustine, Florida 32085.

Telephone: (904) 829-8205.

SOURCES FOR ADDITIONAL STUDY

Callincos, Constance. *American Aphrodite: Becoming Female in Greek America*. New York: Pella, 1990.

Kunkelman, Gary. *The Religion of Ethnicity: Belief and Belonging in a Greek-American Community*. New York: Garland, 1990.

Moskos, Charles C. *Greek Americans: Struggle and Success*, second edition. New Brunswick, New Jersey: Transaction, 1989.

Mouzaki, Rozanna. *Greek Dances for Americans*. Garden City, New York: Doubleday, 1981.

Pappas, Susan. "The Greek-American Press Marks Its 100th Anniversary This Year," *Editor and Publisher*, September 1992, pp. 18-19.

Rouvelas, Marilyn. *A Guide to Greek Traditions and Customs in America*. Bethesda, Maryland: Attica, 1993.

Salutos, Theodore. *The Greeks in the United States*. Cambridge: Harvard University Press, 1964.

Scourby, Alice. *The Greek Americans*. Boston: Twayne, 1977.

Treasured Greek Proverbs, compiled, edited, and translated by Elaine G. Bucuvalas, Catherine G. Lavrakas, and Poppy G. Stamatos. (1980).

U.S. Department of Commerce, Economics and Statistics Administration. *Ancestry of the Population in the United States, 1990*. Washington, D.C.: Government Printing Office, 1990.

U.S. Department of the Interior, National Park Service, Division of Publications. *Lowell: The Story of an Industrial City*. Washington, D.C.: Government Printing Office, 1990.

GYPSY

by
Evan Heimlich

AMERICANS

Gypsies value luck and health. Ideas about health and illness among the Rom are closely related to a world view (*romania*), which includes notions of good and bad luck, purity and impurity, inclusion and exclusion.

OVERVIEW

Ethnic Gypsies are descendants of an ancient Indian caste that roamed westward. Ethnic Gypsies in the United States from eastern and southern Europe call themselves Rom; those from Great Britain are Romnichals (who may be related to Irish tinkers and travelers); and those from Spain or Mexico may be known as Gitanos. Each group of ethnic Gypsies draws its own line to determine which other groups they consider Gypsy, and which not. Estimates of the total population of ethnic Gypsies in the United States range from 250,000 to one million.

HISTORY

The Gypsies originated in India as the *Dom*, a caste of strolling entertainers who beat drums, sang, and danced. According to Angus Frazier's *The Gypsies*, they spoke a branch of Hindi. Among the vegetarian Hindus (as among the Punjabi and other tribes of India) they constituted a low-caste of meat-eating, dark-skinned, menial workers. Near the end of the ninth century B.C. an Indian King, Shangul, sent 10,000 *Dom* to Persia (now Iran) as minstrel musicians. According to Jean Paul Clébert (*The Gypsies*, translated by Charles Duff [Harmondsworth: Penguin, 1967], p. 40) their remarkable story is recorded in the Persian nation-

This gypsy woman is participating in a traditional dance.

al epic poem, *Shah Nameh* (*Book of Kings*), by poet Firdawsi. In the poem, Bahram Gur, the Persian monarch, has declared that everyone in his kingdom should work only half a day and should spend the other half listening to music, eating, and drinking. He seeks lute players and other Indians to ease the burdensome existence and the tedium of work of his people and requests the Indian King to gather and send 10,000 musicians, which the Indian King does. When the Persian monarch receives his itinerant musicians (male and female), he attempts to turn them into farmers. He assigns them wheat and cattle and the necessary land to provide their own sustenance while amusing his people. However, when the musicians fail to plant the wheat or breed the cattle, and consume the stock instead, the king rebukes them and orders them to pack their possessions onto their asses and support themselves by travelling the countryside.

According to Marlene Sway's *Familiar Strangers*, the name that Gypsies use to refer to themselves, "Rom" originates from the Sanskrit word *Dom*. Literally translated, *Dom* means "a man of low caste who gains his livelihood by singing and dancing." Sway posits that *Dom* probably derived from the sound that a drum makes, and that the "first pariahs may have been the *Dom*, as the term originally described a despised people who were hereditary drum-beaters."

Linguistic evidence indicates that after a hundred years or so of entertaining Persians in the tenth century the *Dom* began to roam far afield. They separated into two major groups and lived as nomads. The first group to leave wandered into Syria, Palestine, and Egypt, eventually spreading throughout the Middle East and North Africa. The second group traveled northward from Persia into Armenia, where they stayed for a long time; after passing through Byzantine Greece, the Northerners reached Eastern Europe. They traveled across Europe, often moving because of harsh treatment. According to Sway, "The inhospitality of the Balkans caused a band of three hundred [of these nomads] to explore more western regions.... Promising reports given by their pioneers inspired massive migrations of these nomads into northern, central, and southern Europe."

The Gypsies approached Europe from Turkish-occupied lands. By the fifteenth century, when Gypsies had reached Western Europe, populations of that region still feared the Turkish domination of the Ottoman Empire. It was in Western Europe that some of these people became known as Gypsies. The term itself probably derives from 'Gypcian, and results from an early confusion of Egypt with Epirus, or Little Egypt, in the Western Byzantine Empire. Eventually, Europeans used "Gypsies" or related words to name not only a particular ethnic group of people, but also other groups of people, unrelated by blood, whose traveling lifestyles made them resemble ethnic Gypsies. For the most part, Gypsies kept to themselves as a people; however, as Matt Salo suggests in his introduction to *Urban Gypsies*, "The existence of a number of Gypsy-like peripatetic groups, some of which (such as British Travellers) have intermarried with Gypsies ... complicate our attempts at classification" of who should not count and who should count as Gypsies. Although purists tend to define the group narrowly, loose classifications of ethnic Gypsies include all nomads who live and identify themselves as Gypsies.

During the fifteenth century, nomadic descendants of the *Dom* spread throughout and beyond Europe. The migrations widely dispersed the small groups, which lost contact with one another; and Matt Salo reports that sufficient cultural and linguistic differentiation occurred so that the groups lost consciousness of themselves as a single people. Around the middle of the nineteenth century, more Gypsies left Eastern Europe, constituting the second wave of migrations westward, northward and southward from there. Crossing many political borders, Eastern European Gypsies began migrating to Mexico, Central and South America, and to a lesser extent, countries in the Caribbean basin. Many of these Gypsies or their descendants arrived in the United States via this Latin American route. Some who came to the United States left, especially after the United States passed restrictive immigration legislation in 1924. Currently, Gypsies live in at least 40 different countries, and may number as many as ten million worldwide.

The two groups of Gypsy Americans about whom scholars know the most are the Rom and the Romnichals. Many of the Rom came to the New World from Russia, or Eastern or Central Europe; the Romnichals came from Great Britain. Although these two groups have much in common, they also are divided by the cultural differences and prejudices between Great Britain and Eastern Europe; the derision with which some Romnichals refer to the Rom reflects this split. The Romnichals came to the United States earlier than the Rom, and ran successful horse-trading operations in New England. The Rom arrived in the United States during the late nineteenth century and filled an American need for fortune-tellers. It is uncertain how many Gypsies are in the United States primarily because many Gypsies entered the country illegally, leaving few records, and were not counted on statistical tables of immigrants. Those who did immigrate legally were recorded by their country of origin and not as Gypsies. Because Gypsies are historically rooted in no nation, mutual mistrust has grown between Gypsies and governments. Gypsies tend to avoid the census taker and are justifiably wary of record-collecting, especially since records on Gypsies enabled the Nazis them to round up and kill one million of them during World War II. According to Rom Gypsy and scholar Ian Hancock, estimates that there are half a million Rom in America. In an October 1994 interview, Sheila Salo, another leading scholar of Gypsy Americans, estimated that America may have as few as 100,000 Rom and perhaps as many Romnichals.

Almost all Gypsies in the United States originated from some part of Europe, although there are a few small groups from elsewhere, such as parts of Asia. Some "black Dutch," from Germany, the Netherlands, and Pennsylvania, intermarried with Romnichals, and pass as white Anglo-Americans. Besides the Eastern Europeans who make up the large group of Rom, there are in the United States two other large groups of Gypsies: the Baschalde (from Slovakia, Hungary, and Carpagia), who may number close to 100,000; and the Romungre (from Hungary and Transylvania) who may number as many as 60,000. There are also some Horchanay, who are historically Muslims from the South Balkans, and a small population of Sinti Gypsies, who came from Northern Europe—Germany, Netherlands, France, Austria, Hungary—where they, like other Gypsies, were targets of the Nazis. There are also Bosnian and Polish Gypsies present in the United States Within the category of Rom Gypsies, there are several subgroups in the United States, such as the Kalderash and Machwaya. One of the most recent immigrations of a Gypsy group is that of the Lovara, which arrived in the 1990s. There are also a few small groups of Romanian Ludar, who may be Gypsies, in addition to the population of Gypsy Americans who emigrated from the Gypsy stronghold within the nation of Romania.

IMMIGRATION WAVES TO THE UNITED STATES

Gypsies have come to the United States for reasons similar to those of other immigrants; however, since European powers have tended to oppose Gypsies, this hostility has hastened Gypsy emigrations. Some Gypsies, though, came before those from Eastern Europe. According to Sway, "Gypsy deportations from England, France, Portugal, and Spain created the genesis of Gypsy life in the New World." Gypsies' social marginality left them little institutional power in Europe. To the deporting nations, sending Gypsies to the colonies let them remove what was seen as a "Gypsy problem." Sway adds that England deported some Gypsies to Barbados and Australia, and by the end of the seventeenth century, every European country with New World holdings followed the practice of deporting Gypsies to the Americas.

Ill will between Gypsies and established powers of civilizations spurred Gypsy emigration, also. Christian churches of Europe institutionalized hostility toward Gypsies, prompting their deportation. Sending Gypsies home was not an option—no nation welcomed them since their origin in India was unknown to the Western world until the eighteenth century. As Sway states, "After wandering in Europe for two hundred years, the Gypsies were citizens of no country and members of no church." Near the end of the nineteenth century, Eastern European emigrants spread throughout Europe and the Western Hemisphere; within this mass movement came the biggest immigrant waves of Gypsies to the United States.

Although Europeans have historically treated Gypsies poorly, Gypsies tended to fare better in Western Europe than in Eastern Europe, where they suffered the extremes of racial prejudice, including enslavement. Still, the New World society extended hope for alleviating social oppression. Some came to the United States via indirect routes. Of Gypsies deported to South American colonies, some migrated North. Some Gypsies were annexed into America with territory itself: for example, Napoleon transported hundreds of Gypsy men to Louisiana during the two-year period before selling the Louisiana Territory to the United States in 1803. More recently, toward the end of the twentieth century, the collapse of communism in Eastern Europe has enabled Gypsies to emigrate more freely, and has generated new waves of Eastern European Gypsies to the United States. Currently, of the estimated ten million Gypsies worldwide, the United States hosts between 250,000 and a million.

SETTLEMENT PATTERNS

Gypsies have resisted pressures from any civilization, including the United States, to have a single name or address. Nomadic Gypsies travel to avoid permanent settlement. By keeping their populations on the move and thinly spread, Gypsies decrease their visibility. They often go where they can make money and balanced nomadism allows groups of Gypsies to maintain their own economic territories. Rather than wander, they tend to travel purposefully from one destination to another. Historically, some families have reportedly traveled in regular circuits, often returning to the same places; others have ranged more widely, following no set route. Hardly ever, though, has travel been either continuous or completely random. Awareness of the best cities, small towns, or rural areas for exploitation has guided all travel. A group might camp for weeks, sometimes months, at especially productive urban areas, returning to these spots year after year.

Gypsy Americans might maintain a sequence of home bases; they often live in mobile homes, settling indefinitely in a trailer park. Gypsy Americans, unlike their European counterparts, tend to remain mobile despite a somewhat restricted range of mobility. Gypsies frequently tear down walls or and enlarge doorways of their homes to combine rooms or make them larger to create a wide open space suitable for the large social gatherings that occur in Rom homes. In *Urban Gypsies*, Carol Silverman notes that Gypsies frequently pass along the houses, apartments, or trailers that they modify to a succession of Gypsy families.

According to Anne Sutherland's essay in *Gypsies, Tinkers and Other Travellers*, "Because they no longer travel in caravans or pitch their tents in the fields of America, many Rom claim that they are no longer nomadic, and they speak with nostalgia about the 'good old days' when they were 'on the road.'" Relative to other Americans, however, many Gypsy Americans tend to travel and to change residences frequently; by non-Gypsy standards, they remain an itinerant people.

The Gypsy population has been participating in American migrations from countryside into cities. Yet, estimates tend to support that the Gypsy American population at any given time is evenly divided between urban and rural areas. Generally, as noted by Silverman, the urbanization of the Rom began as early as the end of the eighteenth century when various groups began to spend the winter months camping in vacant lots on the outskirts of cities, and intensified when "a large number of *Rom* flocked to the cities during the 1920s and 1930s to take advantage of various relief programs, and remained there because of gas rationing and because of increasing business opportunities within the city."

Because Gypsies tend to follow economic opportunities, the most populous cities, such as Los Angeles, San Francisco, New York, Chicago, Boston, Atlanta, Dallas, Houston, Seattle, and Portland, have the largest concentrations of Gypsies. Currently, there are Romnichal strongholds of very conservative Gypsies who reside in Texarkana, southern Arkansas, and other predominantly rural regions. Gypsies also have joined American movement westward. Many live in California.

REVERSE IMMIGRATIONS

Gypsy Americans who can do so often travel to other parts of the Western Hemisphere and to Europe. Many repeatedly visit certain places as part of a set route, including places where their kinfolk lived for generations. Gypsy Americans largely consider Eastern Europe their peoples' home. "In 1933 at the first International Conference on Gypsy Affairs held in Bucharest, Romania," states Sway, "the United Gypsies of Europe asked for a piece of land in Bucharest where Gypsies in trouble could settle. Later in 1937, Janus Kwiek, the 'Gypsy King of Poland,' asked Mussolini to grant the Gypsies a strip of land in Abyssinia (present-day Ethiopia) so they might escape persecution in various host societies."

Many Americans have romanticized Gypsies as exotic foreigners. Some Americans draw on the supposedly romantic appeals of Gypsy traditions—especially traditions of dancing and music-making, lives on the road, and maintaining a traveling culture. Often, established Americans maintain or adopt European prejudices against Gypsies and treat Gypsy immigrants poorly. Just as Europeans have often attributed the fortune-telling skills of Gypsies to "black magic," Gypsy traders have been accused of fencing stolen goods, and of stealing their goods themselves. Laws attempting to deter, prevent, and punish fortune-tellers and thieves in America have singled out Gypsy Americans. According to Sway, until 1930, Virginia legally barred Gypsies from telling fortunes. And in New Jersey in the middle 1980s, special regulations and licensing requirements applied to Gypsies who told fortunes. Gypsy households have been labeled as "dens of thieves" so that charges brought against one resident may apply to any and all. In Mississippi in the middle 1980s, such application of liability "jointly-and-severally" is law. There have also been recent cases in the Pacific Northwest. Police, moreover, tend to regard Gypsies with vigilance and disfavor. As recently as the 1970s, New Hampshire expelled some Gypsies from that state on the grounds merely that they were Gypsies.

The fearsome shadow of attempted genocide of Gypsies in Europe still menaces Gypsies. Gypsy Americans are concerned about worsening oppression of fellow Gypsies, most severely in Eastern Europe. This concern is understandable in light of the first two genocidal massacres: during World War I, Turks killed Gypsies and Armenians; and during the Holocaust, Nazis massacred Gypsies alongside Jews. Because too few people know about the Gypsy victims of the Nazis, Gypsies advocate public recognition of that loss. They attempt to draw attention, too, to the current plight of Eastern European Gypsies. Though the collapse of communist regimes—especially that of Ceauşescu, which conducted sterilizations and other genocidal persecutions of Gypsies—has alleviated some of the worst oppression, "ethnic cleansing" in Eastern Europe is a cause for Gypsy concern.

ACCULTURATION AND ASSIMILATION

Groups of Gypsies are supremely resistant to assimilation. Traditional Gypsy Americans continue to resist the inroads of acculturation, assimilation, and absorption in the United States Even groups such as the Gitanos or Romnichals, despite having lost most of their original language, still maintain a strong sense of ethnic identity and exclusiveness. A major issue facing Gypsy Americans since the 1980s is a worldwide Christian Fundamentalist revival that has swept up Gypsies around the world. As masses of Gypsies practice versions of Pentecostal Christianity, currents of Gypsy culture may be undergoing a sea-change.

Gypsies maintain a powerful group identity, though. Their travelling itself sets them apart from other cultures, as does their common rejection of international borders. Travels of Gypsies and exclusivity of Euro-American cultures have helped maintain a group-identity for Gypsies. Travel itself helps keep Gypsies separate from any settled society, and unrestricted by national boundaries. Gypsy American separation from mainstream America is best evidenced by their general lack of attendance at schools. Until recently, many Gypsies sent their children to schools only until the age of ten. Although Gypsies have adapted to American business ways, many try to limit their acculturation to only those necessary business practices.

Prejudice against Gypsies has strengthend their insolation. One might suppose that economic interactions would disperse the group insularity of Gypsies, if insular social techniques did not pull Gypsies together. These opposing tensions give Gypsies a flexible identity. Gypsy people may seem split between their business life, which focuses outwardly on non-Gypsies, and on the other hand, their social life, which focuses inwardly on only Gypsies.

Gypsy Americans—especially the Romnichals, who can pass as Anglo-Americans—seem to have been more successful in resisting assimilation than other groups. As Silverman notes, some Gypsy Americans may pass as Puerto Ricans, Mexicans, Armenians, Greeks, Arabs, and as other local ethnics in order to obtain jobs, housing, and welfare.

Contemporary urban Rom usually live interspersed among the non-Gypsy population, establishing *ofisi* (fortune-telling parlors) in working areas or in their homes. Their businesses may make many Gypsies seem quite assimilated, and at other times the same Gypsies may seem very traditional. Gypsies have tended to maintain two distinct standards of public behavior, one among themselves, another among outsiders, and Sway points to a "form of body language and interactional style" that Gypsies often use when interacting with non-Gypsies. "A Gypsy's very survival among non-Gypsies often depends on his [or her] ability to conceal as well as exaggerate his Gypsiness at appropriate times," observes Silverman. For example, an appropriate time for a Gypsy to exaggerate Gypsiness is while performing as a musician or fortune-teller for audiences who are known to value Gypsies' exoticism. On the other hand, Silverman adds that "a large part of behaving appropriately as a Gypsy involves knowing when to conceal one's Gypsiness." By passing as someone from a less stigmatized group, one can circumvent anti-Gypsy prejudice. For many, notes Silverman, "the process of boundary crossing [is] a performance strategically enacted for survival."

Gypsies and non-Gypsy Americans tend to have bad impressions of each other. To many Americans, Gypsy Americans seem to be sinister foreigners. To the Gypsies, Sway observes, "non-Gypsies seem cold, selfish, violent," as well as defiled or polluted. However, because Gypsies depend economically on non-Gypsies as customers for their services, they cannot afford to isolate themselves physically from non-Gypsies. Instead, social techniques enable Gypsies to maintain their cultural separateness from the people near whom they live, and with whom they do business. Basically, these techniques consist of taboos. A Gypsy court system enforces the taboos, to effectively limit social interactions with non-Gypsies. Gypsy Americans may bend their taboos by eating in a restaurant with non-Gypsies, and then attend to the taboos by remarking that some uncleanliness made them sick or unlucky.

IMAGES OF GYPSY AMERICANS

Stereotypes of Gypsies have targeted their nomadism, fortune-telling, and their trading. Ethnically, non-Gypsies have stereotyped Gypsies, their cultures, and their skills as exotically different. Non-Gypsies have described Gypsies as a harmful other, lurking within the body of society, with rhetoric that often portrays them as parasites, reproducing uncontrollably. Mainly, Europeans and Americans have stereotyped Gypsies as criminals. As a result, English-speakers say that to defraud, swindle, or cheat someone is to "gyp" them. This sensational image of Gypsies as criminals does not find support from statistical analysis of court records, since conviction rates of Gypsy Americans seem to be lower than rates of other ethnic Americans for rape and murder; and the conviction rate of Gypsies for theft is no higher than the rate for other Americans. However, Hancock points out in his *The Pariah Syndrome* that the association of Gypsies with crime goes deep and is sometimes justified since Gypsies have resorted to theft as a means of survival; but, "much of it is not justified, however, and is the result of exploitation of a stereotype by a popular press which is less interested in the honest Gypsies."

Western stereotypes of Gypsies as criminals arose when Gypsies first entered Europe. Confusion reigned over Europe's attempts to know who the Gypsies were. Matt Salo states in his introductory essay to *Urban Gypsies* that "many early [European] accounts describe Gypsy bands as conglomerations of various segments of the underclass of society," adding that Gypsies were widely thought to be "a motley assemblage of rogues and vagabonds." European Christians, especially, tended to believe that dark-skinned people were evil. Sway suggests that because the Gypsies were dark, strangely dressed, and spoke a language believed to be "a kind of gibberish used to deceive others" lent credence to the fear that they were spies for the Turks and enemies of Christendom.

Their obscure origins, plus their lack of geographic and institutional ties, have made the Gypsy people seem mysterious. Europeans sometimes thought that Gypsies' differences were all part of their scam. Matt Salo recounts that "they were accused of painting their faces with walnut juice to appear darker and to have invented an argot to disguise their speech for criminal purposes." Gypsies' dark skin and language were authentic—the stories about them were invented. Sway points out that "Gypsies themselves have participated in building and spreading myths about themselves, either from a desire to confuse non-Gypsies or through actual ignorance."

Many Europeans and Americans have romanticized Gypsies in literature, music, and folklore; part of the strength of the Gypsy-figure's appeal was that s/he seemed free from the constraints of life in contemporary industrial society. This stereotypical figure's popularity has captured audiences and helped to conceal ethnic Gypsies. In addition to their supposed criminality and freedom, the Gypsies have been portrayed as beautiful, loose, loose-bodied, flexible, and insolent—as in British novelist D. H. Lawrence's portrayal of a Gypsy man in *The Virgin and the Gipsy*, first published in 1931. Desire for the other tends to represent itself culturally as the other's desire; as Hancock notes, "Gypsy women have long been represented as sexual temptresses, and Gypsy men as a sexual threat to non-Gypsy women, in both song and story."

Conversely, the roles of non-Gypsies as customers for Gypsy businesses have contributed to Gypsies' negative stereotypes of non-Gypsies. Primarily, non-Gypsies may be seen as gullible "suckers." To fortune-tellers, furthermore, non-Gypsies tend to seem depraved. "Many regular customers are lonely, mal-adjusted, or both," writes Sway. "They reveal aspects of *gaje* (non-Gypsy) life to the fortune-teller which sound deviant to her; in turn, she tells her family everything she has heard."

Until relatively recently, when some Gypsy activists and scholars have begun to try to present their people in a better light, stereotypes faced little or no opposition. Most Gypsies have resisted attempts to reveal how they "really" are, and lacked the resources (such as literacy) to publish denials of specific claims.

However, many Gypsy Americans are actively trying to debunk oppressive stereotypes of Gypsies and promote a new public image. The film, *King of the Gypsies*, which was "suggested by" the best-selling book by Peter Maas, focuses on the squalor of Gypsy life from the perspective of a Gypsy-born boy who reviles Gypsies. Gypsies have protested the inaccurate and garish portrayals in this film. At the other end of the film spectrum is *Latcho Drom*—a "musical journey from India to Iberia, a seamless anthology of Gypsy music as played by an assortment of professionals on a variety of stringed instruments—sitars, zithers, violins, guitars—against means of percussion that range from small drums to brass vases to paired spoons to castanets," writes J. Hoberman (*Village Voice*, July 26, 1994, p. 47). "The vocals are as wailing and soulful as the rhythms are hypnotic and infectious." Community scenes feature children in Istanbul; an old man sings of the fall of Ceauşescu; a woman sings a lament of Auschwitz. The film ends in Western Europe, with singers, players, and dancers performing in France and Spain.

TRADITIONS AND TABOOS

Gypsies' patterns of kinship structures, traveling, and economics characterize them as an ancient people who have adapted well to modern society. Much scholarship on U.S. Gypsies treats only the Rom; and although other groups differ in some ways, Silverman states that the folk belief or folk religion of all ethnic Gypsies consists mainly of "the taboo system, together with the set of beliefs related to the dead and the supernatural."

Gypsy taboos separate Gypsies—each group of Gypsies—from non-Gypsies, and separate the contamination of the lower half of the adult Gypsy's body (especially the genitals and feet) from the purity of its upper half (especially the head and mouth). The waist divides an adult's body; in fact, the *Romani* word for waist, *maskar*, also means the spatial middle of anything. Since a Gypsy who becomes polluted can be expelled from the community, to avoid pollution, Gypsies try to avoid unpurified things that have touched a body's lower half. Accordingly, a Gypsy who touches his or her lower body should then wash his or her hands to purify them. Similarly, an object that feet have touched, such as shoes and floors, are impure and, by extension, things that touch the floor when someone drops them. Gypsies mark the bottom end of bedcovers with a button or ribbon, to avoid accidentally putting the feet-end on their face.

To Gypsies, it seems non-Gypsies constantly contaminate themselves. Non-Gypsies might neglect to wash their hands after urinating in public restrooms, they may wash underwear together with face towels and even tablecloths, or dry their faces and feet with the same towel. According to Silverman, when non-Gypsies move into a home, "they often replace the entire kitchen area, especially countertops and sinks, to avoid ritual contamination from previous non-Gypsy occupants."

Taboos apply most fully to Gypsies who become adults when they marry. Childbearing potential fully activates taboos for men and especially for women. At birth, the infant is regarded as entirely contaminated or polluted, because s/he came from the lower center of the body. The mother, because of her intensive contact with the infant, is also considered impure. As in other traditional cultures, mother and child are isolated for a period of time and other female members will assume the household duties of washing and cooking. Between infancy and marriage, taboos apply less strictly to children. For adults, taboos, especially those that separate males and females, relax as they become respected elders.

CUISINE

Hancock generalizes that for mobile Gypsies, methods of preparing food have been "contingent on circumstance." Such items as stew, unleavened bread, and fried foods are common, whereas leavened breads and broiled foods, are not. Cleanliness is paramount, though; and, "like Hindus and Muslims, Roma, in Europe more than in America, avoid using the left hand during meals, either to eat with or to pass things" (Ian Hancock, "Romani Foodways," *The World and I*, June 1991, p. 671; cited hereafter as Foodways).

Traditionally, Gypsies eat two meals a day—one upon rising and the other late in the afternoon. Gypsies take time from their "making a living in the *gadji-kanó* or the non-Gypsy milieu," in order to have a meal with other Gypsies and enjoy *khethanipé*—being together (Foodways, p. 672). Gypsies tend to cook and eat foods of the cultures among which they historically lived: so for many Gypsy Americans traditional foods are Eastern European foods. Those who have adopted Eastern Orthodox Catholicism celebrate holidays closely related to the *slava* feast of southeastern Europe, and eat *sarmaa* (cabbage rolls), *gushvada* (cheese strudel), and a ritually sacrificed animal (often a lamb). Gypsies consider these and other strong-tasting foods *baxtaló xabé*, or lucky.

For all Gypsies, eating is important. Gypsies commonly greet an intimate by asking whether or not s/he ate that day, and what. Any weight loss is usually considered unhealthy. If food is lacking, it is associated with bad living, bad luck, poverty, or disease. Conversely, for men especially, weight gain traditionally means good health. The measure of a male's strength, power, or wealth is in his physical stature. Thus a Rom *baro* is a big man physically and politically. A growing awareness of the health risks of obesity tempers some Gypsies' eating.

Eating makes Gypsy social occasions festive, and indicates that those who eat together trust one another. Taboos attempt to bar anybody sickly, unlucky, or otherwise disgraced from joining a meal. Because of these taboos, it is more than impolite for one Gypsy to refuse an offer of food from another. Such refusal would suggest that the offerer is *marimé*, or contaminated. Since Gypsies consider non-Gypsies unclean, in Gypsy homes they serve non-Gypsies from special dishes, utensils, and cups that are kept separate, or disposed of and replaced. Though some Gypsies will eat in certain restaurants, traditionally Gypsies cook for themselves.

CLOTHING

Gypsies have brightly colored costumes often using brilliant reds and yellows. Women often wear dresses with full skirts and men wear baggy pants and loose-fitting shirts. A scarf often adorns a woman's hair or is used as a cumberbund. Women wear much jewelry and the men wear boots and large belts. A married Gypsy woman customarily must cover her hair with a *diklo*, a scarf that is knotted at the nape of the neck. However, many Gypsy women may go bareheaded except when attending traditional communal gatherings.

HOLIDAYS AND FESTIVALS

In addition to religious holidays, Gypsy funerals are the biggest community holidays. Groups of Gypsies travel and gather to mark the passing of one of their own. Marriages are also important gatherings.

HEALTH AND MENTAL HEALTH ISSUES

Gypsies value luck and health. Ideas about health and illness among the Rom are closely related to a world view (*romania*), which includes notions of good and bad luck, purity and impurity, inclusion and exclusion. Sutherland, in an essay entitled "Health and Illness Among the Rom of California," observes that "these basic concepts affect everyday life in many ways including cultural rules about washing, food, clothes, the house, fasting, conducting rituals such as baptism and the slava, and diagnosing illness and prescribing home remedies." In Gypsy custom, ritual purification is the road to health. Much attention goes to avoiding diseases and curing them.

The most powerful Gypsy cure is a substance called *coxai,* or ghost vomit. According to Gypsy legends, *Mamorio* or "little grandmother" is a dirty, sickness-bringing ghost who eats people, then vomits on garbage piles. There, Gypsies find and gather what scientists call slime mold, and bake it with flour into rocks. Gypsies also use *asafoetida,* also referred to as devil's dung, which has a long association with healing and spiritualism in India; according to Sutherland, it has also been used in Western medicine as an antispasmodic, expectorant, and laxative.

Sutherland also recounts several Gypsy cures for common ailments. A salve of pork fat may be used to relieve itching. The juice of chopped onions sprinkled with sugar for a cold or the flu; brown sugar heated in a pan is also good for a child's cold; boiling the combined juice of oranges, lemons, water, and sugar, or mashing a clove of garlic in whiskey and drinking will also relieve a cold. For a mild headache, one might wrap slices of cold cooked potato or tea leaves around the head with a scarf; or for a migraine, put vinegar, or vinegar, garlic, and the juice of an unblemished new potato onto the scarf. For stomach trouble, drink a tea of the common nettle or of spearmint. For arthritis pain, wear copper necklaces or bracelets. For anxiety, sew a piece of fern into your clothes. Sutherland notes that elder Gypsies tend to "fear, understandably, that their grandchildren, who are turning more and more to American medicine, will lose the knowledge they have of herbs and plants, illnesses, and cures."

When a Gypsy falls sick, though, some Gypsy families turn to doctors, either in private practices or at clinics. As Sutherland notes in her essay in *Gypsies, Tinkers and Other Travellers,* "The Rom will often prefer to pay for private medical care with a collection rather than be cared for by a welfare doctor if they feel this care may be better." The Romnichals seem to have been historically prone to respiratory illnesses. In general, Gypsy culture seems to facilitate obesity, and thus heart trouble.

LANGUAGE

Most Gypsies are at least bilingual, speaking the language of the country in which they live as well as some branch of the Gypsy language, *Romani.* Sway observes that "since the Gypsy language has [almost] never been written, it has been easily influenced by the sounds of local languages." The Armenian language strongly influenced that of the Gypsies in their sojourns. Next, modern Greek contributed words to the vocabulary.

The language of the Gypsies was the key that unlocked the mystery of their supposed origin. Sway reports that the discovery that Gypsies originated in India was made by a scholar who noticed a close similarity between the language of the Hungarian Gypsies and the Sanskritized Malayalam of subcontinent Indians. This discovery, by a Hungarian theology student, Istvan Valyi, did not come until the middle of the eighteenth century. Matt Salo suggests that "from the realization that Gypsies indeed had their own language, the step to the recognition of their separate ethnicity followed automatically." Linguistics remains the science that can advance the most defensible claims about genealogies of peoples, including Gypsies.

Matt Salo points to linguistic histories that help account for Gypsies who do not speak *Romani:* groups of Gypsies split when they left the Balkans, leaving behind others, including those who were enslaved. Frazier indicates that currently, some dialects of *Romani* are classified as Armenian, others as Asiatic (other than Armenian), and the rest as European. Groups from each of the language branches are now widespread. And, according to Frazier, the English word, "pal," (first recorded in 1681) is one of the few *Romani* words to have entered the English lexicon.

When non-Gypsies ask Gypsies speaking *Romani* to identify the foreign language, explains Silverman, "Gypsies usually answer Romanian, Greek, or Yugoslavian," to minimize curiosity and prejudice toward them. Among themselves, Gypsies are also said to use a sort of sign language, *patrin*—marks meaningful to themselves but unintelligible to others. They seemingly used these symbols to describe conditions of camps for future campers, as well as to provide information about people in the area that might be useful for those practicing fortune-telling. Furthermore, Gypsies usually use their Gypsy name only among other Gypsies, and adopt an Americanized name for general and official uses. Particularly because many Gypsies pick common names, they are hard to trace.

GREETINGS

P'aves Baxtalo/Baxtali! ("pah-vis bach-tah-low/ bach-tah-lee")—May you be lucky (to a male/ female).

A gypsy wedding party poses for the camera in this 1941 photograph.

FAMILY AND COMMUNITY DYNAMICS

Traditionally Gypsies maintain large extended families. Clans of people numbering in the scores, hundreds, or even thousands gather for weddings, funerals, other feasts, or when an elder falls sick. Although Gypsy communities do not have kings, as such, traditionally a group will represent a man as king to outsiders when it needs one to serve as a figurehead or representative. Often, too, a man and his family will tell hospital staffers that he is "King of the Gypsies" so that he will receive better treatment—the title can help provide an excuse for the hospital to allow the large family to make prolonged visits.

In units bigger than a family and smaller than a tribe, Gypsy families often cluster to travel and make money, forming *kumpanias*—multi-family businesses. During recent decades in the United States, on the other hand, Gypsies have been acculturating more closely to the American model by consolidating nuclear families. Currently, after the birth of their first child, some Gypsy couples may be able to move from the husband's parents' home into their own. This change has given more independence to newly wedded women as daughters-in-law.

Gypsy families and communities divide along gender lines. Men wield public authority over members of their community through the *kris*—

the Gypsy form of court. In its most extreme punishment, a *kris* expels and bars a Gypsy from the community. For most official, public duties with non-Gypsies, too, the men take control. Publicly, traditional Gypsy men treat women as inferiors.

The role of Gypsy women in this tradition is not limited to childbearing: she can influence and communicate with the supernatural world; she can pollute a Gypsy man so that a *kris* will expel him from the community; and she makes and manages most of a family's money. Fortune-tellers, all of whom are female, when successful provide the main income for their families. Men of their families will usually aid the fortune-telling business by helping in some support capacities, as long as they are not part of the "women's work" of talking to customers.

MARRIAGE AND CHILDREN

Gypsies of marriageable age may travel with their parents to meet prospective spouses and arrange a marriage. In making a good match, money, and the ability to earn more of it, tend to be factors more important than romance. A Gypsy who marries a non-Gypsy can expect her community to expel her, permanently. A Gypsy man, however, may eventually get permission to return to his people with his wife. Once married, a new daughter-in-law must subject herself to the commands of her husband's family, until her first pregnancy. With the birth of her first child, she fully enters womanhood.

Gypsy cultural practices attempt to prevent Gypsy children from learning non-Gypsy ways, and to facilitate raising them as Gypsies. Gypsy children, or at least post-adolescents, generally do not go to school, day-care centers, or babysitters who are not friends or relatives. Furthermore, Gypsy culture forbids them to play with non-Gypsies. Instead, they socialize with Gypsies of all ages. Formal schooling, as such, is minimal. Traditionally, Gypsies devalue education from outside their own culture. They educate their own children within extended families. An important reason Gypsies do not like to send their children to school is that they will have to violate Gypsy taboos: they will have to use public restrooms, and the boys and girls will come into contact too closely in classrooms and on playgrounds. Many Gypsy Americans send their children to schools until the age of ten or 11 years, at which time the parents permanently remove them from school.

Children are expected to watch and act like their elders. Rather than bar children from adult life, Gypsies often include them in conversations and business. Children learn the family business, often at home. Many Gypsies marry and become partners in family businesses by their late teens. For example, daughters, but not sons, of a fortune-teller train early to become fortune-tellers. Boys may train to sell cars.

RELIGION

Gypsy spirituality, part of the core culture of Gypsies, derives from Hindu and Zoroastrian concepts of *kintala*—balance and harmony, as between good and evil. When that balance is upset, ancestors send signals to keep people on track. Mysticism of fortune-tellers and tarot readers—though services to non-Gypsies are not the same as Gypsies' own spirituality—has a basis in Gypsy spirituality. Many Gypsies are Christians. Despite the fact that some Gypsies may use Christian symbols and Christian identity for self-preservation and advantage, Gypsy faith in Christianity need not necessarily be doubted.

Historically, toward the beginning of the second millennium B.C., Gypsies invented a story of their origins in Egypt—hence the name, "Gypsies"—which gave many of them safe passage in a hostile Europe. The story claimed that they had been oppressed and forced into idol-worship in Egypt, and that the Pope had ordered them to roam, as penitence for their former unchristianity. This story also played on legends of a common heritage of Gypsies and Jews, which were partly based on actual overlap of these two ethnic cultures in marginal trades and ghettos. Sway indicates that the story of an Egyptian origin convinced Europeans until the early sixteenth century when the church became convinced these "penitents" were frauds. The church moved to isolate its followers from Gypsies: "As early as 1456 excommunication became the punishment for having one's fortune told by a Gypsy.... More effective than the policy of excommunication was the assertion by the Catholic Church that the Gypsies were a cursed people partly responsible for the execution of Christ."

Although European churches have a long history of condemning Gypsies, their magic, and their arranged marriages, most Rom Gypsy Americans are Eastern Orthodox. They celebrate the *pomona* feast for the dead, at which the feasters invite the dead to eat in heaven. Also, preparation for their *slava* feast requires thorough cleaning of the interior of the host's house, its furniture, and its inhabitants, as the host transforms a section of the house into a church. The feast ceremony begins with coffee for the guests, prayer and a candle for the saints.

Today, around the world Christian fundamentalist revival movements have been sweeping through Rom, Romnichal, and other groups of Gypsies. Since the mid-1980s, through Assemblies of God, various American groups have formed Gypsy churches. In Fort Worth, Texas, for example, a church integrates traditional Gypsy faith with Christian Pentecostal ritual.

Gypsies have tended to syncretize or blend their ethnic Gypsy folk religion with more established religions, such as Christianity. Gypsy religious beliefs are mostly unrelated to the business of fortune-telling. Silverman points out that while Gypsies may disbelieve Gypsy "magic," and "often joke about how gullible non-Gypsies are," in some ways, others act as believers; fortune-tellers generally treat their reading room as sacred and may "consult elder Gypsy women who are known to be experts in dream interpretation, card reading, and folk healing". Gypsies use code-names to mention certain evil-spirits to other Gypsies; and Gypsies sometimes cast curses on other Gypsies (or ward them off). Also, states Silverman, Gypsy fortune-tellers use diverse religious iconography to create impressions out of a belief "that good luck and power can come from any the symbols of any religion."

EMPLOYMENT AND ECONOMIC TRADITIONS

Quite often, Gypsy Americans have found their economic niche by making money from other members of the lower classes of U.S. society, usually other ethnic minorities, such as Hispanic Americans, African Americans, and immigrants to America from Eastern and Central Europe.

Mobility and adaptation characterize Gypsy trades. By serving populations they encounter, Gypsies have succeeded in various times and places. From their beginnings, their traditional occupations have kept them dependent on other groups, and at the same time maintained Gypsies' separation. The *Dom* were never agricultural; they were musicians, dancers, and entertainers in ancient India, states Sway, adding that they were also were metalworkers—"the only group in ancient India to work with iron, a metal considered dangerous according to Indian religious belief."

The need for mobility shaped their livelihoods. In their essay in *Urban Gypsies*, Matt and Sheila Salo explain that "the main features of all occupations were that they were independent pursuits, required little overhead, had a ubiquitous clientele, and could be pursued while traveling" in urban and rural areas. Moreover, Gypsies have adapted to different locales and periods. Silverman discusses a change in occupations in twentieth century America that parallels the urbanization of the Rom. After their arrival in the 1880s, the Rom followed nomadic European trades such as coppersmithing, refining, and dealing in horses for the males, and begging or fortune-telling for the females. They would camp in the country and interact mostly with the rural population, venturing into the cities only to sell their services and purchase necessities. As the automobile supplanted horse travel, the Rom became used-car dealers and repairmen, occupations that they still pursue. When metalworking skills became less important, Gypsies learned new trades, including the selling of items such as watches and jewelry.

As Sutherland points out in *Gypsies, Tinkers and Other Travellers*, "In the *kumpania* men and women cooperate with each other in exploiting the economic resources of their area." Although jobs may be exploited by an individual, the Rom prefer to work in groups called *wortacha*, or partners. These groups always comprise members of the same sex, however, women often take along children of either sex. *Wortacha* may also include young unmarried Gypsies who learn the skills of the adults. Adults work as equals, dividing expenses and profits equally. As a token of respect for an elder, an extra amount may be given, but unmarried trainees receive only what others will give them. The Rom do not earn wages from another Rom. As a rule, Gypsies profit from non-Gypsies only. In the United States and other countries (including England and Wales), Gypsy Americans divide geographic territories to minimize competition between Gypsy businesses.

Gypsies, supremely mobile and profit-making traders, became dealers of vehicles. Romnichals took an early American role as horse traders, and achieved particular success in Boston. According to Matt and Sheila Salo, "During World War I, Gypsies brought teams of their horses to the Great Plains to help harvest crops. For a while at least, the label 'horse trader' or 'horse dealer' seemed almost synonymous with 'Gypsy.' The colorful wagons used by Romnichals to advertise their presence to any community they entered further reinforced this identification by the professionally painted side panels depicting idealized horses and the horse trading life." The pride of Romnichals in their ability to trade horses is reflected in the carved figures of horses on the tombstones of horse dealers, say Matt and Sheila Salo. Many of the Rom, who arrived in America after the horse trade's heyday, sell cars. Other mobile service contributions of the Gypsies have included driveway blacktopping, house painting, and tinsmithing. Gypsy tinkers, who were mostly Romanian-speaking Gypsies, were essential to various industries such as confectioneries, because they re-tinned large mixing bowls and other machinery on-site. They also worked in bakeries, laundries, and anywhere steam jackets operated.

By the 1930s the Rom group of Gypsy Americans virtually controlled the business of fortune-telling. Their advertisements and shop windows have their undeniable place on American boardwalks, roads, and streets. Gypsy mysticism, as represented in fortune-teller costumes and props such as the crystal ball and tarot deck, have impacted on American culture directly, and through their media representations and imitations, such as the likes of commercially produced Ouija boards. Gypsies have maintained a presence and influence in America's quasi-religious, commercially mystical functions.

MUSIC AND MINSTRELSY

Worldwide, Gypsies are most famous for their contributions as musicians. In the United States, Hungarian Slovak Gypsies, mostly violists, have played popular Hungarian music at immigrant weddings. Historically, Gypsies have contributed to music Americans play. Flamenco, which Gypsies are credited with creating in Spain, has its place in America, particularly in the Southwest. Django Rheinhardt, a well-known European Gypsy who contributed to American culture is perhaps the all-time greatest jazz guitarist. Furthermore, Klezmer music of Jewish immigrants overlaps with music of Eastern European Gypsies, especially in oriental, flatted-seventh chords played on a violin or clarinet.

There are intriguing parallels between Gypsies and African Americans in European and American cultural history. The rhythmic innovations that Gypsies brought to Europe were not only Asiatic and Middle Eastern, but also African, at least North African; similarly, African Americans brought innovations of African music to America. Some Gypsies owned slaves or employed African American laborers and stevedores (loaders/unloaders). According to legend, some of these men had eloped with Gypsy daughters. When African American ex-slave minstrels first attempted to taste the freedom of the road in post-Reconstruction America, some claimed to adopt the ethnicity, or at least the title, of Gypsies (Konrad Bercovici, "The American Gypsy," *Century Magazine*, 103, 1922, pp. 507-519). In popular American musical traditions of jazz, blues, and rock, the Gypsy has remained a powerful referent.

FORTUNE-TELLERS

In the United States, Rom Gypsies have dominated a niche for fortune-tellers, who are also known as palmists, readers, or advisers. "Fortune-telling actually includes elements of folk psychotherapy and folk healing," made into a business to serve non-Gypsies, writes Silverman, who adds that one fortune-teller describes her relationship with her customers in this way: "All they need is confidence and strength and a friend and that's what I am." Some customers come only once, and others make themselves more valuable by returning. A reader will try to establish a steady relationship with the customer, whether in person, by telephone, or by mail. Readers will also try to use the customer's language, usually English or Spanish. Moreover, readers often adopt and advertise names for themselves that help them claim the ethnicity of their clientele; and/or, they choose an ethnicity renowned for mystical perception, such as an Asian, African, or Native American one. Fortune-tellers set up shop where they can make money. Often, they serve a working-class clientele composed of other ethnic minorities. They tend to choose visible locales where they can operate freely: New York supports a great many fortune-tellers, while Los Angeles (where more Gypsies sell real estate and cars) has relatively few because of strict laws governing fortune-telling. Daughters of successful fortune-tellers traditionally become

fortune-tellers whether or not they are interested. Their family business is part of their household.

PUBLIC ASSISTANCE

It is difficult to determine with much accuracy the percentage of Gypsy Americans on public assistance. For Rom Gypsy Americans, receiving public assistance is part of what they do, the role they perform. Gypsy community leaders can control any Gypsy's access to public assistance in their territory by reporting renegades or outsiders for fraud.

POLITICS AND GOVERNMENT

Aside from benefits it provides, American government tends to hinder Gypsies. Some states and districts maintain policies and statutes that prohibit fortune-tellers, require them to pay hundreds of dollars for annual licenses, or otherwise control activities in which Gypsies engage. Despite the unconstitutionality of such measures, some rules apply specifically to Gypsies, by name. One excuse for this discrimination is the confusion between ethnic Gypsies and vagrants. Additionally, Silverman indicates that many police have little toleration for Gypsies. Truant officers, too, bother Gypsies by continually trying to locate Gypsy children.

INDIVIDUAL AND GROUP CONTRIBUTIONS

CULTURE

Brian Vessey-Fitzgerald, who authored *The Gypsies of England*; Jane Carlisle, Thomas's wife; Rita Sackville West; David Birkenhead Smith; and scholar Ian Hancock.

PERFORMING ARTS

Many Gypsy contributors to American culture have been performers. Among Romnichal (English Gypsies) who lived some in America, we can count Charlie Chaplin and Rita Hayworth. Ava Gardner, Michael Cain, and Sean Connery are reported to have Gypsy ancestry. Freddy Prince, the late singer of rock group Queen, was on one side Hungarian Gypsy.

MEDIA

PRINT

Gypsies and Travelling People.
Contact: Don Kennington or David Barton, Editors.
Address: Capital Planning Information Ltd., 52 High Street, Stamford, Lincolnshire PE9 2LG, England.
Telephone: 780-57300.
Fax: 780-54333.

The World and I.
Contact: Dr. Ian F. Hancock.
Address: P.O. Box 822, Manchaca, Texas 78652-0822.
Telephone: (512) 282-1286.

ORGANIZATIONS AND ASSOCIATIONS

Baschalde.
Contact: Bill Douna.
Telephone: (612) 926-8281.

Gypsy Folk Ensemble.
Also performs for school assemblies.

Contact: Preston Ashbourne.
Address: 3265 Motor Avenue, Los Angeles, California 90034.

Gypsy Lore Society.
Publishes the *Journal of the Gypsy Lore Society.*

Contact: Sheila Salo, Treasurer.
Address: 5607 Greenleaf Road, Cheverly, Maryland 20785.
Telephone: (301) 341-1261.

International Romani Church.
Address: P.O. Box 17222, Wichita, Kansas 67217.

International Romani Union (IRU).
Works to foster unity among members; promotes human rights and obligations; advocates protection and preservation of Romani culture and language. Publishes the quarterly *Buhazi*, the bimonthly *Lacio Drom*, the bi-weekly *Nevipens Romani*, the monthly *Romano Nevipen*, the monthly *Rrom po Drom*, and the quarterly newspaper *Scharotl*.

Contact: Dr. Ian F. Hancock, President.
Address: P.O. Box 822, Manchaca, Texas 78652-0822.
Telephone: (512) 282-1286.

U.S. Romani Council.
Address: 528 Madeira, S.E., Suite 1, Albuquerque, New Mexico 87108.

MUSEUMS AND RESEARCH CENTERS

Texas Romani Archives, University of Texas at Austin.
Address: Calhoun Hall 501, Austin, Texas 78712.

Victor Weybright Archives of Gypsy Studies.
Contact: Sheila Salo, Manager.
Address: 5607 Greenleaf Road, Cheverly, Maryland 20785.
Telephone: (301) 341-1261.

SOURCES FOR ADDITIONAL STUDY

Frazier, Angus. *The Gypsies.* Cambridge, Massachusetts: Blackwell, 1992.

Gypsies and Travelers in North America: An Annotated Bibliography, compiled by William G. Lockwood and Sheila Salo. Cheverly, Maryland: The Gypsy Lore Society, 1994.

Hancock, Ian. *The Pariah Syndrome: An Account of Gypsy Slavery and Persecution.* Ann Arbor, Michigan: Karoma Publishers, 1987.

Miller, Carol. "The American Rom and the Ideology of Defilement," in *Gypsies, Tinkers and Other Travellers*, edited by Farnham Rehfisch. New York: Harcourt, Brace Jovanovich, 1975; pp. 41-54.

Salo, Matt, and Sheila Salo. "Romnichal Economic and Social Organization in Urban New England 1850-1930," *Urban Gypsies* (special issue of *Urban Anthropology*), Volume 11, No. 3-4 (fall-winter) 1982.

Silverman, Carol. "Everyday Drama: Impression Management of Urban Gypsies," *Urban Gypsies* (special issue of *Urban Anthropology*), Volume 11, No. 3-4 (fall-winter) 1982.

Sutherland, Anne. "The American Rom: A Case of Economic Adaptation," in *Gypsies, Tinkers and Other Travellers*, edited by Farnham Rehfisch. New York: Harcourt, Brace Jovanovich, 1975; pp. 1-40.

————. *Gypsies: The Hidden Americans*. London: Tavistock Publications, 1975.

————. "Health and Illness Among the Rom of California," *The Journal of the Gypsy Lore Society*, February 1992.

Sway, Marlene. *Familiar Strangers: Gypsy Life in America*. Chicago: University of Illinois Press, 1988.

Tyrner-Stastny, Gabrielle. *The Gypsy in Northwest America*. Olympia: Washington State American Revolution Bicentennial Commission, 1977.

Urban Gypsies (special issue of *Urban Anthropology*), introduction by Matt Salo, Volume 11, No. 3-4 (fall-winter), 1982.

Yoors, Jan. *Crossing* (autobiography). New York: Simon and Schuster, 1971.

By the 1920s, most immigrants had resolved to stay permanently in the United States. They established families, had American-born children, and became intimately involved in the social lives of their churches, fraternal societies, and cultural institutions that in the past served as their extended families.

HUNGARIAN AMERICANS

by

Steven Béla Várdy

and

Thomas Szendrey

OVERVIEW

Hungary is a small landlocked country in the Carpathian Basin of Central Europe. It is about the size of Indiana (35,919 square miles, or 93,030 square kilometers) with twice the latter's population. It is bounded by Slovakia in the north, Ukraine in the northeast, Romania in the east, the former Yugoslavia (Serbia, Croatia, Slovenia) in the south, and Austria in the west.

Hungary is inhabited almost exclusively by Hungarians (Magyars), who constitute 96.1 percent of its population. The remaining 3.9 percent is made up of Germans, Slovaks, South Slavs, Gypsies, and Romanians. Since the dismemberment of Greater Hungary after World War II—complemented by several waves of overseas emigration—about one-third of all Hungarians live abroad. The majority of them live in parts of former Greater Hungary in such newly created or enlarged neighboring states as Romania (more than two million), Slovakia (700,000), the former Yugoslavia (500,000), Ukraine (200,000), and Austria (50,000). Another two million reside in Western Europe, the Americas, and Australia—the majority of them in the United States.

According to statistics compiled in 1992, 67.8 percent of Hungarians are Catholic, 20.9 percent Calvinist (Reformed), and 4.2 percent Lutheran (Evangelical). The three religious groups together make up 92.9 percent of the population. Of the remaining portion, 2.3 percent belong to several minor denominations (Greek or Byzantine Catholic, Orthodox Christian, Baptist, and Adventist), while 4.8 percent claim no religious affiliation. Jews, who in 1941 constituted 4.3 percent of Hungary's population, do not show up in these statistics. This is in part because the Holocaust or subsequent emigration to Israel decimated their ranks and in part because of the reluctance of some to identify themselves as Jews. Learned estimates, however, put their numbers close to 100,000 (about one percent of the country's population), which still makes them the largest Jewish community in East Central Europe. As the result of half a century of communist rule, relatively few people practice their religion in Hungary. The religious revival following the collapse of communism, however—which includes the return of organized religious education—is in the process of changing this lack of attention to religion.

HISTORY

Medieval Hungarian traditions count even the fifth-century Huns among the Magyars' ancestors, but their immediate forebears arrived in the Carpathian Basin as late as the seventh century. Known as the "late Avars," they established the center of their empire in the region that is part of modern Hungary. The last of several Magyar migratory waves took place in the late ninth century, when under the leadership of Prince Árpád, they conquered this region, gradually extending their rule over the entire Carpathian Basin.

In A.D. 1000, one of Árpád's successors, Stephen I (king of Hungary 997-1038; canonized 1083) Christianized his people and made Hungary part of the Western Christian world. During the next four centuries, the Hungarians continued to expand beyond the Carpathian Basin, especially into the northern Balkans. At the end of the eleventh century they conquered and annexed Croatia as an autonomous kingdom, while in the twelfth and thirteenth centuries they extended their influence over Bosnia, Dalmatia, and northern Serbia—largely at the expense of the declining Byzantine Empire. Moreover, in the fourteenth century, under the Angevin rulers Charles Robert (who ruled from 1308 until 1342) and Louis the Great (who ruled from 1342 to 1382), they expanded their control over the newly formed Vlach (Romanian) principalities of Wallachia and Moldavia and for a brief period (1370-1382) even over Poland. With the expansion of the Ottoman Turkish Empire into the Balkans in the late fourteenth and fifteenth centuries, Hungarian influence over the northern Balkans declined and was replaced by that of the Turks. Even so, Hungary still experienced moments of greatness, particularly under Regent John Hunyadi (who ruled from 1444 to 1456) and his son King Matthias Corvinus (who ruled from 1458 to 1490). Matthias even conquered Moravia and eastern Austria (including Vienna) and also established a brilliant Renaissance royal court at Buda (now part of Budapest).

Medieval Hungary's greatness ended with its defeat at the hands of the Ottoman Turks at the Battle of Mohács in 1526. Turkish conquest was followed by the country's trisection, which lasted for nearly two centuries. Western and northwestern Hungary ("Royal Hungary") became part of the Habsburg Empire ruled from Vienna; central Hungary was integrated into the Ottoman Turkish Empire; and eastern Hungary evolved into the autonomous principality of Transylvania, whose semi-independence under Turkish suzerainty ended with the country's reconquest and reunification by the Habsburgs of Vienna in the late seventeenth and early eighteenth centuries.

Although dominated by Vienna throughout the eighteenth and nineteenth centuries, Hungary retained considerable autonomy within the Habsburg Empire. In the mid-nineteenth century the Habsburgs and the Hungarians clashed in the Hungarian Revolution and War of Independence (1848-1849), and two decades later they united in the Austro-Hungarian Compromise of 1867. This compromise—engineered by Francis Deák (1803-1876) and Emperor Franz Joseph (who ruled from 1848 to 1916)—resulted in the dual state of Austria-Hungary, which played a significant role in European power-politics until nationality problems and involvement in World War I on the German side resulted in its dissolution in 1918-1919.

The demise of Austria-Hungary was accompanied by the dismemberment of historic Hungary, codified in the Peace Treaty of Trianon in 1920. This treaty turned Hungary into a small truncated country, with only 28.5 percent of its former territory (35,900 square miles versus 125,600 square miles) and 36.5 percent of its former population (7.6 million versus 20.9 million). Trianon Hungary became "a kingdom without a king" under the regency of Admiral Nicholas

These Hungarian refugees were part of the U.S. Navy's "sea lift," which helped Hungarians fleeing their homeland after the 1956 Soviet military crackdown.

Horthy (who ruled from 1920 to 1944), who devoted most of the country's energies to the effort to regain at least some of Hungary's territorial losses. These efforts did result in temporary territorial gains in 1938-1941, but as these gains were achieved with German and Italian help, they landed Hungary in the unfortunate German alliance during World War II.

After the war Hungary again was reduced in size and became one of the communist-dominated Soviet satellite states under the leadership of the Stalinist dictator, Mátyás Rákosi (who ruled from 1945 to 1956). Communist excesses and the relaxation that followed Stalin's death in 1953 led to the Hungarian Revolution of 1956, the most significant anti-Soviet uprising of the postwar period. Put down by Soviet military intervention, it was followed by a brief period of retribution and then by a new communist regime under János Kádár (who ruled from 1956 to 1988), who initiated a policy of political liberalization (1962) and economic reform (known as the New Economic

Mechanism of 1968). By the 1970s these reforms—supported by generous Western loans—made Hungary and its system of "goulash communism" the envy of the communist world. In the 1980s, however, the system began to flounder, and economic problems resurfaced. These problems, together with Mikhail Gorbachev's reforms in the Soviet Union, undermined the Kádár regime. Kádár was ousted in 1988, and in 1989 Hungary came under the control of reform communists, who, unable to control the situation, relinquished power in 1990. They were replaced by a new multiparty government under the leadership of the Hungarian Democratic Forum (HDF), headed by József Antall (who ruled from 1990 to 1993). The HDF regime immediately began to transform Hungary from a communist to a democratic state, but the economic and social problems it encountered—rapid social polarization, the collapse of the protective social welfare system, and pauperization of a large segment of the society—proved to be too much. The HDF government was also plagued by amateurism in leadership. Voted out of office in May 1994, it was replaced in July of the same year by a coalition of the Hungarian Socialist Party and the Federation of Free Democrats. The new prime minister is the ex-Communist Gyula Horn (1932-), who had served as Hungary's foreign minister during the peaceful transition from communism to democracy in 1989-1990.

HUNGARIANS IN THE UNITED STATES

According to Hungarian tradition, the first Hungarian to reach the shores of America was a certain Tyrker who had arrived with the Viking chief Eric the Red around A.D. 1000. This is alleged to have happened concurrently with Stephen I's transformation of Hungary into a Christian kingdom. If the Tyrker story is discounted, the first documented Hungarian to land in America was the learned scholar Stephen Parmenius of Buda (c. 1555-1583), who participated in Sir Humphrey Gilbert's expedition in 1583 and later drowned off the coast of Newfoundland.

The next two and one-half centuries belonged to the explorers, missionaries, and adventurers who came to North America in increasing numbers during the colonial and early national periods. The most noted among the latter was Colonel Michael de Kováts (1724-1779), a member of the Pulaski Legion during the Revolutionary War, who is generally credited with being one of the founders of the American cavalry. The late eighteenth and early nineteenth century also saw the arrival of the first sporadic settlers, most of whom came from the middle and upper classes, were motivated by personal reasons to immigrate, and usually settled in such coastal cities as Boston, New York, Philadelphia, Charleston, and New Orleans. In the 1830s and 1840s came a number of learned travelers, including Sándor Bölöni-Farkas (1795-1842) and Ágoston Haraszthy (1812-1869), both of whom wrote influential books about their experiences in the New World under the identical title *Journey to North America* (published in 1834 and 1844, respectively). In 1844 Haraszthy returned permanently with his family and became the founder of California viticulture. The two decades prior to the Hungarian Revolution of 1848 also saw the initial scholarly contacts between the Hungarian Academy of Science and the American Philosophical Society.

The long period of individual migration was replaced in 1849-1850 by the first Hungarian group immigration to America. These were the so-called "Forty-niners," who emigrated to escape retribution by Austrian authorities after the defeat of the Hungarian Revolution of 1848. Several thousand strong, the numbers included only educated men, many of them from the gentry class (middle nobility), who found it difficult to adjust to America's frontier society. A large number of them joined the Union armies during the Civil War, and a few of them returned to Hungary during the 1860s and 1870s, but most of them became a part of American society. Many of the latter rose to important positions, usually in fields other than their original calling.

The next wave was the turn-of-the-century "Great Economic Immigration" that landed about 1.7 million Hungarian citizens, among them 650,000-700,000 real Hungarians (Magyars), on American shores. These immigrants came almost solely for economic reasons, and they represented the lowest and poorest segment of the population.

"When we were getting off of Ellis Island, we had all sorts of tags on us. Now that I think of it, we must have looked like marked-down merchandise in Gimbel's basement store or something."

Anna Vida in 1921, cited in *Ellis Island: An Illustrated History of the Immigrant Experience*, edited by Ivan Chermayeff et al. (New York: Macmillan, 1991).

The outbreak of World War I in 1914 halted mass migration, while the exclusionary U.S. immigration laws of 1921 and 1924 pushed the Hungarian quota down to under 1,000 per year. This situation did not change until the new Immigration Law, the Hart-Celler Act of 1965, ended the quota system. Yet, during the intervening four decades, there were a number of nonquota admissions, which brought completely different types of Hungarian immigrants to American shores. These included the refugee intellectuals (2,000 to 3,000) of the 1930s, who were fleeing the spread of Nazism; the post-World War II political immigrants or the so-called displaced persons or DPs (17,000), who came under the Displaced Persons Acts of 1948 and 1950; and the "Fifty-sixers" or Freedom Fighters (38,000), who left Hungary after the failed Revolution of 1956. Although the combined numbers of these last three groups (60,000) were less than 10 percent of that of the turn-of-the-century economic immigrants, their impact on American society was much more significant.

SETTLEMENT PATTERNS

Although the turn-of-the-century economic immigrants were from rural areas, almost all of them settled in the industrial cities and mining regions of the northeastern United States. According to one set of statistics, of all the Hungarians (Magyars) in the United States in 1920, fewer than 0.2 percent were engaged in agriculture. Virtually all of them worked in mining and industry—most of them in the unskilled or semiskilled category. This was primarily because the majority of them came to America not as immigrants but as migrant workers who intended to repatriate to Hungary. Their goal was to return with enough accumulated capital to be able to buy land and thus become prosperous farmers. To do this, however, they had to work in industry, where work was readily available, because during the Gilded Age the rapidly expanding American industrial establishment was in grave need of cheap immigrant labor.

Most of the immigrants were never able to fulfill their original goal of repatriation, although perhaps as many as 25 percent did return permanently. Factors contributing to this included their inability to accumulate the capital to buy enough land; the difficulties they encountered in readjusting to Hungary's class-conscious society; the influence of their American-born children who viewed Hungary as an alien land; and most important, Hungary's post-World War I dismemberment, which transferred the immediate homelands of most of the immigrants to such newly created states as Czechoslovakia or Yugoslavia or to the much-enlarged Romania. They did not wish to join the ranks of Hungarians who had been forcibly transferred to these states, two of which had gone out of existence twice since their creation (Czechoslovakia and Yugoslavia) and one of which had become the home base of postwar Europe's most oppressive and chauvinistic communist regime (Romania).

According to the 1920 U.S. Census, 945,801 persons in the United States either had been born in Hungary or had Hungarian-born parents, slightly over half of whom (495,845 or 52.9 percent) were Magyars. In 1922 the Hungarian-born Magyars numbered 474,000, of whom 427,500 (90 percent) were concentrated in 10 northeastern states: New York (95,400), Ohio (88,000), Pennsylvania (86,000), New Jersey (47,300), Illinois (40,000), Michigan (26,200), Connecticut (14,800), Wisconsin (11,600), Indiana (10,900), and West Virginia (7,300). They congregated in this region because of the coal mines of Pennsylvania, northern West Virginia, and southeastern Ohio, as well as because of the steel mills, textile mills, and machine factories of Pittsburgh, Cleveland, Youngstown, Chicago, Philadelphia, and the Greater New York area.

This settlement pattern remained unchanged until the 1960s when—partially because of the coming of the more mobile political immigrants, and partially because of the general population shift in previous decades—many Hungarians began to move to the West and to the South. The younger and more daring souls flooded to California and Texas, while the retirees favored Florida. Thus, by 1980 the Hungarian population of these states rose, respectively, to 165,000, 28,000, and 90,000.

RELATIONS WITH ANGLO-AMERICAN SOCIETY

The relationship of the Hungarians to Anglo-American society varied with the diverse waves of immigrants. The Forty-niners, also known as the "Kossuth immigrants" (after the leader of the revolution, Lajos Kossuth), had been received with awe and respect. Because of their gentry-based background and education, they established the image of the Hungarians as a "nation of nobles." This image was undermined by the turn-of-the-century economic poor and uneducated. They were the ones who unwittingly created the negative "Hunky" image of Hungarians, which then was transferred to all of the East and Southeast European immigrants. This image survived well into the post-World War II period, even though by that time the intellectual immigrants of the 1930s and the political immigrants of the 1950s began to diversify the immigrants' social composition. Although far fewer in number, these newer immigrants were the ones who gave birth to the revised Hungarian image that Laura Fermi, the author of the highly praised study *Illustrious Immigrants* (1968), defined as the "mystery of the Hungarian talent." This was a natural by-product of the fact that many of these intellectual and political immigrants made impressive achievements that had a measurable impact on American society.

KEY ISSUES FOR THE FUTURE

The key issue at this time is one of survival and of relationship to Hungary. The third-, fourth-, and fifth-generation descendants of the economic immigrants have already melted into American society. Most of them have lost their ability to speak Hungarian and no longer have a true identity of themselves as Hungarians. Most have only a minimal acquaintance with modern Hungary and know very little about Hungarian traditions. This is somewhat true of the post-World War II immigrants as well, even though a sizable percentage of their American-born offspring does speak Hungarian and has some knowledge of Hungarian culture. Moreover, in light of the collapse of communism in 1989-1990, a significant number of them have found their way back to the land of their ancestors. This was and is being done largely in the form of employment with some of the major American or Western European corporations that have established branches in Hungary. This temporary return does create a set of new ties, but because of the radical transformation of Hungarian society during the four decades of communist rule, the experience is not always positive.

Despite renewed contacts with the homeland, Hungarian Americans are losing their struggle to survive as a separate ethnic group in America. This is evident both in their declining numbers, as well as in the decreasing number of their ethnic institutions, churches, cultural organizations, and fraternal organizations. This phenomenon is best seen when comparing the census statistics of 1980 with those of 1990. The number of those who claimed to be fully or primarily Hungarian during those two census years has declined by nearly 11 percent (from 1,776,902 to 1,582,302), while the number of those who speak primarily Hungarian in their families has dropped by almost 18 percent (from 180,000 to 147,902). During the same period Greater Pittsburgh alone lost about half a dozen Hungarian churches; the remaining ones are struggling for survival. The same fate befell Hungarian cultural and social organizations of western Pennsylvania, few of which are active today. This trend appears to be equally true for the entire Northeast, embracing the above-mentioned 10 states. It should be noted here, however, that this decline is not as evident in California and Florida, which experienced a rapid growth of Hungarians from the 1960s through the 1990s. More recently, however, even California experienced a 3.5 percent decline in its Hungarian population (from 164,903 to 159,121), and Florida gained 11.4 percent only because of its extreme popularity with retirees (from 89,587 to 99,822).

ACCULTURATION AND ASSIMILATION

Notwithstanding earlier immigrations, the Hungarian presence in the United States was estab-lished by the large mass of rural immigrants in the three decades before World War I. These immigrants fostered their Hungarian identity and a sense of community because of their social, cultural, and psychological needs and also because of Anglo-American society's unwillingness to accept them. The same cannot be said of their American-born children, who tended to assimilate at a rapid pace. They were driven by the socioeconomic drawing power of American society, as well as by their own conscious desire to separate themselves from the world of their simple immigrant parents. Most of them managed to move up a notch or two in social status, but perhaps for this very reason many of them also left the ethnic communities founded by their parents. Their efforts to assimilate, however, were not fully successful, for although native born, they were still viewed as outsiders by the Anglo-American majority.

The situation changed significantly with the second native-born generation, whose rise to adulthood coincided with the birth of the "ethnic revolution" of the 1960s. Their embracing of this revolution led to the rediscovery of their ethnic roots. It was impeded, however, by their inability to speak Hungarian and by the gradual disintegration of viable Hungarian ethnic communities, a disintegration that began precisely at the start of this ethnic revolution. At present, most self-contained Hungarian American communities are in the process of final dissolution. A few of their cultural and religious institutions still exist, but they serve only the needs of the older generation, and very briefly those of some of the new arrivals. This dying-out process is best demonstrated in the institutional life of the oldest and largest Hungarian Catholic church and parish in the United States, St. Elizabeth of Cleveland (founded in 1892), where the ratio of burials to baptisms is nearly 20 to one.

The turn-of-the-century immigrants and their descendants provided the foundations of Hungarian American life, but their role and influence were much more limited than those of the later waves, who brought with them a high level of learning and a strong sense of historical and national consciousness. The latter were less prone to buckle under assimilative social pressures. Moreover, if they assimilated, they did so consciously. Most of them, however, retained a large degree of dual identity, which they also passed on to their second- and third-generation descendants. The latter usually moved rapidly into American professional and business circles and—

with the exception of those in the vicinity of greater New York, Cleveland, Chicago, and Los Angeles—were forced to live outside the influence of their ethnic communities. Thus, they experienced their Hungarian identity in isolation. This sense of isolation has permeated the lives of most upward-moving professionals, especially since the 1960s. Consequently, their success or lack thereof in passing their traditions on to their offspring depended and still largely depends on their dedication to the idea of dual identity. But because relatively few had the time to deal with this issue, the next generation is rapidly losing its facility to speak Hungarian and along with it its true Hungarian identity.

American-born offspring of the various immigrant waves still practice some of their folk traditions, partially during social events held at their churches and social clubs, but mostly during major folk festivals and "Hungarian Days" that are still celebrated in such large centers of Hungarian life as New Brunswick, New Jersey; Pittsburgh; and Cleveland. Although declining in numbers, the quality of these major performances has actually improved in recent years because of closer contact with Hungary and Hungarian professionals.

Misconceptions about Hungary and the Hungarians abound in the United States, although this is much less true today than in the early part of the century when they were often misidentified as Mongols or Gypsies. This was due in part to American society's minimum knowledge about Central and Eastern Europe and in part to conscious distortions by politically motivated propagandists. Today, the situation has improved significantly because of the impact of the Hungarian Revolution of 1956 and because of the enhanced number and quality of publications about Hungary, produced mostly by the American-educated offspring of the political immigrants. This improvement, however, is more noticeable among the educated classes than among the general public.

HOLIDAYS

Hungarian Americans generally celebrate three major national holidays: March 15 (Revolution of 1848), August 20 (Saint Stephen's Day), and October 23 (Revolution of 1956). These celebrations may combine patriotic and religious elements. There is no such thing as a specifically Hungarian American holiday, perhaps because

the attention of most unassimilated Hungarian Americans is focused on the mother country.

HEALTH AND MENTAL HEALTH ISSUES

Hungary has the highest suicide rate in the world (45-48 per 100,000). The factors connected with this suicide rate, however, appear to be limited to Hungarian society, and Hungarian Americans are no more prone to mental health problems than are other ethnic groups in the United States.

The Hungarian medical profession is of high quality, even though it does not have access to much of the modern equipment available in the United States. This does not prevent Hungarian physicians from being among the best educated, as is demonstrated by, among other things, the virtually nonexistent failure rate of Hungarian medical students on American medical examinations. This holds true both for Hungarians who have emigrated after their medical training in Hungary and Hungarian Americans who attend Hungarian medical schools and then return to take their examinations in the United States.

LANGUAGE

Hungarian is classified as a Finno-Ugric language and is part of the larger Ural-Altaic linguistic family. The most distinctive characteristic of these languages is that they are agglutinative—that is, words are extended into complex expressions through the use of prefixes and suffixes. One example will conveniently serve to illustrate. The meaning of a single word, *szent* (saint), can be changed by adding numerous prefixes and suffixes as follows (hyphens indicate the additions): *szent-ség* (sanctity), *szent-ség-ed* (your sanctity), *szent-ség-eid-del* (with your sanctity), *szent-ség-eid-del* (with your sanctities), *meg-szent-ségel-és-ed* (your sanctification), *meg-szent-ség-telenít-hetetlen-ség-ed-del* (with your ability to withstand desanctification).

The closest linguistic relatives of the Hungarians are the Finns and the Estonians, but the Hungarians are also distantly related to the Turkic peoples. This is due both to their common roots and to the renewal of contacts through the mixing of Finno-Ugric and Turkic tribes during the first nine centuries of the Christian Era.

Before the conquest of Hungary, the Hungarians had their own runic script. After their conversion to Christianity, they borrowed the Latin liturgical language and alphabet and adapted this alphabet to the phonetic properties of the Hungarian language. This was done by doubling up letters to represent a single sound: "cs" ("ch"), "gy" ("dy"), "ly" ("y"), "ny" (soft "n"), "sz" ("s"), "ty" (soft "t"), "zs" ("zh"), "dzs" ("dzh"); or by adding diacritical marks ("á," "é," "í," "ö," "ő," "ü," "ű"). In many instances the accent marks not only signify the pronunciation but also alter the meaning of the word—for example: *sor* (row), *sör* (beer); *bor* (wine), *bör* (skin); *sas* (eagle), *sás* (sedge); *szar* (excrement), *szár* (stem). The meaning of a single word can be changed several times simply by adding or subtracting a diacritical mark—for example: *kerek* (round), *kerék* (wheel), *kérek* (I am requesting), *kérék* (I have requested).

The English language has had an impact on how Hungarian Americans speak Hungarian. This was particularly true for the less educated immigrants, who readily mixed their simple Hungarian with working-class English. Thus, they rapidly developed a language of their own known as "Hunglish" (Hungarian English), which introduced English words into the Hungarian, but transformed them to fit Hungarian pronunciation and orthography: *trén* (train), *plész* (place), *szalon* (saloon), *bedrőm* (bedroom), *atrec* (address), *tájm* (time), *szendsztón* (sandstone), *gud báj* (good-bye), *foriner* (foreigner), *fandri* (foundry), *fanesz* (furnace), *bakszi* (box), *burdos* (boarder), *burdosház* (boarding house), *görl* (girl), *groszeri* (grocery).

There was also a reverse version of Hunglish that may be called "Engarian" (English Hungarian), which adjusted the primitive English to the ears of the immigrants. The result was two hodgepodge languages that were barely comprehensible to Hungarians or Americans who did not speak both languages—for example: *Szé, miszter, gimi order, maj hen trók brók!* (Say, Mister, give me the order. My hand truck broke.). Such usage is no longer common, largely because the Americanized offspring of the turn-of-the-century immigrants have switched to English but also because the more educated post-World War II immigrants never really acquired it.

GREETINGS AND POPULAR EXPRESSIONS

Common greetings are as follows (all words are pronounced with the accent on the first syllable): *Jó reggelt* ("yo reggelt")—Good morning; *Jó napot* ("yo nahpote")—Good day; *Jó estét* ("yo eshtayt") —Good evening; *Jó éjszakát* ("yo aysahkaht")—

Good night; *Kezitcsókolom* ("kezeet choakholohm")—I kiss your hand; *Szervusz* or *Szerbusz* ("servoos, serboos")—Hello, Hi; *Szia* ("seeyah") —Hi, Hello; *Viszontlátásra* ("veesoant-lahtahshrah")—Good-bye, See you again; *Isten áldjon meg* ("eeshten ahldyoan meg")—God bless you. Other popular expressions include: *Boldog újévet* ("bohldogh ooy-ayveth")—Happy New Year; *Kellemes húsvétot* ("kellehmesh hooshvaytoth")—Happy Easter; *Kellemes karácsonyi ünnepeket* ("kellehmesh karahchoanyi ünnepeketh")— Merry Christmas; *Boldog ünnepeket* ("bohldogh ünnepeketh")—Happy Holidays; *Egészségedre* ("eggayshaygedreh")—To your health (spoken when toasting).

FAMILY AND COMMUNITY DYNAMICS

After the early and predominantly male phases of economic immigration abated, Hungarian American immigrant communities assumed a traditional and stable family structure. By the 1920s, most immigrants had resolved to stay permanently in the United States. They established families, had American-born children, and became intimately involved in the social lives of their churches, fraternal societies, and cultural institutions that in the past served as their extended families. The structure survived almost intact into the 1960s, although with only limited participation by the political immigrants of the interwar and postwar periods. Unable to agree on a common platform with the earlier economic immigrants, the latter usually founded their own organizations and pursued their familial and social activities within these more politically oriented groups.

With the exception of the relatively few immigrants who came during the 1960s through the 1980s—many of them from the Hungarian-inhabited regions surrounding Hungary—very few Hungarians have ever received public assistance. Traditionally, accepting handouts has been perceived in Hungarian society as an admission of failure. This view was much less prevalent among the more recent immigrants, who had become accustomed to state assistance under the communist social system.

Immigrant life and ethnic experience in America transformed basic traditional patterns of family life, resulting in a hybrid set of customs. In terms of everyday existence, Hungarian family life conforms to American patterns, but with a greater emphasis on education. The role of women has been enhanced compared with the still male-dominated Hungarian model. Adjustment to American custom is also evident in the area of dating, marriage, and divorce. Until a generation ago, dating practices were very strict and circumscribed. More recently, they have loosened, as has the commitment to a lasting marriage. Thus, whereas a generation ago divorce among Hungarian immigrants was rare, today it is almost as common as it is for American society as a whole.

Philanthropic activities among Hungarian Americans tend to be aimed at specific groups of Hungarians. During the past three decades, these were oriented almost exclusively toward the Hungarian minorities in the areas surrounding Hungary. There are, of course, exceptions to the rule, but these exceptions are usually connected with the philanthropic activities of the few super-rich, the best-known of whom is the billionaire investor George Soros.

RELIGION

Hungary has been a Roman Catholic country since its conversion to Christianity in the late tenth and early eleventh centuries. This religious uniformity was shattered only in the sixteenth century, when Protestantism entered the country and spread, especially in its Calvinist form. After a century of intense struggle, Catholicism remained strong in the country's western and central regions, while Calvinism came to dominate its eastern regions. This Catholic-Calvinist rivalry was complicated somewhat by the presence of a significant minority of Lutherans (Evangelicals), Jews, Greek/Byzantine Catholics, and Unitarians, as well as by a few other small Christian sects. Yet, in spite of its losses to rival faiths, Roman Catholicism retained its dominant position as Hungary's only official "state religion" until the communist takeover in 1948.

The religious divisions in Hungary also came to be reflected in Hungarian American society. The Calvinists were the first to establish their pioneer congregations in 1891 in Cleveland and in Pittsburgh, to be followed in 1892 by the Roman Catholics (St. Elizabeth of Hungary Church, Cleveland) and in 1907 by the Lutherans (Cleveland). These early congregations soon sprouted scores of other Hungarian churches throughout the Northeast. As a result, by the 1930s Hungarian Americans had nearly 140 Calvinist, more than 60 Roman Catholic, and about ten Lutheran churches, as well as perhaps two dozen other prayer houses. Although the Calvinists had the greatest number of churches, their congregations were small, and as such they represented only one-third as many faithful as did the Roman Catholics.

Roman Catholics, Calvinists, and Lutherans together constituted slightly over 90 percent of all religious affiliations of Hungarian Americans. The other eight to ten percent was made up of smaller denominations including the Byzantine Catholics, Jews, Baptists, and Adventists. Because of their small numbers, however, none of the latter had more than a limited and passing influence on Hungarian American life.

The religious practices of Hungarian Roman Catholics and Protestants in the United States are basically identical to those of their coreligionists in Hungary and are also similar to the practices of their American counterparts. Although religious practices did not change after emigration, the social significance of the congregations and the position and the role of the parish priests and pastors underwent significant changes. In Hungary the religious congregations and their priests or ministers were supported by their respective mother churches through an obligatory religious tax. As a result these congregations were centrally controlled, with little or no input from the members of the congregations. This was particularly true of the Roman Catholic Church, which had retained its monarchical structure from the Middle Ages. Although Calvinist and Lutheran congregations did elect their pastors even in Hungary, the powers of the presbytery (church council) were much more limited than in the United States. This was true not only because of the somewhat authoritarian nature of traditional Hungarian society but also because the pastors did not depend on the financial support of their parishioners. In Hungary, therefore, it was the priests and the ministers who controlled the congregation, and not vice versa.

After emigration, this relationship changed significantly. Much of the control over church affairs slipped into the hands of the members of the church council. This change in the power relationship was due both to the lack of state support for religion and to the fact that now the members of the congregations were paying for the upkeep of their churches and their pastors.

Just as the role of the church leaders had changed, the function of the church had also changed. Traditionally, American churches have

A Hungarian refugee

reunites with his family in

a New Jersey airport in

1957.

always combined religious and social functions—a phenomenon that was largely unknown in Europe. This American tradition was accepted by the immigrant churches, which consequently ceased to function solely as houses of prayer. They now also assumed the role of social clubs, where members of the congregation combined their search for spiritual salvation with an ongoing attempt to fulfill their earthly social needs. As such, immigrant churches lost some of the sanctity of their Old World counterparts.

The climax of Hungarian religious life in America was reached in the period between the 1920s and 1960s. By the 1970s, however, a process of slow decay had set in, which during the 1980s had accelerated to the point where several Hungarian ethnic churches were closing their doors every year.

During the past 100 years of Hungarian religious life in the United States, all denominations have been plagued by dissension, but none more

so that the Hungarian Calvinist (Reformed) Church. Within the first quarter century after having taken root in America, this dissension has led to the establishment of several competing Calvinist denominations—a process that resulted in a new subdenomination as late as 1982. While some of these conflicts and fragmentations were of an ideological and administrative nature (e.g., their relationship to the mother church in Hungary), most of them were really the result of personal animosity among the clergy. American social practices make it easy for anyone to establish a new church, while personality conflicts and group squabbles often result in institutional divorces. At the moment Hungarian Calvinists are still divided into a half dozen rival and competing churches that are held together only by the awareness of their common roots and by their membership in the Hungarian Reformed Federation (HRF). Founded in 1898 as a fraternal association, the HRF also serves as a force of unity among Hungarian Calvinists.

Employment and Economic Traditions

Hungarian immigrants have been involved in all facets of American economic life, with the level of their employment depending for the most part on their social background. Those who came before the mid-nineteenth century were individual adventurers who were well prepared for all eventualities in the New World. Although few in numbers, most of those who stayed proved to be successful. Some of them became well-known merchants in Philadelphia, Baltimore, and New Orleans, while others became well-respected professors at American universities. Whatever they did, they did it well, for they could rely on a good education and on the self-assurance common to well-born individuals.

To a large degree this was also true for the 3,000 to 4,000 Forty-niners who immigrated after the defeat of the Hungarian Revolution of 1848. Belonging mostly to the gentry, they had no intention of becoming dirt farmers or laborers in America. They spread Hungary's image as the land of a valiant "noble nation," but only a minority were able to adjust to America's pioneer society. This was true even though a few of them also became involved in the establishment of Hungarian colonies in the West, such as László Újházy (1795-1870), a high-ranking official of the revolutionary government, who founded New Buda in Iowa in 1852. After trying their hands at many things, a thousand of the Forty-niners joined the Union armies in the Civil War, after which a good number of them went into diplomatic service or into various major business ventures in the West.

The next wave of immigrants came during the late nineteenth and early twentieth centuries with the intention of repatriating after four or five years with enough capital to make themselves into prosperous farmers. Few of them achieved this goal, and virtually all of them became unskilled or semiskilled workers in America's bustling industries. They were the peons of America's Gilded Age, who contributed their brawn to American coal mines and steel smelters, and who produced the mythical Hungarian American hero, Joe Magarac, who could bend steel bars with his bare hands.

Each of the next four immigration waves contributed to the abatement of this stereotype. These waves comprised the interwar "intellectual immigrants"; the post-World War II "political immigrants"; the Fifty-sixers; and finally the political-economic immigrants of the past four decades. Given their achievements in Europe, the intellectual immigrants moved immediately into the highest American intellectual and scientific circles and almost overnight created the myth of the uniqueness of Hungarian talent.

The political immigrants, or DPs, represented the military-legal-administrative leadership of interwar Hungary and had few transferable skills; thus, many of them were forced to engage in physical labor. Yet, their learning, cultural background, and personal bearing immediately revealed to their fellow American workers that they were of a different caliber. Many of them eventually did manage to transfer to white-collar work, although it was largely their American-educated children who moved up rapidly into the professions.

The Fifty-sixers differed from the DPs in their relative youth, orientation toward transferable technical and practical skills, and diminished cultural background—the product of a decade of communist restructuring of Hungarian society. Yet they and the American-educated children of the DPs produced a class of professionals that penetrated all aspects of American scientific, scholarly, artistic, literary, and business life.

The final immigration wave began during the 1960s and is still going on today. It is characterized by a slow but gradual influx of professionals and professionally oriented individuals. During the 1960s through the 1980s, political persecution was the ostensible motive for their immigration. Since the collapse of communism, they have come as needed professionals.

According to a recent survey by the *New York Times*, Hungarians are not among the most highly regarded ethnic groups in America, but they are certainly among the most successful. They have also managed to eradicate the Hunky stereotype that was unwittingly transmitted by their less fortunate predecessors.

Politics and Government

The political activism of the Hungarians in America reaches back to the mid-nineteenth century, when Lajos Kossuth (1802-1894) visited the United States (1851-1852) and in a highly celebrated tour of the country urged Americans to intervene on behalf of defeated Hungary by supporting Hungary's struggle against Austria. Although the Hungarian statesman's presence created a veritable "Kossuth craze" in America, the results were disappointing. Despite its outward expression of sympathy, the U.S. government was unwilling to budge from its policy of isolationism. Although unsuccessful in its political aims, Kossuth's presence did create a positive image of Hungary, as well as stir up pro-Hungarian sentiment among the American public. The image and sentiment survived until the turn of the century. The final blow to the Kossuth-inspired image came during World War I, when Austria-Hungary sided with imperial Germany.

Although the Austro-Hungarian Empire disappeared and historic Hungary was dismembered after the war, anti-Hungarian sentiment resurfaced after Hungary's forced alliance with Italy and Germany during World War II. Following the war, Hungary came to be regarded as a Soviet satellite. The daring anti-Soviet uprising of 1956 once again stirred pro-Hungarian sentiment. The American image of Hungary has been improving ever since, both because Hungary was among the first of the Soviet-dominated nations to liberalize economically and politically during the 1960s and because of the increasingly sophisticated political activism of Hungarian American lobby groups.

Hungarians established several mutual aid societies in the second half of the nineteenth century, but not until 1906 did they create the first successful political organization, the American-Hungarian Federation (AHF), which is still in existence. The twin goals of the AHF were to protect the interests of the Hungarian immigrants and to promote the cause of Hungary in the United States. During the first decade of its existence, the AHF worked toward these goals in close cooperation with Hungary. During World War I, particularly after the United States entered the war on the opposite side, this task became impossible. Following the war the AHF proved unsuccessful in its efforts to influence American foreign policy on postwar treaties. Yet, during the interwar period—in conjunction with the largest Hungarian fraternal organizations (i.e., Verhovay, Rákóczi, Bridgeport, the Reformed Federation)—it conducted a steady propaganda campaign to revise the unfair terms of the Treaty of Trianon (1920). This task became increasingly difficult during the late 1930s, when Hungary began to regain some of its former territory with the help of Germany and Italy.

The darkest and most difficult period in Hungarian political activism came during World War II, when the AHF and the major fraternal organizations were forced to defend Hungary's territorial gains while maintaining their support for the American war effort. To prove their loyalty to the United States, more than 50,000 Hungarians served in the U.S. armed forces, and all Hungarian American organizations bought U.S. defense bonds and made repeated declarations of allegiance. Toward the end of the war, they organized the American-Hungarian Relief Committee, whose members undertook a major effort to send aid to their devastated homeland, as well as to hundreds of thousands of Hungarians who had been trapped in German and Austrian refugee camps. Moreover, in 1948 and 1950, the AHF and the major Hungarian fraternal societies supported the passage of the two Displaced Persons Acts that brought almost 18,000 Hungarian political refugees to the United States.

The appearance of the post-World War II political immigrants—the DPs during the early 1950s and the Fifty-sixers after the Revolution of 1956—created a completely new situation. Much better educated and more involved politically than most of their predecessors, the newcomers created their own organizations. Some of the most vocal and active of these associations included the American branch of the Fraternal Association of Hungarian Veterans (1947), the Cleveland-based Committee for Liberation (1951), and the Hungarian National Committee (1948)—the last of which was viewed by the U.S. government as a virtual government in exile.

The appearance of the Fifty-sixers added a new color to this political spectrum. Although a number of them joined existing DP organizations, many of them also founded their own associations. The most important of these was the Hungarian Freedom Fighter's Federation (1957), although very soon it was joined by others with nearly identical names. During the 1970s several minority-oriented organizations were created specifically to help the cause of the increasingly oppressed Hungarian minorities in the neighboring states. These included the Committee for Human Rights in Romania, the Transylvania World Federation, the Transylvanian Committee, and the Hungarian Human Rights Committee, all of which were especially concerned with the plight of the Hungarian minorities under the oppressive rule of the communist Ceauşescu regime in Romania.

From the late 1950s through the early 1980s, most of the nonminority-oriented organizations were concerned primarily with the liberation of Hungary and then with soliciting U.S. government help to undermine the communist regime. Throughout this period the politically active new immigrants had little concern for American domestic politics; their attention was turned to Hungary. Thus, after becoming citizens, they usually voted with the Republican Party, which they perceived to be tougher on communism. As opposed to them, the turn-of-the-century economic immigrants and their American-born descendants paid only lip service to Hungary. They were much more concerned with domestic politics, and with bread-and-butter issues, than with the problems of communism. Thus, they voted mostly Democratic.

The rise of a new generation among the political immigrants during the 1970s and 1980s also produced some changes. On the one hand, the American-born or American-educated members of the younger generations became involved in U.S. domestic politics in both political parties. On the other hand, they began to assume a much more realistic approach toward Hungary and its "goulash communism." Some of them assumed the leadership of the AHF and carried their pragmatism into its politics. While understandable, this act split the AHF and brought about the foundation of the National Federation of Hungarian Americans (NFHA) in 1984, and subsequently several rival organizations, including the very active and influential Hungarian American Coalition (HAC) in 1992.

The collapse of communism and the rise of a nationalist government under the Hungarian Democratic Forum (1989-90) produced a general euphoria among Hungarian Americans, and also an upsurge in their desire to help their homeland. The euphoria coincided with Hungary's unheard of popularity in the world for its role in undermining communism. This euphoria and popularity, however, did not last. The country's social and economic problems produced a general disillusionment that was also felt by Hungarian Americans, many of whose hopes also remained unrealized.

At present, most Hungarian Americans have become American citizens and are heavily involved in the political life of both U.S. political parties. At the same time they still display considerable interest in Hungary. Even though somewhat disillusioned with the way things are going in Hungary, they continue to pursue pro-Hungarian lobbying efforts through several umbrella organizations (AHF, NFHA, HAC), as well as through their presence in the U.S. Congress. The most visible and active among the Hungarian congressional representatives is the Fifty-sixer Tom Lantos (1928-) from California (1980-), who in recent years has become increasingly involved in Hungarian-related political activities.

MILITARY

Relative to their size as an ethnic group, more Hungarian Americans served in the Civil War than any other nationality. Of the approximately 4,000 Hungarians in the United States (including women and children) at the outbreak of the war in 1861, more than 800—at least three-fourths of the adult male population—served in the Union armies. Among them were two major generals, five brigadier generals, 15 colonels and lieutenant colonels, 13 majors, 12 captains, about four dozen first and second lieutenants, and scores of noncommissioned officers.

The most prominent of the officers was Major General Julius H. Stahel (1825-1912)—known in Hungary before his emigration as Gyula Számvald. General Stahel became a close confidant of President Lincoln and the first Hungarian recipient of the Congressional Medal of Honor. Among the nearly 1,000 Hungarians in the Union Army was the young Joseph Pulitzer (1817-1911), who subsequently became the king of American journalism and the founder of the famous literary prize that bears his name.

INDIVIDUAL AND GROUP CONTRIBUTIONS

Following Hungary's dismemberment after World War I, many educated Hungarians—engineers, physicians, sociologists, educators, and lawyers—came to the United States to pursue their livelihood. In the 1930s their numbers were increased by those fleeing the spread of fascism in Central Europe. In this category were numerous internationally known scientists, social scientists, musicologists, artists, filmmakers, and other persons of unusual talent.

ECONOMICS

From the late nineteenth century, Hungarians have made important contributions to U.S. industry and finance. Two of the earliest entrepreneurs were the Black (Schwartz) and Kundtz families. The Black family founded a series of garment factories and department stores, while Tivador Kundtz (1852-1937) established the White Machine factory. These two families employed and aided thousands of fellow immigrant Hungarians.

Modern entrepreneurs include the billionaire financier George Soros (1930-), who has played a significant role in the transformation of the former Soviet world through philanthropic efforts such as the establishment of the Budapest- and Prague-based Central European University; and Andrew Grove (born András Gróf; 1936-), who as the founder and president of Intel Corporation created the world's largest manufacturer of computer chips.

FILM AND ENTERTAINMENT

Two Hungarians were influential in the development of the Hollywood film industry: Adolph Zukor (1873-1976), the founder of Paramount Pictures; and William Fox (1879-1952), the founder of Twentieth Century-Fox. Zukor and Fox transformed the stylish Biedermeier culture of the Austro-Hungarian Empire into the glamorous society portrayed in Hollywood film.

Other pioneers in the film industry included directors/producers Michael Curtiz (born Michael Kertész; 1888-1962), Sir Alexander Korda (1893-1956), George Cukor (1899-1983), and Joseph Pasternak (1901-), as well as film stars Leslie Howard (born Árpád Steiner; 1893-1943), Bela Lugosi (1883-1956) of Dracula fame, Tony Curtis (born Bernard Schwartz; 1925-), and the Gabor sisters, Zsa-Zsa, Eva, and Magda. In this category also belongs the magician Harry Houdini (born Erich Weisz; 1874-1926).

MUSIC

By the time the internationally known composers Béla Bartók (1881-1945) and Ernő Dohnányi (1877-1960) emigrated in the 1940s, the American cultural scene was already peopled by such Hungarian composers as Fritz Reiner (1888-1963), George Szell (1897-1970), Eugene Ormandy (1899-1985), Antal Dorati (1906-1988), and Sir Georg Solti (1912-). Hungarians were also present on Broadway in popular American musicals. The best-loved of them was Sigmund Romberg (1887-1951), who was perhaps the most successful transplanter of the Viennese and the Budapest operetta. Also significant was the contribution of Miklós Rózsa (1907-), who worked with Sir Alexander Korda and wrote the music to some of the great American films.

SCIENCE AND MATHEMATICS

Three Hungarians assisted Enrico Fermi with the breakthroughs in atomic fission that resulted in the development of the atomic bomb: Leo Szilard (1898-1964), Eugene Wigner (1902-1995), and Edward Teller (1908-). Other major contributors are Theodore von Kármán (1881-1963), father of the heat and quantum theory; mathematician and father of the computer Johann von Neumann (1903-1957); and Zoltán Bay (1900-1992), the pioneer in radar astronomy.

George Pólya (1887-1985) and Gábor Szegő (1895-1985) were responsible for making Stanford University one of the world's premier centers of mathematics. A much younger exponent of finite mathematics and its application, John George Kemény (1926-) later became the president of Dartmouth College.

Other leading Hungarian scientists included the Nobel laureates Georg Karl Hevesy (1855-1966), Albert Szent-Györgyi (1893-1986), Georg von Békésy (1899-1972), and Dennis Gabor (1900-1979). The list also includes several members of the Polányi family: the social philosopher Karl Polányi (1886-1964), the physicist-philosopher Michael Polányi (1891-1976), as well as the latter's son, John Charles Polányi (1926-), who won the Nobel Prize for chemistry in 1986.

MEDIA

PRINT

Amerikai-Kanadai Magyar Élet (American-Canadian Hungarian Life).
Founded in 1959 as *Amerikai Magyar Élet*, this weekly has been under the control of Bishop Tibor Dömötör of the Free Hungarian Reformed Church since 1986.

Contact: Elizabeth Schmidt, Managing Editor.
Address: 2637 Copley Road, Akron, Ohio 44321.

Telephone: (216) 666-2637.

Fax: (216) 666-4746.

Amerikai Magyar Szó(American Hungarian Word).

Weekly newspaper printed in Hungarian.

Contact: Z. Deak, Editor.

Address: 130 East 16th Street, New York, New York 10003.

Telephone: (212) 254-0397.

Californiai Magyarság (California Hungarians).

Founded in 1924 as a middle-of-the-road regional newspaper, it is now a national paper that has retained its moderate stance.

Contact: Mária Fényes, Editor and Publisher.

Address: 207 South Western Avenue, Suite 201, Los Angeles, California 90004.

Telephone: (213) 463-3473.

Fax: (213) 384-7642.

Hungarian Insights.

A quarterly publication that provides news and information on Hungarian culture, history, and business.

Contact: Lel Somogyi, Editor.

Address: 6020 Pearl Road, Cleveland, Ohio 44130.

Telephone: (216) 842-4651.

Hungarian Studies Newsletter.

Quarterly publication of the American Hungarian Foundation; publishes news of the Foundation as well as information for English-speaking scholars concerned with Hungarian studies.

Contact: August J. Molnar, Editor.

Address: American Hungarian Foundation, P.O. Box 1084, New Brunswick, New Jersey 08903.

Telephone: (201) 846-5777.

Magyar Elet (Hungarian Life).

An independent weekly newspaper published in Hungarian and circulated throughout Canada and the United States.

Contact: Laszlo Schnee, Editor.

Address: 21 Vaughan Road, Suite 201, Toronto, Ontario, Canada M6G 2N2.

Telephone: (416) 652-6370.

Fax: (416) 652-6370.

Magyarok Vasárnapja (Hungarians' Sunday).

Founded in Cleveland in 1894, for its first hundred years this paper was called Katolikus Magyarok Vasárnapja (Catholic Hungarians' Sunday). Since the change in ownership in 1993, it has lost its religious character and has become the voice of populist nationalism.

Contact: Loránt Szász, Editor and Publisher.

Address: P.O. Box 4442, Thousand Oaks, California 91359.

Telephone: (818) 707-1548.

Fax: (818) 597-9867.

Szabadság (Liberty).

Published for the East Coast readership under the title Amerikai Magyar Népszava (American Hungarian People's Voice), the two papers, which were founded in 1891 and 1899 respectively, were once rivals, but after the owner-editor of Szabadság bought its rival in 1949, they were gradually merged into a single paper under two different titles.

Contact: Eva Nadai, Editor; or, Judith Fliegler, English Editor.

Address: 8140 Mayfield Road, Cleveland, Ohio 44026-2441.

Telephone: (216) 729-7200.

Fax: (216) 729-7250.

Új Világ (New World).

Founded in 1971, this paper was a neutral middle-of-the-road weekly until the early 1990s, when it became the voice of the right wing.

Contact: Viktor K. Molnár, Editor and Publisher.

Address: 15005 South Vermont Avenue, Gardena, California 90247.

Telephone: (310) 719-1078.

Fax: (310) 719-8918.

William Penn Life.

Founded in 1965 to replace an earlier Hungarian-language version, Vehovayak Lapj (Verhovay News), it is a small English-language monthly geared toward the William Penn Association, the largest Hungarian fraternal organization in America. Its influence is limited to its membership, which is made up largely of third- and fourth-generation descendants of the turn-of-the-century economic immigrants.

Contact: Elmer E. Vargo, Editor.

Address: William Penn Association, 709 Brighton Road, Pittsburgh, Pennsylvania 15233-1821.

Telephone: (412) 231-2979.
Fax: (412) 231-8535.

TELEVISION

The Nationality Broadcasting Network.
Located in Cleveland, this network broadcasts Hungarian programs everyday via satellite throughout North America.

Contact: Miklós Kossányi, President.
Address: 11906 Madison Avenue, Cleveland, Ohio.
Telephone: (216) 221-0330.
Fax: (216) 221-3638.

ORGANIZATIONS AND ASSOCIATIONS

American Hungarian Federation (AHF) (Amerikai Magyar Szövetség [AMSZ]).
Founded in Cleveland in 1906, the AHF is the oldest umbrella organization of Hungarian Americans. After being based in Washington, D.C., from the 1940s to the 1970s, in the early 1980s it transferred its office to Akron. Following an internal controversy that resulted in the formation of the rival National Federation of American Hungarians in 1984, the AHF is now the second-largest Hungarian American umbrella organization, with about 55 member organizations. Like its rival organizations, it conducts lobbying activities on behalf of Hungarian causes.

Contact: Rev. Tibor Dömötör, President.
Address: 2631 Copley Road, Akron, Ohio 44321.
Telephone: (216) 666-9777.
Fax: (216) 666-4746.

American Hungarian Folklore Centrum (AHFC).
Supports and promotes Hungarian studies and folk culture within the scholarly and public life of America.

Contact: Kalman Magyar, Director.
Address: P.O. Box 262, Bogota, New Jersey 07603.
Telephone: (201) 836-4869.

American Hungarian Reformed Federation (AHRF) (Amerikai Magyar Református Egyesület [AMRE]).
Founded in 1898, the AHRF is the second-largest and only religiously based Hungarian fraternal association in existence. It has about 20,000 members, and although it is now primarily an insurance company, it continues to support Hungarian cultural activities and also engages in some lobbying efforts on behalf of Hungarian causes.

Contact: George Dózsa, President.
Address: 2001 Massachusetts Avenue, N.W., Washington, D.C., 20036-1011.
Telephone: (202) 328-2630.
Fax: (202) 228-7984.

Hungarian American Coalition (HAC) (Magyar-Amerikai Koalíció [MAK]).
Founded in 1992, the HAC is the most recent of the Hungarian umbrella organizations. Politically, it has a moderate-centrist, pragmatic orientation. It attempts to carry out an effective lobbying effort on behalf of Hungarian causes in Washington, D.C.

Contact: Edit Lauer, President.
Address: Suite 850, 818 Connecticut Avenue, N.W., Washington, D.C. 20006.

Hungarian Association of Cleveland (Cleveland Magyar Társaság).
Founded in 1958 in Austria and transferred to Cleveland in 1952, the Hungarian Association has been the most influential organization of the post-World War II immigrants, or DPs. Since 1961 it has organized annual congresses (the proceedings of which are published in its yearbook *Krónika*). In 1965 it sponsored the foundation of the Árpád Academy (*Árpád Akadémia*) to recognize the scholarly, scientific, and artistic achievements of Hungarians throughout the world. In 1990 it was responsible for the establishment of one of the rival umbrella organizations of the American Hungarian Federation, the National Federation of Hungarian Americans (NFHA) (Magyar Amerikaiak Országos Szövetsége [MAOSZ]). The Hungarian Association of Cleveland and its member organizations are ideologically conservative, representing essentially the views of interwar Hungary. The HAC functions and publishes primarily in Hungarian.

Contact: Gyula Nádas, President.
Address: 1450 Grace Avenue, Cleveland, Ohio 44107.
Telephone: (216) 226-4089.

Hungarian Cultural Foundation (HCF).
Interested in preserving Hungarian cultural heritage in the United States and elsewhere in the English-speaking world.

Contact: Joseph Ertavy-Barath, President.
Address: P.O. Box 364, Stone Mountain, Georgia 30086.
Telephone: (404) 377-2600.

Hungarian Scout Association in Exile (HSAE) (Külföldi Magyar Cserkészszövetség).

Founded in 1947 in Germany and transferred to the United States in 1951, the HSAE is a worldwide organization, with well over a hundred scout troops, whose goal is to uphold the traditions of Hungarian scouting in the Hungarian language.

Contact: Gábor Bodnár, President.
Address: Post Office Box 68, Garfield, New Jersey 07026.
Telephone: (201) 772-8810.
Fax: (201) 772-5145.

National Federation of Hungarian Americans (NFAH) (Amerikai Magyarok Országos Szövetség).

Founded in 1984, as a splinter group of the much older American-Hungarian Federation, the NFAH has since grown into the largest umbrella organization of Hungarian Americans, with more than one hundred institutional members. Its primary function is to serve as a lobby group for Hungarian and Hungarian American causes in Washington, D.C., and to aid Hungary's transformation toward democracy.

Contact: László Pásztor, National President.
Address: 717 Second Street, N.E., Washington, D.C., 20002.
Telephone: (202) 546-3003.
Fax: (202) 543-8425; or, (202) 547-0392.

William Penn Association (WPA).

Founded in 1886, as the Verhovay Aid Association, the WPA is the largest Hungarian fraternal association in North America. It assumed its present name in 1955, when it absorbed its largest rival, the Rákóczi Federation of Bridgeport, Connecticut. Although primarily an insurance company, the WPA still sponsors certain Hungarian cultural functions. Recently, the WPA has transferred much of its archives and library to the Hungarian Heritage Center of New Brunswick, New Jersey.

Contact: Elmer E. Vargo, National President.
Address: 709 Brighton Road, Pittsburgh, Pennsylvania 15233-1821.
Telephone: (412) 231-2979.
Fax: (412) 231-8538.

MUSEUMS AND RESEARCH CENTERS

American-Hungarian Foundation (AHF), Hungarian Heritage Center.

Founded in 1955, the AHF has grown into a major Hungarian cultural foundation that operates the Hungarian Heritage Center in New Brunswick, New Jersey. In addition to its museum and visitors' center, the Hungarian Heritage Center possesses one of the largest collections of archival materials relating to Hungarian Americans, as well as one of the largest Hungarica libraries in the United States (40,000 volumes). The library is by far the best source of material on the Hungarian American past.

Contact: August J. Molnar, President.
Address: 300 Somerset Street, New Brunswick, New Jersey 08903-1084.
Telephone: (908) 846-5777.
Fax: (908) 249-7033.

Hungarian Chair, Department of Uralic and Altaic Studies, Indiana University.

Founded in 1979 within the confines of an internationally known Department of Uralic and Altaic Studies that developed during the 1950s, the Hungarian Chair is in charge of the only Ph.D.-oriented Hungarian Studies program in North America. It draws heavily on the expertise of the other members of the department, as well as on Indiana University's multidisciplinary Russian and East European Institute and its strong library collection in Hungarian (25,000 volumes) and Russian and East European (200,000 volumes) material. It is also in charge of organizing several conferences every year, as well as publishing books and periodicals in the field of Hungarian studies. The only other Hungarian chair in North America is at the University of Toronto and publishes the *Hungarian Studies Review*.

Contact: Hungarian Chair Professor.
Address: Department of Uralic and Altaic Studies, Indiana University, Bloomington, Indiana 47405-2401.
Telephone: (812) 855-2223.
Fax: (812) 855-7500.

Hungarian Institute, Rutgers University.

Founded in 1992 with the financial support of the Hungarian government, the Hungarian Institute is in an early stage of development and at the moment is involved only in undergraduate education. It draws heavily on the intellectual and library resources of Rutgers University (Hungarica, 2,000 volumes), as well as on the library of the nearby American-Hungarian Foundation (Hungarica, 40,000 volumes).

Address: Rutgers University, New Brunswick, New Jersey 08903-5049.

Telephone: (908) 932-1367.

Fax: (908) 932-6723.

Several North American libraries have strong Hungarica collections, the most noteworthy of which are: the Library of Congress (60,000 volumes); Columbia University (50,000 volumes); Indiana University (25,000 volumes); University of Chicago (25,000 volumes, including the newly acquired Szathmáry Library and Archives); Harvard University (20,000 volumes); Stanford University and the Hoover Institution (20,000 volumes); New York Public Library (20,000 volumes); University of Illinois (15,000 volumes); University of Toronto (10,000 volumes); Yale University (10,000 volumes); and at least another half dozen libraries with collections of between 5,000 and 10,000 volumes (Berkeley, Cornell, Duke, Notre Dame, UCLA, University of Washington).

Hungarian Reformed Federation Library and Archives, Bethlen Home.
The Bethlen Home is the center of American Hungarian Calvinism. Located about 50 miles east of Pittsburgh, it houses an Old Age Home and the Archives of the Hungarian Reformed Church, including the papers of all dissolved congregations. The Bethlen Home also has a significant library of Hungarian American materials. The annual meetings of the Hungarian Reformed Federation (founded in 1898 and based in Washington, D.C.) also take place there, with the representatives of all Reformed congregations, irrespective of their current affiliations, in attendance.

Contact: The Reverend Paul Kovács, Director.

Address: P.O. Box 657, Ligonier, Pennsylvania 15658.

Telephone: (412) 238-6711.

Fax: (412) 238-3175.

SOURCES FOR ADDITIONAL STUDY

Lengyel, Emil. *Americans from Hungary.* Philadelphia and New York: J. B. Lippincott, 1948; reprinted, Westport, Connecticut: Greenwood, 1974.

McGuire, James Patrick. *The Hungarian Texans.* San Antonio: University of Texas, Institute of Texan Culture, 1993.

Papp, Susan M. *Hungarian Americans and Their Communities in Cleveland.* Cleveland: Cleveland Ethnic Heritage Studies, Cleveland State University, 1981.

Puskás, Julianna. *From Hungary to the United States, 1880-1914.* Budapest: Akadémiai Kiadó, 1982.

Tezla, Albert. *The Hazardous Quest: Hungarian Immigrants in the United States, 1895-1920.* Budapest: Corvina, 1993.

Várdy, Steven Béla. *Clio's Art in Hungary and in Hungarian-America.* New York: Columbia University Press, 1985.

———. *The Hungarian-Americans.* Boston: Twayne, 1985.

———. *The Hungarian Americans: The Hungarian Experience in North America.* New York and Philadelphia: Chelsea House, 1990.

Várdy, Steven Béla, and Agnes Huszár Várdy. *The Austro-Hungarian Mind: At Home and Abroad.* New York: Columbia University Press, 1989.

BOOKS

Alba, Richard. *Ethnic Identity: The Transformation of White America*. New Haven, Connecticut: Yale University Press, 1990.

   Discusses relations between white and ethnic minority groups in contemporary American society.

Albyn, Carol Lisa, and Lois Sinako Webb. *The Multicultural Cookbook for Students*. Phoenix, Arizona: The Oryx Press, 1993.

   Covers the cuisines of 122 countries, providing at least two traditional recipes per country. Glossary of terms.

Ashabranner, Brent. *Still a Nation of Immigrants*. New York: Cobble Hill Books/Dutton, 1993.

   Illuminates recent trends in American immigration. Photographs.

Beard, Timothy Field. *How to Find Your Family Roots*. New York: McGraw-Hill, 1977.

   Guide for tracing ethnic backgrounds in America and abroad (180 countries).

Bernardo, Stephanie. *The Ethnic Almanac*. New York: Doubleday, 1981.

   Reference source covering 40 ethnic groups that includes statistical data, short essays, biographies, customs, and bibliographies.

Boland, Emily. *An American Christmas: A Celebration of Our Heredity from around the World*. New York: Philosophical Library, 1989.

   Explores the ethnic folklore, customs, and social life of several ethnic groups.

Brown, Francis J., and Joseph Roucek. *One America: The History, Contributions, and Present Problems of Our Racial and National Minorities*. New York: Prentice Hall, 1952.

   Reference book covering almost 100 ethnic groups that includes information on immigration, settlement, and major contributions, as well as statistical data and bibliographies.

Bruhn, Wolfgang, and Max Tilke. *A Pictorial History of Costume*. London: A. Zwemmer, 1955.

   Contains excellent color illustrations of ethnic costumes from Europe, Asia, and Africa.

Buenker, John, and Lorman Ratner. *Multiculturalism in the United States: A Comparative Guide to Acculturation and Ethnicity*. New York: Greenwood Press, 1992.

   Discusses minority groups in America, focusing on pluralism and ethnic relations.

Buttlar, Lois, and Lubomyr R. Wynar. *Building Ethnic Collections: An Annotated Guide for School Media Centers and Public Libraries*. Littleton, Colorado: Libraries Unlimited, 1977.

   Recommends books covering over 50 ethnic groups.

Cardasco, Francesco. *American Ethnic Groups, the European Heritage: A Bibliography of Doctoral Dissertations at American Universities*. Metuchen, New Jersey: Scarecrow Press, 1981.

   Lists over 1,400 dissertations that cover 30 ethnic groups.

Casey, Betty. *International Folk Dancing, USA*. Garden City, New York: Doubleday, 1981.

   Describes folk dancing in several European, Asian, and Latin American countries. Illustrated.

Champion, Selwyn G. *Racial Proverbs: A Selection of the World's Proverbs Arranged Linguistically*. New York: Macmillan, 1965.

   Offers hundreds of proverbs from 27 countries.

Chiswick, Barry. *Immigration, Language, and Ethnicity: Canada and the United States*. Washington, D.C.: AEI Press, 1994.

   Explores immigration patterns, ethnic and linguistic minorities, and language policy in both countries.

Coppa, Frank J., and Thomas J. Curran, eds. *The Immigrant Experience in America*. Boston: Twayne, 1976.

   Provides historical coverage of European, Hispanic, and Asian immigration to the United States.

Daniels, Roger. *Coming to America: A History of Immigration and Ethnicity in American Life*. New York: Harper-Collins, 1990.

   Historical overview of immigration and settlement patterns in the United States. Photographs.

Davis, Hillary. *Celebrate: Traditional Ethnic Entertaining in America*. New York: Crescent Books, 1992.

   Explores the folklore, festivals, cookery, and heritage of various ethnic groups.

Dinnerstein, Leonard. *Ethnic Americans: A History of Immigration*, third edition. New York: Harper & Row, 1988.

   Historical overview of immigration and ethnic relations.

Dinnerstein, Leonard et al. *Natives and Strangers: Blacks, Indians, and Immigrants in America*, second edition. New York: Oxford University Press, 1990.

Historical account of various ethnic groups in the United States and their relationships with one another. Illustrated.

Di Pietro, Robert. *Ethnic Perspectives in American Literature: Selected Essays on the European Contribution*. New York: Modern Languages Association, 1983.

Illuminates European ethnic groups. Bibliography.

Dunbar, Nelia, and Brian Rajewski, eds. *Countries of the World and Their Leaders Yearbook*. 2 vols. Detroit: Gale Research, 1995.

Comprehensive study of more than 200 countries that includes information on religion, education, media, and politics and government.

Eiseman, Alberta. *From Many Lands*. New York: Atheneum, 1970.

Documents the immigrant experiences from the past 200 years through journals, newspapers, and literature.

Ferraro, Thomas J. *Ethnic Passages: Literary Immigrants in Twentieth Century America*. Chicago: Chicago University Press, 1993.

Discusses the impact of emigration and immigration on twentieth-century American fiction.

Friedman, Lester D. *Unspeakable Images: Ethnicity and the American Cinema*. Urbana: University of Illinois Press, 1991.

Traces ethnic influences in American motion pictures.

Georges, Robert A. *American and Canadian Immigrant Folklore: An Annotated Bibliography*. Hartford, Connecticut: Garland Press, 1982.

Includes coverage of 50 ethnic groups, primarily Europeans, but also Asian and African peoples.

Gold, Milton J., and Carl Grant. *In Praise of Diversity: A Resource Book for Multicultural Education*. Washington, D.C.: Association of Teacher Educators, 1977.

Contains essays praising various cultures and ethnic groups for their contributions to American society.

Greene, Victor R. *American Immigrant Leaders, 1800-1910: Marginality and Identity*. Baltimore, Maryland: Johns Hopkins University, 1987.

Recognizes Irish, German, Norwegian, Swedish, Jewish, Polish, and Italian leaders in various fields. Bibliography.

Handlin, Oscar. *The Uprooted: The Epic Story of the Great Migrations that Made the American People*. Boston: Little Brown, 1990.

Reference source that compares immigrant groups, emphasizing how they altered American culture.

Hecker, Melvin. *Ethnic America, 1970-1977: Updating the Ethnic Chronology Series*. Dobbs Ferry, New York: Oceana Publications, 1979.

Provides chronology information on 31 ethnic groups.

Hoerder, Dick. *The Immigrant Labor Press in North America, 1840s-1970s: An Annotated Bibliography*. New York: Greenwood Press, 1987.

Includes essays, statistical data, and bibliographies on 30 ethnic groups, most of which are European.

Hutchinson, Edward Prince. *Immigrants and Their Children, 1850-1950*. New York: Wiley, 1956.

Comprehensive study illuminating the generation gaps within numerous ethnic groups over the past 100 years, focusing on economic, social, professional, and linguistic issues.

James, J.P., and E. James. *We the People of America: An Atlas of America's Ethnic Diversity*. New York: Macmillan, 1988.

Identifies American ethnic groups on national, regional, and city scales, providing good annotations, maps, and statistical data based on the 1980 U.S. Census.

Johnson, Harry A. *Ethnic American Minorities: A Guide to Media and Materials*. New York: R & R Bowker, 1976.

Includes audio-visual aids, catalogs, and bibliographies.

Katz, William Loren. *The Great Migrations, 1880s-1912*. Austin, Texas: Raintree, Steck-Vaughn, 1993.

Recounts major immigration waves from Europe, the Middle East, and Asia.

Kivisto, Peter. *The Ethnic Enigma: The Salience of Ethnicity for European Origin Groups*. Philadelphia: The Balch Institute Press, 1989.

Addresses ethnic relations between European American groups.

Kraus, Barbara. *The Barbara Kraus International Cook Book: Fabulous Meals from the Cuisines of More than 100 Countries*. New York: Perigree Books, 1991.

Contains typical dishes indexed by the names of meals and by country. Bibliography.

Lieberson, Stanley. *From Many Strands: Ethnic and Racial Groups in Contemporary America*. New York: Russell Sage Foundation, 1988.

Analysis of American ethnic and racial groups based on 1980 U.S. Census data.

Liebman, Lance. *Ethnic Relations in America*. Englewood Cliffs, New Jersey: Prentice-Hall, 1982.

Provides essays on ethnic history, immigration, and language, as well as political and legal issues.

McCabe, Cynthia Jaffe. *The American Experience: Contemporary Immigrant Artists*. New York: Independent Curators; Philadelphia: The Balch Institute for Ethnic Studies, 1985.

Examines the artistic contributions of various ethnic groups in America.

Manoogian, Sylvia, and Natalia Bezugloff. *Directory of Language Collections in North American Public Libraries*. Chicago: American Library Association, 1986.

Locates language collections in over 200 libraries, arranging them by foreign language and by geographic location.

Mead, Frank S. *Handbook of Denominations in the United States*, nineteenth edition. Nashville, Tennessee: Abingdon Press, 1990.

Reference source that includes the religious bodies of several American ethnic groups.

Melton, J. Gordon, ed. *Encyclopedia of American Religions*, fourth edition. Detroit: Gale Research, 1993.

Offers comprehensive coverage of over 1700 religious groups.

————. *Directory of Religious Organizations in the United States*, third edition. Detroit: Gale Research, 1993.
> Provides information on over 2,500 religious organizations.

Miller, Sally. *The Ethnic Press in the United States: A Historical Analysis and Handbook.* New York: Greenwood Press, 1987.
> Furnishes essays and bibliographies on over 25 ethnic groups.

Miller, Wayne Charles. *A Comprehensive Bibliography for the Study of American Minorities.* 2 vols. New York: New York University Press, 1976.
> Covers several dozen ethnic groups (not only minorities) in short essays and bibliographies.

————. *A Handbook of American Minorities.* New York: New York University Press, 1976.
> A condensed version of *A Comprehensive Bibliography for the Study of American Minorities* (1976) by the same author that is useful for quick reference.

Morrison, Joan, and Charlote Fox Zabusky. *American Mosaic: The Immigrant Experience in the Words of Those Who Lived It.* Pittsburgh, Pennsylvania: University of Pittsburgh Press, 1980.
> Collection of experiences by American immigrants from Europe, Asia, the Middle East, South America, and South Africa.

Newman, Jaqueline. *Melting Pot: An Annotated Bibliography and Guide to Food and Nutrition Information for Ethnic Groups in America.* New York: Garland Publications, 1993.
> Contains information on the food habits, cookery, and nutrition of several dozen American ethnic groups.

Parillo, Vincent. *Strangers to These Shores: Race and Ethnic Relations in the United States*, fourth edition. New York: Macmillan, 1990.
> Examines America's pluralism in a multiracial society, covering more than 100 ethnic groups.

Pozzetta, George. *Folklore, Culture, and the Immigrant.* New York: Garland, 1991.
> Discusses immigration, ethnicity, and acculturation in the United States.

Racinet, Albert. *The Historical Encyclopedia of Costumes.* New York: Facts on File, 1988.
> Includes traditional costumes from Africa, Asia, Europe, Oceania, and North America. Illustrated.

Santoli, Al. *New Americans: An Oral History, Immigrants and Refugees in the U.S. Today.* New York: Viking Press, 1988.
> Personal accounts of American immigrants from several ethnic groups.

Schwartz, Carol, and Rebecca Turner, eds. *Encyclopedia of Associations.* 3 vols. Detroit: Gale Research, 1994.
> Reference source covering over 100 ethnic organizations.

Shenton, James P. *Ethnic Groups in American Life.* New York: Arno Press, 1978.
> Contains reproduced articles from *The New York Times* dealing with American ethnic groups and their concerns.

Sowell, Thomas. *Ethnic America: A History.* New York: Basic Books, 1981.
> *Standard Periodical Directory.* New York: Oxbridge Press, 1995.
> Annual directory containing English and bilingual titles that covers over 60 American ethnic groups.

Statistical Abstract of the United States. Washington, D.C.: U.S. Bureau of the Census, 1995.
> Reference source published annually that presents immigration statistics by country of origin along with comparative data dating back to the nineteenth century.

Stave, Bruce, and John Sutherland. *From the Old Country: An Oral History of European Migration to America.* New York: Twain Publishers, 1994.
> Furnishes oral histories from the 1930s through the 1970s, including discussions on crossing the ocean, work, family, love and marriage, community life, and other topics.

Thernstrom, Stephan et al. *Harvard Encyclopedia of American Ethnic Groups.* Cambridge, Massachusetts: Belknap Press/Harvard University Press, 1980.
> Scholarly source covering over 100 ethnic groups that includes discussions of immigration, settlement, organizations, religions, and major contributions. Bibliographies.

Tilke, Max. *National Costumes from East Europe, Africa and Asia.* New York: Hastings House, 1978.
> Treats various ethnic groups. Color illustrations.

Tilton, Jeff Todd. *Worlds of Music: An Introduction to the Music of the World's Peoples.* New York: Schirmer Books, 1992.
> Addresses Native American, African American, European, Asian, Latin American, and American (folk) music.

Upton, Dell. *America's Architectural Roots: Ethnic Groups that Built America.* Washington, D.C.: Preservation Press, 1986.
> Provides examples of American ethnic architecture. Illustrated.

U.S. Census of the Population and Housing. Washington, D.C.: U.S. Bureau of the Census, 1991-1992.
> Contains the latest numerical data on American ethnic groups, their geographical location, language preservation, and other relevant topics.

Wasserman, Fred. *Ellis Island: An Illustrated History of the Immigrant Experience.* New York: Macmillan, 1991.
> Records the experiences of individuals who entered America through Ellis Island through photographs.

Wasserman, Paul, and Alice Kennington, eds. *Ethnic Information Sources of the United States*, second edition. 2 vols. Detroit: Gale Research, 1995.
> Comprehensive source covering over 120 American ethnic groups that includes organizations, periodicals, research centers, radio, and other subjects. Bibliography.

Wasserman, Paul et al. *Festival Sourcebook.* Detroit: Gale Research, 1977.
> Includes discussions of ethnic celebrations.

Waters, Mary C. *Ethnic Options: Choosing Identities in America*. Berkeley: University of California Press, 1990.

Reviews the ethnic composition of America, focusing on mixed marriages and the freedom to choose ethnic backgrounds.

Wertsman, Vladimir F. *What's Cooking in Multicultural America: 400 Ethnic Cuisines at Your Finger Tips*. Metuchen, New Jersey: Scarecrow Press, 1995.

Presents cuisines from every continent, including 120 Native American tribes. Annotated bibliographies.

———. *Career Opportunities for Bilinguals and Multilinguals: A Directory of Resources in Education, Employment, and Business*, second edition. Metuchen, New Jersey: Scarecrow Press, 1994.

Employment guide that identifies educational institutions specializing in languages and targets prospective employers in the United States and abroad who are interested in hiring individuals with language skills.

Westin, Jeane Eddy. *Finding Your Roots: How Every American Can Trace His Ancestors at Home and Abroad*. Los Angeles: J.P. Tarcher, 1977.

Guide for tracing one's background in the United States and beyond.

Wilde, Larry. *Larry Wilde's Complete Book of Ethnic Humor*. New York: Bell Publishing Co./Crown Publishers, 1984.

Reveals the ethnic wisdom, expressed through humor, of various ethnic groups.

Williams, Robin Murphy. *Mutual Accomodation: Ethnic Conflict and Cooperation*. Minneapolis: University of Minnesota Press, 1977.

Explores intercultural communication.

Wittke, Carol Frederick. *We Who Built America: The Saga of the Immigrant*. Rev. ed. Cleveland, Ohio: Case Western University, 1967.

Provides concise coverage of several American ethnic groups.

Wynar, Lubomyr. *Encyclopedic Directory of Ethnic Newspapers and Periodicals in the United States*. Littleton, Colorado: Libraries Unlimited, 1976.

Pioneer work covering over 50 ethnic groups.

———. *Guide to Ethnic Museums, Libraries and Archives in the United States*. Kent, Ohio: Kent State University, 1978.

Includes information on over 60 ethnic groups.

———. *Ethnic Film Strip Guide for Libraries and Media Centers*. Littleton, Colorado: Libraries Unlimited, 1980.

Covers several dozen groups.

———. *Encyclopedic Directory of Ethnic Organizations in the United States*. Littleton, Colorado: Libraries Unlimited, 1985.

Contains information on over 70 ethnic groups.

Yinger, J. Milton. *Ethnicity: Source of Strength; Source of Conflict*. New York: State University of New York Press, 1994.

Evaluates the pros and cons of ethnicity, ethnic relations, and assimilation.

PERIODICALS

Emie Bulletin (1976-). New York: Ethnic Materials Information Exchange Round Table/ALA Queens College Graduate School of Library and Information Studies. Quarterly.

Multiethnic coverage featuring short articles, bibliographies, and book reviews.

Ethnic Forum (1980-). Kent, Ohio: Center of Study of Ethnic Publications, Kent State University. Semi-Annual.

Contains essays on American ethnic groups, book reviews, and bibliographies.

Ethnic Groups (1976-). New York: Gordon & Breach Science Publishers. Quarterly.

Treats ethnic identity, social, and cultural policies.

Ethnic Newswatch (1992-). Stamford, Connecticut: Softline Information. Quarterly.

CD-ROM containing articles form over 90 ethnic and minority newspapers and magazines.

Ethnic Resource Guide (1975-). Bloomington: Ethnic Heritage Studies Program, Indiana University. Annual.

Provides articles on African American and European groups.

Explorations in Ethnic Studies (1978-). Tempe: National Association of Ethnic Studies, Arizona State University. Monthly.

Focuses on cultural activity and inter-ethnic group relations.

Melus (1973-). Huntington, West Virginia: Society of Multicultural Literature in the USA, Marshall University. Quarterly.

Studies ethnicity in American literature and media.

Multicultural Review (1990-). Westport, Connecticut: Greenwood Publishers. Quarterly.

Contains articles, book reviews, and bibliographies, providing excellent coverage of numerous American ethnic groups.

Archipenko, Alexander **II:** 606

architecture **I:** 30, 34, 47, 52-53, 69, 107, 178, 192, 196, 211, 217, 259, 271 **II:** 404, 450, 478, 536, 563, 565, 576

Ardoin, Amédé **I:** 13

Are You Being Served **I:** 185

Arendt, Hannah **II:** 366

Argentina **I:** 17, 184 **II:** 543-545, 572, 594, 604

Arizona **I:** 56, 97, 197, 203 **II:** 333, 344, 501, 537, 544-545, 619

Arkansas **I:** 265, 282 **II:** 395, 496

Arlington Heights, Illinois **I:** 93

Armenia **I:** 18, 280 **II:** 553, 581 **III:** 19

Armenian Americans **II:** 587

Armenian Library and Museum of America **II:** 572

Armenian Network of America **I:** 97

Armour, Philip Danforth **I:** 227

Arnheim, Michigan **I:** 215

Art Center **II:** 469

Arthur Graphic Clarion **I:** 42

Asen II **I:** 80

Ashland, Michigan **I:** 151

Asian Exclusion Act **I:** 205

Asimov, Isaac **II:** 366

Askov, Minnesota **I:** 148

Associated Press **I:** 241, 273

Association Canado-Américaine **I:** 239, 245, 247

Association for the Advancement of Dutch American Studies **I:** 169

Association of Romanian Catholics of America **II:** 469

Assumption College **I:** 234-235, 242, 247-248

Astor, John Jacob **I:** 258

Astoria, New York **I:** 128, 275, 277 **II:** 406

Astoria, Oregon **I:** 189, 204

Athanas, Anthony **I:** 24

Athens **I:** 262-263, 274, 276-277 **II:** 496

Atlanta, Georgia **I:** 265

Atlantic Ocean **I:** 217 **II:** 440, 486

Atlantic Seaboard **I:** 179, 232

Attell, Abe **II:** 366

Attic **I:** 267-268

Audubon, John James **I:** 227

Auel, Jean **I:** 212

Augustana Lutheran Synod **I:** 208

Augustine, Hermann **I:** 131

Auschwitz **I:** 285

Austin, Texas **I:** 292 **II:** 381

Australia **I:** 47, 93, 177, 185, 281, 294 **II:** 373, 407, 529, 545, 571, 594, 604, 613

Australian Open **I:** 141

Austria **I:** 7, 44-56, 60, 67, 84, 130-131, 139, 249-250, 281, 294-295, 305, 309 **II:** 331, 351, 373, 424, 473, 499, 528-530, 570, 593-594, 603 **III:** 26

Austria-Hungary **I:** 82, 96, 117, 124-125, 127, 295, 305 **II:** 351, 499

Austrian American Club **I:** 56

Austrian American Council **I:** 55-56

Austrian Americans **I:** 45-56

Austrian Benevolent Society **I:** 123

Austrian Broadcasting Company **I:** 55

Austrian Cultural Institute **I:** 55-56

Austrian Empire **I:** 45-46 **II:** 500, 529, 594

Austrian Society of Arizona **I:** 56

Austrian-American Federation, Inc. **I:** 55

Austrians **I:** 44-56, 96, 117, 119-120, 123, 131-133, 138, 297, 305 **II:** 426, 432, 499-501, 504, 529-531, 535, 573, 593-595, 603

Austro-Hungarian Empire **I:** 45-46, 51-52, 95-96, 101, 117, 295, 305, 307, 311 **II:** 457, 471, 473, 499-501, 508, 516, 595

Autio, Rudy **I:** 211

Azores **II:** 440-441, 443, 447-449, 454 **IV:** 368

B

Bacall, Lauren **II:** 365

Bacharach, Burt **II:** 366

Bacon, Francis **I:** 173

Bad Ischl, Austria **I:** 53

Baden **I:** 251

Baekeland, Leo **I:** 76

Bahriany, Ivan **II:** 607

Baja California **I:** 119

Baker, Herman **I:** 168

Balanchine, George **II:** 482

Balch, Emily Greene **I:** 128

Balkan Peninsula **I:** 19, 79, 81, 116-118 **II:** 457

Balkan Wars **I:** 82-83, 91, 265 **II:** 499, 502

Balkans **I:** 25, 79-81, 93, 117-118, 124, 280-281, 287, 295 **II:** 351, 473, 497, 499-500, 509, 528, 592

Baltic Americans **II:** 393

Baltic Republics **I:** 187, 190, 197 **II:** 384, 389, 395

Baltic Sea **I:** 187 **II:** 371-372, 384, 423, 472, 556

Baltimore Orioles **I:** 127

Baltimore, Maryland **I:** 64, 191 **II:** 496

Bandelier, Adolphe **II:** 578

Baptism **I:** 11, 28, 39, 89, 110, 137, 269, 271, 286 **II:** 404, 462-464, 575, 617

Baptist churches **I:** 100, 179, 183 **II:** 464, 602

Baraga, Frederic **I:** 46 **II:** 530, 537

Barbados **I:** 281

Barbu, Valer **II:** 467

Barbulescu, Constanin **II:** 468

Brussels, Belgium **I:** 72, 76, 78, 243
Bruun, Ulrikka Feldtman **II:** 420
Bryan, Violet Harrington **I:** 106, 114
Bryant, Lane **II:** 393
Brynner, Julius **II:** 577
Bryson, Bill **I:** 186
Bucharest, Romania **II:** 456
Buchwald, Art **II:** 365
Buckley, William F. **II:** 326
Budapest, Hungary **I:** 119
Budweiser **I:** 12, 139
Buffalo, New York **II:** 435, 607
Buisson, Benjamin **I:** 225
Bukovac, Vlaho **I:** 127
Bulgaria **I:** 79-93, 262 **II:** 456, 473, 497, 499, 581 **III:** 78
Bulgarian American Chamber of Commerce **I:** 93
Bulgarian American Enterprise Fund **I:** 93
Bulgarian Americans **I:** 80-94
Bulgarian Eastern Orthodox Mission **I:** 90
Bulgarian Exarchate **I:** 81
Bulgarian National Committee **I:** 91
Bulgarian National Front **I:** 91, 93
Bulgarian Orthodox Church **I:** 79-81, 90
Bulgarian People's Union **I:** 91
Bulgarian Revolutionary Central Committee **I:** 81
Bulgarian Socialist Labor Federation **I:** 91
Bulgarian Socialist Party **I:** 82
Bulgars **I:** 80 **II:** 582
Bull, Ole **II:** 419
Bunyan, Paul **I:** 242
Bureau of Indian Affairs **I:** 70 **II:** 327
Burgundy **I:** 67, 160 **II:** 441
Burke, Virginia **I:** 260
Burlamaqui, Jean Jacques **II:** 576
Burlington, Vermont **I:** 245
Burns, George **II:** 365
Burns, Robert **II:** 494, 496
Burton, Richard **II:** 618
Busella, Florea **II:** 465
Butkas, Dick **II:** 394
Butler, Pierce **II:** 327
Byelorussian American Women Association **I:** 65
Byelorussian American Youth Organization **I:** 65
Byelorussian Autocephalous Orthodox Church **I:** 65
Byelorussian Congress Committee **I:** 65
Byzantine Catholic Seminary **I:** 98
Byzantine Empire **I:** 16, 80, 100, 263, 280, 295 **II:** 582
Byzantine Rite Catholic Church **I:** 97, 100, 102 **II:** 385
Byzantium **I:** 80, 117, 263 **II:** 498, 582

C

Cabaret **I:** 242 **II:** 343
Cable Television Network **I:** 276
Cabot, John **II:** 332
Cabral, João Sérgio Alvares **II:** 452
Cabrini, Francesca Xavier **II:** 344
Cadillac **I:** 232
Cagney, James **II:** 326
Cahill, George D. **II:** 330
Cajun Country Guide **I:** 13
Caledonia **I:** 133
California Gold Rush **I:** 201, 222 **II:** 323
California **I:** 18, 27, 47, 53-56, 64, 84, 93, 97, 100, 113, 119, 121, 124-128, 141, 143, 146, 148, 151, 153-155, 157, 162, 178, 180, 185-186, 189, 196, 199, 201-203, 209, 211, 214, 222-223, 227, 229, 235, 254, 258-260, 265, 273, 282, 286, 292-293, 297-299, 306, 308 **II:** 323, 327, 329, 333, 352, 365, 367-368, 372, 380, 382-383, 387, 395, 406, 411, 420, 437, 443-445, 449-455, 457, 459, 465, 468-469, 472, 474, 478, 482-484, 487, 496, 504, 506, 509-513, 531, 536-537, 542, 544-545, 547-548, 550-555, 558, 566, 572, 575-576, 579, 594, 604, 614-615, 617, 620
California State University **I:** 186
Calkins, Mary Whiton **II:** 619
Callas, Maria **I:** 274
Calvin College **I:** 164, 169-170
Calvin Theological Seminary **I:** 169
Calvin, John **I:** 169, 218 **II:** 492
Calvinism **I:** 138, 170-171, 294, 302-303, 311 **II:** 489, 617
Cambrian **I:** 172
Cambridge, Massachusetts **I:** 26, 260, 292 **II:** 555, 580, 590, 608
Canaan **II:** 350, 366
Canada **I:** 1, 3, 22, 42-43, 47, 64, 76, 83, 90, 93, 104, 107, 145, 148, 154, 169-170, 177, 184, 191, 197-198, 214, 220-223, 228-237, 239-241, 243, 245-247, 308 **II:** 316, 330, 373, 395, 397, 410, 421, 452, 458, 464, 470, 487, 495, 504, 506, 513-514, 525-526, 529-530, 538, 572, 577, 594, 603, 605-606, 609, 612, 615, 619-620
Canadian Americans **I:** 220
Canal Street **I:** 108
Canal Zone **I:** 76
Canary Islands **IV:** 434
Candlemas **I:** 237
Cankar, Ivan **II:** 529
Canterbury **I:** 173
Canuck **I:** 243
Cape Breton Island **I:** 232
Capek, Thomas **II:** 527

capitalism **I:** 82, 166-167 **II:** 325, 332, 466, 472, 492, 565

Capone, Al **II:** 334

Capp, Andy **I:** 181

Capra, Frank **II:** 336, 343

Caprivi, Leo **II:** 529

Carbondale **II:** 568-569

Cardozo, Benjamin **II:** 365

Carey, Mathew **II:** 326

Caribbean Sea **II:** 372

Carmen **II:** 451, 546

Carnegie Foundation **I:** 125

Carnegie Hall **I:** 122 **II:** 488, 537, 605

Carnival **I:** 7-8, 48 **II:** 445

Carol I **II:** 457, 461

Carol II **II:** 457

Caroll, Christina **II:** 467

Caron, Leslie **I:** 226

Carpathian Mountains **I:** 80, 95, 117, 131 **II:** 516

Carpatho-Russian American Center **I:** 99, 104

Carpatho-Russian Orthodox Diocesan Seminary **I:** 98

Carpatho-Rusyn Research Center **I:** 98-99, 104

Carpatho-Rusyn Roman Catholics **I:** 100

Carpatho-Rusyn Society **I:** 99, 103-104

Carpatho-Rusyns **I:** 58, 95-104 **II:** 473-474, 478-479, 515, 522, 592, 602-603

Carrel, Alexis **I:** 227

Carrière, Joseph Medard **I:** 241

Carter, Jimmy **II:** 434

Cartier, Jacques **I:** 221, 231

Caruso, Enrico **I:** 126

Casals, Pablo **II:** 552

Caspian Sea **I:** 145

Cassavetes, John **I:** 273

Cathedral of St. George **I:** 25

Cather, Willa **I:** 137, 143

Catholic church **I:** 8, 10, 22, 28, 49, 75, 97, 100, 102-103, 111, 117, 127, 138, 166, 218, 222, 231, 239, 257, 289, 299, 302 **II:** 321-323, 327, 340, 344, 387-388, 391, 404, 426, 428, 442, 449, 464, 469, 498, 522, 547, 550, 561, 575, 602, 608

Catholic Family Life Insurance **I:** 239

Catholic Mass **I:** 73, 124 **II:** 403

Catholic Raphael Society **I:** 253

Catholic schools **I:** 111, 256 **II:** 322, 431, 534

Catholicism **I:** 11, 51, 58, 97, 100, 103, 111, 116, 124, 145, 173, 218, 221, 237, 286, 302 **II:** 317, 321-322, 340-341, 385, 387, 390-391, 396, 424, 427, 501, 516, 523, 525-526, 579, 592

Celts **I:** 9, 45, 67, 160, 173, 178, 218 **II:** 314-315, 320, 328, 441, 485-486, 495-496, 611, 615-617

Cenarrusa, Pete **II:** 553

Census Bureau **I:** 3, 202, 207, 220 **II:** 377, 386

Center for Acadian and Creole Folklore **I:** 14-15

Center for Austrian Studies **I:** 56

Center for Belgian Culture **I:** 77

Center Franco-Américain **I:** 245, 247

Central Intelligence Agency **II:** 510

Cermak, Anton Joseph **I:** 141

Cernan, Eugene A. **I:** 141

Ceuta **IV:** 434

Chada, Joseph **I:** 139, 143

Challenger **I:** 10

Champaign, Illinois **II:** 609

Champlain, Samuel de **I:** 221, 231

Channel Islands **I:** 174

Chaplin, Charlie **I:** 291

Charlemagne **I:** 45, 67, 249-250

Charleroi **I:** 68

Charles I **I:** 173, 183 **II:** 315, 442, 486

Charles IV **I:** 131

Charles Robert **I:** 295

Charles V **I:** 45, 160

Charleston, South Carolina **II:** 576

Chartier, Armand **I:** 242

Chartist **I:** 177

Chase, Loretta **I:** 25

Chereshnovsky, Michael **II:** 606

Cherry Hill, New Jersey **I:** 276

Chervenkov, Vulko **I:** 82

Cheslav **II:** 498

Chester, Montana **I:** 189

Chevalley, Montreux **II:** 576

Cheviot Hills **I:** 172

Chevrolet, Louis Joseph **II:** 578

Chicago Bears **I:** 141 **II:** 394, 606

Chicago Black Hawks **I:** 127, 142 **II:** 524, 606

Chicago Cubs **I:** 25, 274

Chicago Opera Ballet **I:** 140

Chicago Public Library **I:** 20 **II:** 389

Chicago Symphony Orchestra **I:** 141, 212 **II:** 605

Chicago Tribune **I:** 243

Chicago, Illinois **I:** 56, 61, 84, 93, 127, 142, 228, 259, 275-278 **II:** 328, 346-347, 367, 394-397, 435-438, 468, 483, 512-514, 539, 561, 567-568, 579, 607, 609

Chicopee Falls, Massachusetts **I:** 241

Children's Day **II:** 507

China **I:** 120 **II:** 440, 473, 537

Chinese for Affirmative Action **I:** 128

Chino, Eusebio **II:** 332, 344

Chios **I:** 264-265

Life in America **I:** 18, 247, 293, 303 **II:** 410, 422, 467

Lilith **I:** 273

Lincoln, Abraham **I:** 46, 204, 257 **II:** 417, 420, 512, 552, 563, 566, 601, 619

Lind, Jenny **II:** 566

Lind, John **II:** 563

Lindbergh, Charles Jr. **II:** 565

Lindbergh, Charles Sr. **II:** 564-565

Lindfors, Viveca **II:** 566

Linn, Charles **I:** 201, 211

Lithuania **I:** 57-60, 188, 190, 198, 254 **II:** 371, 383-393, 395-397, 424, 434, 473, 556, 592 **IV:** 279

Lithuanian American Community **I:** 224 **II:** 388-397

Lithuanian American Council **I:** 224 **II:** 396

Lithuanian Americans **I:** 194 **II:** 385-397

Lithuanian National Foundation **II:** 396

Lithuanian Roman Catholic Alliance of America **II:** 396

Lithuanian World Community **II:** 395-396

Loewe, Frederick **I:** 50, 54

Loewi, Otto **I:** 54, 258

Lombardi, Vincent **II:** 345

London, Jack **I:** 119 **II:** 619

Londos, Jimmy **I:** 274

Longfellow, Henry Wadsworth **I:** 226

Louisiana **I:** 1-9, 11-15, 105-107, 109, 111-115, 119, 220-224, 227-229, 232, 248, 254, 282 **II:** 333, 347, 510, 544, 581

Lovell, James **I:** 141

Luckman, Sid **II:** 367

Ludvigh, Samuel **I:** 46

Lugonja, Vladimir **II:** 504

Lugosi, Bela **I:** 307

Lukas, Anthony J. **II:** 365

Lunt, Alfred **I:** 213

Luria, Salvador **II:** 345

Lutheran church **I:** 145, 152-156, 193, 198, 201, 204, 208, 212, 214-216 **II:** 373, 378-379, 382-383, 391, 415-416, 522, 534, 563

Luxembourg **IV:** 286

Lysenko, Mykola **II:** 597

M

Mabinogion **II:** 616

MacArthur, General Douglas **II:** 327

Macedonia **I:** 16, 79, 81-83, 91-93, 262, 265 **II:** 457 **IV:** 294

Macedonian Political Organization **I:** 91

MacMonnies, Frederick **II:** 494

Madeira **IV:** 368

Madrid, Spain **II:** 543

Magnusson, Warren **II:** 564

Mailer, Norman **II:** 365

Maine **I:** 1, 9, 15, 44, 176, 180, 197, 211, 213, 231-232, 234-235, 239-248 **II:** 313, 433, 481, 485, 558, 580

Maislin, Albert **II:** 393

Makarova, Natalia **II:** 482

Makedonska Tribuna **I:** 91, 93

Maki, Dennis **I:** 212

Makinen, Markin **I:** 212

Malamud, Bernard **II:** 365

Malden, Karl **II:** 511

Malinowski, Bronislaw **II:** 433

Malkovich, John **II:** 511

Malta **II:** 398-400, 402-407 **IV:** 303

Maltese Americans **II:** 399-407

Mamet, David **II:** 366

Manfred, Frederick **I:** 168

Mangione, Jerre **II:** 343, 348

Manhattan **I:** 67, 74, 92, 258 **II:** 341, 343, 345, 352, 451, 467, 604

Manoliu-Manea, Maria **II:** 466

Manuel I **II:** 441

Manuel II **II:** 442

Maravich, Pete **II:** 512

Marciano, Rocky **II:** 345

Marculescu, Yolanda **II:** 467

Marcus, Jacob Rader **II:** 364

Mardin, Arif **II:** 588

Margrethe I **I:** 145

Margrethe II **I:** 145-146, 152

Marie **I:** 9, 113, 224, 227, 238 **II:** 336, 466, 541

Mark, Hermann Francis **I:** 55

Marquette, Jacques **I:** 233

Marshall, John **II:** 619

Martin, Peter **I:** 154

Martin, Sylvia Wene **II:** 367

Martin, Tony **II:** 451

Martinu, Bohuslav **I:** 141

Marx, Chico **II:** 365

Marx, Groucho **II:** 365

Marx, Gummo **II:** 365

Marx, Harpo **II:** 365

Marx, Zeppo **II:** 365

Mary of Scotland **II:** 493

Maryland **I:** 16, 64-66, 131, 159, 175-176, 178, 191, 197, 274, 278, 292 **II:** 315, 381-383, 433, 435, 443, 496, 511, 531, 557, 563-564, 584, 589, 613, 621

Massachusetts **I:** 2, 17-18, 22-27, 61, 76, 104, 175-176, 179-180, 202-204, 214-215, 221, 223, 226-228, 231, 234-235, 237, 239-248, 260, 265, 270-271, 274-276, 292, 309 **II:** 325, 328-330, 333, 345-346, 368-369, 372, 374-375, 380, 386-387, 436, 443-445, 450-

Mount Allegro **II:** 343
Mountain of Winter **I:** 212
Mourning Becomes Electra **I:** 273
Mouw, Richard **I:** 169
Mr. Deeds Goes to Town **II:** 343
Mr. Smith Goes to Washington **II:** 343, 493
Mucha, Alphonse **I:** 142
Muilenburg, James **I:** 169
Mulder, Arnold **I:** 168
Muni, Paul **I:** 55
Munich Agreement **II:** 516
Munk, Jens **I:** 146
Murad I **II:** 498
Murgas, Joseph **I:** 141
Murphy, Audie **II:** 327
Museum of Modern Art **I:** 24, 53, 103 **II:** 468
Musial, Stan **I:** 141 **II:** 434
Muste, A. J. **I:** 168
Mutimir **II:** 498
Mylonas, George **I:** 273

N

Nabokov, Vladimir **II:** 481
Nadeau, Gabriel **I:** 237
Nagel, Ernest **II:** 364
Nalley, Marcus **I:** 126
Napoleonic Era **I:** 160
Napoleonic Wars **I:** 45, 145, 225, 251 **II:** 399, 409, 544
Nashreeye B'nei Torah **II:** 367
Nassi, Thomas **I:** 24
Nast, Thomas **I:** 258
National Aeronautics and Space Administration **I:** 58
National Association for the Advancement of Colored People **I:** 53
National Association of Franco-Americans **I:** 228
National Baseball League **II:** 343
National Committee for Amish Religious Freedom **I:** 43
National Croatian Society **I:** 124
National Football League **I:** 155, 274 **II:** 394
National Hockey League **II:** 381, 479, 606
National Lithuanian Society of America **II:** 396
National Public Radio **I:** 214 **II:** 467, 495
National Security Council **II:** 434, 510
National Slovak Society **II:** 525-526
National Welsh American Foundation **II:** 620
Native Americans **I:** 7, 46, 51, 67, 75, 108, 118-119, 140, 155, 205 **II:** 488, 537, 577
Navratilova, Martina **I:** 141
Neagoe, Peter **II:** 467
Neble, Sophus **I:** 154

Nebraska **I:** 133, 136-138, 143, 147-148, 151-157, 253-254, 256 **II:** 327, 530, 558, 564, 566, 569
Necessary Roughness **I:** 24
Negulesco, Jean **II:** 466
Nelsen, Ancher **I:** 154
Nelson, Knute **II:** 420
Nelson, Nelson Olson **II:** 419
Nemanja, Stefan **II:** 498
Nemerov, Howard **II:** 366
Nesmith, Michael **II:** 494
Nestorovych, Volodymyr **II:** 605
Netherland-America Foundation **I:** 170
Netherlands **I:** 28, 33, 45, 66-68, 71, 146, 159-160, 162-166, 169-171, 249-250, 281 **II:** 326, 351, 420, 496 **IV:** 322
Neumann, John Nepomuk **I:** 46
Neutra, Richard **I:** 53
Nevada **I:** 120, 265 **II:** 420, 423, 501, 545, 549, 553-555
Never the Twain Shall Meet **II:** 380
New Amsterdam **I:** 160, 164, 167, 176 **II:** 351
New Brunswick **I:** 1, 3, 65, 114, 164, 169, 171, 230-231, 246, 278, 300, 308, 310-311 **II:** 438
New England **I:** 2-3, 9, 15, 23-24, 26, 43, 167, 176-177, 179, 182-183, 196, 209, 215, 221, 233-235, 237-248, 265, 271, 281, 292 **II:** 315, 323, 333, 443, 445, 449, 454, 487, 584, 611, 614
New Hampshire **I:** 43, 53, 176, 180, 223, 228, 234-235, 240-244, 246-247, 265, 283 **II:** 454
New Jersey **I:** 18, 23, 47, 55, 61, 63-65, 67, 96-97, 99-100, 103-104, 152, 159, 162, 164-165, 169, 171, 176, 180, 189, 197-199, 222, 241, 247-248, 276-278, 283, 298, 300, 303, 308-311 **II:** 330, 333, 338, 345-346, 348-349, 365, 386-387, 406, 438, 443, 450, 453, 459, 474, 478, 483, 518, 522, 525-526, 545, 550, 561, 572, 576, 578, 584, 594-595, 599, 603-604, 607, 610, 619-620
New Mexico **I:** 203, 211, 292 **II:** 408, 544-545, 550, 552
New Netherland Colony **I:** 166
New Year's Day **I:** 32, 70, 87, 236, 267 **II:** 337, 402, 460, 585
New York **I:** 11, 13, 15, 18, 20-27, 29, 46-47, 53-56, 60-61, 63-65, 67-68, 76-78, 83-84, 87, 91-94, 96-100, 103-104, 113-114, 122-123, 126-130, 132-133, 136, 138-139, 141, 143, 146, 148, 153-158, 160-164, 166, 170-172, 176-180, 185-186, 189-193, 197-199, 201-202, 209, 211-214, 216, 221-222, 226-229, 231, 234-235, 242-244, 246, 248, 252-255,

Palestine Aid Society of America **I:** 9, 13, 15, 237

Palestine **I:** 280 **II:** 349-350, 355-356, 363-364, 541

Paloheimo, Yrjö **I:** 211

Panama Canal **I:** 76

Panama **I:** 76 **II:** 511

Panic, Milan **II:** 512

Pano, Nicholas **I:** 24

Papadopoulos, Colonel George **I:** 264

Papana, Alexandru **II:** 468

Papnicolaou, George **I:** 274

Parkhurst, Helen **II:** 618

Parti Québecois **I:** 233

Partridge, Captain George **I:** 274

Passover **II:** 355

Pasternak, Joseph **I:** 307

Pastore, John O. **II:** 344

Pauli, Wolfgang **I:** 54

Pavlovskis, Valdis **II:** 380

Paxinou, Katina **I:** 273

Pecheniha-Ouglitzky, Paul **II:** 605

Pelikan, Jaroslav **I:** 140

Peloquin, C. Alexander **I:** 244

Penn, William **I:** 138, 251, 308, 310 **II:** 487, 613

Pennsylvania **I:** 18, 29-31, 33-35, 37, 39-40, 42-43, 47, 52, 61, 67-68, 77, 84, 90, 96-102, 104, 121, 124, 127-128, 138, 143, 146, 175-176, 178, 180, 183, 210, 221-222, 251, 253-255, 257, 259-261, 265, 274, 281, 298-299, 308, 310-311 **II:** 315, 325, 327, 333, 346-347, 365, 372-373, 379, 382-383, 386-387, 391-392, 394-397, 405-406, 437, 459, 465, 474, 478-479, 487-488, 495-496, 501-502, 506, 511-513, 518, 521-527, 530, 532, 534, 536, 538, 540, 545, 550, 553, 563, 567-568, 571, 573, 575, 577-580, 593-595, 597, 602-604, 606-608, 612-615

Pentecost **I:** 32, 62, 271 **II:** 447

Pereira, William L. **II:** 450

Perlea, Ionel **II:** 467

Perlman, Itzhak **II:** 366

Persia **I:** 263, 279-280 **II:** 582

Peter I **II:** 441, 592

Peter I Island **IV:** 337

Peter, George **I:** 52

Peters, Steven **I:** 25

Petersen, William **I:** 155

Peterson, Rudolph **II:** 565

Petrakis, Henry Mark **I:** 274

Petrovic, Karadjordje **II:** 498-499

Petrunkevitch, Alexander **II:** 482

Pevny, B. **II:** 605

Peyton Place **I:** 243

Philadelphia Story, The **II:** 493

Philadelphia, Pennsylvania **I:** 84, 255 **II:** 346-347, 382, 394, 397, 526, 567-568, 579, 607-608

Philipp, Emanuel Lorenz **II:** 577

Phillip II **I:** 160

Phoenix, Arizona **I:** 56 **II:** 619

Pilsudski, Josef **II:** 424

Pipa, Arshi **I:** 23, 25

Piszek, Edward J. **II:** 433

Pitcairn Island **IV:** 483

Plante, Annie David **I:** 243

Plantinga, Alvin **I:** 169

Plantinga, Cornelius **I:** 169

Podres, Johnny **II:** 394

Poe, Edgar Allan **II:** 326, 468

Poland **I:** 45, 57-60, 95-96, 102, 104, 117, 130-131, 163, 188, 249-250, 254, 283, 295 **II:** 351, 384-385, 390, 393, 423-439, 472-473, 515-516, 556-557, 591-593, 595-597, 602, 604, 608 **IV:** 352

Polányi, John Charles **I:** 307

Polányi, Karl **I:** 307

Polányi, Michael **I:** 307

Polish American Congress **II:** 427, 433, 437

Polish American Historical Association **II:** 435, 437-438

Polish Americans **II:** 389, 423-439

Polish Genealogical Society of America **II:** 437

Polish National Alliance of the United States **II:** 437

Polish Surname Network **II:** 437

Pollak, Gustav **I:** 53

Pólya, George **I:** 307

Pomutz, George **II:** 457

Pone, Gundaris **II:** 381

Popa, Lieutenant Eleanor **II:** 465

Porgy and Bess **II:** 366

Porter, Sylvia **II:** 365

Portugal **I:** 218, 281 **II:** 350, 356, 440-443, 445-448, 451-455, 543 **IV:** 368

Portuguese Americans **II:** 441-455

Pothier, Aram J. **I:** 240

Powderly, Terrence V. **II:** 325

Power, Tyrone **II:** 326

Praeger, Frederik Amos **I:** 53

Pregl, Frederic **II:** 529, 537

Preminger, Otto **I:** 47, 55

Presanctified Gifts **I:** 270

Presbyterian Church **I:** 74, 138 **II:** 449, 492, 495

Preseren, France **II:** 529

Preska, Margaret **I:** 211

Prifti, Peter R. **I:** 24

Primeau, Ernest J. **I:** 239

Primo Maggio **I:** 48 **II:** 334, 402

Skopec, Andreas **II:** 530

slavery **I:** 2-4, 46, 76, 105-106, 109, 111-112, 117-118, 140, 146, 176, 291-292 **II:** 350, 487, 493, 498, 508, 563, 593, 619

Slovak Americans **I:** 140 **II:** 516-527

Slovak **I:** 44, 98, 102, 130-132, 138, 140, 143, 290, 294 **II:** 430, 505, 515-527, 531, 593

Slovak World Congress **II:** 526

Slovakia **I:** 95-96, 98, 102-103, 124, 130-131, 140, 281, 294 **II:** 423, 456, 473, 515-516, 519, 523-526, 528, 591 **IV:** 411

Slovene **I:** 117-118, 125 **II:** 499-500, 530, 532, 538, 540-541

Slovene National Benefit Society **II:** 538, 540

Slovenia **I:** 116-118, 124, 294 **II:** 331, 500, 509, 528-530, 533-534, 536, 538-541 **IV:** 420

Slovenian Americans **I:** 125 **II:** 528-541

Slovenian National Directory **II:** 538

Slovenian Research Center of America **II:** 536, 540-541

Slovenian Women's Union **II:** 539-540

Slovenska Drzava **II:** 538

Smedes, Lewis B. **I:** 169

Smibert, John **II:** 494

Smith, Alfred Emanuel **II:** 324

Smithmeyer, John L. **I:** 53

socialism **I:** 139, 141, 193, 202, 208, 210 **II:** 363, 369, 372, 392, 481, 564

Société Historique Franco-Américaine **I:** 228, 247

Society for Armenian Studies **I:** 301

Sole Savage **I:** 274

Solidarity **I:** 1, 4-5, 30, 164, 258 **II:** 331, 339, 389, 393, 395, 412, 425, 433, 559

Solitude **I:** 25

Solti, Georg **I:** 307

Solvay, Ernest Rebecq **I:** 76

Solzhenitzyn, Aleksander **II:** 481

Son of the Moon **I:** 126

Sonnets de guerre **I:** 243

Sontag, Susan **II:** 366

Sorokin, Pitirim **II:** 482

Soros, George **I:** 302, 307

Sound of Music, The **II:** 366

Sousa, John Philip **II:** 451

South Carolina **I:** 2, 221 **II:** 457, 487, 496, 571, 576

South Dakota **I:** 147-148, 154-155, 162, 189, 202, 254 **II:** 413, 416, 434, 465, 575

South Slavic Americans **I:** 125

Soviet Union **I:** 25, 45, 57, 82, 95, 102, 117, 131, 146, 188, 194, 196, 201, 203, 211, 251, 296 **II:** 352, 372, 377-378, 380, 385-386, 392, 424-427, 457, 471-479, 481, 484, 499, 552, 590-591

Spain **I:** 2-3, 25, 45, 67, 106, 118, 160, 217-218, 232, 249, 251, 257, 279, 281, 285, 290 **II:** 332, 350-351, 356, 405, 440-442, 448, 486, 542-552, 554, 571, 606 **IV:** 434

Spanish Americans **II:** 542-555

Spanish-American War **I:** 210, 274 **II:** 419, 457, 543, 546

Spellman, Francis Joseph **II:** 327

Spielberg, Steven **II:** 365

Spingarn, Joel Elias **I:** 53

Spitz, Mark **II:** 367

Spock, Benjamin **I:** 169

Spring Festival **II:** 550

Springsteen, Bruce **I:** 168

St. Anthony **I:** 111 **II:** 534

St. Basil **I:** 270

St. David **II:** 611, 614, 617, 620-621

St. Demetrius's Day **I:** 87

St. Elijah's Day **I:** 87

St. Germain, Fernand J. **I:** 241

St. John's Eve **I:** 191, 206 **II:** 375-376, 422, 559

St. Jude **I:** 111

St. Louis Cardinals **I:** 141, 274 **II:** 345

St. Louis, Missouri **I:** 84, 141 **II:** 503

St. Nicholas's Day **I:** 87

St. Paul, Minnesota **I:** 142-143, 199, 215, 278 **II:** 329, 348, 383, 397, 421, 526, 561, 568, 619

St. Peter **I:** 111 **II:** 402, 561

Stahel, Julius H. **I:** 306

Stallone, Sylvester **II:** 343

Stamatos, Poppy G. **I:** 278

Stanceu, Charlie **II:** 468

Stars and Harp **II:** 328

Staub, Peter **II:** 572

Stefan, Joseph **II:** 529

Steinmetz, Charles **I:** 259

Stella, Frank **II:** 345

Stephanopoulos, George **I:** 272, 274

Stephen I **I:** 295, 297

Stephens, Alice Barber **II:** 618

stereotypes **I:** 42, 48, 84, 163, 181, 205, 265, 284-285, 304 **II:** 317, 333, 337, 353, 412, 428, 546, 562

Stern, Otto **I:** 258

Stewart, Anita **II:** 380

Stewart, James **II:** 493

Stokowski, Leopold **II:** 434

Stone, I. F. **II:** 365

Stowe, Harriet Beecher **II:** 618-619

Strank, Michael **II:** 524

Strauss, Leo **II:** 366

Stravinsky, Igor **II:** 482

Streetcar Named Desire, A **I:** 273 **II:** 511, 604

Struve, Gleb **II:** 481

Stuart, Gilbert **II:** 494
Stuart, James **II:** 486
Stuyvesant, Peter **I:** 160 **II:** 351
Sullivan, Ed **II:** 326
Sullivan, John L. **II:** 327
Sunni Muslims **II:** 588
Suomalainen Kansallis Raittius Veljeysseura **I:** 209
Sutter, John August **I:** 258 **II:** 572
Sutton, George Paul **I:** 54
Svalbard **IV:** 337
Svecenski, Louis **I:** 126
Swados, Elizabeth **II:** 394
Sweden **I:** 144-145, 188-189, 191, 198, 200-201, 214 **II:** 372-373, 408-409, 419, 421, 556-569, 592 **IV:** 448
Swedes' Day **II:** 559
Swedish Americans **I:** 208 **II:** 557-569
Swedish **I:** 131, 145-146, 150, 152, 188-189, 191, 200, 202-203, 207-208, 211, 255 **II:** 372, 377, 409, 411-412, 414, 421, 556-569, 592
Swiss American Historical Society **I:** 268 **II:** 578-580
Swiss American **II:** 573-574, 578-580
Switzerland **I:** 28, 44, 75, 217, 249 **II:** 331, 528, 570-574, 576-580, 583 **IV:** 462
Syria **I:** 18, 280 **II:** 349, 581
Szell, George **I:** 307
Szent-Györgyi, Albert **I:** 307
Szilard, Leo **I:** 259, 307 **II:** 366

T

Take All to Nebraska **I:** 154
Talese, Gay **II:** 343
Talon, Jean **I:** 231
Tanguay, Eva **I:** 242
Teller, Edward **I:** 259, 307
Tennessee **I:** 79, 114, 151 **II:** 468, 490-491, 572
Teodoresco, Eugen **II:** 457
Teodorescu, Iosif **II:** 468
Ternina, Milka **I:** 126
Tesich, Steve **II:** 511
Tesla, Nikola **II:** 511, 514
Tétrault, Maximilienne **I:** 241
Texas **I:** 4, 7, 11-12, 15, 56, 126-127, 133, 137-138, 140, 142, 148, 154, 178, 185, 203, 217, 222, 253-254, 257, 260, 265, 289, 292, 298, 311 **II:** 367, 381, 411, 426, 452, 487, 489, 493-494, 511, 531, 544, 558, 565, 581, 584
Thessaloniki **I:** 262
Thirty Years War **I:** 250
Thoeny, Wilhelm **I:** 53
Thomas, Carey **II:** 618

Thompson, James **II:** 564
Thoreau, Henry David **I:** 226
Threatening Shadows **I:** 126
Three Circles of Light **II:** 343
Three Coins in a Fountain **II:** 466
Tight White Collar, The **I:** 243
Time Warner Cable **I:** 277
Times of Acadiana, The **I:** 14, 113
Tirana, Bardhyl Rifat **I:** 25
Titanic **II:** 466
Tito, Marshal **I:** 117
Tkach, Joseph W. **I:** 103
Tobago **II:** 372
Tobin, Daniel **II:** 327
Tokle, Torger **II:** 420
Tolstoy, Alexandra **II:** 477
Toronto **I:** 22, 63-64, 104, 128, 191, 197-198, 215, 230, 308, 310-311 **II:** 381, 495, 514, 526, 529, 538, 606, 609
Tosca **I:** 126, 274
Toth, Alexis **I:** 100, 103 **II:** 478, 602
Tracy, Spencer **II:** 326
Trailing Geronimo **I:** 120
Trajan **II:** 457
Transylvania **I:** 281, 295, 305 **II:** 457-460, 466
Treasure of the Sierra Madre, The **II:** 493
treaties **I:** 2, 45, 59, 67, 75, 81, 118, 145, 153, 218-219, 226, 232, 250, 263, 295, 305 **II:** 315, 372, 409, 442, 486, 592
Tremblay, Pierre-Amedee **I:** 243
Tremblay, Rémi **I:** 241, 243
Trifan, Marioara **II:** 467
Triffin, Robert **I:** 75
Trinidad **II:** 449
Truman, Harry S **I:** 140, 257 **II:** 364, 429, 466
Tsakiris, George **I:** 273
Tsina, Eftalia **I:** 24
Tsongas, Paul Efthemios **I:** 274
Tuchman, Barbara **II:** 364
Tunney, Gene **II:** 327
Turchin, John Basil **II:** 481
Turkey **I:** 16, 18-19, 32, 79-82, 84, 91, 117, 250, 263, 265, 272 **II:** 354, 405, 473, 519, 529, 581-590, 596
Turkish Americans **II:** 582-590
Turkish Daily News—Almanac **II:** 589
Turkish Independence Day **II:** 587
Turkish Newsletter **II:** 589
Turkish Women's League of America **II:** 590
Turpinen, Viola **I:** 212
Twelfth Night **I:** 236, 248 **II:** 547
Twentieth Century Spanish Association of America **II:** 554
Twice a Man **I:** 273
Tytla, William **II:** 605